THE PARALEGAL'S GUIDE TO FAMILY LAW AND PRACTICE

By Grace A. Luppino, Esq.
and
Justine FitzGerald Miller, Esq.

Prentice Hall

Upper Saddle River, New Jersey 07458

Library of Congress Cataloging-in-Publication Data
Luppino, Grace A.
    Family law and practice : the paralegal's guide / Grace A. Luppino, Justine FitzGerald Miller.
       p. cm.
    Includes index.
    ISBN 0-13-901125-0
    1. Domestic relations—United States. I. Miller, Justine FitzGerald. II. Title.
KF505.Z9 L87 2002
346.7301'5—dc21   00-047862

Executive Editor: *Elizabeth Sugg*
Production Editor: *Lori Dalberg, Carlisle Publishers Services*
Production Liaison: *Eileen O'Sullivan*
Director of Manufacturing & Production: *Bruce Johnson*
Managing Editor: *Mary Carnis*
Manufacturing Buyer: *Cathleen Petersen*
Senior Design Coordinator: *Miguel Ortiz*
Cover Designer: *Marianne Frasco*
Marketing Manager: *Tim Peyton*
Editorial Assistant: *Anita Rhodes*
Interior Design and Composition: *Carlisle Communications, Ltd.*
Printing and Binding: *Courier Westford*

Prentice-Hall International (UK) Limited, *London*
Prentice-Hall of Australia Pty. Limited, *Sydney*
Prentice-Hall of Canada Inc., *Toronto*
Prentice-Hall Hispanoamericana, S.A., *Mexico*
Prentice-Hall of India Private Limited, *New Delhi*
Prentice-Hall of Japan, Inc., *Tokyo*
Prentice-Hall Singapore Pte. Ltd.
Editora Prentice-Hall do Brasil, Ltda., *Rio de Janeiro*

113631172

10 9 8 7 6 5 4 3
ISBN 0-13-901125-0

DEDICATION

This book is dedicated to Margaretann Antonelli, my niece Grace, and my nephews Rocco and Jhonnatan, and to my legal mentors: Elizabeth Gleason, Herbert L. Grayson, Mary Moers Wenig, Patricia Buck Wolf, and Gerald Zuckerman.

Grace A. Luppino

Dedicated to my children, Justine and George.

Justine FitzGerald Miller

CONTENTS

CHAPTER 7   CHILD CUSTODY, VISITATION, AND RIGHTS OF THIRD PARTIES   145

CHAPTER 8   CHILD SUPPORT   167

CHAPTER 9   THE CLIENT INTERVIEW   189

CHAPTER 10 INITIAL AND RESPONSIVE PLEADINGS 224

▼

CHAPTER 13 SEPARATION AGREEMENTS 317

PREFACE

This book evolved from the need to have an understandable, interesting, and relevant textbook from which to teach and a book that would prepare paralegal students to respond successfully to the numerous demands in a real-world family law practice.

The goal of this book is to thoroughly prepare students in the areas of family law that they are most likely to encounter in the real world. Therefore, the major emphasis in this book is on the theoretical, procedural, and practical aspects of the divorce process with its attendant issues such as alimony, property distribution, child custody, and child support, as well as other matters arising after the divorce occurs, such as postjudgment modifications of orders for custody, child support, and alimony.

The book is logically ordered to guide the student through the various theories underlying family law and the procedures that translate these theories into practice. There is a balance between chapters on theory and chapters that focus on practice. For instance, Chapter 1, "Introduction to Family Law Practice," addresses the practical aspects of working as a paralegal in a family law practice. Chapter 2, "The Roots and Traditions of American Family Law," provides an historical backdrop for the emergence of the changing and evolving theory of family law, including the changing views on the nature of marriage, and the role of women and children in a family.

Chapter 3, "Ethics in Family Law," presents a mix of theory and practice in that it outlines the legal professional code of ethics and how it applies to a family law setting. This chapter includes cases involving paralegals who violated various rules of ethics such as the divorce paralegal who slept with the client's husband and revealed confidential information regarding the case to him during the course of their affair.

Chapter 4 deals with the issues of prenuptial agreements, cohabitation and same-sex marriage. Chapters 5 through 8 provide a black letter law overview of the four major areas encountered in the practice of family law: alimony, property and debt distribution, child custody, and child support. Along with a recitation of the rules, these chapters provide the theoretical justification for each rule and also provide excerpts of interesting and entertaining cases that demonstrate how some courts apply the legal principles of family law to decide disputes over the myriad of issues these areas embrace.

Chapters 9 through 15 focus exclusively on practice and the paralegal's role in the process. These chapters contain examples of the type of documents prepared throughout the divorce process. These chapters also present model complaints, motions, orders, and agreements which the paralegal can modify to the requirements of his or her jurisdiction. Also included are selections of legal documents filed by celebrities, for example, Lucille Ball's divorce complaint against Desi Arnaz. The appendixes include Madonna and Sean Penn's separation agreement.

Finally, Chapter 16 addresses the issue of state intervention in family matters, such as child abuse and neglect, termination of parental rights, and adoption.

Although this book is national in scope, we have tried to provide cases, statutes, and forms from various jurisdictions. However, the need for students to become familiar with and knowledgeable about the law, procedure, and documents in their own jurisdiction is paramount. This need is addressed in the end-of-chapter exercises that require students to go out in the field—to their courthouses and law libraries—and acquire hands-on experience with their jurisdiction's statutes, cases, forms, and procedural rules.

It is our hope that this book will be a long-time companion to the paralegal student who finds employment in a family law practice.

Grace A. Luppino
Justine FitzGerald Miller

A C K N O W L E D G M E N T S

We wish to thank the following people for their support and encouragement in making this book a reality:

Dana Meltzer and Elizabeth Sugg at Prentice Hall; our colleagues and students at Branford Hall Career Institute and Briarwood College; Dawn A. Chuley for her expertise on distance learning and Internet research; Heather Bell for preparing the transparencies and distance learning portion of this book and her expertise on Internet research; Connie Luppino for her photocopying; Margaretann Antonelli for her many errands and meals; Katharine Hunt for her expertise and assistance in preparing the final manuscript; our friends and families; and to the following paralegal students for their legal research: Diane Allen, Sherrian Benson, Kelly Butler, Christy Cash, Domenica Colavolpe, Laurie Coppola, Raymond Daley, Lori DiGiovanni, Connie Esposito, Mia Garmizo, Andrew Gister, Cheryl Granoff, Joann Gleason, Gail LaGreca, Deanna Lozowski, Susan McClintock, Linda McCue, Cynthia McQueen, Mary Notarangelo, Joann O'Leary, Melanie Rieder, Margaret Sabilla, Christine Van Vliet, and Elizabeth Young.

Our special thanks to paralegal Pamela Robicheau for her countless hours of legal research, editing, and preparation of the manuscript. This book could not have been completed without her hard work, expertise, and devotion to this project.

Special thanks to the American Bar Association, the National Association of Legal Associates, Inc., W. Kelsea Wilbur Eckert, and the National Conference of Commissioners on Uniform State Laws for their permission to reprint documents in this book.

Grace A. Luppino
Justine FitzGerald Miller

C H A P T E R

1

INTRODUCTION TO FAMILY LAW PRACTICE

KEY TERMS

Mediation   Settlement

Family law is one of the most interesting, exciting, and dynamic areas of legal practice. If you like boxing, wrestling, or any of the other pugilistic arts, you will certainly enjoy being part of a legal team that tackles the knotty problems and ever-changing cultural, social, and economic issues that affect the American family.

Family law as a specialty evolved slowly, but now, in many jurisdictions, family law cases occupy more space on the civil court docket than any other type of matter. This increase has occurred because of changes in our society during the past forty years that have affected attitudes toward marriage, family, divorce, and parenting.

During the first half of the twentieth century in the United States, divorce was far less common than it is today. At the turn of the twentieth century, less than one in twenty marriages ended in divorce; since the mid-1970s, for every two marriages that took place in a given year, one divorce has occurred. Today, more than one-half of children under the age of eighteen are growing up in one-parent homes. As a result of this trend, many law firms devote their practice exclusively to family law; for other firms, the practice of family law comprises a large segment of the work produced. Both types of law firms increasingly employ paralegals in their family law department. These paraprofessionals, with the guidance of their supervisory attorneys, complete the myriad of tasks needed to provide thorough and effective representation to clients on family matters.

FIGURE 1–1
A paralegal who is both competent and enthusiastic about family law practice can provide valuable assistance to attorneys.

A paralegal who is both competent in and enthusiastic about family law practice can provide valuable assistance to attorneys who spend all or most of their time practicing family law. Employment opportunities for paralegals in this field of law will abound as long as individuals continue to seek attorneys to help them resolve their marital and family conflicts, and as long as there are paralegals whose training has provided them with a solid background in both family law theory and practice. The goal of this book is to provide the paralegal student, in a comprehensive and understandable manner, with just that type of theoretical and practical education.

FAMILY LAW THEORY

Family law theory provides the analytical framework for the body of substantive law used in courts to decide marital and family-related matters. These laws determine, regulate, and enforce the obligations of marriage and parenthood. They are made by the the legislative branch as state legislators fashion and enact statutes and upheld by the judicial branch as judges make decisions in the courtroom. These common law and statutory decisions are not made arbitrarily, nor are they made in a vacuum without considering what is taking place in the society in which the laws will be enforced. When a law is being made, it is fashioned in a way that promotes the dominant views of the time on the proper, fair, or most enlightened way to handle the issues at hand. Legislation and judicial opinions reflect the values and attitudes of society. These values and attitudes produce the ideas that provide the theory or underlying rationale for resolving a legal issue in a particular manner. As values and attitudes change and as society acquires new information and knowledge related to various aspects of family law issues, new theories emerge and replace the earlier rationales for resolving disputes.

In the area of family law, courts and legislatures use many different approaches to address marital disputes and the issues arising from such disputes. These issues include

▼ Support and maintenance of family members,

▼ Care and custody of minor children, and

▼ Division of property upon the breakup of the marital unit.

Over time, family law theory has grown and evolved as society has changed. The history of American family law presented in the next chapter demonstrates how differently family law issues have been treated during different time periods.

FAMILY LAW PRACTICE

COURT PROCEDURES

In every jurisdiction, the judicial system provides specific procedures for bringing disputed substantive family law issues before the court. These procedures include

▼ Procedures for initiating family-related actions in a court,

▼ Procedures for acquiring and presenting evidentiary information,

▼ Procedures for providing temporary solutions to issues of support, custody, and visitation while a matter is pending, and

▼ Procedures for enforcing or modifying a court's orders.

Every state or jurisdiction has its own particular set of procedural rules to follow in the practice of family law. These rules are part of the jurisdiction's larger body of civil procedural law that governs how private parties may enforce their substantive legal rights through the court system. In the practice of family law, knowledge of the family court's procedural rules is essential.

OFFICE PROCEDURES

It is equally essential to know the procedures that a law firm uses within its office to handle family law matters. Every law office has its own particular methods and practices for the following aspects of managing family law cases:

▼ Obtaining and recording information from clients,

▼ Setting up files,

▼ Preparing legal documents for filing in court,

▼ Docketing court dates,

▼ Recording the amount of time spent working on each file, and

▼ Billing clients for work done.

APPLYING FAMILY LAW THEORY TO FAMILY LAW PRACTICE

It is also very important to understand how family law theory is actually applied in the real world of family law practice. In many instances in a marital dispute, the issues such as property division, alimony, child support, and even child custody are worked out by the parties in a manner that is not consistent with the prevailing theoretical view or even the substantive statutory or common law guidelines. This happens when the parties work out an agreement to settle their differences.

SETTLEMENT

Occasionally, spouses who have agreed to end their marriage are able to work out an agreement between themselves to resolve each of the issues arising from the marital breakup. This informal process of dispute resolution is called **settlement.** The parties themselves negotiate areas of disagreement and, through compromise, reach an agreement to present to the court. In doing so, each party usually forfeits a portion of what they might be fully entitled to in a court of law in exchange for a concession from the opposing party. This manner of settling family disputes may be accomplished by the parties acting alone or with the assistance of their attorneys.

MEDIATION

Family or marital disputes may also be settled by the alternate dispute resolution procedure known as **mediation.** With the assistance of a trained mediator, who is either court provided and free or privately engaged and paid, the parties meet and attempt to resolve the issues surrounding the dissolution of their marriage. Mediators are not judges. They may suggest but not order solutions. The mediator attempts to have the parties participate in a give-and-take process to resolve the outstanding issues. If the parties come to an agreement in the mediation sessions, the agreement is not binding on them if they shortly afterward change their minds. However, if the parties incorporate the solutions agreed to in the mediation proceedings into a formal settlement document that is presented to the court and the court approves and enacts the agreement as a court order, the parties are then bound by it.

When the parties cannot forge an agreement on their own, the law is strictly applied on some or all of the issues involved. The parties go to trial and a judge, after hearing each side's arguments and reviewing their evidence, makes the decisions on how the disputed issues will be handled. These decisions become court orders that the parties must follow. Not infrequently, the party who has been least open to negotiation and compromise finds that the court's decision is far less favorable to him- or herself than the proposed settlement.

When the parties have agreed to a settlement and, forgoing a trial, present their agreement to the court, the judge does not have to automatically approve the

FIGURE 1–2
With the assistance of a trained mediator, the parties attempt to resolve the issues surrounding the dissolution of their marriage.

agreement and make it an order. Judges in family court have a great deal of discretion in deciding whether or not to approve an agreement that the parties present to the court. If an agreement appears to be particularly one-sided, arousing the suspicion that the less favored spouse may have been coerced into signing the agreement, a judge may refuse to accept the unfair portions of the agreement and instead enter more equitable orders.

THE FAMILY PRACTITIONER'S ROLE IN THE DISSOLUTION PROCESS

The practice of family law involves as much negotiating as it does litigating. For instance, a common saying is that there are no winners in a divorce, and the children are the biggest losers. The family practice law firm that strives to favorably resolve its client's legal problems in a manner that creates the least amount of additional damage and pain to all individuals affected—and does so successfully—provides the greatest degree of service to the client. Whether the service involves the initial divorce proceeding, or a subsequent need to enforce or modify the alimony, child support, or custody order, the family practice lawyer who can meet the client's objectives with the least amount of court intervention will serve a client well.

All litigation is adversarial and can only escalate hostility between the adverse parties. In a family law practice, the clients' need for legal assistance arises from discord in the most personal and intimate areas of their lives. Much attention and concern should be given to the manner in which the controversy is handled and the consequences for all concerned of mishandling or insensitively handling the issues underlying the dispute. All staff members of the law office should be aware of the need to handle delicate matters with great care. With the very high divorce rate that exists today, both the many members of the court system and attorneys who practice a considerable amount of family law have become adept at treating all parties with respect and with understanding of the turmoil that accompanies the breakup of a marriage.

Divorces are much easier to obtain in the new millenium than they were in the 1890s. Most of the stigma attached to divorce has disappeared, and today's communities offer many resources to help divorcing spouses and their children deal with the difficult changes taking place. Community support for families going through this type of crisis is readily available today because of our society's acceptance of divorce. This was not always the case. For many centuries and for a number of decades in the twentieth century, there was enormous pressure from social, cultural, and certain religious institutions to preserve the marital union and nuclear family at almost any cost. The following chapter provides an historical glimpse of the nature of marriage and divorce over time and the values and attitudes that contributed to past and present views of both marriage and divorce.

REVIEW QUESTIONS

1. Why has the specialty of family law practice grown during the last thirty years?
2. Name the two areas in which a paralegal needs training in family law.
3. Discuss the family law practitioner's role in the dissolution process.
4. Name the sources of substantive law that regulate the practice of family law.

5. Name the sources of procedural law that govern the practice of family law.

6. How do changing social ideas and moral values affect the status of substantive family law?

7. Name three issues family courts address in a family law dispute.

8. Name three types of family law conflicts in which the judicial system provides specific procedures to bring the matter before the court.

9. Name three typical office procedures used in a family law practice.

10. In a family law matter, how do the procedures of settlement and mediation operate and what is their value to resolving conflicts between spouses or the nonmarital parents of minor children?

EXERCISES

1. Go to your local public library and locate United States Census figures for 1950, 1970, 1990 and 2000. For each of those years, locate the divorce rate per marriages and the number of one-parent households. Prepare a written summary of this information.

2. Go to your local law library and locate the statutes for your state and the specific title, chapters, or sections of those statutes that address substantive family law matters. Photocopy these. Prepare a written summary of each statute regulating family law, identifying the statute name and statute number and describing briefly the area of family law the statute addresses.

3. Go to your local law library and locate the case law digest for your state. Find the digest topic that addresses family law. Prepare a summary of this digest topic, including the name of the major sections and subsections of the topic, and describe the type of issues that the cases in this section and subsection address.

4. Locate a copy of the rules of court or the practice book for your state. Locate the section that contains procedural rules for the practice of family law. Prepare a written summary that briefly describes the content of the procedural rules in this section.

5. Call the clerk's office of a state court in your area and ask to speak to the family law clerk or the supervisor of the family relations division of the court. Ask the clerk or supervisor if the court offers free and either mandatory or optional participation in mediation services for parties involved in a dissolution or custody dispute.

2

THE ROOTS AND TRADITIONS OF AMERICAN FAMILY LAW

KEY TERMS

Alienation of affection
Annulment
Breach of promise to marry
Legal separation

No-fault divorce
Paternity action
Separate maintenance

Much of American legal tradition has its roots in the common law decisions of England. However, centuries before the creation of the English common law, ancient legal systems developed rules to govern the rights and responsibilities of spouses and other family members. These ancient rules left their mark on later legal systems. In ancient Greece, a married woman was chattel, the legal property of her husband with no rights of her own. For centuries afterward, marriage was a formal arrangement in society in which women were subservient to men. Although in various cultures, at different points in history, women did possess some legal rights, they generally occupied a legal status that was inferior to that of men. In the United States, it was not until the passage of the Married Women's Property Acts that American women were allowed to own property in their own name. For this and many other equally compelling reasons, women were often reluctant to initiate legal proceedings to end their marriages.

Marriage, for many centuries, was a very strong social institution that contributed to the stability of society. Christianity transformed marriage from a mere social institution into a sacrament, a holy union lasting for eternity—"What God has brought together, let no man put asunder." Marriage was a legally and morally sanctioned relationship between a man and a woman, functioning as one social and economic unit. Spouses were responsible for the care of each other and jointly responsible for the care and maintenance of children, the issue of their union. However, divorce was not unheard of even in the earliest of times. In ancient times, a form of divorce took place when a woman left her husband or when a husband cast out his wife. In both instances, the husband remained in the family home and retained possession and control of the children of the marriage since they were regarded as chattel, pieces of personal property owned by the husband. In the Christian Western European civilizations of the Middle Ages, church and state were intertwined and the state enforced the doctrines of the Christian church, including the proscription against divorce.

Until the mid-1500s, there was one Christian church for all of Western Europe. This was the Roman Catholic Church with its seat of power vested in the Pope in Rome. In the 1530s when King Henry VIII wished to divorce his queen, Catherine of Aragon, and marry Anne Boleyn, the Roman Catholic Church refused to give Henry VIII a dispensation to divorce and remarry. Henry VIII, as the head of the church in England, broke from Rome and established the Church of England. During the second half of the 16th century, several different religious groups arose in England, Scotland, Germany, and France, eventually resulting in the establishment of many new Christian sects, separate from the Church of Rome, which became branches of the Protestant movement. Originally, in the European countries where Protestantism prevailed, the church and state continued their close connection and the national religion became the prevailing Protestant denomination in the country. For instance, in Scotland, the established religion was Presbyterianism. In the American colonies settled by the Puritans, such as the Massachusetts Bay Colony, Puritanism became the state religion. In other of the thirteen original American colonies such as Virginia and the Carolinas, which were settled by Englishmen who remained loyal to the established Church of England, the Anglican religion became the official religion of the colony. However, despite the continuing connection of church and state, many of the now largely Protestant European nations and the Protestant colonies in America allowed at least what came to be called civil divorce. On the other hand, in the European countries where Roman Catholicism remained either the state religion or the religion embraced by the majority of inhabitants, civil divorce was much slower in coming. In Italy and the Republic of Ireland, civil divorce was not legally authorized until the second half of the twentieth century!

MARRIAGE, DIVORCE, AND FAMILY LAW FROM COLONIAL AMERICA TO THE TWENTIETH CENTURY

In colonial America, although marriage was regarded as a sacred union, the Puritans, who had settled the New England colonies, recognized and allowed divorce. They also sanctioned a form of legal separation known as "divorce of bed and board" under which the couple's sacred union remained intact but they no longer cohabited. When a couple divorced or separated, colonial governments imposed on the husband the continuing obligation of economic support of his wife and their children.

When the thirteen original colonies broke away from England and formed a new nation, the state governments assumed the power to legally authorize and legally dissolve marriages. The new American nation provided specifically for the separation of church and state in its Constitution. There was to be no national religion nor were any of the new states allowed to establish any one religion as the official religion of that state. Henceforth, marriage and divorce as civil matters became separated from marriage and divorce as religious issues. In the eyes of the state, marriage was now viewed as a civil contract between two parties.

Under the marriage contract, each party had obligations to the other party. When one of the parties failed to perform an obligation of the marriage, he or she had breached the marital contract. The nonbreaching party could sue for a termination of the marriage contract and for damages from the other party as compensation for the harm caused by the breach. If the nonbreaching or "innocent" party proved that the marital contract had been breached, the court could terminate the marriage and, under the civil law, both parties were free to remarry. The state, through its court system, could order the offending or breaching party to compensate the other party and enter orders for the continuing support of the minor children of the marriage.

When each state government established either legislative or common law grounds for establishing breach of the marriage contract, these were commonly referred to as the grounds for divorce. When the female spouse alleged and proved grounds for divorce, the court almost always ordered the male spouse to continue to provide financial support to his former wife and his children. In many instances, even when a husband brought and won a divorce action against his wife, if the wife had been financially dependent on her husband for subsistence, the court ordered the husband to continue to provide for her financial support. However, enforcing these obligations was not always possible. Many ex-husbands disappeared from the court's jurisdiction and many divorced women and their children suffered economic deprivation and frequently social isolation as well. As long as women lacked the ability to support themselves, divorce was not a practical alternative. Societal pressures from many avenues, including the church, the extended family, and the local community were also exerted to keep the family intact.

Political and economic forces also promoted the advantages of staying married. During the eighteenth century and for a good part of the nineteenth century, the intact family was the basic economic unit of the new American nation. When the United States was mainly an agrarian society, its financial health and political strength depended on the production and sale of agricultural products from thousands of small family farms. All family members were essential to the operation of these farms. Family members, even young children, contributed to the economic advancement of their family and the nation by performing one or more of the many chores needed to keep the farm running.

THE INDUSTRIAL REVOLUTION AND THE FAMILY

The Industrial Revolution of the nineteenth century gave rise to the factory system in the United States and shifted the centers of economic activity from the country towns to the cities. In the early and middle years of the nineteenth century, many individuals left the family farms in the New England and Middle Atlantic states to work in the cities. Throughout the second half of the 1800s the large influx of immigrants from Europe added to the population of urban centers.

Frequently mothers, fathers, and even young children worked in city factories. Eventually laws were passed to protect children from working at early ages.

Some women then began to stay at home to care for their children. When this occurred, the husband became the person primarily responsible for the family's financial support. He also usually became the family member with predominant economic power. Men had the ability to obtain credit in their own names, whereas women could only obtain credit under their husband's, father's, or brother's signature. Even married women who continued to work in mills and factories and later in offices and stores had inferior economic power because these women were frequently paid far less than their male counterparts. Single women fared no better in the workplace. In fact, except for low-paying jobs in factories or low-paying positions as domestic servants, there were few employment opportunities for women in nineteenth-century America.

As time went by, "respectable" married women were not expected to work. Even well-educated, married women who, when single, had held positions as schoolteachers or nursing professionals had few or no opportunities to work for

FIGURE 2–1
As time went by, respectable married women were not expected to work, but rather stay home, do housework, and take care of the children.

pay. Many school systems prohibited married women from working as teachers; other school systems would not hire women with young children. Hospitals frequently instituted similar exclusionary policies for staff nurses.

As a result of these constraints, married women did not often consider divorce as a solution to a failing or unhappy marriage. Many women feared that they would have no means of supporting themselves or their children. Further, divorce carried a social stigma. Divorced women were not well accepted in many communities. The children of divorced mothers were often excluded from neighborhood play and not welcome in the homes of their friends who came from intact families.

Despite the many negative consequences of divorce for both women and men, and especially for children, the divorce rates rose at a slow but steady pace throughout the nineteenth century and into the early decades of the twentieth century. In the 1880s, one out of sixteen American marriages ended in divorce.

FAMILY LAW FROM THE DAWN OF THE TWENTIETH CENTURY TO THE PRESENT DAY

By 1900, there was one divorce for every twelve marriages. Undoubtedly, industrialization and urbanization played some part in this increase, if for no other reason than that these social and economic developments decreased the value of the intact family as an economic unit while providing women a meager increase in opportunities for paid employment outside the home.

However, divorce did occur during the first half of the twentieth century. Courts, when granting a divorce, usually ordered a husband to make weekly alimony payments and support payments for the maintenance of his former spouse and his children. Mothers were always awarded custody of children unless they were deemed in some way unfit or unless they abandoned the children and did not seek custody. Society continued to frown on divorce. To get a legal divorce, one party had to bring a civil suit and prove one of a limited number of grounds before the court would grant a decree of divorce. Typically, most states granted a divorce if one party proved the other committed adultery, abandoned them, or was a habitual drunkard. Eventually many states added grounds known as intolerable cruelty and mental cruelty. Even if parties agreed to divorce, one party had to sue the other party alleging one of these grounds. If the other party did not challenge the allegations, the judge would grant a divorce.

TYPES OF ACTIONS IN THE AREA OF FAMILY LAW

At the turn of the century, the number of suits for divorce, although increasing, still represented a small percentage of the legal actions that were marriage or family related. Some of these other related matters, such as actions to establish paternity, continue to be a part of today's family court calendar. Other actions such as petitions for annulment or actions for legal separation and spousal maintenance have greatly decreased, and yet other actions, such as suits for breach of promise to marry and alienation of affections, have virtually disappeared from the court's dockets.

BREACH OF PROMISE TO MARRY

The **breach of promise to marry** action is an excellent example of a legal action whose time has passed because of changed moral and social attitudes. Throughout the nineteenth century and for the first few decades of the twentieth century, a woman could and frequently did sue a man for breach of promise if the man had promised to marry her and failed to do so. Lawsuits were frequently filed for breach of promise in instances where a man made the promise to marry a woman and, relying on the promise, the woman engaged in sexual intercourse with the man and subsequently became pregnant. When the man refused to marry the woman she brought a suit for breach of promise.

"Breach of Promise"—The Distressed Damsel's Remedy

The following cases deal with actions for the breach of a promise to marry. They clearly demonstrate that this legal action was a creature of the times. The opinion rendered in the 1818 case of *Wightman v. Coates* sets out the important legal, social, and moral reasons for court authority and intervention to uphold the legality of the contract to marry and to impose money damages on a party who breaches this contract. This opinion also set out the evidentiary standard for proving that such a promise-to-marry contract existed and that the promise was broken and, hence, the contract breached.

FIGURE 2–2
Legal actions called *breach of promise to marry* were frequently filed by women who were left standing at the altar.

Where is he?

WIGHTMAN V. COATES

15 Mass. 1, 8 Am. Dec. 77 (1818)

Supreme Judicial Court of Massachusetts

Assumpsit on a promise to marry the plaintiff, and a breach thereof by refusal, and having married another woman. . . .

PARKER, C. J., delivered the opinion of the Court. Respectable counsel having expressed doubts upon the point reserved in this case, and having also suggested an opinion that the action was of a nature to be discountenanced rather than favored, we have given more consideration to the case than our impression of the merits of the objections would have required.

We can conceive of no more suitable ground of application to the tribunals of justice for compensation, than that of a violated promise to enter into a contract, on the faithful performance of which the interest of all civilized countries so essentially depends. When two parties, of suitable age to contract, agree to pledge their faith to each other, and thus withdraw themselves from that intercourse with society which might probably lead to a similar connection with another,—the affections being so far interested as to render a subsequent engagement not probable or desirable,—and one of the parties wantonly and capriciously refuses to execute the contract which is thus commenced, the injury may be serious, and circumstances may often justify a claim of pecuniary indemnification. . . .

As to the technical ground upon which the objection to the verdict now rests, we entertain no doubts. The exception taken is that there was no direct evidence of an express promise of marriage made by the defendant. The objection implies that there was indirect evidence from which such a promise may have been inferred; and the jury were instructed that if, from the letters written by the defendant, as well as his conduct, they believed that a mutual engagement subsisted between the parties, they ought to find for the plaintiff. They made the inference, and without doubt it was justly drawn. . . .

A mutual engagement must be proved, to support this action; but it may be proved by those circumstances which usually accompany such a connection. No case has been cited in support of the defendant's objection. On the contrary, it is very clear, from all the *English* cases, that a promise may be inferred, and the direct proof is not necessary. . . .

Judgment on the verdict.

Almost 100 years after *Wightman v. Coates* praised the action on breach of promise as a societal necessity, American courts were still providing remedies for "damsels in distress." However, an issue had arisen and it was not always clear how to handle it.

In the case of *Rieger v. Abrams,* a woman who was grievously wronged had pursued remedies in two separate lawsuits. In one, she sought damages for seduction under a tort theory. After this action was completed, she sued her seducer for breach of his promise to marry her. The trial court decided that she had already had her day in court because the seduction suit was based on the same dastardly behavior of her former lover. The wronged woman appealed this decision to the Supreme Court of Washington State. That court upheld the decision saying that her breach of promise claim was barred by the legal principle of *res judicata* (Latin for "the thing has already been adjudicated and ruled on").

This case is important because it established limits to the number of legal penalties that can be levied for this type of wrongful conduct. But it is also interesting because of the colorful language used to describe the dastardly conduct of the deceptive suitor and the humiliating aftereffects the naïve damsel suffered at the scoundrel's hands.

RIEGER V. ABRAMS

98 WASH. 72, 167 PAC. 76 (1917)

SUPREME COURT OF WASHINGTON

PARKER, J.

The plaintiff, Mattie Rieger, seeks recovery of damages from the defendant, Robert Abrams, for breach of promise of marriage which she alleges was made by him and accepted by her. Judgment was rendered by the superior court for King county in his favor, denying the relief prayed for by her, upon the facts admitted in the pleadings. The judgment was rendered upon motion made in that behalf, and rested upon the theory that the facts so admitted showed that, in another action prosecuted by her in that court, a judgment was rendered which became a final adjudication of her rights in the premises. From this disposition of the cause the plaintiff has appealed to this court. . . .

. . . Appellant in her final amended complaint in this action, after alleging that at all times in question both she and respondent were over 21 years old and unmarried, alleges:

"That on or about the 1st day of August, 1915, at said city of Seattle, defendant proposed marriage to plaintiff, and upon his urgent solicitations, representations to plaintiff, and his request the plaintiff thereafter, to wit, on or about the 15th day of August, 1915, in good faith, accepted said proposal, and she and said defendant thereupon mutually and verbally agreed, in consideration of love and affection, and of reasons aforesaid, to intermarry each with the other, within a reasonable time thereafter, which defendant then and there represented to plaintiff would be as soon as he could arrange his business affairs therefor, not longer than three or four weeks from said last mentioned date. . . . That on or about the 1st day of September, 1915, at the city of Seattle, the defendant, by reason of the relation and confidence which plaintiff had learned to repose in him as aforesaid, and by reason of the affection which she had grown to feel for him, and of their constant association together, and by reason of defendant's promise and their engagement to marry, did then and there by many endearments and solicitations, and under promise of marriage, and by subtly inducing plaintiff to drink intoxicating liquors, to wit, beer and wine to the extent of stupefying and intoxicating her, and against plaintiff's consent and insistent remonstrance, wickedly seduce, debauch, and carnally know her, and thereafter, by repeated promises to early marriage, induced plaintiff to continue said sexual intercourse with said defendant, whereby she became sick and pregnant with child. . . . That at all times prior to said last-mentioned date, plaintiff had been a chaste and virtuous woman, happy in her self-esteem and the confidence and esteem of her said child and friends, and theretofore

having at all times bourne an unquestioned reputation for chastity and virtue. . . . That said defendant has disregarded, and still disregards, his said promise of marriage with said plaintiff as aforesaid, and has not taken with her to be his wife, although reasonable time for the purpose has long since elapsed, and though frequently requested by said plaintiff, said defendant, on or about the ____ day of January, A.D. 1916, positively refused to make his said promises good, he has hitherto refused, and still refuses, to marry the plaintiff. . . . That by reason of said defendant's failure to keep and perform his promise and agreement to marry this plaintiff, she has lost all the advantage and social position which said marriage afforded her, and caused her to suffer great pain, humiliation, mental anguish, and mortification, all to her great damage in the sum of $50,000."

Respondent in his final second amended answer to appellant's amended complaint, after denying the allegations thereof above quoted, alleges as a second affirmative defense facts showing the commencement and prosecution to final judgment in the superior court for King county of an action by appellant against him as follows:

[The Washington Supreme Court then quotes from the final amended complaint which the wronged woman had filed in an earlier suit for seduction which she won and in which she was awarded $500.00 in damages. The complaint stated the same sad facts.

The woman's lawyers argued that her lover was liable to her in both the previous seduction suit, a tort action, and the current breach of promise matter, a civil action. The Washington Supreme Court thought otherwise.]

. . . We are unable to read appellant's final amended complaint in the former action and her final amended complaint in this action and reach any other conclusion than that they plead in substance the same facts upon which recovery is sought, and upon which judgment was awarded her, in the former action. We find alleged in each of these complaints the same promise of marriage, the same continued course of illicit relations induced by the promise of marriage, and the same breach of the promise of marriage, each of which facts is pleaded in each of the complaints with substantially equal precision and given substantially equal prominence therein. It seems plain to us that appellant has in each of these actions pleaded facts so related to each other that her right of recovery in each thereof must be considered as resting upon the same alleged wrong.

We do not overlook the fact that the real question here for consideration is whether or not the claim of damage made by appellant for breach of promise of marriage was rendered res judicata against her by the judgment rendered in her favor in the former action, instead of the converse of the proposition. Nor do we overlook the fact that seduction does not necessarily involve a breach of promise of marriage, though the latter is probably the most common inducement put forward to effect seduction. Of course, where seduction is induced apart from a promise of marriage, a recovery of damages therefor by the one seduced would not be a bar to recovery by her of damages for a breach of such promise. It may be also conceded that, where damages for seduction are recovered by a parent or some one entitled thereto other than the one seduced, such recovery would not be a bar under any circumstances to her recovery for breach of promise of marriage. But our present problem is not so conditioned. We have here the identical parties to both actions. We have here the identical facts in each action, in substance, finally pleaded by appellant as a basis for her recovery. It is true she alleged in the former action that she was damaged because of the seduction, and in this one that she is damaged because of the breach of promise of marriage. These allegations, we think, however, must be regarded as only her conclusions and claims as to the extent of her damage. Both of these would have been equally appropriate concluding allegations in her complaint in each of the actions, and would not have changed the facts upon which her recovery must in its final analysis rest. So far as the question of res adjudicata is concerned, we think it is of no consequence as to whether the plaintiff may in her complaint evidence her intention to proceed upon the theory of recovering damages for seduction or for breach of promise of marriage, assuming of course that the facts alleged are so related as to show but one wrong, as we think the pleadings in appellant's former action and in this action do show. . . .

We conclude that appellant has had her day in court upon all of the issues here presented, and that the judgment rendered in the former action res judicata of all her rights in the premises. A trial of this action upon the issues raised by the final pleadings filed herein would be but a retrial of the issues finally raised by the pleadings, and upon which judgment was rendered in the former action.

The judgment is affirmed.

"Lack of Virtue" Before and During the Engagement—The Most Effective Defense to a Breach of Promise Action

> In 1936, the Court of Appeals of Kentucky reversed the lower court's judgment awarding damages in a breach of promise action because the woman's sexual encounters with other men both prior to and during the engagement period invalidated the engagement agreement. In this decision, which clearly reflects an earlier time's strong disapproval of a woman's rights to sexual freedom, the court found that, because of the woman's "lewd and lascivious conduct," there was no "contract of marriage."

BARRETT V. VANDER-MUELEN

264 KY. 441, 94 S.W.2D 983 (1936)

COURT OF APPEALS OF KENTUCKY

OPINION OF THE COURT BY STANLEY, COMMISSIONER—REVERSING.

This appeal is from a judgment for $15,000 on account of a breach of promise to marry. . . .

The plaintiff pleaded and proved a mutual promise to marry was made in October, 1930, and after a series of postponements, the engagement was broken by the defendant in January or in June, 1933. The defendant denied both in pleading and proof ever having promised to marry the plaintiff. He also alleged that both before and after the time stated in the petition that the engagement was entered into, the plaintiff was and is a woman of bad moral character and not virtuous, which was unknown to the defendant at all times, and "the defendant especially pleads and relies upon the bad character and morals and lack of virtue of the plaintiff in bar" of her claim and right of recovery. That was traversed. It is admitted in pleading and proof that the parties had engaged in repeated sexual relations. Testimony was admitted which tended to prove immorality and misconduct on the part of the plaintiff with other men *after* the date of the alleged contract to marry. The defendant testified that he was ignorant of all of that prior to the institution of this suit. It is not necessary to notice the pleading or evidence further.

However, the court excluded evidence of particular occasions of immorality on the part of the plaintiff with other men *prior* to the time she testified the engagement to marry was entered into. The appellant maintains this was error. The appellee's responsive argument is that since the defendant was ignorant of the claimed meretricious conduct, her incontinence or unchastity could not and did not cause the breach; hence the evidence was irrelevant and incompetent. 9 CJ 337; *Edmonds v. Hughes,* 115 Ky. 561, 74 S.W. 283, 24 Ky. Law Rep. 2467; *Watson v Bean,* 208 Ky. 295, 270 S.W. 801. We think appellee misconstrues the rule.

It is the legal as well as moral duty of persons who have plighted mutual vows to marry to preserve themselves during betrothal pure and blameless; and if a betrothed woman prostitutes her person to another man, it will mar her action for breach of the marriage contract. Contracts to marry, like contracts of marriage, are peculiar and distinguishable from ordinary contracts, since they establish a relation of extreme confidence between the parties and alter their status. The presumption of virtue always exists. If upon the strength of that presumption and in innocence of any misconduct one enters into an agreement to marry, and it develops that the other contracting party was not of that purity of virtue so impliedly represented and relied upon, there is fraud which vitiates the contract and the right of renunciation at any time arises. If such misconduct after marriage is sufficient in law to justify a divorce, a fortiori, it is a sufficient justification for not marrying. So it is that the guilt of one party and the innocence of the other constitutes for the latter a complete defense to an action for breach of contract; but conduct merely immodest, falling short of actual unchastity, does not. . . . And this is so even if the defendant did not know of plaintiff's unchastity until after the action is brought. *Colburn v. Marble,* 196 Mass. 376, 82 N.E. 28, 134 Am. St. Rep. 564. The law is thus stated in Schouler, Marriage, etc., section 1293. . . .

In this case the plaintiff's claims were that she was virtuous and the defendant had promised to marry her and refused, while the defendant's contentions were that she was unchaste and there was no promise. With these conflicting propositions, the evidence of unchastity of the one both before and after the engagement, and of innocence of the other was competent. Hence the rejection of the evidence was prejudicial error.

The second instruction given was as follows:

"If you believe from the evidence that the defendant, Thomas L. Barrett, agreed and promised to marry the plaintiff, Bessie Vander-Muelen, and she accepted said proposal, as set out in instruction No.1, and if you further believe from the evidence that the plaintiff, Bessie Vander-Muelen, had been guilty of such lewd and lascivious conduct as proved her to be unchaste, then you will consider such fact, if such is the fact, in mitigation of the damages, if any, that you will award to the plaintiff under instruction No. 3."

Evidence of unchastity or of bad reputation for virtue both before and after the engagement is competent for the purpose of reducing the recovery or in mitigation of damages where the defendant had knowledge of it. 4 R.C.L. 173. Under the respective claims of the parties, the defendant's being that plaintiff was guilty and he ignorant, such an instruction was improper.

The defendant offered the following instruction, which was refused: "If you believe from the evidence that before or after the plaintiff claims to have become engaged to marry the defendant, that said plaintiff was a lewd, unvirtuous, or immoral woman, and this fact was unknown to the defendant, then the law is for the defendant and you shall so find, even though you may believe that there was a contract of marriage between the plaintiff and the defendant."

This instruction was substantially correct, and it, or one like it, should have been given. Strictly speaking, there was no "contract of marriage," but a claimed contract to marry.

It is not necessary and we do not pass upon any other question raised. Wherefore, the judgment is reversed.

ALIENATION OF AFFECTION

In the early years of this century, the husband or the wife could sue a third party for becoming romantically or sexually involved with his or her spouse and interfering with or breaking up the marriage. This type of action, known as **alienation of affection,** has also met its demise because of changing cultural attitudes about the causes for marital breakups and because of more liberal attitudes toward not only divorce but also toward marital infidelity.

COMMON LAW MARRIAGE DISSOLUTIONS

By the end of the nineteenth century, the institution known as common law marriage was recognized in most states in the United States as a legal form of marriage that carried with it all of the rights and obligations of a ceremonial and statutorily memorialized union. Common law marriages were numerous in frontier states and in rural areas where the parties were often geographically distant from the county or municipal offices that issued marriage licenses. However, common law marriages also existed in urban areas. Today, many states have statutorily abolished common law marriage. Legal proceedings that affect common law marriages are becoming increasingly rare because so few states permit or recognize the formation of a common law marriage within their boundaries. However, states that do recognize common law marriages do adjudicate their dissolution. In addition, some states do not recognize the formation of a common law marriage within the state, but will recognize as legally valid a common law marriage formed in a state where common law marriage is legal. In these states, the courts will adjudicate the dissolution of these marriages as long as other jurisdictional requirements have been met.

What Is a Common Law Marriage?

In states where common law marriage is legal, a relationship is recognized as a common law marriage when two individuals live together and hold themselves out to the world as husband and wife. Each party must possess the legal capacity to marry. For example, each party must be mentally competent, of legal age, and neither party can be already married to another.

A valid common law marriage is as legally binding as a ceremonial marriage and children who are the issue of such a union are legitimate.

Why Choose Common Law Marriage

People may opt for a common law marriage for these reasons:

▼ *Convenience.* In the nineteenth century, while the frontier was being settled, parties pledged themselves to each other without benefit of clergy or state officials because they were miles away from either religious or governmental institutions.

▼ *Personal preference.* Some couples opposed and wished to avoid intrusion by either church or state. For instance, in the early decades of the twentieth century, many free-spirited individuals known as *Bohemians* lived in the Greenwich Village section of New York and scorned the legal and religious trappings of conventional society as bourgeois and artificial. Their common law marriages were often political or societal statements. Some Bohemians went even further with their protests and embraced living together instead of any legally binding arrangement.

▼ *Poverty.* Some couples simply had no money for a church wedding or for an official ceremony and the attendant costs of a marriage license and blood tests.

ANNULMENT

Annulments are alive and well in the United States today as the accompanying recent and much-publicized case illustrates. The winning contestant on the short-lived "Who Wants to Marry a Millionaire" television show soon discovered that sometimes it's not easier to *stay* married to a rich man than a poor man.

1   COMA

2   JOHN D. HANOVER, ESQ., Nevada Bar No. 6672
     RICHARD A. CALEEL, ESQ., Nevada Bar No. 6585
3   LAW OFFICES OF JOHN D. HANOVER
     3753 Howard Hughes Parkway, Suite 200
4   Las Vegas, Nevada 89109
     Telephone: (702) 836-8499
5

6   Attorneys for Plaintiff

7

8
                       EIGHTH JUDICIAL DISTRICT COURT
9
                         CLARK COUNTY, NEVADA
10

11
)
12   Darva Conger.   )
)
13   Plaintiff,   )
)
14   vs.   )   CASE NO. D251297
)   DEPT NO. C
15   Richard Scott Rockwell,   )
)
16   Defendant.   )
)
17   _____)

18

19   COMPLAINT FOR ANNULMENT

20

21   I.

22   Plaintiff entered into marriage ceremony in the City of Las Vegas, County of

23   Clark, State of Nevada, on or about the 8th day of February 2000, having first secured a

24   marriage license from the County Clerk of Clark County Nevada.

25

26   II.

27   There are no minor children the issue of said purported marriage.

28

                      DOCUMENT PREPARED ON RECYCLED PAPER

III.

There is no community property of the parties hereto.

IV.

The marriage has not been consummated and the parties to the marriage have not cohabitated at any time.

V.

The grounds for the annulment are fraud, pursuant to N.R.S. 125.340, and all equitable grounds pursuant to N.R.S. §125.350, including, but not limited to, mutual mistake in that the contract of marriage does not express the true intentions of the parties with regard to the marriage.

VI.

Plaintiff was a contestant on a televised show entitled "Who Wants to Marry A Millionaire" which was broadcast on February 15, 2000 (hereinafter the "Show"). The producers of the Show and the Fox Network (hereinafter "Fox"), the network that aired the Show, brought fifty female contestants to Las Vegas, Nevada, from all over the United States to compete on the Show for "the opportunity to marry a millionaire" and in exchange for certain gifts and prizes. The Defendant was the "millionaire" for whom the contestants competed. Each of the fifty contestants applied for a marriage license in Nevada so that if chose, the Show could conclude with a marriage ceremony, to be broadcast live, purporting to unite the perfect strangers as man and wife. The wedding ceremony, and the contest, were intended to draw millions of viewers and thereby generate significant revenues for the producers of the Show and Fox. Neither the contestants nor the Show's producers seriously contemplated creating a proper marriage. In fact, the Show's producers and Fox had each of the contestants and the defendant sign

1   an annulment agreement prior to the Show as a guaranty of the contestants' right to an

2   annulment.

3

4   VII.

5   *As part of the Show and for entertainment purposes,* Plaintiff and Defendant

6   agreed to be married on television with the understanding that the marriage was not of

7   legal force and effect and could be annulled following the show's televised broadcast.

8   Plaintiff, at the time she entered into the marriage, did not intend to become the actual

9   wife of the Defendant in law or in fact. Plaintiff is informed and believes that Defendant

10   did not intend to become the husband of Plaintiff in law or fact.

11

12   VIII.

13   At the time she entered into the purported marriage, Plaintiff relied in good faith

14   on the erroneous assertions of the Defendant and/or the Show's producers regarding

15   Defendant and his background. Defendant and/or the Show's producers misrepresented

16   material facts regarding Defendant's personality and his background to Plaintiff. Plaintiff

17   was unaware that Defendant had a history of problems with his prior girlfriends and was

18   the subject of at least one restraining order for threatening and dangerous behavior. Had

19   Plaintiff known the true and complete material facts at the time she entered into the

20   purported marriage, she would not have taken the action that she did. Plaintiff could not

21   reasonably discover the true facts regarding Defendant prior so the marriage since even

22   Defendant's identity was concealed from her until its revelation on live television just

23   moments before the purported marriage.

24

25   IX.

26   The marriage is the result of a mutual mistake of fact and was entered into solely

27   for an entertainment purpose. The parties did not intend that the marriage should be of

28

1   operative legal force or effect. Moreover, Plaintiff's purported consent is invalidated by

2   the misrepresentations upon which she reasonably relied.

3

4   WHEREFORE, Plaintiff prays that said purported marriage of plaintiff and

5   defendant may be, by an Order of the above-entitled Court, declared to be null and void

6   *ab initio* for the reasons hereinabove set forth, and for such other and further relief as to

7   the Court may deem just and proper.

8

9   DATED: March 3, 2000   LAW OFFICES OF JOHN D. HANOVER

10

11   By: *John D. Hanover*

12   John D. Hanover, Esq., Bar No. 6672

13   Richard A. Caleel, Esq., Bar No. 6585

14   3753 Howard Hughes Parkway

15   Suite 200

16   Las Vegas, NV 89109

17   Telephone (702)836-8489

18   Attorney for Plaintiff

19

20

21

22

23

24

25

26

27

28

Although *annulment* is not a totally unfamiliar term to the average layperson, most persons do not know how an annulment differs from a marital dissolution or divorce action. The legal theory underlying an annulment action is quite different from the action for divorce or dissolution of marriage. A person institutes a divorce or dissolution of marriage action to end a valid existing marriage. A person initiates an annulment proceeding to obtain a judicial decision that a valid marriage does not exist nor ever existed between that person and another party.

Just as a common law marriage may be legally formed without a formal ceremony, a formal ceremony does not always establish legal marriage. In an annulment action the court is called on to legally declare that despite ceremonial and state procedures, no legal marriage was formed or exists. A court may grant an annulment even if the parties obtained a marriage license and went through a marriage ceremony providing that the petitioning party alleges and proves that at the time of the marriage ceremony, an impediment existed to the forming of a legally valid marriage. The petitioning party must introduce evidence of facts or circumstance which the state legislature or state common law has determined constitute an impediment to the forming of a valid marital union.

Typical grounds for annulment can include incapacity because of minority age status, mental incompetence, one or both parties' involvement in the existence of a still legally valid marriage, the inability of one party to consummate the marital union through sexual intercourse, and fraud that is material to the decision to marry (such as lying about one's reproductive ability, withholding knowledge of one's own infertility, or withholding material information about one's criminal history or the state of one's health).

A person seeking an annulment must be one of the parties to the marriage, unless a party is legally a minor or mentally incompetent. In such instance, the party's parent, legal guardian, or conservator can bring the action. The person bringing the annulment action must institute an annulment proceeding in a family court.

Grounds for Annulment

As just summarized, a court can annul a marriage on proof of one of the following grounds:

1. Lack of capacity to enter into a valid marriage because:

    a. One or both parties were underage or were already married.
    b. One or both of the parties were not legally mentally competent.
    c. The couple is too closely related by blood.
    d. The couple is physically unable to consummate the marriage.

2. Lack of proper intent in that:

    a. One or both spouses were mentally disabled to the extent of *not* being able to understand or appreciate the nature of marriage.
    b. One or both parties were entering the marriage with no intention of entering a marital relationship or living in the marriage. For instance, at one time in the United States, a noncitizen could acquire U.S. citizenship by marrying a U.S. citizen. In many cases the citizen agreed to the marriage for monetary compensation, and sometimes did not meet the other person until the day of the ceremony and never saw the person again.

3. *Duress.* One party or both parties were forced into marriage by parents or others under threat of death or bodily harm.

4. *Fraud.* One party married the other party without knowing vital information about the other party, which, if it had been disclosed prior to the marriage, would have resulted in the first party not wishing to marry the other. Examples include failure to disclose infertility, a criminal history of felonious conduct, an incurable illness, or a history of severe mental illness.

Void versus Voidable Marriage

When a court is satisfied that the petitioning party has proven that a legal impediment existed at the time the marriage ceremony took place, the court may declare a marriage null and void. In some jurisdictions, where only certain grounds are proven, the court may be limited to declaring the marriage "voidable" rather than "void." For instance, where a petitioning party has brought an annulment action based on the legal incapacity due to minority age, if both parties are now of legal age, the court may issue a decision giving the petitioning party the legal right to void the marriage. However, if that party has reconsidered their decision to annul the marriage, the marriage may continue because the court will not void the marriage on its own initiative. Conversely, a court will always declare a marriage null and void on proof that one or both parties entered into a prior valid marriage and is still legally married to the party of the prior marriage.

LEGAL SEPARATION

An action for a **legal separation** is similar to a divorce or dissolution action in that specific grounds must be alleged and proven. The grounds that can be alleged are usually the same grounds that can be alleged in a divorce proceeding. Historically, an action for legal separation was brought by a spouse who desired to avoid the legal, social, or religious ramifications of a divorce but nevertheless wished to live apart from the other spouse. Legal separations are not as common today, but the action has survived and is still available to the spouse who wishes to pursue that course of action rather than divorce.

Courts granting legal separations may, when appropriate, order one spouse to provide for the financial support of the other spouse by making periodic payments to the spouse. Most courts will order the noncustodial spouse to pay child support to the custodial spouse for the minor children. Courts may also order an equitable distribution of marital property or may incorporate into the separation decree the parties' separation agreement in which the parties themselves have negotiated a division of the marital estate.

After a legal separation, both parties retain certain marital rights and obligations which are extinguished after a divorce is final. For instance, a spouse may still have to provide medical insurance coverage for the other spouse and will still be able to have that spouse covered under any family policy. Similarly, if an individual's pension plan, on that individual's death, calls for the payment of either a lump sum or partial or full periodic pension payments to the person's spouse, the spouse who has obtained a legal separation rather than a divorce will be eligible for such a benefit. In addition, if one party to a legal separation dies intestate, his or her spouse will be entitled to a statutory spousal share of the estate. If the deceased spouse had a will, then the other spouse may elect to receive either what was bequeathed to him or her in the will or to receive the statutory spousal share, and will usually select whichever amount is greater.

A legal separation also places limitations on spouses. The most restrictive limitation is that because the parties are still legally married, neither party is free to remarry.

SEPARATE MAINTENANCE

An action for **separate maintenance** is similar to a legal separation. The marriage is still valid and neither party is legally free to remarry. In addition, an action for separate maintenance affirms the continuation of the marriage and enforces the legal obligations of each spouse in the marriage. An action for separate maintenance does not expressly or necessarily authorize a husband or wife to live apart; however, a wife's refusal to cohabit with her husband is sanctioned and authorized. Actions for separate maintenance are less common today than in the nineteenth century and during the first half of the twentieth century. Sometimes they were initiated by a wife whose husband was about to go abroad or to another part of this country to work or to perform military service. On other occasions, the action for separation was a precursor to a divorce action brought during a period of marital discord or during a trial separation.

PATERNITY ACTIONS

Paternity actions are alive and well in the United States. In such a proceeding, the petitioning party, usually the child's mother, requests that the court hold a hearing to establish whether a particular man is the child's biological father. In many jurisdictions, a child born during an existing valid marriage is presumed to be the child of the husband. This presumption can be overcome by a conclusive showing that the husband had no access to the child's mother during the period of possible conception, by proof that the father was sterile during that period, or by medical evidence, such as the results of a blood test or DNA test that clearly rule out the husband as the biological father. When the mother of a child is unmarried at the time of a child's birth, the party seeking to establish the child's paternity may request that the court order a DNA testing of the possible father.

THE TRANSITION TO CONTEMPORARY FAMILY LAW THEORY AND PRACTICE

By the 1960s attitudes toward divorce were changing. Many young people no longer feared the severe sanctions imposed by their religious faith. Also, some religious groups took a more compassionate view of couples in a bad marriage. Traditional religious institutions lost much influence over individuals and society in the 1960s when people began to question all aspects of American culture, including women's roles and women's rights, constraints on employment opportunities for women, and constraints on sexual freedom and reproductive choices.

Prior to the 1960s, fault played a central role in both the granting of divorce and in the determination of the amounts set for alimony awards and the distribution of marital property. Beginning in the mid-1960s and growing strong in the 1970s, public support emerged for what came to be known as **no-fault divorce.** Beginning in the 1970s, a number of state legislatures modified existing divorce laws to include the ground that the marital union or marital relationship had broken down irretrievably. This ground did not place fault for the breakdown on either party. The spouse seeking the divorce and bringing the legal action had merely to testify under oath that the marriage had broken down irretrievably and that there was no possibility of reconciliation. This change plus the many societal changes mentioned earlier resulted in many more divorces than previously.

In addition, the 1970s witnessed the beginnings of a trend toward awarding custody to fathers even when mothers were not deemed unfit. Many custody battles ensued as mothers' work schedules paralleled fathers' in terms of time spent away from home.

Divorce actions also increased dramatically in segments of the married population where individuals previously never considered severing their marital ties. Older women, frequently with the support of and at the urging of their adult children, sought divorces after decades of troubled marriages. These women demanded a fair share not only of what they and their husbands had acquired during the marriage, but also a fair share of their husbands' pensions and Social Security benefits.

Another development arising from new social conditions dealt with health care provisions. With the advent of comprehensive health insurance and the skyrocketing costs of health care, courts routinely ordered the noncustodial spouse, often the father, to maintain his minor children and sometimes his former spouse on his health plan. Women with superior health plans through their employers also sometimes were required to cover former spouses and children even if they were not the children's custodial parent. Further, with women making large salaries, men began to seek alimony from former wives and courts began awarding it to them!

The increase in the number of divorces gave rise to an increase in second and third marriages. With this higher rate of divorce and remarriage, prenuptial agreements also increased in both number and complexity.

The trend toward easy and frequent divorce continued through the 1980s and 1990s. The mid-1990s saw the beginnings of social and political action to once again make divorces harder to obtain. Laws surrounding the severing of the marital relationship may well come full circle by the twenty-first century!

Family Law Attorneys Reject Return to Fault-Based Divorce Finds ABA Survey

WASHINGTON, DC, Oct. 18—Eighty-four percent of family lawyers oppose rescinding no-fault divorce laws according to a survey released today by the American Bar Association Section of Family Law.

"No-fault" divorce, available in some form in all 50 states, allows spouses to divorce without the assignment of blame. Prior to the adoption of no-fault laws in the 1970s, spouses were required to establish such fault-based grounds as adultery or mental or physical cruelty to obtain a divorce.

Legislatures in states such as Idaho, Michigan, and Iowa are among those currently examining their divorce laws and considering new legislation that is termed more "pro-family." Proposals typically include the establishment or extension of waiting periods before the divorce can be finalized; special education for parents so they understand the impact of divorce on their children; and returning to fault-based divorces. "Bad idea" say most of the more than 1,400 attorneys who responded to the ABA survey, when asked if there should be a return to fault-based divorce.

Continued on next page

The overwhelming majority of respondents, nearly 84 percent, say they do not support a return to fault-based divorces. Further, more than two-thirds (69 percent) of the respondents do not agree that there is a direct correlation between the increase in the divorce rate in this country and the advent of the no-fault divorce 20 years ago.

"Divorce is one of the most complex issues of our time," says Los Angeles attorney Ira Lurvey, chair of the 11,000-member ABA Family Law Section. "No single magic bullet is the answer. Fault was taken out of divorce 25 years ago to promote harmony and reduce fighting. Putting it back in will do little more than return those evils, plus an increased divorce rate. We don't get progress by going back to the past."

However, nearly one-third (30 percent) of respondents support two systems of divorce based on whether the divorcing spouses were parents, while 66 percent do not support such a differentiation.

Respondents indicate support for the idea that no-fault divorce helps families weather the storm of divorce better than they did under fault-based systems.

Two-thirds of respondents (67 percent) agree that no-fault divorces are typically quicker than fault-based divorces; More than two-thirds indicate that no-fault divorces are less expensive than fault divorces (69 percent); and 65 percent agree that no-fault divorces typically are less acrimonious than fault divorces.

Proponents of a return to fault-based divorce say it will cure a host of ills related to the dissolution of marriage. Most respondents in the ABA survey, however, disagree. When asked whether or not these problems would be solved by divorce by fault the percentage of lawyers saying "no" were:

financial disparity between the divorcing spouses—women consistently fare worse (86 percent);

the abandonment of the family by those who are unwilling or cannot abide the mandatory waiting periods currently in place in 24 states (88 percent); and

unfairness to victims of domestic violence who occasionally are treated with bias by the courts and/or in the mediation process (85 percent).

"What may help is a retraining program for all of us. We live in a world of false expectations and mixed messages. Marriage is not necessarily bells and whistles forever. It is hard work, caring and being selfless. Those are commodities often in short supply these days," said Lurvey. Respondents are more split on whether no-fault divorces are emotionally easier on the children involved. While nearly 58 percent agree that no-fault divorces are emotionally easier on children from the marriage, more than one-third (37 percent) do not agree.

When asked to consider the impact of no-fault divorce on the fathers' rights movement in custody, just over one-fourth (26 percent) of survey participants agree that no-fault divorce is more equitable in custody, while 59 percent do not agree.

More than half of respondents (54 percent) agree that judges still do consider fault in divorce today.

"Judges do consider fault, and in some states are required to do so, but almost exclusively in the division of property, not in granting the divorce," said Lurvey.

The survey of approximately 6,000 of the nation's top matrimonial lawyers was conducted via fax. 1,462 attorneys participated in the survey, yielding an approximate response rate of 24 percent.

REVIEW QUESTIONS

1. What status did the Greek legal system assign to a married woman?

2. How did the Married Women's Act of 1913 improve the status of women?

3. How did Christianity view marriage?

4. How did the rise of the various branches of Protestant religions change the concepts of marriage and divorce?

5. What was "divorce of bed and board"?

6. How did marriage and divorce become civil matters instead of religious matters in the American colonies?

7. Early in U.S. history, how was the issue of spousal support and child support handled?

8. How was a marital dissolution or divorce action similar to a breach of contract action?

9. What is meant by *grounds* for divorce and what were some of the grounds for divorce in the early years of the United States?

10. What were the early social and economic factors that discouraged a woman from seeking a dissolution of her marriage?

11. How did the Industrial Revolution change the character of the American family?

12. How did the Industrial Revolution affect a married woman's economic position?

13. In early America, why was divorce considered a stigma?

14. What were the most frequently used grounds for divorce in 1900?

15. Name two family law court actions that have virtually disappeared.

EXERCISES

1. Go to your local public library. Look in the history section for a book on the history of marriage. Review this book and summarize information found on marriage, divorce, and the rights of spouses and children at various periods in history and in various countries and civilizations. Also find a social history of ancient Greece, medieval England, nineteenth-century England, and colonial America. Summarize information on marriage and family rights and obligations for these time periods.

2. Go to your law library and locate your state's statute books from 1900, 1920, 1940, and 1950. Find the sections that deal with marriage, divorce, annulments, and paternity. Write a summary of the various statutes from each period and what changes were made from edition to edition.

3. Go to your local law library. Find your state's digest of cases. Locate the topics that deal with divorce, custody, annulment, and paternity. Find case summaries on each of these subjects for cases between 1800 and 1960. In case law reporters, find and copy older cases on as many of these four subjects as possible. Summarize three to five older cases and show how the law changed between 1800 and 1960 on any or all of these four subjects.

4. At your local law library, find a copy of the Married Women's Act of 1913 and provide a written summary of its main points.

5. At your local law library, find an older case dealing with the issue of alienation of affection or breach of promise. Prepare a case brief.

3 CHAPTER

ETHICS IN FAMILY LAW

KEY TERMS

Administrative Procedure Act

Attorney/client privilege

Authorized practice of law

Billable hours

Code

Competency

Complaint

Confidentiality

Conflict of interest

Contingent fees

Costs

Costs of litigation

Deep pocket

Disciplinary board

Earned retainer

Ethical wall

Fee

Fee agreement

Flat fee

Former client–current Opponent

Freelance paralegal

Grievance

Grievance committees

Hourly basis

Integrated bar association

Legal advice

Living expenses

Model Rules of Professional Conduct

Multiple representation

National Association of Legal Assistants, Inc.

National Federation of Paralegal Associations

Padding

Premium

Pro hac vice

Pro per

Pro se

Reciprocity

Release

Respondeat superior	Time slip
Retainer	Unauthorized practice of law
Rules of ethics	Unearned retainer
Sanction	Vicarious liability
Solicitation	Work product
Time sheet	

During the course of a typical workday, the family law paralegal will come in contact with a variety of people: clients, supervising attorneys, office staff, opposing counsel and their staff, sheriffs, lay and expert witnesses, and court personnel. In addition, they will also encounter a variety of situations in which they will have to make decisions regarding their professional conduct. Whatever paralegals do or say during the course of their employment will impact the client, their supervisor, and themselves. The statutes regulating the unauthorized practice of law and the rules of ethics are two aspects of the law that paralegals must become familiar with in order to conduct themselves properly on a daily basis. This chapter addresses the principles regulating paralegal conduct and provides paralegals with guidelines that will help them maneuver confidently through their busy schedules.

AUTHORIZED PRACTICE OF LAW

Every state has enacted statutes that establish the requirements necessary to obtain a license to "practice law" in that jurisdiction. The general criteria for obtaining a license to practice law require that an individual be a graduate of an accredited law school, possess a good moral character, and successfully pass the state bar exam. Once all statutory requirements have been met, the individual is admitted to the bar of that state and is **authorized to practice law** in that state only. If he or she wishes to practice law in another jurisdiction, he or she must meet that particular state's requirements for admission to the bar. This may include taking another bar exam. Some states do not require an attorney licensed to practice in another jurisdiction to take the state bar exam. One state may extend to attorneys in a different state the right to practice law in its jurisdiction in exchange for the other state's granting the same privilege to attorneys in their state. This is called **reciprocity.**

A state may allow out-of-state attorneys to practice law in its jurisdiction as long as the attorney has been practicing law in another state for a specified time and is a member in good standing of that state's bar. Other requirements must also be met, but they vary from state to state. A state may also grant an attorney special permission to handle one particular case. This is known as appearing ***pro hac vice.***

FIGURE 3–1
Statutory require-
ments for obtaining a
license to practice law
are imposed to protect
the public from
unqualified legal
representation.

UNAUTHORIZED PRACTICE OF LAW

Statutory requirements for obtaining a license to practice law are imposed to protect the public from unqualified legal representation. Although there has been
considerable discussion about licensing paralegals, as of 2000 no state had yet enacted such requirements. Even if paralegals were to be licensed by the state, they
could not engage in the practice of law. Only those individuals who have met the
state's statutory criteria may engage in the activities that constitute the practice of
law.

In addition to statutes regulating the practice of law, most jurisdictions have
enacted laws prohibiting the **unauthorized practice of law** or "UPL statutes,"
as they are commonly referred to in the paralegal profession. These statutes define
the unauthorized practice of law. Violation of the UPL statutes is a criminal offense. This means that a nonattorney can be prosecuted in criminal court for engaging in any activity that a UPL statute prohibits.

STATUTES

Illustrated below are the UPL statutes of Connecticut, Florida, California, and Texas. Each statute imposes a criminal penalty for its violation.

CONNECTICUT GENERAL STATUTES

SEC. 51-88. *Practice of law by persons not attorneys.*
(a) A person who has not been admitted as an attorney under the provisions of section 51-80 shall not: (1) Practice law or appear as an attorney-at-law for another, in any court of record in this state, (2) make it a business to practice law, or appear as an attorney-at-law for another in any such court, (3) make it a business to solicit employment for an attorney-at-law, (4) hold himself out to the public as being entitled to practice law, (5) assume to be an attorney-at-law, (6) assume, use or advertise the title of lawyer, attorney and counselor-at-law, attorney-at-law, counselor-at-law, attorney, counselor, attorney and counselor, or an equivalent term, in such manner as to convey the impression that he is a legal practitioner of law, or (7) advertise that he, either alone or with others, owns, conducts or maintains a law office, or office or place of business of any kind for the practice of law

(b) Any person who violates any provision of this section shall be fined not more than two hundred and fifty dollars or imprisoned not more than two months or both. . . .

FLORIDA STATUTES ANNOTATED (WEST)

454.23 PENALTIES. Any person not licensed or otherwise authorized by the Supreme Court of Florida who shall practice law or assume or hold himself or herself out to the public as qualified to practice in this state, or who willfully pretends to be, or willfully takes or uses any name, title, addition, or description implying that he or she is qualified, or recognized by law as qualified, to act as a lawyer in this state, and any person entitled to practice who shall violate any provisions of this chapter, shall be guilty of a misdemeanor of the first degree, punishable as provided in s. 775.082 or s. 775.083.

CALIFORNIA CODE

*BUSINESS AND PROFESSIONS CODE
SECTION 6125-6126*

6125. No person shall practice law in California unless the person is an active member of the State Bar.

6126. (a) Any person advertising or holding himself or herself out as practicing or entitled to practice law or otherwise practicing law who is not an active member of the State Bar, is guilty of a misdemeanor.

VERNON'S TEXAS CODES ANNOTATED

SEC. 38.123. *Unauthorized Practice of Law*
(a) A person commits an offense if, with intent to obtain an economic benefit for himself or herself, the person:

(1) contracts with any person to represent that person with regard to personal causes of action for property damages or personal injury;

(2) advises any person as to the person's rights and the advisability of making claims for personal injuries or property damages;

(3) advises any person as to whether or not to accept an offered sum of money in settlement of claims for personal injuries or property damages;

(4) enters into any contract with another person to represent that person in personal injury or property damage matters on a contingent fee basis with an attempted assignment of a portion of the person's cause of action; or

(5) enters into any contract with a third person which purports to grant the exclusive right to select and retain legal counsel to represent the individual in any legal proceeding.

(b) This section does not apply to a person currently licensed to practice law in this state, another state, or a foreign country and in good standing with the State Bar of Texas and the state bar or licensing authority of any and all states and foreign countries where licensed.

(c) Except as provided by Subsection (d) of this section, an offense under Subsection (a) of this section is a Class A misdemeanor.

(d) An offense under Subsection (a) of this section is a felony of the third degree if it is shown on the trial of the offense that the defendant has previously been convicted under Subsection (a) of this section.

UPL VIOLATIONS

Violations of the UPL statute may have additional consequences for the paralegal, including civil liability, and may give rise to disciplinary proceedings against the supervising attorney, which is addressed later in this chapter. The paralegal may also suffer loss of employment and experience difficulty finding a new job if word gets around in the legal community that the paralegal has engaged in the unauthorized practice of law. The activities discussed in the following subsections define the practice of law.

Representing Someone in Court or at Administrative Proceedings

Only attorneys are allowed to represent clients in court proceedings or administrative proceedings unless a specific state or federal statute or regulation allows a nonattorney to appear. There are limited circumstances in which a nonattorney may represent another person. The **Administrative Procedure Act,** 5 U.S.C.A. § 555 (1967), is a federal statute that allows a person appearing before a federal administrative agency to be represented by an attorney or, if the agency permits, "by other qualified individual." This means that you must consult the federal statutes and regulations to determine (1) if the particular agency allows nonattorneys to practice before it and, if so, (2) what requirements the nonattorney must meet in order to be deemed a "qualified representative" (i.e., testing, applications). Examples of agencies that allow nonattorneys to practice before them on an administrative level are the Internal Revenue Service, Social Security Administration, and Immigration and Naturalization Service.

Many states have similar statutes that allow nonattorneys to represent individuals before state agencies. In addition, nonattorneys are always allowed to represent themselves before any court or administrative body. These individuals who represent themselves are known as *pro se* or *pro per* litigants.

Legal Advice

This involves advising a client of his or her specific legal rights and responsibilities, and either predicting an outcome or recommending that the client pursue a particular course of action. Paralegals must be very careful so that they do not render **legal advice,** either to clients or to the public in general. A paralegal may experience pressure from family, friends, or clients to render a legal opinion. The best way to avoid this is to tell the individual that the rendering of legal advice by a nonattorney is a violation of the law and that the paralegal may be subject to criminal prosecution.

Paralegals are allowed to relay legal advice from the attorney to the client but must be careful not to add any additional advice to the clients that was not mentioned by the attorney. Paralegals must also be careful not to put legal advice in letters to a client that are signed by the paralegal and not the attorney.

Preparation of Legal Documents and Pleadings

Paralegals may prepare legal documents and pleadings under the supervision of attorneys. It is the responsibility of the attorney to review the documents and make sure they have been drafted correctly. The attorney is also responsible for signing legal documents and pleadings. Paralegals may sign a letter, but must indicate their paralegal status at the end of the letter. Preparation of legal documents without attorney supervision constitutes the unauthorized practice of law.

Lawyer's Supervision Required

In the following case, a paralegal advertised to prepare uncontested divorce papers for clients. The U.S. District Court was not swayed by the paralegal's constitutional arguments.

FIGURE 3–2
Paralegals may prepare legal documents under the supervision of attorneys.

NADINE O. MONROE V. DANIEL B. HORWITCH ET AL.

820 F. Supp. 682 (D. Conn. 1993)

United States District Court, Connecticut

Ruling on Pending Motions

DORSEY, DISTRICT JUDGE.

Plaintiff sues under 42 U.S.C. § 1983 alleging deprivation of her rights under the United States Constitution. Defendants move to dismiss.

I. BACKGROUND

Facts alleged in the complaint are assumed for purposes of a motion to dismiss. Plaintiff alleges that Conn. Gen. Stat. §51-88,[1] forbidding the unauthorized practice of law, violates the First Amendment, freedom of speech, and the Fourteenth Amendment, equal protection and due process. Plaintiff further alleges that Conn. Gen. Stat. §51-90a(2) and §51-90c(b)[2] unconstitutionally grant defendants, the Statewide Grievance Committee (SGC) and the Statewide Bar Counsel (SBC), respectively, criminal jurisdiction.

In October 1991, plaintiff, a paralegal, advertised an offer to prepare papers for parties representing themselves in uncontested divorce actions. In November 1991, defendant Horwitch, acting for SGC was investigating her, under Conn. Gen. Stat. §51-88, for the unauthorized practice of law. Plaintiff did not testify at a March 1993 hearing, refusing to recognize the SGC's authority to conduct or to subpoena her to said hearing.

The SGC found, based on her advertisement, that plaintiff's actions constituted the unauthorized practice of law. Because plaintiff had ceased running the advertisement and had not served any clientele, the SGC recommended dismissing the complaint without prejudice. It recommended pursuit of the complaint under Practice Book 31(c) if she resumes offering the services.[3] In June 1992, defendant informed plaintiff of the SGC's decision. Plaintiff alleges that since that time, Horwitch has threatened her with prosecution for criminal contempt if she resumes the practice in question. . . .

1. FIRST AMENDMENT FREEDOM OF EXPRESSION

The prohibition against unauthorized practice of law does not violate plaintiff's First Amendment right to freedom of speech . . . (citation omitted). "The practice of law is above that of a mere privilege. It cannot be treated as a matter of grace or favor. But it may be granted only upon fulfillment of certain rigid qualifications established by this court. The defendant had not fulfilled these qualifications and he is not therefore entitled to exercise the privilege bestowed upon those who have . . ." (citation omitted).

FOURTEENTH AMENDMENT

Due process

Statutes forbidding the "unauthorized practice of law" are "sufficiently definite" to withstand constitutional scrutiny . . . (citation omitted). An activity on the "outerboundaries" of the "practice of law" might be impermissibly vague. *Hackin,* 102 Ariz. at 221, 427 P.2d at 913. [P]reparation "of legal documents fall squarely within the boundaries.

. . . Plaintiff's vulnerability to Conn. Gen. Stat. § 51-88 arises from her offer to prepare court documents in uncontested divorce actions. Preparation of legal documents is "commonly understood to be the practice of law." *Grievance Committee v. Dacey,* 222 A.2d at 349. What constitutes "preparation of legal documents" is construed broadly.

---

[1]Conn. Gen. Stat. § 51-88 proscribes the practice of law by persons not attorneys. Subsection (b) provides: "Any person who violates any provision of this section shall be fined not more than two hundred and fifty dollars or imprisoned not more than two months or both."

[2]Conn. Gen. Stat. §§ 51-90a and 51-90c(b) each delineate the powers and duties of the State-wide Bar Committee and Counsel, respectively, to include "investigate and prosecute complaints involving the violation by any person of any provision of section 51-88."

[3]Conn. Prac. Book 31(c) provides in part: "A petition to restrain any person from engaging in the unauthorized practice of law not occurring in the actual presence of the court may be made by written complaint to the superior court in the judicial district where the violation occurs. . . . Such complaint may be prosecuted by the state's attorney, by the statewide bar counsel, or by any member of the bar by direction of the court. . . . Such complaints shall be proceeded with as civil action."

Preparation of instruments, even with *pre-printed forms* involves more than a "mere scrivener's duties" and, therefore, constitutes the practice of law. *State v. Buyers Service Co.*, 292 S.C. 426, 357 S.E.2d 15, 17 (1987). *See also Pulse v. North Am. Land Title Co.*, 218 Mont. 275, 707 P.2d 1105, 1109 (1985) ("drafting or filling in of blanks in printed forms of instruments dealing with land" constitutes the practice of law; *Kennedy v. Bar Ass'n*, 316 Md. 646, 561 A.2d 200, 208 (1989) (preparation of legal documents in patent case constitutes the practice of law). Legal documents purport to allocate legal obligation.

The preparation of documents in simple divorce actions unequivocally constitutes the practice of law. *See United States v. Hardy*, 681 F. Supp, 1326, 1328–29 (N.D. Ill. 1988) ("Common sense dictates that the drafting of even a simple complaint or an uncomplicated petition for dissolution of marriage requires at least some degree of legal knowledge or skill"); *McGiffert v. State ex rel. Stowe*, 366 So. 2d 680, 683 (Ala.1979) ("It would seem to be clear that only a licensed lawyer may obtain an uncontested divorce for another person without violating the statute"); *Florida Bar v. Brumbaugh*, 355 So. 2d. 1186, 1194 (Fla.1978) (assistance in preparation of dissolution of marriage forms constitutes the practice of law; *State Bar v. Cramer*, 399 Mich. 116, 249 N.W.2d 1, 9 (1976) (preparation of a client's no-fault divorce documents constitutes the practice of law). Such documents may assert, fail to assert or acknowledge legal rights.

Equal Protection

. . . The states have a "compelling interest" in the practice of professions. *Goldfarb v. Virginia State Bar*, 421 U.S.

773,793, 95 S. Ct. 2004, 2015–16, 44 L. Ed. 2d. 572 (1975). "As part of their power to protect the public health, safety and other valid interests they have broad power to establish standards for licensing practitioners and regulating the practice of professions." *Id.* The limitation of the practice of law to bar members "protects the public against rendition of legal services by unqualified persons." Conn. Prac. Book Rule 5.5 (comment). Such a limitation constitutes "protection" in that "the public can better be assured of the requisite responsibility and competence if the practice of law is confined to those who are subject to the requirements and regulations imposed upon members of the legal profession." ABA Model Code of Professional Responsibility, EC3-1 (1987).

A lawyer may delegate functions to a paralegal "so long as the lawyer supervises the delegated work and retains responsibility for their work." Conn. Prac. Book Rule 5.5 (comment). Oversight and accountability guarantee, so far as practicable, that the "requirements and regulations" imposed on lawyers will also ensure the quality of work of supervised paralegals (footnotes omitted). Prohibiting unsupervised paralegals from work with legal consequences is rationally related to public protection. *See Lawline v. American Bar Ass'n*, 956 F.2d 1378, 1385–86 (7th Cir. 1992). . . .

VI. CONCLUSION

Defendant's motion to dismiss (document #10) is granted.

Negotiating with Opposing Attorney in Pending Litigation

It is the attorney's job to negotiate with the opposing party's attorney in pending litigation. Paralegals may relay messages between their supervising attorney and opposing counsel, but must be careful not to use their independent judgment in making or accepting offers.

Accepting and Rejecting Cases

Only the attorney can determine whether or not to accept or reject cases. The paralegal must leave this task up to the attorney and cannot use independent judgment in deciding whether or not to accept a case. Paralegals may screen prospective clients upon instruction by attorneys in limited and specific instances. For instance, if a person calls the law office requesting representation in a personal injury matter, and the law office limits its practice to family law, the paralegal may communicate this information to the caller without referring the call to the attorney.

Setting and Collecting Fees

It is the attorney's responsibility to establish fees for legal services or collect fees from delinquent clients.

Maintaining an Office to Render Legal Services

Only attorneys may operate an office for the practice of law. Many paralegals run paralegal services companies, which generally provide paralegal services to attorneys or law firms on an as-needed basis. When a paralegal is retained, the attorney or firm that hired the paralegal will supervise him. In some jurisdictions, paralegal businesses may prepare legal documents for nonattorney individuals but must be careful not to render legal advice in the course of providing this service.

RULES OF ETHICS

Every profession has **rules of ethics.** Rules of ethics are standards of conduct that a profession demands from its members. Adherence to these standards of conduct is not limited only to attorneys. Attorneys often employ other attorneys, law students, paralegals, secretaries, clerks, and investigators to assist them in rendering legal services to clients. Supervising attorneys are obligated to see to it that all those employed by them are cognizant of the rules of ethics. Attorneys also hire **freelance paralegals** who are not employees of the attorney, but independent contractors who work for a number of attorneys on an as-needed basis. Attorneys supervise freelance paralegals in the course of performing each particular assignment. Freelance paralegals are also responsible for knowledge of the rules of ethics.

Attorneys and paralegals must work within the confines of the professional rules of ethics. Rules of ethics govern the manner in which the members of a profession conduct themselves. The legal profession holds itself to a high standard of conduct in order to facilitate a sense of trust and confidence among the general public and to preserve the integrity and respectability of the profession. The legal profession has a set of written rules called a **code** that establishes the guidelines for attorneys in their interactions with clients, courts, staff, and their obligations to the general public.

The American Bar Association (ABA) has established the **Model Rules of Professional Conduct** as a prototype for attorney ethics. Because the ABA is a national, voluntary bar association that does not have jurisdiction to oversee the legal profession, it has written the Model Rules of Professional Conduct (MRPC) as a model for states that wish to adopt them. A majority of the states have adopted the MRPC as their ethical code. Some states have not adopted the MRPC but follow the Model Rules of Professional Responsibility, which is the ABA's older model code.

The legal profession and licensed attorneys are under the control of the state's highest court, commonly referred to in most jurisdictions as the supreme court. Some states have **integrated bar associations** in which membership is mandatory. Other states require attorneys to register and pay fees to state bar associations or to the court or designated agency. State bar associations regulate the legal profession through disciplinary bodies known as **grievance committees** or **disciplinary boards.** These disciplinary bodies may **sanction** or punish attorneys for engaging in conduct that violates the state's code of professional conduct.

If a **complaint** or **grievance** is filed with the disciplinary body, attorneys have the right to a hearing and to an appeals process in order to defend their privilege to practice law in that jurisdiction. Attorney grievance proceedings may result in a variety of dispositions. If the allegations against an attorney are unsubstantiated, the grievance committee may dismiss the complaint. This is equivalent to "dropping the charges." If the allegations against an attorney are substantiated, the attorney may be reprimanded, put on probation, suspended, or even disbarred, depending on the seriousness of the offense.

Paralegals are not members of the bar and cannot join, vote, or hold office. In some jurisdictions paralegals may become associate members. The state agency or authority responsible for disciplining attorneys for unethical conduct does not have the same authority to impose sanctions on paralegals for engaging in unethical behavior. Therefore, it is important for paralegals to have a thorough knowledge of their jurisdiction's rules of professional conduct, which regulate attorneys, and of any ethical guidelines their state has established for paralegals. While national, state, and local paralegal associations like the **National Association of Legal Assistants, Inc.** (NALA) and the **National Federation of Paralegal Associations** (NFPA) have established their own ethical codes, membership in these organizations is voluntary. These organizations do not have any disciplinary authority over paralegals. The most that one of these paralegal associations can do is revoke a paralegal's membership in the association. The complete text of the NALA's Model Standards and Guidelines for Utilization of Legal Assistants is given in Exhibit 3–1 at the end of this chapter.

While the state bar association cannot discipline paralegals for violating the rules of ethics, their supervisors will be held responsible for any unethical conduct by paralegals. Attorneys who employ paralegals are obligated to supervise their employees' conduct and **work product.** Work product consists of the notes, materials, memoranda, and written records generated by the attorney, as well as the written records of the attorney's mental impressions and legal theories concerning the case. Attorneys are also ultimately responsible for the quality and accuracy of their paralegal's work product.

As mentioned, if paralegals violate an ethical rule, it is the attorneys who have to answer to the state disciplinary body, not the paralegals. Although grievance committees can punish only attorneys for unethical conduct, violation of certain ethical rules may expose not only the attorney, but also the paralegal, to civil lawsuits and/or criminal prosecution.

EXAMPLE

Johnny Swift, Esq., and his paralegal, Nona Williams, get bored one afternoon. They conspire to raid the Mary Smith Client Trust Account and go gambling in Atlantic City. They withdraw $50,000 from the account and take off for the casino. They lose the entire $50,000 at the roulette wheel. Mary finds out that her money was stolen by Swift and Williams.

▼   ▼   ▼

What are Mary's remedies?

1. *Grievance.* Smith may file a grievance against Swift with the state disciplinary body. A lawyer is obligated under the ethical rules to safekeep his client's property and to maintain a fiduciary relationship of trust and confidence with the client. Although the grievance committee can reprimand, suspend, or disbar Swift, it has no authority to discipline the paralegal,

Nona Williams. The consequences of a grievance will affect the attorney's privilege to practice law.

2. *Criminal.* Because Williams and Swift conspired to take the client's money, they committed a crime and may be subject to criminal prosecution. If a paralegal knowingly assists an attorney in committing a crime during the course of representation, both the paralegal and the attorney can be prosecuted. If a paralegal commits a crime on her own during the course of employment, both she and the attorney may be prosecuted. The consequence of a criminal prosecution is fine, imprisonment or both, or at the very least a criminal record.

3. *Civil.* Smith may also bring civil action against Swift and Williams alleging both the torts of civil conversion of Smith's money and malpractice. An aggrieved client may sue the attorney for injuries caused by the attorney or paralegal. An attorney and his staff owe a duty to effectively and ethically represent a client. In addition, an attorney is in a fiduciary relationship with the client. In this case, Swift owed Smith a fiduciary duty to safekeep her money. When the attorney breaches that duty and in the course of that breach the client suffers some type of loss, the client can sue the attorney for damages. The duty to Smith was breached when the money was removed from the client's trust account for personal use without the client's consent. Because the client's money was lost, the client was damaged, Smith can sue both Swift and Williams. The consequence of a civil suit is the payment of money damages to the client, if she prevails in the case.

What if Williams acted on her own in this case? Would attorney Swift be civilly responsible for her actions? The answer is yes. An employer is **vicariously liable** or responsible for the negligence and other torts committed by his employees when the acts are committed during the scope of their employment. This is known as the doctrine of ***respondeat superior.*** Even if Williams acted alone in the above scenario, Smith may bring a civil action naming both the attorney and paralegal as defendants.

Although the client may sue both the attorney and the paralegal, the attorney is eventually the best defendant in the case because of his deep pocket. **Deep pocket** is the term applied to characterize the defendant in a lawsuit who has the financial resources to absorb a civil suit for monetary damages. Attorneys ordinarily carry malpractice insurance, which will cover them in civil lawsuits brought by their clients for their negligent acts or mistakes. However, malpractice insurance will not cover an attorney in a civil action based on a criminal act or for an intentional tort. Some states, such as Connecticut and New Jersey, require contributions from attorneys to fund accounts to reimburse clients in this type of situation.

Malpractice insurance usually covers the negligent acts of attorneys and sometimes the negligent actions of the attorney's staff; however, this is not always the case. Paralegals should inquire as to whether or not they are covered under a firm's malpractice insurance. Attorneys pay a **premium,** which is a monetary sum paid on an annual or installment basis for malpractice insurance coverage. The policy is renewable on a yearly basis. Attorneys must notify their malpractice carrier immediately on becoming aware that they have committed an act, error, or omission that could result in a civil lawsuit.

This chapter does not intend to exhaust all of the ethical rules that apply to attorneys. It only provides a general overview of the basic ethical principles paralegals must become familiar with in the course of a family law practice. As stated earlier, paralegals must become thoroughly familiar with the rules of ethics that apply to attorneys in their jurisdiction and any ethical guidelines the state bar associations of their states have developed for them. Ethical codes established by paralegal associations also provide excellent guidelines. Paralegals should review the ethical rules on a regular basis in order to refresh their knowledge and update themselves on any changes in the rules or opinions interpreting them. If a paralegal has even the slightest concern about an ethical issue, the paralegal should always consult with the supervising attorney before taking action. Communication is a good way to minimize problems that could expose the firm to a grievance or malpractice suit. While supervising styles differ in the legal profession, conscientious attorneys will appreciate the paralegal's attention and cautiousness.

There are many ethical challenges in the area of family practice. This area of the law is emotionally draining because it thrusts two people who once shared a life together into an adversarial system that is normally not conducive to amicable resolutions. Almost 50 percent of today's marriages end in divorce, and the proceedings involved may represent the first time a client is exposed to the legal system. Their expectations of what the legal system can do may be based on bad legal advice obtained from talk shows, magazine articles, or friends. When the results of a dissolution case do not live up to these expectations, an attorney may become the target of a disgruntled client. Paralegals should keep this in mind when performing their daily activities and their conduct should conform to a strict adherence to the rules of ethics and UPL statutes.

In addition to knowing and observing ethical boundaries, the following office procedure tips will assist paralegals in protecting their supervising attorneys firm malpractice claims and grievance proceedings:

1. Promptly return client phone calls, log client contact in the client file, and reduce client conversations to a writing to avoid any misunderstandings that can later be used against the attorney or paralegal. The attorney should review the file entries and client correspondence and maintain the attorney/client relationship.

2. Perform assignments in a timely fashion to avoid delays.

3. Identify professional status at all times and explain to those unfamiliar with the paralegal profession the limitations the law has placed on nonattorneys.

4. Keep track of all important court dates and make sure they are appropriately marked in the office master calendar and the attorney's personal calendar promptly.

5. Disclose any conflicts of interest to the attorney relating to the paralegal.

6. Promptly relay client information to the attorney so action can be taken on a client's case.

OVERVIEW OF BASIC ETHICAL PRINCIPLES

CONFIDENTIALITY

The ethical rule of **confidentiality** protects communications between attorneys and their clients. Paralegals working for attorneys, either as employees or freelance independent contractors, are equally obligated to be guardians of client information revealed during the course of representation. Attorneys cannot disclose information related to the representation of a client. There are two exceptions to this rule. The attorney may reveal such information after obtaining the client's consent. This means that the client has given his or her attorney the permission to disclose information to another party. This permission should always be obtained in writing, in the form of a document called a **release,** which the paralegal may be asked to draft. Paralegals should also be very careful when disclosing information under the consent exception. The file should be consulted at all times to verify the existence of a release, to whom the information may be disclosed, and to what extent. Under most circumstances, the attorney may disclose most information to the paralegal who is working on the client's file. The paralegal, as an employee of the attorney or law firm, will have the same obligation to maintain client confidentiality.

Under the second exception, attorneys may reveal client confidences when they have a reasonable belief that clients will engage in conduct that is likely to result in substantial bodily harm or death. The purpose of this rule is to prevent such crimes from occurring rather than reporting them to the authorities after the fact.

EXAMPLE

During an office visit with his attorney, a very distraught client pulls out a .357 magnum pistol and reveals his plans to kill his wife.

In this scenario, if the attorney reasonably believes that her client will engage in conduct that may result in death or a serious physical injury, she may have an ethical obligation to inform the authorities of her client's plans for the purpose of

FIGURE 3–3
Paralegals should refrain from engaging in unethical conduct such as gossiping about clients' cases.

stopping the crime before it takes place. If however, the client first committed the murder and then broke down and confessed his crime to the lawyer, the attorney is under no ethical obligation to notify anyone! The communications between the attorney and client are confidential, privileged, and protected by law.

Paralegals must take special precautions to protect client confidentiality. If clients arrive early for an office appointment and start talking about their case in the reception area, paralegals should politely instruct clients to wait until they have privacy with the attorney before they discuss their case. Other clients or delivery or repair persons may be within earshot of the client's personal business, and once clients have disclosed information in the presence of a third party that disclosure is not protected by the rules of confidentiality.

Paralegals should also be protective of client files, correspondence, or other materials and should not leave them in open view where other clients or visitors may see them. Therefore, reception areas, interview rooms, and any other area where clients or visitors may roam should be free of client information.

Paralegals should also avoid taking calls from clients while in the presence of other clients. If it is an emergency, the paralegal should use a separate room, which lends itself to privacy. If no separate room is available, the call should be very short and paralegals should not reveal the caller's name or any other information. Care should also be taken when visitors such as repair, delivery, or cleaning personnel are in the office. Again, client documents should be kept out of sight and oral communications should be brief and discreet.

The paralegal who works in a family practice office will often be privy to the most intimate details of a client's marital relationship. Sometimes these details may be shocking, scandalous, or simply humorous or ridiculously funny. The paralegal may be tempted to share with friends or family some of the spicier portions of clients' files. Paralegals should avoid doing so, at all costs! Technically, an attorney, paralegal, or any other employee of a law firm will not violate client confidentiality if they disclose information that is already a matter of public record in the court system or in any other office of public records such as the town land records office or town tax assessor. However, even when questioned about this already public information, the wisest and most prudent course of action for the paralegal to pursue is to refrain from any disclosures of a client's business.

The client's right to confidentiality also extends to the courtroom. Attorneys or paralegals may find themselves summoned to testify in a case involving the client. Whether or not the attorney or paralegal may provide testimony is based on evidentiary rule called the **attorney/client privilege.** In a judicial proceeding, it is up to the client to decide whether or not she will allow the attorney or any of his staff to disclose confidential client information on the witness stand. The client is the holder of the privilege and unless the client consents, the attorney or paralegal must not answer any questions, but simply assert the attorney/client privilege.

CONFLICT OF INTEREST

"You can't serve two masters" best describes this rule of ethics. Attorneys owe their clients a duty of loyalty and must exercise their independent judgment in the course of representation. Any activity that may divide an attorney's loyalty and compromise her independent judgment is a **conflict of interest.** The following subsections present an overview of the various activities that might result in a conflict of interest situation.

Multiple Representation

Sometimes divorcing couples decide to save money by hiring one lawyer to represent both spouses. This is known as **multiple representation** and presents unique ethical problems for attorneys.

Legal Services Out of Control

Not only do we have a serious conflict of interest in the accompanying multiple representation case, but also documents forged by the firm's paralegal!

PETERS V. HYATT LEGAL SERVICES

220 Ga. App. 398, 469 S.E.2d 481 (Ga. App. 1996)

Court of Appeals of Georgia

POPE, PRESIDING JUDGE.

This is the second appearance of this legal malpractice, breach of contract, breach of fiduciary duty, breach of statutory duty case before this court. See *Peters v. Hyatt Legal Svcs.*, 211 Ga. App. 587, 440 S.E.2d 222 (1990). After a bifurcated trial, the jury awarded plaintiff Richard Peters $10,000 in nominal damages, $35,545.10 in attorney's fees and expenses to litigation, and $175,000 in punitive damages against Hyatt Legal Services (Hyatt). The trial court granted Hyatt's motion for judgment notwithstanding the verdict on punitive damages, and Peters appeals.

Richard E. Peters brought suit against Hyatt, Hyatt attorney Linda Gross and the Hyatt legal assistant and notary public Kasonya M. Storey for damages resulting from Hyatt's representation of Peters in an uncontested divorce action. Although defendant Gross died after Peters filed the complaint, she was aware that legal action had been threatened.

Peters and his former wife were married on July 2, 1986, and had one child. Both were enlisted personnel in the United States Army with Mr. Peters stationed in West Germany. In January 1988, Peters discovered his wife in bed with another man. Peters and his wife took steps to separate legally that same month. Counsel for Mrs. Peters in West Germany prepared a proposed settlement agreement which Mrs. Peters executed on June 24, 1988. However, Peters did not agree to the proposed terms and did not sign the agreement.

On October 14, 1988, Peters returned to the United States on military leave to obtain a divorce. He consulted Hyatt attorney Linda Gross, paying $222.50, half the total fee for an uncontested divorce. Peters signed a fee agreement with Hyatt and signed his name on the signature line titled "client."[1] Peters returned to West Germany and expected the paperwork would be sent to him within 30 days, and that he would then receive a bill for the balance of the fee. He testified he told Gross if she provided him with 30 days' notice he expected that he could obtain the military leave necessary to be present in court. When Mrs. Peters asked him about the status of the pending divorce, Peters provided her with the name and address of Gross. Although Peters told his wife he would send the remaining money to Hyatt, Mrs. Peters indicated to him she would satisfy the balance while she was in the United States later in the month. Peters testified he did not authorize his wife to consult with Gross, but only to pay the balance so the divorce could proceed.

In December 1988, Mrs. Peters paid the outstanding balance and Gross began representing her. Although Peters thought that Hyatt continued to represent him, Gross had no contact with him after his initial visit. Instead, Gross filed the complaint for divorce with Mrs. Peters as plaintiff on December 29, 1988, the day after Mrs. Peters went to Hyatt and paid the remainder of the fee. It is undisputed that the acknowledgment of service of the complaint dated December 29, 1988, contains a forged signature of Richard E. Peters, notarized by Kasonya M. Storey, a Hyatt employee. Nor is it disputed that the consent to final hearing dated December 29, 1988, witnessed

---

[1] The Hyatt Legal Services Fee Statement provided. "When half the total attorney fee and costs is paid, we will complete preparation of the paperwork. When your account is paid in full, we will file the case. This is not binding until you make a payment. Your signature allows us to represent you after payment is made."

by Linda M. Gross, the Hyatt attorney, contains a forged signature of Richard E. Peters.

The forged acknowledgment and forged consent were filed with the petition for divorce on December 29, 1988. A final judgment and decree was thereafter entered on January 31, 1989. After Peters discovered the divorce was final, he contacted Hyatt to find out what had transpired and Hyatt informed him that the file had been lost. Peters then obtained the paperwork directly from the court, discovered the forged signatures, and realized something was wrong.

Peters first contends that the trial court erred in granting j.n.o.v. on the issue of punitive damages. We agree. . . .

OCGA § 51-12-5.1(b) provides that "[p]unitive damages may be awarded in only such tort actions in which it is proven by clear and convincing evidence that the defendant's actions showed willful misconduct, malice, fraud, wantonness, oppression, or *that entire want of care which would raise the presumption of conscious indifference to consequences.*" (Emphasis supplied)

Peters presented the following evidence of Hyatt's entire want of care from which the jury could have determined the evidence raised the presumption of conscious indifference to consequences. It is undisputed that the forged documents were at all times in Hyatt's sole custody and control. It is undisputed that Hyatt represented adverse parties in a divorce proceeding without obtaining the informed consent of both. Peters presented evidence of a conflict of interest and breach of fiduciary duty. Mrs. Peters testified that the Army Legal Center refused to represent both her and her husband. Hyatt's own expert testified he would not allow an attorney in his office to represent both parties to a divorce. Peters' expert testified Gross' conduct was "unethical," "improper," "illegal," and constituted a breach of her agreement with Peters. Peters' expert also claimed Gross had a duty to inform Peters of his case. Yet Peters testified that after he paid half the fee, Hyatt never sent him any paperwork or contacted him in any way. Peters also testified that when he returned stateside and contacted Hyatt, he was told his file had been lost. Hyatt's employee, Storey, admitted she sometimes notarized documents without people signing in her presence, a violation of the statutory duty impose by OCGA § 45-17-8(e). No evidence was presented that Hyatt's so-called audit procedure properly detected the conflict problem. For the foregoing reasons, we reject Hyatt's contention that there was insufficient factual evidence to support an award of punitive damages.

Hyatt argues that neither dual representation nor witnessing the forging of Peters' signature supports the imposition of punitive damages because punitive damages are not allowed for violation of an ethical rule. *Allen v. Lefkoff, Duncan, Grimes & Dermer, P.C.,* 265 Ga. 374, 453 S.E.2d 719 (1995). However, Hyatt has distorted the holding of *Allen.* The Supreme Court held that *standing alone,* an alleged violation of the Code of Professional Responsibility or the Standards of Conduct cannot serve as a legal basis for a legal malpractice action. Moreover, evidence of even a potential conflict of interest is sufficient to raise a jury issue on punitive damages in a legal malpractice case. *Read v. Benedict,* 200 Ga. App, 4, 6(2), 406 S.E.2d 488 (1991).

Although attorneys may represent two opposing parties, provided that both parties consent, this could be disastrous in cases involving family relations. Parties may wish to retain a single lawyer's services on the promise that they have come to an agreement as to the distribution of their assets, the disposition of custody, and so on. The parties may represent that they merely need someone to act as a scribe for their agreement and to get them through the court system. The problem is that the amicable divorce of today can turn into the World War III of tomorrow. In addition, a client may find that after having consulted an attorney and learning of his or her legal rights, the agreement originally made with the other spouse may not be in his or her best interest. This puts the lawyer in an awkward position as both an advocate and as a counselor.

The parties may also have revealed confidential information to one attorney that can be used against them later. If attorneys have heard confidential information regarding the case, it would be unethical for them to represent one spouse versus the other. Before hearing any confidential information, attorneys may take on the representation of one spouse and direct the other spouse to obtain independent representation.

Former Client–Current Opponent

Attorneys and paralegals who switch jobs and go from one firm to another present special ethical problems. During their course of employment, attorneys and paralegals are privy to clients' confidential information. Upon switching jobs, an attorney or paralegal may discover that a former client is now the adversary of one of the clients in the new firm.

EXAMPLE

John Doe is a paralegal who works at Law Firm A. Law Firm A represents Mrs. Smith in the divorce matter of Smith v. Smith. John Doe leaves Law Firm A and is now employed at Law Firm B, who represents Mr. Smith in the divorce case. John must immediately inform his new supervisor of the existence of a conflict. Because he previously worked on this case at Law Firm A, he cannot work on the same case in Law Firm B.

If John were allowed to work on the case, the danger exists that he could use the confidential information obtained in Mrs. Smith's case against her interests, in favor of Mr. Smith. Law Firm B must now build an **ethical wall** around John. This means that John cannot discuss the case with anyone in the office, nor can he have access to the file.

Another activity that may raise a conflict of interest is the commonly used tactic by one spouse seeking a divorce to obtain a free consultation from a variety of well-known divorce attorneys in the community. Confidential information is then revealed during the course of these initial consultations so as to preclude their spouses from retaining those attorneys' services. The unscrupulous spouse will then raise a conflict of interest claim alleging that he is the former client of the attorney and request that the attorney be disqualified from representing his spouse. The paralegal should carefully log the names of all clients, even if they just come to the office for an initial consultation, to avoid any conflict of interest challenges.

Sexual Relations with Clients

Attorneys and paralegals should not engage in sexual relations with clients during the course of the client's representation! Clients going through a divorce may be very vulnerable and emotionally devastated. Unfortunately, unscrupulous attorneys take advantage of clients in this position and may engage in romantic relations or actual sexual harassment. Such a dynamic may influence attorneys to act contrary to a client's best interest. Sometimes paralegals work very closely with divorce clients over an extended period of time. The intimacy of working together may lead to a mutual personal attraction. If this attraction is acted on during the course of the representation of the client, the paralegal has put herself in an ethically precarious position. Only after representation has been completed should a paralegal consider having any sort of personal relationship with a client.

Sex and the Legal Assistant

The *Logan* case illustrates the serious breach of client confidentiality and conflict of interest problems involved when a legal assistant has an affair with a client's husband.

GERALDINE L. LOGAN V. HYATT LEGAL PLANS, INC.

874 S.W.2D 548(MO. APP. W.D. 1994)

MISSOURI COURT OF APPEALS, WESTERN DISTRICT

PER CURIAM:

Geraldine Logan appeals from the trial court's order dismissing with prejudice her first amended petition for damages against Hyatt Legal Plans, Inc., a Delaware corporation. Her petition asserted that Hyatt Legal Plans, Inc., is liable for the tortious conduct of Dori Dolinar, a secretary and legal assistant who worked in the "Hyatt Legal Services" office during the time that an attorney in that office represented Logan in an action for dissolution of marriage. The trial court, concluding there could be no basis of vicarious liability against Hyatt Legal Plans, Inc., dismissed the action with prejudice. We now reverse and remand.

Prior to and during the time of her dissolution proceeding in October 1991, Logan was employed by American Telephone & Telegraph (AT&T). One of the benefits offered to eligible non-management AT&T employees was a group legal services plan which provided pre-paid personal legal services. . . .

. . . Logan claims that she was referred to Jay Crotchett of "Hyatt Legal Services" in Kansas City after calling the 800 number listed in the plan. Crotchett was employed in the law office operating under the name "Hyatt Legal Services." Logan apparently assumed that Crotchett was employed by Hyatt.

On May 16, 1991, Logan retained Crotchett as her attorney to represent her in a dissolution proceeding. Although she and her husband, John Gragg, were separated, they both attended the initial meeting at the Hyatt Legal Services office. At that meeting, Logan and Gragg met Dori Dolinar, a secretary and legal assistant, employed by the law firm. Shortly thereafter, Dolinar allegedly began a sexual relationship with Gragg that continued throughout the dissolution proceedings. There is no allegation in the petition that either Jay Crotchett or Allen Lebovitz were aware of Dolinar's involvement with Gragg during Crotchett's representation of Logan. Logan alleges that during the time she was being represented by Crotchett, Dolinar secretly disclosed to Gragg various confidential communications between Logan and her attorney as to her negotiating posture, and that Dolinar counseled and encouraged Gragg to refuse to pay certain portions of the marital debt, to renege on previous commitments, to threaten

bankruptcy, and to refuse any offers of reconciliation with his wife.[1]

Following the dissolution of her marriage, Logan learned of Dolinar's involvement with Gragg and brought suit against Hyatt alleging that the corporation was vicariously liable for the tortious conduct of Dolinar. Hyatt filed a motion to dismiss, contending that Hyatt could have no liability because "Hyatt Legal Services" was a separate entity from Hyatt and that neither Dolinar nor Crotchett were agents or employees of Hyatt. The motion to dismiss was sustained by the court and Logan was granted thirty days to file an amended petition. . . .

. . . An employer may be held liable for the negligent acts or omissions of his employee under the doctrine of respondeat superior if those acts are committed within the scope of employment. *Studebaker v. Nettie's Flower Garden, Inc.*, 842 S.W.2d 227, 229 (Mo. App. 1992). In this case, all of the alleged misconduct of which Logan complains is attributed to Dolinar. The affidavit of Andrew Kohn, General Counsel of Hyatt, asserts that at the time of the alleged misconduct, Dolinar was employed by Allen Lebovitz, a sole proprietor of a law firm using the trade name "Hyatt Legal Services." The affidavit states that Dolinar was not paid and had never been an employee or agent of Hyatt and offers the conclusion that Hyatt had no actual control or right to control the activities of Ms. Dolinar. . . .

. . . On this appeal, Plaintiff argues that, based on the content of the summary plan booklet, defendant is estopped from denying liability for Dolinar's conduct. Plaintiff essentially argues that the content of the summary plan booklet created an impression, upon which plaintiff reasonably relied, that the legal services would be provided by an employee of Hyatt Legal Plans. . . . At this early stage of the case, we will give plaintiff's pleadings (and proposed pleadings) the broadest possible intendment for purposes

---

[1]Logan alleges Dolinar was guilty of various acts of a tortious nature. Some of the alleged tortious conduct is no longer cognizable in Missouri. *See Thomas v. Siddiqui*, 869 S.W.2d 740 (Mo. banc 1994) (where the Missouri Supreme Court abolished the tort of criminal conversation). Stripped to its basics, the claim would seem to be essentially a claim of legal malpractice based on Dolinar's conduct, which was disloyal to Logan.

of our review, in view of the finality of a disposition by summary judgment.

A provision in the plan booklet states that "Hyatt Legal Plans or the law firms providing services under the plan are responsible for all services provided by their attorneys." This provision could be interpreted as a statement that Hyatt *is at least contingently responsible* for legal services provided under the plan. Also, the plan booklet states that service of process "concerning legal services provided under the plan should be directed to" Hyatt. Another provision of the booklet, which concerns liability with regard to legal services and attorney conduct, states: "[y]ou should understand that AT&T, the unions, the Plan and their directors, officers, and employees have no liability for the conduct of any plan attorney or the services provided." This sentence does *not* say that *Hyatt Legal Plans, Inc.* has no liability in connection with such services, and the term "the Plan" is not synonymous with Hyatt Legal Plans, Inc., in the definitions set forth in the booklet (footnote omitted). Since the summary plan booklet is not entirely supportive of the idea that Hyatt has no relationship to Dolinar upon which liability could be imputed, there remained some reasonable question as to the nature of the relationship between Hyatt Legal Plans, Inc. and "Hyatt Legal Services."

Plaintiff's intention to plead a theory of vicarious liability was cut short by the action of the court in dismissing the case without prior notice to plaintiff that the court was considering, in effect, a summary judgment ruling. . . . It is difficult to imagine how plaintiff intends to show that Dolinar's actions were within the scope of her employment or agency when there is no apparent reason to believe that Dolinar's actions were undertaken in the interest of her employer, or were encouraged or tolerated by her employer. Crotchett, who was engaged in representing Logan, ordinarily would have no reason to countenance Dolinar's involvement with Gragg, which was disloyal to Logan and could have interfered with Crotchett's ability to secure a favorable result for Logan. However, we cannot say that it is impossible to imagine a set of facts in which Crotchett or Lebovitz could hypothetically have involved themselves in the matter to such a degree that vicarious liability is appropriate. . . . Plaintiff should be given an opportunity to explore the possibility of any malfeasance by Crotchett or Lebovitz, and to explore the relationship between Hyatt and "Hyatt Legal Services." Consequently, we reverse and remand the case. We conclude that there remain some genuine issues of material fact.

Loaning Money to a Client

Attorneys may advance the **costs of litigation** to a client. These costs include filing fees, sheriff's fees, deposition costs, expert witness fees, and excessive photocopying and mailing costs. **Living expenses,** however, may not be advanced to a client. This includes any monies for client's personal use.

Gifts from a Client

Clients may often show their appreciation by making a gift to attorneys or paralegals. There is nothing wrong with accepting a gift from a client as long as the transferring of that gift does not include the preparation of legal documents like a deed, will, trust, or letter. An attorney may prepare a document that includes in it a bequest or transfer of property to that attorney if the attorney is related to the donor. If the attorney is not related to the donor, it is best for the attorney to send the donor to another lawyer to avoid later allegations of undue influence.

COMMUNICATING WITH OPPOSING PARTY

Attorneys and paralegals may not communicate directly with the opposing party if that party is represented by legal counsel. It is unethical to communicate directly with a represented adversary without the opposing attorney's permission, which is rarely obtained. This ethical rule protects represented individuals from being approached by the opposing party and gathering information to be used against them.

Sometimes defendants who have been served with "divorce papers" may call the plaintiff's attorney and demand to speak to someone. If an opposing party contacts the office by telephone, paralegals should instruct that party to have his or her attorney contact the office. The conversation should go no further.

If an opposing party contacts the office in writing, the paralegal should inform the supervising attorney immediately.

THE PRO SE LITIGANT

As you learned in the previous section, legal professionals cannot communicate with opposing parties if they are represented by counsel; instead they must communicate directly with the opposing party's legal representative. Sometimes, an individual may elect to self-representation, acting as a *pro se* or *pro per* litigant in order to save money, or they may just wish to handle their own representation. It is important to navigate carefully when dealing with persons who are not represented by counsel. First, it is prudent to ask the *pro se* party to forward a letter confirming the self-representation. In addition, if there is a pending proceeding, the opposing party must file an appearance with the court indicating self-representation. The office should request a copy of the appearance from the *pro se* party and verification of its filing through the clerk's office. While this procedure may seem like a cumbersome formality, it enables attorneys to formally confirm the opposing party's status as a *pro se* litigant.

It is also prudent to communicate with a *pro se* party in writing when at all possible so that the office has a record of the communication. While many *pro se* litigants represent themselves with dignity and a high degree of professionalism, some *pro se* litigants abuse the legal system and resort to unethical conduct. Having communications in writing avoids the "he said, she said" situations that can occur when the office relies on telephone communications as opposed to written documentation. When telephone communications do occur, paralegals must carefully log all phone calls to keep the file current.

Attorney and paralegals must also take care not to offer legal advice to *pro se* parties or take unfair advantage of them because of their lack of knowledge of the legal system. Paralegals should also avoid engaging the *pro se* party in any unnecessary communications.

COMPETENCE

Attorneys have a duty to render competent legal representation to their clients. **Competency** is the duty to exercise a reasonable degree of care and skill commonly used by other attorneys engaged in a similar area of practice. Paralegals must also deliver competent services in assisting attorneys in client representation.

Competency is attained by engaging in activities that educate attorneys as to the most efficient and effective manner of representing a particular client. The following activities help educate attorneys:

1. *Attendance at continuing legal education seminars.* Such seminars are provided by local bar associations, local paralegal associations, and by private entities.
2. *Associating with more experienced attorneys.* Experienced attorneys who possess adequate knowledge and skill in their particular area of practice frequently, either informally or through organized legal mentor programs,

share their knowledge and expertise with attorneys who are new to their area of practice.

3. *Consulting statutes, case law, legal periodicals, journals, and other legal publications.* The practice of law is flexible in that attorneys can practice in a variety of areas as long as they become competent in those areas. Paralegals also enjoy this flexibility and work in different areas of practice as long as they too become competent and are supervised by attorneys. The ethical duty of competency is ongoing and imposes on attorneys and paralegals the obligation of continually educating themselves and upgrading their skills.

It is important for paralegals involved in family practice to review their jurisdiction's domestic relations statutes and relevant case law and to attain familiarity with the forms used in their state. State bar associations and local paralegal associations may periodically offer seminars in family practice, of which the paralegal should take full advantage. In addition, state bar publications and legal periodicals focusing on the jurisdictional law and procedures should be read on a regular basis to keep current on changing legal developments.

FIGURE 3–4
It is important for family law paralegals to review their state's domestic relations law and attain familiarity with the forms used in their jurisdiction.

FEES

Attorneys should charge "reasonable" **fees.** The factors considered when determining what is "reasonable" are the skill and experience of the attorney, the simplicity or complexity of the client's matter, the cost of similar service in the community, the result obtained, the reputation of the attorney, and whether the matter is contested or uncontested.

Divorce attorneys may be compensated for their legal services by employing any one of the following fee arrangements:

Flat Fee

Under a **flat fee** arrangement, a fixed dollar amount is agreed on and charged for the entire case. Flat fees are sometimes charged in uncontested divorce cases where the parties have no children, no property, and no disputed issues between them.

Hourly Rates

Attorneys may also charge clients on an **hourly basis.** This means that they will bill the client for each hour of time spent working on a client's file, including, but not limited to, research, drafting documents, phone calls, travel, office visits, trial preparation, and interviewing witnesses. Attorneys often bill in tenth or quarter hours.

Attorneys will also charge for expenses or **costs,** such as filing fees, sheriff's fees, and court reporter fees for transcripts and depositions.

Retainer Arrangement

Another type of fee arrangement is the requiring of a **retainer** prior to the attorney committing himself or herself to representation of a client. A retainer is a payment made in advance to an attorney. The attorney will deposit the retainer in a client trust account and withdraw amounts from the retainer in proportion to the amount of work expended on the client's file. For example, a client gives his attorney a retainer of $2,000 to represent him in a divorce matter. The attorney bills at the rate of $200 an hour. Once the attorney has completed ten hours of work on the case, he is entitled to withdraw the **earned retainer.** If the attorney spent only five hours on the client's case, the attorney would be entitled to an earned retainer of $1,000 and would be obligated to return the **unearned retainer** to the client.

Contingent Fee Arrangement

Attorneys may also be paid under a **contingent fee** arrangement, which entitles attorneys to a percentage of the financial outcome of the case, be it a judgment or settlement. Contingent fee arrangements are frequently used in personal injury cases and in other areas of civil litigation where the plaintiff lacks the financial resources to provide a retainer or pay the customary hourly rates. Many contingent fee arrangements provide that the attorney will receive one-third of the judgment or settlement amount the client recovers. Contingent fees are unethical in divorce cases because they discourage attorneys from accepting a settlement if they do not feel that the offer is adequate enough to cover their fee. They may push the parties to trial in order to seek a better disposition. Under these circumstances, they are acting in their best interests, not the client's.

Fee Agreements: Putting It in Writing

Attorneys should always enter into written **fee agreements** with their clients so as to avoid any confusion regarding the attorney's billing practices. In fact, many jurisdictions require fee agreements between attorneys and clients to be in writing.

The fee agreement should specify the services to be performed by the attorney, the charge to the client, and the costs of litigation to be paid by the client. If the attorney uses paralegals in her law practice, the attorney should specify the paralegal's hourly rate for the performance of paralegal duties and the hourly rate for routine clinical tasks such as excessive photocopying, typing, filing. Charging a client the attorney's rate for performing paralegal or clerical tasks is unethical.

Paralegal Fees

The *McMacklin* case outlines the criteria for setting paralegal fees and the importance of differentiating between attorney, paralegal, and secretarial work in client billing practices.

JAMES H. MCMACKLIN V. MARIANNE C. MCMACKLIN

651 A.2D 778 (1993)

FAMILY COURT OF DELAWARE, NEW CASTLE COUNTY

OPINION

CROMPTON, JUDGE.

The following is my decision regarding attorney's fees in the above-entitled matter. I have reviewed Affidavits for Fees submitted by counsel for both James H. McMacklin (hereinafter "Husband") and Marianne C. McMacklin (hereinafter "Wife"). Wife's total attorney's fees, paralegal fees and costs amount to $12,785.50. Husband's total attorney fees, paralegal fees and costs are $9,768.35.

. . . In the past, Family Court Judges have treated paralegal fees in a variety of ways. Some Judges have permitted them. Others have steadfastly denied them. In my view, paralegal costs should be uniformly allowed, so long as certain information is specifically addressed by the supervising attorney in the fee affidavit presented to the Court.

13 *Del.C* § 1515 is the controlling statute regarding an award of fees following a division of marital assets and debts. That statute reads as follows:

The Court from time to time after considering the financial resources of both parties may order a party to pay all or part of the cost to the other party of maintaining or defending any proceeding under this title and for attor-

ney's fees, including sums for legal services rendered and costs incurred prior to the commencement of the proceeding or after the entry of judgment. The Court may order that the amount be paid directly to the attorney, who may enforce the order in his name.

The phrase "all or part of the costs of the other party of maintaining or defending" has previously been found broad enough to include fees incurred by a legal assistant or paralegal (citation omitted). . . .

. . . The United States Supreme Court has found that the term "attorney's fee" refers not only to the work performed by members of the Bar but also to reasonable fees for the work product of an attorney, which includes the work of paralegals, law clerks and recent law graduates at market rates for their services. *Missouri v. Jenkins*, 491 U.S. 274, 109 S. Ct. 2463, 105 L. Ed. 2d 229 (1989). . . .

. . . Paralegal fees are not a part of the overall overhead of a law firm. Paralegal services are billed separately by attorneys, and these legal assistants have the potential for greatly decreasing litigation expenses and, for that matter, greatly increasing the efficiency of many attorneys. By permitting paralegal fees, the danger of charging these fees off as the attorney's work is hopefully extinguished. By the same token, the danger of charging off a secretary's services as those of a paralegal is very real and present, thereby mandating that certain information be provided by the supervising attorney before paralegal fees can be awarded by this Court in the future. Those criteria are as follows:

1. The time spent by the person in question on the task;

2. The hourly rate as charged to clients (will vary based on expertise and years of experience);

3. The education, training or work experience of the person which enabled him or her to acquire sufficient knowledge of legal concepts. The Court recognizes that not all those who work in a paralegal capacity have a paralegal degree or license, but many of these people do possess expertise, which should be recognized in family law matters;

4. The type of work involved in detail. The work must *not* be purely clerical or secretarial in nature. Such work would fall under costs and may not be charged as paralegal fees at the market rate. The task must contain substantive legal work under the direction or supervision of an attorney such that if that assistant were not present, the work would be performed by the attorney and not a secretary. However, the assistant may not do work that only an attorney is allowed to do under the rules of practice and ethics. Substantive legal work which may be performed by legal assistants and billed at the market rate includes, but is not limited to, such activities as:

(a) Factual investigation, including locating and interviewing witnesses;

(b) Assistance with depositions, interrogations and document preparation;

(c) Compilation of statistical and financial data;

(d) Checking legal citations;

(e) Correspondence with clients/opposing counsel/courts; and

(f) Preparing/reviewing/answering petitions and other pleadings.

. . . Applying the above standards to the two Affidavits received in the matters *sub judice,* it is evident that both of them contain the required information. Both affidavits clearly comply with all four criteria previously discussed. For example, they describe the time spent by the paralegal, the hourly rate, and the education training or work experience of the paralegal. The type of affidavit submitted by Husband's counsel is exactly what this Court expects when reviewing fees. The affidavit of Wife's counsel leaves a bit to be desired in that it merely attaches invoices sent to the client. These invoices are very difficult to read and should be consolidated into one document with a separate affidavit attached by the paralegal. Husband's affidavit complies in every respect, but Wife's affidavit is certainly within the guidelines. Both attorneys have described in detail the type of work performed by the paralegal. This work includes such activities as reviewing depositions, preparing subpoenas, reviewing discovery, assisting in preparing Rule 52(d) Submissions, conferences with clients and correspondence. Clearly the type of work involved is that which would normally have been prepared or accomplished by the attorney and not a secretary.

Having made the decision that paralegal fees are and will be henceforth permissible by this Court, and having also decided that the Affidavits presented by counsel in this specific case rise to the required standards, I nevertheless must make a determination of counsel fees in accordance with 13 *Del. C.* § 1515, supra. . . .

. . . Husband has stated in his answer to Wife's Motion for Counsel Fees that he has no cash available to pay her fees. It is my opinion that his substantial income of approximately $82,000.00 per year versus Wife's income of approximately $35,000.00 per year mandates that he pay 60% of her fees or $7,671.30. This amount is to be added to the lump sum which Husband owes to Wife and is to be paid at the same time.

IT IS SO ORDERED.

In a law office, time is money; therefore there is a lot of emphasis on **billable hours.** This is the amount of time expended on a particular case, which can later be billed to that client. There is a lot of pressure in many firms to achieve a certain number of billable hours on a yearly basis. Attorneys and even paralegals are under similar pressure to produce billable hours. This pressure may lead some attorneys and paralegals to engage in unethical billing practices.

Paralegals record the time spent working on client files on forms called **time sheets** or **time slips.** Time sheets and time slips are used as a record of work performed on behalf of a client that will be billed to them on a periodic basis (see Exhibit 3–2). These documents should include the client's name, file number, spaces to log the date, activity performed on the client's file, and time actually spent. Every time the paralegal performs a task on the client's file, it is important to log the appropriate information on the client's time sheet. The time sheet should be completed at the same time the work is done. Several risks arise if time sheets are not completed in a timely manner. The paralegal may forget to include tasks performed, which would cheat the law firm out of earned revenue. Conversely, the paralegal may increase the time spent on a particular task, which would cheat the client and risk engaging in the unethical practice of **padding.** Padding means unjustifiably increasing the number of hours actually spent on a client's case. Padding is not only fraudulent, but also illegal since you are, in effect, stealing from the client.

Establishing Legal Fees

Just as it is the attorney's role to accept or reject cases, the attorney is also the only one who may set legal fees. Paralegals cannot set legal fees. This is for the attorney to determine after he has consulted with the client. Attorneys are also prohibited from splitting fees with nonattorneys. For example, attorneys and paralegals may not enter into an agreement whereby the paralegal is paid a percentage on each client file. Attorneys may compensate paralegals through a weekly salary or on an hourly basis. In addition, the attorney may also offer the paralegal fringe benefits such as bonuses, retirement plans, and health insurance coverage.

SOLICITATION

Paralegals cannot be paid for cases that they refer to the office. While paralegals may hand out the attorney's business cards and be a source of referral, paralegals cannot be compensated for the cases referred. The ethical rule prohibiting this practice is called **solicitation.** The public commonly uses the phrase "ambulance chasing" to describe this conduct. Attorneys cannot actively seek out persons they know are in need of legal services, either by mail or in person, unless there already exists an attorney/client relationship or a family relationship. However, attorneys may solicit clients if they wish to volunteer their legal services for free. In addition, attorneys may advertise their services to the general public through the media, by having listings and advertisements in the telephone directory and on the Internet, and by having advertising spots on television and the radio.

EXAMPLE 3–1

Standards and guidelines for utilization of paralegals.

NATIONAL ASSOCIATION OF LEGAL ASSISTANTS, INC.

Model Standards and Guidelines for Utilization of Legal Assistants

INTRODUCTION

The purpose of this annotated version of the National Association of Legal Assistants, Inc. Model Standards and Guidelines for the Utilization of Legal Assistants (the "Model," "Standards" and/or the "Guidelines") is to provide references to the existing case law and other authorities where the underlying issues have been considered. The authorities cited will serve as a basis upon which conduct of a legal assistant may be analyzed as proper or improper.

The Guidelines represent a statement of how the legal assistant may function. The Guidelines are not intended to be a comprehensive or exhaustive list of the proper duties of a legal assistant. Rather, they are designed as guides to what may or may not be proper conduct for the legal assistant. In formulating the Guidelines, the reasoning and rules of law in many reported decisions of disciplinary cases and unauthorized practice of law cases have been analyzed and considered. In addition, the provisions of the American Bar Association's Model Rules of Professional Conduct, as well as the ethical promulgations of various state courts and bar associations have been considered in the development of the Guidelines.

These Guidelines form a sound basis for the legal assistant and the supervising attorney to follow. This Model will serve as a comprehensive resource document and as a definitive, well reasoned guide to those considering voluntary standards and guidelines for legal assistants.

▼▲▼▲▼▲▼▲▼▲▼▲▼▲▼▲▼

I. PREAMBLE

Proper utilization of the services of legal assistants contributes to the delivery of cost-effective, high-quality legal services. Legal assistants and the legal profession should be assured that measures exist for identifying legal assistants and their role in assisting attorneys in the delivery of legal services. Therefore, the National Association of Legal Assistants, Inc., hereby adopts these Standards and Guidelines as an educational document for the benefit of legal assistants and the legal profession.

COMMENT

The three most frequently raised questions concerning legal assistants are (1) How do you define a legal assistant; (2) Who is qualified to be identified as a legal assistant; and (3) What duties may a legal assistant perform? The definition adopted in 1984 by the National Association of Legal Assistants answers the first question. The Model sets forth minimum education, training and experience through standards which will assure that an individual utilizing the title "legal assistant" has the qualifications to be held out to the legal community and the public in that capacity. The Guidelines identify those acts which the reported cases hold to be proscribed and give examples of services which the legal assistant may perform under the supervision of a licensed attorney.

These Guidelines constitute a statement relating to services performed by legal assistants, as defined herein, as approved by court decisions and other sources of authority. The purpose of the Guidelines is not to place limitations or restrictions on the legal assistant profession. Rather, the Guidelines are intended to outline for the legal profession an acceptable course of conduct. Voluntary recognition and utilization of the Standards and Guidelines will benefit the entire legal profession and the public it serves.

II. DEFINITION

The National Association of Legal Assistants adopted the following definition in 1984:

Legal assistants, also known as paralegals, are a distinguishable group of persons who assist attorneys in the delivery of legal services. Through formal education, training, and experience, legal assistants have knowledge and expertise regarding the legal system and substantive and procedural law which qualify them to do work of a legal nature under the supervision of an attorney.

COMMENT

This definition emphasizes the knowledge and expertise of legal assistants in substantive and procedural law obtained through education and work experience. It further defines the legal assistant or paralegal as a professional working under the supervision of an attorney as distinguished from a non-lawyer who delivers services directly to the public without any intervention or review of work product by an attorney. Statutes, court rules, case law and bar associations are additional sources for legal assistant or paralegal definitions. In applying the Standards and Guidelines, it is important to remember that they were developed to apply to the legal assistant as defined herein.

Lawyers should refrain from labeling those who do not meet the criteria set forth in this definition, such as secretaries and other administrative staff, as legal assistants.

For billing purposes, the services of a legal secretary are considered part of overhead costs and are not recoverable in fee awards. However, the courts have held that fees for paralegal services are recoverable as long as they are not clerical functions, such as organizing files, copying documents, checking docket, updating files, checking court dates and delivering papers. As established in *Missouri v. Jenkins*, 491 U.S.274, 109 S.Ct. 2463, 2471, n.10 (1989) tasks performed by legal assistants must be substantive in nature which, absent the legal assistant, the attorney would perform.

There are also case law and Supreme Court Rules addressing the issue of a disbarred attorney serving in the capacity of a legal assistant.

III. STANDARDS

A legal assistant should meet certain minimum qualifications. The following standards may be used to determine an individual's qualifications as a legal assistant:

1. Successful completion of the Certified Legal Assistant ("CLA") certifying examination of the National Association of Legal Assistants, Inc.;
2. Graduation from an ABA approved program of study for legal assistants;
3. Graduation from a course of study for legal assistants which is institutionally accredited but not ABA approved, and which requires not less than the equivalent of 60 semester hours of classroom study;
4. Graduation from a course of study for legal assistants, other than those set forth in (2) and (3) above, plus not less than six months of in-house training as a legal assistant;
5. A baccalaureate degree in any field, plus not less than six months in-house training as a legal assistant;
6. A minimum of three years of law-related experience under the supervision of an attorney, including at least six months of in-house training as a legal assistant; or
7. Two years of in-house training as a legal assistant.

For purposes of these Standards, "in-house training as a legal assistant" means attorney education of the employee concerning legal assistant duties and these Guidelines. In addition to review and analysis of assignments, the legal assistant should receive a reasonable amount of instruction directly related to the duties and obligations of the legal assistant.

COMMENT

The Standards set forth suggest minimum qualifications for a legal assistant. These minimum qualifications, as adopted, recognize legal related work backgrounds and formal education backgrounds, both of which provide the legal assistant with a broad base in exposure to and knowledge of the legal profession. This background is necessary to assure the public and the legal profession that the employee identified as a legal assistant is qualified.

The Certified Legal Assistant ("CLA") examination established by NALA in 1976 is a voluntary nationwide certification program for legal assistants. The CLA designation is a statement to the legal profession and the public that the legal assistant has met the high levels of knowledge and professionalism required by NALA's certification program. Continuing education requirements, which all certified legal assistants must meet, assure that high standards are maintained. The CLA designation has been recognized as a means of establishing the qualifications of a legal assistant in supreme court rules, state court and bar association standards and utilization guidelines.

Certification through NALA is available to all legal assistants meeting the educational and experience requirements. Certified Legal Assistants may also pursue advanced specialty certification ("CLAS") in the areas of bankruptcy, civil litigation, probate and estate planning, corporate and business law, criminal law and procedure, real estate, intellectual property, and may also pursue state certification based on state laws and procedures in California, Florida, Louisiana and Texas.[1]

IV. GUIDELINES

These Guidelines relating to standards of performance and professional responsibility are intended to aid legal assistants and attorneys. The ultimate responsibility rests with an attorney who employs legal assistants to educate them with respect to the duties they are assigned and to supervise the manner in which such duties are accomplished.

COMMENT

In general, a legal assistant is allowed to perform any task which is properly delegated and supervised by an attorney, as long as the attorney is ultimately responsible to the client and assumes complete professional responsibility for the work product.

ABA Model Rules of Professional Conduct, Rule 5.3 provides:

With respect to a non-lawyer employed or retained by or associated with a lawyer:

(a) a partner in a law firm shall make reasonable efforts to ensure that the firm has in effect measures giving reasonable assurance that the person's conduct is compatible with the professional obligations of the lawyer;

(b) a lawyer having direct supervisory authority over the non-lawyer shall make reasonable efforts to ensure that the person's conduct is compatible with the professional obligations of the lawyer; and

(c) a lawyer shall be responsible for conduct of such a person that would be a violation of the rules of professional conduct if engaged in by a lawyer if:

(1) the lawyer orders or, with the knowledge of the specific conduct ratifies the conduct involved; or

(2) the lawyer is a partner in the law firm in which the person is employed, or has direct supervisory authority over the person, and knows of the conduct at a time when its consequences

can be avoided or mitigated but fails to take remedial action.

There are many interesting and complex issues involving the use of legal assistants. In any discussion of the proper role of a legal assistant, attention must be directed to what constitutes the practice of law. Proper delegation to legal assistants is further complicated and confused by the lack of an adequate definition of the practice of law.

Kentucky became the first state to adopt a Paralegal Code by Supreme Court Rule. This Code sets forth certain exclusions to the unauthorized practice of law:

For purposes of this rule, the unauthorized practice of law shall not include any service rendered involving legal knowledge or advice, whether representation, counsel or advocacy, in or out of court, rendered in respect to the acts, duties, obligations, liabilities or business relations of the one requiring services where:
A. The client understands that the paralegal is not a lawyer;
B. The lawyer supervises the paralegal in the performance of his or her duties; and
C. The lawyer remains fully responsible for such representation including all actions taken or not taken in connection therewith by the paralegal to the same extent as if such representation had been furnished entirely by the lawyer and all such actions had been taken or not taken directly by the attorney. Paralegal Code, Ky.S.Ct.R3.700, Sub-Rule 2.

South Dakota Supreme Court Rule 97-25 Utilization Rule a(4) states:

The attorney remains responsible for the services performed by the legal assistant to the same extent as though such services had been furnished entirely by the attorney and such actions were those of the attorney.

Guideline 1

Legal assistants should:

1. Disclose their status as legal assistants at the outset of any professional relationship with a client, other attorneys, a court or administrative agency or personnel thereof, or members of the general public;
2. Preserve the confidences and secrets of all clients; and
3. Understand the attorney's Rules of Professional Responsibility and these Guidelines in order to avoid any action which would involve the attorney in a violation of the Rules, or give the appearance of professional impropriety.

COMMENT

Routine early disclosure of the legal assistant's status when dealing with persons outside the attorney's office is necessary to assure that there will be no misunderstanding as to the responsibilities and role of the legal assistant. Disclosure may be made in any way that avoids confusion. If the person dealing with the legal assistant already knows of his/her status, further disclosure is unnecessary. If at any time in written or oral communication the legal assistant becomes aware that the other person may believe the legal assistant is an attorney, immediate disclosure should be made as to the legal assistant's status.

The attorney should exercise care that the legal assistant preserves and refrains from using any confidence or secrets of a client, and should instruct the legal assistant not to disclose or use any such confidences or secrets.

The legal assistant must take any and all steps necessary to prevent conflicts of interest and fully disclose such conflicts to the supervising attorney. Failure to do so may jeopardize both the attorney's representation of the client and the case itself.

Guidelines for the Utilization of Legal Assistant Services adopted December 3, 1994, by the Washington State Bar Association Board of Governors states:

"Guideline 7: A lawyer shall take reasonable measures to prevent conflicts of interest resulting from a legal assistant's other employment or interest insofar as such other employment or interests would present a conflict of interest if it were that of the lawyer."

In Re Complex Asbestos Litigation, 232 Cal. App. 3d 572 (Cal. 1991), addresses the issue wherein a law firm was disqualified due to possession of attorney-client confidences by a legal assistant employee resulting from previous employment by opposing counsel.

The ultimate responsibility for compliance with approved standards of professional conduct rests with the supervising attorney. The burden rests upon the attorney who employs a legal assistant to educate the latter with respect to the duties which may be assigned and then to supervise the manner in which the legal assistant carries out such duties. However, this does not relieve the legal assistant from an independent obligation to refrain from illegal conduct. Additionally, and notwithstanding that the Rules are not binding upon non-lawyers, the very nature of a legal assistant's employment imposes an obligation not to engage in conduct which would involve the supervising attorney in a violation of the Rules.

The attorney must make sufficient background investigation of the prior activities and character and integrity of his or her legal assistants.

Further, the attorney must take all measures necessary to avoid and fully disclose conflicts of interest due to other employment or interests. Failure to do so may jeopardize both the attorney's representation of the client and the case itself.

Legal assistant associations strive to maintain the high level of integrity and competence expected of the legal profession and, further, strive to uphold the high standards of ethics.

NALA's Code of Ethics and Professional Responsibility states:

A legal assistant's conduct is guided by bar associations' codes of professional responsibility and rules of professional conduct.

Guideline 2

Legal assistants should not:

1. Establish attorney-client relationships; set legal fees; give legal opinions or advice; or represent a client before a court, unless authorized to do so by said court; nor

2. Engage in, encourage, or contribute to any act which could constitute the unauthorized practice of law.

COMMENT:

Case law, court rules, codes of ethics and professional responsibilities, as well as bar ethics opinions now hold which acts can and cannot be performed by a legal assistant. Generally, the determination of what acts constitute the unauthorized practice of law is made by State Supreme Courts.

Numerous cases exist relating to the unauthorized practice of law. Courts have gone so far as to prohibit the legal assistant from preparation of divorce kits and assisting in preparation of bankruptcy forms and, more specifically, from providing basic information about procedures and requirements, deciding where information should be placed on forms, and responding to questions from debtors regarding the interpretation or definition of terms.

Cases have identified certain areas in which an attorney has a duty to act, but it is interesting to note that none of these cases state that it is improper for an attorney to have the initial work performed by the legal assistant. This again points out the importance of adequate supervision by the employing attorney.

An attorney can be found to have aided in the unauthorized practice of law when delegating acts which cannot be performed by a legal assistant.

Guideline 3

Legal assistants may perform services for an attorney in the representation of a client, provided:
1. The services performed by the legal assistant do not require the exercise of independent professional legal judgment;
2. The attorney maintains a direct relationship with the client and maintains control of all client matters;
3. The attorney supervises the legal assistant;
4. The attorney remains professionally responsible for all work on behalf of the client, including any actions taken or not taken by the legal assistant in connection therewith; and
5. The services performed supplement, merge with and become the attorney's work product.

COMMENT:

Legal assistants, whether employees or independent contractors, perform services for the attorney in the representation of a client. Attorneys should delegate work to legal assistants commensurate with their knowledge and experience and provide appropriate instruction and supervision concerning the delegated work, as well as ethical acts of their employment. Ultimate responsibility for the work product of a legal assistant rests with the attorney. However, a legal assistant must use discretion and professional judgment and must not render independent legal judgment in place of an attorney.

The work product of a legal assistant is subject to civil rules governing discovery of materials prepared in anticipation of litigation, whether the legal assistant is viewed as an extension of the attorney or as another representative of the party itself Fed. R.Civ. P. 26 (b)(2).

Guideline 4

In the supervision of a legal assistant, consideration should be given to:
1. Designating work assignments that correspond to the legal assistant's abilities, knowledge, training and experience;
2. Educating and training the legal assistant with respect to professional responsibility, local rules and practices, and firm policies,
3. Monitoring the work and professional conduct of the legal assistant to ensure that the work is substantively correct and timely performed;
4. Providing continuing education for the legal assistant in substantive matters through courses, institutes, workshops, seminars and in-house training; and
5. Encouraging and supporting membership and active participation in professional organizations.

COMMENT:

Attorneys are responsible for the actions of their employees in both malpractice and disciplinary proceedings. In the vast majority of cases, the courts have not censured attorneys for a particular act delegated to the legal assistant, but rather, have been critical of and imposed sanctions against attorneys for failure to adequately supervise the legal assistant. The attorney's responsibility for supervision of his or her legal assistant must be more than a willingness to accept responsibility and liability for the legal assistant's work. Supervision of a legal assistant must be offered in both the procedural and substantive legal areas. The attorney must delegate work based upon the education, knowledge and abilities of the legal assistant and must monitor the work product and conduct of the legal assistant to insure that the work performed is substantively correct and competently performed in a professional manner.

Michigan State Board of Commissioners has adopted Guidelines for the Utilization of Legal Assistants (April 23, 1993). These guidelines, in part, encourage employers to support legal assistant participation in continuing education programs to ensure that the legal assistant remains competent in the fields of practice in which the legal assistant is assigned.

The working relationship between the lawyer and the legal assistant should extend to cooperative efforts on public service activities wherever possible. Participation in pro bono activities is encouraged in ABA Guideline 10.

Guideline 5

Except as otherwise provided by statute, court rule or decision, administrative rule or regulation, or the attorney's rules of professional responsibility, and within the preceding parameters and proscriptions, a legal assistant may perform any function delegated by an attorney, including, but not limited to the following:
1. Conduct client interviews and maintain general contact with the client after the establishment of the attorney-client relationship, so long as the client is aware of the status and function of the legal assistant, and the client contact is under the supervision of the attorney.
2. Locate and interview witnesses, so long as the witnesses are aware of the status and function of the legal assistant.

3. Conduct investigations and statistical and documentary research for review by the attorney.
4. Conduct legal research for review by the attorney.
5. Draft legal documents for review by the attorney.
6. Draft correspondence and pleadings for review by and signature of the attorney.
7. Summarize depositions, interrogatories and testimony for review by the attorney.
8. Attend executions of wills, real estate closings, depositions, court or administrative hearings and trials with the attorney.
9. Author and sign letters providing the legal assistant's status is clearly indicated and the correspondence does not contain independent legal opinions or legal advice.

COMMENT:

The United States Supreme Court has recognized the variety of tasks being performed by legal assistants and has noted that use of legal assistants encourages cost-effective delivery of legal services, *Missouri v. Jenkins*, 491 U.S.274, 109 S.Ct.2463, 2471, n. 10 (1989). In Jenkins, the court further held that legal assistant time should be included in compensation for attorney fee awards at the rate in the relevant community to bill legal assistant time.

Courts have held that legal assistant fees are not a part of the overall overhead of a law firm. Legal assistant services are billed separately by attorneys, and decrease litigation expenses. Tasks performed by legal assistants must contain substantive legal work under the direction or supervision of an attorney, such that if the legal assistant were not present, the work would be performed by the attorney.

In *Taylor v. Chubb*, 874 P.2d 806 (Okla. 1994), the Court ruled that attorney fees awarded should include fees for services performed by legal assistants and, further, defined tasks which may be performed by the legal assistant under the supervision of an attorney including, among others: interview clients; draft pleadings and other documents; carry on legal research, both conventional and computer aided; research public records; prepare discovery requests and responses; schedule depositions and prepare notices and subpoenas; summarize depositions and other discovery responses; coordinate and manage document production; locate and interview witnesses; organize pleadings, trial exhibits and other documents; prepare witness and exhibit lists; prepare trial notebooks; prepare for the attendance of witnesses at trial; and assist lawyers at trials.

Except for the specific proscription contained in Guideline 1, the reported cases do not limit the duties which may be performed by a legal assistant under the supervision of the attorney.

An attorney may not split legal fees with a legal assistant, nor pay a legal assistant for the referral of legal business. An attorney may compensate a legal assistant based on the quantity and quality of the legal assistant's work and value of that work to a law practice.

CONCLUSION

These Standards and Guidelines were developed from generally accepted practices. Each supervising attorney must be aware of the specific rules, decisions and statutes applicable to legal assistants within his/her jurisdiction.

---

[1]The United States Supreme Court has addressed the issue concerning the utilization of professional credentials awarded by private organizations. In *Peel v. Attorney Registration and Disciplinary Committee of Illinois*, 496 U. S. 91, 110 S. Ct. 2281 (1990), the Court suggested that a claim of certification is truthful and not misleading if:

1) the claim itself is true;
2) the bases on which certification was awarded are factual and verifiable;
3) the certification in question is available to all professionals in the field who meet relevant, objective and consistently applied standards; and
4) the certification claim does not suggest any greater degree of professional qualification than reasonably may be inferred from an evaluation of the certification program's requirements.

Further, the Court advised that there must be a qualified organization to stand behind the certification process. For a detailed discussion of the Peel decision and the Certified Legal Assistant program, see "The Certified Legal Assistant Credential and Guidelines of the United States Supreme Court," 1996, National Association of Legal Assistants, 1516 S. Boston, #200, Tulsa, OK 74119 or http://www.nala.org

Addendum

For further information, the following cases may be helpful to you:

Duties:
Taylor v. Chubb, 874 P.2d 806 (Okla. 1994)
McMackin v. McMackin, 651 A.2d 778 (Del.Fam Ct 1993)

Work Product:
Fine v. Facet Aerospace Products Co., 133 F.R.D. 439 (S.D.N.Y. 1990)

Unauthorized Practice of Law
Akron Bar Assn. v. Green, 673 N.E.2d 13 07 (Ohio 1997)
In Re Hessinger & Associates, 192 B.R. 211 (N.D. Calif. 1996)
In the Matter of Bright, 171 B.R. 799 (Bkrtcy. E.D. Mich)
Louisiana State Bar Assn v. Edwins, 540 So.2d 294 (La. 1989)

Attorney/Client Privilege
In Re Complex Asbestos Litigation, 232 Cal. App. 3d 572 (Calif. 1991)
Makita Corp. v. US., 819 F. Supp. 1099 (CIT 1993)

Conflicts
In Re Complex Asbestos Litigation, 232 Cal. App. 3d 572 (Calif 1991)
Makita Corp. v. U. S., 819 F. Supp. 1099 (CIT 1993)
Phoenix Founders, Inc. v. Marshall, 887 S.W.2d 831 (Tex. 1994)
Smart Industries v. Superior Court, 876 P. 2d I 1 76 (Ariz. App. Div. 1 1994)

EXHIBIT 3–2   Sample time sheet.

CLIENT _____			PHONE _____	
ADDRESS _____				
DOCKET # _____		IN RE: _____	TYPE OF CASE _____	
NOTES _____				

_____

_____

DATE	IN	OUT	HRS	DESCRIPTION OF SERVICES
	:	:		
	:	:		
	:	:		
	:	:		
	:	:		
	:	:		
	:	:		
	:	:		
	:	:		
	:	:		
	:	:		
	:	:		
	:	:		
	:	:		
	:	:		
	:	:		
	:	:		
	:	:		
	:	:		
	:	:		
	:	:		
	:	:		
	:	:		
	:	:		
	:	:		

TOTAL HRS _____

REVIEW QUESTIONS

1. Why is it important for a paralegal to have a thorough knowledge of ethics?
2. Define the unauthorized practice of law.
3. Name the activities that constitute the practice of law.
4. Are paralegals allowed to prepare legal documents?
5. Define rules of ethics.
6. What is a freelance paralegal?
7. What are the possible consequences of an attorney's breach of ethical standards? What about a paralegal's breach?
8. Define confidentiality.
9. In a divorce matter, what is the problem with one attorney representing both parties?
10. Define conflict of interest.
11. What is an ethical wall?
12. How do lawyers get paid for their services?
13. What is a fee or retainer agreement?
14. What is padding and why should it be avoided?
15. Define solicitation.

EXERCISES

1. Find out what the requirements are for obtaining a license to practice law in your state.

2. Look up the unauthorized practice of law statute in your jurisdiction. How does your state define the "unauthorized practice of law"?

3. Find out what the penalty is in your state for practicing law without a license.

4. Find case law that has interpreted your state's UPL statute. If you can find one that deals with family law matters, write a case brief on it.

5. Locate the Code of Professional Conduct in your state. Cite the source of these rules.

6. Does your state's bar association allow paralegals to become associate members? If so, contact your bar association and request information.

7. Has your state adopted guidelines for paralegals? If so, obtain a copy of those guidelines.

8. Locate your state's rule on confidentiality in the attorney's Code of Professional Conduct. Under what circumstances may an attorney reveal a client's confidential information?

9. Contact your local paralegal association and obtain a membership application. If possible, join the organization and start attending meetings. It is a great way to network and stay current on important issues involving your profession.

10. A paralegal has a duty to be competent. Find out what resources are available in your state that would assist you in fulfilling this ethical obligation.

4 CHAPTER

PRENUPTIAL AGREEMENTS, COHABITATION, AND SAME-SEX MARRIAGE

KEY TERMS

Antenuptial agreement

Beneficiary

Cohabitation agreement

Constructive trust

Defense of Marriage Act

Domestic partnership

Express contract

Expressed trust

Full faith and credit clause

Fundamental right

Implied partnership

Implied trust

Implied-in-fact contact

Marriage statute

Miscegenation laws

Post-nuptial agreement

Premartial agreement

Prenuptial agreement

Public policy

Quasi-contract

Resulting trust

Same-sex marriage

Second glance doctrine

Trustee

Unconscionable

PRENUPTIAL AGREEMENTS

INTRODUCTION

Prior to marriage, the parties involved may choose to enter into a contract that determines their respective rights upon dissolution of the marriage or the death of one of the parties. These arrangements are called **antenuptial agreements, premarital agreements,** or **prenuptial agreements.** A prenuptial agreement is a contract entered into between two parties who intend to marry. Occasionally, this document addresses how the responsibilities and property rights will be handled during the marriage—who will pay the bills, who will support children from a prior marriage, who will pay the mortgage, how the children's upbringing will be handled, and who will care for the children's day-to-day needs. Frequently, the prenuptial agreement focuses on the disposition of the parties' estates in the event of divorce or death.

Once exclusively a staple in the legal arsenal of the rich and famous, more and more couples are now considering prenuptial agreements. These contracts were historically entered into by older men who married younger women. These men wished to protect their assets from potential "gold diggers" who were arguably marrying them for their money. Today, prenuptial agreements are popular among people who are entering into second or third marriages. In these cases, one or both parties may come with baggage. The husband, for instance, may be obligated to pay alimony and child support to the former wife. The wife may have children from a previous relationship. Prenuptial agreements are also used by parties who have more assets or income than their spouse-to-be, and by those who wish to protect the inheritance rights of their adult children. Prenuptial agreements are also considered a means of financial and emotional self-defense in a society with a high divorce rate. In addition, young professionals who have postponed marriage until their thirties or forties resort to prenuptial agreements to protect assets they have accumulated.

Some parties enter into such agreements *after* the marriage has been performed. These contracts are called **post-nuptial agreements** and the elements are similar to those of prenuptial agreements.

A prenuptial agreement is not a very romantic topic to discuss with a prospective partner, even if it can save the parties a great deal of grief in the long run. Money is also a very delicate topic to discuss under any circumstance and even more difficult to interject into a personal relationship. Talk of money can dredge up old childhood wounds and expose embarrassing habits that have formed in adulthood.

Prior to 1970, prenuptial agreements were frowned on by the courts. Judges often found these contracts void against public policy because they contemplated the end of the marital relationship. The state government had an interest in preserving the institution of marriage. The prevailing view was that prenuptial agreements facilitated divorce because they encouraged the spouse in the position to benefit most from the contract to put less effort into preserving the marital relationship. Courts were also protective of women's interests, fearing that men, who traditionally had more assets and business savvy, would leave women destitute in the event of divorce. For many centuries, a woman's traditional position was that of homemaker and child rearer. Many women lacked the education and finances to negotiate on an equal level with men. Prenuptial agreements were introduced into our legal system by men who had greater assets and greater business sophistication in legal matters. The courts feared that if prenuptial agreements were enforced, women would be unable to support themselves and would have to rely on public assistance.

The 1960s and 1970s brought many social changes to the institution of marriage, such as the advent of the women's liberation movement and no-fault divorce. No-fault divorce removed the traditional fault grounds that were once required to be proven by the moving spouse in order to obtain a divorce (i.e., abandonment, adultery, intemperance). The changing role of women propelled them to pursue higher education, greater opportunities in the workplace, and, as a result, economic independence. The women's liberation movement also demanded equal treatment under the law. Courts eventually did away with the legal presumptions that aimed to protect women in the legal system. Judicial attitudes progressed to the point where prenuptial agreements were enforced because it made sense in this era. Prenuptial agreements allowed prospective spouses to enter into a marriage with more predictability since they could now get their legal and financial house in order.

In 1970, the Florida Supreme Court, in *Posner v. Posner*, 233 So.2d 381 (Fla. 1970), paved the way for family courts around the country to hold that prenuptial agreements made in contemplation of marriage were not invalid per se. While the prenuptial agreement in this case was invalidated because of nondisclosure of assets, it was not struck down on public policy grounds. The following *Posner* excerpt illustrates the historical progression of prenuptial agreements in our legal system.

VICTOR POSNER, PETITIONER V. SARI POSNER, RESPONDENT

233 So.2d 381 (1970)

SUPREME COURT OF FLORIDA

MARCH 25, 1970

ROBERTS, JUSTICE.

. . . Both parties had appealed to the appellate court for reversal of the decree of the Chancellor entered in a divorce suit—the wife having appealed from those portions of the decree awarding a divorce to the husband and the sum of $600 per month as alimony to the wife pursuant to the terms of an antenuptial agreement between the two parties. . . .

. . . The three appellate judges . . . each took a different position respecting the antenuptial agreement concerning alimony. Their respective views were (1) that the parties may validly agree upon alimony in an antenuptial agreement but that the trial court is not bound by their agreement; (2) that such an agreement is void as against public policy; and (3) that an antenuptial agreement respecting alimony is entitled to the same consideration and should be just as binding as an antenuptial agreement settling the property rights of the wife in her husband's estate upon his death. They have certified to this court, as one of great public interest, the question of the validity and binding effect of an antenuptial agreement respecting alimony in the event of the divorce or separation of the parties. . . .

. . . At the outset we must recognize that there is a vast difference between a contract made in the market place and one relating to the institution of marriage.

It has long been the rule in a majority of the courts of this country and in this State that contracts intended to facilitate or promote the procurement of a divorce will be declared illegal as contrary to public policy. . . .

. . . At common law. The so-called "matrimonial causes," including divorce, were cognizable only in the

Ecclesiastical Courts. Because of the Church's view of the sanctity of the nuptial tie, a marriage valid in its inception would not be dissolved by an absolute divorce *a vinculo matrimonii,* even for adultery—although such divorces could be granted by an Act of Parliament. Therefore, the divorce was only from bed and board, with an appropriate allowance for sustenance of the wife out of the husband's estate. See Ponder v. Graham, 1851, 4 Fla. 23; *Chitty's Blackstone,* Vol. I, Ch. XV, 432, 431. We have, of course, changed by statute the common-law rule respecting the indissolubility of a marriage valid in its inception; but the concept of marriage as a social institution that is the foundation of the family and of society remains unchanged. . . . Since marriage is of vital interest to society and the state, it has frequently been said that in every divorce suit the state is a third party whose interests take precedence over the private interests of the spouses. . . .

. . . The state's interest in the preservation of the marriage is the basis for the rule that a divorce cannot be awarded by consent of the parties . . . this court said that it "would be aiming a deadly blow at public morals to decree a dissolution of the marriage contract merely because the parties requested it;". . .

. . . And it is the same policy that is the basis for the rule that an antenuptial agreement by which a prospective wife waives or limits her right to alimony or to the property of her husband in the event of a divorce or separation, regardless of who is at fault, has been in some states held to be invalid . . . Crouch v. Crouch, 1964, 53 Tenn.App. 594. . . . The reason that such an agreement is said to "facilitate or promote the procurement of a divorce" was stated in Crouch v. Crouch, *supra,* as follows: "Such contract could induce a mercenary husband to inflict on his wife any wrong he might desire with the knowledge his pecuniary liability would be limited. In other words, a husband could through ill treatment of his wife force her to bring an action for divorce and thereby buy a divorce for a small fee less than he would otherwise have to pay."

Antenuptial or so-called "marriage settlement" contracts by which the parties agree upon and fix the property rights which either spouse will have in the estate of the other upon his or her death have, however, long been recognized as being conducive to marital tranquility and thus in harmony with public policy. See Del Vecchio v. Del Vecchio, Fla.1962, 143 So. 2d 17, in which we prescribed the rules by which the validity of such antenuptial or postnuptial property settlement agreements should be tested. Such an agreement has been upheld after the death of the spouse even though it contained also a provision settling their property rights in the event of divorce or separation – the court concluding that it could not be said this provision "facilitated or tended to induce a separation or divorce." . . .

. . . In this view of an antenuptial agreement that settles the rights of the parties in the event of divorce as well as upon death, it is not inconceivable that a dissatisfied wife—secure in the knowledge that the provisions for alimony contained in the antenuptial agreement could not be enforced against her, but that she would be bound by the provisions limiting or waiving her property rights in the estate of her husband—might provoke her husband into divorcing her in order to collect a large alimony check every month, or a lump-sum award (since, in this State, a wife is entitled to alimony, if needed, even though the divorce is awarded to the husband) rather than take her chances on being remembered generously in her husband's will. In this situation, a valid antenuptial agreement limiting property rights upon death would have the same meretricious effect, insofar as the public policy in question is concerned, as would an antenuptial divorce provision in the circumstances hypothesized in Crouch v. Crouch, *supra,* 385 S.W.2d 288.

There can be no doubt that the institution of marriage is the foundation of the familial and social structure of our Nation and, as such, continues to be of vital interest to the State; but we cannot blind ourselves to the fact that the concept of the "sanctity" of a marriage—as being practically indissoluble, once entered into—held by our ancestors only a few generations ago, has been greatly eroded in the last several decades. This court can take judicial notice of the fact that the ratio of marriages to divorces has reached a disturbing rate in many states; and that a new concept of divorce—in which there is no "guilty" party—is being advocated by many groups and has been adopted by the State of California in a recent revision of its divorce laws providing for the dissolution of a marriage upon pleading and proof of "irreconcilable differences" between the parties, without assessing the fault for the failure of the marriage against either party.

With divorce such a commonplace fact of life, it is fair to assume that many prospective marriage partners, whose property and familial situation is such as to generate a valid antenuptial agreement settling their property rights upon the death of either, might want to consider and discuss also—and agree upon, if possible—the disposition of their property and the alimony rights of the wife in the event their marriage, despite their best efforts, should fail. . . .

We know of no community or society in which the public policy that condemned a husband and wife to a lifetime of misery as an alternative to the opprobrium of divorce still exists. And a tendency to recognize this change in public policy and to give effect to the antenuptial agreements of the parties relating to a divorce is clearly discernable. . . .

. . . We have given careful consideration to the question of whether the change in public policy toward divorce requires a change in the rule respecting antenuptial agreements settling alimony and property rights of the parties upon divorce and have concluded that such agreements should no longer be held to be void *ab initio* as "contrary to public policy." If such an agreement is valid when tested by the stringent rules prescribed in Del Vecchio v. Del Vecchio, *supra,* 143 So. 2d 17, for ante- and post-nuptial agreements settling the property rights of the spouses in the estate of the other upon death, and if, in addition, it is made to appear that the divorce was prosecuted in good faith, on proper grounds, so that, under the rules applicable to postnuptial alimony and property settlement agreements referred to above, it could not be said to facilitate or promote the procurement of a divorce, then it should be held valid as to conditions existing at the time the agreement was made. . . .

LEGAL REQUIREMENTS OF A VALID PRENUPTIAL AGREEMENT

The content of a prenuptial agreement, as well as any other contract, will depend on the intent of the parties. Some are very detailed documents covering specific aspects of married life, such as who will pay the bills and who will do the household chores. Exhibit 4–1 at the end of the chapter shows a sample prenuptial agreement. Prenuptial agreements, however, cannot bind parties during the marriage. For example, assume the parties agree in a prenuptial agreement that the husband will wash the dishes and take out the trash. This provision will not be enforced by the court. The court will not enforce those portions of a prenuptial agreement that govern the spouse's respective duties during an intact marriage. These provisions are useful only to provide the couple with guidelines as to how they wish to conduct their day-to-day affairs.

ACQUIRING THE NECESSARY DOCUMENTATION

The following information should be obtained from the client for review, whether the office is representing the spouse seeking the prenuptial agreement or the spouse reviewing the agreement. For each party, obtain

1. A list of assets and their current fair market value;
2. Income, both earned and unearned;
3. Debts and liabilities;
4. Previous divorce obligations owed to a former spouse, such as the following:
   - ▼ Alimony—What is the amount and duration of payments?
   - ▼ Child support—What is the amount and ages of children?
   - ▼ College expenses—Is the party obligated to pay higher education costs?
   - ▼ Insurance premiums—Must the party pay health, life, or disability insurance premiums?
   - ▼ Qualified Domestic Relations Orders (QDRO)—Are there any future rights to an employee pension that the client will receive or be required to pay out?
   - ▼ Tax obligations—Do either of the parties owe money to a local, state, or federal tax entity?
   - ▼ Lawsuits—Does either party anticipate receiving money damages or a settlement amount from a pending lawsuit?

- ▼ Legal judgments—Have any legal judgments been entered against the parties requiring payment of damages?
- ▼ Credit history—Have there been previous or pending bankruptcies?

WHO SHOULD HAVE A PRENUPTIAL AGREEMENT?

The following parties should consider having a prenuptial agreement prepared:

- ▼ Parties who have children from a previous marriage whose financial interests they wish to protect,
- ▼ Parties who have significant assets or are very well compensated,
- ▼ Parties who anticipate a family inheritance, and
- ▼ Parties who wish to protect their separate property (property acquired prior to marriage).

If a party wants to ensure that assets pass to the children of a previous marriage, a prenuptial agreement is essential. A spouse enjoys statutory protections, such as:

- ▼ An elective statutory share of the deceased spouse's estate (this share is usually elected if the deceased spouse left the surviving spouse nothing or very little in the will);
- ▼ Intestacy succession rights;
- ▼ Homestead rights in the principal; and
- ▼ Widow's allowance.

These rights are automatically conferred on the spouse by virtue of the legal marital status. A spouse may, however, waive these rights in the prenuptial agreement. Without a properly executed prenuptial agreement in effect, a surviving spouse is legally entitled to claim a portion of the deceased spouse's estate. An attorney may advise a client to sign a Qualified Terminal Interest Trust (QTIP). A QTIP is a trust naming the children as beneficiaries of the client's estate while allowing the surviving spouse access to the assets acquired during his or the deceased spouse's lifetime. In addition, the attorney should also advise the client to write a new will, change beneficiary designations on insurance policies, trusts, annuities, and other retirement plans to safeguard the current spouse.

Parties who are well compensated or have significant assets may also seek the protection of a prenuptial agreement. The client may be well advised by the attorney to keep the money he or she has already amassed in a separate account and not to commingle these funds with marital property.

KNOW YOUR STATE LAW

The following jurisdictions have adopted the Uniform Premarital Agreement Act:

Arizona	Iowa	Nevada	Rhode Island
Arkansas	Kansas	New Jersey	South Dakota
California	Maine	North Carolina	Texas
Hawaii	Montana	North Dakota	Utah
Illinois	Nebraska	Oregon	Virginia

The full text of the Uniform Premarital Agreement Act is provided in Appendix A. The model act provides guidelines for parties who wish to enter into a prenuptial agreement. Check your state statutes if you live in a state that has adopted this act.

Other jurisdictions may have adopted a modified version of the model act or have their own state laws addressing this issue. It is essential to check your state's statutory *and* case law, because laws vary from jurisdiction to jurisdiction. California, for instance, does not allow elimination or modification of a spouse's right to receive alimony at the time of divorce. When the California legislature adopted the Uniform Premarital Agreement Act, it refused to codify language that gave the contracting parties the ability to eliminate or modify spousal support payments. In 1998, in *Pendelton v. Fireman* 98 Daily Journal DAR 3087 (1998), the California Appellate Court addressed the issue of spousal support waiver. The parties, a well-educated and well-to-do couple, contracted in a prenuptial agreement that neither one would ask for alimony in the event of a divorce. Both parties were represented by independent counsel at the time of entering into the agreement. Four years later, they found themselves in divorce court. The wife, now asking for alimony, argued that the agreement was void against California public policy. **Public policy** is a belief generally held by a majority of the public as to the desirability or rightness or wrongness of certain behavior. In this case, the trial court agreed with the wife. The California Appellate Court reversed, upholding the waiver on the grounds that California case law rather than the statutory law should prevail on the issue of spousal support and that waivers and limitations no longer violate public policy. The case is currently on appeal before the California Supreme Court.

THE INTENT OF THE PARTIES MUST BE CLEAR

In drafting a prenuptial agreement, it is important to express the intentions of the parties. This requires a clear statement of each party's intent. It may be necessary for the parties' attorneys to prepare and/or review several drafts of the agreement before the final document memorializes each party's intent to his or her own satisfaction and that of the other party.

COMPLIANCE WITH THE STATUTE OF FRAUDS

The Statute of Frauds requires that promises made in contemplation of marriage must be in writing and signed by the party to be charged.

ADEQUATE DISCLOSURE

Prospective spouses have a duty to fully disclose their financial status. This is essential since parties who intend to marry share a confidential relationship and mutual trust. Sometimes a person may not be fully aware of the prospective spouse's financial status. Most jurisdictions require the parties to attach an accurate financial statement to the agreement. The extent of disclosure is different in each state. The safest approach is to provide a detailed disclosure of all income, expenses, assets (fair market value), and liabilities. Each party should also disclose assets in which the party may have a future interest, such as an inheritance or a trust fund distribution.

The paralegal may assist by helping the client to obtain a description and, when appropriate, the fair market value of the following:

- ▼ IRAs, pensions, 401k funds, deferred profit sharing compensation;
- ▼ Securities, stocks, bonds, commodities, real estate;
- ▼ Collectibles (artwork, antiques, guns, coins, stamps, jewelry);
- ▼ Royalties from patents, copyrights, trademarks;
- ▼ Future interests (inheritances, trusts); and
- ▼ Beneficiary designations.

Essentially, the contracting parties should have knowledge of the extent of the other's estate.

ADVICE OF INDEPENDENT COUNSEL

The proponent of the prenuptial agreement must give the other party the opportunity to have an independent attorney of her choice review the agreement. An attorney reviewing a prenuptial agreement will advise a client of what she is legally entitled to as a spouse and what she will be giving up by signing this document. It is not advisable for the attorney drafting a prenuptial agreement to refer the opposing party to an attorney. This may later raise the specter of conflict of interest. Additionally, one lawyer should not draft such an agreement for both parties, because this would also present a conflict.

A prospective spouse should not be pressured into signing a prenuptial agreement. For instance, the document should not be slipped under a bustling bride's nose on the morning of the wedding. A party should have ample opportunity to seek counsel.

FAIRNESS

In order for a prenuptial agreement to be valid, it must not be **unconscionable.** An agreement is unconscionable when it is so unfair to one party that the court will refuse to enforce it. Courts regularly review contracts on the basis of "fairness." In business settings, the parties enter into contracts as arm's length transactions. The courts protect the freedom of contract in business transactions. Prospective spouses, however, are in a confidential relationship and may be pressured into signing for fear that otherwise the marriage will not go forward. Therefore, prospective spouses are more susceptible to undue influence, thus alerting the courts to the possibility of unconscionability.

Courts will generally enforce a prenuptial agreement unless one party can prove that it promotes divorce (e.g., a large, enticing property settlement upon divorce); the contract was entered into with the intent to divorce; or that the agreement was unfairly executed without benefit of independent counsel. A prenuptial agreement will be enforced as long as the proponent of the agreement (the spouse claiming the agreement's enforceability) adequately disclosed income and assets to the opposing spouse and that at the time of entering into the agreement, the opposing spouse was not under undue pressure to sign. In some jurisdictions, the agreement is unenforceable if it was deemed "unfair" at the time of signing.

Assessing the Client's Position Regarding the Enforceability of the Prenuptial Agreement

The law office will either be representing the party who originally proposed that a prenuptial agreement be prepared and executed and now seeks its enforcement or the party who agreed to its execution but who now seeks legal representation to oppose the enforcement. In either case, the first aspect to review is what circumstances existed during the formation of the contract. The court will generally uphold a prenuptial agreement unless the parties possessed unequal bargaining power. If both parties had similar financial and educational backgrounds at the time of the execution, the court will most likely uphold the agreement.

The second aspect to consider is what circumstances exist at the time one of the parties seeks enforcement of the agreement. The courts apply the **"second glance doctrine"** in order to protect spouses from changes in circumstances that occurred since the date of the formation of the prenuptial agreement. The courts will not enforce the contract due to unconscionability if enforcing the contract "today" would be unfair in light of the current circumstances. The contract must be fair and reasonable to the relinquishing spouse. The court may overrule the prenuptial agreement if enforcement would cause a spouse to become a charge of the state or greatly reduce his standard of living.

EXAMPLE

Jonathan and Shannon enter into a prenuptial agreement. Shannon waives away her right to alimony. Later, Shannon gets sick with Parkinson's disease and cannot work or support herself. Is the prenuptial agreement enforceable? No.

Provisions may not take effect for years. Fairness and reasonableness are subjective tests to be determined by the courts after reviewing the totality of circumstances, such as the parties' health, financial status, intellectual and business savvy, existence of dependent children, and current standard of living.

The Contract Must Be Entered Into Voluntarily

Any contract must be a "meeting of the minds." This means that each party must understand and agree to the terms of the contract. If a person is forced to sign a premarital agreement, or is under pressure to sign, or signs for fear that otherwise the marriage will not go forward, the contract can later be declared void by the court.

Jurisdiction

A prenuptial agreement should include a clause indicating which state's law will control. Language such as "This prenuptial agreement shall be construed under the laws of the State of Massachusetts" should be incorporated into the document. Under traditional contract law, when the agreement is silent, the construction and validity of an agreement is determined by the law of the jurisdiction where the agreement was originally signed. Unlike contract law, family law is steeped in public policy concerns and the state reviewing the contract for enforcement has jurisdiction over disputes.

A party may have entered into a prenuptial agreement in a jurisdiction where the terms were valid under that state's laws, but the parties moved to a state that disfavors prenuptial agreements or certain provisions. Under the Uniform Premarital Agreement Act, the law of the state where enforcement of the agreement is sought controls.

UNENFORCEABLE PROVISIONS

The court may invalidate certain provisions of a prenuptial agreement while enforcing others if the children agreement contains provisions for the care, custody, and support of the couple's union. These provisions are usually not enforceable. The court decides these issues according to the "child's best interest standard." Like other contractual arrangements, the court may invalidate some provisions of the prenuptial agreement while enforcing other provisions.

COHABITATION

INTRODUCTION

Cohabitation agreements, either express or implied, are contracts entered into by unmarried individuals who live together or plan to live together. Prior to the late 1970s, cohabiting couples were left to resolve their legal differences by themselves. Courts did not recognize sexual relationships outside of matrimony. These relationships were viewed as void against public policy. The courts also refused to recognize these relationships because recognition would erode the traditional family unit. But our society has seen an increase in the number of couples who have chosen to live together without the benefit of marriage. At one time in our social history, living together was considered scandalous. Now, for heterosexual couples, it is a matter of preference or convenience. For same-sex couples, cohabitation agreements and domestic partnerships (valid in only a few jurisdictions and also available to heterosexual couples) are the only option available since no jurisdiction has legalized same-sex marriage.

WHY COHABITATION?

In the case of heterosexual couples, a variety of reasons exist for choosing a cohabitation arrangement rather than the institution of marriage:

1. Fear of the greater level of commitment and perceived greater level of responsibility that formal marriage appears to bring.
2. Some couples feel the commitment they make to each other to cohabit is just as serious and binding as a formal marriage; however, they are aware that future events could change the relationship and weaken the strength of the commitment. If unforeseen events change the nature of the relationship, it is easier and less expensive to loosen the bonds.

3. Women have attained greater financial independence. This has helped to alleviate the rush to the altar in order to find someone who could care for them financially.

4. Some individuals, male and female, have considerable assets and choose not to marry at all for fear of losing those assets.

5. Some individuals have been through the financial and emotional trauma of a divorce, or even multiple divorces, and have no desire to remarry.

Despite the increased public acceptance of cohabitation, the law still favors traditional marriage. A preference for marriage is reflected throughout state and federal statutory schemes, such as:

▽ Intestate succession;

▽ Right of election;

▽ Disposition of a deceased spouse's body;

▽ Community property and tenancy by the entirety as concurrent ownership schemes;

▽ Loss of consortium damages in civil matters;

▽ Marital privilege protecting communications between spouses in evidentiary proceedings;

▽ Immigration privileges;

▽ Social Security benefits;

▽ Workers' compensation benefits;

▽ Federal and state tax benefits;

▽ Health insurance;

▽ Medical leave; and

▽ Mutual obligation to financially support each other.

Another very important benefit of marriage is access to the family courts to dissolve the relationship. The family courts also have the power to order a division of the assets and impose obligations such as alimony, child support, and custody. Generally, cohabitants, unless they have children together, have no access to the family court and must rely on the civil court to resolve disputes, unless they are able to amicably resolve their differences.

MARVIN V. MARVIN

In response to the very sharp increase in cohabitation arrangements that occurred in the late 1960s and early 1970s, the law had to change to make some accommodations for resolving disputes between cohabiting partners. The first case to recognize the rights of cohabitants was *Marvin v. Marvin*, 18 Cal. 3d 660, 557 P.2d 106, 134 Cal. Rptr. 815 (1976). In Marvin, the plaintiff and the defendant had lived together for a period of seven years. During this period, the plaintiff agreed to give up her career and provide domestic services for the defendant. In exchange, the defendant agreed to financially support the plaintiff and share any assets that were accumulated. This agreement was *not* memorialized in writing.

When the relationship ended, the plaintiff sued the defendant on a contractual basis for support and a division of the assets. The trial court dismissed her case and she appealed. On appeal, the California Supreme Court held that the contract between the parties was valid and remanded the case to the trial court to be judged on its merits. The parties had accumulated approximately one million dollars in assets. However, these assets were titled in the name of the defendant.

The defendant attacked the validity of the contract by raising the long-standing public policy argument. According to the defendant, a contract that included sexual relations was void. The California Supreme Court held that as long as sexual relations were not the sole consideration, the court should disregard that provision and enforce the lawful provisions of the agreement.

The next step was to determine the remedies available to the parties. While *Marvin* is a landmark case in the area of cohabitation, these remedies vary from state to state. First, the court had to decide what type of contract was in effect:

1. **Express contract.** This would require an express agreement between the parties regarding the specific terms. The high court recognized that in a romantic relationship, parties do not generally negotiate the terms of their roles and expectations, let alone reduce them to a writing.

2. **Implied-in-fact contract.** In an implied-in-fact contract, the intention of the parties is inferred by their conduct. For example, a person goes to a restaurant and orders ham and eggs. The waiter brings him his food and he consumes the meal. There is an implied contract that the consumer intends to pay for the meal. In supporting an implied contract action in a cohabitation case, examining the conduct of the parties is essential. How did the parties conduct themselves during their relationship? What contributions, both monetary and nonmonetary, did the parties bring to the relationship? Were assets commingled in joint accounts?

3. **Quasi-contract.** Quasi-contracts are contractual obligations that are imposed upon the parties by the court. No actual contract has been entered into by the parties. The court takes this position when it appears that one party has been so unjustly enriched that the court creates a contract to avoid unfairness to the other party.

4. **Implied partnership.** When a cohabiting couple works on a business enterprise that is owned by one of the parties, the court creates an implied partnership. The court assesses the financial status of the business and distributes the assets and liabilities just as such a distribution would occur upon the dissolution of a business partnership.

5. **Implied trust.** A trust is a legal relationship where one party, the **trustee,** holds legal title to property for the benefit of the **beneficiary.** Most trusts are **expressed trusts,** in which the terms have been negotiated by the parties. Implied trusts are created by the court to avoid an injustice. One type of trust is a **resulting trust.** In a resulting trust, one party provides the funds for property, while title is in the other party's name.

EXAMPLE

Mary has enough money for a down payment on a house, but has poor credit. John has excellent credit and can qualify for a mortgage in his sole name. With Mary's down payment, John agrees to split the mortgage payments and purchases the house, which is titled in his name only. John and Mary move into the house and live there for ten years together. During this time, Mary contributes to the mortgage payments and household expenses. The relationship deteriorates and Mary and John break up. Mary moves out of the house because John has become verbally abusive. Mary may sue for her interest in the house on a resulting trust theory.

▽   ▽   ▽

6. **Constructive trust.** A constructive trust is imposed by the court to avoid unjust enrichment when there is no intent between the parties to create a trust.

While the *Marvin* court established a variety of legal remedies for litigating cohabitants, it did not approve of treating cohabiting couples as married couples:

. . . [W]e take this occasion to point out that the structure of society itself largely depends upon the institution of marriage and nothing we have said in this opinion should be taken to derogate from that institution. [*Marvin v. Marvin*, 557 P.2d 106, 122 (1976)]

SAME-SEX MARRIAGE

INTRODUCTION

Same-sex couples find themselves in the same legal position as cohabiting heterosexual couples. The one difference between the two is that, if they so choose, heterosexual couples have the option of legalizing their union, while same-sex couples do not.

The sexual revolution brought about many social changes, one of which has been the opening of the closet door. The current headlines indicate that members of the gay community are demanding not only social acceptance and equal rights, but also the right to enter into marital relationships. This idea, however, is not yet widely accepted by society, and triggers many emotional reactions from those who wish to preserve the traditional type of marriage—a union between a man and a woman.

Every social movement has a defining moment in its history. The gay liberation movement was born during the Stonewall riots in New York City in 1969. Since then, the gay rights movement has sought to remove the stigma that has so long been attached to this lifestyle. This stigma affects familial, legal, economic, and social aspects for a gay person. Legal and religious institutions in particular have condemned the gay lifestyle. While many state laws have been repealed, there are still laws on the books that criminalize sodomy or other gay conduct. Homosexuality is also considered a sin in many religious traditions.

To date, no state has legalized **same-sex marriage**—a legal marriage between members of the same sex who are entitled to the same rights and privileges as heterosexual married couples.

DOMESTIC PARTNERSHIPS

A **domestic partnership** is an arrangement between same-sex couples or opposite-sex couples who cannot or who choose not to marry, but live together just like a married couple. Several states, including California and Vermont, have

STATUTES

VERMONT STATUTES ANNOTATED TITLE 23, SECTION 1.15

An Act Relating to Domestic Partnerships
§ 1202. Requisites of a Valid Domestic Partnership
For a domestic partnership to be established in Vermont, it shall be necessary that the parties satisfy all of the following criteria:

(1) Have a common residence.
(2) Consider themselves to be members of each other's immediate family.
(3) Agree to be jointly responsible for one another's basic living expenses.
(4) Neither be married nor a member of another domestic partnership.
(5) Not be related by blood in a way that would prevent them from being married to each other as prohibited by chapter 1 of this title.
(6) Each be at least 18 years old.
(7) Each be competent to enter into a contract.
(8) Each sign a declaration of a domestic partnership as provided for in section 1203 of this title.

enacted Domestic Partnership Acts, which protect each party in the event of a breakdown of the relationship. A domestic partnership agreement works like a prenuptial agreement in that it spells out who is responsible for what in the event of a breakup.

MARRIAGE STATUTES

Every state has a **marriage statute.** This is a law passed by a state legislature that indicates who may marry. This is the same statute that tells us, for instance, that a man cannot marry his niece because they are too close in consanguinity and this union could violate public policy. Marriage statutes vary from state to state. Some statutes explicitly forbid a marriage between members of the same sex by specifying that marriage must be between a man and a woman. In these jurisdictions, same-sex marriages are prohibited.

In other jurisdictions, the marriage statute is silent as to who may marry. When the statute is silent as to definitions, these jurisdictions also prohibit same-sex marriage because they apply the "plain meaning" and dictionary definition of the word "marriage."

THE LEGAL BATTLE FOR RECOGNITION OF SAME-SEX MARRIAGE

The advocates of same-sex marriage contend that the prohibition against same-sex marriage violates the Establishment Clause of the First Amendment of the Constitution because the state is establishing a religion (i.e., the prohibition reflects Judeo-Christian biblical views against homosexual conduct). Courts have rejected this argument, ruling that a legitimate governmental interest is served by prohibiting marriages between members of the same sex. It is the view of many courts that states should sanction only marriages that are capable of procreating—reproducing children. The courts have also believed that preserving the traditional family unit will discourage children and youth from viewing homosexuality as an acceptable lifestyle.

THE FOURTEENTH AMENDMENT ARGUMENT

Marriage is considered a **fundamental right** in our system of jurisprudence. Advocates of same-sex marriage have argued that denying homosexuals the right to marry on the basis of their sex violates the Fourteenth Amendment. A classification resulting in the denial of a fundamental right may only be upheld where it is necessary to accomplish a compelling state interest and achievement of that goal cannot be done by less restrictive means.

In 1967, the U.S. Supreme Court struck down a Virginia statute that prohibited interracial marriages. This statute and similar legislation were know as **miscegenation laws** and were enforced in many states. The Virginia statute at the time read as follows:

> All marriages between a white person and a colored person shall be absolutely void without any decree of divorce or other legal process. (Virginia Code Ann. 750-57)

In *Loving v. Virginia*, 388 U.S. 1 (1967), the Supreme Court held that marriage is a fundamental right which cannot be restricted by states unless there is a compelling state interest. Courts have rejected this application of this holding to decide the legality of same-sex marriage and routinely uphold laws passed by state legislatures that prohibit same-sex marriage. Many courts employ the rationale that upholding such statutes discourages the illegal activity of sodomy and encourages procreation.

THE STATE EQUAL RIGHTS AMENDMENT ARGUMENT

Another theory of attack used by same-sex marriage advocates has been states' Equal Rights Amendments.

> Equality of rights under the law shall not be denied or abridged on account of sex. (Ex. **Colo.Const.Art. II Section 29.**)

A state's Equal Rights Amendment would bar sex-based classifications, even though the classification may be based on a compelling state interest. There is no federal Equal Rights Amendment (ERA). Efforts to pass an ERA to the U.S. Constitution failed on several occasions with protestors alleging that it would lead to women serving in military combat, unisex toilets, and . . . same-sex marriage.

One state that has received a lot of attention in the same-sex marriage controversy has been Hawaii, particularly because of the case of *Baehr v. Miike* (formerly Baehr v. Lewin), 74 Haw. 530, 852 P.2d 44 (1993). Hawaii was the first state in the country in which a court of law was asked to determine if same-sex couples have the right to a legally recognized marriage. In December 1990, several same-sex couples applied for marriage licenses and were denied. The couples filed a lawsuit against the Hawaii State Department of Health contending that the marriage statute was unconstitutional because it prohibited same-sex couples from obtaining marriage licenses on the basis of sex and sexual orientation. In October 1991, the plaintiffs' complaint was dismissed by the trial court on the grounds of failure to state a claim on which relief could be granted. The plaintiffs appealed this decision to the Supreme Court of Hawaii. On May 1, 1993, Hawaii's highest court stunned the nation when it reversed the trial court's ruling and remanded the case for a new trial. The court held that restrictions on same-sex marriages may violate the state's Equal Protection Clause because it prohibited same-sex couples from obtaining a marriage license on the basis of gender. Couples were entitled to protection under the state's Equal Rights Amendment and could not be denied a marriage license based on compelling state interests. This would require the legal test of strict scrutiny.

On remand, it was up to the Hawaii State attorney general to prove a compelling state interest—that the state of Hawaii was justified in its restrictions. The state's position was that marriage is for the promotion and rearing of children by heterosexuals only. It is in the children's best interest to be raised by their biological parents and states have interests in promoting the development of children.

The plaintiffs presented expert testimony that confirmed that children of gay parents are no different developmentally than children raised by heterosexual couples. In addition, the plaintiffs argued that the State's argument is flawed because the state places children in foster care and because many children are raised in single-parent homes.

While the *Baehr* case progressed through the Hawaiian court system, the Hawaii Legislature in 1994 reacted to the decision by amending its marriage statute to expressly state that marriage is between a man and a woman.

 **STATUTES**

Hawaii Revised Statutes §572-1

§572-1 Requisites of valid marriage contract. In order to make valid the marriage contract, which shall be only between a man and a woman, it shall be necessary that:

(1) The respective parties do not stand in relation to each other of ancestor and descendant of any degree whatsoever, brother and sister of the half as well as the whole blood, uncle and niece, aunt and nephew, whether the relationship is the result of the issue of parents married or not married to each other;

(2) Each of the parties at the time of contracting the marriage is at least sixteen years of age; provided that with the written approval of the family court of the circuit within which the minor resides, it shall be lawful for a person under the age of sixteen years, but in no event under the age of fifteen years, to marry, subject to 572-2;

(3) The man does not at the time have any lawful wife living and that the woman does not at the time have any lawful husband living;

(4) Consent of neither party to the marriage has been obtained by force, duress, or fraud;

(5) Neither of the parties is a person afflicted with any loathsome disease concealed from, and unknown to, the other party;

(6) The man and woman to be married in the State shall have duly obtained a license for that purpose from the agent appointed to grant marriage licenses; and

(7) The marriage ceremony be performed in the State by a person or society with a valid license to solemnize marriages and the man and the woman to be married and the person performing the marriage ceremony by all physically present at the same place and time for the marriage ceremony.

In December 1996, the trial court ruled in favor of the plaintiffs and issued an injunction ordering the state to issue marriage licenses to the same-sex couples. The next day, the state filed a motion to stay the injunctions until the State had the opportunity to appeal the case. The motion was granted and no licenses were issued to the plaintiffs.

In April 1997, The Hawaii legislature closed this issue by passing a constitutional amendment stating that the legislature could limit marriage to a man and a woman.

NINIA BAEHR, GENORA DANCEL, TAMMY RODRIGUES, ANTOINETTE PREGIL, PAT LAGON, JOSEPH MELILLO, V. LAWRENCE MIIKE, DIRECTOR OF THE DEPARTMENT OF HEALTH, STATE OF HAWAII

SUPREME COURT OF THE STATE OF HAWAII

CIV. NO 91-1394-05

FILED ON DECEMBER 11, 1995

SUMMARY OF DISPOSITION ORDER

Pursuant to Hawaii Rules of Evidence (HRE) Rules 201 and 202 (1993), this court takes judicial notice of the following: On April 29, 1997, both houses of the Hawaii legislature passed, upon final reading, House Bill No. 117 proposing an amendment to the Hawaii Constitution (the marriage amendment). *See* 1997b House Journal at 922; 1997 Senate Journal at 766. The bill proposed the addition of the following language to article I of the Constitution: "**Section 23.** The legislature shall have the power to reserve marriage to opposite-sex couples." *See* 1997 Haw. Sess. L. H.B. 117 §2, at 1247. The marriage amendment was ratified by the electorate in November, 1998.

In light of the foregoing, and upon carefully reviewing the record and the briefs and supplemental briefs submitted by the parties and amicus curiae and having given due consideration to the arguments made and the issues raised by the parties, we resolve the defendant-appellant Lawrence Miike's appeal as follows:

On December 11, 1996, the first circuit court entered judgment in favor of plaintiffs-appellees Ninia Baehr, Genora Dancel, Tammy Rodrigues, Antoinette Pregil, Pat Lagon, and Joseph Melillo (collectively, "the plaintiffs") and against Miike, ruling (1) that the sex-based classification in Hawaii Revised Statutes (HRS) §572-1 (1985) was "unconstitutional" by virtue of being "in violation of the equal protection clause of article I, section 5 of the Hawaii Constitution," (2) that Miike, his agents, and any person acting in concert with or by or through Miike were enjoined from denying an application for a marriage license because applicants were of the same sex, and (3) that costs should be awarded against Miike and in favor of the plaintiffs. The circuit court subsequently stayed enforcement of the injunction against Miike.

The passage of the marriage amendment placed HRS §572-1 on new footing. The marriage amendment validated HRS §572-1 by taking the statute out of the ambit of the equal protection clause of the Hawaii Constitution, at least insofar as the statute, both on its face and as applied, purported to limit access to the marital status to opposite-sex couples. Accordingly, whether or not in the past it was violative of the equal protection clause in the foregoing respect, HRS §572-1 no longer is. In light of the marriage amendment, HRS §572-1 must be given full force and effect.

The plaintiffs seek a limited scope of relief in the present lawsuit, i.e., access to applications for marriage licenses and the consequent legally recognized marital status. Inasmuch as HRS §572-1 is now a valid statute, the relief sought by the plaintiffs is unavailable. The marriage amendment has rendered the plaintiffs' complaint moot.

Therefore,

IT IS HEREBY ORDERED that the judgment of the circuit court be reversed and that the case be remanded for entry of judgment in favor of Miike and against the plaintiffs.

IT IS FURTHER ORDERED that the circuit court shall not enter costs or attorney's fees against the plaintiffs.

DATED: Honolulu, Hawaii, December 9, 1999.

Baehr sent shock waves throughout the country. In response, many jurisdictions amended their marriage statutes, defining marriage as a union between a man and a woman. States feared that if Hawaii legalized gay marriage, same-sex partners would go to Hawaii, get married, then return to their state of domicile and demand that their marriage be recognized under the **full faith and credit clause** of the U.S. Constitution. The full faith and credit clause states that states must honor the public acts, records, and judicial proceedings of every other state. U.S. Const. Art. IV, §1. If a heterosexual couple marries in Hawaii, then moves to Ohio, the state of Ohio must legally recognize the marriage.

In May 1996, the U.S. Congress enacted the **Defense of Marriage Act** (DOMA). The act protects the traditional definition of marriage as a union between a man and a woman in the United States Code and bars same-sex couples from enjoying federal benefits, regardless of how their states redefine marriage, either through statute or judicial act. Marriage is referenced in many federal laws such as tax, bankruptcy, immigration, Social Security, and military justice. DOMA also ensures that states would not be forced to recognize same-sex marriages performed in states that have sanctioned such unions.

DEFENSE OF MARRIAGE ACT, 28 U.S.C. SECTION 1738C (1996)

Sec. 2. Powers Reserved to the States.

(a) IN GENERAL—Chapter 115 of title 28 United States Code, is amended by adding after section 1738B the following:

"Sec. 1738C. Certain acts, records, and proceedings and the effect thereof

No State, territory, or possession of the United States, or Indian tribe, shall be required to give effect to any public act, record, or judicial proceeding of any other State, territory, possession, or tribe respecting a relationship between persons of the same sex that is treated as a marriage under the laws of such other State, territory, possession, or tribe, or a right or claim arising from such relationship."

Sec. 3. Definition of Marriage

IN GENERAL – Chapter 1 of Title 1, United States Code, is amended by adding at the end the following:

"Sec. 7. Definition of 'marriage' and 'spouse'

In determining the meaning of any Act of Congress, or of any ruling, regulation, or interpretation of the various administrative bureaus and agencies of the United States, the word 'marriage' means only a legal union between one man and one woman as husband and wife, and the word 'spouse' refers only to a person of the opposite sex who is a husband or a wife."

Another battle for the recognition of same-sex marriage is being waged in the state of Vermont. On December 20, 1999, the Vermont Supreme Court reached a landmark decision is the case of *Baker v. State*. The state's highest court held that three same-sex couples who applied for marriage licenses and were denied had the right to the same benefits of marriage as their heterosexual counterparts—that is, an absolute right to legal marriage benefits under Vermont law. The court extended the Common Benefits Clause of the Vermont Constitution to include the right of same-sex couples to marry. The court also retained jurisdiction in the case. Therefore, if the Vermont legislature is unable to provide a remedy to same-sex couples according to the court's ruling, the court will do so on its own. As of April 2000, the Vermont legislature passed Bill H-847, creating civil unions for same-sex couples. This statute will grant same-sex couples numerous state benefits of marriage, including tax benefits, inheritance rights, and the right to make medical decisions.

STAN BAKER, ET AL. V. STATE OF VERMONT, ET AL.

VERMONT SUPREME COURT

DOCKET NO. 98-032

NOVEMBER TERM, 1998

DECEMBER 20, 1999

AMESTOY, C. J.

May the State of Vermont exclude same-sex couples from the benefits and protections that its laws provide to opposite-sex married couples? That is the fundamental question we address in this appeal, a question that the Court knows arouses deeply-felt religious, moral, and political beliefs. Our constitutional responsibility to consider the legal merits of the issues properly before us provides no exception for the controversial case. The issue before the Court, moreover, does not turn rather on the statutory and constitutional basis for the exclusion of same-sex couples from the more secular benefits and protections offered married couples.

We conclude that under the Common Benefits Clause of the Vermont Constitution, which, in pertinent part, reads that government is, or ought to be, instituted for the common benefit, protection, and security of the people, nation, or community, and not for the particular emolument or advantage of any single person, family, or set of persons, who are a part only of that community, Vt. Const., ch. I, art. 7. Plaintiffs may not be deprived of the statutory benefits and protections afforded persons of the opposite sex who choose to marry. We hold that the State is constitutionally required to extend to same-sex couples the common benefits and protections that flow from marriage under Vermont law. Whether this ultimately takes the form of inclusion within the marriage laws themselves or a parallel "domestic partnership" system or some equivalent statutory alternative, rests with the Legislature. Whatever system is chosen, however, must conform with the constitutional imperative to afford all Vermonters the common benefit, protection, and security of the law.

Plaintiffs are three same-sex couples who have lived together in committed relationships for periods ranging from four to twenty-five years. Two of the couples have raised children together. Each couple applied for a marriage license from their respective town clerk, and each was refused a license as ineligible under the applicable state marriage laws. Plaintiffs thereupon filed this lawsuit against defendants—the State of Vermont, the Towns of Milton and Shelburne, and the City of South Burling-

ton—seeking a declaratory judgment that the refusal to issue them a license violated the marriage statutes and the Vermont Constitution.

The State, joined by Shelburne and South Burlington, moved to dismiss the action on the ground that plaintiffs had failed to state a claim for which relief could be granted. The Town of Milton answered the complaint and subsequently moved for judgment on the pleadings. Plaintiffs opposed the motions and cross-moved for judgment on the pleadings. The trial court granted the State's and Town of Milton's motions, denied plaintiffs' motion, and dismissed the complaint. The court ruled that the marriage statutes could not be construed to permit the issuance of a license to same-sex couples. The court further ruled that the marriage statutes were constitutional because they rationally furthered the State's interest in promoting "the link between procreation and child rearing." This appeal followed.

I. THE STATUTORY CLAIM

Plaintiffs initially contend the trial court erred in concluding that the marriage statutes render them ineligible for a marriage license. It is axiomatic that the principal objective of statutory construction is to discern the legislative intent. . . . While we may explore a variety of sources to discern that intent, it is also a truism of statutory interpretation that where a statute is unambiguous we rely on the plain and ordinary meaning of the words chosen. . . ." . . . [W]e rely on the plain meaning of the words because we presume they reflect the Legislature's intent. . . ."

. . . Vermont's marriage statues are set forth in Chapter 1 of Title 15, entitled "Marriage," which defines the requirements and eligibility for entering into a marriage, and Chapter 105 of Title 18, entitled "Marriage Records and Licenses," which prescribes the forms and procedures for obtaining a license and solemnizing a marriage. Although it is not necessarily the only possible definition there is no doubt the plain and ordinary meaning of "marriage" is the union of one man and one woman as husband and wife. . . .

. . . Further evidence of the legislative assumption that marriage consists of a union of opposite genders may be found in the consanguinity statutes, which expressly prohibit a man from marrying certain female relatives. . . . In addition, the annulment statutes explicitly refer to "husband and wife" . . . as do other statutes relating to married couples. . . .

. . . These statutes, read as a whole, reflect the common understanding that marriage under Vermont law consists of a union between a man and a woman. . . .

II. The Constitutional Claim

Assuming that the marriage statutes preclude their eligibility for a marriage license, plaintiffs contend that the exclusion violates their right to the common benefit and protection of the law guaranteed by Chapter I, Article 7 of the Vermont Constitution. They note that in denying them access to a civil marriage license, the law effectively excludes them from a broad array of legal benefits and protections incident to the marital relation, including access to a spouse's medical, life, and disability insurance, hospital visitation and other medical decision making privileges, spousal support, intestate succession, homestead protections, and many other statutory protections. They claim the trial court erred in upholding the law on the basis that it reasonably served the State's interest in promoting the "link between procreation and child rearing." They argue that the large number of married couples without children, and the increasing incidence of same-sex couples with children, undermines the State's rationale. They note that Vermont law affirmatively guarantees the right to adopt and raise children regardless of the sex of the parents, see 15A V.S.A. §1-102, and challenge the logic of a legislative scheme that recognizes the rights of same-sex partners as parents, yet denies them—and their children—the same security as spouses.

In considering this issue, it is important to emphasize at the outset that it is the Common Benefits Clause of the Vermont Constitution we are construing, rather than its counterpart, the Equal Protection Clause of the Fourteenth Amendment to the United States Constitution. . . .

. . . "[O]ur constitution is not a mere reflection of the federal charter. Historically and textually, it differs from the United States Constitution. It predates the federal counterpart, it extends back to Vermont's days as an independent republic. It is an independent authority, and Vermont's fundamental law."

. . . [W]e turn to the question of whether the exclusion of same-sex couples from the benefits and protections incident to marriage under Vermont law contravenes Article 7. The first step in our analysis is to identify the nature of the statutory classification. As noted, the marriage statutes apply expressly to opposite-sex couples. Thus, the statutes exclude anyone who wishes to marry someone of the same sex.

Next, we must identify the governmental purpose or purposes to be served by the statutory classification. The principal purpose the State advances in support of the excluding of same-sex couples from the legal benefits of marriage is the government's interest in "furthering the link between procreation and child rearing". . . .

. . . [T]he reality today is that increasing numbers of same-sex couples are employing increasingly efficient assisted-reproductive techniques to conceive and raise children. . . . The Vermont Legislature has not only recognized this reality, but has acted affirmatively to remove legal barriers so that same-sex couples may legally adopt and rear the children conceived through such efforts. . . . The State has also acted to expand the domestic relations laws to safeguard the interests of same-sex parents and their children when such couples terminate their domestic relationship. . . .

. . . Therefore, to the extent that the State's purpose in licensing civil marriage was, and is, to legitimize children and provide for their security, the statues plainly exclude many same-sex couples who are no different from opposite-sex couples with respect to these objectives. If anything, the exclusion of same-sex couples from the legal protections incident to marriage exposes their children to the precise risks that the State argues the marriage laws are designed to secure against. In short, the marital exclusion treats persons who are similarly situated for purposes of the law, differently. . . .

. . . The question thus becomes whether the exclusion of a relatively small but significant number of otherwise qualified same-sex couples from the same legal benefits and protections afforded their opposite-sex counterparts contravene the mandates of Article 7. It is, of course, well settled that statutes are not necessarily unconstitutional because they fail to extend legal protection to all who are similarly situated. . . .

. . . While the laws relating to marriage have undergone many changes during the last century, largely toward the goal of equalizing the status of husbands and wives, the benefits of marriage have not diminished in value. On the contrary, the benefits and protections incident to a marriage license under Vermont law have never been greater. They include, for example, the right to receive a portion of the estate of a spouse who dies intestate and protection against disinheritance through elective share provisions, preference in being appointed as the personal representative of a spouse who dies intestate, the right to bring a lawsuit for the wrongful death of a spouse, the right to bring an action for loss of consortium, the right to workers' compensation survivor benefits, the right to spousal benefits statutorily guaranteed to public employees, including health, life, disability, and accident insurance, the opportunity to be covered as a spouse under group life insurance policies issued to an employee, the opportunity to be covered as the insured's spouse under an individual health insurance policy, the right to claim an evidentiary privilege for marital communications, homestead rights and protections, the presumption of joint ownership of property and the concomitant right of survivorship, hospital visitation and other rights incident to the medical treatment of a family member, and the right to receive, and the obligation to provide, spousal support, maintenance, and property division in the event of separation or divorce . . . (citations omitted).

. . . The legal benefits and protections flowing from a marriage license are of such significance that any statutory exclusion must necessarily be grounded on public concerns of sufficient weight, cogency, and authority that the justice of the deprivation cannot seriously be questioned. Considered in light of the extreme logical disjunction between the classification and the stated purposes of the law—protecting children and "furthering the link between procreation and child rearing"—the exclusion falls substantially short of this standard. The laudable governmental goal of promoting a commitment between married couples to promote the security of their children and the community as a whole provides no reasonable basis for denying the legal benefits and protections of marriage to same-sex couples, who are no differently situated with respect to this goal than their opposite-sex counterparts. Promoting a link between procreation and child rearing similarly fails to support the exclusion. . . .

. . . Thus, viewed in the light of history, logic, and experience, we conclude that none of the interests asserted by the State provides a reasonable and just basis for the continued exclusion of same-sex couples from the benefits incident to a civil marriage license under Vermont law.;. . . .

. . . F. Remedy

It is important to state clearly the parameters of today's ruling. Although plaintiffs sought injunctive and declaratory relief designed to secure a marriage license, their claims and arguments here have focused primarily upon the consequences of official exclusion from the statutory benefits, protections, and security incident to marriage under Vermont law. While some future case may attempt to establish that—notwithstanding equal benefits and protections under Vermont law—the denial of a marriage license operates per se to deny constitutionally-protected rights, that is not the claim we address today.

We hold only that plaintiffs are entitled under Chapter I, Article 7, of the Vermont Constitution to obtain the same benefits and protections afforded by Vermont law to married opposite-sex couples. We do not purport to infringe upon the prerogatives of the Legislature to craft an appropriate means of addressing this constitutional mandate, other than to note that the record here refers to a number of potentially constitutional statutory schemes from other jurisdictions. These include what are typically referred to as "domestic partnership" or "registered partnership" acts, which generally establish an alternative legal status to marriage for same-sex couples, impose similar formal requirements and limitations, create a parallel licensing or registration scheme, and extend all or most of the same rights and obligations provided by the law to married partners. . . .

. . . We hold that the current statutory scheme shall remain in effect for a reasonable period of time to enable the Legislature to consider and enact implementing legislation in an orderly and expeditious fashion. . . .

While California passed a domestic partnership act, California Code Family Code §297 *et seq.*, it took a step backward in March 2000 by passing Proposition 22. California's Proposition 22 bars the state from recognizing same-sex marriages performed in other states. It declares that only unions between a man and a woman are valid. Interestingly, this bill was sponsored by Republican State Senator Pete Knight, whose gay son was one of the opponents of the bill.

EXHIBIT 4–1

Sample Prenuptial Agreement (Author unknown)

WHEREAS, the parties are contemplating a legal marriage under the laws of the State of Connecticut; and

WHEREAS, it is their mutual desire to enter into this Agreement whereby they will regulate their relationship toward each other with respect to the property each of them own and in which each of them has an interest;

NOW, therefore, it is agreed as follows:

1. That the properties of any kind or nature, real, personal or mixed, wherever the same may be found, which belong to each party, shall be and forever remain the separate estate of said party, including all interests, rents and profits which may accrue therefrom.

2. That each party shall have at all times the full right and authority, in all respects, the same as each would have if not married, to use, enjoy, mortgage, convey and encumber such property as may belong to him or her.

3. That each party may make such disposition of his or her property as the case may be, by gift or will during his or her lifetime, as each sees fit; and in the event of the decease of one of the parties, the survivor shall have no interest in the property of the estate of the other, either by way of inheritance, succession, family allowance or homestead.

4. That each party, in the event of a legal separation or dissolution of marriage, shall have no right as against the other by other by way of claims for support, alimony, property division, attorney's fees and costs.

5. This Prenuptial Agreement shall be construed under the laws of the State of Connecticut.

Dated this 10th day of May, 2001

_____   _____
(Name)   Witness

_____   _____
(Date)   Witness

_____
(Name)

_____
(Date)

REVIEW QUESTIONS

1. Define prenuptial agreement.
2. Why would a couple contemplating marriage enter into a prenuptial agreement?
3. What are the legal requirements for a valid prenuptial agreement?
4. Why is the advice of independent counsel so important for the purpose of reviewing a prenuptial agreement?
5. Define cohabitation.
6. Why are some couples choosing a cohabitation arrangement as opposed to a more traditional marriage?
7. In the landmark case of *Marvin v. Marvin*, what remedies did the California Supreme Court set forth for cohabitants?
8. List the legal benefits available to couples who are legally married.
9. In your opinion, should same-sex couples be allowed to marry?
10. Define domestic partnership.

EXERCISES

1. Research your state's prenuptial agreement statute. Does your state follow the Uniform Premarital Agreement Act? A modified version? A state version?

2. Review your state's case law on prenuptial agreements. Read and brief a recent case in this area of the law.

3. Research your state's law on cohabitation agreements. What remedies does your state confer on cohabiting couples?

4. Review your state's marriage statute. In your jurisdiction, who may marry? Does your jurisdiction specifically prohibit marriage between persons of the same sex?

5. Does your state recognize domestic partnerships? If so, what rights and responsibilities do domestic partners have in your jurisdiction?

CHAPTER 5

ALIMONY

KEY TERMS

Adultery

Alimony

Alimony in gross

Allowable deduction

Arrearages

Attorney's fees

Canon law

Church court

COBRA

Cohabitation

Contempt proceeding

Cost of living clause

Desertion

Discretion of the court

Divorce

Divorce *a mensa et thoro*

Divorce *a vinculo matrimonii*

Ecclesiastical court

Escalation clause

Family support payments

Front loading

Gross income

Habitual intemperance

Incarceration in a penal institution

Incompatiblilty

Institutionalization for mental illness

Irreconcilable differences

Irremediable breakdown

Irretrievable breakdown

IRS recapture rule

Legal grounds

Lump sum alimony

Married Women's Property Act

Mental cruelty

Modification of alimony

Net income

No-fault divorce laws

Nominal alimony

Pendente lite alimony

Periodic alimony

Permanent alimony   Spousal maintenance
Physical cruelty   Spousal support
Rehabilitative alimony   Wage execution
Reimbursement alimony   Willful contempt
Secular court

Alimony is the term given to a sum of money, or other property, paid by a former spouse to the other former spouse for financial support, pursuant to a court order, temporary or final, in a divorce proceeding. Terms such as **spousal support** or **spousal maintenance** are synonyms for alimony and any one or all of these terms may be used by different jurisdictions in statutory or case law.

HISTORY OF ALIMONY

Historically, married women had no rights to property in their own name or independent of their husbands. They could not control their own income, enter into contracts, buy and sell land, or sue or be sued. Since the United States inherited its legal system from England, we must look to early English law to trace the history of alimony. In England, the ecclesiastical courts or church courts had the power to grant divorces.

ECCLESIASTICAL COURTS

For many centuries throughout Western Europe, **ecclesiastical courts** or **church courts** coexisted with **secular courts** or courts administered by the state. In many European countries, there was an official state church and it was this church that controlled ecclesiastical courts. In England, eventually it was the Church of England or Anglican Church that administered the church courts. These courts had the jurisdiction to hear some matters that could also be heard in the general state courts. In certain areas, however, the ecclesiastical or church court was the exclusive forum for addressing disputes.

Ecclesiastical courts had exclusive jurisdiction over all family-related legal matters. In these matters, the church courts applied **canon law.** The term *canon law* refers to the Church's body of law or rules that determine man's moral obligations to man, to woman, and to God. In England, the Anglican Church retained much of the doctrine and dogma of the Roman Catholic Church, including the proscription against divorce as we known it and the status of matrimony as a sacrament. The "divorces" granted by these courts were not the divorces we are accustomed to today. Our definition of **divorce,** or **divorce *a vinculo matrimonii,*** is the complete severance of the marital relationship, allowing the parties to go their separate ways. This includes the right to remarry. The ecclesiastical courts only granted **divorce *a mensa et thoro,*** which means divorce from bed and board. The result of a divorce *a mensa et thoro* did not sever the marriage; it merely enabled the spouses to live separate and apart. In many religions, marriage is a sacrament not to be entered into lightly. In the eyes of God and the church, only the death of one of the two spouses ended a marriage. The church allowed only widowed persons to enter into new or second marriages.

The church also changed the status of individuals upon marriage in that they were viewed as one entity. This concept influenced the secular law regarding the economic positions of spouses at common law. Upon marriage, husband and wife merged into "one body," the "one" being the husband. By virtue of the marriage ceremony, the spouses entered into a marital contract that imposed the duty of support on the husband. In turn, the wife gave up her rights to control or possess property or earnings that belonged to her. Women did not work outside the home and upon marriage took on the traditional roles of homemaking and rearing the children. This enabled the husband to focus on his career and increase his earning capacity.

Origins of the Alimony Award

Upon granting a divorce *a mensa et thoro*, the ecclesiastical courts ordered the husband to pay "alimony" or support to the wife. Not only was the husband obligated to support the wife during the marriage, this duty was ongoing, even through the separation period. The husband's duty to support the wife upon divorce was not absolute. The wife was entitled to alimony as long as she was an "innocent spouse." If she had caused the breakdown of the marriage, she would get nothing. This would leave the wife with no monetary support. If the husband were at fault for the breakup of the marriage, his punishment obligated him to pay for his fault. Historically, both the theoretical and practical basis for the creation of alimony was to provide compensation for the wife and punish the husband for his wrongdoing.

FIGURE 5–1
In early times, a married couple was viewed as "one body" by the church, that one body being the husband.

ALIMONY IN EARLY AMERICA

The English common law system was adopted by the settlers of America and along with it came the laws regarding the severing of a marriage and the legal disadvantages suffered by married women. The duty of a husband to pay alimony upon divorce was codified in statutes of many American jurisdictions. In the late 1830s, American jurisdictions began passing the **Married Women's Property Acts.** These statutes eliminated the disadvantages of married women and gave them the right to control their own earnings, bring lawsuits, be sued, own their own property, enter into contracts, and function in a legal capacity. As time passed, societal attitudes toward women changed. Women were increasingly joining the workforce and gaining the ability to support themselves. Even though times were changing and more opportunities opened up to women, the American legal system still held on to the husband's duty to support his former wife.

When initiating a divorce action, the plaintiff spouse had to allege a legal reason or ground for requesting a divorce in the complaint or petition for dissolution of marriage. In the early 1970s many jurisdictions began passing **no-fault divorce laws.** Prior to the passage of no-fault laws, a spouse seeking a divorce was required to have **legal grounds**—that is, facts proving that the other spouse was at fault. Some of the fault grounds included:

- **Adultery,**
- **Habitual intemperance,**
- **Desertion,**
- **Mental cruelty,**
- **Physical cruelty,**
- **Incarceration in a penal institution,** and
- **Institutionalization for mental illness.**

The plaintiff spouse was required to produce evidence to prove his case. If the wife was responsible for the breakdown of the marriage, she lost alimony and property. If the husband was at fault, he would probably have to pay alimony and give the wife a considerable portion of property. If the plaintiff spouse could not meet the burden of proof, no divorce would be granted. Parties seeking divorces colluded or conspired together to commit perjury in cases where no fault existed and the parties merely wished to go their separate ways and end an unhappy marriage. The frequency of this type of charade was one of many factors that prompted state legislatures to consider and eventually enact laws that made divorce easier in most circumstances. In 1969, California led the nation in the passage of this country's first no-fault divorce law.

ALIMONY AWARDS IN A NO-FAULT SETTING

Under our current system of no-fault divorce, the courts must first dissolve the marriage. After the marriage is dissolved, the court will then render orders regarding alimony, property division, child support, child custody, and attorney's fees. No-fault divorce means that in order for the court to dissolve a marriage, one of the parties only has to allege that the marriage has broken down and that there is no hope of reconciliation.

Depending on the jurisdiction, the no-fault ground may be referred to as one of the following:

- ▽ **Irreconcilable differences,**
- ▽ **Incompatibility,**
- ▽ **Irretrievable breakdown,** and
- ▽ **Irremediable breakdown.**

While all states have some form of no-fault divorce law, many jurisdictions also allow spouses to allege a fault ground in their divorce pleadings. Whether the issue of fault may be raised in determining alimony or property division depends on the jurisdiction.

Cheating Husband Tries to Cheat Wife!

In this case, the wife was awarded permanent alimony at the trial court level. On appeal, the court found that the husband was unable to meet his burden of proving that his wife was at fault for the breakdown of the marriage and not entitled to alimony. Both the husband and the wife represented themselves on the appeal as *pro per* parties.

ETHEL RAE CORMIER THIBODEAUX v. EUGENE THIBODEAUX

454 S.2d 813 (1984)

COURT OF APPEAL OF LOUISIANA, THIRD CIRCUIT

ETHEL C. THIBODEAUX, IN PRO PER.

EUGENE THIBODEAUX, IN PRO PER.

DOUCET, JUDGE.

Defendant, Eugene Thibodeaux, appeals from a judgment awarding plaintiff, Ethel Rae Cormier Thibodeaux, permanent periodic alimony at the rate of $150.00 per month. . . .

. . . On appeal defendant contends that the trial court erred in not finding that plaintiff was at fault in causing the dissolution of the marriage, thus precluding her from receiving permanent alimony. In the alternative, defendant asserts that the trial court erred in finding that the plaintiff did not have sufficient means for support such as would entitle her to an award of $150.00 per month in alimony.

Permanent periodic alimony may be awarded a spouse who had not been at fault and has not sufficient means for support. La.C.C. art. 160; *Lamb v. Lamb,* 460 So. 2d 634 (La. App. 3rd Cir. 1984); *Silas v. Silas,* 399 So. 2d 779 (La. App. 3rd Cir. 1981). The burden of proof is on the party seeking alimony to show that he or she is without fault in

causing the dissolution of the marriage and that he or she is in necessitous circumstances and in need of support. *Lamb v. Lamb,* supra. A trial court's finding of fact on the issue of fault will not be disturbed on appeal unless it is clearly wrong. *Pearce v. Pearce,* 348 So. 2d 75 (La. App. 3rd Cir. 1977); *Boudreaux v. Boudreaux,* 460 So. 2d 722 (La. App. 3rd Cir. 1983). . . .

. . . Defendant bases his allegations of fault on (1) cruel treatment by his wife, C.C. art. 138(3); and/or (2) her public defamation of him, C.C. art. 138(4). C.C. art. 138(3) provides that cruel treatment by one of the spouses towards the other must be of such a nature as to render their living together insupportable. In addition, the jurisprudence holds that the fault sufficient to preclude a spouse from receiving permanent alimony must be a serious and independent contributory or proximate cause of the dissolution of the marriage. *Pearce v. Pearce,* supra; *Lamb v. Lamb,* supra.

Defendant cites as cruel treatment accusations by his wife that he was dating other women. The defendant testified that almost every week his wife would accuse him of seeing other women, usually when he "came home late from work." Defendant flatly denied dating or seeing other women. Plaintiff testified that she suspected defendant was seeing other women and that she accused him of this—but not every week. Plaintiff and her thirteen-year-old daughter both testified that, as they were returning from church services one evening at approximately 10:00 p.m., they happened to see the defendant and a former girlfriend of his coming out of the front door of her residence. Defendant denied this allegation. Plaintiff also admitted that she had accused defendant of dating her brother's girlfriend.

The parties physically separated when plaintiff and her two children moved out of the family home. This step was taken approximately one week after defendant began hiding the household cookware so that plaintiff could not prepare meals. This was never specifically denied by defendant. There was evidence that shortly before plaintiff left, defendant disconnected the air conditioner—this was in the month of August. Defendant claimed that he only did this during the day when no one was home to save on his utility bill. However, plaintiff claims that defendant told her that he could not afford to support her and his girlfriend and that he wanted her out of the house. In other words, plaintiff claimed that defendant drove her out of the house. On a couple of occasions, plaintiff's son heard defendant tell his mother that he didn't want her in the home.

From this evidence the trial court concluded that the plaintiff was free from fault. The trial judge's reasons for this finding are not clear. However, from the evidence in the record before us we are unable to say that this conclusion of the trial court was clearly wrong. The record furnishes a basis for finding that the plaintiff's accusations of extra-marital activity were not totally unfounded and therefore would not constitute cruel treatment. A wife who observes her husband and his ex-girlfriend leaving her residence together at 10:00 p.m. is justified in having her suspicions aroused. Moreover, it appears that the reason for the marital breakup rests on the shoulders of defendant who by his actions drove plaintiff from the family home. In addition, defendant testified at trial that he would welcome the plaintiff back but she refuses to return. Thus, by defendant's own testimony, the accusations made by his wife could not be considered a serious and independent contributory or proximate cause of the marital breakup.

Defendant next contends that the plaintiff publicly defamed him, and under La.C.C. art. 138(4), and the applicable jurisprudence, this constitutes fault sufficient to preclude her from receiving alimony. We will examine the issue of defamation even though, as we have discussed above with reference to alleged cruel treatment (accusations of infidelity), any public defamation could not, we feel, have been contributory or proximate cause of the marital breakup.

To establish a public defamation as contemplated in C.C. art. 138(4) it is necessary to prove the alleged defamatory statement was: (1) false; (2) made publicly to a person to whom the accuser has no legitimate excuse to talk about the subject of the accusation; (3) not made in good faith; and (4) made with malice (citation omitted).

As we have previously discussed, plaintiff's accusations were not totally unfounded and her suspicions were justifiably aroused. However, without regard to truth or falsity, there is no evidence that any statements made to others by the plaintiff were made with malice. Plaintiff, a beautician, apparently confided to her fellow beautician her belief that defendant was dating other women. There is nothing in the record to suggest that this was done with malice or was anything other than one person seeking sympathy or advice from another. A fellow employee of defendant testified that while he was working one day plaintiff came and asked him if "that woman" left. On another occasion as this same individual was walking past the parties' residence, plaintiff asked him "what woman Eugene was talking to." Again, we can discern no evidence of malice on the part of the plaintiff in making these vague inquiries and there is nothing to indicate that plaintiff acted other than in good faith. In view of these facts and circumstances and the applicable law and jurisprudence we find no error in the trial court's failure to find fault on the part of the plaintiff on the grounds of public defamation. . . .

. . . Considering the evidence as a whole we are unable to find any abuse of discretion in the trial court's awarding plaintiff permanent periodic alimony in the amount of $150 per month.

For the reasons assigned, we affirm the judgment of the trial court.

AFFIRMED.

The 1960s and 1970s also saw a change in society's view of men, women, and marriage. More opportunities were available to women so they could become economically self-sufficient. In addition marriage was no longer viewed as a master/servant relationship, but rather an economic partnership, where the contributions of the wife as homemaker were also gaining a new respect.

The modern view of marriage is much like that of a business partnership, whereupon dissolution of the entity, the partners are entitled to a fair division of the marital assets. The courts prefer property division awards as opposed to alimony because the parties can make a "clean break" and go their separate ways, much like business partners. Alimony does not coincide with this modern view of marriage because there is still a legal tie between former spouses.

While most states gender neutralized their alimony statutes on their own initiative, other states resisted until court intervention required such a change. For instance, the Supreme Court of the United States in *Orr v. Orr*, 440 U.S. 268 (1979), held that an Alabama statute imposing the obligation on the husband alone to pay alimony was unconstitutional in that it violated the Fourteenth Amendment's Equal Protection Clause. While the court may impose the duty to pay alimony on either spouse, the reality is that women are still earning less than men and comprise the majority of alimony recipients today. Spouses most likely to obtain alimony for a significant period of time are those who have been in long-term marriages (over ten years), have given up career opportunities to raise a family and care for the home, or those that are ill or have a disability and cannot work. Alimony may also be awarded to a spouse for a limited period of time, allowing the opportunity to become self-sufficient. Alimony is also appropriate if the parties do not have substantial assets and periodic payments would provide for the needs of a spouse. It is also crucial that the payor spouse be employed and have a stable work record. When substantial property is involved, property division is preferred for the purpose of allowing parties to make a clean break. From the ecclesiastical view to present, we have seen alimony evolve from a punishment to compensate a spouse for the bad acts of another, to a vehicle for providing economic support for a spouse.

Parties are free to negotiate an agreement regarding the amount of alimony to be paid. If the parties cannot agree, the court must make that decision. The determination of alimony is within the **discretion of the court.** This means that the court has the power to make the alimony decision and that an appellate court will not reverse that decision unless the judge somehow abused his discretion. The parties are also free to agree to a waiver, meaning that they will not seek an alimony award in the divorce case. Consider the following excerpt from *Lawsuits of the Rich and Famous:*

> But husbands are no longer the only ones being taken to the proverbial cleaners. *Good Morning America's* Joan Lunden irked some feminists in 1992 when she expressed ire over the $18,000 per month which she was told to hand over to Michael Krauss, 54, her husband of 14 years. A Westchester County judge also deemed that Ms. Lunden was also liable for the mortgage on the couple's 10-room house, as well as property taxes, fuel, electricity, cable TV bills, and payments on his life and health insurance. Hardcore women's libbers, who think that professional women should accept the spankings which sometimes come with professional territory, were miffed when the ordinarily good-natured hostess snarled, "This is a deplorable and shameful statement on how working women are treated."
>
> Feminist attorney Gloria Allred saw justice in the decision, telling *People* magazine, "If we want to make advances in women's rights, we can't deny men their rights." But the National Organization for Women came to Lunden's defense, saying she was the victim of "the judicial version of 'Gotcha!'" Then, as if to pour salt on the wound, Lunden told *Redbook* magazine that she had sometimes superseded her ex-husband's ego, even on trivial matters; "Michael always wanted the reservations in his name. But with my name we would call at the last minute and still get a good table at a busy restaurant. . . ."

Ms. Lunden's remarks sparked responses from advocates for men's rights in the 1990's. Sidney Siller, founder and president of the National Organization for Men, a New York lawyer and the author of a men's rights column for *Penthouse* magazine, told the *San Francisco Chronicle*, "The peal of anguish that went up from women after the Joan Lunden case smacked of hypocrisy. There's not a level playing ground in the courts for men. . . . I've got one case on appeal, a man who is a disabled World War II veteran. His wife is working as an executive. For 40 years of marriage, she was always the main support, while he did work in houses they bought and sold. The judge denied him alimony because he had become an alcoholic. He would have been responsible for her, clearly, if the situation had been reversed."

If the Joan Lunden case constituted a reversal, then consider the $10 million which aerobics empress Jane Fonda has handed over to California Assemblyman Tom Hayden, even though Hayden himself reportedly only earns about $50,000 annually (Ms. Fonda, now married to cable entrepreneur and Atlanta Braves owner Ted Turner, is worth between $60 million and $100 million); or contemplate the $75,000 Goldie Hawn paid to get away from hubby Gus Trikonis in 1976, only to turn about five years later and relinquish half of her assets to spouse number two, Bill Hudson.

Or take the 1991 divorce case of Jane Seymour. In May of that year, the Santa Monica Superior Court awarded her husband, real estate developer David Flynn, $10,000 a month through 1994, plus coverage by Seymour of $500,000 in debts owed by Flynn's company and half the value of their $5 million Santa Barbara home, their furniture and their art.

Georgia beauty Kim Basinger is another wife caught up in the divorce courts' new-found sense of equity. In 1988, afraid that her ex-husband would go to the tabloids with tales of what he termed her "flamboyant affairs," she forked over to him $64,000 in support and the keys to their $700,000 Los Angeles home.

Likewise stung was designer Mary McFadden, 56, who in 1992 paid Kohle Yohannan, 26, her husband of a mere 22 months, $100,000 in alimony. According to *Parade Magazine,* things got nasty in that one when Yohannan claimed he had been "the victim of a much older, selfish alcoholic woman." She bit back, calling him a "spaced-out delinquent," a "known homosexual," and alleging that he was unable to consummate their marriage.

The mud began to fly, too, in the early rounds of divorce proceedings between Roseanne and Tom Arnold, in 1994. She renewed claims of spousal abuse by Tom and provided photographs of bruises she said were inflicted by her husband; she also resubmitted documents she said she had earlier withdrawn because she was afraid of Arnold. As for Arnold, he followed the lead of Flynn, Yohannan and others when he declared that he was unemployed and would need $100,000 per month in support. He also alleged that Roseanne had "plundered" his belongings and thrown his wardrobe into the pool at their Brentwood mansion.

Excerpt from *Lawsuits of the Rich and Famous* by W. Kelsea Wilbur Eckert and Jeff Trippe, pp. 34–36. Used with permission.

DETERMINING ALIMONY

State alimony statutes set forth a list of criteria to be weighed by the judge in evaluating whether or not an award of alimony is appropriate. Although the court considers each statutory factor, it does not have to give each factor equal weight. The court may focus on any number of factors depending on the circumstances of the case.

The California and Florida statutes presented below outline an example of statutory criteria considered by the family courts in determining whether an alimony award is appropriate.

STATUTES

WEST'S ANNOTATED CALIFORNIA CIVIL CODE

§ 4320. Determination of amount due for support; circumstances

in ordering spousal support under this part, the court shall consider all of the following circumstances:

(a) The extent to which the earning capacity of each party is sufficient to maintain the standard of living established during the marriage, taking into account all of the following:

   (1) The marketable skills of the supported party and the job market for those skills; the time and expenses required for the supported party to acquire the appropriate education or training to develop those skills; and the possible need for retraining or education to acquire other, more marketable skills or employment.

   (2) The extent to which the supported party's present or future earning capacity is impaired by periods of unemployment that were incurred during the marriage to permit the supported party to devote time to domestic duties.

(b) The extent to which the supported party contributed to the attainment of an education, training, a career position, or a license by the supporting party.

(c) The ability to pay of the supporting party, taking into account the supporting party's earning capacity, earned and unearned income, assets, and standard of living.

(d) The needs of each party based on the standard of living established during the marriage.

(e) The obligations and assets, including the separate property of each party.

(f) The duration of the marriage.

(g) The ability of the supported party to engage in gainful employment without unduly interfering with the interests of dependent children in the custody of the party.

(h) The age and health of the parties.

(i) The immediate and specific tax consequences to each party.

(j) Any other factors the court determines are just and equitable.

FLORIDA STATUTES ANNOTATED (WEST)

61.08 Alimony

(1) In a proceeding for dissolution of marriage, the court may grant alimony to either party, which alimony may be rehabilitative or permanent in nature. In any award of alimony, the court may order periodic payments or payments in lump sum or both. The court may consider the adultery of either spouse or the circumstances thereof in determining the amount of alimony, if any, to be awarded. In all dissolution actions, the court shall include findings of fact relative to the factors enumerated in subsection (2) supporting an award or denial of alimony.

(2) In determining a proper award of alimony or maintenance, the court shall consider all relevant economic factors, including but not limited to:

   (a) The standard of living established during the marriage.

   (b) The duration of the marriage.

   (c) The age and the physical and emotional condition of each party.

   (d) The financial resources of each party, the nonmarital and the marital assets and liabilities distributed to each.

   (e) When applicable, the time necessary for either party to acquire sufficient education or training to enable such party to find appropriate employment.

   (f) The contribution of each party to the marriage, including, but not limited to, services rendered in homemaking, childcare, education, and career building of the other party.

   (g) All sources of income available to either party.

The court may consider any other factor necessary to do equity and justice between the parties.

(3) To the extent necessary to protect an award of alimony, the court may order any party who is ordered to pay alimony to purchase or maintain a life insurance policy or a bond, or to otherwise secure such alimony award with any other assets which may be suitable for that purpose. . . .

Statutory criteria are also important in negotiations. Lawyers will prepare with the statute in mind, looking at each factor in light of the facts under the particular client's case. If the jurisdiction's alimony statute does not enumerate criteria for determining alimony, it is important to check local case law. In considering an alimony award, the courts will examine the payor's ability to pay versus the recipient spouse's needs.

Balancing Need versus Ability to Pay

> While Mr. Adkins, an attorney, clearly had the ability to pay, Mrs. Adkins failed to demonstrate her need for alimony to the court.

▽

PAMELA S. ADKINS v. MILTON R. ADKINS

650 So.2d 61 (1994)

FLORIDA DISTRICT COURT OF APPEALS, THIRD DISTRICT

HUBBART, JUDGE.

This is an appeal by the wife, Pamela S. Adkins, and a cross-appeal by the husband, Milton R. Adkins, from an amended final judgment of marriage dissolution entered after a non-jury trial. For the reasons which follow, we affirm in part and reverse in part.

The wife on the main appeal raises a multitude of points which center around two general arguments containing a large number of related subpoints. . . . Second, it is urged that the trial court erred in failing to award the wife alimony and attorney's fees. . . .

. . . I. In the instant case, the parties married in 1978; it was the second marriage for both parties. There were no children borne of the marriage and the husband filed for dissolution of the marriage in 1987. The trial court made the following relevant findings in the amended final judgment under review:

. . . Each party entered this marriage with substantial assets. The Husband has estimated his net worth to approximate Five Hundred Thousand Dollars ($500,000.00), and the Wife has estimated hers to approximate Two Hundred Fifty Thousand Dollars ($250,000.00). Among the assets owned by the Husband was his home located at 3502 Alhambra Circle, Coral Gables, Florida, its furnishings, various investment properties, and a pension plan.

During the course of marriage, the parties, by agreement, maintained separate bank accounts, separate accounting records, and separate business interests. The Wife inherited from family members substantial assets consisting primarily of real estate and tillable farmland and having a net worth of approximately Two Million Dollars. During this marriage, the Wife managed her inherited property, churned her stock holdings profitably, and reinvested the profits of her labor in other property interests including income-producing property in North Carolina and a Shoney's Restaurant in South Carolina. At no time did the Wife share with her husband the fruits of her labor or the profits resulting therefrom. In fact, the Wife requested that the Husband reimburse her for any and all expenses she incurred from which the Husband and/or one of his assets may have derived a benefit.

The Husband worked diligently during this marriage to provide the Wife with a comfortable lifestyle. She was provided with a maid five days a week, a beautiful home, and an environment which included trips to Europe and elsewhere. In return for his labor, the Husband asked the Wife to abide by her premarital promise to provide a "nest," using the Wife's words, to be his companion and friend, and to be there when he returned from work. Instead, the Wife, for reasons unexplained, chose to lead a singular and self-gratifying lifestyle. For example, she would disappear from the home without notice or explanation for days, weeks, or even for months at a time. She hesitated to be a homemaker in any of the traditional senses. Although these responsibilities are not required by today's environment, they were the responsibilities that were promised by the Wife to the Husband and they were the reasons that he was induced to marry her in the first instance. He had hoped to marry at last and forever and expressed to his wife his need for a warm, comfortable, and stable homeplace. The Wife argues that she redecorated the home and was responsible for the addition of a porch during the course of the marriage. The Husband does not deny that the Wife practiced her hobby of decorating, but does deny that such enhanced the value of his premarital asset or in any way provided a "substantial contribution" during the course of this marriage. The Court finds that the labors of the Wife were insubstantial and not the cause of any enhancement in the value of the Husband's home. As such, the Husband's home and contents were and shall remain an asset owned solely by him free of any claim or encumbrance in favor or the Wife. . . .

. . . With respect to the denial of wife's request for alimony, the trial court made the following relevant findings in the amended final judgment:

"The Wife has advanced a claim for the award of temporary, permanent, rehabilitative, and/or lump-sum alimony, in this cause. In support of her request, she states that she has lost her job and is presently receiving unemployment compensation as a result. While receiving unemployment compensation, the Court finds that the Wife has a net worth in excess of Two Million Dollars. In fact, while completing the weekly form work required by the Bureau of Unemployment Compensation, the Wife has managed and maintained her stock portfolio, reinvested moneys received through the sale of a small portion of real estate, effected a tax-free exchange of her South Carolina assets for investment property in North Carolina, and has acquired an interest in a Shoney's Restaurant. In short, the Wife is gainfully employed at this time, managing her substantial estate. The Court finds that the Wife fails to demonstrate the need or entitlement to receive alimony from the Husband. In fact, at no time during the long pendency of this case did the Wife request and receive alimony or support from the Husband."

Given the substantial wealth and income-producing property of the Wife, the relatively high earning capacity of the Wife, and the relatively short-term nature of this marriage, we see no abuse of the trials court's discretion in denying the Wife's request for alimony. For the same reason, we see no abuse of discretion in the trial court's denial of attorney's fees for the Wife. At the very least, reasonable people may differ as to the propriety of the trial court's ruling in this respect (citations omitted).

RESOURCES FOR ALIMONY

Ability to pay involves an evaluation of the resources available to the payor spouse. The court looks at the following resources of a payor spouse:

▼ Income from principal employment;
▼ Income from any additional employment;
▼ Income from rental property;
▼ Investment income;
▼ Income from royalties, copyrights, patents, and trademark rights; and
▼ Pension income.

To determine the amount of resources available, the court looks at the payor spouse's **net income.** Taxes, debts, and allowable expenses must be deducted from the spouse's **gross income.** Gross income refers to sum of all available sources of income. Net income is the dollar amount remaining after **allowable deductions** have been subtracted. These amounts must be carefully scrutinized because manipulation of these figures may occur during the course of the dissolution action. Some spouses intentionally reduce their income during the pendency of the case. They may refrain from taking promotions or raises, purposely cut down hours, drastically reduce commissions, get rid of a part-time job, or seek employment where they are paid cash "under the table." The payor spouse may also negotiate more fringe benefits from an employer for the purpose of showing less monetary compensation. The challenge for the payee spouse is to produce enough evidence to prove that the reduction in income was intentionally manipulated for the purpose of showing a smaller income. In this situation, it is essential that the discovery materials be reviewed carefully to determine whether the payor is living far beyond his or her means. Debts and expenses should also be scrutinized. Transfers to third parties, such as loans to family members and relatives, should also be looked on with suspicion. The question that must be asked is, was this debt or expense acquired in good faith?

DETERMINING SPOUSAL NEED

A spouse is entitled to an alimony award sufficient enough to support him or her in the standard of living to which he or she had grown accustomed during the marriage. If the office represents the spouse seeking alimony, instruct the client to keep a log of attempts to find work. It may be very crucial to preserve that information for trial later. Has spouse had difficulty finding work due to lack of marketable skills or age discrimination?

The client should also keep a log of all their expenses during the course of the divorce case. Later on, the paralegal may review and help clarify how much money the client needs to live. As stated earlier in this chapter, more and more frequently, women are perfectly able to reenter the workforce and become self-supporting. Family courts take this into consideration when making alimony awards. The trend is to award no alimony at all or alimony that is short in duration. The courts will also look at the property available for division between the spouses. If there is a sufficient amount of property to distribute, then the courts are less likely to award alimony.

Alimony may also be awarded where the payee spouse has custody of small children and cannot work full time. Because day care can be very expensive, it may make more economic sense for the courts to make an alimony award at least until the children have reached the age where they are in school full time. The custodial parent will then have more opportunities to seek employment outside the home.

An award of alimony is highly probable in the case of an older homemaker who lacks the skills to go into the workforce or in the case of a spouse who is in poor health. The courts want to prevent a spouse from becoming a "charge on the state;" that is, from having to apply for welfare and be supported by the taxpayers.

BALANCING PROPERTY DIVISION, CHILD SUPPORT, AND ALIMONY

Courts do not make alimony awards in a vacuum. Judges balance property division, child support, and alimony in order to reach an adequate resolution given the resources of the parties and their particular circumstances. Property awards divide the marital assets. Child support awards provide money paid to the custodial spouse for the benefit of the children. When there is an adequate amount of property, a property award may be more attractive especially if payor spouse's income or employment is unstable. If a spouse is steadily employed and income is stable, alimony may be a better choice. Some jurisdictions have even codified consideration of the property award in their alimony statutes. A higher child support award may be preferable in certain cases because the custodial parent does not have to declare child support payments as income for tax purposes. On the other hand, child support terminates when the child reaches the age of majority. The spouse is then left only with the more modest alimony payment.

FIGURE 5–2
A court may reduce an alimony award once a payee spouse has entered the workforce and is gainfully employed.

TYPES OF ALIMONY

The court may order alimony during the pendency of the divorce action and at the time that it renders its final orders at the divorce trial or other judgment. At the time of making the final orders, the court may award or the parties may agree to either permanent, rehabilitative, or reimbursement alimony. This section describes the different types of alimony with which the paralegal should become familiar.

PENDENTE LITE ALIMONY

Pendente lite **alimony** or temporary alimony awards are payments made during the pendency of the divorce with the purpose of providing temporary financial support for the spouse. In order for a court to make a temporary alimony award, the payor spouse must be served with notice, be physically present in court, and be given the opportunity to be heard and present his or her side of the case.

The Florida, Massachusetts, and Alabama statutes cited below are examples of the family courts' statutory power to provide temporary support for spouses.

STATUTES

FLORIDA STATUTES ANNOTATED (WEST)

61.71. Alimony pendente lite; suit money
In every proceeding for dissolution of the marriage, a party may claim alimony and suit money in the petition or by motion, and if the petition is well founded, the court shall allow a reasonable sum therefor. If a party in any proceeding for dissolution of marriage claims alimony or suit money in his or her answer or by motion, and the answer or motion is well founded, the court shall allow a reasonable sum therefor.

MASSACHUSETTS GENERAL LAW'S ANNOTATED (WEST)

§ 17. Pendency of action; allowance; alimony
The court may require either party to pay into court for the use of the other party during the pendency or the action an amount to enable him to maintain or defend the action, and to pay to him alimony during the pendency of the action. When the court makes an order for alimony on behalf of a party, and such party is not a member of a private group health insurance plan, the court shall include in such order for alimony a provision relating to health insurance, which provision shall be in accordance with section thirty-four.

CODE OF ALABAMA

§ 30-2-50. Allowance for support during pendency of action.
Pending an action for divorce, the court may make an allowance for the support of either spouse out of the estate of the other spouse, suitable to the spouse's estate and the condition in life of the parties, for a period of time not longer than necessary for the prosecution of the complaint for divorce.

FINAL ORDERS

Permanent Alimony

Permanent alimony is the term applied to court-ordered payments that are to be made to a spouse on a regular and periodic basis and that terminate only upon the death, remarriage, or cohabitation of the other spouse or upon court order. Permanent alimony is awarded with less frequency today. Women have increasingly joined the workforce and developed marketable employment skills to help them become self-sufficient. If you recall the historical discussion regarding the extension of the husband's duty to support after awarding divorce *a mensa et thoro,* you will see that the expanded role of women in the workplace has made permanent alimony a rare disposition in today's divorce courts. Spouses who are more likely to receive permanent alimony awards are those who have been in long-term marriages, those unable to acquire marketable skills, and those who are ill or have a disability. It is highly unlikely for spouses in these cases to be able to go to work and earn enough to adequately support themselves.

Permanent Alimony to the Rescue

In the following case, the appellate court found that the wife was entitled to permanent alimony and remanded the case so that the trial court could determine the amount. The court again balances need versus the ability to pay and Mrs. Kirkland wins the balancing act.

BETTY F. KIRKLAND v. JOE RAY KIRKLAND

568 So. 2d 494 (Fla. App. 1st Dist. 1990)

District Court of Appeal of Florida, First District

ERVIN, JUDGE.

Appellant, Betty F. Kirkland, appeals the trial court's judgment dissolving the marriage between her and her former husband, appellee Joe Ray Kirkland. She contends that the court erred. . . in failing to award the wife permanent periodic and rehabilitative alimony; and in refusing to require the husband to pay the wife's attorney's fees. We reverse the trial court's . . . denial of permanent, periodic alimony to the wife. . . .

. . . Finally, although we find no error in the trial court's denial of rehabilitative alimony to the former wife, we cannot make a similar conclusion regarding the court's failure to grant her permanent, periodic alimony. We consider that the former wife is entitled to an award of permanent, periodic alimony, in addition to the $4,000 lump-sum alimony awarded to her. Under *Canakaris v. Canakaris*, 382 So. 2d 1197 (Fla.1980), a court must evaluate the need of one spouse and the ability of the other to pay in determining whether to grant the petitioning spouse an award of permanent, periodic alimony. In the present case, wife was a homemaker during most of the marriage, although she was briefly employed as a secretary. She obtained some schooling to improve her secretarial skills. Early in the marriage, the husband obtained a master's degree in education. At the time of the final hearing, the wife was employed at a convenience store earning $497.12 per month. By the time of the attorney's fee hearing she was a correctional officer earning $5.89 per hour, or $779.37 net income per month. Husband's net salary as director of vocational education in Columbia County was $2,743.00 per month. Based on a comparison of the parties' incomes and the court's distribution of assets, the trial court erred in failing to award the wife permanent alimony.

Although the trial court was no doubt correct, based upon the evidence before it, in concluding that the "[w]ife has sufficient skills, education and training which would enable her to earn wages sufficient to support herself." This is not the proper criterion for determining a spouse's entitlement to an award of permanent, periodic alimony. As the Supreme Court observed in *Canakaris*, "Permanent periodic alimony is used to provide the needs and the necessities of life to a former spouse as they have been established by the marriage of the parties." *Canakaris*, 382 So. 2d at 1201. At forty-five years of age, with secretarial skills, it is highly doubtful that the former wife will be able to attain the style of life to which she had become accustomed while living with her former husband. If the trial court's award to the wife remains unchanged, her standard of living will be significantly reduced from that which she enjoyed during the marriage, while the husband's will remain virtually the same and perhaps even improve once he has satisfied the parties' short-term debts. *See Harrison v. Harrison*, 540 So. 2d 230, 231 (Fla. 1st DCA 1989) (trial court "must ensure that neither spouse passes from misfortune to prosperity or from prosperity to misfortune.") Because the former husband has not shown that he lacks the resources to pay a periodic alimony award, the trial court on remand shall determine a proper award of permanent alimony to the wife. Pursuant to Section 61.08, Florida Statutes (1989). . . .

. . . AFFIRMED in part, REVERSED in part, and REMANDED.

Rehabilitative Alimony

The frequency of **rehabilitative alimony** awards reflects the current legal trend of providing short-term, financial support to a former spouse. Rehabilitative alimony is awarded for a limited period of time to give the spouse the opportunity to become self-sufficient. In determining whether this type of alimony is appropriate, the crucial question to be answered is whether this spouse has the *ability* to become self-sufficient. For the traditional housewife who finds herself divorced after many years of marriage, and has never worked outside the home, this may not be possible; nor is it feasible for a disabled or ill spouse. In many cases however, the spouse either has marketable skills or has the ability to obtain them within a reasonable period of time. Under these circumstances an award of rehabilitative alimony would provide the spouse with some financial assistance while she gets back on her feet.

Tennis Wife Gets Rehabilitative Alimony

The wife worked on more then her backhand in this marriage! In the end, Mrs. Evans had to join the workforce and establish a plan to become self-sufficient.

FIGURE 5–3
Judges can exercise their discretion when awarding rehabitative alimony while the payee spouse gets back on his or her feet.

EDWIN E. EVANS v. CYNTHIA S. EVANS

559 N.W. 2d 240 (S.D. 1997)

SOUTH DAKOTA SUPREME COURT

GILBERTSON, JUSTICE.

FACTS AND PROCEDURE

Ed and Cyndy were married in June 1973, following completion of Ed's first year of law school. Cyndy had completed her college degree and worked full time from the beginning of the marriage until the parties moved to Sioux Falls in June 1977. At that time Cyndy was expecting her first child. She did not return to the work force.

The parties' lifestyle was such that they belonged to a country club, had household help, and dined out frequently. They generally took two family vacations a year. The record reflects Ed worked many hours, including evenings and some weekends, and was often required to be out of town for days to weeks at a time. Cyndy volunteered her time in community, church, and school-related activities.

The parties have two children, Ashley and Kelsey, who were ages 17 and 14, respectively, at the time of the divorce trial. They attend parochial school and participate in many school and extracurricular activities. They drive late model cars and wear the best brand-named clothing. Cyndy has largely been responsible for coordinating the children's activities. While Ed was not available as much as Cyndy, he too took an interest in their children, assisting them with their homework and driving them to out-of-town functions.

In 1990, the parties began construction of a new home in Sioux Falls which ultimately cost considerably more money than had been originally planned. Around this time, Cyndy discontinued her volunteer activities and devoted her time instead to tennis and other personal interests. The parties admit they had problems with communication; the marriage began to deteriorate. In 1993, Cyndy invited a twenty-seven year old male tennis friend to move into the family's residence without discussing it with Ed and without his knowledge. When Ed learned of his wife's houseguest, he left home for a few days but returned at the children's request. He attempted to improve his relationship with Cyndy, but she showed little interest in attempts and spent evenings out with her friends, returning home in the early morning hours. Ed moved into a separate bedroom to show his displeasure, but the couple did not discuss their problems. By the summer of 1994, Cyndy had ceased attending family vacations, preferring instead to spend time with her friends at Lake Okoboji, while Ed and the children took family vacations without her. In the fall of 1994, Ed learned Cyndy was having an affair with a man who owned a home in Lake Okoboji. Although Cyndy initially denied the affair, she eventually admitted it was true. Upon learning this, Ed moved out of the parties' home.

Ed and Cyndy attempted a reconciliation, Cyndy promising to discontinue the affair and Ed promising to spend less time at work and more time with Cyndy and the children. Ed returned home, bought Cyndy a new car that she wanted, planned a family vacation in Jamaica for Thanksgiving, and purchased tickets for a concert Cyndy wanted to attend in Minneapolis. Within four days of Ed's return home, Cyndy announced she did not intend to stop seeing other men. Ed left home for the last time.

He continued spending time with Cyndy, however, and the family went on the planned vacation and to the concert and shopping trips in Minneapolis. Ed continued to provide spending money and paid the household expenses. He reduced his hours at work. Ed sought counseling and encouraged Cyndy to attend counseling sessions with him, or alone. She refused. Ed eventually gave up trying to reconcile the marriage.

During this period of separation, Ed paid Cyndy $10,000 per month to support her and their children. She stated they could not live on this amount. Ed suggested she sell the house. Cyndy refused and Ed filed the divorce action.

The trial court heard the matter over a four-day period, October 30–31, 1995, and on December 12–13, 1995. The trial court determined issues involving child support, property division, alimony award, and attorney fees. On February 16, 1996, the trial court awarded Ed a divorce on grounds of adultery and dismissed Cyndy's counterclaim. Both parties appealed the judgment of the trial court.

Cyndy raises . . . issues as follows. . . .

. . . 3. Whether the trial court erred in determining the amount of alimony awarded?

ANALYSIS AND DECISION

. . . 3. Whether the trial court erred in determining the amount of alimony awarded?

The trial court awarded Cyndy rehabilitative alimony of $2,500 per month for six months, and $1,000 per month for five years thereafter. Cyndy's vocational expert opined, and the trial court found, that she would be able to earn $25,000 per year within three to five years, after retraining and reentering the work force. Cyndy appeals this award, arguing she is entitled to substantially more alimony. She bases her argument on her years of service to the marriage as a wife and homemaker and the vast discrepancy between earning capabilities of the parties.

Our standard of review of challenges to a trial court's award of alimony is well established. *Dussart v. Dussart,* 1996 S.D. 41, 546 NW2d 109, 111; *DeVries v. DeVries,* 519 N.W.2d 73, 77 (S.D. 1994).

A trial court is vested with discretion in awarding alimony and its decision will not be disturbed unless it clearly appears the trial court abused its discretion. Trial courts must consider the following factors when setting an alimony award: (1) the length of the marriage; (2) the parties' respective ages and health; (3) the earning capacity of each party; (4) their financial situations after the property division; (5) their station in life or social standing; and (6) the relative fault in the termination of the marriage. A trial court's findings on these factors must support its legal conclusions. As often stated, an abuse of discretion exists only where discretion has been "exercised to an end or purpose not justified by, and clearly against, reason and evidence."

Additional factors must be considered when the trial court makes an award of rehabilitative alimony. *Saint Pierre v. Saint Pierre,* 357 N.W.2d 250, 252 (S.D. 1984). In awarding rehabilitative or reimbursement alimony, the trial court should be guided by "the amount of supporting spouse's contributions, his or her foregone [sic] opportunities to enhance or improve professional or vocational skills, and the duration of the marriage following completion of the nonsupporting spouse's professional education." *Id.* An award of rehabilitative alimony must be designed to meet an educational need or plan of action whose existence finds some support in the record. *Radigan,* 465 N.W.2d at 486; *Ryken v. Ryken,* 440 N.W.2d 300, 303 (S.D. 1989) *(Ryken I).* "[T]he decision to award 're-imbursement' or 'rehabilitative' alimony, and, if so, in what amount and for what length of time, is committed to the sound discretion of the trial court. The purpose of rehabilitative alimony is to put the supporting spouse in a position to likewise upgrade their own economic marketability." *Studt v. Studt,* 443 N.W.2d 639, 643 (S.D. 1989) (internal citations omitted).

A review of the record in this case demonstrates the trial court's consideration of all the necessary factors, including Cyndy's traditional role of homemaker {4} and the parties discrepancy in earning capabilities. {5} The trial court also considered Cyndy's financial situation after the property division and her fault in the dissolution of the parties' marriage and lack of cooperation in Ed's efforts to save the marriage. In granting a divorce in favor of Ed on the basis of adultery, the trial court had before it numerous examples of uncontested marital misconduct by Cyndy upon which to base its finding of fault:

1.   Moving into the family home a twenty-seven year old male tennis friend without Ed's prior knowledge or consent;

2.   Refusing to attend family vacations as in the past, but rather vacationing at Lake Okoboji with friends;

3.   Having an affair with a man who owned a home at Lake Okoboji;

4.   Refusing to stop seeing other men after Ed found out about the affair, and when Ed attempted reconciliation, and

5.   Refusing to attend when Ed sought counseling and encouraged Cyndy to attend either with him or alone.

The trial court properly concluded that Cyndy's fault was a factor to be taken into account in deciding alimony.

Following division of the marital property, Cyndy leaves the marriage with over one million dollars in assets. Approximately $400,000 of these assets are in the form of cash payments to be paid to Cyndy by Ed either immediately or over a period of the next five years at 7% interest on the unpaid balance. The trial court found that, through conservative investment, Cyndy's liquid assets would provide annual income to her of $40,792, or 3,399 per month, without invading the principal. Following three to five years of wage-earning, this monthly income would rise to $4,782 per month. The trial court specifically noted that Cyndy would not be able to live in the luxurious lifestyle she enjoyed while married to Ed but, at the same time, should not be able to demand excessive long-term support from the husband to whom she did not wish to be married. The trial court concluded Cyndy should be able to live comfortably on the amount awarded. The court acknowledged Cyndy's contribution to the family's accumulation of wealth and her husband's success, and further noted the award was justified due to Cyndy's forgone employment opportunities during the parties' twenty-two year marriage. We cannot say the trial court's award was against reason and the evidence.

Regarding "educational need or plan of action" that must be evidenced from the record for an award of rehabilitative alimony, *Radigan,* 465 N.W.2d at 486, Cyndy presented herself for evaluation by the vocational rehabilitation specialist who testified on her behalf. Following his evaluation, which included a personal interview with Cyndy, taking her educational and work history, and submitting her to various vocational and personality-type testing, this expert concluded Cyndy's best course of action for reentering the work force would be to complete approximately six months of select computer courses at a vocational school and begin work in an entry-level position in the banking field. Cyndy had worked in banking before the parties moved to Sioux Falls in 1977 and her test scores in the vocational evaluation demonstrated a high interest and ability in this area. Her test scores also were high in the fields of business and sales. Although Cyndy did not express to this specialist any specific plans for employment or retraining during their interview, it was noted by the expert at trial that this is not unusual for a person who had not been career-minded during a long marriage and is presently going through a divorce. The vocational rehabilitation specialist testified he and Cyndy discussed assistance with her career development after the divorce.

We affirm on this issue. . . .

Reimbursement Alimony

As the following chapter illustrates, some jurisdictions have categorized a professional or advanced degree acquired during the marriage as marital property. This categorization has enabled the courts to put a monetary value on the degree and to award the nondegreed spouse either money or other property for his or her contributions made during the marriage which enabled the other spouse to obtain the degree. Many jurisdictions however do not categorize a degree as property. This would leave the nondegreed spouse uncompensated for the sacrifices endured in hopes that their family would have a better future. Courts, however, have responded to this injustice by creating the **reimbursement alimony** award. Here, the nondegreed spouse may be "reimbursed" for his or her contribution to the student spouse's attainment of the advanced degree, which results in an enhanced earning capacity. The nondegreed spouse may have helped pay the student spouse's tuition, supported the family while the student spouse was in school, or relocated or put off pursuing his or her own education in hopes that these sacrifices would later pay off in an increased standard of living. In these jurisdictions, the nondegreed spouse is reimbursed for the monetary and nonmonetary efforts that enhanced the other spouse's earning capacity. Reimbursement alimony awards are generally nonmodifiable and nonterminable so as to fully compensate the nondegreed spouse.

I Don't Want Alimony to End!

In *Lalone*, the Supreme Court found that the wife's efforts did not increase her husband's earning capacity, which did not entitle her to reimbursement alimony. In addition, the wife also sought to extend her award of alimony beyond the husband's death and her remarriage. The Court however applied general principles of law and affirmed the lower court's award of alimony in the amount of $1,500 per month for ten years.

IN RE THE MARRIAGE OF GARY L. LALONE AND SHARON M. LALONE

469 N.W.2d 695 (IOWA 1991)

SUPREME COURT OF IOWA

LARSON, JUSTICE.

Sharon Lalone's appeal from decree of dissolution claims error in child support and alimony allowances, division of some of the parties' marital assets, and the allowance of attorney fees. We affirm.

Our review of the evidence is de novo. Gary and Sharon were married in 1972. At that time, Gary had graduated from college with a degree in business administration, and Sharon had attended college part-time. Following their marriage, both parties worked full time. However, since the birth of their first child in 1979, Sharon had worked only part-time, averaging less than $5,000 per year in income. Sharon has assumed the primary responsibilities for the home and child care and is not presently employed outside the home. The children of the parties, at the time of the dissolution, were seven and eleven years of age. Gary was forty, and Sharon was thirty-seven.

In 1982, Gary assumed a management position with a chain of retail clothing stores, advancing to the position of regional manager and manager of the local Storm Lake store. Gary's base salary is $37,200, and he receives family medical and dental benefits from his employer. In addition, a substantial yearly bonus is paid to Gary based on a percentage of the company profits. The bonus is paid each April. Gary's income had averaged in excess of $100,000 for the five years preceding the dissolution. In 1990, his gross income was $144,428.

The parties entered a pretrial stipulation regarding the disposition of some of their assets and agreed on custody and visitation. Sharon received physical care of the children, and Gary received liberal visitation. Physical care and visitation are not issues on appeal. . . .

. . . II. ALIMONY

The district court ordered Gary to pay alimony of $1500 per month for ten years. Alimony would terminate earlier upon the death of either party or Sharon's remarriage. Sharon contends that the court should not have placed any conditions on Gary's alimony obligation, although she does not challenge either the amount or the ten-year limit.

Sharon's argument that she should have been awarded unconditional alimony is based on her argument that it was allowed as "reimbursement" alimony. *See In re Marriage of Francis*, 442 N.W.2d 59, 64 (Iowa 1989). Reimbursement alimony is predicated upon economic sacrifices made by one spouse during the marriage which directly enhances the future earning capacity of the other. Reimbursement alimony is not subject to modification or termination until full payment has been made, except that it will terminate upon the recipient's death. *Id.*

We do not agree that this is reimbursement alimony. This is not a case similar to *Francis*, in which the wife directly increased the husband's earning capacity by assisting in his obtaining a medical degree. In this case, while Sharon worked part-time, her efforts did not directly increase Gary's earning capacity. Rather, the district court found, and we agree, that both Gary and Sharon contributed to the success of the family unit and were rewarded with financial success. We believe that the equal division of the marital property adequately compensated Sharon for any contributions made by her.

Sharon also contends that the alimony should continue beyond the time of her death. Gary responds that, because alimony is based on a need for support, this need would terminate on her death. And, although she contends it should be available for payment to the children, Gary points out that the decree required him to provide $500,000 in life insurance for the benefit of the two children. Further, under Internal Revenue Code section 71(b)(1)(D), periodic payments must cease on the death of the recipient in order to be considered alimony. We agree that alimony should cease on Sharon's death.

As to Sharon's contention that alimony should not terminate on Gary's death, it is the general rule that alimony will terminate upon the death of the payor. *In re Marriage of Bornstein*, 359 N.W.2d 500, 503 (Iowa 1984). Also, as previously noted, the decree provides for life insurance in a substantial amount for the benefit of the children. Inclusion of this amount of money in the family unit, as Gary contends, would substantially alleviate any financial problems arising from Gary's death.

Sharon also complains that the alimony would terminate on her remarriage. Under our law, even if a decree does not provide for automatic termination in remarriage, there is a presumption that alimony will cease in the absence of a showing of extraordinary circumstances. *In re Marriage of Shima*, 360 N.W.2d 827, 828 (Iowa 1985). If Sharon remarries and remains in need of financial assistance, the burden of showing a need for continued alimony should be on her to do so in an application to modify the decree.

We believe the provision terminating alimony on remarriage is reasonable and is in accordance with our existing law. . . .

. . . AFFIRMED

MODES OF ALIMONY PAYMENT

Alimony payments may be made on a **periodic** basis (i.e., weekly), or they may be made in one single payment, known as **lump sum alimony** or **alimony in gross.** Once a spouse receives an award of lump sum alimony, his or her interest has vested. This means that he or she is entitled to the entire amount. This amount may be made in installments, if agreed upon by the parties or ordered by the court.

MODIFICATION OF ALIMONY

Modification of alimony addresses the issue of whether alimony may be either increased or decreased after the original order has been entered. To change or "modify" an alimony award, the party seeking the modification must go back to court and request that the court modify the original order. The moving party must prove that a substantial change of circumstances occurred since the date of the original order and that the change was involuntary. Because the court made the original order, only the court can change the obligations of the parties. For example, *pendente lite* orders may be modified during the *pendente lite* phase as long as the moving party can satisfy his or her burden of proof.

EXAMPLE

John, who is employed at a factory, files for divorce. His wife Mary files a motion for pendente lite *or temporary alimony. Based on her need and John's ability to pay, she is awarded $100 a week. John loses his job and does not pay Mary for ten weeks. John owes Mary $1,000 in alimony* **arrearages** *or "back alimony."*

Upon losing his job, John should have immediately filed a motion for modification with the court. He would then be able to get the original $100 order modified because of a substantial change in circumstances, that is, the loss of his job. Once Mary stops receiving payments, she has the right to the arrearage, or amounts due by court order but unpaid. Mary may seek to enforce the original order by returning to court.

Final orders may also be modified upon a showing of a substantial change in circumstances. A party may request an order of one dollar of alimony per year. Obviously, this is only a **nominal alimony** amount; however, a request for such an award is necessary so the party may seek a modification after the entering of a final judgment. If no alimony is awarded to the spouse at the time the divorce decree is entered, he or she will be prohibited from coming back to court and seeking an alimony award in the future, because no basis exists for modifying it. The reason for the one dollar award is so that a nominal amount of alimony will leave the issue of alimony modifiable in the future in the event of a substantial change in circumstances.

Remember that an alimony award may be achieved in one of two ways: by agreement of the parties or by order of the court. When the parties are drafting an agreement, the modifiability of the alimony award must be addressed in the settlement agreement. While the parties may have agreed to the nonmodifiability of alimony and included such a clause in the separation agreement, the court may not enforce such a provision if a spouse would have to go on public assistance and be supported at taxpayers' expense.

Permanent alimony may be modified if there is a substantial change in circumstances. Remarriage automatically terminates permanent alimony in some jurisdictions, and in others, the party seeking the modification must do so through the court. When a former spouse remarries, the new spouse is legally obligated to provide spousal support. **Cohabitation,** which means unmarried parties living together, may also terminate alimony. While cohabiting parties do not have a legal obligation to support each other, sharing expenses may improve the financial position of the divorced spouse; in other cases, it may not. The court must look at requests for modification on a case-by-case basis.

Cohabitation Nixes Alimony Award

The Supreme Court of Connecticut upheld the trial court's termination of the wife's alimony award. The husband was able to prove that the wife's circumstances substantially changed when she moved in with the handyman.

RITA A. LUPIEN v. HERVEY A. LUPIEN

192 CONN. 443, 472 A.2d 18 (CONN. 1984)

SUPREME COURT OF CONNECTICUT

SPEZIALE, CHIEF JUSTICE.

The plaintiff appeals from the judgment to the trial court terminating her award of alimony. Because we hold that the trial court was not clearly erroneous in finding that the plaintiff was living with another person under circumstances that caused such a change of circumstances as to alter her financial needs, there is no error.

The parties were divorced on September 22, 1967, and the defendant was ordered to pay the plaintiff $150 per week periodic alimony. In 1980, the defendant moved to "modify the Judgment by reducing, suspending or terminating the alimony." The defendant claimed, inter alia, that the plaintiff was living with another man under circumstances that caused a change in her financial needs.[1]

Following a hearing on the motion, the trial court found that the plaintiff "is living openly with another man [and] receives support from this other man. . . ." The trial court modified the judgment of 1967 and ordered alimony terminated. The plaintiff appealed and alleges that

there was insufficient evidence to find either that the plaintiff was living with another person or that her living arrangements had caused a change in her financial circumstances. We disagree.

To modify an award of alimony pursuant to General Statute § 46b-86(b), the trial court must find "that the party receiving the periodic alimony is living with another person under circumstances which the court finds should result in the modification, suspension or termination of alimony because the living arrangements cause such a change of circumstances as to alter the financial needs of that party." (Footnote omitted). See *Kaplan v. Kaplan,* 185 Conn. 42, 440 A.2d 252 (1981). The trial court so found but the plaintiff argues that its finding was "clearly erroneous."

The evidence before the court showed that Gilbert Poirier had been living in a room in the plaintiff's home for two years. The plaintiff was paid $30 weekly for food by Poirier and he performed numerous handyman chores for her.[2] These chores included roofing the garage, recon-

---

[1]The defendant also claimed that the plaintiff's employment by Gilbert Poirier had caused a change in the plaintiff's financial circumstances.

[2]The plaintiff's twenty year old son also resided in the house and paid $30 weekly to the plaintiff.

struction of cubicles remaining from the defendant's dental practice, repair and maintenance of a swimming pool, and installation in the plaintiff's house of a wood stove owned by Poirier. Because of lack of finances, the plaintiff had not previously been able to "fix up" the house. Poirier and the plaintiff are "going steady" and "occasionally" have "marital relations." The plaintiff would like to marry him. After finding that the plaintiff and Poirier were "cohabitating" and that "the living arrangements . . . have caused such a change of circumstances as to alter materi-

ally her financial needs," the trial court terminated the alimony award (footnote omitted). . . .

. . . There was evidence in this case to indicate both the plaintiff was living with another person and that this living arrangement caused such change in circumstances as to alter her financial needs. While termination of alimony is a harsh result, we are unable to say that the trial court's findings were clearly erroneous (footnote omitted). . . .

. . . There is no error.

Rehabilitative alimony is generally nonmodifiable; however, some courts retain jurisdiction for the purpose of modification. Lump sum alimony awards are generally not modifiable. This means that the lump sum alimony award is not affected by remarriage or cohabitation and at the death of the payor spouse, the payee spouse may sue the payor's estate for any payments due. Because reimbursement alimony is awarded on the basis of the amount contributed by the nondegreed spouse, it is commonly nonmodifiable.

ESCALATION CLAUSES AND COST OF LIVING INCREASE CLAUSES

In drafting settlement agreement provisions regarding alimony, the parties may include an **escalation clause** or **cost of living clause.** An escalation clause provides for increases in the alimony payments due to the increase of payor's income and an increase in the cost of living. The escalation clause obviates the need for the parties to go back to court for modifications, which will save parties time and money.

MEDICAL INSURANCE

Because alimony involves the support of a former spouse, this chapter would not be complete without a brief discussion of medical insurance. The **Consolidated Omnibus Budget Reconciliation Act (COBRA),** 26 U.S.C. sec. 4980B(f), is a federal law that enables a nonemployee spouse to continue his health insurance coverage provided by his spouse's employer, for a period of three years after the divorce, as long as the nonemployee spouse pays the premium. The children of the marriage may also be covered under COBRA during their dependency on their parents. Either one parent or both will be responsible for providing medical insurance coverage for the children.

State laws also have an impact on medical insurance coverage. Some jurisdictions require a divorced spouse to provide coverage for former spouses who are not able to provide coverage for themselves.

STATUTES

MASSACHUSETTS GENERAL LAWS ANNOTATED (WEST)

§ 34. Alimony or assignment of estate; determination of amount; health insurance.
. . . When the court makes an order for alimony on behalf of a spouse, and such spouse is not covered by a private group health insurance plan, said court shall determine whether the obligor under such order has health insurance on a group plan available to him through an employer or organization that may be extended to cover the spouse for whom support is ordered. When said court has determined that the obligor has such insurance, said court shall include in the support order a requirement that the obligor exercise the option of additional coverage in favor of such spouse

Sometimes the COBRA payments are too high and a spouse may seek health insurance through their employer or other resource.

ATTORNEY'S FEES

It is the responsibility of the respective parties to pay their **attorney's fees.** A common myth still held by many women is that the husband is required to pay her attorney's fees. The case of *Orr v. Orr*, 440 U.S. 268 (1979) declared this statutory requirement unconstitutional. Either party, however, may seek attorney's fees from the other spouse. The standard the court applies in determining attorney's fees is the need of one spouse and the ability to pay of the other spouse.

Most attorneys require clients to pay a retainer before taking on their divorce case and will later seek an award of attorney's fees to reimburse their client. For those who cannot afford a retainer, some attorneys may motion the court at the beginning of the proceedings for an advance award of legal fees to represent the needy spouse. In these cases, it is advisable that the representation of the spouse be contingent upon the granting of the motion for attorney's fees by the court and the receipt of payment. The rules of ethics require that an attorney's fee must be *reasonable.* It is within the court's discretion to determine what is reasonable. When defending the moving party's motion for attorney's fees, it is essential that an itemized bill be requested and that the charges be reviewed.

TERMINATION OF ALIMONY

REMARRIAGE

Alimony usually terminates on remarriage. The underlying policy is that upon remarriage, the new spouse has a duty to support. It would be unfair to allow a divorced spouse, who now has remarried, to receive support from two sources. In some states alimony automatically terminates upon remarriage and payor spouse simply ceases payments. In other states, the parties petition the court for termination of alimony.

COHABITATION

In some states, alimony may be modified when a recipient cohabits with a member of the opposite sex. The problem with cohabitation as opposed to remarriage is that a cohabitant has no legal duty to support. It is important when drafting the settlement agreement to specifically indicate what type of conduct gives rise to a modification.

DEATH

Alimony terminates on the death of either party unless otherwise stated in the settlement agreement or the divorce decree. If support is to be extended beyond death, it can be accomplished by an irrevocable insurance policy on the payor's life, naming payee spouse as beneficiary. Lump sum alimony paid in installments and property division awards do not terminate on the death of the payor spouse.

FIGURE 5–4
Alimony may be modified if an alimony recipient decides to cohabit with a member of the opposite sex.

TAX CONSEQUENCES OF ALIMONY

Alimony payments to a spouse are considered a form of income to the spouse. Therefore, alimony is taxable to the recipient and deductible to the payor. The deductibility of alimony is advantageous to a payor spouse with high earnings. It is very important to obtain the Social Security number of the payor or recipient spouse so your client will have that information available at tax time. If your office is representing the recipient spouse, the attorney may encourage that spouse to pay quarterly estimated taxes to avoid a hefty tax burden at the end of the year.

THE IRS RECAPTURE RULE

In 1986, the Internal Revenue Service defined alimony as a payment made in cash or its equivalent pursuant to a court-ordered divorce agreement that terminates on death. In the past, lawyers would label property division as alimony for the purpose of deducting property distribution payments.

Property settlements are not deductible and by labeling these settlements as alimony, the payor spouse would deduct these payments from his income taxes. The IRS redefined alimony and limited the amount of alimony that can be deducted in the first three years after the divorce. If alimony payments total $15,000 or less per year, they are deductible. If they exceed $15,000, the payor must satisfy complex tax rules for this deduction. If the parties do not wish to have alimony taxed as income or deducted, then it should be indicated in the settlement agreement. This is known as the **IRS recapture rule.** The majority of property settlements in a divorce case are made in the first three years after the divorce. This is known as **front loading.** Lawyers were structuring property settlements by classifying them as "alimony." By calling a property settlement "alimony" the payor client could deduct the amount from income taxes. The IRS monitors alimony payments for front loading. If the majority of payments are made in a period of years, at the year 3 mark, this will indicate that front loading has occurred. The IRS will then seek to *recapture* the tax deduction. To be safe, payments in year 1 should not exceed payments made in year 2 or year 3 by more than 15 percent.

FAMILY SUPPORT PAYMENTS VERSUS SEPARATE PAYMENTS OF ALIMONY AND CHILD SUPPORT

Family support payments is the term given to regular, periodic payments a payor spouse makes to the other spouse for the financial maintenance of both the ex-spouse and children. This amount is not delineated into a portion that comprises spousal alimony and a portion for child support, but rather one sum deemed "family support." Care should be taken so that a reduction of the amount of the family support payment does not occur upon the happening of a child-support related event such as emancipation, employment, or the end of schooling.

The problem lies in determining what is alimony and what is child support. The IRS watches unallocated family support payments carefully. If the unallocated support payment is reduced due to changes in a child's age or needs, the IRS will be able to determine how much has been allocated for alimony and how much has been allocated for child support. If previously, the payor spouse was deducting as alimony payments an amount greater than the IRS subsequent determination of what constituted alimony, the payor spouse will have to pay a back tax and possibly a fine. If a payee spouse claimed as income a lesser amount of the family support payment than was actually allocated for alimony, the payee spouse will owe the IRS back taxes and also probably be subject to a fine.

EFFECTS OF BANKRUPTCY ON ALIMONY, CHILD SUPPORT, AND PROPERTY DIVISION

Alimony and child support awards are not dischargeable under federal bankruptcy law. Property awards, however, are dischargeable. If a bankruptcy action is being contemplated due to high debts, the recipient client should opt for alimony and child support payments instead of property division payments.

PRACTICAL TIPS FOR CLIENTS

▼ Never make alimony or child support payments in cash.

The family attorney and/or the paralegal who has been working with the client should emphasize to the client that it is essential that alimony and child support obligations be paid with either check or money order to preserve proof that payments were actually made. If your client must use cash, tell the client that it is important to get a receipt. Receipt booklets may be purchased at any stationery store. The recipient client may receive alimony payments by being paid directly by the payor or through a **wage execution** where the alimony payment is deducted from the payor spouse's paycheck, or an automatic transfer from payor's bank account occurs.

▼ Keep accurate and complete records of payments.

Clients should be told of the importance of record keeping. Both the payor spouse and the recipient spouse should keep good records for tax purposes, and may want to photocopy checks, money orders, or, if cash is tendered, request a copy of the receipt. The IRS can and may dispute deduction amounts or income received, therefore adequate record keeping is essential.

▼ Recognize the need for lifestyle changes.

The financial reality for the recipient spouse is that alimony may not be enough to live on. It is important for the attorney or the paralegal to review a client's financial information with the client to determine how much he or she will need to live on and whether adjustments need to be made to their lifestyles after the divorce. The client may have to sell assets or find part-time work in order to supplement income. The client may have to go on a budget or cut up credit cards and cancel them with the credit card company in order not to incur any further debt. Consumer credit counseling services may be a good resource for clients who are in over their heads. Displaced homemaker groups may also provide support and budget counseling to help the traditional homemaker through the transition.

FIGURE 5–5
If the IRS decides to dispute alimony allocations, adequate record keeping becomes essential.

ENFORCEMENT OF COURT-ORDERED PAYMENTS

When a party entitled to alimony payments pursuant to a court order is not paid, that party may commence a civil **contempt proceeding** to force the payor spouse to comply with the court's order. This process begins with the recipient spouse filing the appropriate paperwork within that jurisdiction (e.g., a motion for contempt or a citation with an order to show cause). In the proper document, the recipient will state what was awarded in the original order, that the payor spouse has not paid since a specific date, and include a request that the delinquent spouse be found in contempt of court. These documents are served on the payor and filed in the court where the original alimony award was entered. A contempt is an extension of the divorce matter, therefore it is unnecessary to assert personal jurisdiction over the payor spouse. The only requirement is service, notice of the proceedings, and the opportunity to be heard.

Once the parties are in court, it is the payor spouse's burden to prove that she has, in fact, kept up the alimony payments and has the canceled checks or receipts to prove it. If the payor spouse cannot provide such proof, the court will order the payor spouse to pay the arrearage. If the arrearage cannot be paid in a lump sum, the court will make the arrearage payable in installments. The payor will then find herself obligated to make weekly payments on the arrearage in addition to the weekly payments authorized by the original court order.

The filing of a contempt action by the recipient spouse or payee spouse will often precipitate the filing of a modification motion by the payor spouse. This is especially true in cases where the payor spouse has failed to discharge his or her alimony or child support obligation because of unfavorably changed financial circumstances.

EXAMPLE

On August 1, John is ordered by the court to pay $100 per week as alimony to his wife Linda. On October 1, John loses his job due to a layoff at the plant where he works. Four weeks pass and Linda is not paid her court-ordered alimony award. Linda files a contempt action. John is properly served. He meets with his lawyer who immediately files a modification on the basis that there has been a significant change in John's circumstances since the entering of the original alimony order, i.e., John's being laid off.

In this scenario, John will probably not be able to modify his obligation for the arrearage because in most jurisdictions, past alimony amounts due may not be increased or decreased retroactively. Some states *do* allow for retroactive modifications of arrearages, but they are the exception not the rule. Most courts, however, can always modify an alimony order for prospective payments. In John's case, his substantiated showing of his changed circumstances and its negative financial consequences should be sufficient good cause for the court to lower his alimony obligation.

ATTORNEY'S FEES IN CONTEMPT ACTIONS

The recipient spouse, forced to bring a contempt action, may also demand attorney's fees from the delinquent spouse. The recipient spouse will prevail if the payor is found to be in **willful contempt.** The court is likely to find willful contempt if the recipient spouse proves that the payor spouse has the means to make the payments but purposefully and deliberately fails to do so. The court may also find willful contempt if the recipient spouse demonstrates that although financial problems now prevent the payor from complying with the court-ordered alimony obligation, the payor, himself or herself, caused the financial setback either by spending too much, voluntarily leaving their employment, defrauding the recipient spouse, or engaging in some other type of irresponsible conduct.

REVIEW QUESTIONS

1. Define alimony.
2. What is the history of alimony?
3. Can a husband be awarded alimony?
4. Before a court awards alimony, what are the two interests the court must balance?
5. List the resources of a payor spouse that a court may consider in determining alimony.
6. How does a court determine spousal need?
7. What is *pendente lite* alimony?
8. Define permanent alimony and indicate the type of spouse most likely to be awarded this type of alimony.
9. What is rehabilitative alimony and what is its ultimate goal?
10. Define reimbursement alimony.
11. What are the two modes of paying alimony?
12. Under what circumstances may alimony be modified?

13. What is the purpose of an award of one dollar per year?

14. What are the tax consequences of alimony?

15. Explain the IRS recapture rule.

EXERCISES

1. Locate your state's alimony statute and determine what factors the courts consider in making an alimony award.

2. Find your state's statute regarding the determination of attorney's fees in divorce cases. What factors do the courts consider in making such an award?

3. Is *fault* a factor the court may consider in awarding either alimony or attorney's fees in your state? If so, find and brief a recent case where marital fault was considered.

4. Find the modification of alimony statute in your state and determine what criteria must be met before an alimony award is modified.

5. Locate the statute that enables a spouse to bring a contempt action against a delinquent spouse for failing to pay an award of alimony. What must be proven in order to satisfy the contempt statute? What defense may a payor spouse raise under the statute?

PROPERTY AND DEBT DISTRIBUTION

KEY TERMS

Antenuptial agreement

Buyout

Civil code

Community property

Concurrent ownership

Creditor

Debt

Debtor

Disclosure

Dissipation

Equitable distribution

Employee Retirement Income
Security Act (ERISA)

Equity

Fair market value

Goodwill

Hold harmless clause

Joint ownership

Joint tenancy

Marital assets

Marital debts

Marital property

Necessaries

Nonvested

Offset

Partnership

Pension

Personal property

Premarital agreement

Prenuptial agreement

Qualified domestic relations
order (QDRO)

Quasi-community

Real property

Retirement Equity Act (REA)

Right of survivorship

Separate property

Separation agreement

Settlement agreement

Sole ownership

Tax deferred

Tenancy by the entirety

Tenancy in common	Unity of spouses
Title	Valuated
Tracing	Value
Transmutation	Vested

W hile the goal of alimony is to provide a needy spouse with support or "maintenance," the goal of property and debt distribution is to fairly distribute the marital assets and debts between the spouses. Property and debt division are the most contested issues in modern divorce cases, second only to custody disputes. Spouses generally accumulate a myriad of assets and debts during a marriage which may take center stage at a divorce hearing where the central issue is "who gets what?" While asset accumulation is one of the goals of the married couple—especially the fulfilling of the American dream of home ownership—debts are unfortunately also part of the equation. In some marriages, distribution of debt may be the only financial issue to resolve.

This chapter focuses on the issue of property and debts and how they are divided at the time of divorce; therefore, an understanding of basic property principles is essential before proceeding any further.

BASIC PRINCIPLES OF PROPERTY

Property can be classified as either *real* or *personal*. **Real property** is land and anything affixed to it (examples: house, garage, barn, condominium). **Personal property** is anything other than real property that can be touched and is movable (examples: cash, automobiles, bank accounts, jewelry, furniture, clothing, stocks, bonds).

Property can be owned by an individual alone; this is known as **sole ownership.** Property also can be held by two or more persons together; this is known as **concurrent ownership** or **joint ownership.** A sole owner has the right to give, sell, will, encumber, and lease her property. In other words, a sole owner can do anything legal with her property without another's approval. Concurrent owners have rights and responsibilities vis-à-vis each other that differ from jurisdiction to jurisdiction. The most common forms of concurrent or joint ownership are as follows:

- ▽ Tenancy in common,
- ▽ Joint tenancy with right of survivorship,
- ▽ Tenancy by the entirety, and
- ▽ Community property.

Tenancy in Common

Tenants in common each own an undivided interest in the property, have equal rights of use and enjoyment, and may dispose of their share by gift, will, or sale. At the time of a co-owner's death, his share passes to his beneficiaries, if he left a will, or to his heirs under the intestacy succession laws of his state if he dies without a will.

Joint Tenancy

Joint tenants own equal interests in property and at the death of one of the joint tenants, her interest automatically passes to the remaining joint tenant through what is known as the **right of survivorship.** A joint tenant also has the right to sell her interest in the jointly owned property. The sale of one co-owner's interest destroys the right of survivorship; the new co-owner and the remaining tenant now hold the property as tenants in common.

Tenancy by the Entirety

Tenancy by the entirety is a form of co-ownership that can only exist between a husband and wife. It is similar to joint tenancy in that it carries with it the right of survivorship. The main difference, however, is that one tenant may not sever a tenancy by the entirety without the permission of the other co-tenant.

Community Property

In community property states, all property and income acquired during the marriage is deemed to be owned equally by both spouses, subject to certain exceptions. Community property is discussed in more detail later in this chapter.

PROPERTY AND DEBT DISTRIBUTION UPON MARITAL DISSOLUTION

It is the responsibility of each party's attorney to determine the extent and value of the property owned and what the client should be entitled to at the time of divorce. This process begins with the task of determining what property the client and his spouse own, either solely or jointly, regardless of how the property is titled. **Title** indicates a party's ownership interest in property; that is, " whose name is the property in?" A list of property can be developed from information obtained from the client interview and through the formal discovery devices. The term **marital assets** refers to property acquired during a marriage. Here are some examples:

antiques	appliances	artwork
automobiles	bank accounts	boats
bonds	business interests	cash
clothing	collectibles (stamps, coins, etc.)	condominiums
copyrights	credit union accounts	goodwill
heirlooms	household furnishings	insurance
jewelry	judgments	lottery winnings
marital gifts	marital home	mutual funds
pending lawsuits	pension plans (401K, SEP, IRA)	pets
professional degrees	profit-sharing plans	silverware
stocks	tax refunds	time shares
trademarks	trailers	vacation homes

The next two cases presented in this chapter illustrate that marital property is not limited to traditional assets such as the marital home, bank accounts, and automobiles. Marital assets exist in many surprising forms. All it takes is a good legal eye to spot them and a good legal argument to toss them into the marital property pot. In *Campbell,* the court affirmed a long-standing rule defining lottery winnings as marital assets. In *Keedy,* it is the baseball collection that is up for grabs as the court rules that it is a marital asset.

KIMBERLY A. CAMPBELL V. TERRY M. CAMPBELL

213 A.2D 1027, 624 N.Y.S.2D 493 (A.D. 4 DEPT. 1995)

SUPREME COURT, APPELLATE DIVISION, FOURTH DEPARTMENT

MEMORANDUM:

Plaintiff and 10 co-workers agreed that they would take turns purchasing a lottery ticket and that, if any one of them purchased a winning ticket, the proceeds would be shared in 11 equal shares. Plaintiff purchased a lottery ticket on at least one prior occasion, but it was not a winner. A co-worker purchased a winning lottery ticket on October 7, 1992. The jackpot prize was $4.5 million. Because of the policy of the New York State Lotto Commission to recognize only one winner per ticket, the co-worker obtained a Federal taxpayer identification number in the name of a trust and prepared a trust agreement for the disbursement of the lottery proceeds to all 11 co-workers. The trust agreement acknowledges the prior agreement of the parties, and all 11 co-workers executed the trust agreement.

Plaintiff commenced this action for divorce in 1993. Defendant counterclaimed for divorce and moved for an order enjoining and restraining plaintiff from spending or transferring her interest in the lottery proceeds. Defendant maintained that the lottery proceeds were marital property subject to equitable distribution. Supreme Court determined that the co-worker who purchased the winning lottery ticket was under no legal duty to share the proceeds with her co-workers, that the agreement to disburse a share of the proceeds to plaintiff constituted a gift, and that gift constituted plaintiff's separate property.

An agreement to share the proceeds of a lottery is a valid and enforceable agreement (citations omitted). An oral agreement to share proceeds that will be paid over a period of several years does not contravene the Statute of Frauds (citations omitted). The oral agreement to the co-workers was sufficiently definite to be enforced (citation omitted), and the court erred in concluding that the co-worker who purchased the winning ticket was under no legal duty to share the proceeds. Moreover, there is no evidence in the record of donative intent. It is undisputed that the co-worker acted pursuant to the oral agreement.

Domestic Relations Law §236(B)(1)(c) defines marital property as "all property acquired by either or both spouses during the marriage and before . . . commencement of a matrimonial action, regardless of the form in which title is held." Thus, property acquired during the marriage is presumptively marital property, and plaintiff had the burden of showing that it was separate property (citations omitted). Courts have universally held that the proceeds of a winning lottery ticket acquired by a spouse during the marriage constitute marital property (citations omitted). That principle applies to instances where one spouse contributed with third persons to a pool of funds used to purchase lottery tickets and one of the tickets was a winner (citations omitted). The agreement of the co-workers constituted a pooling arrangement, and plaintiff's share of the proceeds constitutes marital property (citations omitted). Thus, we modify the order on appeal by vacating that part denying defendant's motion and by determining that plaintiff's share of the lottery proceeds constitutes marital property.

Because the court determined that the proceeds were separate property, it did not consider whether plaintiff should be enjoined from transferring or otherwise disposing of the proceeds and whether the proceeds should be placed in escrow pending the distribution of marital property. We remit this matter to Supreme Court for determination of defendant's motion.

Order unanimously modified on the law and as modified affirmed without costs and matter remitted to Supreme Court for further proceedings.

IN RE THE MARRIAGE OF MICHAEL H. KEEDY AND CAROL SUE KEEDY

813 P.2D 442 (MONT. 1991)

SUPREME COURT OF MONTANA

GRAY, JUSTICE.

The appellant, Michael Keedy, appeals from the property distribution of the Eleventh Judicial District Court, Flathead County, in this marital dissolution action. We affirm in part, reverse in part, and remand for further proceedings. . . .

. . . The appellant and the respondent, Carol Keedy, were married on May 27, 1973, in Lincoln, Nebraska. At the time of the marriage, Michael's education consisted of a bachelor's degree and a juris doctorate degree; Carol possessed a bachelor's degree in education. Two children were born to the marriage: a son, born on October 29, 1974, and a daughter, born on November 23, 1979.

Throughout the marriage, Michael has been employed as a lobbyist, attorney, legislator and for the past seven years, district court judge. During the marriage Carol worked primarily as a homemaker; she currently teaches at a private school.

The parties separated on April 1, 1989, and brought this matter before the District Court on April 30, 1990. The District Court entered its Amended Findings of Fact, Conclusions of Law, and Order on August 3, 1990. Michael appeals.

The first issue raised on appeal is whether the District Court erred in including the entire baseball card collection as a marital asset.

The baseball card collection consists of approximately 100,000 baseball cards. Michael testified that he began the collection as a boy in 1954 and continued to collect the cards up through 1963. He resumed his card collecting again in 1971 and continued collecting baseball cards after his marriage to Carol in 1973. At trial he introduced into evidence various lists of cards in an attempt to demonstrate which cards he had acquired prior to the marriage and which cards he had acquired after the marriage.

Carol hired an appraiser who estimated the value of the entire collection at $208,000. Michael testified that he believed the collection to be worth $100,000. After struggling with the evidence before it, the District Court abandoned its attempt to determine which cards were brought into the marriage or to place a value on the baseball cards. The court required Michael to divide the collection into two equal piles and allow Carol to select one pile of cards.

Michael argues, first, that the District Court erred in including in the marital estate those baseball cards he

brought into the marriage. He also contends that the current value of such cards is not a product of contribution from the marital effort and should be excluded from the marital estate as his separate property.

This Court has repeatedly held that distribution of marital assets by a district court, where based upon substantial credible evidence, will not be overturned absent a clear abuse of discretion (citation omitted).

Section 40-4-202(1), MCA, requires the courts to, [e]quitably apportion between the parties the property and assets belonging to either or both, however and whenever acquired. . . . In dividing property acquired prior to the marriage; . . . property acquired in exchange for property acquired before the marriage. . . ; [and] *the increased value of property acquired prior to marriage;* . . . the court shall consider those contributions of the other spouse to the marriage, including:

(a) the nonmonetary contribution of a homemaker;

(b) the *extent to which such contributions have facilitated the maintenance of this property;* and

(c) whether or not the property division serves as an alternative to maintenance arrangements. (Emphasis supplied)

The District Court properly determined that the baseball card collection was a marital asset, however, it erred in not crediting Michael with the value, at the time of the marriage, of the cards he brought into the marriage.

The value of the premarital cards at the *time of the marriage* was undisputed between the parties. Michael testified that the value of the collection at the time of the marriage, or shortly thereafter, was approximately $5,000. Carol herself proposed in her Trial Memorandum, that in order "to equitably divide the property, the [District] Court should award $5,000.00 to the Petitioner to represent the value of the baseball card collection that he brought into the marriage."

In considering the factors presented in § 40-4-202(1), MCA, it becomes apparent that the value of the premarital cards is not properly a part of the marital estate. The undisputed amount of $5,000 could not have been contributed to in any way by Carol.

However, the appreciation in value of the cards, including the premarital cards, properly could be included in the marital estate under §40-4-202(1), MCA, if the evidence supported spousal contribution to that appreciated value. Michael argues that the increase in value of the premarital baseball cards was not related to any marital contribution from Carol. We disagree.

In the present case, substantial credible evidence exists to support the finding that Carol contributed to the maintenance and growth of the collection. Evidence shows that she encouraged Michael to collect the cards, participated in the collection by buying foods associated with particular cards, and on at least one occasion, protected the cards from a flood while Michael was away from home. Testimony also indicated that Michael's card purchases strained the family budget at times, with the family sacrificing other items in order to build the collection.

It was not erroneous, under these circumstances, for the District Court to find that Carol contributed to the maintenance and growth of the card collection and, therefore, that she is entitled to share in the postmarital appreciation in value.

Thus, we hold that it was proper to include the baseball card collection as part of the marital estate, but that the District Court erred in failing to credit Michael with the undisputed value of $5,000 for the baseball cards he brought into the marriage. . . .

. . . Affirmed in part, reversed in part, and remanded to the District Court for further proceedings consistent with this opinion.

TURNAGE, C.J. and HARRISON, HUNT, McDO-NOUGH, and WEBER, JJ., concur.

TRIEWEILLER, Justice, concurring in part and dissenting in part.

Dog Visitation?

Enforcement and supervision of pet visitation clauses would open the floodgates to litigation over pet-related problems. Traditionally, the courts have held that pets are personal property and will award the pet to either spouse at the time of the dissolution.

RONALD GREG BENNETT V. KATHRYN R. BENNETT

655 So. 2d 109 (Fla. App. 1 Dist. 1995)

District Court of Appeal of Florida, First District

WOLF, JUDGE.

Husband, Ronald Greg Bennett, appeals from a final judgment of dissolution of marriage which, among other things, awarded custody of the parties' dog, "Roddy." The husband asserts that (1) the trial court erred in awarding the former wife visitation with the parties' dog, and (2) the trial court erred in modifying the final judgment to increase the former wife's visitation rights with the dog. We find that the trial court lacked authority to order visitation with personal property; the dog would properly be dealt with through the equitable distribution process.

A brief recitation of the procedural history will demonstrate the morass a trial court may find itself in by extending the right of visitation to personal property. The parties stipulated to all issues in the final judgment of dissolution of marriage except which party would receive possession of the parties' dog, "Roddy." After a hearing, the trial court found that the husband should have possession of the dog and that the wife should be able to take the dog for visitation every other weekend and every other Christmas.

The former husband contested this decision and filed a motion for rehearing alleging that the dog was a premarital asset. He also filed a motion for relief from final judgment and an amended motion for rehearing. The wife replied and filed a motion to strike former husband's amended motion for rehearing and a motion for contempt. The former wife requested that the trial court transfer custody of the dog because the former husband was refusing to comply with the trial court's order concerning visitation with the dog.

A hearing on these motions was held on September 27, 1993. The wife's counsel filed an ore tenus motion requesting the trial court to change custody, or in the alternative, change visitation. The trial court denied the former husband's motion for rehearing and granted the former wife's ore tenus motion to change visitation. Thus, the trial court's ruling on visitation now reads:

7. *Dog, Roddy:* The former husband, RONALD GREGORY BENNETT, shall have custody of the parties' dog "Roddy" and the former wife, KATHRYN R. BENNETT n/k/a KATHRYN R. ROGERS, shall have visitation every other month beginning October 1, 1993. The visitation shall begin on the first day of the month and end on the last day of the month.

Based on the history of this case, there is every reason to believe that there will be continued squabbling between the parties concerning the dog.

While a dog may be considered by many to be a member of the family, under Florida law, animals are considered to be personal property. *County of Pasco v. Riehl,* 620 So. 2d 229 (Fla.2d DCA 1993), and *Levine v. Knowles,* 197 So. 2d 329 (Fla.3d DCA 1967). There is no authority which provides for a trial court to grant custody or visitation pertaining to personal property. §61.075, Fla.Stat. (1993).

While several states have given family pets special status within dissolution proceedings (for example, *see Arrington v. Arrington,* 613 S.W.2d 565 (Tex. Civ. App. 1981)), we think such a course is unwise. Determinations as to custody and visitation lead to continuing enforcement and supervision problems (as evidenced by the proceedings in the instant case). Our courts are overwhelmed with the supervision of custody, visitation, and support matters related to the protection of our children. We cannot undertake the same responsibility as to animals.

While the trial judge was endeavoring to reach a fair solution under difficult circumstances, we must reverse the order relating to the custody of "Roddy," and remand for the trial court to award the animal pursuant to the dictates or the equitable distribution statute.

WEBSTER and MICKLE, J.J., concur.

Debts are also part of the marital acquisition equation and must be identified as well as assets. **Marital debts** are the liabilities incurred by either spouse during the marriage. Examples of marital debts are as follows:

assessments	court judgments	credit card balances
loans	mortgages	tuitions
unpaid taxes	unreimbursed medical expenses	

Credit Card Crazy

In *Szesny,* the husband incurred debt of $82,000 as a result of his out-of-control spending. The Appellate Court of Illinois found no error with the lower court's ruling imposing the entire debt to the husband.

JAMES A. SZESNY V. TARYN SZESNY

197 ILL. APP. 3D 966, 145 ILL. DEC. 452, 557 N.E.2D 222 (ILL. APP. 1 DIST. 1990)

APPELLATE COURT OF ILLINOIS, FIRST DISTRICT, SIXTH DIVISION

PRESIDING JUSTICE LAPORTA DELIVERED THE OPINION OF THE COURT:

Respondent appeals from a Judgment of Dissolution of Marriage, claiming that the trial court abused its discretion in imposing almost the entire marital debt of over $82,000 upon him. . . . We affirm as to the distribution of the marital debt. . . .

. . . The parties were married on November 1, 1980 in Chicago Heights, Illinois. From the time of their marriage

until late in 1984, they lived with Respondent's mother, paying no rent and making no monetary contributions to the household. In 1984 the couple purchased a house, borrowing the money needed for earnest money deposit ($5,000) and for a down payment ($20,000) from the bank where Respondent worked. The loans were secured by one-year lump-sum notes and liens on the cars of Respondent's mother and sister. The remaining $70,000 of the purchase price came in the form of a purchase money mortgage against the house, also held by the bank where Respondent worked.

Petitioner testified that after they purchased the house, their standard of living went down; they did not go out as often and went to "cheap places." Petitioner testified that she told Respondent that their credit cards should be destroyed and she destroyed several of them herself. Respondent testified that he opened new charge accounts and took the cash advances to pay off other charge accounts. Petitioner testified that she did not sign for these credit cards although some of them bore her name.

Respondent testified that their standard of living did not abate, and in fact their living expenses increased dramatically. Their consumer debt jumped from nothing to $40,000 in 1984, with $20,000 owed on charge cards at the end of 1985, $43,000 owed at the end of 1986, and over $70,000 owed at the end of 1987. The current debt is approximately $82,000. Respondent testified that various loans were taken out in an effort to retire some of the debt. He also admitted to "playing the field" with their joint checking account, by hoping that deposits would arrive in time to cancel overdrafts.

Petitioner testified that she would attempt to "force the balance" of their checking account registers at the end of each month, but this was difficult because Respondent would not record all transactions, would use counter checks instead of those provided for their account, and would not report deposits. When Petitioner questioned Respondent about the entries, they would argue and he would beat her. Respondent admitted that he did not always tell Petitioner about a deposit but testified that he always made a notation in the check register, and that Petitioner would ask him about them when reconciling the checkbook. . . .

. . . Respondent's first argument is that the trial court inequitably distributed the marital assets and debts by granting all assets to Petitioner and assessing all debts against Respondent. The trial judge found no appreciable marital assets, that Petitioner possessed only a triply-refinanced 1984 Mazda and a vanity which had been a gift from Respondent, and that Respondent retained what little marital property remained. Respondent argues that this decision is arbitrary and an abuse of the trial court's discretion. . . .

. . . However, in the case here the trial court specifically found that Respondent was solely responsible for the over $82,000 in debt. There was testimony that after they purchased the marital home, Petitioner drastically reduced her expenditures while Respondent maintained or increased his. The trial court noted that Respondent would go out at night without his wife and child; that he belonged to a health club; that Respondent opened charge accounts without Petitioner's knowledge or permission; that Respondent spent money on clothing for himself and at fine restaurants; that he gave money to his mother; that Respondent borrowed money but did not use it to reduce the marital debt; and that he "in effect kited his account in consumer debts." The trial court also found that Petitioner spent minimal amounts on clothing, ate in fast food restaurants, and in one year was responsible for less than one-twelfth of their total expenses.

Dissipation can occur prior to dissolution. (*Partyka*, 158 Ill. App. 3d at 549, 110 Ill. Dec. at 503, 511 N.E.2d at 680.) The key is whether one spouse uses marital property for his or her own benefit for a purpose unrelated to the marriage. (*Malters*, 133 Ill. App. 3d at 181–182, 88 Ill. Dec. at 469, 478 N.E.2d at 1077.) When one party is charged with dissipation, he must prove by clear and convincing evidence that the questioned expenditures were made for a marital purpose (citations omitted). . . . Unsupported statements that the funds were used for marital purposes are insufficient (citation omitted).

The trial court here noted that Respondent claimed to have spent the money for family expenses but that he could produce only a few credit card statements for insignificant amounts. The court also noted that Respondent opened credit card accounts without Petitioner's permission, even though her name was used, and that Respondent retained total control of these accounts, having the statements sent to his mother's house. Where one spouse has sole access to funds or incurs debt without the knowledge of the other, that spouse can be held to have dissipated marital assets and can be held responsible for the entire debt (citations omitted). Here Respondent had sole access to the credit cards used to incur the debt, and for that reason the trial court properly found that he alone would be held responsible. . . .

. . . We affirm the distribution of marital debt as ordered by the trial court. . . .

THE DISTINCTION BETWEEN SEPARATE AND MARITAL PROPERTY

Once a list of a client's property and debts has been prepared, the next step is to divide the property into two categories: separate property and marital property. **Separate property** is property acquired by a spouse *prior* to the marriage or after the marriage by a gift, inheritance, or will, designated to that particular spouse alone. **Marital property** can be defined as property and/or income acquired during the marriage.

Hey . . . That's My Parent's Money

A common struggle in many divorce cases involves the down payment on the marital home. Kind parents who sometimes give money for the purchase of the home may find themselves in the middle of the separate versus marital property dilemma.

SHIRLEY R. COHEN V. HAROLD L. COHEN

474 P.2D 792 (1970)

SUPREME COURT OF COLORADO

GROVES, JUSTICE.

This proceeding arises out of a divorce action brought by the wife. The parties appear here in the same order as in the trial court and are referred to as plaintiff and defendant. The alleged error relates to the division of property and the award of alimony and attorney's fees to the plaintiff. We affirm. . . .

. . . The plaintiff's principal contention is that the court erred in finding that a monetary gift made by the defendant's parents was a gift to the defendant rather than to the plaintiff. Prior to the marriage the defendant's father executed two checks payable to the plaintiff in the respective amounts of $6,000 and $5,000. The defendant's parents specified that the proceeds were to be applied towards the purchase of a home to be occupied by the parties, and the money was so applied. After executing the checks the father gave them to the defendant, who pre-

sented them to the plaintiff. The plaintiff endorsed the checks to the defendant and returned them to him. The defendant's father testified that he made the checks payable to the plaintiff on the advice of his accountant, who apparently thought this might cause a saving of gift tax. (The gift tax of $11,000 was later declared to the taxing authorities as having been made to the defendant.)

The court found that this was a gift by the defendant's parents to the defendant and that the plaintiff was not entitled to any portion of the $11,000 in the property division. The testimony was in conflict, but there is ample evidence to support the finding of the trial court as to the intent with respect to the gifts, and we should not and will not disturb that finding. . . .

Judgment affirmed.

HODGES, KELLEY and LEE, JJ., concur.

Remember that the definition of marital property excludes separate property. The issue of title or "whose name is property in" is unimportant. For instance, if the marital home was purchased during the marriage but title is solely in the wife's name as evidenced by the deed, it is still considered marital property. Both wife *and* husband have an interest in the home, regardless of whose name is on the deed. The family courts have statutory power to award property in a divorce matter regardless of the title interest.

The underlying policy behind the judicial authority statutes is that marriage is a **partnership.** In a business partnership, the partners pool their expertise, efforts, and resources to make the business operative and profitable. Similarly, during a marriage, the efforts and personal and financial resources of the parties are pooled for the benefit of the marital partnership. When the marriage has ended, each spouse has an interest in whatever has accumulated during the course of this partnership.

The task of defining separate and marital is an important part of the divorce process. The court will award separate property to the spouse entitled to its ownership. Once the separate property is parceled out to respective spouses, the marital property becomes one of the focal points of the divorce litigation. Whatever goes into the marital property pot is up for grabs. In some states, like Connecticut, the court may award *any* of the spouses' property, separate or marital, in the course of the divorce proceedings to either spouse, regardless of whether the property is separate or marital.

STATUTES

Relief is also provided in jurisdictions that make distinctions between separate and marital property, if doing so would result in an unjust or unfair result.

CONNECTICUT GENERAL STATUTES ANNOTATED (WEST)

§ 46B-81.

(a) At the time of entering a decree of annulling or dissolving a marriage or for legal separation pursuant to a complaint under section 46b-45, the superior court may assign to either the husband or wife all or any part of the estate of the other. The court may pass title to real property to either party or to a third person or may order the sale of such real property, without any act by either the husband or the wife, when in the judgment of the court it is the proper mode to carry the decree into effect. . . .

(c) In fixing the nature and value of the property, if any, to be assigned, the court, after hearing the witnesses, if any, of each party, except as provided in subsection (a) of section 46b-51, shall consider the length of marriage, the causes for the annulment, dissolution of the marriage or legal separation, the age, health, station, occupation, amount and sources of income, vocational skills, employability, estate, liabilities and needs of each of the parties and the opportunity of each for future acquisition of capital assets and income. The court shall also consider the contribution of each of the parties in the acquisition, preservation or appreciation in value of their respective estates.

Frequently it is easy to determine what property belongs in the separate property category and what belongs in the marital property category; in other instances, the distinctions are not as clear. Separate property loses its separate classification and attains the marital property distinction when it is

▼ Titled jointly,

▼ Used for the purpose of supporting the marriage,

▼ Becomes so commingled with marital property that its separate origin cannot be traced.

This transformation of separate property to marital property is known as **transmutation.** The process of determining when the asset was acquired by tracking its origin is called **tracing.** Tracing helps determine whether the property is separate or marital property. Tracing is not as easy as it sounds. The determination of what is separate or marital property may depend on who your office is representing, and may ultimately have to be decided by the courts if the parties cannot agree.

Whenever separate property is transmuted, the attempts at making a solid distinction between separate and marital property become blurry and tracing will be problematic. Determining when a separate asset exactly makes the transition to marital property may be very difficult. When a couple marries, it is usually their intent to share their resources and work in unison for the benefit of the marital partnership. Marriages are not entered into with the intent of tracking and recording every penny or every hour of labor performed in the acquisition of those marital assets. Therefore, the issue of whether a questionable asset is classified as separate or marital property may have to be resolved by the family court.

VALUATION OF ASSETS

Once the property has been classified as either separate or marital property, the next step is to determine its **value;** that is, what is the marital property worth? What is the property's fair market value? **Fair market value** is the price a buyer is willing to pay a seller in exchange for the property.

Several methods are available to determine the value of marital property. Sometimes the parties are in agreement with the value of an asset and will mutually agree to a monetary figure. This consensus is very common with automobiles and the marital home. While many family homes are owned outright, others have outstanding mortgages and taxes due. Here, it is important to determine how much *equity* the parties have in the property. **Equity** is the fair market value of the property minus any encumbrances (i.e., mortgages, taxes, and liens).

FIGURE 6–1
A family home is often part of the marital property and attorneys need to determine how much equity the parties have in it.

EXAMPLE

John and Mary are married and they own a four-bedroom house. The fair market value of the marital home is $250,000. The outstanding mortgage due is $125,000, and property taxes due are $5,000. The equity is determined as follows:

FMV	**$250,000**
(less) Outstanding Mortgage & Property Taxes	**$130,000**
Equity	**$120,000**

The paralegal can verify the equity portion of the property by obtaining a release from the client authorizing the office to obtain information from the client's bank. Bank records can also help determine the value of various bank accounts. The values of stock, bonds, mutual funds, and other investments can be obtained from reviewing *The Wall Street Journal* or other financial publications.

RETAINING EXPERTS FOR VALUATION OF PROPERTY

If the parties cannot agree or are unable to determine the value of a marital asset, an expert can be retained. A family practice should always keep at its disposal a list of experts commonly used in family matters. The paralegal may assume the responsibility of maintaining a file folder on each expert, which should include an up-to-date résumé, list of fees, and area of expertise. Experts include accountants,

FIGURE 6–2
Expert witnesses can help settle disputes about the value of marital assets.

appraisers, actuaries, bank counselors, domestic violence counselors, financial planners, pension valuators, social workers, psychiatrists, and psychologists.

If an expert is needed, either spouse or both should file a motion for appointment of an expert with the court. If the parties are in agreement, they can present the agreement to the court and put it on the record.

If they are not in agreement, the court will decide. The court will order the appointment of a disinterested expert, identify the specific property to be assessed, determine who will pay the expert, and how the expert will be paid.

EFFECT OF PRENUPTIAL AGREEMENTS ON PROPERTY DISTRIBUTION

Prior to marriage, the parties may have determined their respective property rights in a written document called a **prenuptial, premarital,** or **antenuptial agreement** (see Chapter 4). This is a contract entered into by the prospective spouses regarding their rights during the marriage and in the event of a divorce. It is essential to determine whether a client has entered into one of these agreements and to obtain a copy. Most courts will enforce these agreements provided that certain conditions existed at the time of their execution and circumstances have not substantially changed since the signing of the agreement. Premarital agreements must be in writing. There must be a full **disclosure** of all assets. This means that the parties must disclose the full extent and current values of all assets. The parties must also have an adequate opportunity to seek independent counsel before signing a premarital agreement.

In the absence of a premarital or prenuptial agreement, divorcing spouses are free to negotiate between themselves how property is to be distributed, and then enter into a mutually consensual agreement regarding the division of their marital assets and marital debts, as well as child custody and support, alimony, visitation, and attorney's fees. If the parties are unwilling to negotiate, or if negotiation on some or all aspects of the marital dissolution fails, the court will decide the outcome of the unresolved issues.

RESOLVING THE ISSUE OF PROPERTY DISTRIBUTION: CONTESTED OR UNCONTESTED

When the parties are able to negotiate a plan they find mutually acceptable, a **settlement agreement** or **separation agreement** is drafted and signed by both parties, thus obviating the need for a long court battle. Courts prefer agreements because the parties are more likely to be content with a settlement they have voluntarily negotiated and crafted. The court will not change or question an agreement unless it appears to be unfair or against public policy. The court will generally approve the agreement upon determining that it was entered into voluntarily and that it is fair and equitable. Courts also prefer agreements because it keeps the court docket moving by disposing of cases without protracted judicial proceedings and thus conserves judicial resources.

When the parties are unable to reach an agreement, it is up to the court to resolve the property dispute. Trial courts have great discretion in their decision-making powers. A trial court is in the best position to observe the demeanor of the parties. A trial court's decision will not be reversed on appeal unless the appellant can convince the higher court that the trial court abused its discretion by either misapplying the law or by making erroneous rulings regarding the admission of evidence.

When resolving disputes over the division of property, the courts will first make an award of separate property to the owner spouse. The definition of separate versus marital property may be one of the first areas of contention in the trial. Once the marital property pot has been defined, the court will divide the property according to the jurisdiction's property distribution statute. Family law paralegals must become familiar with their jurisdictions' statutes and the case law interpreting those statutes.

JURISDICTIONAL APPROACHES TO PROPERTY DISTRIBUTION

In the United States, two systems are used to dictate the division of marital property upon the dissolution of marriage: *equitable distribution* and *community property distribution.*

Equitable Distribution

As mentioned in earlier sections of this book, our system of jurisprudence is based on the English common law. The English common law system was also the approach used to determine the division of marital property upon dissolution of a marriage. Upon marriage, a husband and wife merged into a single legal entity—the husband. This was known as the **unity of spouses.** At common law, married women had no separate legal identity. A married woman could not own or manage her own property, she could not sue or be sued, nor could she control her wages. As time passed, and attitudes toward married women changed, state legislatures in the United States, toward the end of the 1800s, enacted the Married Women's Property Acts. These statutes removed the common law disabilities that prevented married women from owning and managing their own resources.

Although these statutes made it possible for women to own their own property, the divorce law did not change along with the new status of married women. Property acquired during the marriage was divided on the basis of who supplied the funds to purchase the property and possessed title. Traditionally married women did not work outside the home. Husbands bought the property, retained title and ownership, and upon divorce, walked away with the lion's share of the assets. While jointly held property was divided between the spouses, the courts had no power to award property solely owned by one spouse to the nontitle spouse. States legislatures eventually saw the inequity and harshness of this method of property division and enacted statutes allowing family courts to distribute property acquired during marriage on the basis of equity or fairness, as opposed to ownership. This is known as the **equitable distribution** system of dividing marital property. Family courts in equitable distribution states, in determining how property is to be divided between a divorcing couple, must evaluate each spouse's interest in the marital property on an individual or case-by-case basis. Equitable distribution state statutes enumerate statutory factors that the courts must consider in the division of marital assets and debts. The courts, however, are not required to give equal weight to each factor, and have the discretion to make decisions based on the merits of the particular case before them.

Most jurisdictions in the United States follow the equitable distribution system of property division. However, several states, particularly those located in the American Southwest, and originally settled by Spanish and French colonists, adhere to the distribution system known as community property.

COMMUNITY PROPERTY

In **community property** jurisdictions, property acquired during the marriage belongs equally to each spouse, unless it has been excluded as separate property. California's property division statute provides that the court will "equally" divide the community estate of the parties.

 **STATUTES**

CALIFORNIA CIVIL CODE ANNOTATED (WEST)

§ 2550. **MANNER OF DIVISION OF COMMUNITY**

Except upon the written agreement of the parties, or on oral stipulation of the parties in open court, or as otherwise provided in this division, in a proceeding for dissolution of marriage or for legal separation of the parties, the court shall, either in its judgment of dissolution of the marriage, in its judgment of legal separation of the parties, or at a later time if it expressly reserves jurisdiction to make such a property division, divide the community estate of the parties equally.

The community property arrangement is based on Spanish and French concepts of marital property as codified in the *code civile* or **civil code,** the system of law existing on the European mainland, as opposed to the common law system of England.

The nine states that use the community property system are mostly situated in the West and Southwest region of the United States. The community property states are (see Figure 6–3):

Arizona	New Mexico
California	Texas
Idaho	Washington
Louisiana	Wisconsin
Nevada	

The community property system assumes that both husband and wife contribute to the accumulation of marital assets. This concept valued the work of the husband who traditionally worked outside the home as well as that of the stay-at-home spouse who took care of the home and the children. The husband, however, had the right to control the community property, until such statutory provisions were found to violate the Equal Protection Clause of the U.S. Constitution. Upon acquisition of any asset or income during the marriage, both spouses acquire an equal interest in the property, regardless of who supplied the funds for its acquisition. Because each spouse is deemed to have contributed to the acquisition of the marital assets (and also the marital debts), the assets and debts are divided on a 50/50 basis upon divorce. The various community property states allow for deviations or application of the equitable distribution system after the property has been divided on a 50/50 basis.

STATUTES

Arizona and California also recognize what is known as **quasi-community.** If a married couple acquires property in a noncommunity property state and then moves to a community property jurisdiction, upon divorce, the property is considered community property. Therefore, community property carries its distinctiveness over state lines.

NEVADA REVISED STATUTES ANNOTATED

ALIMONY AND ADJUDICATION OF PROPERTY RIGHTS; AWARD OF ATTORNEY'S FEE;

Except as otherwise provided in NRS 125, 155 and unless the action is contrary to a premarital agreement between the parties which is enforceable pursuant to chapter 123A of NRSl

1. In granting a divorce, the court: . . .

(b) Shall, to the extent practicable, make an equal disposition of the community property of the parties, except that the court may make an unequal disposition of the community property in such proportions as it deems just if the court finds a compelling reason to do so and sets forth in writing the reasons for making the unequal disposition.

2. Except as otherwise provided in this subsection, in granting a divorce, the court shall dispose of any property held in joint tenancy in the manner set forth in subsection 1 for the disposition of community property. If a party has made a contribution of separate property to the acquisition or improvement of property held in joint tenancy, the court may provide for the reimbursement of that party for his contribution. The amount of reimbursement must not exceed the amount of the contribution of separate property that can be traced to the acquisition or improvement of property held in joint tenancy, without interest of any adjustment because of an increase in the value of the property held in joint tenancy. The amount of the reimbursement must not exceed the value, at the time of the disposition of the property held in joint tenancy for which the contribution of separate property was made. In determining whether to provide for the reimbursement, in whole or in part, of a party who has contributed separate property, the court shall consider:

(a) The intention of the parties in placing the property in joint tenancy;

(b) The length of the marriage;

(c) Any other factor which the court deems relevant in making a just and equitable disposition of that property.

As used in this subsection, "contribution" includes a down payment, a payment for the acquisition or improvement of property, and a payment reducing the principal of a loan used to finance the purchase or improvement of property. The term does not include a payment of interest on a loan used to finance the purchase or improvement of property, or a payment made for maintenance, insurance or taxes on property.

3. Whether or not application for suit money has been made under the provisions of NRS 125.040, the court may award a reasonable attorney's fee to either party to an action for divorce if those fees are in issue under the pleadings.

4. In granting a divorce, the court may also set apart such portion of the husband's separate property for the wife's support, the wife's separate property for the husband's support or the separate property of either spouses for the support of their children as is deemed just and equitable. . . .

FIGURE 6–3
Most of the community property states are located in the West and Southwest.

Community Property States: Arizona, Nevada, California, Washington, Wisconsin, Idaho, Louisiana, New Mexico, Texas

If you are a practicing paralegal in a community property state, it is essential that you become familiar with the intricacies of the community property laws in your state, as they differ from jurisdiction to jurisdiction.

THE NOT-SO-OBVIOUS ASSETS OF MARRIAGE—GOODWILL, PENSIONS, AND PROFESSIONAL DEGREES

Introduction

It is important that all marital assets be identified. The client must inform his or her attorney regarding all actual or potential assets so that the client's attorney can determine what rights, if any, the client may have in the asset. Some marital assets are not so obvious because they are not present in tangible form, i.e. something we can see and touch. These intangible assets however may have substantial value and it would be considered legal malpractice not to identify, valuate, and seek a fair division for the client. Some of the major intangible marital assets include goodwill, pension and the professional degree.

GOODWILL

Goodwill is a term used to describe the ability of a business or professional to attract future customers and repeat business due to a good reputation in the community. A dollar value on goodwill can be determined by an expert. Many states identify goodwill as marital property if a business or career has been enhanced during the marriage. A spouse who assists the other spouse in achieving that reputation may be entitled to share in the enhanced earning capacity that reputation will bring. Even where a spouse has stayed at home as a traditional homemaker, her contribution to the marital partnership has enabled her husband to pursue his business endeavors and create the goodwill that has enhanced his business reputation in the community. Therefore, in many states, she is entitled to a portion of the goodwill value of the business.

In calculating goodwill, it is essential that an expert be obtained to valuate this asset. Exhibit 6–1 illustrates a letter from an accounting firm enlisted to calculate the celebrity goodwill of comedian Jim Carrey. The letter details the documents necessary to make such a calculation. Other states are not as willing to define goodwill as marital property because reputation is not an "asset."

The Goodwill of Bethany Foot Clinic

In this case of first impression, the Supreme Court of Oklahoma held that the goodwill of a medical sole proprietorship was a marital asset and its value subject to division by the family courts.

FIGURE 6–4
Goodwill that results from having run a successful business is considered marital property in some states.

ROBERT J. TRACZYK V. KATHLEEN M. TRACZYK

891 P.2d 1277 (Okla. 1995)

Supreme Court of Oklahoma

SIMMS, JUSTICE.

Husband first takes issue with the trial court considering the goodwill of his medical practice as marital property. He testified that there was no goodwill because he was the reason the patients came to the Bethany Foot Clinic and "not very many" of the patients would stay at the Bethany Foot Clinic with a new doctor if Husband sold it.

The professional practice of one spouse is an appropriate element of the marital property to be divided between the parties where it is jointly-acquired property. *Ford v. Ford*, 766 P.2d 950 (Okla. 1988); *Carpenter v. Carpenter*, 657 P.2d 646 (Okla. 1983). The issue before us is whether goodwill of Husband's podiatry practice may be considered in determining the value of the practice. . . .

. . . Pursuant to 60 O.S.1991, §§315 and 316, goodwill of a business is defined as "the expectation of continued public patronage," and is considered property transferable like any other property. *See also Freeling v. Wood*, 361 P.2d 1061, 1063 (Okla. 1961). ("The 'good will' value of any business is the value that results from the *probability that old customers will continue to trade with an established concern*. . . . [Such] good will of a business may be sold.") (Emphasis supplied); *Travis v. Travis*, 795 P.2d 96,97 (Okla. 1990) (quoting *Freeling); Mocnik v. Mocnik*, 838 P.2d 500, 504 (Okla. 1992) (quoting *Travis*). . . .

In determining the value of the Bethany Foot Clinic, the expert witness consulted the Goodwill Registry, "an accumulation of information concerning sales of medical related practices by experts." From this publication, the expert determined that of the most recent purchases of podiatry clinics, an average of thirty-two percent (32%) of the podiatry patients stay with the clinic after it is sold to a new doctor. The range from which he obtained the average was 21% to 44% of clients staying. Noting that the traditional method used in valuing a medical practice is the previous year's gross income, the expert then took the previous year's gross income at the clinic ($324,201.51) and multiplied it by the 32% figure to arrive at a goodwill value of $103,744.00 Adding this to the value of the remaining business assets, the expert found the total value of the Bethany Foot Clinic to be $152,605.44. The trial court accepted this valuation and used it in determining how much alimony in lieu of property division to award.

We find that the trial court did not err in considering the goodwill of the Bethany Foot Clinic as a factor in determining the value of the clinic as marital property. The goodwill of the Bethany Foot Clinic is distinct from the personal reputation of Dr. Traczyk. Although many of Dr. Traczyk's patients would not continue to patronize the Bethany Foot Clinic were Dr. Traczyk to sell to another podiatrist, competent evidence indicates that many would stay. Indeed, Dr. Traczyk may use the goodwill as a selling point to potential purchasers.

"If goodwill is to be divided as an asset, its value should be determined either by an agreement or *by its fair market value*. Both of these methods are widely accepted for valuing goodwill. *See* annotation, 78 A.L.R.4th 853, 860–71 (1987). *Mocnik*, 838 P.2d at 505." . . .

. . . Husband further argues that by both allowing goodwill to be divided as marital property and awarding support alimony, the trial court has charged him twice for his future income. We first reiterate that the goodwill of the Bethany Foot Clinic is not properly characterized as future income. Rather, it is an asset of the clinic.

Husband, though, disagrees with the distinction between future income and assets. He asserts two cases cited in *Travis* resolve the issue of "double-dipping" into his future income. However, we find these cases, *Holbrook v. Holbrook*, 103 Wis. 2d 327, 309 N.W.2d 343 (1981) and *Beasley v. Beasley*, 359 Pa. Super. 20, 518 A.2d 545 (1986), *allocatur denied*, 516 Pa. 631, 533 A.2d 90 (1987), unpersuasive because, as *Travis* indicates, they both concerned the goodwill of law practices where such goodwill was related to the reputation of the lawyer. In other words, *Holbrook* and *Beasley* are distinguishable because they did not involve a professional practice with transferable goodwill as the case at bar did.

The goodwill of the Bethany Foot Clinic was valued as an asset and was a factor in determining the total value of the business for property division purposes. This goodwill was part of the property which should be divided between the parties; Wife had a right to receive her share of the property. 43 O.S.1991, §121. On the other hand, the award of *support alimony* was a separate determination based upon Husband's ability to pay and Wife's demonstrated need. *Johnson v. Johnson*, 674 P.2d 539 (Okla. 1983). Although the property division is permanent and irrevocable, the award of support alimony is subject to modification upon a showing of substantial change in circumstances, i.e. Husband's ability and/or Wife's demonstrated need. 43 O.S.1991, §134; *Clifton v. Clifton*, 801 P.2d 693 (Okla. 1990).

"[S]upport alimony is not alimony in lieu of a division. Support alimony is exactly what its name implies, alimony for support and maintenance. Alimony *in lieu of a division* is given for satisfaction of a property division obligation. These are distinct obligations and the acceptance of one does not by implication waive the right of the other." *Greer v. Greer,* 807 P.2d 791, 794 (Okla. 1991) (Emphasis in original). By awarding support alimony and including goodwill in the value of the business for property division purposes, the trial court did not "double dip" into Husband's future income. Both awards, one for support alimony and one for alimony in lieu of property division were proper and distinct from the other. We find no error in the trial court's valuation of the marital property and award of alimony in lieu of property division. . . .

PENSIONS

Next to the marital home, a **pension** may very often be the largest asset available for distribution upon divorce. A pension is a retirement benefit acquired by an employee. At the time of retirement, the employee is entitled to receive the pension funds, either by periodic payments or in a lump sum. Pension may be funded either through contributions from the employer, employee, or a combination of both. A spouse seeking a portion of the employee spouse's pension is only entitled to the portion of the pension acquired during the marriage.

A pension is either **vested** or **nonvested.** While an employee is entitled to walk away from her job with the contribution made by her during her period of employment, she will only be entitled to the funds contributed by the employer if her pension has vested. A vested pension entitles the employee to the employer's contribution portion provided that the employee has worked for the employer for an enumerated number of years. Once the employee has reached the specific benchmark, her right to the employer contribution attaches and she is entitled to the pension. If she leaves her employment with an unvested pension, the right to the employer portion of the funds has not yet attached. In a divorce case, a vested pension should be considered marital property. An unvested pension represents a future expectancy interest. If an unvested employee leaves her employer before the vesting period, a divorcing spouse may only be entitled to a portion of the employee spouse's contributions.

Whether your office is representing the employee spouse or the nonemployee spouse, it is necessary to obtain the following information, either through discovery or the client interview:

1. Name, address, and telephone number of the plan administrator,
2. Copy of the pension plan, and
3. A computer printout of monies paid into the plan by the client.

A pension must be **valuated.** This means that the value or worth of the pension must be determined. Valuation will provide the attorney with a dollar amount attached to the pension so that the client's interests in marital property can be adequately protected. Numerous pension valuation services are available to family law attorneys. Many advertise in professional publications directed at the family bar. These services employ experts trained at valuing pensions and determining their fair market value. If the parties wish to forego the valuation of the pension because of the added expense, a clause in the settlement agreement indicating that the valuation was waived is essential to protect the attorney from a malpractice claim.

Once a pension has been valuated, the attorneys for the parties must determine how this asset will be divided. This will depend on what other types of marital assets are available for distribution. If there is very little cash or other assets to distribute, the parties may seek to obtain a **Qualified Domestic Relations Order (QDRO).** This is a court order served on the pension administrator ordering the plan to distribute a specified portion of the pension funds to the nonemployee spouse. Appendix B includes two QDROs prepared in the divorce of comedian Jim Carrey and his wife, Melissa.

While state law dictates property division, federal law controls retirement benefits. When addressing the distribution of pension funds, employers must comply with the **Employee Retirement Income Security Act (ERISA).** ERISA is a federal statute passed in 1974 to protect employees and their pensions in case an employer declares bankruptcy or goes out of business. This law governs retirement pay and pension benefits. ERISA was amended by the **Retirement Equity Act (REA)** of 1984. This federal statute determines the manner in which states may divide a pension at the time of divorce and its requirements must be complied with in order for the QDRO to be valid. If the QDRO is invalid, the plan will not release any funds.

Pensions, either through an employer or self-directed (i.e., an IRA a spouse may have started on his own at a local bank), are **tax deferred.** This means that taxes on the income produced by the pension will not be paid until the monies are withdrawn at the time of retirement. If these funds are withdrawn prior to retirement, tax penalties will be imposed. An accountant should be consulted to determine the tax liability of liquidating any deferred compensation plan. The tax liability should be determined in advance so as to negotiate a payment of taxes due between the spouses. If the tax consequences are overlooked, the employee spouse could be in for a big surprise come tax time.

An employee spouse may not wish to have her pension distributed. If there are ample funds, the parties may agree to a **buyout.** In this scenario, the pension will be valuated, and the employee spouse will give cash to the nonemployee spouse, in exchange for any interest he may have in her pension. This would allow the employee spouse's pension to remain untouched. The parties may also agree to **offset** the pension with other assets. For example, the employee spouse may agree to transfer her interest in the marital home or other marital assets in exchange for the full ownership of her pension benefits.

Federal law requires that the employee spouse name the nonemployee spouse as a beneficiary of his retirement benefits. Once the marriage has been severed by a court, the client should be advised to change the beneficiary designation immediately. A certified copy of the judgment or certificate of dissolution complete with a court seal should be filed with the pension plan along with any necessary form required by the particular plan.

The Garbage Man's Disability Pension

In 1991, the New York Court of Appeals held that a portion of a Department of Sanitation worker's disability pension was marital property and have subject to equitable distribution.

GERALD A. DOLAN V. LOIS A. DOLAN

583 N.E.2D 908, 577 N.Y.S.2D 195 (N.Y. 1991)

NEW YORK COURT OF APPEALS

ALEXANDER, J.

On this appeal, plaintiff-husband challenges the Appellate Division's affirmance of Supreme Court's determination that a portion of his ordinary disability pension received from the New York City Employee's Retirement System is marital property and thus subject to equitable distribution pursuant to Part B Section 236 of the Domestic Relations Law. We conclude that inasmuch as a portion of that ordinary disability pension represents deferred compensation related to length of employment occurring during the marriage, it constitutes marital property subject to equitable distribution. Thus, there should be an affirmance.

The parties to this litigation were married on July 23, 1966. Three children were born of the union. In 1969, plaintiff became employed by the New York City Department of Sanitation. Nine years later he injured his back when he fell from a sanitation truck. He could not work at all for approximately five weeks and was unable to perform his normal work routine when he returned to work. Eventually, he was retired on an ordinary disability pension pursuant to Section 13-167 of New York City Administrative Code, effective April 17, 1980. At the time of his retirement, he had accumulated approximately eleven years of service with the Department of Sanitation, thus entitling him to pension benefits of $811.84 per month from the New York City Employee's Retirement System. He subsequently became employed by Marist College where he then enrolled as a full-time student.

. . . The court concluded that 47.62% of plaintiff's ordinary disability pension was marital property subject to equitable distribution and that the remaining 52.38% was disability payment, and thus, was separate property not subject to equitable distribution.

In order to determine the allocation between retirement benefits and disability benefits, the court compared the pension benefit plaintiff would have received had he retired normally with the allowance plaintiff received under the ordinary disability retirement provision. If plaintiff had fifteen years of service, he would have had vested regular pension benefits (see, NYS Admin Code §13-173.1) computed under the formula for determining normal retirement allowances, and his pension would have been considerably less—it would have equaled 47.62% of what he received under the ordinary disability plan. Supreme Court concluded that 47.62% of the ordinary disability was pure pension, and thus was marital property of which defendant was entitled

to 50%. The court also determined that defendant was entitled to 23.81% of any future increase in the monthly pension payment as well as retroactive pension payments from the date of the commencement of the action.

The Appellate Division affirmed Supreme Court's determination in all respects concluding that because the ordinary disability pension benefits plaintiff was receiving has a ten-year service requirement, such benefits were not solely compensation for injuries but were, in part, an award for length of service. It also concluded that the method used by Supreme Court to determine defendant's award was proper (—AD2d—). For reasons set forth below, we affirm.

The New York Legislature has determined that marital property shall include "all property acquired by either or both spouses during the marriage and before the execution of a separate agreement or the commencement of a matrimonial action" (Domestic Relations Law §236 [B][1][d]). This Court has previously determined that pension benefits or vested rights to those benefits, except to the extent that they are earned or acquired before marriage or after commencement of a matrimonial action, constitute marital property (see, *Majauskas v. Majauskas*, 61 NY2d 481, 490). That determination was consistent with the intent of the Legislature as embodied in DRL §236(B)(5)(d)(4) and accords with our understanding that a pension benefit is, in essence, a form of deferred compensation derived from employment and an asset of the marriage that both spouses expect to enjoy at a future date (*Damiano v. Damiano*, 94 AD2d 132, 137). Allowing one spouse to share the pension benefit the other obtains through employment and considering such benefits to be marital property is also consistent with the concept of equitable distribution which rests largely on the view that marriage is, among other things, an economic partnership to which each party has made a contribution (id. at 138).

However, any compensation a spouse receives for personal injuries is not considered marital property and is not subject to equitable distribution (DRL §236 [B][1][d][2]). Thus a number of courts in this state have distinguished a "retirement pension" from a pure "disability pension" noting that the former is subject to equitable distribution whereas the latter, received as compensation for personal injuries, is not (see *Mylette v. Mylette*, 163 AD2d 43m revg, 140 Misc 2d 607; *West v. West*, 101 AD2d 834, after remittur, 115 AD2d 601; *Newell v. Newell*, 121 Misc 2d 586).

Plaintiff argues that his disability pension should not be subject to equitable distribution. He points to the fact that he was not eligible to receive a normal retirement pension because he had not been employed a sufficient number of years to be vested. Thus, had he retired without a disability in April 1980, he would have received no pension benefit. He contends that the pension benefits he receives are based merely upon his disability and should not be considered Marital property. These arguments are unavailing.

Plaintiff was retired pursuant to the retirement for ordinary disability provision of Section 13-167 of the New York City Administrative Code, which entitles a member of the city civil service to receive an ordinary disability pension if he or she "is physically or mentally incapacitated for the performance of duty and ought to be retired," provided he or she "has had ten or more years of duty-service and was a member or otherwise in city-service in each of the ten years next preceding his or her retirement" (NYC Admin Code §13-167 [a][1]). Thus, an employee may receive an ordinary disability pension even if the disability was not the result of a job-related accident, provided the employee satisfies the length of service requirement.

By contrast, a civil service member qualifying for a pension for "accident disability" does not have to satisfy a length of service requirement. Rather, the only requirement for entitlement to an "accident disability" pension is that the employee be "physically or mentally incapacitated for the performance of city-service, as a natural and proximate result of such city-service," and that the "disability was not the result of willful negligence" on the part of the employee (NYC Admin Code §113-168). Thus, the statutory scheme distinguishes between eligibility for "regular," "ordinary disability" and "accidental disability" pensions on the basis of length of service; entitlement to a "regular" pension vests upon 15 years of service (NYC Admin Code §13-173.1) and an "ordinary disability" pension upon 10 years of service (NYC Admin Code §13-167[a][1]), while there exists no length of service requirement for an "accidental disability" pension.

As indicated previously, it is firmly established in our jurisprudence that an employee's interest in " 'pension rights', the rights commonly accorded an employee and his or her spouse in a pension plan, . . . except to the extent that [that interest] is earned before marriage or after commencement of a matrimonial action, is marital property" (*Majauskas v. Majauskas*, 61 NY2d 481, 490, supra), the pension benefits constituting a form of deferred compensation derived from employment (*West v. West*, 101 AD2d 834, supra). In the typical pension plan, the employees' rights are incremental in that for each month or year of service, the employee receives credit which will enter into the computation of what the pension plan will pay to the employee (*Majauskas v. Majauskas*, supra at 490).

It is clear from the length of service requirement for the ordinary disability pension at issue here that plaintiff is being compensated for his length of service to the Department of Sanitation in addition to being compensated for the injuries he sustained. Indeed, implicit in the service requirement for this ordinary disability pension is the desire to provide employees whose injuries have prevented them from working until normal retirement age with some form of compensation for their injuries while also awarding them a portion of the deferred compensation to which they would have been entitled but for the injuries (see e.g. *Mylette v. Mylette*, 163 AD2d 463, 465 supra). Thus, to the extent plaintiff's ordinary disability pension represents deferred compensation, it is indistinguishable from a retirement pension and therefore, to that extent, is subject to equitable distribution (see e.g. *Mylette v. Mylette*, 163 AD2d 463, 463 supra; *West v. West*, 101 AD2d 834, supra; *Newell v. Newell*, 121 Misc 2d 586, supra; see generally, Annotation, Pension or Retirement Benefits as Subject to Award or Division by Court in Settlement of Property Rights Between Spouses, 94 ALR3d 176 §13).

Accordingly, the order of the Appellate Division should be affirmed, with costs.

Order affirmed with costs. Opinion by Judge Alexander. Chief Judge Wachtler and Judges Simons, Kaye, Titone, Hancock, and Bellacosa concur.

PROFESSIONAL DEGREE

In a marital partnership, spouses often make sacrifices of time, energy, and financial resources for the future good of the partnership. One of the sacrifices often made is putting a spouse through school. Many spouses who make the decision to seek a professional degree or license do so with the commitment and support of the other spouse. This decision may require moving to another city or town or sometimes another country. It also can involve the decision of the nonstudent spouse to give up, either permanently or temporarily, his or her own professional goals while the student spouse pursues his or her goals. It can involve the nonstudent spouse working as the sole breadwinner in order to allow the student spouse time to focus on scholastic endeavors. It can also involve a drastic change in lifestyle in which the student spouse devotes a majority of his or her time on studies at the expense of spending quality time with the family. It can also involve financial sacrifices in terms of money needed for books, tuition, and debt incurred for academic loans. These sacrifices are made in hopes that a professional or advanced degree will provide the family unit with a more prosperous future in which homes and other assets may be purchased, children educated, and retirement plans funded.

Despite these high hopes and dreams of a higher standard of living, many nonstudent spouses upon graduation have found themselves served with divorce papers while the student spouse embarks on a new career, with newfound friends and, sometimes, new romantic love interests! Some states have classified a professional degree as marital property if it was obtained during the marriage. In these jurisdictions, a nonstudent spouse who makes monetary and nonmonetary contributions that enhance the other spouse's earning potential may claim a portion of the value of the professional degree as marital property. An expert can provide a monetary figure representing the value of a professional degree. The court will then award a portion of the value to the nonstudent spouse pursuant to the state's property division laws. Other jurisdictions have refused to recognize the professional degree as a marital asset. Courts have even extended the professional degree as property theory to any artistic or athletic skill developed during the marriage which enhances the participant spouse's earning capacity. To compensate the nonstudent spouse, however, some states have awarded reimbursement alimony to the nonstudent spouse for his or her efforts and contributions toward the attainment of the spouse's enhanced earning capacity.

FIGURE 6–5
Some jurisdictions consider an advanced degree to be marital property if it was obtained during the marriage.

WIFE'S SLAM DUNK

In *Marriage of Anderson*, the court held that an NBA player's contract signed by the husband for the 1988–1989 season was marital property and subject to equitable distribution.

IN RE THE MARRIAGE OF BERNADETTE K. ANDERSON AND RICHARD A. ANDERSON

811 P.2D 419 (COLO.APP. 1990)

COLORADO COURT OF APPEALS, DIV. II.

OPINION BY JUDGE ROTHENBERG.

In this dissolution of marriage action, Bernadette K. Anderson (wife) appeals from permanent orders entered relating to distribution of property and maintenance. We reverse and remand with directions.

The principal issue on appeal is whether husband's player contract with a professional basketball team constitutes marital property subject to division.

At the time of the decree on March 1, 1989, husband was currently under a three-year contract with the Portland Trail Blazers for the 1988–89, 1989–90 and 1990–91 seasons. According to the contract, he was to receive three yearly lump-sum payments totaling 1.5 million dollars. On October 5, 1988 and December 1, 1988, he received the first payment which totaled $267,000 after taxes. Remaining payments of $475,000 and $575,000 were payable December 1989 and December 1990, respectively.

The NBA player contract in issue was never made part of the trial court record, but testimony of both husband and his attorney-agent indicated that the contract guaranteed payment: (1) if he died; (2) if he sustained injury during an NBA game or an official practice session; (3) if he had a mental breakdown or disability; (4) if he was terminated for lack of skill; or (5) if he were traded or waived by the team. Payment was not guaranteed if he sustained a physical disability from an injury unrelated to an NBA game or practice, or if he failed to pass a physical exam at the beginning of each season.

Husband testified that he used part of the $267,000 received to pay marital debts, child support maintenance and mortgage payments on the parties' townhouse. At the time of the permanent orders, however, he still had $150,000 in treasury securities and $14,000 in his checking account.

The trial court ruled that husband's NBA contract including the $267,000 payment already received by husband was not marital property, but was income belonging to the husband for husband's future services. On appeal, wife argues that husband's NBA contract is marital property, and she relies heavily on cases holding that a spouse's compensation which is deferred until after the dissolution, but fully earned during the marriage, is marital property (citations omitted). . . .

. . . In our view, the money already received by husband during the marriage is not future income. It is cash on hand and therefore marital property subject to division. Accordingly, we hold that the money paid under the contract for the 1988–89 season and not expended for marital purposes as of the date of the dissolution *is* marital property subject to equitable distribution, and the trial court erred in ruling otherwise.

However, as to the final two years of husband's contract, we hold that those payments to be received for the 1989–90 and 1990–91 seasons do not constitute property; rather, they constitute future income. *See In re Marriage of Faulkner, supra.*

Section 14-10-113, C.R.S. (1987 Rel.Vol.6B) requires a trial court to consider three separate issues regarding the equitable distribution of assets in a dissolution: (1) It must characterize the asset and determine whether it is property; (2) it must then allocate the asset as separate property of one spouse or as marital property; and (3) finally, it must distribute the property equitably (citation omitted). . . .

On remand, the court should consider all relevant factors in distributing the marital property here including the contribution of each spouse during the marriage, the fact of their separation, and any dissipation of marital property (citation omitted). . . .

. . . The judgment as to maintenance and division of property is reversed, and the cause is remanded to the trial court for further proceedings not inconsistent with the views expressed herein.

TURSI and HUME, J.J., concur.

DISTRIBUTION OF THE MARITAL DEBTS

Division of the marital debts is as important as division of the marital assets. Many failed marriages have no assets, but only debts to parcel out between the parties. A **debt** is a sum of money owed to a party called a **creditor.** The party responsible for the debt is called a **debtor.**

Debts must be identified and classified as either separate or marital debt. Then the obligation to pay is imposed on the respective spouses according to state law. Like separate property, debts incurred by a spouse prior to marriage belong to that spouse. A creditor in this case may only attach separate property to satisfy a debt incurred before the marriage. If no separate property exists, the creditor may then seek to attach marital property for satisfaction of the debt.

Debts incurred during the course of the marriage are considered marital debts. Just as spouses are jointly entitled to share in the fruits of the marriage, they will also be jointly responsible for the debts incurred during the marriage, regardless of whether the debt was incurred by one spouse or both. During the course of the marriage, couples will incur debts for **necessaries** such as food, clothing, shelter and medical care. As long as a debt for necessaries is incurred during the marriage, both spouses are responsible for the debt. This obligation to provide for the necessaries of the family was historically imposed on the husband. Today, both husbands and wives are mutually responsible for providing the essentials to their families. A creditor due an obligation regarding a necessary may seek an attachment of marital property. Note that in the *Szesny* case, illustrated earlier in this chapter, the husband was held repsonsible for debts incurred during the marriage that were not classified as necessaries. Husband had dissipated the marital assets and it would have been unfair for the court to hold the wife responsible for the husband's wrongdoing.

During the divorce process, the parties are free to negotiate regarding which spouse will assume a particular debt. If there is no dispute, a separation agreement will be drafted and the debt clauses will specify the debts to be assumed by the respective parties. The debt section should also include a **hold harmless clause.** A hold harmless clause indicates that a particular spouse will be responsible for a debt incurred during the marriage, that he will be solely responsible for its payment, and that the other spouse shall be free and clear of any obligation regarding that debt. This agreement, however, is not binding on a creditor. A creditor who is due a debt incurred during the marriage may sue one or both spouses regardless of what the separation agreement indicates. The hold harmless clause allows the spouse who got "stuck" paying the debt to turn around and seek repayment from the spouse initially obligated under the separation agreement. Remember also that, although the creditor may only sue the spouse who incurred the debt during marriage, if judgment is granted in favor of the creditor, the creditor may seek to enforce the judgment against the marital assets of the marriage, assets in which the other spouse has an interest. After a divorce, a creditor can still seek to satisfy the debt by pursuing the spouse most able to pay the debt.

If the court must determine the allocation of debts, the spouse's ability to pay and assets available will be considered.

DISSIPATION OF MARITAL ASSETS

Just as each spouse during the period of a marriage may contribute to the acquisition, enhancement, preservation, and appreciation of the marital estate, so either or both spouses may *dissipate* or waste away marital assets. **Dissipation** or depletion of the marital assets can occur in one or more of the following ways:

- ▼ Overspending during the course of an intact marriage.
- ▼ Overspending in contemplation of divorce.
- ▼ Overspending upon formal or informal notice of impending divorce.
- ▼ Destroying, giving away, or selling a spouse's property.

Activities that constitute dissipation include running up credit card debt, depleting or closing out joint checking and savings accounts, making suspicious loans to relatives, purchasing "big ticket" items with cash, gambling, and making high-risk or highly speculative investments.

When making property distribution awards in a dissolution proceeding, the court will take into consideration each spouse's role in and responsibility for the dissipation of marital assets. The court may punish the wrongdoing spouse by requiring the spouse to compensate the other spouse for the waste. This may be accomplished either by awarding the innocent spouse a larger percentage of the marital property or by ordering the wrongdoing spouse to pay to the other spouse an amount of cash equal to the monetary value of the assets depleted.

Motorcycle Madness

Let's discuss the *Click* case. In defiance of a court order, Mr. Click took the Clicks' Gold Wing motorcycle and had an accident, which left him comatose. The Gold Wing was destroyed in the accident, leaving Mrs. Click to argue that her husband had dissipated a marital asset.

▼

IN RE MARRIAGE OF WANDA CLICK AND ROBERT CLICK

169 ILL. APP. 3D 48, 119 ILL. DEC. 701, 523 N.E.2D 169 (ILL. APP. 2 DIST. 1988)

APPELLATE COURT OF ILLINOIS, SECOND DISTRICT

JUSTICE UNVERZAGT DELIVERED THE OPINION OF THE COURT.

Petitioner, Wanda Click, appeals from the property distribution portion of an order entered by the circuit court of Kane County dissolving her marriage to Robert Click. While petitioner's action was pending, Robert was critically injured in a motorcycle accident. He has been in a coma since May 4, 1986. The trial court consolidated the dissolution action with an action by Robert's

mother, Jacquelyn Click, to have Robert adjudicated a disabled adult and to have a guardian appointed for him. Jacquelyn was subsequently appointed guardian of Robert's person and estate, and she participated in the property division portion of the dissolution proceeding on his behalf.

Wanda initially sought to enforce a settlement agreement which she alleged the parties had reached before Robert's accident. The court rejected that claim, however, concluding that Wanda had not sufficiently established the terms of the alleged agreement to allow it to be enforced. On March 19,1987, the court entered an order dissolving the marriage and dividing the marital property. The court noted that, according to Wanda, Robert was a professional thief who had only occasionally been "gainfully employed" during the marriage. Wanda worked only part-time during the marriage. The court found the testimony regarding the parties' earnings to be incredible as the evidence demonstrated that they had acquired assets far in excess of their reported income. The property division portion of the order directed the sale of the marital residence, in which Wanda was residing, and an equal distribution of the proceeds between the parties. It awarded Robert the proceeds of a worker's compensation claim involving an employment-related injury he had received, the proceeds of a pending action concerning his motorcycle accident, the salvage value of the Gold Wing motorcycle on which he was injured, a motorcycle trailer, and a number of personal items. It awarded Wanda a 1983 automobile, a smaller motorcycle, an aluminum boat, and some personal items. Wanda was additionally required to reimburse Robert for some of his furnishings which she sold after his accident, and for some charges she made to his credit cards. The court also ordered the equal division of any property contained in a safe deposit box and an equal division of the sale proceeds of a speedboat "if it is ever located," which Wanda claimed Robert had bought. The court directed the guardian to sell all of the assets assigned to Robert and to use the proceeds for his care. The court reserved the issue of future maintenance for Robert.

On appeal, Wanda alleges that: . . . (2) the evidence demonstrated that Robert had dissipated a marital asset by destroying the Gold Wing motorcycle. . . .

. . . Petitioner next contends that the court erred in rejecting her claim that Robert dissipated a marital asset when he took the Gold Wing motorcycle in contravention of a court order and then destroyed it in the accident that left him comatose. Dissipation of marital assets is generally defined as "the use of marital property for the sole benefit of one of the spouses for a purpose unrelated to the marriage at a time that the marriage is undergoing an irreconcilable breakdown" (citations omitted). While petitioner correctly asserts that courts have occasionally found a dissipation of assets where the dissipating spouse has derived no personal benefit from his or her actions (see, *e.g.*, *In re Marriage of Siegel* (1984), 123 Ill. App. 3d 710, 719, 79 Ill. Dec. 219, 463 N.E.2d 773), we know of no authority, nor has petitioner cited any, which would permit a party to be held accountable for a dissipation which is not only detrimental to both parties, but purely unintentional as well. Robert violated a court order in taking the motorcycle – conduct which would ordinarily have resulted in the court's imposition of contempt sanctions against him. (See generally *In re G.B.* (1981), 88 Ill. 2d 36, 41, 58 Ill. Dec. 845, 420 N.E.2d 1096 (regarding a court's inherent contempt power).) There was no evidence to suggest that his injury and the destruction of the motorcycle were anything other than accidental, however, and we therefore conclude that the court correctly found that he did not dissipate a marital asset . . .

. . . Judgment affirmed.

NASH and REINHARD, JJ., concur.

During the pendency of a divorce or dissolution action, each spouse may have some access to the marital assets. During that period, each spouse has the right to use some portion of marital funds to pay for legitimate expenses, including the payment of reasonable legal fees in conjunction with the divorce action. Divorcing spouses may also use marital funds to pay certain personal expenses which they always paid from the funds during the course of the marriage. Such expenses may include individual property tax bills for each spouse's automobile, automobile insurance and health insurance premiums, expenses for unexpected, emergency home repairs, dental work, reasonable expenses of the minor children, and, of course, reasonable expenditures for necessaries such as food, clothing, and shelter.

FIGURE 6–6
A spouse may be required to replace monies dissipated during the course of a marriage dissolution action.

EXHIBIT 6–1
Calculating goodwill.

IRA W. BRODSKY, C.P.A.
EDWARD J. LIEBERMAN, C.P.A.
PHOEBE H. SHAW, C.P.A.
JOSEPH S. SWEENEY, C.P.A.
RICHARD B. TAYLOR, C.P.A.

TAYLOR AND **LIEBERMAN**

AN ACCOUNTANCY CORPORATION

10890 WILSHIRE BOULEVARD · SUITE 1100

LOS ANGELES, CALIFORNIA 90024

TELEPHONE
(310) 479-9920

TELECOPIER
(310) 474-2733

June 30, 1994

Brenda A. Beswick, Attorney at Law
Trope and Trope
12121 Wilshire Boulevard
Suite 801
Los Angeles, CA 90025

Re: Marriage of Carrey

Dear Brenda:

The following is a list of the initial documents and
information which we will need to begin our work regarding the
calculation of goodwill for the above-stated matter:

<u>JAMES CARREY</u>

1.   Cash flow and income tax projections for 1994.

2.   All contracts, agreements, and related amendments in effect
      from the date of marriage through the most current date
      available, <u>except</u> those previously provided, as follows:
      a.   "Night Life"
      b.   "Peggy Sue Got Married"
      c.   "Earth Girls are Easy"
      d.   "Jim Carrey Special"
      e.   "Doing Time on Maple"
      f.   "Ace Ventura"
      g.   "The Mask"
      h.   "In Living Color"
      i.   "Dumb and Dumber"
      j.   United Talent Agency contract dated March 12, 1993

3.   Listing of all written, published, produced and/or performed
      works including date written and/or started, date completed
      and compensation received beginning August 29, 1984 through
      the most current date available.

<u>JIMMY-GENE, INC.</u>

3.   Corporate tax returns for the period beginning August 29,
      1984 through August 31, 1989.

4.   Financial statements for the period beginning September 1,
      1993 through the most current date available.

EXHIBIT __B__

EXHIBIT 6–1
Continued

Brenda Beswick, Attorney at Law
June 30, 1994
Page 2

5.   All contracts, agreements, and related amendments in effect
     from August 29, 1984 through the most current date
     available, <u>except</u> those previously listed in #2 above.

PIT BULL PRODUCTIONS, INC.

6.   Financial statements for the period beginning January 1,
     1994, through the most current date available.

7.   All contracts, agreements, and related amendments in effect
     from December 13, 1993, through the most current date
     available, <u>except</u> those previously listed in #2 above.

AGENTS

8.   Schedule of all meetings or telephone discussions regarding
     television, film or other projects whether or not offered or
     accepted. The schedule should include dates and terms of
     compensation beginning March 28, 1987 through the most
     current date available.

     This request is not intended to be an all inclusive list of
documents necessary to perform our work. Review of the above
information may reveal items which warrant further inquiries and
documentation in order to complete our assignment.

     Please contact me with any questions you may have.

                              Sincerely,

                              Phoebe H. Shaw
                              Phoebe H. Shaw

PHS:tgw:L063094

REVIEW QUESTIONS

1. Define real and personal property.
2. What are the most common forms of concurrent or joint ownership?
3. What is title?
4. Explain the difference between separate property and marital property.
5. Define transmutation and the three circumstances in which separate property is transmuted.
6. What is tracing?
7. How are marital assets valuated? How is equity determined?
8. Explain the effect of premarital agreements on property distribution.
9. Explain the main difference between equitable distribution states and community property law states.
10. What were the Married Women's Property Acts and how did they change the property rights of married women?
11. Name the nine community property states.
12. Explain the difference between a vested pension and a nonvested pension.
13. What is a QDRO?
14. How are marital debts distributed in a divorce action?
15. Define the dissipation of marital assets.

EXERCISES

1. Find your state's property distribution statute and determine whether you live in a community property distribution or equitable distribution jurisdiction.

2. Does your state's property distribution statute distinguish between separate and marital property or may both estates be considered by the courts in making a property award?

3. How does your state define separate property and marital property?

4. List the statutory factors the courts must consider in making a property distribution award. Is fault a consideration?

5. Review your state's statutory and case law and determine how your jurisdiction treats the professional degree. Is it considered marital property or is yours a reimbursement alimony state?

CHAPTER 7

CHILD CUSTODY, VISITATION, AND RIGHTS OF THIRD PARTIES

KEY TERMS:

Best interest of the child	Primary caretaker
Best interest standard	Psychological parent
Custodial parent	Reasonable rights of visitation
Expert witness	Shared physical custody
Family relations unit	Sole custody
Fixed schedule	Split custody
Family services division	Standing
Joint custody	Supervised visitation
Legal custody	Tender years doctrine
Noncustodial parent	Third-party intervenor
Patria potestas	Unsupervised visitation
Physical custody	Visitation rights

When a family unit is intact, both parents enjoy physical and legal custody of their children. Both parents are the children's legal guardians and, as such, have the right to make decisions regarding their children's health, education, and welfare. This is known as **legal custody.** In addition, both parents have actual physical possession of the children in that the children reside with them. This is known as **physical custody.** If the family unit dissolves, and husband and wife begin living separately, formal arrangements must be made for the care and custody of the children either through a stipulated agreement by the parents that is approved of by the court and made an order, or through a determination made and ordered by the court, when a mutually agreed-on arrangement is not possible. In either case, court orders will be entered and will address the issues of both legal custody and physical custody.

Throughout history, society's legal systems have used various ways to decide child custody issues. At times, societies and their legal systems have had very cut and dry and inflexible rules for awarding the guardianship and/or legal and physical custody of children to one parent or the other when the marital unit was dissolved.

A HISTORICAL PERSPECTIVE ON CUSTODY

THE AGE OF PATERNAL DOMINANCE

In ancient civilizations, fathers possessed absolute right to the possession of their children. This right was known as *patria potestas.* Centuries later, at English common law, the father's right of possession still prevailed. In both England and the United States, until the early nineteenth century, according to traditional concepts of property law and the law of child custody, children were chattels, the private property of the estate of their fathers. The father had complete authority over his children and controlled their education, discipline, and upbringing. If the parent's marriage broke down, upon its dissolution, the father had a superior right to custody. In a few present-day patriarchal societies, the right of *patria potestas* prevails; however, most contemporary societies have long discarded this custom.

THE SHIFT TO MATERNAL CONTROL

By the end of the nineteenth century many societal changes had occurred which shifted the preference from father to mother in custody determinations. The Industrial Revolution played a significant role in this shift. When families lived on and operated the family farm as an economic enterprise, the father of the family occupied the leadership role and made decisions that affected every aspect and detail of the lives of the other family members. In addition, the father was almost always physically with the children. He was able to direct and supervise their upbringing since his place of work was also the family's home. With the coming of the factory system and people's migration to urban areas, the father began to work out of the home and the mother became the manager of the household and children.

It was during this time period that the traditional roles of father as breadwinner and mother as homemaker emerged. With the mother dominant at home and responsible for meeting the children's needs throughout the day, the viewpoint developed that a mother's continuing presence was indispensable for the physical and emotional well-being of the minor children. For many years, the courts routinely awarded custody to the mother even if the father opposed this choice unless the father or another relative seeking custody could prove that the mother was unfit to care for the child. The theoretical justification for the placing of children with their mother was known as the "tender years" doctrine.

THE TENDER YEARS DOCTRINE

The **tender years doctrine** was based on the assumption that young children needed to be and were better off being cared for by their mothers than by anyone else. Fathers were not viewed as being equipped to deal with the care of infants and young children. Children of tender years included children ages twelve and under. However, custody of children between age twelve and the age of majority was also almost always awarded to their mothers. Occasionally, custody of an older son might be awarded to his father, either because the mother could not control the child, the son wished to live with the father, or the mother and father agreed that the father would have custody of the older child.

The practice of routinely granting custody to the mother continued until the early 1970s, a decade that witnessed a great increase in the incidents of awarding custody to the father and also heralded the advent of joint custody and split custody as alternatives to **sole custody** by either parent. This change occurred as the primacy of the tender years doctrine declined and was replaced by the **best interest of the child** standard. The **"best interest" standard** opened the contest for custody not only to fathers but to other potential caregivers when the child's well-being or interests could be best served by such a custody determination.

FIGURE 7–1
Until the 1970s, custody was traditionally awarded to mothers as a result of the tender years doctrine.

EQUALIZING THE CUSTODIAL PLAYING FIELD: THE TRANSITION FROM "TENDER YEARS" TO "BEST INTEREST"

As noted earlier, the 1960s and 1970s brought many societal changes including an increase in the number of mothers who worked outside the home during marriage and/or upon marital dissolution.

Prior to these decades, when a marriage broke up, the mother was most often a nonworking spouse who in many instances had never had a paying job. The father worked outside of the home, and was the family's only source of economic support. Upon dissolution of the marriage, the court usually awarded the nonworking spouse alimony, intending among other things, to provide the wife with the unearned income she would need to maintain the household and remain at home to raise the children to adulthood. Giving custody to fathers generally was not a viable option, because fathers had to work to support themselves, their former spouses, and the children.

With the advent of greater and better paying job opportunities for women, many mothers went to work. Therefore, in situations where both husband and wife were considered fit parents, the wife was no longer the undisputed choice for custody, especially if she worked outside of the home. Courts had adhered to the belief that children of "tender years" always belonged with their mothers because young children needed personal care throughout the day and stay-at-home mothers were available to do it.

Once mothers went to work and left the child care to a nanny, an older sibling, other relative, or a day care center, they no longer presented a more favorable choice than the working father who could also engage similar resources to care for the child. The child's well-being or interests were no longer necessarily best served by awarding sole custody to the mother. Fathers who desired custody and who were keenly aware of these changed conditions could now present arguments to the court that were very logical, persuasive, and, above all, successfully resulted in an award of custody to fathers.

FIGURE 7–2
After the shift from the tender years doctrine to the best interest standard, fathers began to be awarded custody more often than in the past.

Frequently, at the heart of the successful father's argument was the contention that the children would be better off with the father. Many fathers' attorneys, phrasing this concept in a more intellectually sophisticated manner, reminded the court that the "best interests of the child" should determine the custody disposition and that the interests of their client's child would be best served by placing the child with his or her father. Courts, for many years, had been able to routinely apply the tender years doctrine with such conviction because the courts believed that maternal custody promoted the children's best interest. That is no longer true.

THE BEST INTEREST STANDARD AS THE ULTIMATE DETERMINANT

By the end of the 1970s, the best interest of the child had become a very significant factor that most jurisdictions considered. This trend continued and by the 1990s, virtually all jurisdictions had abandoned the blanket or automatic tender years presumption of maternal custody in favor of identifying what determination would promote the child's best interests. The application of the best interest standard not only determined who would have custody but also whether custody would be sole custody, shared custody, or split custody.

THE BROADER RESULTS OF APPLYING THE BEST INTEREST STANDARD

Once the tender years doctrine lost favor and the shift away from always awarding sole custody to the mother occurred, there was another shift, as well, from always awarding custody to only one parent. When both parents worked, sometimes courts believed that both parents should be jointly responsible for the children's financial maintenance and for the children's physical and emotional care, and the joint custody practice began to emerge.

JOINT CUSTODY

By the 1970s fathers had begun to assume a more intimate role in parenting their children even when these offspring were infants. Fathers were involved in many more aspects of their child's upbringing. Upon marital dissolution, these fathers wished to remain involved and frequently, although not always, their ex-spouse, the child's mother, wanted them involved as well. This attitude gave rise to and support for the practice of **joint custody.**

Parents having joint custody are jointly or equally responsible for the financial, emotional, educational, and health-related needs of their children. They have an equal responsibility and an equal degree of say in deciding how to meet the various needs of their children. Joint custody will only be successful if the parents can communicate effectively with each other and put aside personal feelings toward each other when dealing with issues relating to the children, be flexible enough to compromise when each party has a different view on how to handle some aspect of the child's upbringing, and be able to negotiate to arrive at an adequate solution when conflicts arise.

If parents cannot function smoothly with one another, then joint custody will not be in the children's best interest, because it will produce an ongoing atmosphere of friction. Every major decision will be a struggle. In this type of situation, the interest of the child will be better served by awarding one parent sole custody and affording the other parent liberal visitation rights, provided that the custodial parent's authority will not otherwise thwart or impair the noncustodial parent's relationship with the child.

TYPES OF JOINT CUSTODY

Generally there are two types of joint custody:

▼ Joint custody with primary physical custody in one parent or
▼ Joint custody with shared physical custody.

JOINT CUSTODY WITH PHYSICAL CUSTODY IN ONE PARENT

Under this arrangement, both parents share legal custody of the children. Both parents have equal say in making decisions regarding the child's upbringing; however, one parent has exclusive physical custody of the child. This means that the child permanently resides with one parent, the **custodial parent,** and has but one legal and actual residence for purposes of attending school, etc. The child may visit the other parent, the **noncustodial parent,** frequently and may stay for long periods of visitation such as summer or holidays and school vacation. Nevertheless, the child's primary residence is with the custodial parent. In this instance because the parent with whom the child primarily resides has expenses for the child's daily needs, the joint but noncustodial parent will be ordered to pay child support to the custodial parent to be used for the physical maintenance of the child. Child support is discussed in detail in Chapter 8.

SHARED PHYSICAL JOINT CUSTODY

This arrangement succeeds most often when each parent resides geographically close to each other and close to the child's school, church, doctor, and site of the child's recreational activities. Under **shared physical custody** arrangements, the child resides with one parent a certain number of days a week and a certain number days with the other parent. The child for all intents and purposes has a dual residence. Usually neither parent pays the other parent child support because both parents share expenses. If one parent is financially more able than the other parent to provide for the child, the more affluent parent gives the less financially able parent money to cover the child's needs while the child is physically in the other's custody. Joint custody with shared physical custody is different from split custody.

SPLIT CUSTODY

A split custodial arrangement is less frequently used than other types of custody dispositions. Under the practice of **split custody,** one parent has sole custody of the child for a part of the calendar year, each year, and the other parent has sole

FIGURE 7–3
As more mothers
began working and
earning wages, courts
began to award joint
custody, allowing both
parents to remain
involved with their
children's upbringing.

custody for the remaining portion of the year. Sometimes under a split custody arrangement, the split will be equal; each parent will have custody of the child for six months. During that time period, the parent will have sole custody of the child and complete physical custody of the child.

Sometimes split custody means that one parent has sole custody and physical custody of the child during the school year and the other parent has sole and physical custody of the child for the summer months. Each parent has full authority to make decisions regarding the child's health, education, discipline, recreation, and welfare. This arrangement differs from joint custody with shared physical custody in that parents with joint custody with shared physical custody must consult the other custodial parent regarding at least major decisions regarding health, education, and welfare. For instance, if while a child residing for the school year with the mother under joint custody physical or otherwise decided to have the child undergo elective surgery for removal of tonsils and adenoids, if the father who had joint custody did not agree that such removal was the best medically appropriate alternative, then the parents would have to reach some type of agreement before surgery could be performed. Under a split custodial arrangement, the parent enjoying their physical custody time could have the child undergo elective surgery without the legal consent of the other parent.

Split custody was actually a compromise before the 1970s. For several decades during the first half of the twentieth century, courts entered orders for a split custodial arrangement in instances either where both parents requested it or where the court felt that such a "Solomon" type of disposition was the fairest under the circumstances. In the 1960s and 1970s the arrangement occurred mainly when parents lived in different parts of the country or in different countries. Split custody can be very disruptive and undermine the child's need for continuity and stability in his or her relationships and environment. This type of arrangement is used very little today. Today, most, if not all, courts apply the "best interest of the child" standard to decisions regarding custody, and the current prevailing view is that split custody is detrimental to a child's best interest.

Another type of split custody arrangement may involve the splitting of siblings. One parent would be awarded custody of one or more children, and the other parent would have custody of the others. Courts generally frown on splitting up siblings. Keeping brothers and sisters together provides the children with some level of stability at a time when the breakup of their parents is traumatic for them to handle. There are some instances, however, where splitting the siblings may actually be in the best interest of the children, as one parent may be better able to control, discipline, or care for a particular child.

FIGURE 7–4
Courts prefer not to break up siblings when a marriage dissolves, because keeping brothers and sisters together provides children with some level of stability during this rough period.

HOW TO DETERMINE WHAT IS IN THE CHILD'S BEST INTEREST

The shift from the tender years doctrine to the best interest standard came about in the 1970s and remains the preferred standard today. However, legal and psychological experts differ on the factor or factors to apply in determining "best interest."

As mentioned earlier, the 1970s saw a shift away from always awarding custody solely to the mother. When both parents worked outside the home and had to rely on other individuals to care for children while they worked, sometimes a consideration of each parent's circumstances revealed that the child would be better off with the working father rather than the working mother, or that one of the two forms of joint custody would most benefit the child.

The discipline of child development and child psychology grew tremendously during the 1960s and 1970s. The knowledge gained from these fields and the criteria that emerged were applied to the making of custodial decisions on a regular basis. Courts increasingly referred the issue of custody to the court's **family relations unit** or **family services division.** In this unit, trained social workers conducted studies and applied child development and child psychology concepts to make custody and visitation recommendations. Further, working parents frequently employed their own psychologist and psychiatrists to evaluate their children and testify on their behalf in court as **expert witnesses.**

FACTORS CONSIDERED IN DETERMINING BEST INTEREST

State statutory schemes articulate the factors used by family court judges in determining the preferable placement of a child in a disputed custody action. An excerpt of Arizona's custody statute illustrates the factors considered in determining the best interest of the child.

STATUTES

ARIZONA REVISED STATUTES ANNOTATED (WEST)

25.403.   CUSTODY; BEST INTEREST OF CHILD. . . .

A. The court shall determine custody, either originally or upon petition for modification, in accordance with the best interests of the child. The court shall consider all relevant factors, including:

1. The wishes of the child's parent or parents as to custody.
2. The wishes of the child as to the custodian.
3. The interaction and interrelationship of the child with the child's parent or parents, the child's siblings and any other person who may significantly affect the child's best interest.
4. The child's adjustment to home, school and community.
5. The mental and physical health of all individuals involved.
6. Which parent is more likely to allow the child frequent and meaningful continuing contact with the other parent.
7. If one parent, both parents, or neither parent has provided primary care of the child.
8. The nature and extent of coercion or duress used by a parent in obtaining an agreement regarding custody.
9. Whether a parent has complied with Chapter 3 article 5 of this title. . . .

Family court judges have broad discretion in resolving issues of child custody and visitation. The court must not only assess a parent's ability to provide a child with the necessities of life such as food, clothing, and shelter, but also with nurturing, love, and affection. Certain factors have emerged as essential indicators of whether a certain custodial disposition is in the child's best interest.

PSYCHOLOGICAL PARENT

Where both parties are equally fit, a court may order a custody study to ascertain which parent is the child's **psychological parent.** Often, the parent who has had the child since the child's birth and/or who has spent the most meaningful time with the child, has bonded most fully with the child, and who has provided the most psychological nurturing of the child is considered the psychological parent. Custody is frequently awarded to the psychological parent because it is considered harmful to wrest the child away from the individual whom the child considers his psychological parent, the one with whom he has the strongest bonds.

PRIMARY CARETAKER

Courts frequently decide that custody should be awarded to the child's **primary caretaker.** The primary caretaker is the individual who has done most of the significant parenting of the child since birth or for the several preceding years. The primary caretaker is usually the child's psychological parent also. The primary caretaker standard is in effect similar, if not identical, to the psychological parent concept.

The Primary Caretaker Rule

An excerpt from the following case illustrates the factors used by courts in identifying a child's "primary caretaker."

DEBRA PASCALE V. JAMES PASCALE

660 A.2D 485 (N.J. 1995)

SUPREME COURT OF NEW JERSEY

. . . In cases of only joint legal custody, the roles that both parents play in their children's lives differ depending on their custodial functions. In common parlance, a parent who does not have physical custody over her child is the "non-custodial parent" and the one with sole residential or physical custody is the "custodial parent." Because those terms fail to describe custodial functions accurately, we adopt today the term "primary caretaker" to refer to the "custodial parent" and the term "secondary caretaker" to refer to the "non-custodial parent." Although both roles create responsibility over children of divorce, the primary caretaker has the greater physical and emotional role. Because the role of "primary care-taker" can be filled by men or women, the concept has gained widespread acceptance in custody determination. . . . Indeed, many state courts often determine custody based on the concept of "primary caretaker." E.g. *Burchard v. Garay,* 724 P.2d 486 (Cal. 1986); *Maureen F. G. v. George W. G.,* 445 A.2d 934 (Del. 1982); *Agudo v. Agudo,* 411 So. 2d 249 (Fla. Dist. Ct. App. 1982); *Rolde v. Rolde,* 425 N.E.2d 388 (Mass. App. Ct. 1981); *Maxfield v. Maxfield,* 452 N.W.2d 219 (Minn. 1990); *Riaz v. Riaz,* 789 S.W.2d 224 (Mo. App. Ct. 1990); *Burleigh v. Burleigh,* 650 P.2d 753 (Mont. 1982); *Crum v. Crum,* 505 N.Y.S.2d 656 (App. Div. 1986); *Moore v. Moore,* 574 A.2d 105 (Pa.Super. Ct. 1990); *Pusey v. Pusey,* 728 P.2d 117 (Utah 1986);

Harris v. Harris, 546 A.2d 208 (Vt. 1988); *Garska v. McCoy*, 278 S.E.2d 357 (W. Va. 1981).

In one of the earliest cases using the concept of "primary caretaker," the Supreme Court of Appeals of West Virginia articulated the many tasks that make one parent the primary, rather than secondary, caretaker: preparing and planning of meals; bathing, grooming, and dressing; purchasing, cleaning and caring for clothes; medical care, including nursing and general trips to physicians; arranging for social interaction among peers; arranging alternative care, i.e., babysitting or daycare; putting child to bed at night, attending to child in the middle of the night and waking the child in the morning; disciplining; and educating the child in a religious or cultural manner. *Garska, supra,* 278 S.E.2d at 363. . . .

CHILD'S PREFERENCE

Some parents have the mistaken belief that a child's preference is the determining factor in a custody dispute. Courts are well aware that parents may pressure children, shower them with gifts, or avoid disciplining them in an effort to win their favor in a custody fight. While courts will consider the child's wishes as to whom she would prefer as a custodian, this is only one factor in a list of many which must be balanced in the best interest equation. States vary in terms of the age at which they will consider the child's wishes or the maturity level necessary for the child to form an intelligent decision.

The Right to Decide

The *Harbin* case illustrates Georgia's child preference statute, which allows a child of fourteen years of age the right to decide his custodian, unless that custodian is deemed to be unfit.

ALICE JACKSON HARBIN V. ALLEN THOMAS HARBIN

238 GA. 109, 230 S.E.2D 889 (GA. 1976)

SUPREME COURT OF GEORGIA

PER CURIAM.

This is an appeal from the denial of a petition to change custody. It was brought by the appellant-mother against the appellee-father who had been granted custody in a divorce action in 1972. There are three sons aged 15, 14 and 12 years. This appeal involves only the elder two children who have elected to live with the appellant. . . . In the divorce action the mother was found to be unfit to have custody. A previous petition to change custody was denied in 1974 with a finding that there was no evidence of the mother's rehabilitation. . . .

Appellant contends that since her children over 14 years of age had elected to live with her, the trial court erred in ruling that she had the burden of persuasion as to her fitness to have custody. Appellant concedes that absent such an election by a child over 14 years of age, the moving party has the burden of showing a change of conditions materially affecting the welfare of the child. However, it is argued that once a 14-year-old child makes an election to live with one parent, the other parent has the burden of showing the selected parent is unfit to have custody. Appellant relies on Code Ann. §74-107 which provides, ". . . where the child has reached the age of 14 years, such child shall have the right to select the parent with whom such child desires to live and such selection shall be controlling unless the parent so selected is determined not to be a fit and proper person to have the custody of said child." Code Ann. §30-127 contains the same provision. . . .

. . . The mother who was the parent selected by the children presented evidence of her fitness to have custody. The father who has custody of the children presented evidence of the mother's unfitness by introducing the record of their 1972 divorce action and the 1974 judgment finding no evidence of rehabilitation. In our opinion the critical issue here is whether the 1972 divorce record and the later 1974 decree are, as contended in enumeration of error #3, inadmissible as evidence of the mother's unfitness. If this evidence is inadmissible then there is no evidence of the mother's unfitness and she is entitled to custody under Code Ann.§74-107 and Code Ann.§30-127.

In *Adams v. Adams*, supra, it is stated, "It is not a new or novel concept that a minor child may well be capable of making a wise selection. . . . Under the Act of 1962 (Ga.L.1962, pp. 713–715) [Amendment to Code Ann. §74-107 and Code Ann. §30-127] no parental right of custody by judgment or decree can defeat the right of a child reaching 14 years of age 'to select the parent with whom such child desires to live.' " This case together with a careful reading of the 1962 Act, which is now incorporated into Code Ann. §30-127, persuades us that a child of 14 years or more was mature enough to select the parent with whom he desired to live and that this right of selection was controlling despite previous adjudications of unfitness. Therefore, it is our conclusion that such child's right of selection can only be defeated by a showing of present unfitness. . . . Accordingly, there is no evidence of the present unfitness of the appellant-mother to have custody. The judgment of the trial court must be reversed. The case is remanded for further hearing to permit the appellee to present evidence of appellant's present unfitness to have custody of her two children over 14 years of age.

Judgment reversed.

PARENTS' PHYSICAL AND MENTAL HEALTH

A particular physical or mental health problem does not automatically render a parent unfit. The courts focus will be on how the parent's particular condition affects his or her ability to provide the necessary care and supervision for the child.

RELIGION

The Establishment Clause of the U.S. Constitution prohibits a court from favoring one religion over another in a custody or visitation dispute. A court is also prohibited from favoring a parent who practices a particular faith over another parent who may have no religious beliefs or affiliations. However, a court may consider the issue of religion when it affects the best interest of the child. If a child has participated in religious training throughout her lifetime, the court may determine that it is in the child's best interest for her to continue her training and may favor the parent who is most willing or able to facilitate the child's involvement. A court may consider religion when the beliefs and practices of the religion may harm the child, such as parents avoiding medical treatment for a sick child, excessive door-to-door solicitation, prolonged meditation or prayer services, excessive corporal punishment, or illegal activities.

PARENTAL CONDUCT

A parent's conduct is a factor considered by the courts when the parent's behavior negatively affects the best interest of the child and the parent's ability to provide the child with the appropriate care and supervision. For instance, if a parent has a drug or alcohol problem that interferes with his or her ability to parent, the court may consider the parent's conduct as sufficient grounds to deny custody or place limits on visitation. While adulterous conduct during the marriage and cohabitation with a member of the opposite sex do not present sufficient grounds to deny custody, the court may still consider the effect of the parent's conduct on the child. Many courts have indicated that they do not intend to punish the parent for their behavior, but rather to protect the child's best interests.

In cases where the custodial parent remarries, the court may also consider the child's relationship with the stepparent and new siblings in making a custody determination. Also, while many courts do not consider a parent's sexual preference as an impediment to custody, other courts still deny custody to or limit visitation for gay parents. Fears still exist that children will be "converted" to a gay lifestyle if they are exposed to it as an acceptable alternative or that their friends will ridicule them.

Mother's Sexual Preference

In the *Charpentier* case, although the mother did not contest a decree granting custody to the father, she did dispute the financial orders entered by the trial court claiming that the lower court was unduly influenced by her lifestyle. This case illustrates the trial court's concern with the effect of the mother's lifestyle and her same-sex partner's mental illness on the children.

REAL J. F .CHARPENTIER V. CATHY A. CHARPENTIER

206 CONN. 150, 536 A.2D 948 (CONN. 1998)

SUPREME COURT OF CONNECTICUT

SHEA, J.

. . . The parties were married on October 2, 1967. During the marriage five children were born, ranging in age from five to twelve at the time of judgment. The marriage was dissolved on August 22, 1986 by the Honorable Joseph Bogdanski, state trial referee, acting as the trial court. The trial court awarded the plaintiff husband, Real J. F. Charpentier, custody of the five children, and granted a right of reasonable visitation to the defendant wife. The defendant has not contested the custody decree. . . .

. . . A major contention of the defendant is that the trial court's financial orders were impermissibly influenced by her admitted lesbian sexual preference. We conclude that the trial court's financial orders were not so premised, but instead reasonably reflected the economic burden imposed on the plaintiff by the custody decree as the parent primarily responsible for raising five young children.

The defendant does not dispute engaging in an adulterous relationship with another woman, M, before the parties' separation. In December, 1984, while the plaintiff was hospitalized for seven days for viral pneumonia, the defendant moved M into the family home to live there amidst the five children. When the plaintiff returned home to recuperate, the defendant would leave each night to spend time with M. In February, 1985, the plaintiff moved out of the house. Within one day, the defendant had invited M again to live in the house with her and the children.

There is some indication in the record that the trial court might have been influenced by the defendant's lesbian sexual preference when it awarded custody of the children to their father, although the trial court was also much concerned with the abusive behavior of M toward the children. The trial court stated: "In spite of the dissolution action, there does not appear to be hostility or anger displayed by the parties to each other, and it is apparent that both parents deeply love their children. It further appears that both parents are capable of raising five children alone. The problem here is the presence in the homestead of a third party [M]. The children all blame her for the breakup of their parent's marriage. They feel they are second best to her, and feel that their mother prefers to spend more time with her than with them. They have spoken of their concerns regarding the open display of affection between two lesbian women in the home and their desire not to have this done in front of their friends. As the children grow older they will have to struggle with a home life that is quite different from those of their peers. [M] has displayed difficulty in dealing with stress by impulsively attempting suicide or requesting in-patient hospitalization. The children have complained of her yelling at them and slapping them. It is not clear at this time how much stress and tension she can tolerate, and a household of five children can produce a chaotic environment."

We construe the references in the memorandum of decision to the defendant's lesbian relationship as indicating concern of the trial court not with her sexual orientation per se but with its effect upon the children, who had observed in the home inappropriate displays of physical affection between their mother and M, who had twice been institutionalized for mental problems, had been diagnosed as a schizophrenic, and had a history of suicide attempts, to continue to reside in the home with the children, especially when left alone to care for them. In awarding custody, the trial court ordered that M not be present during the defendant's visitation. . . .

Evidence of violence inflicted by one parent over another is also a factor for the court to consider in a custody or visitation dispute. Some states have even legislated consideration of domestic violence in custody or visitation cases, as illustrated by the following Arizona statute.

STATUTES

ARIZONA REVISED STATUTES ANNOTATED (WEST)

25-403 (B) . . . The court shall consider evidence of domestic violence being contrary to the best interests of the child. If the court finds that domestic violence has occurred, the court shall make arrangements for visitation that best protects the child and the abused spouse from further harm. The person who has committed an act of domestic violence has the burden of proving that visitation will not endanger the child or significantly impair the child's emotional development. . . .

The Battle over Sydney and Justin Simpson

While O. J. Simpson was acquitted in criminal court of murdering his ex-wife, Nicole Brown Simpson, the California Court of Appeals held that the family court judge who awarded Simpson custody of his children on his release from prison should have waited for the verdict in the wrongful death suit before making a custody decision. On November 10, 1998, the appellate court reversed the family court's decision on the grounds that evidence of Nicole's murder should have been considered and remanded the case for a new custody hearing.

GUARDIANSHIP OF SYDNEY SIMPSON, ET AL.

COURT OF APPEALS OF THE STATE OF CALIFORNIA

FOURTH APPELLATE DISTRICT, DIVISION THREE

NOVEMBER 10, 1998

Appeal from a judgment of the Superior Court of Orange County, Nancy Wieben Stock, Judge. Reversed and remanded. . . .

I. INTRODUCTION

A guardianship was established for Sydney and Justin Simpson after their father, O.J. Simpson, was jailed on the charge of murdering Nicole Brown Simpson, their mother, and another victim, Ron Goldman. We need not go into the details of the killings, but certain, basic well-reported—and undisputed—facts about them are unavoidably relevant to the proceeding before us now; Nicole's throat had been slit, and she had been left in a pool of blood at her own doorstep while her children, Sydney and Justin, lay sleeping in the house. It was only a happenstance that the neighbors discovered the body first, sparing the children the horror of finding their dead mother. Whoever committed this crime must have acted in extreme rage and anger and been oblivious to the possibility that the victim's children might discover the body.

After his acquittal in a criminal trial, Simpson requested termination of the guardianship. At the hearing on the termination, the guardians sought to introduce evidence regarding the circumstances of Nicole Simpson's murder. The trial court refused to consider any of it holding that the guardians had waived the issue by not listing any "murder witnesses" on their witness list.

At the time of this guardianship proceeding, the father also faced a *civil* trial in which the plaintiffs sought to establish his liability for the death of the mother. The guardians' attorneys apparently hoped the civil case would conclude in time for the court to take note of its results, which would not only spare their clients great expense, but also save the court the necessity of a prolonged examination of the murder evidence. The court, however, did not wait for the conclusion of the civil case (which, as is common knowledge, ended with a judgment of the father's liability), explaining in its written order that the civil case could not have thrown any light on the guardianship termination anyway, because, in its opinion, the civil case entailed a lower standard of proof than the one involved in the guardianship proceeding. In any event, that case is itself not yet final for issue preclusion

purposes, so the trial court could not take judicial notice of its *result.*

While we understand the incredible pressure the court was under, the fact remains that it made a number of errors. These errors require reversal of the order terminating the guardianship.

First and foremost, the grisly circumstances of the murder itself simply could not be ignored, even if consideration of them would have taken some time. We acknowledge, of course, that consideration of the "murder issue" (as it is sometimes, rather understatedly, referred to in the briefs) would have necessitated a longer trial. However, because the court sat as a court of *equity*, dealing with the *interests of children*, not a court of criminal law in which the standard is guilt beyond a reasonable doubt, there was no need for reenactment of the so-called trial of the century. Consideration of the murder issue would have been conducted by a judge in a well-secured courthouse with the actual proceedings barred to the public, with the power to control the presentation of evidence and prevent unnecessary distraction and delay. With the cooperation of the parties at least, much of the evidence could easily have been presented by way of excerpts from the transcripts in the criminal and civil cases. Had the court considered the murder issue, there would have been no jury, no endless sidebar conferences, and no media distractions. Judges cannot avoid the single most important and relevant issue in a case—particularly a case involving children and the possibility of violence—just because trying that issue will take time. The standard is whether the consumption of time is "undue." (Evid. Code, §352.). . . .

II. THE HISTORY OF THE GUARDIANSHIP

Sydney and Justin's mother, Nicole, and Ronald Goldman were murdered on June 12, 1994. Five days later Simpson was arrested for the crime. On the day of his arrest Simpson signed a document giving temporary care of Sydney and Justin to their maternal grandparents, Louis and Juditha Brown; later, on July 27, 1994, the Browns petitioned the trial court to be appointed guardians of Sydney and Justin. Several months later, on October 7, 1994, the court made a formal order appointing the Browns as the children's guardians.

Simpson's incarceration lasted some 17 months. When released he promptly filed a petition to terminate the guardianship pursuant to section 1601 of the Probate Code, asserting that in light of his release there was "no further need" for the guardianship. . . .

III. DISCUSSION

A. THE EVIDENCE BEARING ON "THE MURDER ISSUE"

1. *The Relevance of the Evidence*

Let us get right to the point. The murder of Sydney and Justin's mother was an extraordinarily violent act showing callous disregard for them. *If* Simpson committed the crime, that information was highly relevant to whether the children should be returned to him. . . .

. . . It may reasonably be inferred from the almost universally known circumstances of the killing that the crime evidenced great violence and rage. We by no means must conclude that Simpson committed the crime to say that *if* he did, that fact was certainly relevant to show a *propensity toward violence* on his part.

As a matter of case law, as well as common sense, the question of whether one parent has actually murdered the other is about as relevant as it is possible to imagine in any case involving whether the surviving parent should be allowed any form of child custody. *In re Sarah H.* (1980)

106 Cal. App. 3d 326 is particularly instructive in this regard. There, the father was a "hard-drinking ranch hand" who "had been a good father to all his children." (*Id.* at pp. 331–332 (conc. opn. of Reynoso, J.).) However, he had a tendency to become violent when drunk; indeed, as the court put it. "alcohol-induced violence was consistent with the father's character." (*Id.* at p. 330.) He beat the mother to death in one of his drunken rages (he was later found guilty of voluntary manslaughter after a no contest plea), and his tendency to such violence was held to constitute substantial evidence justifying not only the establishment of a guardianship—much less its continuation—but also the actual *termination* of *all* parental rights in a dependency proceeding because detriment beyond a reasonable doubt had been shown. (*Id.* at pp. 328–329.). . . .

. . . Finally, the analogous case of *Guardianship of Smith* (1957) 147 Cal. App. 2d 686 is also instructive. There the mother was tried and, like Simpson, acquitted of the murder of the other parent arising out of his death in a car bomb planted by the mother's paramour. Despite the acquittal, the trial judge allowed the entire record of a murder trial to be admitted into evidence, and the evidence contained in that record formed the basis of a decision to maintain the guardianship, which was then upheld on appeal. (See *id.* at p. 699.)

It is clear, then, that evidence of whether Simpson killed Sydney and Justin's mother was not only relevant to the termination of the guardianship, it was so relevant that it could not be reasonably ignored. . . .

VISITATION RIGHTS

A noncustodial parent has the right to frequently spend time with the child unless the court finds that visitation in some way endangers the child's emotional, mental, moral, or physical health. Family courts will award **visitation rights** to a parent in this position. The parties may agree to a visitation schedule or it may be determined by the courts if the parties reach a stalemate.

There are two types of visitation schedules: **reasonable rights of visitation** or a **fixed schedule.** Reasonable visitation is a very flexible arrangement that requires the parties to work out their own schedule. This works best when the parties can reasonably coordinate visitation between themselves. This requires the ability to communicate and the willingness to put aside their differences for the benefit of the children. Some divorce decrees will include this provision and as soon as the ink dries the parties are back in court. Sometimes the custodial parent will set up obstacles to the noncustodial parent's visitation rights. The noncustodial parent may also disrupt the "reasonable" visitation schedule by showing up at the custodial parent's home at inconvenient days and times (especially when the custodial parent becomes romantically involved with someone else!). At this point, one of the parties returns to court for the purpose of enforcing visitation or modifying the existing "reasonable" rights of visitation to a more definite schedule.

Fixed schedules are definite dates and time frames set aside for the purpose of allowing a noncustodial parent to visit with the child. Fixed schedules should spell out the days and hours on which a noncustodial parent may see the child. In addition, it is also a good idea to deal with holidays, birthdays, vacations, reasonable hours for phone calls, and other details so as to avoid conflict between the parties.

In some hostile divorces, the law office will often hear complaints from the client on the day following visitation. For example, custodial parents may call screaming about the noncustodial parent's failure to either pick up or return the child on time. In the latter scenario, some custodial parents will go so far as to call the police when the noncustodial parent is only delayed by several minutes! Custodial parents may also complain that the child looks dirty, has not eaten, or acts out after visitation. Some go further by making allegations regarding child sexual abuse. Noncustodial parents may raise similar concerns, in addition to complaints about the child not being available for visits because the custodial parent has taken it upon himself not to make the child available.

When a client calls with visitation complaints and the attorney is not available, the paralegal should take detailed notes regarding the client's concerns and inform the attorney. Remember not to give legal advice! Clients may be very agitated and may push the paralegal in a moment of desperation. Be polite and courteous, but do not give advice even if you know the answer. Let the attorney handle it.

A paralegal should also be familiar with the difference between unsupervised and supervised visitation. **Unsupervised visitation** permits a noncustodial parent to freely visit with the child without others present, wherever she reasonably wishes to take the child and engage in child-appropriate activities. **Supervised visitation** limits a parent's visitation rights in that it dictates restrictions surrounding the visits. Supervised visitation may be ordered in cases where a noncustodial parent has certain problems that question her ability to properly supervise the child. Parents who have substance abuse problems, mental or physical issues, a history of domestic violence, or are too immature to care for the child on their own may be required to have another person present during the visits at a designated time and place. This person can sometimes be the custodial parent unless there is a history of domestic violence or problems with the parents' interaction. In this case, a neutral third party would be the best solution.

RIGHTS OF THIRD PARTIES

As a rule, a court may not enter an order permitting a third party legally enforceable visitation rights. As with most rules, however, exceptions exist.

In a divorce case, the husband and wife are the only legally recognizable parties to the action. When an individual who is neither mother nor father seeks to have visitation, if the family unit is intact, a third party has no standing to bring an action in court.

Standing is a legal term. It determines whether a party has a legal right to request an adjudication of the issues in a legal dispute. However, where the family unit is no longer intact, there are instances where a third party has standing to

FIGURE 7–5
Every jurisdiction has
enacted statutes that
permit grandparents
to seek visitation or
custody rights with
minor grandchildren,
where the family unit
is no longer intact.

petition the court for custody or visitation. Every jurisdiction has enacted statutes permitting grandparents to intervene in divorce cases and request visitation or custody of the minor children. Once the court grants third parties a legal right to be heard in the proceedings, they are considered **third-party intervenors.**

Protecting the Intact Family

The *Castagno* case outlines the common law and statutory changes that allowed grandparents into divorce court. The courts, however, will not intrude on an intact family and will allow parents to make the decision regarding the grandparents' access to the children.

JEAN T. CASTAGNO, ET AL. V. TINA WHOLEAN, ET AL.

239 CONN. 336, 684 A.2D 1181 (CONN. 1996)

SUPREME COURT OF CONNECTICUT

KATZ, J.

The sole issue in this appeal is whether, pursuant to General Statutes §46b-59,[1] the trial court had subject matter jurisdiction to entertain a petition by grandparents for visitation rights with their minor grandchildren when the grandchildren and their parents were not involved in any case or controversy currently before the court and there

---

[1]General Statute §46b-59 provides: "the superior court may grant the right of visitation with respect to any minor child or children to any person, upon an application of such person. Such order shall be according to the court's best judgment upon the facts of the case and subject to such conditions and limitations as it deems equitable, provided the grant of such visitation rights shall not be contingent upon any order of financial support by the court. In making, modifying or terminating such an order, the court shall be guided by the best interest of the child, giving consideration to the wishes of such child if he is of sufficient age and capable of forming an intelligent opinion. Visitation rights granted in accordance with this section shall not be deemed to have created parental rights in the person or persons to whom such visitation rights are granted. The grant of such visitation rights shall not prevent any court of competent jurisdiction from thereafter acting upon the custody of such child, the parental rights with respect to such child or the adoption of such child and any such court may include in its decree an order terminating such visitation rights.

was no claim that the family unit was no longer intact. We conclude that although §46b-59 lacks specific language imposing any threshold requirement, established rules of statutory construction, the context of the statute and its legislative history support the incorporation of a requirement that plaintiffs must demonstrate disruption of the family sufficient to justify state intervention. In the absence of any attempt by the plaintiffs here to satisfy this threshold requirement, we conclude that the trial court lacked jurisdiction to decide the issue of visitation and, therefore, properly dismissed the plaintiffs' action (footnote omitted). Accordingly, we affirm the judgment of the trial court. . . .

. . . The plaintiffs argue that the trial court misconstrued §46b-59 to contain threshold requirements not expressed in the plain language of the statute. Specifically, the plaintiffs claim that the application of §46b-59 is not limited by any threshold requirements, and that the sole criterion for application of the statute is the best interest of the child. Accordingly, the plaintiffs argue that any third party who seeks state intervention, in the form of a court's grant of visitation rights, may petition the court at any time, and need not present any allegations that the minor child's family is no longer intact. The plaintiffs further maintain that, because the language of §46b-59 is clear and unambiguous, it was inappropriate for the trial court to rely on the legislative history of the statute to establish any threshold requirements. We disagree.

We begin with the common law background against which the visitation statutes were enacted. At common law, grandparents, or third parties in general, have no right to visitation. Rather, the decision as to who may or may not have access to a minor child has been deemed an issue of parental prerogative (citations and footnote omitted). The common law reflects the belief that the family unit should be respected, and its autonomy and privacy invaded through court action only in the most pressing circumstances. "That right [of the parents to determine the care, custody, and control of their children] is recognized because it reflects a strong civilization, and because the parental role is now established beyond debate as an enduring American tradition" (citation and footnote omitted). All families may have, at one time or another, unhappy conflicts and disputes among adult relatives that might result in an absence of contact between those adults and their minor relatives—be they grandchildren, nieces or nephews, cousins, etc.—but longstanding tradition holds that, absent compelling circumstances justifying some state intervention in the form or a judicial order, the parents' decision, whether wise or not, prevails. . . .

. . . The right to family autonomy and privacy acknowledged in the common law has been recognized as so fundamental as to merit constitutional protection. Consequently, any legislation affecting it is strictly scrutinized (citation omitted). . . .

. . . The plaintiffs' construction of §46b-59 would allow the court to intrude upon an intact family that has not already opened itself to such intrusion. . . .

A court can order visitation for a man who cohabited with a woman for years and developed a bond as a psychological parent with the woman's child. Both parties jointly raised the child for four years and the courts have held that a stepparent has standing to seek visitation rights after the man and woman separated, despite the fact that the man was not the child's biological father, did not adopt the child, and had never married the child's biological mother.

Courts also hold that a third party or the state has standing to seek custody of a child if the child has been neglected or abused.

STATUS OF UNMARRIED PARENTS AND THEIR RIGHTS AND RESPONSIBILITIES

Unmarried parents have the same rights and responsibilities as married parents. When an unmarried couple is living together with their biological child, each parent is considered to be the legal guardian of the child. When an unmarried couple splits up, each parent is still considered to be the child's legal guardian unless one of the parents brings a legal action to obtain sole or joint legal custody. Most states have enacted statutes that authorize an unmarried parent to go into court and request that the court enter a custody order which both parents must honor. Usually the party bringing the action into court is the parent with whom the child is residing. That parent seeks to have the court invest him or her with either sole custody or joint legal custody with physical custody in that party. This petitioning party may also request that the court enter an order for payment of child support by the parent who does not reside with the child.

When a parent brings an action for custody and/or child support, the parent must arrange for legal service of the action on the other parent to give the parent notice that this action is taking place. When the other parent is served with legal process, that parent may obtain legal counsel to represent his or her interests, choose to represent himself or herself by entering a *pro se* appearance, or simply do nothing. Frequently, the parent served with a custody action, through counsel, will negotiate to have the petitioning parent agree to joint legal custody with physical custody in the petitioning parent. Sometimes the other parent will threaten to seek sole custody if the petitioning party does not agree to joint legal custody. Occasionally the other parent will seek sole custody not as a strategic tactic but because the other parent wants the child to reside with him or her.

If parents cannot come to an agreement regarding custody, the court will usually refer the matter to the family relations division of the court. Family relations officers will conduct an investigation or study to decide what custodial disposition will best promote the child's interests. Most states have statutes or case law providing that there is a presumption that joint legal custody best serves the child's interests. However, this presumption is rebuttable. If family relations officers conclude that the parents are unable to communicate productively to make joint decisions for their child's health, education, and welfare, the family relations division will recommend that one parent have sole custody and that the other parent have visitation in a manner consistent with the child's well-being.

If the court awards one parent sole custody or enters an order for joint legal custody with legal residence invested in one parent, the court, upon motion from the custodial parent, will also order the noncustodial parent to pay child support. In states that have established uniform child support guidelines, these guidelines will be applied in the same manner they are applied to determine child support for divorcing parents. Child support is discussed in more detail in Chapter 8.

THE ABSENT PARENT

When a parent bringing a custody and support action cannot locate the other parent, the requirement of providing that parent notice is met by publishing a legal notice of the action in a newspaper with a circulation in the geographical area in which the other parent was last known to reside. If the absent parent does not appear at the court proceeding, the court will usually enter an order of sole custody in favor of the petitioning parent. Depending on the rules of the jurisdiction, the court may or may not enter an order for child support. In those states that use uniform child support guidelines and apply a formula based on each parent's income to determine the amount of child support payments, the court will not make a child support order against a nonappearing or absent parent.

CHALLENGES TO CHILD SUPPORT ORDERS

When a child's mother seeks child support from a man whom she never married or a man who was not legally her husband when the child was born, the man whom she alleges is the child's father may deny that he is the child's biological father and demand a paternity test.

PATERNITY ISSUES

Before the advent of DNA tissue analysis, a test to determine paternity could only eliminate a man as a child's father. If the man was not eliminated, the court would look at other factors to decide whether or not he was the father.

Most states have common law holdings that there is a rebuttable presumption that a child born to a woman during the existence of a legally valid marriage is the child of the husband. This presumption may be overcome upon a showing that during the period of conception the husband had no access to the child's mother or was sterile at that time or otherwise medically incapable of fathering a child.

For an unmarried mother, the task of proving paternity was even harder. Frequently, the determination rested on the subjective opinion of the judge. With the advent of DNA testing, a near foolproof method of determining paternity has emerged.

A father contesting paternity may request a DNA test. This test uses several genetic markers to identity genetic similarities between the putative father and the child. If the test shows a likelihood of paternity of 91 percent or better, most courts make a determination that the putative father is the child's biological father. The father will be ordered to pay child support. He will also have the right to reasonable visitation with his child, and, if he wishes, he may seek legal custody of the child then or at any future time during the child's minority.

REVIEW QUESTIONS

1. What is the difference between physical custody and legal custody?

2. How does sole custody differ from joint legal custody with physical custody awarded to only one parent?

3. Define the tender years doctrine.

4. How does the tender years doctrine differ from the best interest standard?

5. Describe the reasoning courts have employed to argue that applying the tender years doctrine also serves the best interest of the child.

6. Describe the types of situations that have arisen where applying the tender years doctrine may not be in the best interest of the child.

7. What were the early exceptions courts made to apply the tender years approach to child custody?

8. What was the right of *patria potestas?*

9. How did the rise of the Industrial Revolution support the tender years doctrine?

10. What changes in the 1970s forced courts to reconsider the preference of applying the tender years doctrine when making custody decisions?

11. When and how did the practice of joint custody develop?

12. How did the best interest approach to awarding child custody emerge?

13. What is a split custody arrangement?

14. What are the drawbacks to split custody?

15. Explain when and why joint legal custody with shared physical custody is awarded.

16. Under what circumstances will joint legal and physical custody be in the best interest of the child?

17. Define the terms *psychological parent* and *primary caretaker.*

18. Describe a situation where the primary caretaker is also the psychological parent and describe a situation where the primary caretaker is *not* also the psychological parent.

19. What is the difference between a court order for reasonable visitation and a court order for specific visitation?

20. When may courts order visitation for a third party? Give examples of persons who might seek and obtain third-party visitation rights.

21. Define the term *standing* and discuss when the issue of standing might arise in a custody proceeding.

22. Under what circumstances might the state seek custody of a child?

23. When may a custody order be changed or modified?

EXERCISES

1. In your local law library, locate the sections in your state's statutes that discuss the issue of joint custody. Copy the section and write a brief summary of the main points of the statute.

2. In your local law library, find the treatises on family law. Locate a treatise that discusses the tender years doctrine and the shift to the best interest standard. Provide a brief written summary of the treatise.

3. In your local law library, locate the index to legal periodicals and find a law review article from the 1970s that advocates the practice of joint custody. Provide a written summary of the article.

4. In your local law library, find a recent case in your state's law digest where the court awarded sole custody in a dispute and a case where the court awarded joint custody. Also find a case law summary of a case since the 1980s where the court awarded custody to the father rather than the mother. Also find a case where the court awarded custody to the grandparents rather than to either parent. Prepare a brief written summary on each case.

CHAPTER 8

CHILD SUPPORT

KEY TERMS

Administrative enforcement

Arrearage

Bureau of Support Enforcement (IV-D agency)

Capias

Child Support Enforcement and Establishment of Paternity Act

Child support guidelines

Combined net income

Contempt hearing

Deviation from the guidelines

Motion for contempt

Motion for modification of child support

National Conference of Commissioners on Uniform State Laws

Parent locator services

Postmajority support agreement

Revised Uniform Reciprocal Enforcement of Support Act (RURESA)

Total net income

Uniform Interstate Family Support Act (UIFSA)

Uniform Reciprocal Enforcement of Support Act (URESA)

The marital obligation to financially support and maintain minor children who are issue of a marriage does not cease for either parent upon dissolution of the marriage. Both parents are expected to provide economic support for their children. The dissolution decree will include an order for financial support of each child until such child reaches age eighteen, the age of majority.

Traditionally, when parents divorced, the father was usually the primary or sole breadwinner. Sole custody was awarded to the mother while support came from the noncustodial parent, usually the father. Today, the noncustodial parent continues to have an obligation for child support. In addition, even where parents have joint custody, courts will order the parent with whom the child does not make his or her primary residence to make child support payments to the parent with whom the child resides.

CHILD SUPPORT GUIDELINES: FEDERALLY MANDATED REQUIREMENTS

Today many courts apply statutorily enacted formulas to determine the amount the noncustodial parent must pay for the support of each child. These are known as **child support guidelines.** Appendix C of this book contains an example of the state of Connecticut's child support and arrearage guidelines. Statutes establishing these guidelines were passed by state legislatures as a result of federal mandates to do so.

This Arizona statute legislates the state's child support guidelines and sets forth the criteria for establishing those guidelines.

 **S T A T U T E S**

ARIZONA REVISED STATUTES ANNOTATED (WEST)

25-320 The supreme court shall establish guidelines for determining the amount of child support. The amount resulting from the application of these guidelines shall be the amount of child support ordered unless a written finding is made, based on criteria approved by the supreme court, that application of the guidelines would be inappropriate or unjust in a particular case. The supreme court shall review the guidelines at least once every four years to ensure that their application results in the determination of appropriate child support amounts. The guidelines and criteria for deviation from them shall be based on all relevant factors, including:

1. The financial resources and needs of the child.
2. The financial resources and needs of the custodial parent.
3. The standard of living the child would have enjoyed had the marriage not been dissolved.
4. The physical and emotional condition of the child, and the child's educational needs.
5. The financial resources and needs of the noncustodial parent.
6. Excessive or abnormal expenditures, destruction, concealment or fraudulent disposition of community, joint tenancy and other property held in common.
7. The duration of visitation and related expenses. . . .

In the mid-1980s the federal government through its appropriate agencies studied court-ordered child support awards made in various jurisdictions throughout the country. The federal study revealed that the amounts that many, if not in fact most, courts ordered noncustodial parents to pay toward the support of their children were far too low to keep up with then-spiraling inflation and too little to meet the children's needs. Absent any uniform and rational guidelines, the amounts set for child support rested on the judge's discretion. Many judges set arbitrary amounts that were usually too low to make much of a difference in the custodial parent's ability to financially maintain the children in the family. Many judges ordered minimal child support payments because of their belief that the noncustodial parent would not pay anything substantial.

As a result of this practice, many single-parent homes existed at or below the poverty line. Single parents, usually single mothers, were forced to rely on government assistance for survival. The federal government, by mandating each state to adopt uniform and rational child support guidelines sought to return the child support obligation back where it belonged, namely, with both parents—noncustodial as well as custodial. States were required to base child support awards on numerical guidelines rather than judicial whims. State legislatures enacted laws to require a uniform method of determining child support, and formula tables and child support guideline worksheets were created by each jurisdiction to execute these legislative enactments.

DETERMINING EACH PARENT'S OBLIGATION FOR CHILD SUPPORT

Most jurisdictions in the United States have complied with the federal mandate and have a system for determining the exact amount a noncustodial parent must pay, given that parent's financial circumstances and the financial circumstances of the custodial parent. In addition, the states complying with the federal mandate have developed child support worksheets that assist parties in the calculation of this obligation. Exhibit 8–1 illustrates Connecticut's worksheet and Exhibit 8–2 gives samples of New York's worksheet. Each parent's income is a factor, as is the cost of living in the geographical area and the age and needs of each child. Each parent's net income is added together to arrive at a **combined** or **total net income** figure. A preset percentage is applied to this figure to establish how much of this combined income should be allocated for the financial maintenance of the child or for each of the children. The amount arrived at is often termed the child maintenance figure. Then, a formula is applied to determine how much of this amount must be paid by the noncustodial parent. For instance, if each parent has the same amount of net income, the court, upon applying the guidelines, will order the noncustodial parent to pay child support equal to one-half of the child maintenance figure. Similarly, if a noncustodial parent's net income is three times as high as that of the custodial parent, the noncustodial parent must pay three-fourths of the child maintenance figure, leaving the custodial parent to supply the other one-fourth needed.

Some states consider each parent's gross income as a starting point, rather than net income. Some states also consider other factors in addition to income to determine child support obligations. For instance, Massachusetts also considers each parent's assets and other resources, the number of children in a household, and the age of each child for whom support is to be ordered.

FIGURE 8–1
Many states have set
guidelines for deter-
mining how much
each parent should
pay in child support
after a divorce.

Determining a Parent's Income

The *Rosenbloom* case involves a father's appeal of the trial court's increase in his
child support obligation pursuant to the mother's post-judgment motion to modify. After the divorce, the mother remarried. The Louisiana Court of Appeal held
that, under Louisiana law, a court may consider the benefits a parent derives from
remarriage in determining the combined monthly income of the parties in arriving at the child support obligation.

D. STEPHEN ROSENBLOOM V. RENEE BAUCHET (KUTCHER), WIFE OF D. STEPHEN ROSENBLOOM

654 So. 2d 877 (La. App. 4 Cir. 1995)

COURT OF APPEAL OF LOUISIANA, FOURTH DISTRICT

. . . Mr. Rosenbloom next argues that the trial judge erred
in calculating the award. Specifically, he argues that she
erred in extrapolating a figure where the combined
monthly income for the parties exceeded the maximum
under the child support guidelines set forth at LSA-R.S.
9:315.10(B), resulting in an excessive award. Mr. Rosenbloom also contends that the award is excessive because
the trial judge failed to consider that Mrs. Kutcher's circumstances had improved after her marriage to Mr.
Kutcher.

With regard to the children of the marriage, both the father and the mother have the obligation to support. Support is to be granted considering the needs of the person to whom it is due, and the circumstances of those who are obligated to pay it (citation omitted). The court may consider as income the benefits a party derives from remarriage, expense-sharing, or other sources. LSA-R.S. 9:315(6)(c). In arriving at an award, the totality of relevant circumstances must by considered (citation omitted). LSA-R.S. 9:315.10(B) provides:

If the combined adjusted gross income of the parties exceeds the highest level specified in the schedule contained in R.S. 9:315.14, the court shall use its discretion in setting the amount of the basic child support obligation, but in no event shall it be less than the highest amount set forth in the schedule.

Under the clear provisions of LSA-R.S. 9:315.10(B), the trial court has discretion in setting the amount of child support when the combined adjusted gross income of the parties exceeds the highest figure provided in the schedule, and its judgment in such matters will not be disturbed in the absence of a showing of an abuse of that discretion (citation omitted).

In the instant case, the trial court used the combined monthly income of the parties in calculating the award. The trial judge determined that Mr. Rosenbloom's monthly income was $39,891.50, by dividing his 1993 gross income of $478,698.00 by 12. As to Mrs. Kutcher's monthly income, the trial judge correctly considered the living expenses incident to her second marriage. The trial judge stated:

[t]he Court notes that in the case of Mrs. Kutcher that she has no single source of income of her own other than approximately 5,000 dollars a year that she earns. The bulk of her income comes from (A) what the Court will describe as an expense sharing that she receives the benefits from her current spouse, Robert Kutcher. And under R.S. 9:315(6)(c)—the law tells us that the Court can only consider as income the benefits a party derives from expense sharing or other sources. However, in determining the benefits of expense sharing the Court shall not consider the income of another spouse regardless of the remarriage existence except to the extent that such income is used directly to reduce the costs of a party's actual expenses.

So, consequently, to determine what Mrs. Kutcher's income is, the Court has to make a determination as to the benefits she receives from Mr. Kutcher. And that part of the statute also says, with regard to the party's actual expenses, his contribution to her actual expenses would not come from his gross income but from his net income.

The judge then correctly determined that Mrs. Kutcher's monthly income was $9,040.12.

MODIFICATION OF CHILD SUPPORT ORDERS

The order for child support entered at the time of dissolution can be modified if there is a substantial change in the financial circumstances of either party. If the paying party suffers a downward shift in income, that party may file a motion with the court to modify the child support to reflect his or her decreased ability to pay. Sometimes a court will not decrease the amount and direct the financially strapped party to economize in other areas of life. This is frequently the case where the custodial parent's income was not substantial at the time of dissolution and has not increased or has in fact decreased. On the other hand, if the custodial parent's income has increased or was substantial to begin with, the court may grant the noncustodial parent's request for a lowering of the amount of periodic child support payments.

In the states where statutory guidelines are used, and a formula is applied to determine each parent's contribution toward the dollar amount needed for the support of the child, if the noncustodial parent's income has dropped, then the court may decide that a greater proportion of the custodial parent's income shall be dedicated to child support and that the noncustodial parent's financial obligation will decrease. Conversely, if the noncustodial parent's income has risen substantially, the custodial spouse may bring a **motion for modification of child support** requesting the court to order the noncustodial parent to pay higher periodic child support payments, so that less of the custodial parent's income will be needed for the child. The court will grant this motion if the custodial parent demonstrates the need for additional support. Even if the children are being adequately provided for under the prevailing order, if the noncustodial parent's income has risen dramatically and includes many discretionary income dollars, the court may see fit to order a higher support obligation providing the court is given proper information on how this extra money will be put to use for the child's benefit.

In jurisdictions where child support guidelines are applied, statutory maximum and minimum limits usually exist for contributions by each parent. However, if the parties agree between themselves that one party or the other will pay more or less of the statutorily determined amount, frequently courts will allow this **deviation from the guidelines** providing that the parties present the court with a good reason for the departure and providing that allowing the deviation does not appear to financially deprive the child.

Tennis, Anyone?

In this section, we revisit the *Evans* case illustrated earlier in Chapter 5. This excerpt deals with determining child support obligation when the income of the parents exceeds the state's child support guidelines.

EDWIN E. EVANS V. CYNTHIA S. EVANS

1997 S.D. 16, 559 N.W.2D 240 (S.D. 1997)

SUPREME COURT OF SOUTH DAKOTA

. . . ANALYSIS AND DECISION

1   Whether the trial court abused its discretion in failing to consider the children's actual needs and standard of living in setting child support?

SDCL 25-7-6.2 provides guidelines that trial courts must follow in setting child support amounts. However, where the parties' income exceeds the statutory guidelines, SDCL 25-7-6.9 provides the child support obligation "shall be established at an appropriate level, taking into account the actual needs and standard of living of the child" (citation omitted). . . .

. . . Cyndy sought $5,000 per month in child support, however, she produced an exhibit which listed expenses of $4,410 per month. Itemized, this figure included:

$400	for food
580	for vehicle expenses
110	per month for medical expenses
550	per month for educational expenses
500	per month for vacations
100	per month for dining out
550	for entertainment and allowances
200	for clothing purchases
1,300	for tennis expenses (Kelsey only) (clothes, supplies, lessons, tournament travel)
60	for piano lessons
25	for beauty shop expenses
25	for cosmetics expenses
10	for newspapers and subscriptions
$4,410	

The trial court ruled at an interim hearing that $1,300 per month for tennis expenses was clearly excessive and Ed would not be required to pay this expense. . . .

. . . Subtracting the $1,300 per month tennis expense from Cyndy's itemized living expenses for the children leaves a balance of $2,185 per month. The trial court ordered Ed to pay child support in this amount, plus pay $500 per month in allowances directly to the children, and $600 per month for their tuition at parochial school, and provide health insurance for each child, for a total child support obligation of $3,505 per month.[1] The trial court noted that Ed had agreed to pay the children's allowances, parochial school tuition, medical insurance, and college expenses. The trial court noted this child support award still provided a "luxurious lifestyle" for the two girls.[2]

On appeal, Cyndy notes the amount of Ed's child support obligation, as determined by the trial court, is approximately 12% of his $25,000 net monthly income. Cyndy argues the trial court made two errors: 1) it applied the wrong legal standard by focusing on the children's needs rather than their standard of living; and 2) it substituted its personal judgment of what the children's standard of living should be, for the standard set by the parties themselves during their marriage.

In the trial court's memorandum decision, it cited "the needs of the children and the father's ability to pay" as the standard for determining child support obligations above

the statutory guidelines. It then stated that because the father's ability to pay was not at issue in this case, the only consideration need be the "reasonable needs of the children." This solitary consideration does not reflect the standard set by statute and prior case law. As noted above, the trial court's inquiry is to take into account the actual needs and standard of living of the children. However, the record reflects the trial court did not apply only the reasonable needs of the children and that it did consider their standard of living in making its determination. A trial court is not required to accept either party's claimed expenses. To do so would remove the trial court's discretion in setting child support obligations where the parties' income exceeds the guidelines set forth in SDCL 25-7-6.2. Cyndy has the burden of proving her claimed expenses reflect the children's needs and standard of living (citation omitted).

Cyndy's claim of $1,300 per month ($15,600 annually) for tennis expenses is a projected expense for only one of the couple's daughters, which includes Cyndy's traveling expenses to accompany her daughter. Ed points out, which Cyndy does not dispute, that this projected expense is $6,760 per year more than was spent in 1995 for Kelsey to travel and participate in tournaments in several states. Ed also notes, which Cyndy does not dispute, that this projection is based in part on daughter Ashley's involvement with tennis, which she severely curtailed after her sixteenth birthday. At the time of this appeal, Kelsey is fifteen years old. As such, Cyndy has failed to prove the $1,300 per month is reflective of Kelsey's standard of living prior to the couple's divorce. (citation omitted). . . . The trial court did not abuse its discretion in ordering support in an amount that will adequately care for the children's actual needs and permit them to enjoy a standard of living commensurate with that prior to their parents' divorce (citation omitted). . . .

---

[1] We note several of these items the trial court ordered Ed to pay *in addition to* the $2,185 total amount were already included in the $2,185 total in Cyndy's list of expenses. Therefore, the amount actually awarded is closer to the amount requested by Cyndy than she argues in her appeal to this Court.

[2] Supplemental information in Ed's brief to this Court notes his older daughter graduated from high school in May 1996 and is currently enrolled in a private college in Minnesota. Ed continues to pay Cyndy the amount ordered by the trial court for two children and has not moved for a reduction of that amount.

CHILD SUPPORT ENFORCEMENT

CIVIL ENFORCEMENT

If a noncustodial parent fails to pay all or part of the child support obligation, the custodial parent may file a **motion for contempt.** This motion will alert the court to the other party's failure to comply with the court's earlier support order and will request that the court provide relief by ordering the other party to pay the back child support owed as well as the attorney's fees the custodial parent has expended to bring the deficiency to the court's attention. If the noncustodial parent does not appear at the **contempt hearing,** the court may order what is known as a **capias.** A capias is a document empowering a sheriff to arrest the

FIGURE 8–2
If a parent continually neglects to pay child support, administrative enforcement may become the only solution.

nonappearing, noncustodial parent and bring him or her to jail and to court. However, if the noncustodial parent cannot be located by a sheriff or other court officer, the custodial parent may turn to administrative enforcement. Administrative enforcement also comes into the picture when the custodial parent is receiving government assistance or when the noncustodial parent has left the jurisdiction.

ADMINISTRATIVE ENFORCEMENT

The term **administrative enforcement** refers to action by a state or federal agency. Many states have **Bureaus of Support Enforcement** or **IV-D agencies** (pronounced "four-d agencies"). These agencies are state agencies mandated by federal law, pursuant to the **Child Support Enforcement and Establishment of Paternity Act** passed by Congress in 1974. Their purpose is to facilitate the entry and enforcement of child support orders on a state-by-state basis. These agencies provide four services: (1) location of noncustodial parents through **parent locator services,** which are statutorily empowered to search the records of state and federal agencies such as the state's department of motor vehicles, or department of revenue services and/or the federal government's Social Security Administration and the Internal Revenue Service; (2) establishment of the paternity of children through testing of putative fathers; (3) facilitation of the entry of support orders following the location of the noncustodial parent or following the establishment of paternity; and (4) the enforcement of existing orders.

INTERSTATE ENFORCEMENT OF CHILD SUPPORT OBLIGATIONS

While the federal government has taken steps to ensure that the individual state governments address the entry and enforcement of child support orders within their borders, there have also been initiatives to enforce a noncustodial parent's child support obligations when that parent has crossed state lines. In the 1950s, the **National Conference of Commissioners on Uniform State Laws,** a commission that drafts model acts that states may choose to adopt, drafted a model act known as the **Uniform Reciprocal Enforcement of Support Act (URESA)** (see Appendix D). Subsequently many states adopted this act and its revised version, the **Revised Uniform Reciprocal Enforcement of Support Act (RURESA)** of 1968 (see Appendix E). Both of these acts authorize an interstate procedure for the collection of child support.

Under the acts' provisions, a custodial parent may ultimately obtain child support from the noncustodial parent residing in another state by instituting the following procedure: First, the custodial parent with a support order goes to his state court for enforcement of the order; the support enforcement division of the court or the IV-D agency forwards the support petition to the office of support division of the court in which the noncustodial parent resides. That court will schedule a hearing and notice the noncustodial parent to appear before the court. That court will enter its own support order in which it applies its own state's guidelines. Depending on that state's support determination formula, the amount of support in this order may be greater or less than, or the same as the amount ordered in the original or initiating state. If the noncustodial parent fails to abide by this court order, the custodial parent can arrange for contempt proceedings in this court without having to travel to that state or hire private counsel.

The process of interstate enforcement has been recently modified in many jurisdictions. These jurisdictions have adopted the 1992 model enforcement act and its 1996 amendment known as the **Uniform Interstate Family Support Act (UIFSA)** (see Appendix F). Under this new act, the noncustodial parent's state must honor the original support and may not enter a new order or modify the existing order to conform to its guidelines for determining the amount of support. Only the custodial parent's state court may modify its own order, unless the parties agree to the modification in writing or both parties have moved to the new state, thus giving the new state court jurisdiction over the matter.

SEPARATION OF THE CHILD SUPPORT ORDER OBLIGATION FROM THE RIGHT TO VISITATION

Just as a noncustodial parent has an obligation to support her minor children, so the custodial parent must comply with the court's order giving the noncustodial parent reasonable visitation.

These obligations are separate obligations, independent of one another, and the default on one obligation by one parent will not excuse the default of the other parent on his obligation. If a noncustodial parent ceases to pay child support, the custodial parent may not withhold visitation; and if a custodial parent refuses to make the minor children available for visitation, the noncustodial parent is not excused from paying child support.

FIGURE 8–3
Child support and visitation rights are separate obligations, so the default of one of these obligations by a parent does allow the other parent to default on his own obligation.

Each party may seek to remedy the respective default by filing a motion for contempt of a court order. The injured party may request that the offending party be held in contempt of court and be ordered to resume her obligation. As mentioned above, frequently the party bringing the motion for contempt will request and receive an order from the court that the offending party pay the costs and reasonable attorney's fees of the injured party. An attorney's fee award is made on the rationale that the party bringing the action would not have incurred the expense of representation had the other party fulfilled his legal obligation.

ASPECTS OF SUPPORT ORDERS

Sometimes support orders contain obligations beyond a periodic monetary payment. For instance, a judge may order a noncustodial parent to provide medical coverage to all children until they reach the age of majority. Also, when parties negotiate an agreement that one party shall pay private school tuition for all children during minority, this provision will be incorporated into the separation agreement. If the parent refuses to pay for tuition during minority, the other party may file a motion for contempt to enforce this agreed-to obligation. If the offending party counters this motion for contempt with a motion to modify the obligation for tuition because of changed financial circumstance, the court will not even consider a modification unless the separation agreement provided an accommodation for the event of changed circumstances. Further, the court will always order the party to pay the past-due amount. A past-due amount is termed an **arrearage.**

POSTMAJORITY CHILD SUPPORT

Prior to 1970, the age of majority in most states was twenty-one. When parties agreed or when a judge ordered a parent to pay children's college costs, failure to do so constituted contempt as long as the child was under the age of twenty-one. This enabled courts to enforce at least two and often three years of college tuition.

In 1970, many states lowered the age of majority to eighteen. Family courts charged with adjudicating disputes on payments for the minor child no longer had jurisdiction to enforce a provision in a separation agreement which obligated a non-custodial parent to pay college tuition for a child who had reached the age of eighteen. Because most children do not even start college until they are over the age of eighteen, this change wreaked havoc in splintered families where agreements long counted on were no longer worth the legal paper on which they were written.

To remedy this situation, eventually a number of state legislatures passed laws that provided henceforth—but not retroactively—that (1) divorcing parties could include a provision in their separation agreement for the postmajority support of children and (2) request that this provision along with the rest of the agreement be enacted into the divorce decree. The new statutes provided that if such a provision was enacted into the order of divorce or dissolution, then the family court had jurisdiction to enforce the clause.

STATUTES

CONNECTICUT GENERAL STATUTES 466-66.

. . . If the agreement is in writing and provides for the care, education, maintenance or support of a child beyond the age of eighteen, it may also be incorporated or otherwise made a part of any such order and shall be enforceable to the same extent as any other provision of such order or decree. . . .

Postmajority support agreements frequently address payment for college tuition or other postsecondary education; payment for the maintenance of postmajority adult children with special needs; and the payment of medical and dental insurance coverage on dependent adult children while they are students or when they are newly employed but not yet eligible for coverage at work. These types of postmajority support provisions are realistic in our current society because young adults frequently continue to have the need for some form of financial support from their family of origin. In instances where both the custodial and the noncustodial parent shared the support obligation during the child's minority, both parents should be required to continue with this obligation if they previously agreed to do so in their separation agreement.

FIGURE 8–4
Postmajority support agreements for college expenses came about as a result of the age of majority being lowered from twenty-one to eighteen during the 1970s.

EXHIBIT 8–1

Sample child support worksheet: Connecticut.

CONNECTICUT CHILD SUPPORT AND ARREARAGE GUIDELINES
WORKSHEET A – Page 1

_____   _____   _____
MOTHER   FATHER   NAME OF CUSTODIAN

COURT_____ D.N./CASE NO. _____ NUMBER OF CHILDREN ____

CHILD'S NAME   DATE OF BIRTH   CHILD'S NAME   DATE OF BIRTH

_____ _____   _____ _____
_____ _____   _____ _____
_____ _____   _____ _____

	I. Net Income Computation (Weekly amounts)	MOTHER	FATHER
1.	Gross income (attach verification)	$_____	$_____
2.	Number of exemptions for tax purposes	_____	_____
3.	Federal income tax	$_____	$_____
4.	State and local income tax	$_____	$_____
5.	Social security tax or mandatory retirement	$_____	$_____
6.	Health insurance premiums (other than child)	$_____	$_____
7.	Union dues or fees	$_____	$_____
8.	Unreimbursed work-related day care	$_____	$_____
9.	Other alimony and child support orders	$_____	$_____
10.	Sum of lines 3 - 9	$_____	$_____
11.	Net income (line 1 minus line 10)	$_____	$_____

II. Current Support Determination

12.	Combined net weekly income (nearest $10.00)	$_____	
13.	Basic obligation (from schedule)	$_____	
14.	Check here if noncustodial parent is a low-income obligor (see instructions)	_____	
15.	Child's health insurance premium	$_____	$_____
16.	Total obligation (Line 13 minus noncustodial parent's line 15 amount if line 14 is checked; line 13 plus line 15 total for all other cases)	$_____	
17.	Each parent's decimal share of line 12 (If line 14 is checked, skip this line and line 19, and enter the line 16 amount in the noncustodial parent's column on line 18.)	_____	_____
18.	Each parent's share of the total obligation (Line 17 times line 16 for each parent)	$_____	$_____
19.	Health insurance premium adjustment	$_____	$_____
20.	Social security benefits adjustment	$_____	$_____
21.	Sum of lines 19 and 20 (for each parent)	$_____	$_____
22.	Recommended support amounts (Line 18 minus line 21)	$_____	$_____
23.	Current support order (Noncustodial parent(s) only. If different from line 22 amount, explain in section VI.)	$_____	$_____

GO TO THE NEXT PAGE

EXHIBIT 8–1
Continued

CONNECTICUT CHILD SUPPORT AND ARREARAGE GUIDELINES
WORKSHEET A – Page 2

III. Total Arrearage Determination

24. Delinquencies on current support orders $_____

25. Unpaid court-ordered arrearages $_____

26. Past-due support (not court-ordered) $_____

27. Total arrearage (sum of lines 24 through 26) $_____

IV. Arrearage Payment Determination

28. Current support order from line 23 (or imputed
     support obligation for IV-D arrearages owed to
     the state or if child living with obligor) $_____

29. Twenty percent (20%) of line 28
     (or fifty percent (50%) of line 28 if
     there is no child under age 18) $_____

30. Noncustodial parent's line 11 amount $_____

31. Fifty-five percent (55%) of line 30 $_____

32. Line 31 minus line 28 $_____

33. Line 28 plus $145 $_____

34. Line 30 minus line 33 $_____

35. Recommended arrearage payment $_____

     (Smallest of lines 29, 32, and 34; or $5.00/month if child living with
     obligor and obligor's gross income is not more than 250% of poverty level;
     or the lesser of $5.00/week or line 34 for low-income obligor. If arrear-
     ages are owed to the state and the family, $5.00/month of this amount is
     allocated to the state, and the balance to the family.)

36. Arrearage payment order (At least $5.00/month
     unless line 34 is less than $1.00. If different
     from line 35, explain in section VI.) $_____

V. Order Summary

37. Current support order $_____

38. Arrearage payment order $_____ $_____
                                                    to state   to family

39. Total arrearage $_____ $_____
                                                    to state   to family

40. Total weekly support order
     (Line 37 plus line 38 total) $_____

VI. Deviation Criteria Applied

41. Reasons for deviation from current support and/or arrearage guidelines:

     _____

     _____

     _____

     _____

     _____

_____   _____   _____
Prepared by   Title   Date

EXHIBIT 8–2
Sample child support worksheet: New York.

SUPREME COURT OF THE STATE OF NEW YORK

1 COUNTY OF _____

--X

2

3   Index No.:

                          Plaintiff,

                                                          CHILD SUPPORT
         -- against --   **WORKSHEET**

4

                          Defendant

--X

This worksheet is submitted by Plaintiff who is the *custodial/noncustodial* parent in the above captioned action. All numbers used are YEARLY figures; weekly or monthly amounts have been converted to annualized numbers. [References are to DRL Section 240(1-b)].

                                                    FATHER   MOTHER

5 **STEP 1** MANDATORY PARENTAL INCOME

    1. Gross (total) income (as reported on most recent Federal tax return, or as computed in accordance with Internal Revenue Code and regulations) [(b)(5)(i)]: _____ _____

    The following items MUST be added if not already included in Line 1:

    2. Investment income [(b)(5)(ii)]: _____ _____
    3. Workers' compensation [(b)(5)(iii)(A)]: _____ _____
    4. Disability benefits [(b)(5)(iii)(B)]: _____ _____
    5. Unemployment insurance benefits [(b)(5)(iii)(C)]: _____ _____
    6. Social Security benefits [(b)(5)(iii)(D)]: _____ _____
    7. Veterans' benefits [(b)(5)(iii)(E)]: _____ _____
    8. Pension/retirement income [(b)(5)(iii)(F)]: _____ _____
    9. Fellowships and stipends [(b)(5)(iii)(G)]: _____ _____
    10. Annuity payments [(b)(5)(iii)(H)]: _____ _____
    11. If self-employed, depreciation greater than straight-line depreciation used in determining business income or investment credit: (b)(5)(vi)(A)]: _____
    12. If self-employed, entertainment and travel allowances deducted from business income to the extent the allowances reduce personal expenditures [(b)(5)(vi)(B)]: _____
    13. Former income voluntarily reduced to avoid child support [(b)(5)(v)]: _____ _____
    14. Income voluntarily deferred [(b)(5)(iii)]: _____ _____

List how you obtained the defendant's income for these calculations:_____

_____

    A. TOTAL MANDATORY INCOME: _____ _____

(Form UD-8)

EXHIBIT 8–2
Continued

---

6   <u>**STEP 2**</u> NON-MANDATORY PARENTAL INCOME

    15. Income attributable to non-income producing assets [(b)(5)(iv)(A)]:   _____ _____
    16. Employment benefits that confer personal economic benefits
        (such as meals, lodging, memberships, autos, etc.) [(b)(5)(iv)(B)]:   _____ _____
    17. Fringe benefits of employment [(b)(5)(iv)(C)]:   _____ _____
    18. Money, goods and services provided by relatives and
        friends: (b)(5)(iv)(D)]:   _____ _____

    B. TOTAL NON-MANDATORY INCOME: _____ _____

7   **C. TOTAL INCOME** (add Line A + Line B):   ======= =======

8   <u>**STEP 3**</u> DEDUCTIONS

    19. Expenses of investment income listed on line 2 [(b)(5)(ii)]:   _____ _____
    20. Unreimbursed business expenses that do not reduce personal
        expenditures [(b)(5)(vii)(A)]:   _____ _____
    21. Alimony or maintenance actually paid to
        a former spouse: [(b)(5)(vii)(B)]:   _____ _____
    22. Alimony or maintenance paid to the other parent but only
        if child support will increase when alimony stops [(b)(5)(vii)(C)]:   _____ _____
    23. Child support actually paid to other children the parent
        is legally obligated to support [(b)(5)(vii)(D)]:   _____ _____
    24. Public assistance [(b)(5)(vii)(E)]:   _____ _____
    25. Supplemental security income [(b)(5)(vii)(F)]:   _____ _____
    26. New York City or Yonkers income or earnings taxes actually paid
        [(b)(5)(vii)(G)]:   _____ _____
    27. Social Security taxes (FICA) actually paid [(b)(5)(vii)(H)]:   _____ _____

9   **D. TOTAL DEDUCTIONS**:   _____ _____

10   **E. FATHER'S INCOME** (Line C minus Line D):   _____

11   **F. MOTHER'S INCOME** (Line C minus Line D):   _____

<u>**STEP 4**</u> [(b)(4)]

12   **G. COMBINED PARENTAL INCOME** (Line E + Line F):   =======

(Form UD-8)

EXHIBIT 8–2
Continued

STEP 5 [(b)(3) and (c)(2)]

MULTIPLY Line G (up to $80,000) by the proper percentage (17% for 1 child, 25% for 2 children, 29% for 3 children, 31% for 4 children, or 35% (minimum) for 5 or more children) and insert in Line H.

13   **H. COMBINED CHILD SUPPORT**: . . . .   ========

14   **STEP 6** [(c)(2)]

I. DIVIDE the noncustodial parent's amount on Line E or Line F: _____
   by the amount of Line G: _____
   to obtain the percentage allocated **to the noncustodial parent**:   _____ %

STEP 7 [(c)(2)]

15   **J. MULTIPLY line H by Line I**:   _____

STEP 8 [(c)(3)]

16   **K. DECIDE the amount of child support to be paid**
     on any combined parental income exceeding $80,000
     per year using the percentages in STEP 5 or the
     factors in STEP 11-C or both: _____

17   **L. ADD Line J and Line K**:   _____

This is the amount of child support to be paid by the noncustodial parent to the custodial parent for all costs of the children, except for child care expenses, health care expenses, and college, post-secondary, private, special or enriched education.

STEP 9 SPECIAL NUMERICAL FACTORS

18   CHILD CARE EXPENSES

M. Cost of child care resulting from custodial parent's:
   __working; __attending elementary education; __attending secondary education; __attending higher education; __attending vocational training leading to employment: [(c)(4)] __seeking work [(c)(6)]:   _____

(Form UD-8)

EXHIBIT 8–2
Continued

---

19   **N. MULTIPLY Line M by Line I:**   _____

This is the amount the noncustodial parent must contribute to the custodial parent for child care.

HEALTH EXPENSES [(c)(5)]

20   **O. Reasonable future health care expenses
        not covered by insurance:**   _____

21   **P. MULTIPLY Line O by Line I:**   _____

This is the amount the noncustodial parent must contribute to the custodial parent for health care or pay directly to the health care provider.

22   **Q. EDUCATIONAL EXPENSE**
        If appropriate, see STEP 11(b) [(c)(7)]   _____

23   **STEP 10** LOW INCOME EXEMPTIONS [(d)]

         R. Insert amount of noncustodial parent's income from Line E or Line F: _____

         S. Add amounts on Lines L, N, P and Q
         (This total is "basic child support"):   _____

         T. SUBTRACT Line S from Line R: ════════

                  If Line T is more than the self-support reserve for this current year, then the low income exemptions do not apply and child support remains as determined in STEPS 8 and 9. If so, go to STEP 11. The self-support reserve is 135% of the official Federal poverty level for a single person household as promulgated by the U.S. Dept. of Health and Human Services and modified on April 1st of each year.

                  If Line T is less than the Federal poverty level for this current year, then complete Lines U, V and W.

24   **U. Insert amount of non-custodial parent's income from Line E or Line F:**   _____

25   **V. Self-support reserve**   _____

26   **W. Subtract Line V from Line U:**   ════════

(Form UD-8)

EXHIBIT 8–2
Continued

If Line W is more than $300 per year, the Line W is the amount of basic child support. If Line W is less than $300 per year, then basic child support must be a minimum of $300 per year. The defendant may attempt to show that he/she cannot pay this minimum amount.

If Line T is greater than Federal poverty level for 1997, but is less than the self-support reserve, then complete Lines X, Y and Z.

27 X. **Insert amount of noncustodial parent's income from Line E or Line F:** _____

28 Y. **Self-support reserve:** _____

29 Z. **SUBTRACT Line Y from Line X:** _____

If Line Z is more than $600 per year, then Line Z is the amount of basic child support. If Line Z is less than $600 per year, then basic child support must be a minimum of $600 per year. The defendant may attempt to show that he/she cannot pay the minimum amount.

30 **STEP 11** NON-NUMERICAL FACTORS

(a) NON-RECURRING INCOME [(e)]

A portion of non-recurring income, such as life insurance proceeds, gifts and inheritances or lottery winnings, may be allocated to child support. The law does not mention a specific percentage for such non-recurring income. Such support is not modified by the low income exemptions. Enter any relevant information:

(b) EDUCATIONAL EXPENSES [(c)(7)]

New York's child support law does not contain a specific percentage method to determine how parents should share the cost of education of their children. Traditionally, the courts have considered both parents' complete financial circumstances in deciding who pays how much. The most important elements of financial circumstances are income, reasonable expenses, and financial resources such as savings and investments. Enter any relevant information:

(c) ADDITIONAL FACTORS [(f)]

Section 240(1-b) of the Domestic Relations Law lists 10 factors that should be considered in deciding on the amount of child support for (i) combined incomes of more than $80,000 per year or (ii) to vary the numerical result of these steps because the result is "unjust or inappropriate."

(Form UD-8)

EXHIBIT 8–2
Continued

These factors are:

1. The financial resources of the parents and the child.
2. The physical and emotional health of the child and his/her special needs and aptitudes.
3. The standard of living the child would have enjoyed if the marriage or household was not dissolved.
4. The tax consequences to the parents.
5. The non-monetary contributions the parents will make toward the care and well-being of the child.
6. The educational needs of the parents.
7. The fact that the gross income of one parent is substantially less than the gross income of the other parent.
8. The needs of the other children of the noncustodial parent for whom the noncustodial parent is providing support, but only (a) if Line 22 is not deducted; (b) after considering the financial resources of any other person obligated to support the other children; and (c) if the resources available to support the other children are less then the resources available to support the children involved in this matter.
9. If a child is not on public assistance, the amount of extraordinary costs of visitation (such as out-of-state travel) or extended visits (other than the usual two to four week summer visits), but only if the custodial parent's expenses are substantially reduced by the visitation involved.
10. Any other factor the court decides is relevant.

Enter any relevant information:_____

_____

_____

NON-JUDICIAL DETERMINATION OF CHILD SUPPORT [(h)]

Outside of court, parents are free to agree to any amount of support, so long as they sign a statement that they have been advised of the provisions of Section 240(1-b) of the Domestic Relations Law. However, the court cannot approve agreements of less than $300 per year. This minimum is not per child, meaning that the minimum for three (3) children is $300 per year, not $900 per year. In addition, the courts retain discretion over awards of child support.

The foregoing have been carefully read by the undersigned, who states that they are true and correct.

31

_____
Plaintiff

(Form UD-8)

EXHIBIT 8–2
Continued

STATE OF NEW YORK, COUNTY OF _____ , ss.:

32   I, _____ , being duly sworn, depose and say that: I am the Plaintiff in this
action; I have read this Child Support Worksheet and I know its contents; they are true to my own
knowledge, except as to the matters stated to be upon information and belief, and as to those I believe
them to be true.

_____

Plaintiff

Sworn to before me on
_____ , 19___

(Form UD-8)

REVIEW QUESTIONS

1. Why do noncustodial parents have an obligation to support their children?

2. What are child support guidelines?

3. What circumstances gave rise to the development and establishment of child support guidelines?

4. What is meant by deviation from the child support guidelines?

5. When might a court enter a child support order that deviates from the child support guidelines?

6. What are the factors a court might consider in determining a parent's child support obligation?

7. When may child support orders be modified?

8. How does a parent obtain a modification of a child support order?

9. When a noncustodial parent fails to make child support payments as ordered, what remedy is available to the custodial parent?

10. May a custodial parent withhold visitation to a noncustodial parent who is not making child support payments? Why or why not?

11. What is a capias and when will the court order a capias in a child support proceeding?

12. When does an administrative agency become involved in enforcing a child support order?

13. What are Bureaus of Support Enforcement or IV-D agencies?

14. What methods are used to establish paternity?

15. What is the purpose of the Uniform Reciprocal Enforcement of Support Act?

16. Under URESA, what steps must a parent take to enforce a child support order in a different state than the state in which the order was made?

17. What is the Uniform Interstate Family Support Act? How does this act differ from the Uniform Reciprocal Enforcement of Support Act in the type of remedies it provides?

18. What is a child support arrearage?

19. How does the court provide for payment of a child support arrearage?

20. What is postmajority child support?

21. When can a family court enforce an order for postmajority child support?

22. Describe a family situation in which divorcing parties might agree to a postmajority child support provision in their separation agreement?

23. Why has the issue of providing for postmajority child support and giving courts jurisdiction to enforce postmajority child support become important in the last twenty-five years?

EXERCISES

1. Go to your local law library and, in your state's statutes, find the statute which authorizes the creation of family support guidelines and the statute establishing the formula used to determine a noncustodial parent's child support obligations. Summarize the method authorized in your state.

2. Use the following facts and your state's established child support obligation formula to compute the noncustodial parent's obligation for one child, two children, and three children: The custodial parent's net weekly income is $550. The noncustodial parent's net weekly income is $700.

3. Go to the clerk's office at the state court in your jurisdiction and obtain preprinted financial affidavit forms if available. On one form, put in figures for a hypothetical custodial parent and, in the other, put in figures for a hypothetical noncustodial parent. Use your state's guidelines to come up with the noncustodial parent's required obligation to one and two children. Make an argument for a deviation from the guidelines to enable the noncustodial parent to pay less or to persuade the court that the noncustodial parent should pay more.

4. Find out from your state's government information line whether your state has a support enforcement agency. If so, contact and interview a support enforcement officer. Prepare a written summary of the services the agency provides where an in-state parent has failed to make child support payments and whether this agency offers assistance in collecting child support payments from a defaulting noncustodial parent who lives outside of the state.

CHAPTER 9

THE CLIENT INTERVIEW

KEY TERMS

Financial worksheet

Initial client intake form

Initial client interview

Jurisdictional requirement

Legal advice

Retainer agreement

Retainer letter

THE PARALEGAL'S ROLE IN THE INITIAL SCREENING PROCESS

The divorce process begins with a potential client contacting the law office for the purpose of obtaining legal representation in the dissolution of his marriage. Clients also seek attorney representation in obtaining some type of postjudgment remedy such as contempt actions and modification proceedings. The client's first contact with the law office will ordinarily be through the telephone. Family law paralegals may often find themselves answering the phone and fielding phone calls from prospective clients.

Use of an **initial client intake form** will help the paralegal obtain important information during the prospective client's first call to the family law office (see Exhibit 9–1). The initial client intake form will aid the paralegal in obtaining data from the client and relaying information to the client. In addition to the prospective client's name, address, phone number and reasons for seeking an attorney, the paralegal may:

1. Schedule an appointment for the client with the attorney, and log the appointment in the attorney's master calendar system and in the attorney's individual daily diary.

2. Inform the client of the cost of an initial consultation (which is determined by the attorney). If the initial consultation is free, inform the client of the time limits of this initial meeting.

3. Give the client travel instructions to the office and tell them where to park.

4. If the prospective client was served with legal papers or has received any correspondence regarding possible litigation, tell the client to bring this material to the initial interview.

FIGURE 9–1
Many clients' first contact with a law office will be made via telephone.

PREPARING FOR THE CLIENT INTERVIEW

The next step in the divorce process is the **initial client interview.** The initial interview is the first meeting between the client and the attorney.

The purposes of the initial interview are as follows:

1. To give the client the opportunity to meet the attorney.
2. To give the client some preliminary legal advice regarding his problem.
3. To give the attorney and the attorney's support staff (the attorney's secretary, paralegal, and law clerks) an opportunity to become acquainted with the client.
4. To enable the attorney to establish a relationship of trust and confidence with the client.
5. To give the attorney the opportunity to discuss fees and fee payment arrangements with the client, and to determine and communicate to the client the scope of the attorney's representation.
6. To give the attorney the chance to assess the client's needs and determine whether he or she is willing and able to represent this particular client.
7. To enable the attorney to obtain enough information to commence the client's legal action.

UNDERSTANDING THE EMOTIONAL ASPECTS OF DIVORCE

Before proceeding further with a discussion of the interview process, it is important for the paralegal to comprehend the emotional aspects of divorce. Marriages are entered into with high expectations. They can range from mutual promises to be faithful to each other and stay together forever, to somber resolves to maintain a sober and responsible lifestyle, to undying pledges to always be there for each other to provide emotional support, financial support, intimacy, companionship, love, caring, and mutual respect. When a client is at the threshold of seeking legal representation in a divorce matter, it is important to understand that some of the expectations of marriage have been shattered in one way or another.

An impending divorce signals the rupture of a dream. This event can literally turn a client's life upside down, and start them on an emotional roller coaster. Throughout the process, clients experience everything from anger, jealousy, rage, and hopelessness to depression, frustration, and distrust. Furthermore, the adversarial nature of our legal system and litigious family law practitioners can exacerbate an already volatile situation.

Paralegals will have contact with clients at various stages in the divorce process, either by phone or in person. The paralegal should provide emotional support for a stressed-out client in a professional and limited manner. While a paralegal should acknowledge clients' feelings and give them an opportunity to express themselves, it may be appropriate, in some cases, to refer a client to a therapist or support group. It is not the function of the law office to provide therapeutic services to clients. The law office must remain within the confines of its role to provide legal services efficiently and competently and refer clients to therapists when they are in need of professional mental health services.

DEVELOPING A RELATIONSHIP OF TRUST AND CONFIDENCE

One of the most important goals of the client interview is developing a relationship of trust and confidence with the client. At the beginning of the interview, the client should be assured that all communications with the office are strictly confidential. While the ethical standard of confidentiality applies to any situation where an attorney/client relationship has been established, it is particularly important to verbally explain this duty to a client, especially a family law client. Divorce or family-related matters may present very sensitive issues that a client may be too embarrassed to discuss with an attorney or paralegal. Assure the client that the information will not be disclosed to third parties unless the client has consented or the disclosure is required by one of the exceptions to the confidentiality rule. A thorough knowledge of your state's confidentiality rule is extremely important.

A proficiently managed law office and a competent staff responding to clients' needs also helps inspire trust and confidence. Returning phone calls and following through on promises made to clients is essential. If you have told a client that documents will be forwarded for her review, do so. Take good notes when speaking with a client, either in person or on the telephone. Transfer any tasks to be completed on behalf of the client to your "Things to Do" list. This will ensure that this information will not get lost and that these tasks will be completed. Attorneys are very busy and may also need to be reminded to complete certain tasks or return a client's phone call.

DEVELOPING GOOD LISTENING SKILLS

A good interviewer develops listening skills over time and experience with a variety of clients. There are, however, some techniques that are worth discussing and applying when interviewing a client. One such technique is active listening. When interviewing a client, it is important to pay close attention to what they are saying and to convey to him that you are actually listening. If the interviewer is not engaged in the interview the mind may wander and vital information that could be useful to the client's case will be missed. The following are some guidelines to help you develop active listening skills:

1. *Refrain from passing judgment on your clients.* You will encounter clients with a wide range of life experiences and backgrounds that may conflict with your own values. It is not your function to judge the client, but rather to assist the attorney in the client's representation. You may empathize with the client, if appropriate, but refrain from expressing an opinion on their choices or lifestyle.

2. *Be aware of your body language.* We communicate nonverbally through the use of our bodies. As interviewers, it is important that we maintain eye contact with the client. If you keep looking at the clock, for instance, it may show that you are either bored or in a rush. Maintaining eye contact shows that you are interested in what the client has to say. Another way to show a client that you are engaged in the conversation is to be conscious of your body position. Avoid placing barriers (i.e., a desk) between you and the client. Sit across from the client at a reasonable distance and lean forward to show interest. Clients also com-

municate with body language. There are numerous books on the market which can help you learn how to interpret visual cues and how to respond to them.

3. *Provide feedback.* Repeat some key facts back to the client or summarize a series of events. Politely do this during a break in the conversation. This conveys that you are actually hearing what they are saying and gives the client the opportunity to correct any misunderstandings.

4. *Empathize with your clients.* Be sensitive to your client's emotional needs and acknowledge his feelings. Do not, however, share your personal experiences. Not only is this unprofessional, but getting too personal will disrupt your professional relationships. If you find that interviewing divorce clients raises certain issues in your own life, seek professional help or a support group.

PREINTERVIEW PREPARATIONS

Determine the scope of the interview with your supervisor. Is the client seeking a divorce or is it a postjudgment matter? Next make sure that the interviewing room or area is private, neat, and free from confidential information pertaining to other clients. Facial tissues are also important to have on hand in case the client becomes emotional. You will also need a copy of the preprinted form used by your office, a legal pad for notes, and any releases or other documents necessary.

THE CLIENT INTERVIEW

THE CLIENT'S ARRIVAL

When the client arrives, make sure that you are not interrupted. Greet the client with a smile and a handshake. Introduce yourself and identify your paralegal status. Take the client's coat and engage in small talk in order to put the client at ease. Chatting about the weather or asking if the client had difficulty locating the office are some ways of initiating a conversation. Many offices keep hot and cold beverages for their clients' enjoyment. Offer the client something to drink if this is the procedure in your office.

THE ACTUAL INTERVIEW

Once the client is comfortably seated, explain your role. Tell the client that for her own protection, the ethical rules of the state prohibit you from giving legal advice.

The client's communication level will dictate how you approach the interview. Some clients are more verbal than others. For clients who talks too much, it is important to focus them on the purpose of the interview. Others are very nervous and need to be prompted with a lot of questions. Give the client an overview of the interview process and tell her that it is important that you hear her story and collect the necessary data. Tell the client that you will be taking notes so that you can preserve the information for the file.

Gathering Information

Start with open-ended questions that will illicit more than a one-word response. For instance:

- ▼ "You contacted us about a divorce matter. Could you tell me what is going on in your marriage?"
- ▼ "What can we help you with today?"

These questions will encourage the client to start talking.

Tape recording client interviews is not recommended. When the recorder is on, your mind will relax knowing that you are getting all the information on tape. The problem is that you may not be alert to sections of the interview where you need to ask questions. Focus on the client and listen. Only when you listen can you ask relevant questions. Jot down notes about questions or areas on which you may want the client to elaborate.

Narrowing Issues

Once you have a general idea of the client's situation, it is time to focus on specific issues. For example:

- ▼ "Can you elaborate on your child's educational problems?"
- ▼ "You mentioned that your wife was unfaithful during your marriage. Can you be more specific?"

Once you have a general picture of the marriage and the causes of the breakdown it is now time to focus on the preprinted form. Say to the client, "I think I have enough for now. I'd like to go through our questionnaire so that we can take down some important information the attorney will need in order to adequately represent you."

Concluding the Interview

Tell the client what will happen next: "I'll pass this information on to Attorney Jones" or "We'll draft the initial document and send you a copy." Take care of any documents that need to be signed at this time, such as releases or retainer agreements. (Retainer agreements are discussed later in this chapter.)

Explain to the clients what is expected from them. Do they need to gather additional information? Do they need to perform certain tasks? Ask the clients if they have any questions and tell them to feel free to call the office.

Whenever conducting a client interview, the interviewer must remember to obtain the essential information: where, when, who, what, why, and how. If a client has trouble remembering specific facts such as date, time, and place, it may be helpful to have the client go through his personal calendar, which may jar his memory. In addition to the initial interview, paralegals will often conduct subsequent follow-up interviews with the client during the course of the attorney's representation of the client. The basic skills of listening, actively asking questions, and gathering information from the client are equally as important in follow-up interviews.

REFERRING CLIENT TO SUPPORT SERVICES

Referring a client to a therapist or support group must be done in a sensitive, diplomatic manner, to avoid insulting or talking down to a client. Fortunately the stigma of consulting a counseling professional or support group has waned in recent years, but it still may be difficult for some clients to accept. A good way to broach the subject is to ask the client if they think it would help them to talk to someone about their feelings. It is also helpful to convey to the client that during periods of extreme stress, many individuals seek the professional help of an objective ear who can provide them with some healing advice.

Encouraging a client to seek counseling can also help the client cope throughout the divorce process, which will have its ups and downs. The client who is getting professional help and has a sounding board will be stronger and better emotionally able to handle the divorce process. This client will rely less on the divorce process to solve their emotional problems. This client will also rely less on the legal staff to address his or her emotional needs, thus allowing the law office to concentrate on the client's legal matter.

A family law paralegal should become familiar with the local services available to clients. Local newspapers, hotline telephone information lines, and hospitals can provide appropriate referrals. A client should also be encouraged to explore her medical insurance coverage to determine whether or not such services are provided under her plan. If insurance will not cover therapy or the client is without insurance and cannot afford to pay a private therapist, the law office can make the client aware of agencies that offer sliding scale counseling services and of community support groups that are free or that charge a nominal fee to help defray the cost of the meeting space.

The paralegal should create a list of resources, updating it regularly, that provides a quick reference for client referrals. The list should include a variety of services for an array of clients needs such as domestic violence services, twelve-step groups, substance abuse counselors, support groups, displaced homemaker services, mental health clinics, pastoral counselors, and private mental health counselors. Clients themselves may also have resources available to them that they have not considered. They may have had a friend who went through a divorce and can recommend either a therapist or support group. Other clients may be in the position to take advantage of employee assistance programs at their place of employment. If a client has religious affiliations, these institutions may also provide services or referrals to the client.

The paralegal should keep the following client information in a Rolodex or other type of filing system:

▼ Name of agency,
▼ Address,
▼ Phone number,
▼ Name of contact person, and
▼ What services are provided, dates, times, and cost.

Some organizations or professionals may also provide the office with business cards or brochures describing their services, which can be distributed to clients.

REFERRALS FOR CHILDREN

In addition to assisting and encouraging the client to seek professional help, an inquiry should also be made regarding the status of the children. Divorce is devastating for most children and their needs should be addressed, because this stressful event may have long-term effects on them. In addition to information hotlines, schools may also provide resources for children whose parents are going through a divorce.

CONDUCTING THE INITIAL INTERVIEW

No set rule dictates who should conduct the initial client interview. It will depend on the preference of the supervising attorney or, in an emergency situation, who is available. In some offices, the attorney will conduct the initial interview; in others, the paralegal will be the first person with whom the client has contact. The most ideal situation is to have both the attorney and the paralegal available for the client.

The presence of the attorney during the initial client interview is extremely important. Attorneys can perform a function that a paralegal cannot: give **legal advice.** A client seeking a divorce from a spouse will have many questions regarding how the law will impact on *their* particular case and how it will effect *their* family. **Legal advice can only be provided by an attorney.** Giving legal advice means that you are applying the law to a particular client's particular circumstances and either predicting an outcome or advising the client to take a particular course of action. A paralegal may relay legal advice from the lawyer to the client, may provide nonlegal advice, and may give information by describing the law. Once the paralegal has applied the specific facts of the client's case, the paralegal has crossed the line into the unauthorized practice of law. Any paralegal conducting *any* client interview must be very careful to refrain from giving legal advice to the client.

In offices where the attorney conducts the initial interview, the attorney will obtain enough information to commence the representation of the client. This information will then be passed on to the paralegal, who will begin the drafting of the initial pleadings. Sometimes the attorney will introduce the paralegal to the client so they may become acquainted and the role of the paralegal in the representation of the client explained.

In some law offices, both the attorney and paralegal are present at the initial interview. This enables the client to observe the attorney and paralegal as a team working toward the client's representation. The attorney can explain the paralegal's role and allow the client and paralegal to form a professional relationship that will benefit the client. Because family attorneys are often in court representing clients, the client may find the paralegal more accessible. The paralegal will have a considerable amount of contact with the client during the divorce process for purposes of gathering information, drafting documents, answering client phone calls, and relaying messages from the attorney. A client's ability to communicate with the attorney, even through the paralegal, will increase the client's satisfaction and decrease his level of anxiety. A client who has to wait until the attorney gets around to answering his phone calls or attending to his case will be a frustrated and dissatisfied customer.

FIGURE 9–2
A paralegal may conduct the initial interview, but must refrain from ever giving legal advice. That can only be done by the attorney.

In some law offices, the paralegal will conduct the initial interview. In this situation, the paralegal must be ever so careful not to render legal advice in the course of the interview. Even though a paralegal may know the answer to the client's question and be 100% correct, she must resist the temptation. In some instances, either unexpected or planned, the paralegal may be conducting the initial interview alone. For instance, a client will have a scheduled appointment with the attorney and the attorney is delayed in court. If this happens, the paralegal should contact the client to reschedule the appointment. If the client is already en route to the office, the paralegal will have to take over the initial interview. The paralegal should politely explain that the attorney has been delayed and that she will instead obtain all the necessary information, but that the client will be contacted later that day by the attorney who will answer all legal questions.

MAINTAINING A HIGH DEGREE OF PROFESSIONALISM

At all times during *any* client contact, the paralegal should maintain a professional demeanor. It is important that boundaries be set with the client so as to keep the relationship on a professional level at all times. Paralegals should never discuss personal information with the client either about themselves, the attorney, or the law firm. Paralegals should also refrain from making moral judgments about clients and telling them what to do with their lives. The paralegal must always remember that the goal of the law office is to process the client's matter and achieve the client's ultimate legal goals. Client's other needs should be provided for by mental health professionals or the client's support network.

PREPARING FOR THE CLIENT INTERVIEW

The paralegal should make adequate preparations for the client interview. The actual time and date of the interview will have been set in advance at the time the client made the initial contact with the office. The paralegal should check the office calendar in order to refresh his recollection as to the name of the client and the date and time of the appointment. Steps should be taken to make the interview area neat and tidy and ensure that other client's files and correspondence are kept out of view for confidentiality purposes. The paralegal should also make sure that a box of tissues is readily available for the client's convenience in the event the client becomes emotional.

Upon the client's arrival, they should be greeted as "Mr.____" or "Ms.____." The paralegal should introduce herself and indicate her professional status; for example, "I am Mary Jones, a paralegal with this office." The client may be nervous at the first meeting so the paralegal may want to engage the client in light conversation regarding the weather or compliment a client's outfit and offer the client a beverage to ease the client's anxiety.

FUNDAMENTALS OF CLIENT INTERVIEWING IN THE FAMILY LAW OFFICE

At the outset of the interview, the paralegal should explain his role in the family law office. Some clients will not be familiar with the paralegal profession and will need to be educated on what services the paralegal provides under the supervision of an attorney. The paralegal should also make it clear to the client that he cannot give legal advice. The issues of confidentiality should also be addressed. The client should be ensured that all communications made to any law office personnel are confidential, barring certain exceptions, particular to the jurisdiction's rules of ethics.

It is also important to encourage the client to disclose all information, whether positive or negative, to the attorney and paralegal. Clients will often withhold embarrassing or damaging information for fear of being judged by the interviewer. It is imperative that the client disclose any information that can impact the divorce proceedings. If the attorney is made aware of this information in advance, she will be better equipped to deal with it instead of being surprised on the day of trial, or having the opposing side ambush her in the course of negotiation. Learning about negative information at an advanced stage in the proceedings may be too late, and the attorney may be unable to counteract its effects.

Once the client is comfortably seated, the paralegal may encourage him or her to give a brief synopsis of the problem. At this time, the paralegal should not take notes, because it is important to actively listen and develop a trust relationship with the client. The paralegal should get a general idea of what caused the breakdown of the marriage, the extent of the marital estate, and the number and ages of the children. Tape recorders should be avoided because the interviewer tends to relax and be less active if he is aware that a machine is preserving the data. This will make him less interactive with the client and he may fail to ask probing questions.

Once some general information has been exchanged, the paralegal should tell the client that he will have to obtain some essential information in order for the office to adequately represent the client. Then the paralegal can use a preprinted form as a guideline for obtaining the necessary information. Moving to the use of a form too quickly may insult a client and give him or her the impression that the office is sterile and uncaring.

OBTAINING ESSENTIAL INFORMATION FROM THE CLIENT

One of the primary purposes of the initial interview is to obtain enough information to commence representation of the client in her family matter. Most family law offices use preprinted initial intake sheets to garner these facts from the client (see Exhibit 9–2). The advantage of a preprinted form is that the paralegal will not miss obtaining any relevant information because the form serves as a guideline. A legal pad should also be kept on hand to jot down other notes in the course of the interview.

Some paralegals may find themselves working for new attorneys or attorneys with very busy schedules that have not had the opportunity to draft preprinted forms. In such a case, the following is an overview of what information the initial interview should elicit about both spouses:

1. *Name.* The names of both the client spouse and the other spouse should be obtained and spelled correctly. The wife's maiden name should also be elicited.

2. *Current address.* Physical address is important for the purpose of personal or abode service. Post office boxes or mailbox services are not sufficient for service, but the client may request that correspondence be forwarded to a P.O. box for security purposes. For example, the client may fear that his correspondence will be intercepted by his spouse or other third party. The office should have a system of alerting any office personnel who happen to pick up the file on any given day that care should be taken in terms of forwarding correspondence to the client, perhaps using a special colored sticker to serve as a "red flag."

3. *Telephone numbers.* Obtain home and work numbers. Sometimes clients cannot receive phone calls at work so you should avoid making calls to their workplace, except in emergency situations. On the other hand, some clients may not be comfortable receiving calls at home if they are still residing with their spouse, especially in cases where domestic violence is a problem. Clients may also request that you leave phone messages with family members or friends, while others will use beepers in this electronic age to keep attorney communications confidential.

4. *Jurisdiction.* How long has the client resided in the state? Each state has a **jurisdictional requirement** indicating how long a party must reside in the state before the state courts have the power to dissolve the marriage.

5. *Social Security numbers.* Social Security numbers are useful for many reasons. Some jurisdictions may require Social Security numbers on initial pleadings. They are also important for tax purposes or when engaging the services of an investigator to conduct asset searches or track down a "deadbeat" parent. Social Security numbers are also useful in debt collection proceedings against delinquent clients.

6. *Military service.* Did either spouse serve in the military? This question is important, because military pensions may qualify as marital property. Also, if a spouse is currently in the military, care must be taken so service of process will be adequate.

7. *Employer.* Where is the client employed? What is the address? What is the client's occupation? How long has the client been employed in his current position? Similarly, where is the client's spouse employed and what is her occupation? This information will be helpful for purposes of service, subpoenaing employment records, and obtaining pension information.

8. *Date and place of marriage.* This will establish where and when the marriage took place.

FIGURE 9–3
The initial interview should include a question about military service, because military pensions may qualify as marital property, and knowledge of military service helps ensure proper service of process.

9. *Education, race, and age.* This data may be necessary for statistical information to be made available to the state's bureau of vital statistics. Education will also indicate how far a client has gone through school, which may be relevant in terms of his ability to earn income.

10. *City or state welfare assistance.* Has the state or city welfare system ever provided financial support for the spouse and the children? Many jurisdictions require this information and require that the governmental entity be notified of the proceedings and appear for purposes collecting monies owed to them.

11. *Date of separation.* When did the parties separate and what were the reasons for the separation?

12. *Cause of breakdown of the marriage.* All jurisdictions have adopted some form of no-fault divorce where the grounds for divorce are commonly referred to as irretrievable breakdown or irreconcilable differences. It is still important, however, to illicit the cause of the breakdown of the marriage from the client.

13. *Reconciliation.* Is there any hope of reconciliation? Divorce is a devastating life event, not only for the spouses, but more importantly for the children. It is the ethical responsibility of the attorney or paralegal to make sure that a divorce is what the client wants. Most clients who have made their way to an attorney's office are confident in their decision to dissolve the marriage. A client who is reluctant or may be having second thoughts should be encouraged to seek professional counseling services.

14. *Children.* How many children were born during the marriage? What are their names and dates of birth? Were any children born to the spouses prior to their marriage? Were there any children born to the spouses during the marriage who are not issue of the marriage? Is the wife pregnant? These questions are important to ask for purpose of allocating child support responsibilities and determining the custody and visitation rights of the parents. Paternity may also be at issue if challenged.

15. *Previous marriage(s).* Was either of the parties previously married? How, why, and when did the previous marriage(s) end? Is the spouse currently paying alimony or child support to a former spouse pursuant to a court order? What, if any, orders are in effect?

16. *Prenuptial agreement.* Did the parties sign a prenuptial agreement? If the answer is yes, be sure to obtain a copy from the client. The existence of a prenuptial agreement will raise several issues. Is the agreement valid? What rights did the parties give up? What did they obligate themselves to do?

17. *Was a divorce action previously initiated in the course of this marriage?* If the client tells you that a divorce was previously initiated, the paralegal should review any paperwork the client may have. The paralegal should then follow it up with a review of the court file in the appropriate courthouse where the actions were filed. The client may be surprised to find out that he may already be divorced or that the initial pleadings may have been filed. If the file is still active, a client seeking a divorce may save on filing and sheriff's fees. If this is the case, the filing of responses will be sufficient.

18. *Disability/illness.* The interviewer should ask whether either spouse or children suffer from any disabilities or illnesses. Issues regarding medical care and expenses, insurance coverage, and support may require special attention.

19. *Date of the interview.* When did the interview take place?

20. *Name of the interviewer.* Who conducted the interview?

21. *Source of referral.* Who referred the client to the attorney? This will help track the attorneys advertising dollars and zero in on where business is being generated. Thank you cards or letters should be sent to individuals and organizations who refer business to the office.

22. *Legal fees.* If the attorney is conducting the interview, she will quote the client a fee for her services. If the paralegal is conducting the interview, he cannot quote a fee. Remember that a paralegal cannot set fees; this is the attorney's responsibility. In this instance, inform the client that he can discuss the fee structure with the attorney.

23. *Type of relief.* The interviewer should ask the client what type of legal relief he is seeking as a result of the family action. First and foremost, the attorney must determine the legal cause of action to be filed. Does the client want a dissolution of marriage, legal separation, or annulment? An attorney's legal advice is essential in making this selection. Additional relief includes child custody, child support, property and debt distribution, alimony, and attorney's fees.

FIGURE 9–4
The initial interview should include questions about any disabilities or illnesses from which the spouse or children suffer to ensure that proper attention is paid to any such special circumstances.

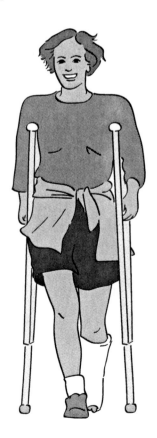

24. *Name change.* A wife may seek to resume the use of her maiden name as part of the final divorce decree. It was a long-standing custom for women to assume their husband's surname upon marriage. Some states went as far as requiring women to assume their husband's last names through court decisions. Gender discrimination laws however, prohibit this judicial mandate. The Equal Protection Clause of the U.S. Constitution prohibits states from requiring women to assume the husband's surname since their is no rational basis for women, but not men, to change their last names upon marriage. Today, women are free to follow custom or to retain their own maiden names. Some couples create a new last name using the wife's maiden name and the husband's surname. A married woman's legal name is determined by what she actually calls herself *after* the marriage ceremony. She is basically free to use whatever she pleases as long as her choice is not intended to defraud her creditors or use her name for unlawful purposes. In preparing the initial divorce pleadings, the wife may include restoration of her maiden name in her prayer for relief. The court will automatically grant the wife's wishes despite objections from the husband. Some women choose to retain their husband's surname as a matter of preference. Many women with young children choose to retain their married name until the children have finished school and may later return to court to restore their maiden name. Change of name after the divorce is final is considered a postjudgment matter. The wife must file a petition in the proper state court. A hearing date is scheduled by the court and a notice is published in the legal section of the newspaper. Courts generally allow former spouses to change their names as long as the change is not being made to advance fraudulent or illegal purposes. The wife must then obtain a certified copy of the court's final decree and notify her creditors and the Social Security Administration of the change. The children of the marriage will also assume their biological father's last name. Problems arise when the wife remarries. Sometimes the children develop a close relationship with their new stepfather and wish to take his name. Mothers may also push for a change of the children's last names for various reasons. Because the change of names, even for minor children, requires a court hearing, the biological father must be notified of the proceedings. If the parties disagree regarding the children's name change, the court will have to decide. The court will determine whether the name change is in the children's best interest. The court will focus on the wishes of the parents, stepparent, and children, and on the name that has been historically used by the child. While the best interest standard is often applied, many courts still believe that it is in the children's best interest to use their biological father's surname.

Whenever conducting any client interview the interviewer must remember to obtain the essential information: where, when, who, what, why, and how. If a client has trouble remembering specific facts such as date, time, and place, it may be helpful to have the client go through their personal calendar, which may jar their memory. In addition to the initial interview, paralegals will often conduct subsequent follow-up interviews with the client during the course of the attorney's representation of the client. The basic skills of listening, actively asking questions, and gathering information from the client are equally as important in follow-up interviews.

Once the initial interview form has been completed, the attorney or paralegal may give the client a **financial worksheet** to take home and fill out (see Exhibit 9–3). This worksheet should focus on the client's income, expenses, assets, and liabilities, be they joint or separate. The financial worksheet will enable the attorney to begin assessing the extent of the marital estate. The client should also be instructed to write a history of the marriage, which will be helpful in illuminating issues that may be of relevance in the divorce action. The client should be instructed to complete these documents before the next meeting.

If the paralegal has conducted the interview without the attorney present, an appointment should be scheduled for a meeting with the attorney, which will enable the client to obtain legal advice and go over the material obtained by the paralegal at the initial interview. The attorney can also address the legal course of action to be taken and review the fee structure.

If the attorney has conducted the interview with or without the presence of the paralegal, he will now turn over the initial interview form to the paralegal for the purpose of having the paralegal draft the initial pleadings.

REPRESENTING THE DEFENDANT SPOUSE

In a family law practice, the office will either be representing the plaintiff or the defendant spouse. With a plaintiff spouse, the divorce proceedings are basically starting at square one, which requires the drafting and service of the writ, summons, and complaint. When representing the defendant spouse, the paralegal must make sure in initial phone consultation to instruct the client to bring in any papers that were served on her and all correspondence received in conjunction with the divorce matter. At the initial interview he must make sure to photocopy all paperwork the client brings. Determine whether service was properly made either through abode or in-hand service. He may also want to go over the complaint or petition with the client to determine whether the information contained is accurate. This will enable the paralegal to obtain the data necessary to prepare the responsive pleadings.

PREPARING RELEASES

Another task the paralegal may be asked to perform is to prepare a release of information or have the client sign a preprinted release. As explained in Chapter 3, the confidential relationship of the attorney and client, such as the doctor and patient, prohibits the professional from disclosing information without the client's consent. In family matters, an attorney may need a client's consent to communicate with any one of the following:

- Client's physician or therapist,
- Children's pediatrician, teachers, or therapists,
- Client's accountant,
- Client's employer, and
- Hospital or treatment centers.

The paralegal should be sure to check the federal and state statutes that concern the release of confidential information, especially when dealing with drug treatment or HIV- and AIDS-related information (see Exhibits 9–4 and 9–5).

FIGURE 9–5
The paralegal should photocopy documents pertaining to the divorce matter that have been provided by the client, especially those papers served on a defendant client by a plaintiff client.

THE RETAINER LETTER

Before the client interview ends, the supervising attorney will review the law office's fee schedule for providing legal services to clients. The law firm's projected costs for handling a dissolution matter or any other related family law matter should be disclosed with realistic figures presented. The client should fully understand the financial obligation he or she is undertaking by retaining the law firm and must be willing to assume this obligation. The client must also feel comfortable in other respects with having that particular law firm provide representation. Similarly, the law firm and the individual attorney who will be in charge of the case must also feel comfortable taking on the client. Sometimes an attorney may have reservations about dealing with a particular client. The attorney may feel that the prospective client may not honor the financial arrangement to be made, or the attorney may sense that the client is not being honest in disclosing information about marital assets, in revealing events leading up to the dissolution, or in revealing events that could cause controversy about the client's fitness as a custodial parent. If, on the other hand, neither the attorney nor the prospective client have such reservations, then the relationship will be formalized. The law office will prepare a retainer letter for the prospective client to sign. Once this document is executed, the law firm will actively begin work on the client file.

A **retainer letter** or **retainer agreement** is a contract between the law firm and the client whereby the law firm agrees to provide specified legal services in exchange for monetary compensation (see Exhibit 9–6). As discussed in an earlier chapter, there are different types of fee arrangements, such as flat fees, contingency fees, and hourly fees assessed for time spent working on the file.

Most of the time, in a complex family matter, firms charge by the hour. When this is the case, the retainer letter will state the firm's hourly rate schedule. There may be one hourly rate specified for work done on the file by a partner, a different and lower hourly rate for work done by associates in the firm, and there will be hourly rates listed for work done by paralegals and law clerks.

The retainer letter will also specify the terms of payment. If interest or late fees are to be charged for tardy payments, that fact will be stated and agreed to. Sometimes a retainer letter will state that if a client defaults on payment of a balance owed, the firm may take legal actions and the client will be responsible for attorney's fees and collection costs. The retainer letter, as a contract, is signed by both parties. Each party has rights and obligations. Like other legal contracts, if either party breaches the agreement by failing to execute their obligations, the injured party may seek relief in the court system.

Retainer letters should not be entered into lightly by either the client or the law firm. The client must consider whether he or she can afford the anticipated cost of representation. The attorney must gauge whether the prospective client actually has the financial means to pay for services. In addition, the attorney must decide whether his or her firm has the legal expertise and technical resources to properly handle a case of the complexity and time the matter requires.

If the prospective client and the law firm agree to go forward with representation of the client, the parties will sign the agreement. When the retainer letter is finalized, the attorney in charge of the file will assign a staff person to prepare the documents that will initiate the court action that is contemplated.

EXHIBIT 9–1
Sample initial telephone interview.

Client Intake Form
Initial Telephone Interview/Family Matters

Date_____

Referred by: ____Friend/coworker/relative

____Legal referral source

Interviewed by:_____

____Yellow Pages

____Bar association

____Other:_____

1. Client's Name:_____

    Address:_____

    City/State/Zip:_____

    Phone: Work_____   Home_____

2. Reason for Calling: Dissolution_____   Postjudgment_____

3. Client's Occupation:_____

    Employer:_____

    Yearly income:_____

4. Length of Marriage:_____   Date Married:_____

5. Number of Children and Ages:_____

6. Brief Description of Assets:_____

7. Are there issues of:____ adultery ____alcoholism/drug abuse

    _____domestic violence _____gambling

8. Initial appointment scheduled for: Date:_____ Time:_____

    With Attorney:_____

Inform the client of the following:

   Directions to the office and parking instructions

   Bring the following documents: _____ Marriage certificate

   _____ Copy of deed

   _____ Current pay stub

   _____ Income tax returns

   _____ Police incident reports

   _____ List of assets and debts

   _____ Certified copy of judgment (if postjudgment)

   _____ Separation agreement (if postjudgment)

EXHIBIT 9–2
Sample preprinted initial client interview form.

<h2 style="text-align:center">Client Intake Form
Initial Interview/Family Matters</h2>

Date_____

Check one:_____ Dissolution of Marriage   Representing: _____Plaintiff

_____ Legal Separation   _____Defendant

_____ Annulment   _____Third party

_____ Postjudgment   Intervenor

   I. *General Information:*

   A. Client's Name:_____   Maiden Name:_____

        Address: _____

        City/State/Zip:_____

        Phone: (Home) _____ (Work) _____ Best time to call:_____

        DOB _____ Place of birth:_____

        SSN _____ Race:_____

        Education:_____ Military Service:_____

   B.   Spouse's Name:_____ MaidenName: _____

        Address: _____

        City/State/Zip:_____

        Phone: (Home)_____ (Work) _____

        Best time to call:_____

        DOB _____ Place of birth:_____

        SSN _____ Race:_____

        Education:_____ Military Service:_____

        Represented by:_____

        _____

        _____

   II. *History of the Marriage:*

   A.   Place of marriage:_____

        Date of marriage:_____ Date of separation:_____

        Reason for breakdown: _____

EXHIBIT 9–2
Continued

B. Children born of the marriage:

Name   D.O.B.   Birthplace

_____

_____

_____

Is wife currently pregnant? _____Yes _____No

C. Public Assistance:

Have you or your spouse ever received public assistance?_____

Are you or your spouse currently receiving public assistance? _____

D. Employment:

Client's Employer:_____

    Address:_____

    City/State/Zip:_____

Occupation: _____

Years Employed:_____ Salary:_____

Benefits: _____

Spouse's Employer:_____

    Address:_____

    City/State/Zip:_____

Occupation: _____

Years Employed:_____ Salary:_____

Benefits: _____

E. What would you describe as the cause of the breakdown of your marriage?

Have you or your spouse sought marital counseling?

Is there any hope of reconciliation?

Did you sign a prenuptial agreement?

F. Have you or your spouse had any prior marriages?

EXHIBIT 9–2
Continued

    G. Disability/Illness (either spouse/children):_____

    H. How long have you resided in this state?

III. *Client Claims:*

Pendente lite	*Final orders*
_____ Alimony	_____ Dissolution of marriage
_____ Child custody	_____ Legal separation
_____ Child support	_____ Annulment
_____ Visitation	_____ Alimony
_____ Attorney's fees	_____ Property division
_____ Exclusive possession	_____ Child custody ___ Sole
of the marital residence	___ Joint
_____ Restraining order	_____ Visitation
_____ Other	_____ Attorney's fees
_____	_____ Name change to:_____
	_____ Contempt citation
	_____ Modification
	_____ Other:
	_____

IV. *Postjudgment Matters*

    Contempt Citations

        Date of the original order: _____

        Court where order entered: _____

        Original order: _____

        Date of last payment: _____

    Modification:

        Date of the original order: _____

        Court where order entered: _____

        Original order: _____

        Modification sought: _____

        Specify the substantial change in circumstances since the date of the original order:

EXHIBIT 9–2
Continued

V.   *Service of Process*

Where to serve spouse:_____

Best time to serve:_____ a.m./p.m.

Brief description of spouse:_____

_____

Description of spouse's car: _____

VI. *Documents to Prepare*

_____ Summons/complaint   _____ Financial affidavit

_____ *Pendente lite* motions   _____ Lis pendens

_____ Subpoena   _____ Contempt citation

_____ Reopen and modify judgment

_____ Other: _____

VII. *Legal Fees*

Fee quoted: $_____   Costs: $_____

Initial retainer amount required before services are commenced: $ _____

Terms of payment: _____

Fee agreement signed? _____ Yes_____ No

VIII. *Referral Source*

_____ Friend/coworker/relative   _____ Legal referral service

_____ Yellow Pages   _____ Bar association

_____ Other _____

EXHIBIT 9–3
Sample financial worksheet to determine assets and liabilities.

Financial Worksheet

Client's name: _____ Date: _____

I. *INCOME*

(Indicate weekly income and deductions. If paid monthly, divide monthly figure by 4.3 to determine weekly amount.)

A. Gross weekly income:

Salary, wages, commissions: $_____

Bonuses   _____

Tips   _____

Pensions/retirement   _____

Public assistance   _____

Social Security   _____

Unemployment insurance   _____

Disability   _____

Dividends/interest   _____

Rental income   _____

Alimony/child support   _____

Other: _____   _____

TOTAL GROSS WEEKLY INCOME $_____

B. Deductions

Federal withholding tax $_____

State withholding tax   _____

F.I.C.A.   _____

Medicare   _____

Health insurance   _____

Union dues   _____

Credit union   _____

Pension   _____

Other: _____   _____

TOTAL WEEKLY DEDUCTIONS $_____

TOTAL NET WEEKLY INCOME $_____

(A minus B)

EXHIBIT 9–3
Continued

II. *EXPENSES*

(Indicate weekly expenses. If expenses incurred on a monthly basis, divide monthly figure by 4.3 to determine weekly amount.)

A. Rent/Mortgage/Household

   1. Rent/mortgage   \$_____

   2. Homeowner's/renter's insurance   _____

   3. Property taxes   _____

   4. Household repairs   _____

   5. Trash collection   _____

   6. Other:_____   _____

       TOTAL RENT/MORTGAGE/HOUSEHOLD   \$_____

B. Utilities

   1. Electricity   \$_____

   2. Heat   _____

   3. Gas   _____

   4. Telephone   _____

   5. Water   _____

   6. Cable TV   _____

   7. Other:_____   \$_____

       TOTAL UTILITIES   \$_____

C. Groceries   \$_____

D. Clothing   \$_____

E. Dry Cleaning/Laundry   \$_____

F. Transportation

   1. Car payments   \$_____

   2. Parking   _____

   3. Tolls   _____

   4. Gas/oil   _____

   5. Repairs   _____

   6. Car taxes   _____

   7. License/registration/emissions   _____

EXHIBIT 9–3
Continued

  8. Bus   _____

  9. Train   _____

  10. Car insurance   _____

  11. Other:_____   _____

    TOTAL TRANSPORTATION $_____

G. Medical (out-of pocket expenses)

  1. Medical insurance $_____

  2. Dental insurance   _____

  3. Doctor visits   _____

  4. Dentist visits   _____

  5. Prescriptions/medicine   _____

  6. Optometrist   _____

  7. Orthodontist   _____

  8. Counseling/therapy   _____

  9. Other:_____   _____

  TOTAL MEDICAL $_____

H. Life Insurance Premium $_____

I. Children's Expenses

  1. School lunches $_____

  2. School books/school supplies   _____

  3. Tutors   _____

  4. School tuition   _____

  5. Camps   _____

  6. Class trips   _____

  7. Lessons (piano, karate, etc.)   _____

  8. Allowance   _____

  9. Religious instruction   _____

  10. Day care/babysitter   _____

    TOTAL CHILDREN'S EXPENSES $_____

EXHIBIT 9–3
Continued

J. Payment on Outstanding Debts

   1. Credit cards:_____ $_____

          _____   _____

          _____   _____

          _____   _____

   2. Student loans   _____

   3. Installment contracts   _____

   4. Personal loans   _____

   TOTAL PAYMENTS ON OUTSTANDING $_____
   DEBTS

K. Miscellaneous Expenses

   1. Haircuts $_____

   2. Newspapers/magazines   _____

   3. Eyeglasses   _____

   4. Charitable contributions   _____

   5. Subscriptions   _____

   6. Gifts   _____

   7. Bank fees   _____

   8. Postage   _____

   9. Vacations   _____

   10. Entertainment   _____

   11. Pet care   _____

   12. Cigarettes   _____

   13. Toiletries   _____

   14. Other:_____   _____

   TOTAL MISCELLANEOUS EXPENSES $_____

TOTAL EXPENSES $_____

EXHIBIT 9–3
Continued

III. *ASSETS*

(Provide the following information for each home, vacation home, condominium, farm, or parcel of real estate.)

A. Real Estate:

1. Address:_____

    City/State/Zip: _____

2. Date acquired:_____

3. Mortgage institution:_____

4. How is property owned? (specify exact names on deed)

    _____

    _____

    _____

5. Estimated value $_____

6. Outstanding mortgage   _____

7. Equity   _____

TOTAL REAL ESTATE $_____

(Include only your one-half undivided interest if property jointly owned.)

B. Bank/Checking Accounts

Name of Bank	Account Number	How Held (Joint or Individual)	Balance
_____	_____	_____	$_____
_____	_____	_____	_____
_____	_____	_____	_____
_____	_____	_____	_____

TOTAL BANK/CHECKING ACCOUNTS $_____

C. Stocks and Bonds

Number of Shares	Company or Fund	Value
_____	_____	$_____
_____	_____	$_____
_____	_____	$_____

TOTAL STOCKS and BONDS $_____

EXHIBIT 9–3
Continued

D. Deferred Compensation (401k, SEP, Keogh, IRA, etc.)

(provide the following information for each plan)

1. Name of company:_____

2. Name of plan:_____

3. Account number:_____

4. Estimated value:_____

5. Name and address of plan administrator:_____

_____

_____

TOTAL DEFERRED COMPENSATION $ _____

E. Motor Vehicles (provide the following information for each motor vehicle, including boats, airplanes, and motorcycles).

1. Year:_____

2. Model:_____

3. Estimated value $_____

4. Loan balance   _____

5. Equity   _____

TOTAL MOTOR VEHICLES $_____

F. Business Interests

1. Name of business:_____

2. Type of business:_____

3. Type of business interest: _____ Sole proprietorship

    _____ Partnership

    _____ Limited liability corporation

    _____ Professional corporation

    _____ Joint venture

    _____ Corporation

4. Estimated value of your interest $_____

TOTAL BUSINESS INTERESTS $_____

EXHIBIT 9–3
Continued

G. Insurance

Insured	Company	Beneficiary	Face Value	Cash Surrender Value
_____	_____	_____	$ _____	$_____
_____	_____	_____	$ _____	$_____
_____	_____	_____	$ _____	$_____

TOTAL CASH SURRENDER VALUE (minus loans) $ _____

H. Personal Property

   1. Household furniture $ _____

   2. Antiques   _____

   3. Jewelry   _____

   4. Artwork   _____

   5. Collectibles   _____

   6. Stereo/electronic equipment   _____

   7. Clothing   _____

   8. Furs   _____

   9. Family heirlooms   _____

  10. Silver   _____

  11. Crystal   _____

  12. Other_____   _____

     _____   _____

     _____   _____

    TOTAL PERSONAL PROPERTY $_____

TOTAL ASSETS $_____

EXHIBIT 9–3
Continued

IV.   LIABILITIES

Outstanding Debts

Date Debt Incurred	Creditor	Incurred by	Monthly Payment	Current Balance
_____	_____	_____	$_____	$_____
_____	_____	_____	$_____	$_____
_____	_____	_____	$_____	$_____
_____	_____	_____	$_____	$_____
TOTAL LIABILITIES				$_____

EXAMPLE 9–4
Sample information release form.

Authorization for Release of Information

I, EVELYN BRONSON, of NEW HAVEN, CONNECTICUT, hereby give permission to DOREEN HUNT, CPA of NEW HAVEN, CONNECTICUT, to allow my attorney, GRACE A. LUPPINO, to review, inspect, and otherwise photocopy any documents or files, or obtain any information pertaining to me currently in my accountant's possession.

_____
Evelyn Bronson

_____
Date

_____
Witness

EXAMPLE 9–5
Sample medical information release form.

Medical Authorization for Release of Information

I, EVELYN BRONSON of NEW HAVEN, CONNECTICUT, hereby give permission to CLAYTON REEVES, M.D., of NEW HAVEN, CONNECTICUT, to permit my attorney, GRACE A. LUPPINO, to review, inspect, and otherwise photocopy my medical records, including laboratory records and reports, all tests of any type and all of my records pertaining to medical care, history, condition, treatment, diagnosis, prognosis, etiology, and expenses.

_____

Evelyn Bronson

_____

Date

_____

Witness

EXAMPLE 9–6
Sample retainer agreement (author unknown).

Retainer Agreement

A. EVELYN BRONSON ("Client") hereby employs GRACE A. LUPPINO, an attorney licensed to practice law in the State of Connecticut ("Attorney"), to represent her in a dissolution of marriage action: RODNEY BRONSON v. EVELYN BRONSON, Docket No. FA 96-123456.

B. In consideration of the services rendered, the Client shall pay the Attorney in the following manner:

   1. The Attorney shall commence work on the Client's dissolution matter upon receipt of an initial retainer of $3,000.00 (Three Thousand dollars) from the Client.

   2. The total number of hours expended by the Attorney will be billed at a rate of $200.00 (Two Hundred dollars) per hour.

   3. Upon expending the initial retainer, the Attorney shall bill the Client for any additional hours expended at a rate of $200.00 (Two Hundred dollars) per hour.

   4. Upon completion or termination of the Attorney's representation of Client, the Attorney shall return any unearned retainer to the Client.

C. The Client shall pay for all costs and expenses incurred by the Attorney in the course of representing the Client. Costs and expenses include, but are not limited to, court entry fees, sheriff's fees, process server fees, transcripts, subpoenas, and expert witnesses.

D. The Client authorizes the Attorney to engage the services of accountants, appraisers, evaluators, investigators, court reporters, sheriffs, experts, and process servers deemed necessary by the Attorney in rendering legal services to the Client. (The Client shall be directly responsible for the fees and bills of these service providers.) The Attorney shall obtain the Client's approval prior to engaging the services of such persons or incurring such costs and expenses.

E. The Attorney shall bill the Client for all legal fees, costs, and expenses on a monthly basis. Such bill shall be paid by the Client within 30 days from the date of the invoice.

F. If this Agreement is terminated by the Client prior to completion of the Attorney's services, the Client shall pay any Attorney's fees, costs, and expenses accrued to that date.

G. The Attorney shall not be required to deliver any reports, investigations, appraisals, evaluations, or other documents prepared by third parties that have not been paid for by the Client.

H. In the event that the Attorney must enforce this Agreement through any legal collection proceedings, the Attorney shall be entitled to recover reasonable attorney's fees and court costs in conjunction with such proceeding.

The undersigned parties have read the above Agreement and agree to abide by its terms and conditions.

Signed this _____ day of _____, 2001.

_____
Evelyn Bronson, Client

_____
Grace A. Luppino, Esq. Attorney

REVIEW QUESTIONS

1. Explain the purpose of using an initial client intake form.
2. What is the initial interview and what is its purpose?
3. Why is it important for the family law paralegal to comprehend the emotional aspects of divorce?
4. Explain the importance of locating appropriate support services for divorce clients.
5. Describe the community resources and services about which the family law paralegal should be aware.
6. What information should the paralegal keep on file regarding community resources and services?
7. Why are referrals for children important?
8. During the initial interview, how should the paralegal respond to clients' questions regarding the legal status of their cases? Explain.
9. What steps should the paralegal take in preparing for the initial interview?
10. Prepare an overview of the information that will be obtained on both spouses during the initial interview.
11. What is a financial worksheet?
12. Explain the differences between conducting an initial interview with a plaintiff spouse or with a defendant spouse.
13. What is the purpose of a retainer letter?
14. What terms should be specified in the retainer agreement?
15. After the initial interview has been completed and the retainer agreement is signed, what is the next step in the divorce process?

EXERCISES

1. Using the information in given in this chapter, draft an initial client intake form.

2. Go to your local library or use the Internet to find a book or articles on the emotional aspects of divorce and the effects of divorce on children. This exercise will broaden one's understanding and appreciation of what clients experience during this process.

3. Make a list of community resources that can be used for client referrals.

4. What resources are available in your community for children of divorce?

5. Does your jurisdiction require retainer agreements? If so, what provisions does your state require to be included in each retainer agreement?

10

CHAPTER

INITIAL AND RESPONSIVE PLEADINGS

KEY TERMS

Abode	Order to show cause
Affidavit	*Pendente lite* motion
Affidavit of publication	Petition
Answer	Petitioner
Appearance	Plaintiff spouse
Application for a prejudgment Remedy	Pleading
	Prayer for relief
Body	Pre-return date relief
Caption	Request for an order attaching
Complaint	Known assets
Contempt	Respondent
Court-entry fee	Return date
Cross-complaint	Rules of court
Default judgment	Service by publication
Defendant spouse	Sheriff's return
Dissipation	Subscription
Filing fee	Summons
Juris number	Temporary restraining order
Motion for disclosure of assets	Verification
Notice to appear for a Deposition to disclose assets	

Following the client interview and the signing of the retainer letter, the supervising attorney on the file will delegate to an appropriate staff member the responsibility of preparing the documents that must be filed with the court to initiate the divorce proceeding or other desired family-related suit.

PROCESSING THE DISSOLUTION ACTION

Every jurisdiction has its own rules for the processing of a dissolution or divorce action. The paralegal must become thoroughly familiar with the jurisdictional procedural rules that govern the preparation and filing of dissolution documents, including the prescribed format for these papers as well as the time frames specified for initiating and responding to each document. This information can be found in the jurisdiction's official publications containing the procedural rules of the jurisdiction, commonly known as the **rules of court.** Additional or supplemental information can also frequently be found in the state's official statutory code.

A dissolution is a civil action. As with all civil lawsuits, the action is commenced when the opposing party is served with a document known as either the **complaint** or the **petition.** Whether this document is called a complaint or a petition depends

FIGURE 10–1
Civil lawsuits begin with the filing of a complaint or petition.

on the jurisdiction's preference for one term or the other. In the state of Connecticut, the initial document in a family action is called the complaint, whereas in New York the same document is called a petition. In jurisdictions where the term *complaint* is used, the party commencing the action is called the **plaintiff** and the party against whom the action is brought is called the **defendant.** In jurisdictions where the term *petition* is used, the commencing party is called the **petitioner** and party against whom the action is being brought is called the **respondent.**

INITIAL PLEADINGS IN A DISSOLUTION ACTION

THE PLEADINGS

The documents that state the plaintiff's claims giving rise to the dissolution action and the defendant's responses or defenses to such claims are documents known as **pleadings.** The pleadings in any litigation matter include a *summons* and *complaint* or *petition;* and an *answer, special defenses, counterclaims,* and *cross-claims.*

THE COMPLAINT

The initial pleading filed in a dissolution matter is the **complaint.** As mentioned above, sometimes the initial pleading is called the **petition.** However, because the more commonly used term is complaint, that term will be used here. A document known as a **summons** usually accompanies the complaint. In most jurisdictions, the summons is a one-page preprinted form on which the names and addresses of parties and the name and address of the court are inserted (see Exhibit 10–1). The summons directs the defendant to appear in court and answer the allegations in the complaint. The spouse bringing the dissolution of marriage action is designated as the **plaintiff spouse.** The spouse against whom the dissolution proceeding is brought is designated as the **defendant spouse.** The plaintiff spouse will initiate the legal proceeding.

The law firm representing the plaintiff spouse will file the pleading known as the complaint. In this document, the plaintiff spouse will allege that grounds exist for a divorce, recite these grounds, and request that the court grant a divorce and enter orders regarding the distribution of marital property and, when appropriate, orders relating to child custody, alimony, and child support and orders addressing any other form of relief the spouse has requested.

FORM OF THE DISSOLUTION COMPLAINT

A dissolution or divorce complaint has distinct sections. They are the *caption,* the *body,* the *prayer,* and the *subscription* (some jurisdictions also require a *verification).*

The Caption

The **caption** refers to the initial section of the complaint, which contains the names of the parties, the name and division of the court, the return date of the action and the date the complaint was drawn up. The **return date** is a date in the near future by which the complaint must be returned to the court clerk's office and filed with the court, along with a check for whatever filing fee the jurisdiction requires to process the complaint. A heading is also included to indicate that the document being drafted is a "complaint."

RETURN DATE: August 15, 2001 :	SUPERIOR COURT
RODNEY BRONSON :	JUDICIAL DISTRICT OF NEW HAVEN
v. :	AT NEW HAVEN
EVELYN BRONSON :	July 15, 2001

The Body

The **body** of the complaint contains the necessary factual information that establishes the jurisdiction of the court and identifies the grounds on which the divorce is being sought. In addition, other mandatory information in the body of the complaint includes the names and addresses of the parties, their date and place of marriage, and the names of all minor children born during the period of the marriage.

Complaint

1. The parties intermarried on March 28, 1986, at Woodbridge, Connecticut.

2. The wife's maiden name was EVELYN CONNER.

3. One of the parties has resided in the state of Connecticut for at least twelve months preceding the filing of the complaint.

4. The marriage of the parties has broken down irretrievably and there is no hope of reconciliation.

5. The parties have two minor children born issue of this marriage:

   Marlise Bronson   D.O.B. June 7, 1987

   Sydney Bronson   D.O.B. August 6, 1988

6. No other minor children have been born to the wife since the date of the marriage.

7. Neither party has been the recipient of any form of public assistance.

Prayer for Relief

The **prayer for relief** section of the complaint contains the plaintiff's request for a dissolution and for court orders, when appropriate, regarding property distribution, alimony, child custody, support of the minor children, and the wife's request for restoration of her maiden name. Certain jurisdictions require very specific detail regarding the nature and extent of relief sought while others require a more general statement. In either case, however, it is always a good idea to include a "catch-all" phrase such as "and such other relief as the court deems fair and equitable."

WHEREFORE, the plaintiff claims,

1. A dissolution of marriage

2. Custody of the minor children

3. Child support

4. Alimony

5. An equitable distribution of the marital assets, debts, and liabilities

6. Attorney's fees

7. Such other relief as the court deems fair and equitable.

The Subscription and Verification

The **subscription** and/or **verification** section of the complaint is included to confirm the truth and accuracy of the allegations and to confirm the veracity of the party making these allegations. The subscription contains the signature of the attorney filing the complaint, along with the attorney's address, phone number, and license number, known in some jurisdictions as the **juris number.** When an attorney signs a complaint, the attorney is representing or *subscribing* that to the best of the attorney's knowledge, the facts contained within are true and accurate. In some jurisdictions, the plaintiff bringing the action is also required to sign the complaint and to attest to its veracity. In these instances, the plaintiff will sign a sworn statement, under oath, that the facts contained in the allegations are true. By so doing, the plaintiff is *verifying* that the information is accurate and true. Hence their swearing and signing is termed the verification. A verified complaint used in the state of New York is illustrated in Exhibit 10–2.

THE PLAINTIFF,
RODNEY BRONSON

BY:_____
    Justine F. Miller, Esq.
    His Attorney
    22 Park Place
    New Haven, CT 06511
    (203) 555-4444
    Juries No. 313133

Exhibit 10–3 includes the complaint for dissolution of marriage filed by Lucille Ball against Desi Arnaz on March 3, 1960, in Los Angeles, California.

PREPRINTED COMPLAINT FORM

The computer age has revolutionized the court record-keeping system. Entire court case files are now being kept on disk. This phenomenon has given rise to the creation and use of many preprinted forms in lieu of manuscripted or individually drafted documents. Many jurisdictions are beginning to require that attorneys fit their pleading information into blank portions of uniform preprinted forms which can easily be scanned into the computerized case files in the courthouse. Therefore, the complaint, which is computer compatible now, will contain all of the sections listed above, but these sections will be compressed into the sections of the preprinted complaint form. An example of a preprinted form appears in Exhibit 10–4, which illustrates a complaint for dissolution of marriage in the case of actor Kevin Costner and his former wife Cynthia.

PRE-RETURN DATE RELIEF

Sometimes, a plaintiff spouse needs and may seek immediate relief or court intervention known as **prereturn date relief.** The plaintiff spouse may have serious and real concerns that the act of serving the dissolution complaint on the defendant spouse may cause the defendant spouse to take certain immediate initiatives that will either damage the plaintiff spouse economically or harm the plaintiff physically and/or emotionally.

For instance, when the plaintiff spouse serves a dissolution complaint in which that spouse seeks, as part of the dissolution action, a division of the marital assets and/or alimony and child support, the defendant spouse may attempt to move, hide, or dispose of assets that would be considered assets of the marital union to avoid having to share them or "split" them in their value with the plaintiff spouse.

FIGURE 10–2
Nowadays, pleadings are submitted on preprinted forms that can be easily and quickly scanned into computers at the courthouse.

There may also be assets acquired during the marriage where title rests completely with one partner or the other. For example, title to each family car will usually be in the name of only one spouse. In many jurisdictions, inheritances bequeathed to one spouse or gifts given solely to one spouse are not marital assets. However, practically every other possession acquired during the marriage is a joint asset. The plaintiff spouse may have concerns that the defendant spouse will dispose of bona fide joint property that is not legally registered to both parties. For instance, the defendant spouse may sell an expensive car purchased with marital funds and pocket or bury the money. The defendant spouse who has equal signing power or a joint checking account, a joint savings account, joint CD certificates, or joint stock accounts may attempt to withdraw the contents of these accounts upon being served with divorce papers. To avoid this **dissipation** or squandering of assets, the plaintiff spouse may file along with the dissolution complaint an **application for a prejudgment remedy** to attach marital assets during the period pending litigation.

In many jurisdictions, a plaintiff spouse may apply for an attachment of known joint assets. Sometimes the court will grant a temporary attachment until there is a hearing on the matter; at other times the hearing must occur before even a temporary or *pendente lite* order is issued.

Sometimes a defendant spouse owns a business that the plaintiff spouse has had little hands-on involvement with and, hence, does not know the actual value of the business. The plaintiff spouse may also serve on the defendant, along with a **request for an order attaching known assets,** a **motion for disclosure of assets** to be made under oath. If the plaintiff is not satisfied with the disclosure, later in the discovery phase of the dissolution suit, the plaintiff may serve the defendant with a **notice to appear for a deposition to disclose assets.** In this deposition, the defendant spouse will be questioned, under oath, on the previous disclosure to determine whether it completely reveals all of the defendant's assets.

The format, language, and other requirements for drafting attachment documents vary from jurisdiction to jurisdiction. A paralegal must check local court rules to ensure that the proper format is complied with. Sometimes the local rules or the local practice book has an annotated edition that contains sample forms. Otherwise, litigation form books may be available for the particular state family court system where the action is to be filed. These form books will enable the paralegal to tailor the documents to fit the jurisdiction.

TEMPORARY RESTRAINING ORDER

Sometimes when a plaintiff spouse has decided to file a dissolution action, the plaintiff spouse fears that notice of this action will trigger a response in the defendant spouse which includes being physically and verbally abusive to the plaintiff and possibly to the children as well. A plaintiff spouse may be afraid to return to the family home while the defendant continues to reside there.

Under these circumstances, if the fear is justified, the plaintiff may seek pre-return date relief in the form of a court-ordered **temporary restraining order** to restrain the defendant spouse from entering the family home for a significant number of days. In the application for such a restraining order, the plaintiff spouse will include a signed, sworn statement known as an **affidavit** that certain prior events have occurred and support the plaintiff spouse's belief that a restraining order is needed to keep the spouse safe from grave harm the defendant would otherwise inflict. A set of specific legal documents must be filed with the court in order for the court to consider the plaintiff's request for a restraining order. A paralegal must know what documents are included in this set and be especially careful to include everything needed and to make sure each document is factually and procedurally correct.

Exhibit 10–5 contains a sample set of documents for requesting a temporary restraining order. In addition, Appendix G includes a sample restraining order and affidavit filed by comedienne Roseanne against her former husband Tom Arnold. Again, students should seek model documents from their own jurisdictions to ensure procedural compliance.

SERVICE OF PROCESS OF THE DIVORCE COMPLAINT

Once the law office has prepared the divorce or dissolution summons and complaint, the paralegal may be responsible for seeing that these documents are properly served on the defendant. In most jurisdictions, the divorce complaint, just like the complaint in a regular civil lawsuit, must be served on the defendant named in the action by a statutorily authorized process server. In some jurisdictions, these individuals are called sheriffs or constables, while in other states they are simply referred to as licensed process servers.

A paralegal will contact the office of the sheriff or process server to confirm that the person is available and willing to handle the matter. The paralegal will mail or hand-deliver the papers to be served, or the sheriff, constable, or process server will come to the law office and pick up the papers.

The process server must locate the party to be served and complete service either by delivering the true and attested copies of legal process into the hand of the party, known as **personal service,** or leaving the papers in the hands of a competent adult at the residence or **abode** of the party to be served. Once service is completed, the sheriff or process server will mail or hand-deliver to the law office the original of the summons and complaint along with his written **sheriff's return** in which he affirms that on a specified date, he served the defendant by leaving with the defendant in his hands, at his abode or by mail, a true and attested copy of the summons and complaint. Exhibit 10–6 illustrates California's Proof of Service of Summons in the Costner divorce. The sheriff's or server's bill for services rendered normally accompanies the return.

After the sheriff or process server returns the summons and complaint to the law office, these documents must be brought to the court and filed, along with a fee, known in most jurisdictions as a **filing fee** or a **court-entry fee.** In addition, an increasing number of jurisdictions now require that accompanying documents be filed at the same time as the complaint. These accompanying documents may include a financial affidavit, a custody affidavit, and stipulations regarding the irretrievable breakdown of the marriage.

Once a complaint has been filed, the clerk will assign the case a docket number. This number will be used on all further communications from the court. In addition, the parties should now replace the return date category with the case number in the caption section of all future documents filed with the court in this matter.

FIGURE 10–3
A divorce complaint
must be served on a
defendant by statuto-
rily authorized process
server, which is often
a sheriff or constable.

RESPONSIVE PLEADINGS TO THE DISSOLUTION COMPLAINT

When a spouse is served with divorce or dissolution papers, the spouse must decide what type of responsive action to take or whether to respond at all. The dissolution summons will command the defendant spouse to appear before the court
on or before a certain date, and to do so not by appearing in person, but by filing
a written appearance form or by having the defendant spouse's attorney file a
written **appearance** on his or her behalf.

    If the defendant spouse fails to file an appearance, depending on the court rules
of the particular jurisdiction, the judicial system will handle this failure in one of two
or three different ways. In many states, the defendant spouse's failure to file an appearance can result ultimately in a **default judgment** being entered against that
person. This means that the plaintiff spouse will "win" the dissolution or divorce suit
by default; that is, the plaintiff spouse will be granted a divorce. In addition, if the
court has personal jurisdiction over the defendant spouse, the court, even in the absence of the defendant, may order both spousal support and child support. In this
event, the defendant will be notified by mail of the court's orders. If the defendant

does not make the court-ordered payments and is still within the jurisdiction, the plaintiff spouse may serve the defendant with additional legal papers. These papers, often collectively called an **order to show cause,** will require the defendant to appear under penalty of civil arrest and to show cause or offer a good reason why the defendant should not be penalized or held in **contempt** for not making the court-ordered payments. In this instance, if the defendant spouse again fails to appear in court, the court may and usually will order a capias, which is actually an arrest warrant for committing a civil violation, in this case, a violation of a court order.

If a plaintiff spouse seeks a divorce from a spouse who has fled the jurisdiction or who may still be in the jurisdiction but is "whereabouts unknown" as far as a place of abode or place of employment, then the plaintiff spouse may have a sheriff or process server serve the defendant by what is known as **service by publication.** The sheriff will put a legal notice in the legal notices section of a newspaper in the city, town, or general area where the defendant was last known to reside or where the defendant is thought to be residing. This legal notice will, in fact, be a printing of the text of the divorce or dissolution complaint. Once the notice is published and the newspaper sends the sheriff its **affidavit of publication,** the sheriff will make a return noting the service by publication and return the complaint to the law firm for filing in court. Under these circumstances, after the appropriate waiting period, the plaintiff may seek to have the court formally dissolve the marriage. The plaintiff will appear on a certain date, the court will note that the defendant, served by publication, has failed to appear. The defendant spouse will be defaulted and the divorce or dissolution will be granted. However, the court will not have the authority to enter orders for alimony or child support because the court has no personal jurisdiction over the defendant spouse.

The case of the nonappearing spouse is the exception rather than the rule. Most often, the defendant spouse obtains the services of an attorney who files a written appearance on behalf of the defendant spouse, and who also files responsive pleadings to the dissolution complaint. Naturally, the defendant spouse must contact an attorney or a law firm and have an initial interview with the attorney or firm's officer. The client interview of the defendant spouse will proceed in a manner that is similar to the interview process described for the plaintiff spouse in Chapter 9. If an agreement is reached regarding representation, the defendant spouse will sign a retainer letter with the law office, pay a retainer fee, and the office will begin to draft the responsive pleadings. This task will be delegated to the family law paralegal.

THE APPEARANCE AND THE ANSWER

As mentioned above, the attorney or firm representing the defendant spouse must file an appearance. This appearance is a one-page form that lists the name of the case, the return date, the name of the party being represented, the fact that the party is the defendant in the action, and the name, address, phone number, and juris number of the attorney or law firm. A sample of a typical appearance form is provided in Exhibit 10–7.

The next document to be filed is the **answer.** The answer, like the complaint, will have a caption containing the name of the case and the return date. It will also have a body where each of the allegations contained in the numbered paragraphs in the complaint is responded to. The defendant spouse will either admit or deny each allegation or, in appropriate instances, will state that he or she lacks the necessary information or knowledge on which to form a response. Exhibit 10–8 illustrates a preprinted answer form.

The next section of the answer is the prayer section. In this section, the defendant spouse will make known his or her requests regarding alimony, child support, child custody, and/or visitation. For instance, a defendant spouse may admit that the marriage has broken down irretrievably in the response to the allegations section. However, in the prayer section, the defendant may signal his or her opposition to the plaintiff spouse's requests by requesting full custody of the minor child or children and by requesting child support and alimony. On the other hand, if the defendant spouse does not object to the plaintiff spouse's request for custody, the defendant spouse will request reasonable visitation rights. If the defendant spouse does not wish any alimony, the defendant will remain silent on this issue and deal with the question of the plaintiff spouse's requests for alimony and child support at a later time in the proceedings. The defendant spouse should always request an equitable division of marital property and should request such other relief as the court deems fair and equitable.

The answer, like the complaint, has a subscription section, which lists the defendant spouse's attorney's name and other identifying information. In some jurisdictions, the defendant spouse, like the plaintiff spouse in the complaint, may have to provide a signed and sworn-to verification of the answer.

THE CROSS-COMPLAINT

In most jurisdictions, the defendant-spouse has the right to file an additional pleading called a **cross-complaint.** In the cross-complaint, the defendant spouse assumes the role of a plaintiff by bringing a cross-action or countersuit for dissolution in which the party makes allegations and asks the court to grant him or her the relief of a dissolution or divorce and orders regarding custody, child support, alimony, and property division. Since the advent of no-fault divorce and the fault-neutral ground of irretrievable marital breakdown, cross-complaints have been rarities. Previously, when divorces were granted only on allegation and proof of a fault-based ground or grounds, the spouse sued for divorce on the grounds of mental cruelty or adultery or another negative ground and was frequently countersued by his or her spouse, who alleged a ground of equally negative conduct. This practice has virtually disappeared except in instances where the divorce is very bitter and where either the marital property is extensive or where the custody of the children is hotly contested. A sample cross-complaint appears in Exhibit 10–9. This form serves the purpose for both complaints and cross-complaints in that it contains virtually the same information. If a cross-complaint is filed, then the original plaintiff spouse must file an answer to this pleading that responds to all allegations and contains its own request for relief.

Once all of the above-mentioned documents have been filed with the court, the pleadings are closed, and the pleading phase of the dissolution process is over. Even if the parties have no areas of disagreement, there will be a statutory waiting period before the divorce is granted. In the meantime, whether the parties are in agreement or not, there will be hearings to provide for temporary relief to the parties while the divorce is pending. During this pendency period, the court will entertain motions regarding alimony, child support, child custody, and other pertinent issues. These motions are known as *pendente lite* **motions** and are discussed in the next chapter.

EXHIBIT 10–1
Sample summons.

SUMMONS
FAMILY ACTIONS
JD-FM-3 Rev. 6-94
C.G.S. 52-45a, Pr. Bk 49

STATE OF CONNECTICUT
SUPERIOR COURT

INSTRUCTIONS

CASE TYPE CODES
F00 Dissolution of Marriage
F10 Legal Separation
F20 Annulment
F90 All Other

1. Prepare on typewriter; sign original summons (top sheet) and conform the copies of the summons (sheets 2 and 3).
2. Attach the original summons to the original complaint, and attach a copy of the summons to each copy of the complaint.
3. After service has been made by proper officer, file original papers and officer's return with the clerk of the court at least six days before the return date.
4. Do not use this form for actions in which an attachment or garnishment is being sought or for petitions for paternity or for support orders, or for actions in which an application for relief from abuse is being sought.

TO: Any proper officer
BY AUTHORITY OF THE STATE OF CONNECTICUT, you are hereby commanded to make due and legal service of this Summons and attached Complaint.

JUDICIAL DISTRICT OF	AT (Town)	RETURN DATE (Mo., day, yr.)	
ADDRESS OF COURT (No., Street, City)		CASE TYPE (From code list above) Major ____ Minor ____	PTY NO.
PLAINTIFF'S NAME (Last, First, Middle Initial)	PLAINTIFF'S ADDRESS (No., Street, Town, Zip Code)		01
DEFENDANT'S NAME (Last, First, Middle Initial)	DEFENDANT'S ADDRESS (If known)(No., Street, Town, Zip Code)		50

NOTICE TO THE ABOVE-NAMED DEFENDANT

1. You are being sued.
2. This paper is a Summons in a lawsuit.
3. The Complaint attached to these papers states the claims that the Plaintiff is making against you in this lawsuit.
4. To respond to this Summons, or to be informed of further proceedings, you or your attorney must file a form called an "Appearance" with the Clerk of the above-named Court at the above Court address on or before the second day after the above Return Date.

5. If you or your attorney do not file a written "Appearance" form on time, the Court may enter judgment against you for the relief requested in the Complaint, which may result in temporary or permanent orders without further notice.
6. The "Appearance" form may be obtained at the above Court address.
7. If you have questions about the Summons and Complaint, you should consult an attorney promptly. The Clerk of Court is not permitted to give advice on legal questions.

DATE	SIGNED (Sign and "X" proper box)	☐ Comm. of Superior Court ☐ Assistant Clerk	TYPE IN NAME OF PERSON SIGNING AT LEFT	
FOR THE PLAINTIFF Please enter the appearance of:	NAME OF ATTORNEY OR LAW FIRM (If pro se, name of plaintiff)			JURIS NO. (If atty. or law firm)
MAILING ADDRESS (No., Street, Town, Zip Code)				TELEPHONE NUMBER
SIGNED (Plaintiff, if pro se or attorney for Plaintiff)				

IF THIS SUMMONS IS SIGNED BY A CLERK:

a. The signing has been done so that the Plaintiff will not be denied access to the courts.
b. It is the responsibility of the Plaintiff to see that service is made in the manner provided by law.
c. The clerk is not permitted to give any legal advice in connection with any lawsuit.
d. The clerk signing this summons at the request of the Plaintiff is not responsible in any way for any errors or omissions in the Summons, any allegations contained in the Complaint, or the service thereof.

	FOR COURT USE
	FILE DATE

I hereby certify I have read and understand the above.	SIGNED (Plaintiff, if pro se)	DATE SIGNED	DOCKET NO.

SUMMONS, Family Actions

235

EXHIBIT 10–2

Sample of a verified complaint.

SUPREME COURT OF THE STATE OF NEW YORK

1 **COUNTY OF** _____

---X

2 3   Index No.:

Plaintiff,

-against-   **VERIFIED COMPLAINT**

ACTION FOR DIVORCE

4

Defendant.

---X

5   Plaintiff *herein* / *by* _____, complaining of the Defendant, alleges:

6   **FIRST:** The Plaintiff and the Defendant were married on the date of _____ in the City, Town or Village of _____, in the County of _____, State of _____.

7   **SECOND:**

     ☐ The Plaintiff has lived in New York State for a continuous period in excess of two years immediately preceding the commencement of this action.

     ☐ The Defendant has lived in New York State for a continuous period in excess of two years immediately preceding the commencement of this action.

     ☐ The Plaintiff has lived in New York State for a continuous period in excess of one year and:
         a. ☐ the parties were married in New York State.
         b. ☐ the Plaintiff has lived as husband and wife in New York State with the Defendant.
         c. ☐ the Defendant also has resided in New York State for a continuous period in excess of one year.
         d. ☐ the cause of action occurred in New York State.

     ☐ The Defendant has lived in New York State for a continuous period in excess of one year and:
         a. ☐ the parties were married in New York State.
         b. ☐ the Defendant has lived as husband and wife in New York State with the Plaintiff.
         c. ☐ the cause of action occurred in New York State.

     ☐ The cause of action occurred in New York State and both parties were residents thereof at the time of the commencement of this action.

(Form UD-2)

EXHIBIT 10–2
Continued

8   **THIRD:** There *is (are)* _____ child(ren) of the marriage under the age of twenty-one (21),   namely:

9   <u>Name and Social Security Number</u>   <u>Date of Birth</u>   <u>Address</u>

　　　_____   _____   _____
　　　_____   _____   _____
　　　_____   _____   _____

10   The Plaintiff's address is _____, and social security number is _____. The Defendant's address is _____ _____, and social security number is _____.

11   The parties are covered by the following group health plans:

　　　　<u>Plaintiff</u>　　　　　　　　　　　　　**<u>Defendant</u>**

Group Health Plan:_____   Group Health Plan:_____
Address:_____   Address:_____
Identification Number:_____   Identification Number:_____
Plan Administrator:_____   Plan Administrator:_____
Type of Coverage:_____   Type of Coverage:_____

Group Health Plan:_____   Group Health Plan:_____
Address:_____   Address:_____
Identification Number:_____   Idendification Number:_____
Plan Administrator:_____   Plan Administrator:_____
Type of Coverage:_____   Type of Coverage:_____

12   **FOURTH:** The grounds for divorce are _____ and are based on the following incidents:_____
_____
_____
_____

13   **FIFTH:** There is no judgment in any court for a divorce in favor of either party and against the other and no other matrimonial action for divorce between the parties is pending in any court of competent jurisdiction.

14   **SIXTH:** The marriage was   *not*   performed by a clergyman, minister or by a leader of the Society for Ethical Culture.
- *To the best of my knowledge I have taken all steps solely within my power to remove any barrier to the Defendant's marriage.*
- *I will take prior to the entry of final judgment all steps solely within my power to the best of my knowledge to remove any barrier to the Defendant's remarriage.*
- *The Defendant has waived in writing the requirements of DRL §253.*

(Form UD-2)

EXHIBIT 10–2
Continued

15   **WHEREFORE,** Plaintiff demands judgment against the Defendant as follows: A judgment dissolving the marriage between the parties and_____

_____

_____

16   Dated:_____   _____

17   *Attorney for* Plaintiff:

18   STATE OF NEW YORK, COUNTY OF _____ ss:

     I am the Plaintiff in the within action for a divorce. I have read the foregoing complaint and know the contents thereof.   The contents are true to my own knowledge except as to matters therein stated to be alleged upon information and belief, and as to those matters I believe them to be true.

Sworn to before me on   _____
_____, 19____   Plaintiff

(Form UD-2)

EXHIBIT 10–3

Sample complaint for dissolution.

```
 1   GANG, TYRE, RUDIN & BROWN          FILED           1
     6400 Sunset Building                                2
 2   Los Angeles 28, California     MAR 3 - 1960         3
     HOllywood 3-4863              HAROLD J. OSTLY, County Clerk
 3                                  By  Hn Singletary    4
     Attorneys for Plaintiff                DEPUTY
 4                                                       5
 5                                                       6
 6                                                       7
 7
 8        IN THE SUPERIOR COURT OF THE STATE OF CALIFORNIA   8
 9          IN AND FOR THE COUNTY OF LOS ANGELES            9
10                                                         10
11   LUCILLE BALL ARNAZ,          )                        11
                                  )
12          Plaintiff,            )   SMD. No. _____   12
                                  )
13          -vs.-                 )   COMPLAINT FOR DIVORCE 13
                                  )
14   DESIDERIO ALBERTO ARNAZ, III,)   (Extreme Cruelty)    14
                                  )
15          Defendant.            )                        15
     _____ )
16        Plaintiff complains of defendant and alleges:   16
17                     I.                                  17
18        Plaintiff and defendant were intermarried in    18
19   Greenwich, Connecticut on November 30, 1940.         19
20                    II.                                  20
21        Plaintiff alleges that she has been a resident of   21
22   the County of Los Angeles for more than three years, and of   22
23   the State of California for more than one year next preceding   23
24   the filing of this complaint.                        24
25                    III.                                 25
26        Plaintiff alleges the following facts as required   26
27   by Section 426(a) of the Code of Civil Procedure of the State   27
28   of California:                                       28
29        1.   The parties were intermarried in Greenwich,   29
30   Connecticut.                                         30
31        2.   The date of said marriage was November 30, 1940.   31
32        3.   The date of separation was February 26, 1960.   32
```

EXHIBIT 10-3

Continued

1   4. The time elapsing between the date of marriage   1

2 and the date of separation is nineteen years and three months.   2

3   5. There are two children the issue of said   3

4 marriage, to-wit, Lucie Desiree Arnaz, age 8-1/2 years, and   4

5 Desiderio Alberto Arnaz, IV, age 7 years.   5

6   IV.   6

7   Defendant has been guilty of extreme cruelty to   7

8 plaintiff. As a direct result of such cruelty and conduct   8

9 of defendant, defendant has wrongfully inflicted grievous   9

10 mental suffering upon plaintiff.   10

11   V.   11

12   Plaintiff and defendant are owners of community   12

13 property and there is certain separate property owned by both   13

14 plaintiff and defendant. Plaintiff and defendant have ne-   14

15 gotiated, except in certain minor particulars, a Property   15

16 Settlement Agreement with respect to their property rights   16

17 and interests and their marital rights and obligations. If   17

18 said Property Settlement Agreement is executed by the parties   18

19 prior to the trial of the within action, plaintiff believes   19

20 the same will be fair, just and equitable and will submit the   20

21 same to the Court for approval.   21

22   VI.   22

23   Plaintiff is a fit and proper person to have the   23

24 care and custody of minor children of the parties, subject to   24

25 the right of reasonable visitation of said children by de-   25

26 fendant. The Property Settlement Agreement which the parties   26

27 have negotiated, as hereinabove alleged, will contain pro-   27

28 visions with respect to the support, maintenance and education   28

29 of said minor children which plaintiff believes will be fair,   29

30 just and reasonable, but which provisions shall be subject   30

31 to modification by further order of this Court.   31

32   WHEREFORE, plaintiff prays judgment as follows: 32

EXHIBIT 10–3
Continued

1.   That the bonds of matrimony now existing between plaintiff and defendant be dissolved.

2.   That the custody of said minor children be awarded to plaintiff, subject to the right of reasonable visitation by defendant.

3.   That the Property Settlement Agreement, to be executed by the parties prior to the trial of this action, be approved, confirmed and ratified by the Court and that the parties be ordered to comply with the executory terms and provisions of such agreement.

4.   That the defendant be directed to pay the plaintiff for the support, maintenance and education of the children of plaintiff and defendant such sum as the parties may agree upon in such Property Settlement Agreement, until further order of the Court.

5.   For such other and further relief as the Court may deem equitable in the premises.

GANG, TYRE, RUDIN & BROWN

By _Milton A. Rudin_

Attorneys for Plaintiff

EXHIBIT 10–4
Sample preprinted form illustrating a complaint for dissolution of marriage.

ATTORNEY OR PARTY WITHOUT ATTORNEY (Name and ... g Address): TELEPHONE NO.: (310) 477-5450

GERALD L. FRIEDMAN PROFESSIONAL CORPORAT
State Bar No. 033401
11400 W. Olympic Boulevard, Ninth Floor
Los Angeles, California 90064-1565

ATTORNEY FOR (Name): PETITIONER

FOR COURT USE ONLY

FILED
LOS ANG...
NOV - 4 1994
EDWARD ...
BY G. MENDIZABAL, DEPUTY

SUPERIOR COURT OF CALIFORNIA, COUNTY OF LOS ANGELES
STREET ADDRESS: 111 North Hill Street
MAILING ADDRESS: 111 North Hill Street
CITY AND ZIP CODE: Los Angeles, California 90012
BRANCH NAME: Central District

MARRIAGE OF
PETITIONER: CYNTHIA R. COSTNER
RESPONDENT: KEVIN M. COSTNER

PETITION FOR
[X] Dissolution of Marriage
[ ] Legal Separation
[ ] Nullity of Marriage
[X] And Declaration Under Uniform Child Custody Jurisdiction Act

CASE NUMBER: BD203807

1. RESIDENCE (Dissolution only) [X] Petitioner [ ] Respondent has been a resident of this state for at least six months and of this county for at least three months immediately preceding the filing of this Petition for Dissolution of Marriage.

2. STATISTICAL FACTS
    a. Date of Marriage: February 11, 1978
    b. Date of Separation: June 23, 1994
    c. Period between marriage and separation
       Years: 16   Months: 4
    d. Petitioner's Social Security No.: To Be Furnished
    e. Respondent's Social Security No.: To Be Furnished

3. DECLARATION REGARDING MINOR CHILDREN OF THIS MARRIAGE FOR WHOM SUPPORT MAY BE ORDERED OR WHO MAY BE SUBJECT TO CUSTODY OR VISITATION ORDERS
    a. [ ] There are no minor children.
    b. [X] The minor children are:

Child's name	Birthdate	Age	Sex
Anne C. Costner	4/15/84	10	F
Lily M. Costner	8/4/86	8	F
Joe T. Costner	1/31/88	6	M

    c. IF THERE ARE MINOR CHILDREN, COMPLETE EITHER (1) OR (2)
    (1) [X] Each child named in 3b is currently living with [X] petitioner [ ] respondent
       in the following county (specify): Los Angeles
       During the last five years each child has lived in no state other than California and with no person other than petitioner or respondent or both. Petitioner has not participated in any capacity in any litigation or proceeding in any state concerning custody of any minor child of this marriage. Petitioner has no information of any pending custody proceeding or of any person not a party to this proceeding who has physical custody or claims to have custody or or visitation rights concerning any minor child of this marriage.
    (2) [ ] A completed Declaration Under Uniform Child Custody Jurisdiction Act is attached.

4. [X] Petitioner requests confirmation as separate assets and obligations the items listed
    [ ] In Attachment 4   [X] below:
       Item   Confirm to
       Per Agreement of the parties   Each of the parties

(Continued on reverse)

Form Adopted by Rule 1281
Judicial Council of California
1281 (Rev. January 1, 1994)

PETITION
(Family Law)

Family Code, §§ 2330, 3409
Cal. Rules of Court, rule 1215

ORIGINAL

EXHIBIT 10–4
Continued

ORIGINAL

MARRIAGE OF (last name, first name of parties):	CASE NUMBER:
COSTNER, CYNTHIA R. and KEVIN M.	

5. DECLARATION REGARDING COMMUNITY AND QUASI-COMMUNITY ASSETS AND OBLIGATIONS AS CURRENTLY KNOWN

   a. ☐ There are no such assets or obligations subject to disposition by the court in this proceeding.

   b. ☒ All such assets and obligations have been disposed of by written agreement.

   c. ☐ All such assets and obligations are listed ☐ in Attachment 5 ☐ below (specify):

6. Petitioner requests

   a. ☒ Dissolution of the marriage based on
      (1) ☒ irreconcilable differences. FC 2310(a)
      (2) ☐ incurable insanity. FC 2310(b)

   b. ☐ Legal separation of the parties based on
      (1) ☐ irreconcilable differences. FC 2310(a)
      (2) ☐ incurable insanity. FC 2310(b)

   c. ☐ Nullity of void marriage based on
      (1) ☐ incestuous marriage. FC 2200
      (2) ☐ bigamous marriage. FC 2201

   d. ☐ Nullity of voidable marriage based on
      (1) ☐ petitioner's age at time of marriage. FC 2210(a)
      (2) ☐ prior existing marriage. FC 2210(b)
      (3) ☐ unsound mind. FC 2210(c)
      (4) ☐ fraud. FC 2210(d)
      (5) ☐ force. FC 2210(e)
      (6) ☐ physical incapacity. FC 2210(f)

7. Petitioner requests that the court grant the above relief and make injunctive (including restraining) and other orders as follows:

		Petitioner	Respondent	Joint	Other
a.	Legal custody of children to Per Agreement of the parties	☐	☐	☒	☐
b.	Physical custody of children to Per Agreement of the parties	☐	☐	☒	☐
c.	Child visitation be granted to Per Agreement of the parties	☐	☐	☐	☐
	☐ supervised as to (specify):				
d.	Spousal support payable by (wage assignment will be issued)	☐	☐		
e.	Attorney fees and costs payable by Per Agreement of parties	☐	☐		
f.	☐ Terminate the court's jurisdiction (ability) to award spousal support to respondent.				
g.	☒ Property rights be determined. Per Agreement of the parties				
h.	☐ Wife's former name be restored (specify):				
i.	☐ Other (specify):				

8. If there are minor children of this marriage, the court will make orders for the support of the children without further notice to either party. A wage assignment will be issued.

9. ' I have read the restraining orders on the back of the Summons, and I understand that they apply to me when this petition is filed.

I declare under penalty of perjury under the laws of the State of California that the foregoing is true and correct.

Date: October 25, 1994

                                     ► ✓ _Cynthia R. Cost_
                                        (SIGNATURE OF PETITIONER)

                            CYNTHIA R. COSTNER

GERALD L. FRIEDMAN   ► _Gerald L. Friedman_
(TYPE OR PRINT NAME OF ATTORNEY)   (SIGNATURE OF ATTORNEY FOR PETITIONER)

NOTICE: Please review your will, insurance policies, retirement benefit plans, credit cards, other credit accounts and credit reports, and other matters you may want to change in view of the dissolution or annulment of your marriage, or your legal separation. However, some changes may require the agreement of your spouse or a court order (see Family Code sections 231-235).

1281 (Rev. January 1, 1994)

PETITION
(Family Law)

Page two

EXHIBIT 10–5
Sample documents requesting a temporary restraining order.

STATE OF CONNECTICUT
SUPERIOR COURT

**APPLICATION FOR
RELIEF FROM ABUSE** JD-FM-78 Rev. 6-89 C.G.S. 46b-15, 52-259

INSTRUCTIONS TO APPLICANT	1. Prepare on typewriter or print in ink. 2. File completed original with the clerk of court.

INSTRUCTIONS TO CLERK	1. Assign a hearing date not later than 14 days from filing date.
	2. If Ex Parte Order entered, retain original for court file and distribute 5 copies as follows:
	  • One copy to respondent • One copy to Family Division • Two certified copies to applicant
	  • One certified copy to appropriate law enforcement agency WITHIN FORTY-EIGHT (48) HOURS OF ISSUANCE OF THIS ORDER.

TO: The Superior Court   AT *(Address of court)*

☐ "X" here if a Protective Order has been entered affecting any person who is a party to this application.

PROVIDE NAMES OF ATTORNEYS FOR ANY PARTY CONNECTED WITH THIS ACTION

NAME OF APPLICANT *(Your name)*   ADDRESS WHERE MAIL WILL REACH YOU

NAME AND ADDRESS OF RESPONDENT *(Person against whom you are bringing this case)*   RESPONDENT'S TELEPHONE NO. *(If known)*

RESPONDENT IS: ("X" all that apply)

☐ my spouse   ☐ my child
☐ my former spouse   ☐ a person 18 or over related to me by blood or marriage
☐ parent of my child   ☐ a person 16 or over with whom I reside or with whom I have resided
☐ my parent   ☐ a caretaker who is providing shelter in his or her residence to a person 60 years of age or older

AFFIDAVIT

I, the above-named applicant, represent that the information contained herein is correct and that I have been subjected to a continuous threat of present physical pain or physical injury by the respondent named above. *(You must attach an affidavit made under oath which includes a statement of the conditions from which you seek relief. Include specific examples with dates.)*

Wherefore I request that the court enjoin the respondent from:

☐ IMPOSING ANY RESTRAINT ON ME
☐ ASSAULTING, MOLESTING, SEXUALLY ASSAULTING OR, ATTACKING ME
☐ ENTERING THE FAMILY DWELLING OR MY CURRENT DWELLING, TO WIT:
  (NOTE: The address provided here will be included on any orders entered by the court. If you do not wish to divulge your address, do not complete this box. However, failure to include this information may limit the protection afforded you by the restraining order.)
  ADDRESS OF DWELLING

and that the court order the following additional relief:

☐ THAT THE COURT DO THE FOLLOWING: _____

_____

_____

| ☐ THAT THE RELIEF REQUESTED ABOVE EXTEND TO THE FOLLOWING DEPENDENT CHILDREN AND/OR OTHER PERSONS: *(Specify names and relationship to applicant)* | **FOR COURT USE ONLY**
DOCKET NO.

FILE DATE |

(CONTINUED ON REVERSE SIDE)

EXHIBIT 10–5
Continued

☐ AWARD ME TEMPORARY CUSTODY OF THE FOLLOWING MINOR CHILD(REN) WHO IS (ARE) ALSO THE CHILD(REN) OF THE RESPONDENT:

	NAME	DATE OF BIRTH		NAME	DATE OF BIRTH
1.			4.		
2.			5.		
3.			6.		

REQUEST FOR EX PARTE RELIEF

☐ I believe there is an immediate and present physical danger to me and therefore request that relief be ordered immediately. I understand that the court will schedule a hearing no later than 14 days after such order is entered on the question of continuing such temporary order. I also understand that such temporary order is only effective until the time of the hearing to be scheduled and that a postponement of such hearing which is requested and granted will not continue such order except upon agreement of the parties or by order of the court for good cause shown.

I understand that the relief requested, other than relief ordered ex parte, may be ordered for a period of up to 90 days but that such order may, upon motion be extended beyond 90 days by the court.

SIGNED (Applicant)	Subscribed and sworn to before me:	(Judge, Asst. Clerk, Notary, Comm. Sup. Ct.)	ON (Date)

ORDER FOR HEARING AND NOTICE

The foregoing application having been presented to the court, it is hereby ordered that a hearing be held thereon at the court location shown below, and that the applicant give notice to the respondent of this application and order and of the date and time set for the hearing not less than five days before the date of the hearing.

JUDICIAL DISTRICT OF	ADDRESS OF COURT (Number, street and town)	DATE AND TIME OF HEARING

DATE AT (Town)	ON (Date)	BY ORDER OF THE COURT:	SIGNED (Assistant Clerk)

TO ANY PROPER OFFICER,
    By authority of the State of Connecticut you are hereby commanded to serve a true and attested copy of the foregoing application and order upon the respondent according to law not less than five days before the hearing date shown above.

DATED AT (Town)	ON (Date)	SIGNED (Asst. Clerk, Comm. of Sup. Ct.)

NOTICE TO RESPONDENT

A hearing on this application for relief from abuse has been scheduled by the court. At this hearing, the court may order relief as requested in this application. If you wish to be heard concerning this application, you should appear at the above court location on the date and time shown above.

EXHIBIT 10–5

Continued

EX PARTE RESTRAINING ORDER

Having considered the application for relief from abuse and affidavit filed by the applicant named herein, it is hereby ordered effective immediately:

☐ 1. That the respondent refrain from imposing any restraint on the applicant.

☐ 2. That the respondent refrain from assaulting, molesting, sexually assaulting or attacking the applicant.

☐ 3. That the respondent refrain from entering the dwelling of the applicant.

ADDRESS OF DWELLING

☐ 4. That the custody of the minor child(ren) who is/are issue of the applicant and the respondent, specifically:

NAME(S) OF CHILD(REN)

is granted to _____ subject to visitation rights granted to

_____ as follows: _____

_____

_____

☐ 5. And it is further ordered: _____

_____

_____

_____

_____

_____

An EX PARTE ORDER is only effective until the hearing date unless extended by agreement of the parties or by order of the court for good cause shown.

This order may be extended by the court beyond 90 days. In accordance with General Statute section 53a-107, entering or remaining in a building or any other premises in violation of this order constitutes criminal trespass in the first degree. This is a criminal offense punishable by a term of imprisonment of not more than one year, a fine of not more than one thousand dollars or both.

SIGNED (Judge)	DATE	DATE OF HEARING

CERTIFICATION

STATE OF CONNECTICUT

Judicial District of _____ ss. _____

I hereby certify that the foregoing is a true copy of the application, order for hearing and notice and ex parte restraining order in the herein-named cause, as on file and of record appears.

In witness whereof, I have hereunto set my hand and the seal

of said court on _____

_____
Clerk of the Superior Court

EXHIBIT 10–5

Continued

RETURN OF SERVICE

STATE OF CONNECTICUT

JUDICIAL DISTRICT OF	NAME OF RESPONDENT	DATE
SS.		

Then and there by virtue of the foregoing, I left with and in the hands of the above-named respondent a true and attested copy of the original application, order for hearing and notice and ex parte restraining order.

The within and foregoing is the original application, order for hearing and notice and ex parte restraining order with my doings thereon endorsed.

Attest _____

(Name and Title)

FEES

COPY _____

ENDORSEMENT _____

SERVICE _____

TRAVEL _____

TOTAL _____

EXHIBIT 10–6

Sample proof of service document.

MARRIAGE OF (last name, first name of parties):	CASE NUMBER:
COSTNER, Cynthia R. and Kevin M.	BD 203 807

Serve a copy of the documents on the person to be served. Complete the proof of service. Attach it to the original documents. File them with the court.

PROOF OF SERVICE OF SUMMONS (Family Law)

1. I served the Summons with Standard Restraining Orders (Family Law), blank Response, and Petition (Family Law) on respondent (name): **Kevin M. Costner**
   a. with (1) [XX] blank Confidential Counseling Statement   (4) [XX] ~~completed~~ blank Income and
   (2) [ ] Order to Show Cause and Application   Expense Declarations
   (3) [ ] blank Responsive Declaration   (5) [ ] completed and blank Property Declarations
                                                              (6) [XX] Other (specify): **Certificate of Assignment**

   b. [ ] By leaving copies with (name and title or relationship to person served):

   c. [ ] By delivery at [ ] home [ ] business
   (1) Date of: (3) Address:
   (2) Time of:

   d. [XX] By mailing (1) Date of: 11/7/94   (2) Place of: **Los Angeles, CA**

2. Manner of service: (Check proper box)
   a. [ ] **Personal service.** By personally delivering copies to the person served. (CCP 415.10)
   b. [ ] **Substituted service on natural person, minor, incompetent.** By leaving copies at the dwelling house, usual place of abode, or usual place of business of the person served in the presence of a competent member of the household or a person apparently in charge of the office or place of business, at least 18 years of age, who was informed of the general nature of the papers, and thereafter mailing (by first-class mail, postage prepaid) copies to the person served at the place where the copies were left. (CCP 415.20(b)) (Attach separate declaration stating acts relied on to establish reasonable diligence in first attempting personal service.)
   c. [XX] **Mail and acknowledge service.** By mailing (by first-class mail or airmail) copies to the person served, together with two copies of the form of notice and acknowledgment and a return envelope, postage prepaid, addressed to the sender. (CCP 415.30) (Attach completed acknowledgment of receipt.)
   d. [ ] **Certified or registered mail service.** By mailing to address outside California (by registered or certified airmail with return receipt requested) copies to the person served. (CCP 415.40) (Attach signed return receipt or other evidence of actual delivery to the person served.)
   e. [ ] **Other** (specify code section):
   [ ] Additional page is attached.

3. The NOTICE TO THE PERSON SERVED on the summons was completed as follows (CCP 412.30, 415.10, and 474):
   a. [XX] as an individual
   b. [ ] on behalf of Respondent
   under [ ] CCP 416.90 (Individual) [ ] CCP 416.70 (Ward or Conservatee) [ ] CCP 416.60 (Minor)
   [ ] Other (specify):
   c. [ ] by personal delivery on (date):

4. At the time of service I was at least 18 years of age and not a party to this action.
5. Fee for service: $ –0–
6. Person serving:
   a. [XX] Not a registered California process server.   e. [ ] California sheriff, marshal, or constable.
   b. [ ] Registered California process server.   f. Name, address, and telephone number and, if
   c. [ ] Employee or independent contractor of a   applicable, county of registration and number:
      registered California process server.   Gerald L. Friedman
   d. [ ] Exempt from registration under Bus. & Prof.   11400 W. Olympic Blvd., 9th Fl.
      Code section 22350(b).   Los Angeles, CA 90064-1565
                                                              (310) 477-5450

I declare under penalty of perjury under the laws of the State   (For California sheriff, marshal, or constable use only)
of California that the foregoing is true and correct.   I certify that the foregoing is true and correct.
Date: 4-26-95   Date:

▶ *Gerald L. Friedman*   ▶
      (SIGNATURE)   (SIGNATURE)

Form Adopted by Rule 1283.5   **PROOF OF SERVICE OF SUMMONS**
Judicial Council of California   **(Family Law)**
1283.5 [New January 1, 1991]
          1283.5   BD108

EXHIBIT 10–7

Sample appearance form.

APPEARANCE

JD-CL-12 Rev. 6-98

Pr. Bk. §§ 3-1 thru 3-6, 3-8

STATE OF CONNECTICUT
SUPERIOR COURT

INSTRUCTIONS

1. *Judicial District Court Locations:* In any action returnable to a Judicial District court location, file only the original with the clerk. In criminal actions see instruction #3.
2. *Geographical Area Locations:* In any action returnable to a Geographical Area court location, except criminal actions, file original and sufficient copies for each party to the action with the clerk. In criminal actions see instruction #3.
3. *In Criminal and Motor Vehicle Actions (Pr. Bk. Secs. 3-4, 3-5):* Mail or deliver a copy of the appearance to the prosecuting authority, complete the certification at bottom and file original with the clerk.
4. *In Summary Process Actions:* In addition to instruction #1 or #2 above, mail a copy to the attorney for the plaintiff, or if there is no such attorney, to the plaintiff and complete the certification below.
5. For *"In-lieu-of"* Appearances (Pr. Bk. Sec. 3-8): Complete the certification below.
6. Pursuant to Pr. Bk. Sec. 17-20, if a party who has been defaulted for failure to appear files an appearance prior to the entry of judgment after default, the default shall automatically be set aside by the clerk.
7. *In Juvenile Matters:* Do not use this form. Use form JD-JM-13 Appearance, Juvenile Matters.

DOCKET NO.
RETURN DATE

NAME OF CASE *(FIRST-NAMED PLAINTIFF VS. FIRST- NAMED DEFENDANT)*

☐ Judicial District	☐ Housing Session	☐ G.A. No. ____	ADDRESS OF COURT *(No., street, town and zip code)*

▼ **PLEASE ENTER THE APPEARANCE OF** ▼

NAME OF OFFICIAL, FIRM, PROFESSIONAL CORP., INDIVIDUAL ATTY., OR PRO SE PARTY *(See "Notice to Pro Se Parties" at bottom)*

MAILING ADDRESS *(No., street, P.O. Box)*		JURIS NO. *(If applicable)*
CITY/TOWN	STATE ZIP CODE	TELEPHONE NO.

in the above-entitled case for: *("X" one of the following)*

FAX NO.

☐ The Plaintiff.
☐ All Plaintiffs
☐ The following Plaintiff(s) only: _____

☐ The Defendant.
☐ The Defendant for the purpose of the bail hearing only *(in criminal and motor vehicle cases only).*
☐ All Defendants.
☐ The following Defendant(s) only: _____

Note: If other counsel have already appeared for the party or parties indicated above, state whether this appearance is:

☐ In lieu of appearance of attorney or firm _____ already on file (P.B. Sec. 3-8) **OR**

☐ In addition to appearance already on file.   *(Name)*

SIGNED *(Individual attorney or pro se party)* X	NAME OF PERSON SIGNING AT LEFT *(Print or type)*	DATE SIGNED

CERTIFICATION	*FOR COURT USE ONLY*

This certification must be completed in summary process cases (Pr. Bk. Sec. 3-5(a)); for *"in lieu of"* appearances (Pr. Bk. Sec. 3-8); and in criminal cases (Pr. Bk. Sec. 3-5(d)).

I hereby certify that a copy of the above was mailed/delivered to:

☐ All counsel and pro se parties of record. *(For summary process and criminal actions)*
☐ Counsel or the party whose appearance is to be replaced. *(For "in lieu of" appearances)*

SIGNED *(Individual attorney or pro se party)* X	DATE COPY(IES) MAILED OR DELIVERED
NAME OF EACH PARTY SERVED *	ADDRESS AT WHICH SERVICE WAS MADE

* If necessary, attach additional sheet with names of each party served and the address at which service was made.

> **NOTICE TO PRO SE PARTIES**
> A pro se party is a person who represents himself or herself. It is your responsibility to inform the Clerk's Office if you have a change of address.

APPEARANCE

EXHIBIT 10–8

Sample preprinted answer form.

DIVORCE (DISSOLUTION OF MARRIAGE) ANSWER JD-FM-160 New 6-98 P.B. § 25-9	STATE OF CONNECTICUT SUPERIOR COURT **INSTRUCTIONS** Complete the form below and file it with the Court Clerk. If you are the defendant, you must also file an Appearance form (JD-CL-12). You may also file a Cross-Complaint (JD-FM-159) to tell the Court what you want the judge to order.	COURT USE ONLY **ANSWER**

☐ **Answer to Divorce (Dissolution of Marriage) Complaint**

☐ **Answer to Divorce (Dissolution of Marriage) Cross-Complaint**

JUDICIAL DISTRICT OF	AT (Town)	RETURN DATE (Mo., day, yr.)
PLAINTIFF'S NAME (Last, First, Middle Initial)	**DEFENDANT'S NAME** (Last, First, Middle Initial)	DOCKET NO.

Number each line in the chart below to match the numbered paragraphs in the Complaint or Cross-Complaint (example: 1, 2, 3, 4, 5a, 5b). Use as many lines as you need. For each paragraph, mark an "X" for Agree, Disagree, or Do Not Know

PARAGRAPH. NO.	AGREE	DISAGREE	DO NOT KNOW

The Court is asked to order: *(Check all that apply)*

☐ A divorce (dissolution of marriage)   ☐ Name change to _____

☐ A fair division of property and debts   ☐ Sole custody

☐ Alimony   ☐ Joint legal custody:

☐ Child Support   ☐ Shared residence

☐ Visitation   ☐ Primary residence with:

_____

And anything else the Court thinks is fair.

I certify that this Answer is true to the best of my knowledge and that a copy of this Answer will be mailed or delivered TODAY to anyone who has filed an Appearance form in this case.

SIGNATURE	PRINTED NAME	DATE SIGNED

ADDRESS (No., street, town or city, zip code)

NAME AND ADDRESS OF EACH PERSON TO WHOM A COPY WAS MAILED OR DELIVERED

EXHIBIT 10–9
Sample cross-complaint.

**DIVORCE (DISSOLUTION OF MARRIAGE)
COMPLAINT/CROSS COMPLAINT**
JD-FM-159 New 10-97
C.G.S. §46b-40, et seq.
P.B. § 1201, et seq.

**STATE OF CONNECTICUT
SUPERIOR COURT**

CROSS COMPLAINT CODE ONLY
CRSCMP

☐ *Complaint: Complete this form. Attach a completed Summons (JD-FM-3) and Notice of Automatic
Court Orders (JD-FM-158).*

☐ *Cross Complaint: Complete this form and attach to the Answer (JD-FM-160) unless it is already filed.*

JUDICIAL DISTRICT OF	AT *(Town)*	RETURN DATE *(Month, day, year)*
PLAINTIFF'S NAME *(Last, First, Middle Initial)*	DEFENDANT'S NAME *(Last, First, Middle Initial)*	
1. WIFE'S BIRTH NAME *(First, Middle Initial, Last)*	2. HUSBAND'S NAME *(First, Middle Initial, Last)*	
3. DATE OF MARRIAGE	4. TOWN AND STATE, OR COUNTRY WHERE MARRIAGE TOOK PLACE	

5. *(Check all that apply)*

☐ The husband or the wife has lived in Connecticut for at least twelve months before the filing of this divorce complaint or before the divorce will become final.

☐ The husband or the wife lived in Connecticut at the time of the marriage, moved away, and then returned to Connecticut, planning to live here permanently.

☐ The marriage broke down after the wife or the husband moved to Connecticut.

6. A divorce is being sought because: *(Check all that apply)*

☐ This marriage has broken down irretrievably and there is no possibility of getting back together. **(No fault divorce)**

☐ Other *(must be reason(s) listed in Connecticut General Statute § 46b-40(c)):*

_____

_____

Check and complete all that apply for items 7-13. Attach additional sheets if needed.

7. ☐ No children were born to the wife after the date of this marriage.

8. ☐ The following children have been born to the wife before, on or after the date of this marriage and the husband is the father. (List only children under 18 years old or 18 and still in high school.)

NAME OF CHILD *(First, middle, last)*	DATE OF BIRTH *(Month, day year)*

9. ☐ The following children were born to the wife **after** the date of the marriage and the husband **is not the father.** *(List only children under 18 years old or 18 and still in high school.)*

NAME OF CHILD *(First, middle, last)*	DATE OF BIRTH *(Month, day, year)*

(OVER)

EXHIBIT 10–9

Continued

10. ☐ The wife is pregnant with a child due to be born on (date) _____ .

      The father of this unborn child is (check one)   ☐ the husband   ☐ not the husband   ☐ unknown.

11. If there is a court order about any child listed above, name the child(ren) below and the person or agency awarded custody or providing support:

CHILD'S NAME	NAME OF PERSON OR AGENCY
CHILD'S NAME	NAME OF PERSON OR AGENCY
CHILD'S NAME	NAME OF PERSON OR AGENCY

12. The husband, the wife, or any of the children listed above has received financial support from the State of Connecticut. *(Check one)*   ☐ Yes   ☐ No   ☐ Do not know
If yes, send a copy of this Complaint and the Notice of Automatic Court Orders to the Assistant Attorney General, 55 Elm Street, Hartford, CT 06106.

13. The husband, the wife, or any of the children listed above has received financial support from a city or town in Connecticut. *(Check one)*   ☐ Yes *(State city or town:_____)*   ☐ No   ☐ Do not know

The Court is asked to order: *(Check all that apply)*

☐ A divorce (dissolution of marriage)   ☐ Name change to _____

☐ A fair division of property and debts   ☐ Sole custody

☐ Alimony   ☐ Joint legal custody:

☐ Child Support   ☐ Shared residence

☐ Visitation   ☐ Primary residence with:

         And anything else the Court thinks is fair.

SIGNATURE	PRINT NAME OF PERSON SIGNING	DATE SIGNED
ADDRESS		TELEPHONE

- *IF THIS IS A COMPLAINT, ATTACH A COPY OF THE AUTOMATIC COURT ORDERS BEFORE SERVING A COPY ON THE DEFENDANT.*

- *IF THIS IS A CROSS COMPLAINT, YOU MUST MAIL OR DELIVER A COPY TO ANYONE WHO HAS FILED AN APPEARANCE AND YOU MUST COMPLETE THE CERTIFICATION BELOW.*

I certify the following:

DATE COPY MAILED OR DELIVERED	SIGNATURE
NAME OF EACH PERSON SERVED*	ADDRESS WHERE SERVICE WAS MADE (*No., street, town, zip code)**

*If necessary, attach additional sheet with names of each party served and the address at which service was made.

JD-FM-159 (Back) New 10-97

REVIEW QUESTIONS

1. What are procedural rules?
2. What are the rules of court?
3. How is a dissolution or divorce proceeding commenced?
4. Define the terms *plaintiff* and *defendant* and discuss how and to whom these terms apply in a family law proceeding.
5. Name each of the pleadings filed in a dissolution or divorce proceeding and identify which party files each of the pleadings.
6. What is a summons?
7. List the sections of a dissolution or divorce complaint.
8. What is a return date?
9. Define the term *filing fee*.
10. What is the name of the complaint section that lists the relief the plaintiff seeks?
11. What does the family law attorney represent to the court when she signs the complaint? What is the signing called and where does it occur in the complaint?
12. What is the verification section of the complaint?
13. What is meant by pre-return date relief?
14. List three types of pre-return date relief that a plaintiff might request.
15. Give three examples of assets that either party might wish to hide or dispose of when served with divorce papers.
16. What is an application for a prejudgment remedy?
17. Describe a motion for disclosure of assets. Which party usually files this document?
18. What is a deposition to disclose assets and under what circumstances might a party use this procedure?
19. What can the plaintiff spouse do to protect him- or herself from any physical or verbal abuse that the defendant spouse might attempt to inflict on the plaintiff spouse?
20. What are the paralegal's responsibilities for arranging service of the dissolution or divorce complaint?
21. What information should the paralegal provide to the sheriff or constable to ensure that the divorce or dissolution complaint will be served in a proper and timely manner?
22. What is the difference between *personal service* and *abode service?*
23. What does a sheriff include on his return?
24. What is a court appearance form and what information must be included on it?
25. What happens in a dissolution proceeding if a defendant fails to file an appearance?
26. What is service by publication and when is this form of service used in a dissolution or divorce action?
27. What are the disadvantages for the plaintiff spouse who obtains a divorce decree in a proceeding where the defendant spouse has failed to enter an appearance?
28. Name and describe the pleading that the appearing defendant spouse files in response to the dissolution or divorce complaint. In which section of this pleading does the respondent spouse make his or her request for relief?
29. What is a cross-complaint, when is it filed, and who files it?
30. Describe how matters such as child support, child custody, and alimony are handled between the time the dissolution or divorce complaint is served and the time the court enters a final decree of dissolution or divorce.

EXERCISES

1. Locate a copy of the rules of court for your jurisdiction. Find the section of procedural rules for family matters. List the section numbers that govern the filing of the dissolution complaint and the answer to the complaint. Also, locate the sections that deal with service of the complaint, service of the answer, and time limits for the respondent to file an appearance and answer. Summarize each section.

2. In the family matters section of the rules of court for your jurisdiction, see if the topic of the return date is addressed. If so, list the section number and summarize it. If not, look in the book's index for the section that contains the rules for proceedings in the civil division of the court. Find the approximate section number on return dates; list and summarize this section.

3. In your state's statutes, locate the title or chapter dealing with family matters. List and summarize the statutory sections that deal with the filing and serving of the complaint and answer.

4. In your state's statutes family matters section, find, list, and summarize the sections that address when and where the family court has the jurisdiction to hear a matter and what conditions are needed for a family law court to have jurisdiction over a respondent spouse.

5. In your local law library, find the forms or form books that contain sample complaints and answers as they appear in your state or jurisdiction. Prepare a complaint and answer using these forms as a model.

6. Using your state's statutes, your state's rules of court, and any helpful form books, prepare all the documents needed to file an application for a prejudgment remedy in a family matter in your jurisdiction.

7. Prepare an affidavit to be used in applying for a temporary restraining order (TRO) in a family law matter. Be sure to include sufficient compelling facts to ensure that the TRO will be granted.

PENDENTE LITE MOTIONS AND ORDERS

KEY TERMS

Body

Caption

Certification

Child support guidelines

Cooling-off period

Court calendar

Custody affidavit

Deny

Docket control system

Grant

Motion day

Motion for alimony, *pendente lite*

Motion for child support, *pendente lite*

Motion for contempt

Motion for counsel fees

Motion for custody, *pendente lite*

Motion for exclusive possession of the marital residence, *pendente lite*

Motion for modification

Motion for payment of mortgage payments and insurance premiums, *pendente lite*

Motion for use of motor vehicle, *pendente lite*

Motion for visitation

Motion to freeze marital assets

Motion to restrain party from entering marital residence

Moving party

Order

Pendente lite motion

Pro per

Pro se

Restraining order

Short calendar

Signature (subscription)

In the United States, there is no such thing as an instant divorce. Every jurisdiction has some type of **cooling-off period** that must elapse before a final divorce decree may be entered. The term *cooling-off period* refers to the statutorily mandated time period following the initiation of divorce proceedings during which no final decree may be entered. This period usually runs for a number of months depending on the jurisdiction.

In many instances, the divorce decree is not issued immediately after the cooling-off period has expired. This is so because divorce presents many complex issues that the parties must resolve or the court must resolve for them. In addition, the parties' respective attorneys' calendars must be accommodated and the court calendar must be considered. The judicial system provides vehicles through which the parties may seek and obtain court orders to determine how the obligations of the marriage partnership may be fulfilled during the time frame. One spouse or the other may use such vehicles to obtain relief on the issues of spousal support, maintenance and custody of the minor children, use of the family residence, protection from an abusive or violent spouse, and arrangements for paying bills to creditors for obligations the marital unit incurred.

The paralegal working in a family law practice plays an important role in facilitating relief for his or her client. Specific documents must be prepared and filed with the court to provide temporary relief for the client seeking such assistance. These documents are called *pendent lite* **motions.**

PENDENTE LITE MOTIONS

Pendente lite is a Latin term meaning "during the litigation." The term *temporary* is also used interchangeably when describing *pendente lite* motions. While a divorce action is pending, the court, upon a party's motion, will consider entering certain orders with which the parties must comply from the time the order is entered until the entry of final orders at the time of the divorce decree.

ANATOMY OF A MOTION

The family law division of every U.S. jurisdiction has certain requirements regarding the form and manner in which motions should be filed. The local rules of practice provide guidelines and sometimes sample forms to follow. In addition, law libraries have many types of form books, which display typical motions, and law offices typically have forms on disk and hardcopy, which can be modified for use in specific cases.

Although specifics vary from jurisdiction to jurisdiction and from case to case, motions have general features common to all jurisdictions: All motions have a *caption,* a *body* and a *signature* or *subscription* section; further, most state court systems require a separate *order* page and a *certification* page.

CAPTION

The **caption** section of a motion must have the docket number, the names of the parties, the name of the court, its geographical location, and the date the motion was filed. This information is arranged either in a block form or modified block form. The action will also contain the title or heading of the motion. The title will appear a few spaces down from the other information and usually will be centered and either underlined, printed in bold, or both.

EXAMPLE

DOCKET NO. FA 96-123456	:	SUPERIOR COURT
BRONSON, RODNEY HAVEN	:	JUDICIAL DISTRICT OF NEW
v.	:	AT NEW HAVEN
BRONSON, EVELYN	:	AUGUST 15, 2000

MOTION FOR RETURN OF PERSONAL PROPERTY

▼   ▼   ▼

BODY

The **body** of the motion identifies the party filing the motion, the relief specifically requested, and the grounds or basis on which relief is requested.

EXAMPLE

The plaintiff-husband respectfully moves for an order requiring the defendant-wife to turn over to the plaintiff-husband and permit him to retrieve from the marital house, the following items of personal property:

1. Golf clubs

2. Grandmother's rocking chair

▼   ▼   ▼

SUBSCRIPTION

The **signature** or **subscription** section lists in block form the designation given to the party in the lawsuit, namely, whether the party is the plaintiff or defendant in the action, the actual name of the party, and then a signature line, the name of the attorney acting on the party's behalf, followed by the attorney's address, license number, and usually her phone number.

If a party is bringing the action himself or herself without benefit of counsel, the party is said to be acting **pro se** or **pro per.** In such a case, the words *pro se* appear underneath the party's name and then the party's own address and phone number are listed.

EXAMPLE

THE PLAINTIFF, RODNEY BRONSON

BY_____
JUSTINE F. MILLER, ESQ.
HIS ATTORNEY
22 PARK PLACE
NEW HAVEN, CT 06511
(203) 861-4444
JURIS NO. 313133

▼   ▼   ▼

ORDER

An **order** is a statement that sets forth the judge's decision on a particular motion before the court. When drafting a motion, an order is included for convenience of the court and may even be required in many jurisdictions.

In many areas of law, the order page of a motion simply contains the title "ORDER" and the following language: "The foregoing motion having been heard, it is hereby ORDERED: GRANTED/DENIED." In family law, the order page frequently contains more specific and more elaborate directives. For instance, the order page accompanying a motion for alimony may contain the statement that the defendant pay to plaintiff spouse the sum of a specific dollar amount at a specific interval, such as $100 a week. The order for child support is usually similarly specific.

Motions for visitation frequently set the number of times for visiting each week and the house where such visits will take place. This is done if the parties have concerns about the duration, frequency, and location of visits, and have not been able to work out these arrangements informally. Where parties have no differences on the issue, an order for reasonable visitation will suffice.

EXAMPLES

ORDER

The foregoing motion having been heard, it is hereby ORDERED:
GRANTED/DENIED
THE COURT

By: _____
Judge

ORDER

The foregoing motion having been heard, it is hereby ORDERED:

That the plaintiff-husband pay to the defendant-wife the sum of $_____

per _____ as alimony pendente lite. This order shall commence on

_____ 20_____ .

THE COURT

By: _____

Judge

▽   ▽   ▽

CERTIFICATION

All parties must receive notice of every motion filed with the court. Court systems recognize the need for efficient and economic service upon parties. Unlike the complaint in a lawsuit, courts do not require most motions to be served by a sheriff or other process server. The typical mode of serving a motion is to file the original of the motion with the clerk of the court either by hand-delivering it or mailing it to the clerk's court address and, on the same day, mailing a copy of the motion to the attorneys appearing for the other parties or to the *pro se* litigant.

The **certification** page of the motion states that a copy of the foregoing (motion and order) was sent on a specific date to all counsel of record and *pro se* appearing parties (if any). This page is signed by the moving party's attorney or by the party, if acting *pro se*. Some local practice rules require that the attorney for the moving party recite the names and addresses of all parties to whom the motion was sent.

EXAMPLE

CERTIFICATION

This is to certify that a true copy of the foregoing motion was mailed, postage prepaid, on this date to all counsel and pro se parties of record on this ____ day of _____, 2000 as follows:

Grace A. Luppino, Esq.
555 Main Avenue
New Haven, CT 06511

_____

Justine F. Miller, Esq.
Commissioner of the Superior Court

Certain motions have additional requirements. On rare occasions, a motion must be served by a process server. However, this usually does not occur during the pendency of the proceeding. Some motions must be filed with an accompanying financial affidavit or an affidavit stating other facts. Other motions will not be accepted by the court for filing without an accompanying memorandum of law setting forth a legal argument for the granting of the motion. Some motions require descriptions of real and personal property when the ownership and location of such property is relevant.

MOST FREQUENTLY USED FAMILY LAW MOTIONS

A number of *pendente lite* or temporary motions are commonly used in family law practice and the paralegal should be familiar with them. They are as follows:

- Motion for alimony,
- Motion for custody of minor children,
- Motion for child support,
- Motion for visitation,
- Motion for counsel fees,
- Motion for exclusive possession of the marital residence,
- Motion for use of motor vehicle,
- Motion for payment of mortgage payments and insurance premiums,
- Motion to restrain party from entering the marital residence (restraining order), and
- Motion to freeze marital assets.

In most family court jurisdictions, the motion practice rules are so flexible that a moving party can create motions to ask the court for an order on various items particular to the party's circumstances. For instance, one party may file a motion for payment of children's secondary school tuition or a motion for joint use of the parties' sailboat.

MOTION FOR ALIMONY

A **motion for alimony** seeks the court to order one spouse to make payments of support to the other spouse. Temporary support payments enable the requesting spouse to meet his or her financial obligations during the pendency of the divorce. Motions for alimony are most common when one spouse has stayed in the home or has earned much less than the other spouse during the marriage (see Exhibit 11–1).

MOTION FOR CUSTODY OF MINOR CHILDREN

A **motion for custody** requests the court to order that one parent have the primary obligation for care and custody of the minor children and the authority to make decisions concerning how the care and maintenance of the children is to be administered. This motion must be taken very seriously by the party who wishes permanent custody of the children. If the pendency period is lengthy, the likelihood of a change in the custody from one parent to the other is very slight because

FIGURE 11–1
Courts do not like to change a child's living arrangements once the child has gotten used to living with one parent.

courts do not make changes in the child's living arrangements after the child has adjusted to being primarily with one parent and is accustomed to that parent's style of parenting. Because the outcome of this motion is so significant, many attorneys pursue this phase of the divorce proceeding with meticulous care and great vigor (see Exhibit 11–2). Whenever a party seeks to obtain custody of a child through a court proceeding, they may be required by state law to file a custody affidavit along with their motion for custody. In this document, signed under oath, the moving party swears that there are no other custody proceedings pending regarding the minor child or children in question.

Motion for Child Support

The party filing a motion for custody frequently also files a **motion for child support,** which seeks an order from the court that the other parent—that is, the noncustodial parent—contribute to the financial support of the children. The court will order the noncustodial parent to pay a specific amount for each child. The court will determine this amount by referring to state-enacted **child support guidelines,** which impose a duty on a noncustodial parent for an amount based on his or her income and the age and number of the minor children. A more detailed discussion of the child support guidelines appears in Chapter 6. State guidelines typically establish an amount for the noncustodial parent to pay after also considering the custodial parent's income and ability to provide for the financial needs of the children (see Exhibit 11–3).

MOTION FOR VISITATION

The noncustodial parent has a right to visitation with the children. Upon motion, the court will address the noncustodial parent's desire for visitation and will tailor the provision in the visitation order to the best interests of the child. It is not unusual for a noncustodial parent's **motion for visitation** to request that the court enter an order for "reasonable visitation" without specifying the breadth or limits of this visitation. An order for "reasonable rights of visitation" leaves much to the discretion of the parties and its success depends on the ability of the soon to be ex-spouses to communicate and negotiate a visitation schedule between themselves. When the parties are unable to do this, a more definite visitation schedule becomes necessary that spells out frequency and duration of visitation, with dates and times of pickup and return specified. Upon a motion for visitation with a detailed schedule, if the court finds that good cause exists, it will order such an arrangement (see Exhibit 11–4).

MOTION FOR COUNSEL FEES

The court has the power, upon **motion for counsel fees** of one of the parties, to order the spouse to pay the reasonable attorney's fees of the moving party. If the court orders reasonable counsel fees, the court will usually specify a dollar amount it deems reasonable. This amount may or may not reflect the actual amount the party will have to pay his or her attorney. Often the court's estimate of "reasonable" falls far below what the client is actually charged.

Sometimes courts choose to deny a motion for counsel fees *pendente lite* and instead indicate that a decision on counsel fees will only be made at the final hearing. Further, when both parties have ample funds or other assets in their own right, the court will not order one party to pay for the other party's legal fees associated with the divorce (see Exhibit 11–5).

MOTION FOR EXCLUSIVE POSSESSION OF THE MARITAL RESIDENCE

The court has the power upon **motion for exclusive possession of the marital residence** by either spouse to order temporary possession of the marital home to the moving spouse. While most couples who own a house own it jointly, the motion is just for possession during the pendency of the lawsuit. This motion determines which of the spouses will live in the family residence until the final divorce decree is entered. At the time of the final decree, the court will recognize each spouse's interest in the property and make equitable orders for the disposition to the residence. Courts are reluctant to order either spouse to leave the family home during the pendency period because of the financial burden it imposes on the spouse having to leave. However, the court will make such an order if the spouses are in agreement as to one spouse leaving or if there are issues of family violence (see Exhibit 11–6).

MOTION FOR USE OF MOTOR VEHICLE

Sometimes household automobiles are titled jointly or in the name of one spouse only. Therefore, the spouse without legal title or sharing title may find it necessary to motion the court to order that one of the family automobiles be designated for his or her use. This motion, a **motion for use of motor vehicle,** like the others typically has an order page attached and is presented to the court usually at the

FIGURE 11–2
A motion can be prepared that provides the moving party with the use of a household automobile.

same time other *pendente lite* motions for alimony, child support, use of the family home, custody, and visitation are addressed (see Exhibit 11–7).

MOTION FOR PAYMENT OF MORTGAGE PAYMENTS AND INSURANCE PREMIUMS

One spouse may make a **motion for payment of mortgage payments and insurance premiums,** which asks the court to order the other spouse to make all or part of the mortgage payment on the family home and also to pay all or part of the insurance premiums needed to keep in effect policies that insure family assets or policies that provide medical or life insurance coverage for the spouses and minor children (see Exhibit 11–8).

RESTRAINING ORDERS

Many judicial systems permit spouses to file a legal document, called a **restraining order,** which requests that the court order the other party to refrain from certain actions or types of conduct or behavior. These orders include a **motion to freeze marital assets,** that is, a restraining order not to deplete the family assets, sell the family home, or any of the family motor vehicles, boats, or other significant articles of personal property; a restraining order freezing the savings or checking account so that neither party may subsequently race to the bank and empty such joint accounts of funds; and a restraining order preventing one party or the other from entering the family home (a **motion to restrain party from entering marital residence**) or harassing or assaulting the other spouse (see Exhibit 11–9).

THE PARALEGAL'S ROLE IN FACILITATING PENDENTE LITE MATTERS

The paralegal in a family law practice will perform many of the steps needed to bring *pendente lite* motions before the court. Frequently, the paralegal will draft all *pendente lite* motions for review by the attorney handling the file and any other documents that must accompany the motions in their respective jurisdiction.

After such review and any possible editing, the paralegal finalizes the motions for filing and makes sure that the appropriate number of copies are created. The paralegal ensures that the motions are filed with the proper court and copies are properly mailed to all necessary parties. The paralegal must make sure that he or she sends the motion to the right court and to the proper division of the court handling family matters.

After the motion is filed with the court, the court clerk will assign the motion a date for a court hearing. The clerk will send a **court calendar** to each attorney or *pro se* party. The court calendar is a small printed booklet or a set of pages that shows a number of cases listed according to parties and docket number (see Exhibit 11–10). Each case has a number, which indicates the order in which cases will be heard. However, the court calendar lists only a starting time for the court day, not for each case, so all attorneys must be there for the call of cases at that starting time even if their case is one of the last to be heard. In many jurisdictions, courts set aside one or two specific days of the week to hear motions brought before the court. Some court systems refer to these times as **motion days,** while other jurisdictions call it **short calendar.**

In every law office at least one staff person has the responsibility of keeping track of when each attorney must be in court. Often this function is delegated to the paralegal. The need to keep track of or docket all court dates is obvious. Failure to appear at a hearing may seriously disadvantage a client, drag out proceedings, and sometimes subject an attorney to a malpractice suit. The need for a **docket control system** is imperative.

FIGURE 11–3
The paralegal may be responsible for making sure the attorney knows when he or she has to appear in court for a hearing.

DOCKET CONTROL SYSTEM

Dates for motions, trials, and other types of hearings come from different sources. In a law office where general litigation is practiced as well as family law, the attorneys may receive calendars from both state and federal courts throughout the state. They may also receive calendars from arbitration bodies and notices of hearings before various commissions and administrative agencies such as the Workers' Compensation Commission, the Commission on Human Rights and Opportunities, and the Unemployment Commission. Calendaring these dates immediately is essential. As soon as these notices arrive, the paralegal must make sure that these hearing dates are entered on the docket control system.

Every law office has a master calendar. In addition, every attorney has his or her own calendar that reflects dates for out-of-court appointments as well as court commitments. The paralegal should enter the court date on the master calendar at once. After this is done, the paralegal should check the responsible attorney's desk calendar to see if there is a conflict and also to enter the date on that attorney's specific calendar. As mentioned previously, the person bringing the motion is known as the **moving party.** The moving party will decide whether to go forward with the motion, that is, appear to argue the motion on the date the court has scheduled. On receipt of a court calendar, the paralegal must first determine whether the motion was brought by an attorney in the firm or by an opposing party. If the motion originated in the paralegal's firm, the paralegal should ask the attorney who brought the motion whether he or she plans to proceed with the motion on the date assigned. If the motion came from an opposing party, the paralegal must find out if the attorney handling the matter for the firm is available to appear at the motion hearing and whether he or she wishes to be there on that date.

If the attorney in the paralegal's firm brought the motion and plans to argue it on the date assigned, the paralegal should call the client to confirm the party's availability for court on that date if the client is needed at the hearing. A letter should be sent to the client confirming the date of the hearing and the necessity of his presence. Then the paralegal must call the office of opposing counsel to notify that attorney that the motion will go forward. If the moving party is the opposing party, the opposing party will notify the paralegal's firm of her intention to go forward or postpone the hearing and the paralegal will communicate this information to necessary individuals.

If the motion is going forward, the paralegal should locate the file prior to the hearing date and make sure that all recently received documents and other pieces of correspondence are appropriately filed. The file should be reviewed and updated on the day before the hearing and the motion should be placed in the front of the court documents section of the file so it will be readily available to the attorney. In addition, the paralegal should confer with the attorney to ensure that other supporting documentation needed at the hearing is put with the file in a manner that is readily available to the attorney at the hearing. The paralegal should prepare the file so that the attorney may review it before the proceeding.

If the parties can reach an agreement on the *pendente lite* motions, they will prepare an agreement, or stipulation, outlining the terms and present it to the court. Exhibit 11–11 illustrates a stipulation regarding *pendente lite* support in the divorce of comedian Jim Carrey and his former wife Melissa.

If the parties cannot agree, they may be required to meet with the court's family services division to assist them in arriving at an agreement. If this is unsuccessful, the court will hold a hearing on the motion. At the hearing the judge will either **grant** or **deny** the motion. If the motion is granted, the court will enter the appropriate orders. The parties are now required to follow the court's order. When the attorney returns from court, the paralegal should review the file to make sure that the motion with orders filled in is properly replaced in the file in the appropriate section.

MOTIONS FOR CONTEMPT AND MODIFICATION

CONTEMPT

When either party does not comply with a court order made in response to a previous motion, the opposing party may seek to have the party comply by filing what is known as a **motion for contempt** (see Exhibit 11–12). The moving party must prove that the noncompliant party willfully violated the court's order. For example, suppose that upon the filing of Mrs. Bronson's motion for visitation, the court enters an order granting Mrs. Bronson reasonable rights of visitation with her minor children. A problem arises when Mrs. Bronson attempts to exercise her rights pursuant to the order and Mr. Bronson refuses to allow her access to the children. Mrs. Bronson's recourse at this stage will be the motion for contempt.

Before drafting the motion for contempt, the paralegal must review the file in order to determine the court's original orders regarding Mrs. Bronson's motion for visitation. The motion for contempt must recite the court's original orders, when they were entered, the judge who entered such orders, and that the noncompliant party is willfully in violation of such order. The motion for contempt must also specify the type of relief sought, which may include a finding of contempt, payment of counsel fees and costs, and possible incarceration. If the motion for contempt addresses financial matters, the paralegal must also include a request for payment of any arrearages due by the spouse in contempt.

MODIFICATION

Sometimes *pendente lite* orders entered by the court are changed when a substantial change in the parties' circumstances occurs from the time the original order was entered. The legal vehicle for making such changes during the *pendente lite* phase is known as the **motion for modification** (see Exhibit 11–13).

For example, suppose that on August 15, 2000, the court grants Mr. Bronson his motion for alimony *pendente lite* and orders Mrs. Bronson to pay him $275 per week. Mrs. Bronson makes weekly payments up to August 22, 2000. On August 25, 2000, Mrs. Bronson loses her job and is not employed again until September 20, 2000. At her new job, Mrs. Bronson earns far less than she did at her previous job. To change the existing order, Mrs. Bronson must file a motion for modification.

Note that while Mrs. Bronson was in the process of job hunting, Mr. Bronson was probably on the phone to his attorney and that office has responded with a motion for contempt against Mrs. Bronson. It is very common for motions for modification and motions for contempt to be filed and addressed simultaneously before the court by the respective parties.

EXHIBIT 11–1

Sample motion for alimony.

DOCKET NO. FA 96-123456	:	SUPERIOR COURT
BRONSON, RODNEY	:	JUDICIAL DISTRICT OF NEW HAVEN
V.	:	AT NEW HAVEN
BRONSON, EVELYN	:	AUGUST 15, 2000

MOTION FOR ALIMONY PENDENTE LITE

The plaintiff-husband in the above-captioned matter respectfully requests that this Court order the defendant-wife to pay to him a reasonable sum for his support during the pendency of this action.

THE PLAINTIFF,
RODNEY BRONSON

BY:_____

     JUSTINE F. MILLER, ESQ.
     HIS ATTORNEY
     22 PARK PLACE
     NEW HAVEN, CT 06511
     (203) 861-4444
     JURIS NO. 313133

ORDER

The foregoing motion having been heard, it is hereby ORDERED:

That the defendant-wife pay to the plaintiff-husband the sum of $_____

per _____ as alimony pendente lite.

This order shall commence on _____, 20_____.

The Court

By:_____
     Judge

CERTIFICATION

This is to certify that a true copy of the foregoing motion was mailed, postage prepaid, on this date to all counsel and pro se parties of record on this _____ day of _____, 2000 as follows:

Grace A. Luppino, Esq.
555 Main Avenue
New Haven, CT 06511

_____
Justine F. Miller, Esq.
Commissioner of the Superior Court

EXHIBIT 11–2
Sample motion for child custody.

DOCKET NO. FA 96-123456	:	SUPERIOR COURT
BRONSON, RODNEY	:	JUDICIAL DISTRICT OF NEW HAVEN
V.	:	AT NEW HAVEN
BRONSON, EVELYN	:	AUGUST 15, 2000

MOTION FOR CHILD CUSTODY PENDENTE LITE

The plaintiff-husband in the above-entitled action respectfully requests that he be awarded sole custody pendente lite of the minor children of the parties with reasonable rights of visitation to the defendant-wife.

THE PLAINTIFF,
RODNEY BRONSON

BY: _____
JUSTINE F. MILLER, ESQ.
HIS ATTORNEY
22 PARK PLACE
NEW HAVEN, CT 06511
(203) 861-4444
JURIS NO. 313133

ORDER

The foregoing motion having been heard, it is hereby ORDERED that sole custody of the minor children be awarded pendente lite to the plaintiff-husband, with reasonable rights of visitation to the defendant-wife.

That these orders shall commence on _____, 20_____.

The Court

By: _____
JUDGE

CERTIFICATION

This is to certify that a true copy of the foregoing motion was mailed, postage prepaid, on this date to all counsel and pro se parties of record on this _____day of _____, 2000 , as follows:

Grace A. Luppino, Esq.
555 Main Avenue
New Haven, CT 06511

_____
Justine F. Miller, Esq.
Commissioner of the Superior Court

EXHIBIT 11–3
Sample motion for child support.

DOCKET NO. FA 96-123456	:	SUPERIOR COURT
BRONSON, RODNEY	:	JUDICIAL DISTRICT OF NEW HAVEN
V.	:	AT NEW HAVEN
BRONSON, EVELYN	:	AUGUST 15, 2000

MOTION FOR CHILD SUPPORT PENDENTE LITE

The plaintiff-husband in the above-referenced matter hereby moves that the Court order the defendant-wife to pay to him a reasonable sum for the care, maintenance, and support of the minor children, pendente lite.

THE PLAINTIFF,
RODNEY BRONSON

BY: _____
JUSTINE F. MILLER, ESQ.
HIS ATTORNEY
22 PARK PLACE
NEW HAVEN, CT 06511
(203) 861-4444
JURIS NO. 313133

ORDER

The foregoing motion having been heard, it is hereby ORDERED:

That the defendant-wife pay to the plaintiff-husband the sum of $_____ per

_____ as child support, pendente lite.

That this order shall commence on _____, 20_____.

THE COURT

BY: _____
JUDGE

CERTIFICATION

This is to certify that a true copy of the foregoing motion was mailed, postage prepaid, on this

date to all counsel and pro se parties of record on this _____ day of _____,

2000, as follows:

Grace A. Luppino, Esq.
555 Main Avenue
New Haven, CT 06511

_____
Justine F. Miller, Esq.
Commissioner of the Superior Court

EXHIBIT 11–4

Sample motion for visitation.

DOCKET NO. FA 96-123456	:	SUPERIOR COURT
BRONSON, RODNEY	:	JUDICIAL DISTRICT OF NEW HAVEN
V.	:	AT NEW HAVEN
BRONSON, EVELYN	:	AUGUST 15, 2000

MOTION FOR VISITATION

The defendant-wife in the above-entitled matter respectfully requests that she be granted reasonable rights of visitation with the minor children of the parties.

THE DEFENDANT,
EVELYN BRONSON

BY: _____
GRACE A. LUPPINO, ESQ.
HER ATTORNEY
555 MAIN AVENUE
NEW HAVEN, CT 06511
(203) 333-3333
JURIS NO. 160000

ORDER

The foregoing motion having been heard, it is hereby ORDERED:

That the defendant-wife shall have reasonable rights of visitation with the minor children of the parties.

That this order shall commence on _____, 20_____.

THE COURT

BY: _____
JUDGE

CERTIFICATION

This is to certify that a true copy of the foregoing motion was mailed, postage prepaid, on this

date to all counsel and pro se parties of record on this _____ day of _____, 2000,

as follows:

Justine F. Miller
22 Park Place
New Haven, CT 06511

_____
Grace A. Luppino, Esq.
Commissioner of the Superior Court

EXHIBIT 11–5
Sample motion for payment of counsel fees.

DOCKET NO. FA 96-123456   :   SUPERIOR COURT

BRONSON, RODNEY   :   JUDICIAL DISTRICT OF NEW HAVEN

V.   :   AT NEW HAVEN

BRONSON, EVELYN   :   AUGUST 15, 2000

MOTION FOR COUNSEL FEES PENDENTE LITE

The defendant-wife in the above-captioned matter hereby moves that the Court order the plaintiff-husband to pay a reasonable sum toward the defendant-wife's counsel fees.

THE DEFENDANT,
EVELYN BRONSON

BY: _____
GRACE A. LUPPINO, ESQ.
HER ATTORNEY
555 MAIN AVENUE
NEW HAVEN, CT 06511
(203) 333-3333
JURIS NO. 160000

ORDER

The foregoing motion having been heard, it is hereby ORDERED:

That the plaintiff-husband pay to the defendant-wife the sum of $_____ as counsel fees, pendente lite.

That these orders shall commence on _____, 20_____.

THE COURT

BY: _____
JUDGE

CERTIFICATION

This is to certify that a true copy of the foregoing motion was mailed, postage prepaid, on this date to all counsel and pro se parties of record on this _____ day of _____, 2000, as follows:

Justine F. Miller
22 Park Place
New Haven, CT 06511

_____
Grace A. Luppino, Esq.
Commissioner of the Superior Court

EXHIBIT 11–6
Sample motion for exclusive possession of marital residence.

DOCKET NO. FA 96-123456	:	SUPERIOR COURT
BRONSON, RODNEY	:	JUDICIAL DISTRICT OF NEW HAVEN
V.	:	AT NEW HAVEN
BRONSON, EVELYN	:	AUGUST 15, 2000

MOTION FOR EXCLUSIVE POSSESSION OF THE MARITAL RESIDENCE

The plaintiff-husband hereby moves that this Court award exclusive possession and use of the family residence at 328 Sycamore Street, New Haven, CT, to the plaintiff-husband.

THE PLAINTIFF,
RODNEY BRONSON

BY: _____
JUSTINE F. MILLER, ESQ.
HIS ATTORNEY
22 PARK PLACE
NEW HAVEN, CT 06511
(203) 861-4444
JURIS NO. 313133

ORDER

The foregoing motion having been heard, it is hereby ORDERED:

GRANTED/DENIED
THE COURT

BY: _____
JUDGE

CERTIFICATION

This is to certify that a true copy of the foregoing motion was mailed, postage prepaid, on this date to all counsel and pro se parties of record on this _____ day of _____, 2000, as follows:

Grace A. Luppino, Esq.
555 Main Avenue
New Haven, CT 06511

_____
Justine F. Miller, Esq.
Commissioner of the Superior Court

EXHIBIT 11–7

Sample motion for use of motor vehicle.

DOCKET NO. FA 96-123456	:	SUPERIOR COURT
BRONSON, RODNEY	:	JUDICIAL DISTRICT OF NEW HAVEN
V.	:	AT NEW HAVEN
BRONSON, EVELYN	:	AUGUST 15, 2000

MOTION FOR USE OF JOINTLY OWNED MOTOR VEHICLE

The defendant-wife in the above-referenced matter respectfully requests that this Court order the plaintiff-husband to make available to her the use of the jointly owned Buick Skylark, which is not being used presently by either party.

THE DEFENDANT,
EVELYN BRONSON

BY: _____
GRACE A. LUPPINO, ESQ.
HER ATTORNEY
555 MAIN AVENUE
NEW HAVEN, CT 06511
(203) 333-3333
JURIS NO. 160000

ORDER

The foregoing motion having been heard, it is hereby ORDERED:

GRANTED/DENIED
THE COURT

BY: _____
JUDGE

CERTIFICATION

This is to certify that a true copy of the foregoing motion was mailed, postage prepaid, on this date to all counsel and pro se parties of record on this _____ day of _____, 2000, as follows:

Justine F. Miller
22 Park Place
New Haven, CT 06511

_____
Grace A. Luppino, Esq.
Commissioner of the Superior Court

EXHIBIT 11–8
Sample motion for payment of mortgage and insurance premiums.

DOCKET NO. FA 96-123456	:	SUPERIOR COURT
BRONSON, RODNEY	:	JUDICIAL DISTRICT OF NEW HAVEN
V.	:	AT NEW HAVEN
BRONSON, EVELYN	:	AUGUST 15, 2000

MOTION FOR PAYMENT OF MORTGAGE AND HEALTH INSURANCE PREMIUMS, PENDENTE LITE

The plaintiff-husband in the above-referenced matter respectfully requests that the Court enter an order pendente lite that the defendant-wife make monthly mortgage payments on the family home and make monthly payments for health insurance premiums for the plaintiff-husband and minor children.

In support hereof, the plaintiff-husband represents as follows:

1. Prior to the institution of this action, the defendant-wife made monthly payments on the family home located at 328 Sycamore Street, New Haven, Connecticut.

2. The plaintiff-husband and the minor children continue to reside at the above-mentioned premises and intend to remain there while this matter is pending.

3. The plaintiff-husband lacks adequate financial resources to pay the monthly mortgage payment at this time; and if the defendant-wife fails to pay the mortgage, the parties will lose this jointly owned asset of the marriage, and the plaintiff-husband and the minor children will be without housing.

4. Prior to the institution of this action, the defendant-wife paid monthly health insurance premiums for a health plan covering herself, the plaintiff-husband and the minor children.

5. The plaintiff-husband lacks adequate financial resources to pay monthly health insurance premiums for himself and the minor children; if the defendant-wife fails to pay monthly health premiums, the plaintiff-husband and minor children will lack health insurance during the pendency of this action.

WHEREFORE, the plaintiff requests that the Court order the defendant-wife to continue to make the monthly mortgage payments on the family home and continue to pay monthly health insurance premiums for the plaintiff-husband and minor children throughout the pendency of this action.

THE PLAINTIFF,
RODNEY BRONSON

BY: _____
JUSTINE F. MILLER, ESQ.
HIS ATTORNEY
22 PARK PLACE
NEW HAVEN, CT 06511
(203) 861-4444
JURIS NO. 313133

EXHIBIT 11–8
Continued

ORDER

The foregoing motion having been heard, it is hereby ORDERED:

GRANTED/DENIED

THE COURT

BY: _____
JUDGE

CERTIFICATION

This is to certify that a true copy of the foregoing motion was mailed, postage prepaid, on this date to all counsel and pro se parties of record on this _____ day of _____, 2000, as follows:

Grace A. Luppino, Esq.
555 Main Avenue
New Haven, CT 06511

_____
Justine F. Miller, Esq.
Commissioner of the Superior Court

EXHIBIT 11–9
Sample restraining order.

DOCKET NO. FA 96-123456 : SUPERIOR COURT

BRONSON, RODNEY : JUDICIAL DISTRICT OF NEW HAVEN

V. : AT NEW HAVEN

BRONSON, EVELYN : AUGUST 15, 2000

MOTION TO RESTRAIN

The defendant-wife in the above-entitled action respectfully represents what the plaintiff-husband has, within his control, significant cash and property assets of the marriage. The defendant-wife desires to secure all assets of the marriage so they will be available for a decree of equitable distribution pursuant to applicable state law.

WHEREFORE, the defendant-wife moves for an order restraining the plaintiff-husband from removing, sequestering, hiding, transferring, disposing of and/or selling, encumbering, liening, mortgaging, or otherwise disposing of any assets during the course of this action.

THE DEFENDANT,
EVELYN BRONSON

BY: _____
GRACE A. LUPPINO, ESQ.
HER ATTORNEY
555 MAIN AVENUE
NEW HAVEN, CT 06511
(203) 333-3333
JURIS NO. 160000

ORDER

The foregoing motion having been heard, it is hereby ORDERED:

GRANTED/DENIED
THE COURT

BY: _____
JUDGE

CERTIFICATION

This is to certify that a true copy of the foregoing motion was mailed, postage prepaid, on this

date to all counsel and pro se parties of record on this _____ day of _____, 2000, as follows:

Justine F. Miller
22 Park Place
New Haven, CT 06522

_____
Grace A. Luppino, Esq.
Commissioner of the Superior Court

EXHIBIT 11–10
Sample court calendar.

NNH$$$sh2

Judicial District of New Haven
SUPERIOR COURT
Short Calendar
235 Church Street—New Haven
9:30 A.M.

NOTICE — MARKING CASES

IN ORDER FOR A CASE TO BE ASSIGNED TO A JUDGE, COUN-SEL/PRO SE PARTIES MUST TELEPHONE THE SHORT CALENDAR MARKING LINE AT (203) 789-7648 AND MARK THE CASE "READY". The marking line is open from 9:30 a.m. Wednesday to 11:00 a.m. Friday of the week prior to every calendar. In the event a state holiday falls on the Friday immediately preceding the calendar, the marking line will close at 11:00 a.m. Thursday of the week prior to the calendar. Movants must indicate on the marking line whether the case being marked is on Short Calendar No. 2 or Short Calendar No. 5.

Counsel/pro se parties must give timely notice to each other of all markings. In addition, notice must be given to the Attorney General's Office at (860) 808-5150 if any party is receiving or has received Public Assistance. Failure to do so will result in the matter not being heard. If conflicting markings are made, the last one

(Notice Continued on Last Column)

11/30/98 09.30
FAMILY
QUESTIONS OF LAW ARG.

0246821 S   MOAN-SOMMERS,LOUISE
FA-86   V. SOMMERS,JOHN S
(1)
J. CHIARELLI   PRO SE
R.K. WALSH
ARG   126.50 MOT OPEN/MODIFY JUDGMENT
ARG   127.00 MOT PROTECTIVE ORDER
ARG   128.00 MOT RESTRAINING ORDER
ARG × 129.00 MOTION TO STRIKE

0416827 S   WALKER,HILTON L
FA-98   V. WALKER,DENEEDA
(2)
PRO SE   CT.L.S.WATERBURY
ARG   102.00 MOTION TO DISMISS

0415891 S   SANDORA,DEBORAH I
FA-98   V. SANDORA,EDMOND M
(3)
NOYES & M PC   DEY S & A LLC
ARG   103.00 MOTION FOR COUNSEL FEES
ARG   104.00 MOTION FOR SANCTIONS
ARG   105.00 MOTION FOR STAY
ARG × 106.00 MOTION TO DISMISS

GA× 0415498 S BOND,GILBERT I
FA-98   V. BOND,ANITA L
(4)
PECK & PECK   RW CALLAHAN
ARG × 117.00 MOTION TO DISMISS
ARG   118.00 MOTION FOR STAY
ARG   120.00 MOTION FOR ORDER

11/30/98 09.30
FAMILY
DISCLOSURES ARG.

0419070 S   BIATOWAS,JANE
FA-98   V. BIATOWAS,STANLEY
(5)
ESPOSITO J J PC   KOLB C & E PC
ARG   104.00 MOT EXTEND TIME-DSCOVERY

0416274 S   POTTS,CAROLYN
FA-98   V. POTTS,PHILIP
(6)
G. H. KAHN   NOYES & M PC
ARG   103.00 MOT EXTEND TIME-DSCOVERY

11/30/98 09.30
FAMILY - DORMANCY
DORMANCY BY COURT ORDER

0414106 S   ESPOSITO,MICHAEL A
FA-98   V. ESPOSITO,LAURA C
(7)
GREAVES & S LLC   BERNBLUM & GREEN
110.00 MOT OPEN DISMISSAL JDGMT

0413732 S   LONERGAN,JENNIFER
FA-98   V. LONERGAN,CHRISTOPHER
(8)
GENTILE C & N LL   PRO SE
103.00 MOT OPEN DISMISSAL JDGMT

0414139 S   HELLER,ERICK
FA-98   V. HELLER,CHERIE
(9)
R.TIETJEN   PRO SE
102.00 MOT OPEN DISMISSAL JDGMT

0414743 S   HOLLAND,MARY C
FA-98   V. HOLLAND,THIMUEL
(10)
PRO SE   PRO SE
AAG GG WILLIAMS
103.00 MOT OPEN DISMISSAL JDGMT

0412747 S   DUBE,KATHRYN M
FA-98   V. DUDE,HENRY G
(11)
PRO SE   HEFFERNAN & F LL
105.00 MOT OPEN DISMISSAL JDGMT

11/30/98 09.30
FAMILY
MISCELLANEOUS ARG.

0418500 S   TORRES,ESTHER
FA-98   V. TEJEDA,RAMON
(12)
MOSCOWITZ C & K   NO APPEARANCE
ARG × 101.00 MOT CUSTODY-PD LITE
ARG   102.00 MOT FOR SUPPORT-PD LITE

0414301 S   GOLUB, BETH A
FA-98   V. GOLUB, ERIC
(13)
BROZDOWSKI P L L   PRO SE
ARG × 105.00 MOTION FOR ORDER
ARG   106.00 MOTION FOR ORDER
ARG   107.00 MOTION FOR COUNSEL FEES

0419602 S   BENEVENTO,ELLEN L
FA-98   V. BENEVENTO,VINCENT J
(14)
T.R.BAINER   NO APPEARANCE
ARG × 101.00 MOT FOR ALIMONY-PD LITE
ARG   102.00 MOT CUSTODY-PD LITE
ARG   103.00 MOT FOR SUPPORT-PD LITE
ARG   104.00 MOTION FOR POSSESSION
ARG   105.00 MOTION FOR COUNSEL FEES

0415503 S   CARABETTA,LINDA S
FA-98   V. CARABETTA,GARY LYNN
(15)
D.POLAN   BUDLONG & ASSOCI
ARG   109.00 OBJECTION TO MOTION

0345804 S   DUBE,RACHEL
FA-93   V. FREDERICKS,ROBERT
(16)
GESMONDE P S & P   PRO SE
G. H. KAHN   J. CHIARELLI
ARG   189.00 MOT DETERMINE ARREARAGE

0287705 S   PICCOLO,KEVIN M
FA-89   V. PICCOLO,DEBRA A
(17)
PRO SE   PRO SE
HF VOLPE
ARG   180.00 MOT REFER TO FRD

0395706 S   BURRIS, ROBERT
FA-97   V. BURRIS, MAUREEN
(18)
PRO SE   PRO SE
JW AUGER   LEGAL CLINIC
JE HUDSON
SUPPORT ENF UNIT
ARG   128.00 MOTION FOR COUNSEL FEES

0273107 S   WALTER,TERRI
FA-88   V. WALTER,NOEL DAVIS
(19)
W.J. NULSEN   PRO SE
ARG   138.00 MOT OPEN/MODIFY JUDGMENT

0405610 S   LANE, REGINA E.
FA-95   V. LANE, KENNETH H.
(20)
PRO SE   PRO SE
L. PARLEY
J. M. KELLEY
L.J. COSTANTINI
ARG   580.00 MOT WITHDRAW APPEARANCE

0373911 S   WILLIAMS,FELICIA
FA-95   V. WILLIAMS,ROBERT J
(21)
M.I. OLMER   ADELMAN L OFFICE
ARG   148.00 MOT PERMISSION WD APPRNC

0402512 S   MUELLER,STEVEN K
FA-97   V. MUELLER,CHARISSE G
(22)
R.S. FRIEDMAN   E.J. DOLAN
ARG   107.00 MOTION FOR VISITATION

0412912 S   VANWILGEN,STEPHANIJA
FA-98   V. VANWILGEN,AART III
(23)
MURPHY MAUREEN   ULLMAN P & SKLAV
AA WALLACE
ARG   112.00 MOT CUSTODY-PD LITE

0390614 S   COX, SHAWN D.
FA-96   V. COX, STEVEN P.
(24)
H.D.MURPHY   E.J. DOLAN
ARG   117.50 MOT OPEN/MODIFY JUDGMENT

0365115 S   GLENN,BARBARA
FA-94   V. GLENN,JOSEPH K
(25)
PRO SE   GJ SACHS
CHILD SPT ENF A   M.F. BRUNSWICK
ARG   125.00 MOT OPEN/MODIFY JUDGMENT

0415615 S   GOULET, RAYMOND III
FA-98   V. REYNOLDS, WENDY
(26)
DIANA C T & COMO   H.A.LAWRENCE
L. PARLEY
ARG   120.00 MOTION FOR MODIFICATION

0385316 S   KUNTZ, SUSAN
FA-96   V. KUNTZ, THOMAS
(27)
GOLDBLATT G & R   V. MCMANUS, JR.
ARG   110.50 MOT OPEN/MODIFY JUDGMENT

0418422 S   DICICCO,JANICE
FA-98   V. DICICCO,MARVIN J
(28)
J. CHIARELLI   J. E. SPODNICK
ARG × 101.00 MOTION FOR POSSESSION
ARG   102.00 MOTION FOR INJUNCTION
ARG   103.00 MOT FOR TRANSPORTATION
ARG   104.00 MOTION FOR ORDER
ARG   106.00 MOT FOR ALIMONY-PD LITE

NEW HAVEN   COLUMN   1
SHORT CAL NO. 2   COLUMN   2   COLUMN   3

EXHIBIT 11–10

Continued

```
0419223 S      GOLD,INGRID
FA-98      V. GOLD,LOUIS
               ( 29)
S.O.LEBAS              F. L. CIRILLO
ARG * 101.01 MOT FOR SUPPORT-PD LITE
ARG   101.02 MOT FOR ALIMONY-PD LITE
---------------------------------------------
0406424 S      EDWARDS,MARK R      ET AL
FA-97      V. EDWARDS,BONNIE
               ( 30)
ADELMAN L OFFICE         D.R. DANIELS
                         AAG AS GUIDO
                         WALLACE & O LLC
ARG * 147.00 MOTION FOR MODIFICATION
ARG   148.00 MOTION FOR ORDER
ARG   149.00 MOT FOR SUPPORT-PD LITE
ARG   150.00 MOTION FOR ORDER
---------------------------------------------
0416924 S      JEFFERSON,LOUIS
FA-98      V. JEFFERSON,KIMBERLY L
               ( 31)
PRO SE                 PRO SE
ARG * 102.00 MOT FOR ORDER PEND LITE
ARG   103.00 MOT FOR ORDER PEND LITE
---------------------------------------------
0418524 S      SARGENT,DOREEN
FA-98      V. SARGENT,ERNEST
               ( 32)
F. M. GLYNN            NO APPEARANCE
ARG * 101.01 MOT CUSTODY-PD LITE
ARG   101.02 MOT FOR SUPPORT-PD LITE
ARG   102.00 MOT FOR ALIMONY-PD LITE
---------------------------------------------
0365225 S      KASSHEIMER,MICHAEL
FA-94      V. KASSHEIMER,SUSAN A
               ( 33)
DUMARK & LINDSAY       SOUSA R C & ASSO
ARG   121.00 MOTION FOR MODIFICATION
---------------------------------------------
0414527 S      HERNANDEZ,OTTO R
FA-98      V. IRIZARRY,MARIA
               ( 34)
D. L. DENVIR           M.DOODY
ARG * 112.00 MOT MOD SUPPORT P/L
ARG   112.50 MOT MOD VIS P/L
---------------------------------------------
0418127 S      D'AMICO,LYNNE L
FA-98      V. D'AMICO,SALVATORE G
               ( 35)
N.M. LEGINSKY          PRO SE
ARG   101.00 MOT FOR ORDER PEND LITE
---------------------------------------------
0418527 S      MAZZELLA,ANNA MARIA
FA-98      V. MAZZELLA,WILLIAM
               ( 36)
CANTOR F R & G P       NO APPEARANCE
ARG * 101.00 MOT FOR ALIMONY-PD LITE
ARG   102.01 MOT CUSTODY-PD LITE
ARG   102.02 MOT FOR SUPPORT-PD LITE
ARG   103.00 MOTION FOR POSSESSION
---------------------------------------------
0412728 S      SPEARMAN,PATTI
FA-98      V. WILLIAMS,CHRISTOPHER
               ( 37)
PRO SE                 NO APPEARANCE
C.E.FRONTIS
ARG   106.00 MOTION FOR CONTINUANCE
---------------------------------------------
0419329 S      GUISTINELLO,SUSAN
FA-98      V. GUISTINELLO,ANTHONY
               ( 38)
NOYES & M PC           AA WALLACE
ARG * 103.00 MOT IMMEDIATE HEARING
ARG   105.01 MOT CUSTODY-PD LITE
ARG   105.02 MOT JOINT CUSTODY
ARG   106.00 MOTION FOR POSSESSION
ARG   107.00 MOT FOR ALIMONY-PD LITE
ARG   108.00 MOT FOR SUPPORT-PD LITE
ARG   109.00 MOTION FOR ORDER
ARG   110.00 MOTION FOR POSSESSION
ARG   111.00 MOT APPT GUARDIAN AD LIT
---------------------------------------------
0387930 S      CLOSE,MEAD A
FA-96      V. CLOSE,JOYCE
               ( 39)
JACOBS G B & D P       PRO SE
                    WINNICK R & C LL
                    AAG AS GUIDO
ARG * 119.00 MOT OPEN/MODIFY JUDGMENT
ARG   121.00 MOTION FOR ORDER
---------------------------------------------


NY* 0416631 S  BONITO,SUSAN Z
FA-98      V. ZISEK,MICHAEL
               ( 40)
AMENDOLA &N.           PRO SE
ARG   109.00 MOT FOR SUPPORT-PD LITE
---------------------------------------------
0418431 S      PELLERIN,CAROL
FA-98      V. PELLERIN,DAVID J
               ( 41)
D. L. DENVIR           P. E. RICCIARDI
ARG * 102.01 MOT CUSTODY-PD LITE
ARG   102.02 MOT FOR SUPPORT-PD LITE
ARG   102.50 MOTION FOR ORDER
---------------------------------------------
0419432 S      MATTEO,GINA
FA-98      V. MATTEO,JOHN
               ( 42)
JACOBS G B & D P       NO APPEARANCE
ARG   101.00 MOT FOR SUPPORT-PD LITE
ARG   102.01 MOT CUSTODY-PD LITE
ARG   102.02 MOTION FOR VISITATION
ARG   103.00 MOTION FOR POSSESSION
---------------------------------------------
0419533 S      DAY,LISA
FA-98      V. DAY,DAVID JR
               ( 43)
FARRELL & LESLIE       NO APPEARANCE
ARG   101.00 MOTION FOR ORDER
---------------------------------------------
0385434 S      PICHE,DONALD
FA-96      V. PICHE, ROSE
               ( 44)
R.M.KESSLER            PRO SE
                       MA WIELER
ARG   107.00 MOT OPEN/MODIFY JUDGMENT
---------------------------------------------
0372136 S      ALLISON,ROBERT J
FA-95      V. ALLISON,KATHLEEN T
               ( 45)
G. BATTISTOLI          PRO SE
                       SUSMAN D & S PC
ARG   121.00 MOT OPEN/MODIFY JUDGMENT
---------------------------------------------
0265836 S      CONSIGLIO, BARBARA A
FA-87      V. CONSIGLIO, VINCENT J
               ( 46)
SCHETTINO & T.         PRO SE
SUPPORT ENF UNIT       ADELMAN L OFFICE
ARG * 139.00 OBJECTION TO MOTION
ARG   140.00 MOT OPEN/MODIFY JUDGMENT
---------------------------------------------
0321937 S      KAUFFMAN,JANET ANN
FA-91      V. KAUFFMAN,BRUCE D
               ( 47)
PRO SE                 MCNAMARA & GOODM
N.R.NESI
J. L. WELTY
ARG   134.00 MOT OPEN/MODIFY JUDGMENT
---------------------------------------------
0409338 S      ROCZYNSKI,LYDIA
FA-98      V. ROCZYNSKI,DARREN J
               ( 48)
RM STUTMAN             ADELMAN L OFFICE
ARG   133.00 MOT PERMISSION WD APPRNC
---------------------------------------------
0419040 S      MCDANIEL,RAUN M
FA-98      V. MCDANIEL,DONALD G
               ( 49)
C NEWMAN               GESMONDE P S & P
ARG * 107.00 MOT JOINT CUSTODY
ARG   108.00 MOTION FOR ACCOUNTING
---------------------------------------------
0363542 S      GAMM, JOHN
FA-94      V. GAMM, INGRID
               ( 50)
GOLDBLATT G & R
                       WEINSTEIN & W PC
                       ULLMAN P & SKLAV
                       VOTRE A A PC
ARG   172.00 MOTION FOR COUNSEL FEES
---------------------------------------------
0397542 S      SAVAGE,MARY ELLEN
FA-97      V. ELLIOTT, E.DONALD
               ( 51)
RUBIN & E.             AMENDOLA & A LLC
ARG * 124.00 MOT APPOINT ATTORNEY
ARG   126.00 MOT RETURN PERSONAL ITEM
---------------------------------------------
0415643 S      CORNING,TERRI
FA-98      V. OWENS,KENNETH
               ( 52)
HARRINGTON & FOR       PRO SE
                       B.H. COX
                                 ---CONTINUED


ARG * 103.01 MOT CUSTODY-PD LITE
ARG   103.02 MOT FOR SUPPORT-PD LITE
---------------------------------------------
0388143 S      BALDWIN,ALISA
FA-96      V. CLARK,STERLING
               ( 53)
M KOSSAR               PRO SE
ARG   103.00 RULE OPEN/MODIFY JDGHENT
---------------------------------------------
0417444 S      HOGFELDT,SHARON A
FA-98      V. HOGFELDT,KARL
               ( 54)
GOULD & G PC           NO APPEARANCE
ARG   103.00 MOTION FOR ORDER
---------------------------------------------
0417544 S      WILDER,GAYLE
FA-98      V. WILDER,REGINALD
               ( 55)
LEVY & S LLC           PRO SE
                       PARRETT P P & C
ARG   113.00 MOTION FOR MODIFICATION
---------------------------------------------
0419245 S      BUCCI,CYNTHIA
FA-98      V. BUCCI,JOSEPH
               ( 56)
NOYES & M PC           NO APPEARANCE
ARG * 101.00 MOT ALIMNY-CUSTDY-SUPPRT
ARG   102.00 MOTION FOR ORDER
ARG   103.00 MOTION FOR COUNSEL FEES
---------------------------------------------
0416846 S      GALLI,DANIELLA
FA-98      V. SOEHNLEIN,PAUL
               ( 57)
BROZDOWSKI P L L       PRO SE
ARG   102.00 MOT APPOINT CONCILIATOR
---------------------------------------------
0415149 S      SANTARPIA,ROBERT
FA-98      V. SANTARPIA,VALERIE
               ( 58)
RUBIN & E.             PRO SE
ARG   110.00 MOTION TO SEAL FILE
---------------------------------------------
0381451 S      ROBLES, LISA J.
FA-95      V. ROBLES, WILSON
               ( 59)
MF VOLPE               CASHMAN W H & AS
ARG   128.00 MOTION FOR ORDER
---------------------------------------------
0399752 S      ERRANTE, STEVEN
FA-97      V. ERRANTE, NANCY
               ( 60)
LYNCH T K & E PC       G. H. KAHN
COUGHLIN & M.
ARG   135.00 MOT PROTECTIVE ORDER
ARG   136.00 MOT PROTECTIVE ORDER
ARG * 137.00 MOTION FOR ORDER
---------------------------------------------
0416953 S      MOCCIO,SHERI
FA-98      V. MOCCIO,ROBERT
               ( 61)
J. CHIARELLI           PARRETT P P & C
ARG * 101.00 MOTION FOR POSSESSION
ARG   102.00 MOT RETURN PERSONAL ITEM
ARG   103.00 MOT FOR ALIMONY-PD LITE
ARG   104.00 MOTION FOR ORDER
ARG   105.00 MOTION FOR COUNSEL FEES
ARG   106.00 MOT FOR TRANSPORTATION
ARG   107.00 MOTION FOR INJUNCTION
ARG   109.00 MOTION FOR POSSESSION
ARG   110.00 MOT EXTEND TIME-DSCOVERY
---------------------------------------------
0416554 S      FITZGERALD,JOHN D
FA-98      V. FITZGERALD,SUZANNE
               ( 62)
KOLB C & E PC          NOYES & M PC
ARG * 101.00 MOT ALIMNY-CUSTDY-SUPPRT
ARG   102.00 MOTION FOR COUNSEL FEES
ARG   103.00 MOTION FOR ORDER
ARG   104.00 MOTION FOR POSSESSION
ARG   105.00 REQUEST FOR CONCILIATION
---------------------------------------------
0399254 S      LEETE, LINDA
FA-97      V. LEETE, BRADFORD
               ( 63)
R.TIETJEN              J. A. KEYES
AAG AS GUIDO           HARRINGTON & FOR
ARG * 124.00 MOT FOR SUPPORT-PD LITE
ARG   125.00 MOTION FOR ORDER
---------------------------------------------
0415655 S      SMITH,DION H
FA-98      V. SMITH,MICHELE L
               ( 64)
                                 ---CONTINUED
```

EXHIBIT 11-10
Continued

COLUMN 7

```
D. L. DENVIR                CELLA M & WILLIA
   ARG   112.00 MOTION FOR MODIFICATION
0261057 S      MURRAY,TERESA A
FA-87        V. MURRAY,THOMAS W SR
                    ( 65)
J. CHIARELLI              PARRETT P P & C
   ARG x 139.00 MOTION FOR SANCTIONS
   ARG   140.00 MOTION FOR SANCTIONS

   0404657 S     KARATZAS,TINA
FA-97        V. KARATZAS,DINO
                    ( 66)
TYLER, C. & A.            COHEN G I L O OF
   ARG   111.00 MOTION FOR SANCTIONS

0414757 S      BRACERO,MELISSA
FA-98        V. BRACERO,MARIO J
                    ( 67)
ADELMAN L OFFICE             DL WRIGHT
   ARG   113.00 MOTION FOR MODIFICATION

0350459 S      SASSO,WARREN
FA-93        V. SASSO,SUSAN B
                    ( 68)
M.F. BRUNSWICK            M.H.LERNER
PERELMUTTER & P.          WEIGAND M & A PC
   ARG   212.00 MOTION FOR MODIFICATION

0390959 S      MAGNAN,EILENE
FA-96        V. MAGNAN, LEONARD J.
                    ( 69)
CANTOR F R & G P          D.POLAN
COHEN & THOMAS
YOLEN & P LLC
   ARG   157.00 MOT PERMISSION WD APPRNC

0403360 S      LAFASCIANO,TRACY
FA-97        V. LAFASCIANO,JASON
                    ( 70)
PRO SE                    GESMONDE P S & P
ANNUNZIATA A PC
AAG AS GUIDO
   ARG   125.00 MOT OPEN/MODIFY JUDGMENT

0419360 S      BASCOM,MICHELE
FA-98        V. BASCOM,DAVID M
                    ( 71)
FARRELL & LESLIE          NO APPEARANCE
   ARG x 101.00 MOT FOR SUPPORT-PD LITE
   ARG   102.00 MOT FOR ALIMONY-PD LITE

0419661 S      SPERANDEO,RALPH A JR
FA-98        V. SPERANDEO,MARGARET R
                    ( 72)
WE SKIPTUNAS              NO APPEARANCE
   ARG   101.00 MOT CUSTODY-PD LITE

0416262 S      LABANARA,PATRICIA A
FA-98        V. LABANARA,ROBERT L
                    ( 73)
CANTOR F R & G P          DH BROWN
   ARG x 101.00 MOT FOR ALIMONY-PD LITE
   ARG   102.00 MOTION FOR POSSESSION

0397662 S      CLARK,JENNIFER (CT)
FA-97        V. NOONAN, MICHAEL
                    ( 74)
PRO SE                    T.R.BAINER
H.I.MENDELSOHN
CADDEN I & IVERS
AAG AS GUIDO
CHILD SPT ENF A
   ARG x 118.00 RULE OPEN/MODIFY JDGMENT
   ARG   119.00 MOT PERMISSION WD APPRNC

0257962 S      CONSOLATORE, DAWN
FA-87        V. CONSOLATORE, ROBERT
                    ( 75)
PRO SE                    PARRETT P P & C
ANTOLLINO,A & S.
   ARG   124.00 MOTION FOR ORDER

0377963 S      QUIELLO,OLIVIA
FA-95        V. QUIELLO,MICHAEL J
                    ( 76)
BERDON Y & M PC           E.J. DOLAN
                          JACOBS G B & D P
                          KOLB C & E PC
   ARG   119.00 MOT OPEN/MODIFY JUDGMENT
```

COLUMN 8

```
0418464 S      DOSTIE,LISA
FA-98        V. HURTEAU,THOMAS W
                    ( 77)
PRO SE                    MIRTO K & B PC
   ARG   106.00 MOT OPEN/MODIFY JUDGMENT

0418465 S      VACCARO,PAUL D
FA-98        V. VACCARO,ANN T
                    ( 78)
KOLB C & E PC             O'DONNELL J L OF
   ARG x 111.00 MOT EXTEND TIME
   ARG   112.00 MOTION FOR MODIFICATION

   0404266 S     SAUERBRUNN,PAULA
FA-97        V. SAUERBRUNN,FREDERICK
                    ( 79)
D.W.CELOTTO,JR.           LASALA, W. & W.
N.EISENHANDLER
   ARG x 122.00 MOT JOINT CUSTODY
   ARG   123.00 MOTION FOR POSSESSION
   ARG   124.00 MOTION FOR ORDER

0359266 S      RICHMOND,WILLIAM M
FA-94        V. RICHMOND,NORMAJEAN
                    ( 80)
J. CHIARELLI              BERNBLUM & GREEN
   ARG   138.00 MOTION FOR ORDER

0280467 S      HARMS,SHEILA
FA-89        V. HARMS,EDWARD
                    ( 81)
JACOBS G B & D P          TYLER, C. & A.
   ARG   126.00 MOT OPEN/MODIFY JUDGMENT

0417667 S      MEHTA,VARSHA
FA-98        V. MEHTA,PRASHANT
                    ( 82)
GESMONDE P S & P          COUGHLIN & M.
   ARG x 101.00 MOT FOR SUPPORT-PD LITE
   ARG   102.00 MOT FOR ALIMONY-PD LITE
   ARG   103.00 MOT JOINT CUSTODY

0389467 S      LAZROVE,STEVEN
FA-96        V. LAZROVE,ANNE
                    ( 83)
COHEN G I L O OF          TYLER, C. & A.
   ARG   132.00 MOT REFER TO FRD

0405467 S      BARNETT,SCOTT
FA-97        V. BARNETT,PAMELA
                    ( 84)
SCHEIRER & GELLE          BERSHTEIN B & B
   ARG   130.00 MOT PERMISSION WD APPRNC

0367268 S      TEODOSIO,ROBIN L
FA-94        V. TEODOSIO,FRANK V
                    ( 85)
V LILBURN                 SOLOHON K & W PC
   ARG x 122.00 MOTION FOR COUNSEL FEES
   ARG   123.00 MOT REFER TO FRD
   ARG   124.00 MOT OPEN/MODIFY JUDGMENT
   ARG   125.00 MOT OPEN/MODIFY JUDGMENT

0415369 S      WADE,MICHAEL G
FA-98        V. FORD-WADE,ANNIE E
                    ( 86)
LS DRESSLER              NO APPEARANCE
   ARG   101.00 MOT FOR RECONCILIATION

0391871 S      CLUKEY, GENEVIEVE S.
FA-96        V. CLUKEY, THOMAS F.
                    ( 87)
RUBIN & E.               GOLDBLATT G & R
JACOBS G B & D P         PARRETT P P & C
   ARG x 235.01 MOT FOR ALIMONY-PD LITE
   ARG   235.02 MOT FOR SUPPORT-PD LITE
   ARG   236.00 OBJECTION TO MOTION
   ARG   237.00 MOTION FOR COUNSEL FEES

0418671 S      FOSTER,LINDA L
FA-98        V. FOSTER,GLENN P
                    ( 88)
L.L. LEVY                 M.BELLEZZA
   ARG x 101.01 MOT FOR ALIMONY-PD LITE
   ARG   101.02 MOTION FOR ALLOWANCE

PA= 0402673 S MILLER,PAMELA ROBYN
FA-97        V. MILLER,PAUL BRIAN
                    ( 89)
ADELMAN L OFFICE          CANTOR F R & G P
   ARG   112.00 MOTION FOR COUNSEL FEES
```

COLUMN 9

```
0419273 S      COLEMAN,DAWN
FA-98        V. COLEHAN,WILLIAM L
                    ( 90)
PRO SE                    NO APPEARANCE
   ARG   101.00 MOT FOR ORDER PEND LITE

0419573 S      SPARANO,DEBRA
FA-98        V. SPARANO,DANIEL SR
                    ( 91)
NOYES & M PC              NO APPEARANCE
   ARG   001.06 MOTION FOR COUNSEL FEES

0418675 S      GUIMARES,ALBERT
FA-98        V. SMITH,LYDIA A
                    ( 92)
VISHNO R & V PC           RR KLASKIN
   ARG x 102.01 MOT FOR ALIMONY-PD LITE
   ARG   102.02 MOTION FOR COUNSEL FEES

0412676 S      FRECKELTON,ERICKA A
FA-98        V. FRECKELTON,LEONARD
                    ( 93)
LAMBOLEY L FIRM           NO APPEARANCE
L.MARLOW
   ARG x 108.00 MOTION FOR COUNSEL FEES
   ARG   109.00 MOTION FOR GENETIC TEST

0394176 S      CRISCUOLO, KIMBERLY
FA-96        V. CRISCUOLO, MARK
                    ( 94)
BERDON Y & M PC           J. F. CIRILLO
                          JC DELANEY
   ARG   131.00 MOT OPEN/MODIFY JUDGMENT

0401377 S      PURPORA,SUZANNE
FA-97        V. PURPORA,DAVID P
                    ( 95)
LYNCH T K & E PC          PRO SE
                          ANDROSKI A & AND
                          R.A. VOLO
   ARG   158.00 MOTION FOR ORDER

0329780 S      ARNEILL, BONNIE P.
FA-92        V. ARNEILL, BRUCE P.
                    ( 96)
SUSMAN D & S PC           J. L. WELTY
   ARG   131.00 MOT PERMISSION WD APPRNC

0400181 S      CLARK, DEBORAH A.
FA-97        V. PERRY, JOHN C.III
                    ( 97)
PRO SE                    PRO SE
JACOBS G B & D P          PT GIORDANO
AAG GM BARTO
GESMONDE P S & P
   ARG   131.00 MOT PERMISSION WD APPRNC

0385281 S      CORVI, PETER A.
FA-96        V. CORVI,PAMELA R.
                    ( 98)
CONN L L S FUND           PRO SE
                          MCMAHON ELIZABET
   ARG   114.00 MOTION FOR MODIFICATION

0419381 S      TUCKER,SUZANNE M
FA-98        V. TUCKER,ALAN R
                    ( 99)
VAVRA N J L OFFI          NO APPEARANCE
   ARG x 101.01 MOT JOINT CUSTODY
   ARG   101.02 MOT CUSTODY-PD LITE
   ARG   101.03 MOT FOR SUPPORT-PD LITE
   ARG   101.04 MOT FOR ALIMONY-PD LITE

0393683 S      THOMPSON, WILLIAM
FA-96        V. THOMPSON, ELIZABETH
                    ( 100)
R. GEE, JR.               A.S.DIBENEDETTO
                          AAG GM BARTO
                          AAG GG WILLIAMS
   ARG x 111.00 MOT RETURN PERSONAL ITEM
   ARG   112.00 MOTION FOR ORDER

0385982 S      RUETTGER,LOUIS M
FA-96        V. RUETTGER,KARY L
                    ( 101)
PRO SE                    PRO SE
J. MIRSKY                 DS GROGINS
                          YOLEN & P LLC
   ARG   121.00 MOTION FOR COUNSEL FEES
```

NEW HAVEN   COLUMN 7   SHORT CAL NO. 2   COLUMN 8   COLUMN 9

EXHIBIT 11–10

Continued

```
0418083 S      ROSEN,JO-ANN
FA-98      V. ROSEN,JAMES
              ( 102)
RUTKIN & O PC          J. L. WELTY
ARG * 101.01 MOT FOR ALIMONY-PD LITE
ARG   101.02 MOT MEDICAL EXPENSES
ARG   101.03 MOTION FOR COUNSEL FEES
ARG   102.00 MOTION FOR ORDER
-------------------------------------
0412284 S      RYAN,BERNADETTE D
FA-98      V. RYAN,EDWARD JOSEPH
              ( 103)
O'DONNELL J L OF        LYNCH T K & E PC
ARG * 113.00 MOTION FOR ORDER
ARG   114.00 MOTION FOR ORDER
-------------------------------------
0280386 S      RICHITELLI,DAWN
FA-89      V. RICHITELLI,MICHAEL
              ( 104)
PHILPOT W M J L        PRO SE
                       MIRTO K & B PC
ARG   136.00 MOT OPEN/MODIFY JUDGMENT
-------------------------------------
0418186 S      PRINDLE,JAQUELINE C
FA-98      V. PRINDLE,BRUCE D
              ( 105)
CELLA M & WILLIA       NO APPEARANCE
ARG   101.00 MOT FOR SUPPORT-PD LITE
-------------------------------------
0419186 S      HUBYK,GREGORY
FA-98      V. HUBYK,PATRICIA
              ( 106)
DINAN & D              PRO SE
                       N.EISENHANDLER
ARG * 101.01 MOT CUSTODY-PD LITE
ARG   101.02 MOT FOR SUPPORT-PD LITE
ARG   101.03 MOT FOR ALIMONY-PD LITE
ARG   101.04 MOTION FOR COUNSEL FEES
ARG   102.01 MOTION FOR POSSESSION
ARG   102.02 MOTION FOR COUNSEL FEES
ARG   105.01 MOT CUSTODY-PD LITE
ARG   105.02 MOT FOR SUPPORT-PD LITE
ARG   105.03 MOTION FOR VISITATION
ARG   105.04 MOT FOR ALIMONY-PD LITE
ARG   106.00 MOTION FOR POSSESSION
ARG   107.00 MOTION FOR COUNSEL FEES
-------------------------------------
0414089 S      GERBE,BARBARA
FA-98      V. BERBE,RAYMOND
              ( 107)
M.SULLIVAN             P. E. RICCIARDI
ARG   106.00 MOTION FOR ORDER
-------------------------------------
0417790 S      KENNEY,CHRISTY
FA-98      V. KENNEY,JOHN
              ( 108)
C.J.RIETHER            NO APPEARANCE
ARG * 101.01 MOT FOR ALIMONY-PD LITE
ARG   101.02 MOTION FOR COUNSEL FEES
-------------------------------------
0419390 S      GUZMAN,SAMUEL
FA-98      V. GUZMAN,MIRIAM
              ( 109)
KINNEY & SECOLA        NO APPEARANCE
ARG   101.00 MOTION FOR VISITATION
-------------------------------------
0417591 S      ANDERSON,THERESA
FA-98      V. ANDERSON,DENIS
              ( 110)
GREENBERG H & C        PRO SE
ARG * 101.00 MOT FOR ALIMONY-PD LITE
ARG   102.01 MOT CUSTODY-PD LITE
ARG   102.02 MOT FOR SUPPORT-PD LITE
ARG   103.00 MOTION FOR POSSESSION
-------------------------------------
0411392 S      CARRANO,ARTHUR T
FA-98      V. CARRANO,HEATHER A
              ( 111)
SOLOMON K & W PC       BOGDANOFF & C LL
ARG   129.00 MOTION FOR MODIFICATION
-------------------------------------
0415692 S      GARTMAN,KENDRA
FA-98      V. GARTMAN,DONALD P III
              ( 112)
G. H. KAHN             KOLESNIK & NORRI
ARG   108.00 OBJECTION TO MOTION
-------------------------------------
0412394 S      NOSAL,MICHELE H
FA-98      V. NOSAL,ANDREW JOHN
              ( 113)
SOLOMON K & W PC       B.A.CHAPLIN
ARG   136.00 MOTION FOR ORDER
-------------------------------------
```

```
0345594 S      HARRIS, DARIN
FA-93      V. HARRIS, ANTHONY
              ( 114)
PRO SE                 PRO SE
ARG   108.00 RULE OPEN/MODIFY JDGMENT
-------------------------------------
0411995 S      LARKIN,DOROTHY
FA-98      V. LARKIN,WILLIAM
              ( 115)
ENGELMAN & WELCH     COHEN G I L O OF
ARG   106.00 MOTION TO COMPEL
-------------------------------------
0416996 S      SWANSON,KAREN
FA-98      V. MCNERNEY,DENNIS
              ( 116)
M.H.LERNER             NO APPEARANCE
ARG   101.00 MOT REFER TO FRD
-------------------------------------
0351197 S      BEAMON, CLAUDETTE J.
FA-93      V. BEAMON, KEVIN E.
              ( 117)
PRO SE                 PRO SE
                       NUGENT & BRYANT
ARG   147.00 MOT OPEN/MODIFY JUDGMENT
-------------------------------------
FPT 0401197 S  ROSEMAN,SHELLEY
FA-97      V. ROSEMAN,MARK
              ( 118)
LEVY & S LLC           PRO SE
S.O.LEBAS              G. M. KAHN
ARG   155.80 MOT OPEN/MODIFY JUDGMENT
-------------------------------------
0418697 S      BISHOP,JONATHAN B
FA-98      V. BISHOP,DIANE E
              ( 119)
H.D.MURPHY             G. BATTISTOLI
ARG * 102.00 MOT FOR ALIMONY-PD LITE
ARG   103.00 MOT RETURN PERSONAL ITEM
-------------------------------------
0383998 S      WILLIAMS,MARCELLE A.
FA-96      V. WILLIAMS,STANLEY A.
              ( 120)
M.H.LERNER             PRO SE
ALBIS & PELLEGRI       E.J. DOLAN
ARG * 149.00 MOTION FOR ORDER
ARG   150.00 MOTION FOR ORDER
-------------------------------------
0398598 S      KACANICH, GARY
FA-98      V. KACANICH, LORRAINE
              ( 121)
COHEN & W PC           G. BATTISTOLI
                       L. PARLEY
ARG   123.00 MOT PERMISSION WD APPRNC
-------------------------------------
0248099 S      CONTESSA,KATHLEEN
FA-86      V. CONTESSA,DOMINIC
              ( 122)
E.J. DOLAN           JACOBS G B & D P
ARG   127.00 MOTION FOR ORDER
-------------------------------------

CHIEF CLERK
```

NOTICE (continued from Column 1)

recorded controls. There is no marking to a later time or separate assignment.

A list of cases marked "Ready" and the judges and courtrooms to whom these cases are assigned, will be posted on the FIRST FLOOR, THIRD FLOOR, AND OUTSIDE THE CLERK'S OFFICE, the preceding Friday afternoon.

FAMILY RELATIONS

Parties must discuss their matter with a counselor from Family Relations when they arrive for their hearing. A Family Relations sign-up sheet is posted on the wall outside of Courtroom 3E for this purpose. Counselors will also be available to discuss pending motions prior to the assigned short calendar date. Call (203) 789-7903 for an appointment.

```
                  COLUMN 10
NEW HAVEN                 SHORT CAL NO. 2          COLUMN 11
```

EXHIBIT 11–11
Sample stipulation regarding temporary support in a divorce case.

<table>
<tr><td>1</td><td colspan="2">SIMKE, CHODOS, SILBERFELD & ANTEAU, INC.</td></tr>
<tr><td>2</td><td colspan="2">6300 Wilshire Boulevard
Suite 9000</td></tr>
<tr><td>3</td><td colspan="2">Los Angeles, California 90048-5202
(213) 653-0211</td></tr>
</table>

FILED

JAN 21 1994

EDWARD ~~~~~~~~, CLERK

H. Hinaga

BY H. HINAGA, DEPUTY

Attorneys for Respondent,
MELISSA JANE CARREY

SUPERIOR COURT OF THE STATE OF CALIFORNIA

FOR THE COUNTY OF LOS ANGELES

In re the Marriage of:)   CASE NO. BD 135 499
)
Petitioner: JAMES EUGENE CARREY   )   STIPULATION RE: PENDENTE
)   LITE SUPPORT
        and   )
)
Respondent: MELISSA JANE CARREY)
)
_____)

WHEREAS, due to the uncertainty of Petitioner's employment that will exist until approximately March 1, 1994; and

WHEREAS, the parties are desirous of entering into a stipulation relative to spousal and child support for income tax purposes; and

WHEREAS, the parties are desirous of establishing some certainty as to spousal and child support for the months of January, February and March of 1994; and

WHEREAS, the parties are agreeable to any such agreement being without prejudice to the contentions of either party,

NOW, THEREFORE, IT IS HEREBY STIPULATED by and between the parties hereto, and joined in by their respective counsel as

10145\stpbl293.car   1

EXHIBIT 11-11

Continued

<u>In re Marriage of Carrey</u>   <u>L.A.S.C. Case No. BD 135 499</u>

follows:

1.   That for the months of January, February and March of 1994, Petitioner shall pay to Respondent, as and for spousal support, the sum of $20,600.00 (Twenty-Thousand, Six-Hundred Dollars) per month, payable one-half (1/2) on the first and one-half (1/2) on the fifteenth days of each month, commencing January 1, 1994, and continuing thereafter through March 15, 1994.

The spousal support paid by Petitioner to Respondent shall be reportable as income by Respondent and deductible by Petitioner for income tax purposes.

2.   That Petitioner shall pay to Respondent, as and for child support of the minor child of the parties, the sum of $5,300.00 (Five-Thousand, Three-Hundred Dollars) per month, payable one-half (1/2) on the first and one-half (1/2) on the fifteenth days of each month, commencing January 1, 1994 and continuing thereafter through the payment on March 15, 1994.

3.   Petitioner shall continue to pay and maintain the existing policies of medical and life insurance for the benefit of Respondent and the minor child.

4.   That with respect to the minor child, the parties shall share equally any non-insurance covered expenses, which shall include at the commencement of 1994, the deductible portions.

5.   Respondent shall be responsible for all of the living expenses of herself and the minor child while in her custody, including but not limited to mortgage payments and real property taxes on the family residence, household expenses and private school expenses for the minor child. Additionally, Respondent

10145\stpbl293.car   2

In re Marriage of Carrey   L.A.S.C. Case No. BD 135 499

shall be responsible for any credit card charges incurred by her after January 1, 1994, and at such time as she receives credit cards which have been issued in her name alone, she will surrender the joint credit cards in her possession.

6.   The aforesaid spousal and child support shall be without prejudice to either party's position, and in the event either party hereafter files an Order to Show Cause proceeding for pendente lite spousal and child support, same shall be retroactive to January 1, 1994, with Petitioner receiving credit for the payments hereinabove set forth.

DATED: ~~December   , 1993~~
        JANUARY 14, 1994
_____
JAMES EUGENE CARREY, Petitioner

DATED: December 6, 1993
_____
MELISSA JANE CARREY, Respondent

APPROVED AS TO FORM AND CONTENT:

_____
NORMAN M. DOLIN, Attorney for
  Petitioner, JAMES EUGENE CARREY

SIMKE, CHODOS, SILBERFELD & ANTEAU, INC.

By_____
RONALD W. ANTEAU, Attorneys for
  Respondent, MELISSA JANE CARREY

10145\stpbl293.car   3

EXHIBIT 11–12
Sample motion for contempt.

DOCKET NO. FA 96-123456	:	SUPERIOR COURT
BRONSON, RODNEY	:	JUDICIAL DISTRICT OF NEW HAVEN
V.	:	AT NEW HAVEN
BRONSON, EVELYN	:	SEPTEMBER 21, 2000

MOTION FOR CONTEMPT

The plaintiff in the above-referenced matter respectfully requests that the court find the defendant in contempt of court for failing to pay plaintiff court-ordered alimony payments. In support hereof, the plaintiff represents as follows:

1. On August 15, 2000, the court ordered the defendant to make weekly pendente lite alimony payments to the plaintiff in the amount of $275.

2. The defendant has failed to make weekly pendente lite alimony payments in any amount since August 29, 2000.

3. The defendant currently owes the plaintiff back pendente lite alimony in the amount of FIVE HUNDRED AND FIFTY DOLLARS ($550).

WHEREFORE, the plaintiff asks that the court find the defendant in contempt of the Court's order of August 15, 2000, and exercises its power to compel defendant to abide by said court order.

THE PLAINTIFF,
RODNEY BRONSON

BY: _____
JUSTINE F. MILLER, ESQ.
HIS ATTORNEY
22 PARK PLACE
NEW HAVEN, CT 06511
(203) 861-4444
JURIS NO. 313133

ORDER

The foregoing motion having been heard, it is hereby ORDERED:

GRANTED/DENIED
THE COURT

BY: _____
JUDGE

EXHIBIT 11–12
Continued

<u>**CERTIFICATION**</u>

This is to certify that a true copy of the foregoing motion was mailed, postage prepaid, on this date to all counsel and pro se parties of record on this _____ day of _____, 2000, as follows:

Grace A. Luppino
555 Main Avenue
New Haven, CT 06511

_____
Justine F. Miller, Esq.
Commissioner of the Superior Court

EXHIBIT 11–13
Sample motion for modification.

DOCKET NO. FA 96-123456	:	SUPERIOR COURT
BRONSON, RODNEY	:	JUDICIAL DISTRICT OF NEW HAVEN
V.	:	AT NEW HAVEN
BRONSON, EVELYN	:	SEPTEMBER 21, 2000

MOTION FOR MODIFICATION OF ALIMONY

The defendant in the above-referenced matter respectfully requests that the Court modify its order for alimony to reflect the defendant's changed financial circumstances.

In support hereof, the defendant represents as follows:

1. On August 15, 2000, this honorable court ordered the defendant to make weekly alimony payments pendente lite to the plaintiff in the amount of $275.

2. The defendant complied with the court's order from the date of its entry through August 22, 2000.

3. On or about August 25, 2000, defendant's employment was terminated and defendant has remained without employment until September 20, 2000.

4. Defendant's income from her present employment is considerably lower than income from defendant's previous position.

5. Defendant is unable to pay plaintiff the weekly amount of $275.

WHEREFORE, the defendant requests that the Court modify its alimony order of August 15, 2000 to reflect the defendant's adversely changed financial circumstances.

THE DEFENDANT,
EVELYN BRONSON

BY: _____
JUSTINE F. MILLER, ESQ.
HIS ATTORNEY
22 PARK PLACE
NEW HAVEN, CT 06511
(203) 861-4444

ORDER

The foregoing motion having been heard, it is hereby ORDERED:

GRANTED/DENIED
THE COURT

BY: _____
JUDGE

EXHIBIT 11–13
Continued

<u>CERTIFICATION</u>

This is to certify that a true copy of the foregoing motion was mailed, postage prepaid, on this date to all counsel and pro se parties of record on this _____ day of _____, 2000, as follows:

Justine F. Miller, Esq.
22 Park Place
New Haven, CT 06511

_____
Grace A. Luppino, Esq.
Commissioner of the Superior Court

REVIEW QUESTIONS

1. What is a statutory cooling-off period?
2. What is meant by the term *pendente lite*?
3. Explain the purpose of a *pendente lite* motion.
4. Name the general features common to motions in all jurisdictions.
5. What information is provided in the caption of a motion?
6. List three motions commonly filed in a divorce proceeding.
7. What is the paralegal's role in facilitating *pendente lite* motions?
8. Explain the purpose of motion days or a short calendar.
9. What is a docket control system?
10. When would a party file a motion for contempt? A motion for modification?

EXERCISES

1. Find out the mandatory cooling-off period for divorce cases in your state. What is the minimum period of time that the parties must wait before the divorce is finalized? Are there any exceptions?

2. Contact the clerk of your local family court to determine when *pendente lite* motions are heard. Arrange to sit in and observe court proceedings on a short calendar or motion day. Make sure you obtain a copy of that day's calendar from the clerk's office so you can follow along.

3. Determine the procedure required in your state for filing *pendente lite* motions. Are you required to file accompanying documents with the motion? What are the time frames for filing motions? What is the procedure for serving motions on the opposing party?

4. Find your state statutes regarding *pendente lite* motions and outline the statutory criteria.

5. What is the required format for *pendente lite* motions in your state?

CHAPTER 12

THE DISCOVERY PROCESS IN FAMILY LAW

KEY TERMS

Capias

Confidential

Confidentiality agreement

Cross-examination

Deponent

Deposition

Direct examination

Discovery

Discovery tool

Duplicative

Financial affidavit

Interrogatories

Irrelevant

Joint stipulation

Malpractice

Memorandum of law

Motion for disclosure of assets

Motion for protective order

Motion to compel examination

Notice of deposition

Notice of filing of interrogatories

Notice of responding to and/or objecting to interrogatories

Objection

Overbroad

Privilege

Redirect

Request

Request for admission

Request for physical or mental examination

Request for production of documents

Requesting party

Responding party

Subpoena

Subpoena duces tecum

The discovery process is an important part of any type of civil suit. **Discovery** is the term used to describe the process or stage in a civil litigation matter during which information is gathered by each party for use in their case against the other party. There are set procedures known as **discovery tools** that the court allows the parties to employ while conducting discovery. The court, upon a motion from one of the parties, may hold the other party in contempt and/or compel the other party to release information held back unless the reluctant party has asserted a valid *objection* or *privilege*.

In a dissolution action, discovery is used to acquire essential information that will lead to an equitable distribution of marital property and to accurately determine each party's income in order to set alimony and child support payments. Finally, discovery can provide the information needed to make wise decisions about what type of custody the court will award and what visitation arrangements are in the child's best interests.

DISCOVERY TOOLS

In any type of lawsuit each party has the right to use any or all of the following discovery vehicles:

- Interrogatories,
- Requests for the production of documents,
- Requests for physical and mental examination,
- Requests for admission, and
- Depositions.

In litigation involving family law matters, most and sometimes all of these general discovery tools are used. Frequently, family law attorneys also employ additional discovery-oriented procedures designed to elicit specific information essential to the resolution of the particular issues involved in a family law matter. Examples include the motion for disclosure of assets and the parties' respective financial affidavits.

What follows is a description of both the general discovery tools common to all types of litigation and the subsidiary discovery vehicles commonly used in family matters. Accompanying each of these descriptions is a summary of the family law paralegal's role and duties in facilitating effective use of each discovery tool and procedure.

INTERROGATORIES

Interrogatories are written questions that one party in a lawsuit serves on any opposing party or parties. The party on whom the interrogatories are served must answer the interrogatories under oath. A party may object to having to answer an interrogatory. **Objections** can be asserted on the grounds that the information sought is **irrelevant, overbroad,** or **duplicative.** A party may also refuse to answer by asserting a privilege. A **privilege** is a court-conferred right permitting parties in a lawsuit to keep confidential any information exchanged between themselves and another person in instances where there was a special type of relationship between themselves and the other person that generated an expectation of trust, confidentiality, and privacy. For instance, the court recognizes

▼ Spousal privilege,

▼ Attorney/client privilege,

▼ Physician/patient (therapist/client) privilege, and

▼ Priest/penitent (clergy/parishioner) privilege.

Interrogatories in a family law proceeding may seek to have the other party identify all banks accounts, stock accounts, and real property held by that party jointly or in his or her name, solely. Interrogatories may contain questions about a spouse's current employment, earned income, bonuses, and health insurance and life insurance coverage. The purpose of these types of interrogatories is to uncover all of the opposing party's assets and sources of earned and unearned income, as well as forms of nonmonetary employment compensation.

Interrogatories may also seek to have the opposing party spouse reveal the names of parties residing with the spouse; the names and addresses of doctors who have treated the spouse or who have treated the minor children when in that spouse's care; and the names of day care providers or other child care workers who have cared for the child or children. Interrogatories must be answered in writing, under oath, and by the party on whom they have been served.

FIGURE 12–1
A party may consider a question "privileged" and refuse to answer it if it deals with a patient/doctor relationship.

Preparation of Interrogatories

The paralegal in a family law practice will often have the task of drafting interrogatories to be served on the opposing party. The paralegal should begin this process by reviewing the client's file and making a list of all areas where information will be needed from the opposing spouse. Then the paralegal, with the supervising attorney's approval, should schedule a meeting with the client.

Prior to the meeting the paralegal prepares a rough draft of the interrogatories or questions to be posed and answered. At the meeting, the client and paralegal review these questions, correct any inaccurate information, and add and delete questions as they agree is appropriate. Following the initial meeting, the paralegal revises the draft of the interrogatories and presents this revised draft to the supervising attorney for review and further revision, if necessary.

Once the supervising attorney completes any needed revisions and signs off on the document, the paralegal prepares the final form of the interrogatories and returns the completed document to the supervising attorney for final review and signature. Once signed, the paralegal ensures that the document is sent to the opposing party's attorney. In most jurisdictions, interrogatories and responses are not filed with the court. Many states, however, require that parties file with the court a **notice of filing of interrogatories** and a **notice of responding to and/or objecting to interrogatories.** The paralegal should learn the jurisdiction's requirements for filing any documents related to interrogatories and responses and time limitations on such filings.

Preparation of Responses to Interrogatories

As mentioned, a party served with interrogatories must answer the interrogatories in writing and under oath, and within a specific time frame. In the oath, the party must state that his answers or responses are true and accurate to the best of his knowledge. This obligation to answer truthfully and accurately does not preclude the law firm from providing a client with assistance in forming and articulating accurate responses or from providing technical assistance in the manuscripting or transcribing of the answers or objections.

When a law firm receives a set of interrogatories for a particular client to answer, frequently the family law paralegal will see to it that the client provides the required responses within the appropriate time frame. The paralegal often copies the interrogatory papers and sends a copy to the client with a cover letter explaining that the client should try to provide answers to all questions as best she can. In this letter the paralegal will also tell the client to mail back her responses as soon as possible. After the client has sent the responses to the law firm, the paralegal reviews the information and then, with the approval of the supervising attorney, calls the client and sets a date for the client to come to the office and meet with the paralegal to discuss and finalize the responses.

At this meeting, the paralegal assists the client in reformulating any answers that are incomplete or that do not really answer the question asked. In addition, the paralegal helps the client delete any information in answers that should be objected to or that are privileged. The paralegal also helps the client delete any information that has not been requested, especially information that, if left in the response, would, in fact, help the other side with their case and hurt the client.

After the client and paralegal have finalized the responses, the paralegal prepares a final document that is reviewed by the supervising attorney. If the supervising attorney has questions or concerns regarding any part of the document, these issues are discussed and resolved. The paralegal then revises the document as needed, and the attorney reviews the revised document.

If everything is in order, the paralegal again arranges for the client to come to the office, review the final document and, subject to any final revisions, the client signs the responses under oath in the presence of two witnesses, and a notary public or officer of the court acknowledges her oath. Once finalized, the paralegal sends the responsive document to the opposing party's counsel and files notice with the court, if such notice is required. A sample set of interrogatories is provided in Exhibit 12–1.

REQUESTS FOR PRODUCTION

Parties may request production and inspection, and often copying, of documents that are relevant to a dissolution action (see Exhibit 12–2). For instance, by means of a **request for production,** one party can request inspection of the other party's federal and state tax returns, canceled checks, bills for the minor children's summer camp or private school, copies of health insurance plans, insurance policies, copies of driver's licenses, pay stubs, and titles to cars, boats, or other recreational vehicles. The party asking to see and, most likely, copy these documents is called the **requesting party.** The party who must produce these documents is known as the **responding party.**

The responding party must produce all documents requested unless he has a valid objection or the documents are privileged, or **confidential,** or the responding party does not have what has been requested and has no idea of where these documents are. Sometimes, a responding party may withhold a document on the grounds that it is confidential. In a family law matter, this issue might arise when the requesting party seeks information relating to the respondent's business, profession, or employment. For the respondent to produce this information, the respondent might be divulging a trade secret, classified work-related data, or even information about an invention for which the respondent is seeking a patent, or about an artistic work the respondent wishes to have copyrighted before revealing it to the public. In instances like this, either or both parties may draft and file with the court a **motion for protective order** and a **confidentiality agreement.** These documents will ensure that although certain confidential information will be disclosed to the opposing party, that party, under penalty of law, must limit disclosure of this information to the court and the parties only and must affirmatively act to protect the confidentiality of the material provided.

Preparation of Requests for Production

The family law paralegal is often the person who prepares the preliminary draft of production requests that the client or the supervising attorney wishes to make. The steps in this process are similar to the steps utilized for preparing interrogatories. The paralegal reviews the file, consults with the attorney and with the client, and also draws on models of production requests from previous similar types of family law actions.

When the opposing party remits documents in response to the request, the paralegal checks off these documents, catalogs them, and prepares a list of documents not produced so that the supervising attorney will know of and can respond to the opposing party's noncompliance.

Preparation of Responses to Requests for Production

The family law paralegal may also be responsible for orchestrating a client's response to the opposing side's production requests. When the law firm receives a request for the production of documents, the paralegal sends a copy to the client just as the paralegal has sent the client a copy of interrogatories served. Because there is only a thirty-day time limit in which to respond to both interrogatories and production requests, the paralegal follows up the letter with a phone call to the client in which the paralegal offers assistance in helping the client to identify and find the requested documents. The paralegal should also meet with the supervising attorney to discuss which documents the attorney wishes to withhold as privileged, which documents the attorney objects to producing, and which documents, if any, the attorney wishes to be shielded by a protective order and confidentiality agreement.

REQUEST FOR PHYSICAL OR PSYCHIATRIC EXAMINATION

In a dissolution action, one party may request that the other party submit to a physical examination and/or a psychiatric evaluation (see Exhibit 12–3). This may occur when the requesting party believes and alleges that the other party's physical or mental status should preclude awarding child custody or unsupervised visitation to the other party.

A party may also file a **request for physical or mental examination** if the opposing party has requested a high amount of alimony on the basis that she is physically unable to work or too emotionally unstable to work, or where the party on her financial affidavit reflects high weekly costs for mental health counseling or therapy.

Finally, in dissolutions involving minor children, the children's mother may request a physical examination of the male spouse to establish paternity of the child for purposes of support, custody, and visitation. The husband/spouse may also request a paternity test if he doubts that he is the natural father of one or more of the children born during the marriage.

Preparation of a Request for a Medical Examination

When a family law paralegal has an initial informational interview with a client, as discussed in an earlier section, the paralegal asks the client to complete a questionnaire that addresses many aspects of the client's marital history and each

FIGURE 12–2
A party to a dissolution may request a mental examination of the other party if the other party claims, for example, an inability to work due to emotional stress.

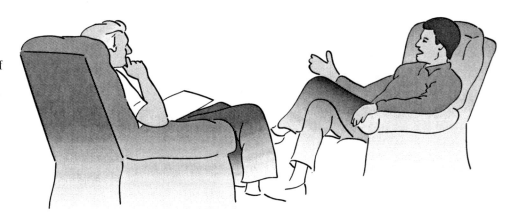

spouse's individual family background, educational attainments, and medical history. After reviewing the client's responses, the paralegal may immediately recognize the existence of one of the above-mentioned circumstances that gives rise to the need for a physical or mental examination of the opposing party. The paralegal should bring this to the attention of the supervising attorney. If the supervising attorney agrees with the paralegal's analysis, she will direct the paralegal to prepare the document for filing in court.

In most jurisdictions, the party desiring such an examination must file a document with the court known as a **request** rather than a motion. A request differs from a motion in that it is automatically granted by the court thirty days after filing, absent the opposing party's objection. The family paralegal files the original of the request document with the court and makes sure that proper service is made on the opposing party's counsel. If no objection is filed within the prescribed time limit and the time limit expires, the paralegal prepares a letter to opposing counsel requesting dates on which to schedule the requested examination or examinations. Absent the timely filing of an objection, the opposing party must submit to the examination within a reasonable amount of time. If the party refuses to do so, the paralegal must alert the supervising attorney of this failure and, with the supervising attorney's approval, file a **motion to compel examination.**

Frequently, an opposing party may object to an examination completely, or object unless there is agreement as to the choice of examiner, agreement as to the extent, nature, and exact purpose of the exam, or the use to which the requesting party will allocate the results. When an objection is filed, the opposing attorneys may be willing to negotiate a compromise and avoid litigating the issue in open court.

If no agreement is reached, the matter is scheduled for a hearing and the paralegal keeps a watchful eye for the court calendar that will be sent to the law firm indicating the date of the hearing. When it arrives, the paralegal will docket the hearing on the calendar. If the scheduled date conflicts with other obligations of the attorney handling the case, the paralegal apprises the supervising attorney, who then decides whether to send another of the firm's attorneys to the hearing or to have the paralegal attempt to reschedule the matter. The paralegal is also responsible for notifying the client of the need to be in court on the hearing date. If the supervising attorney believes that the client will need to offer testimony, the paralegal may schedule a meeting with the client prior to the hearing to review the matter and prepare the client for his appearance on the witness stand.

Preparation of a Response to a Request for a Medical Examination

When the family law firm receives a request that a client be subjected to a physical examination or mental or psychological evaluation, the attorney handling the file may direct the paralegal to communicate the request to the party and arrange for an office conference to discuss the request. After this meeting, the supervising attorney may decide to object to the request or negotiate with opposing counsel to allow the examination subject to agreed-on parameters such as the ones mentioned above.

Usually, a party's attorney will not allow a blanket assent to an examination and the uses to which the results will be applied unless the examination is limited by its own nature and/or unless the client insists on no limitations. The family law paralegal may have the task of drafting a letter to the opposing counsel memorializing the limiting terms parties have agreed to. If no agreement is reached, the

FIGURE 12–3
An attorney may
decide to object to a
request for a medical
examination or may
ask for certain param-
eters to be accepted,
such as naming the
person who will
conduct the examina-
tion.

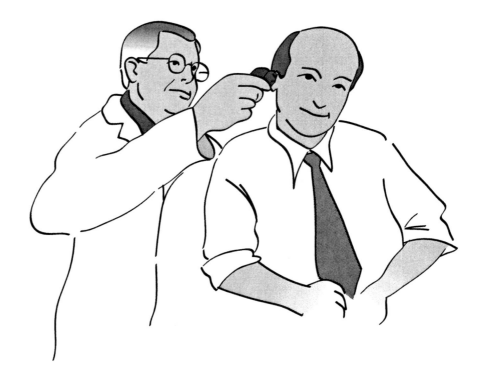

paralegal will, within the thirty-day period, draft and see to the finalization of an objection or objections that must be filed with the court. Once filed, the paralegal will make sure that the court's notice of a hearing on the objections is noted, and docketed on the firm's calendar, and that any need for a continuance is requested in a timely manner.

If a client must submit to a medical examination or mental or psychological evaluation, the paralegal may be the staff person who arranges for the client's appointment, notifies the client of this appointment, and telephones the client a day or two before the appointment to remind the client of this obligation. After the examination, the paralegal should make sure that the firm receives a copy of the examining physician's report and/or a copy of the results of any laboratory tests.

REQUEST FOR ADMISSION

Sometimes either party in a dissolution action may file a **request for admission** of certain facts or events (see Exhibit 12–4). In civil suits, one party may request formally that an opposing party admit the truth of some fact or event that will inevitably be proved at trial. For instance, one party may request that the other party admit that although the other party receives child support for three minor children, the oldest child resides with the noncustodial parent. If one party files a request for admission with the court, and the other party does not object to this request within thirty days after it is filed, the facts or events requested to be admitted are deemed admitted. If the other party does file an objection, then the parties may negotiate a compromise of admissions or, if no compromise is reached, the parties' attorneys will argue their respective positions before the court.

Preparation of a Request for Admissions

The family law paralegal is responsible for recognizing any circumstances listed on the client questionnaire that may necessitate the filing of a request for admission from the opposing party. The paralegal should apprise the supervising attorney of such circumstances and if the supervising attorney agrees that a request for admission of certain facts is in order, then the paralegal may prepare the document, present it to the attorney for review and signing, and see that it is filed properly with the court and that a copy is mailed to the opposing counsel in a timely manner.

Once such a document is filed, the paralegal should watch the calendar to ensure that any objections received from opposing counsel are filed within the thirty-day time limit. If objections are timely filed and the parties' attorneys reach a compromise, the paralegal prepares, for court filing, either a revised request for admissions negotiated and agreed to by both parties, which will be automatically granted after thirty days, or a **joint stipulation** in which the opposing party withdraws its objections subject to the modification of some aspect of the requested admissions.

Preparation of a Response to a Request for Admission

Frequently, when an attorney receives a request for admission from opposing counsel, the attorney will ask the paralegal to contact the client, explain the purpose of a request for admission, describe the nature of the admissions sought, and inquire whether the facts the opposing counsel seeks to have admitted are true and accurate. The paralegal discusses the outcome of this conversation with the supervising attorney, who will decide how to respond to the request. If the paralegal feels that the client needs further explanation or clarification of the request for admissions, the paralegal should convey this to the attorney, who may wish to speak to the client personally before proceeding further. The attorney may direct the paralegal to send the client a copy of the request for admission and a cover letter that requests the client to call the office and set up a time for an office meeting or telephone conference with the attorney to discuss how to proceed.

The paralegal must also monitor the running of the thirty-day objection deadline so that before the time period expires, the attorney confers with opposing counsel and decides whether to allow the admissions or have the paralegal prepare a stipulation, or prepare objections to the request for admission to be heard by the court. If objections are filed and the court schedules a hearing, the paralegal will be responsible for docketing the date and notifying the client. If a scheduling conflict exists, the paralegal may have to notify the office of opposing counsel of this conflict and also notify the court by requesting a continuance for the hearing.

DEPOSITIONS

The need for depositions does not arise in every dissolution case. Depositions are employed primarily when there is a need to identify all of the opposing spouse's assets or when documentation is needed to support one parent's claim that the child's interest will be best served by investing sole custody in that parent, or when a parent wishes to establish the need to severely restrict the other party's visitation rights.

A **deposition** is a procedure in which one party's attorney orally questions an opposing party or a nonparty witness who has sworn under oath to answer all questions truthfully and accurately to the best of their knowledge and ability. The person being deposed is known as the **deponent.** The format of a deposition includes the initial questioning by the deposing party's attorney. This questioning is termed **direct examination.** After the deposing attorney conducts the direct examination, the opposing party's lawyer has the opportunity to cross-examine his or her client. After this **cross-examination,** the deposing attorney may question the deponent on any subject covered in the cross-examination testimony. This questioning is known as **redirect** questioning.

The following individuals must be present at a deposition: the deposing attorney, the opposing party, and the court reporter. The attorney for the opposing party *should* also be present. The deposing party's client may be present and, for practical reasons, should be present. If, however, the deposing party's client in a dissolution suit is terrified of the opposing party, and the deposing lawyer decides that the risks to his or her client's well-being outweigh the value of the client's presence at the deposition, the attorney may choose to depose the opposing party outside the client's presence. The deposing attorney may also decide to have his or her paralegal present to take notes or retrieve documents for direct questioning or cross-examination.

At the deposition of a nonparty witness, all parties must be invited but their presence is not mandatory. Usually the opposing party's lawyer will attend and want the client to also attend. The court reporter must always be present at a deposition.

Deposition Expenses

Depositions are expensive. Therefore, the need for a deposition must be great enough to justify the expense. An attorney will apprise a client of the availability of the deposition as a discovery tool and may strongly recommend deposing the opposing party or a witness or witnesses. However, the decision to depose ultimately rests with the client, who must pay the attorney for time spent preparing for and appearing at the deposition and who must pay the court reporter for transcription services at the deposition and for the typed transcript of the deposition.

FIGURE 12–4
Court reporters are always present at depositions.

Early in a client's representation the attorney should make the client aware of the possible need for depositions and the anticipated costs. An attorney should also tell his client that the opposing spouse's attorney may require that she be deposed. A client may refuse to appear at a deposition once she is noticed. Exhibit 12–5 provides a sample **notice of deposition,** which is served on a party to a lawsuit by sending the notice via first class mail to the party's lawyer.

Once a party has been served, the party through his or her attorney has the following options:

1. Appear at the deposition at the noticed time and place,
2. Negotiate to reschedule the deposition to a time and/or place mutually agreeable to the deposing party and the party being deposed, or
3. Request to have the other party cancel the deposition by offering to negotiate or informally resolve the issue that has given rise to the noticing of a deposition.

If a deposing party's purpose for the deposition is to uncover the opposing party's hidden assets or hidden and ongoing source of income, the party noticed for deposition may decide to amend her financial affidavit to reflect these amounts, thus obviating the need, time, and expense of a deposition, or the party may simply decide to make the opposing spouse a higher property settlement or agree to a higher amount of alimony or child support or both.

Sometimes the simple act of noticing a party for a deposition will produce one or another of these results. Doing so is considered an act of strategy!

The Paralegal's Role in the Deposition

At a minimum, the paralegal in a family law practice is responsible for preparing the notice of deposition, determining the client's availability, and sending copies to all counsel and *pro se* parties. Because a deposition is usually held at the law offices of the deposing attorney, the paralegal must check the availability of the conference room, or in a larger firm, the availability of one of the conference rooms.

Sometimes, either the attorney or the paralegal will call the opposing attorney or their paralegal to agree and reserve in advance the date or dates for the deposition. These dates then appear on the notice of deposition, which must nevertheless be served even if the respective attorneys have agreed to the fact of the deposition and its place, time, and date.

NOTICING OF NONPARTY WITNESSES

The paralegal is also often responsible for preparing the paperwork needed to bring a nonparty witness to a deposition.

To require a nonparty witness to appear at a deposition to be deposed, the deposing lawyer must serve a subpoena on the witness ordering their appearance. A **subpoena** is a legal document signed by an officer of the court that requires the person receiving it to appear under penalty of law at the time, date, and place indicated on the document (see Exhibit 12–6). A sheriff or other indifferent person serves the subpoena on the nonparty witness. In many jurisdictions, the statute requires the sheriff to give the nonparty witness cash or a check to reimburse the nonparty for a percentage of his travel expenses from his home to the site of the deposition. A **subpoena duces tecum** is a subpoena commanding a party or witness, who has in his or her possession, documents that are relevant to a case, to produce them at a motion hearing or trial.

Typically, the paralegal prepares the subpoena and arranges for the sheriff to pick up the subpoena and serve the witness. The paralegal is responsible for giving the sheriff the proper address for the witness and possibly a physical description of the witness. Also, the paralegal should later check with the sheriff to determine if service has indeed been made.

MOTION FOR DISCLOSURE OF ASSETS

Frequently, in conjunction with the taking of a party's deposition, the deposing attorney will file with the court a **motion for disclosure of assets** (see Exhibit 12–7). In this motion, the moving attorney requests the court to order the opposing party to bring to the deposition detailed information on all existing assets and acceptable documentation to substantiate the extent and/or limits of the party's assets. The opposing attorney may object to the granting of this motion, in which case, the court hears arguments from both sides and either grants or denies the motion. If the motion is granted, the party must under penalty of law bring such materials to the deposition. There, the opposing counsel examines the documents and questions the party on various aspects of the information. Naturally, the deponent's attorney will have an opportunity for cross-examination and the deposing attorney may conduct redirect examination on the cross-examination.

If a party's attorney is not deposing the opposing party, the party's attorney may still file a motion for disclosure of assets. If the motion is granted, the opposing party's attorney must see that a written disclosure is made, that it is accompanied by requested documentation, and that the disclosure is made within the court-ordered time frame. If a party fails to fully disclose his or her assets, the opposing counsel may file a motion to hold the party in contempt of a court order. If contempt is proven, the court may order immediate and full disclosure which, if not complied with, may result in the court issuing a **capias,** which is a civil arrest warrant served by a sheriff ordering that officer to take physical custody of the party and bring them to the appropriate corrections facility, that is, *jail,* where they will remain incarcerated until they make arrangements to comply with the court's order for disclosure.

A motion for disclosure of assets in a family law matter typically requests disclosure of all real and personal property owned by a spouse either in her own name or owned jointly with the spouse or with another person or entity. Examples of such assets include bank accounts, certificates of deposit, mutual funds, stocks, boats, cars, and parcels of real estate. The motion for disclosure of assets and the assets it involves is discussed extensively in Chapter 6, which covers property distribution.

Preparation of a Motion for Disclosure of Assets

The family law paralegal is often given the task of drafting the motion for disclosure of assets. The paralegal should review the client intake sheet on which the client has listed assets he believes the other spouse owns. In addition, the paralegal should confer with the client over the phone or in person to review the assets listed and determine whether other categories of assets should also be requested to be disclosed. After the conference, the paralegal drafts the motion and submits it to the supervising attorney for review and possible revision.

Once the final draft of the motion is approved and signed by the supervising attorney, the paralegal files the motion. The court schedules the motion for a hearing that the paralegal then dockets or, if necessary, reschedules through a continuance. If the motion is granted, the paralegal monitors the compliance with the motion and drafts a motion for contempt if disclosure is not made or if disclosure is not complete.

Preparation of a Response to a Motion for Disclosure of Assets

If the opposing party serves the firm's client with a motion for disclosure of assets, the supervising attorney may decide to file with a court a written objection to the motion for disclosure of assets, and may direct the paralegal to draft such an objection and possibly draft a **memorandum of law** supporting the objection. After the supervising attorney reviews and finalizes these documents, the paralegal prepares them in final form, obtains the attorney's signature on them, and sees that the originals of the documents are filed with the court and that copies are properly noticed on opposing counsel.

If the court orders a client to disclose the enumerated assets, the paralegal may be given the task of helping the client list all of the assets and compile, assemble, and organize the substantiating documentation. Once this is done, the paralegal drafts the document containing the disclosed information and documentation, submits it for review and signing to the attorney, transmits the information to opposing counsel, and formally notices the court of the client's compliance.

THE FINANCIAL AFFIDAVIT

Certainly most, if not all, jurisdictions require that both parties in a dissolution or divorce proceeding file a financial affidavit with the court within a specified period of time after the commencement of the proceeding. A **financial affidavit** is a sworn statement that enumerates the party's sources of income, earned and unearned; the party's expenses, necessary and optional; and all of the party's assets and liabilities. As mentioned above, assets include real and personal property, such as cash on hand, cars, furniture, stocks and bonds, rental property, vacation homes, and the interest, if any, in one's primary residence. Liabilities include debts such as credit card balances, student loans, court judgments, mortgages, and balances owned on any and all other secured and unsecured loans.

The party completing the affidavit must provide either a weekly or monthly breakdown of income, expenses, and payments on debts. Whereas in years past the financial affidavit was drafted by a party's attorney, most jurisdictions now provide a preprinted, two-sided "fill-in-the-blanks" form (see Exhibit 12–8). Most family law courts require the filing of this document before resolving any matters of any nature, financial or otherwise, in the pending proceeding. Financial affidavits must always be filed not only in dissolution matters, but also in any subsequent matters involving a change in alimony and child support orders.

Preparation of a Financial Affidavit

The family law office paralegal frequently assists the client in preparation of the financial affidavit. The amount of assistance needed will vary depending on the individual client's level of financial sophistication, her recordkeeping and organizational skills, the quantity and nature of the assets and liabilities involved, and the complexity or simplicity involved in calculating sources of income and essential and nonessential expenses. At the very least, the paralegal will transmit a copy of the financial affidavit form to the client together with a cover letter instructing the client to complete and return the form to the law office together with copies of applicable substantiating documentation such as bills, bank statements, cancelled checks, rental or mortgage payment receipts, pay stubs, and tax returns. When the paralegal receives this information, he may have to see that the amounts reported are broken down into the periodic increments the court requires. For instance, if a client forwards pay stubs that report gross income, deductions, and net income on a bimonthly basis and the jurisdiction requires a weekly breakdown or a monthly breakdown on the affidavit, the paralegal will have to apply arithmetic skills to arrive at and furnish the appropriate figures sought.

In instances where the parties in a dissolution proceeding each earn a moderate income from only one or two sources—for instance, employment compensation and bank account interest—the completion of the financial affidavit is fairly simple. However, when one or both of the divorcing parties have a very high earned income as well as considerable unearned income from several sources, and where the parties, together or separately, have accumulated valuable assets, both tangible and intangible, the completion of a financial affidavit in a manner that accurately and fully reflects each party's financial status is extremely complex. Arriving at proper figures may entail consulting with the client's accountant, financial advisor, and/or investment broker and retaining independent experts to evaluate pension assets and equity in business entities or to appraise tangible personal property such as antiques, expensive household furniture, art work, and other valuable collectibles.

It is extremely important that the financial information obtained be complete and accurate. The paralegal assigned to the file must perform her duties in a very thorough, responsible, and competent manner. Failure to do so could expose the client to allegations of fraud because the financial affidavit is signed under oath. The injured client who has provided honest and full disclosure to the firm handling the matter could seek redress against the firm through an action for professional malpractice and/or breach of fiduciary duty.

The paralegal may also have responsibilities involving the review of the financial affidavit submitted by an opposing party. The paralegal may have to meet with the client to review the other party's affidavit. If the client believes that the opposing spouse has not fully disclosed all assets or sources and amounts of income, or has misrepresented her financial position, the paralegal must report this to the supervising attorney immediately with a summary of the reasons the client has given to support his belief. Subsequently, the attorney may assign the paralegal various tasks designed to properly uncover the opposing party's hidden or undervalued assets and unreported or underreported sources of income.

Again, we cannot stress too strongly that the paralegal must handle these assignments with the utmost care and professionalism. Failure to do so can mislead the supervising attorney who may honestly "miss" identifying and locating all of the opposing party's assets and sources of income. If divorcing parties agree to a financial settlement based on wrong data, the party injured by lack of the right information can and may bring suit against his attorney for negligent legal representation, more commonly known as **malpractice.** The supervising attorney is ultimately responsible for the negligent actions of the law office staff persons assigned to the file and this attorney as well as the entire firm will suffer the consequences. If the attorney has instructed the paralegal in a clear and understandable manner to perform relatively standard procedures for obtaining the additional information sought and the paralegal performs this work in a slipshod or incomplete way, yet leads the supervising attorney to believe that the work has been done in a responsible manner, the paralegal should and most likely will be terminated and may have difficulty obtaining employment in any other law firm.

On the other hand, if an attorney assigns a paralegal work well beyond the paralegal's area of knowledge, training, and expertise and, further, if the attorney fails to review the paralegal's work product before sending it out of the office or relies on the work product to make decisions on the case, the paralegal is blameless. The attorney has committed malpractice and should be dismissed from the firm, but the paralegal should not be held responsible if she completed the assigned work to the best of her training and ability and the supervising attorney failed to review the work before relying on it.

Sometimes an attorney will in good faith assign a paralegal work that is beyond her reach. In this instance, the paralegal and attorney are best served if the paralegal honestly reports her concerns about being able to complete the assignment adequately. The attorney is then put on notice and can either modify the parameters of the assignment or tell the paralegal to complete the assignment as given to the best of her ability, knowing that the results cannot be relied on as a finished product.

EXHIBIT 12–1

Sample interrogatory.

DOCKET NO. FA 96-123456 : SUPERIOR COURT

BRONSON, RODNEY : JUDICIAL DISTRICT OF NEW HAVEN

V. : AT NEW HAVEN

BRONSON, EVELYN : SEPTEMBER 14, 2000

INTERROGATORIES

The plaintiff requests that the defendant answer under oath the following interrogatories within thirty days of the service hereof by serving the same upon counsel for the defendant of this action and that they can be provided by the defendant with substantially greater facility than they can otherwise be obtained by the plaintiff.

1. State whether or not you have any present or future interest in any pension plan, retirement plan, profit sharing plan, stock option plan, deferred income plan, or other similar type of plan, annuity, or fund.

2. If the answer to Interrogatory 1 is yes, please answer the following:

   a. The type of plan, annuity, or fund:

   b. Name of the plan, annuity, or fund:

   c. Account number of the plan, annuity, or fund:

   d. Name and address of the plan administrator, trustee, or custodian:

   e. Age of eligibility for each plan, annuity, or fund:

   f. Date when each plan, fund, or annuity will vest:

EXHIBIT 12–1
Continued

g. Present value of each plan, fund, or annuity:

h. Projected value of plan, fund, or annuity at eligibility age:

i. Date of withdrawal for each plan, fund, or annuity:

j. Amount of benefits upon retirement for each plan, fund, or annuity:

THE PLAINTIFF,
RODNEY BRONSON

BY: _____

JUSTINE F. MILLER, ESQ.
HIS ATTORNEY
22 PARK PLACE
NEW HAVEN, CT 06511
(203) 861-4444
JURIS NO. 313133

The foregoing answers are true to the best of my knowledge and belief.

_____

Rodney Bronson

Subscribed and sworn to me this _____ day of _____, 20__.

_____

Notary Public/
Commissioner of the Superior Court

EXHIBIT 12–1
Continued

ORDER

The foregoing motion having been heard, it is hereby ORDERED:

GRANTED/DENIED

THE COURT

BY: _____

JUDGE

CERTIFICATION

This is to certify that a true copy of the foregoing motion was mailed, postage prepaid, on this date to all counsel and pro se parties of record on this _____ day of _____, 2000, as follows:

Grace A. Luppino, Esq.
555 Main Avenue
New Haven, CT 06511

_____
Justine F. Miller, Esq.
Commissioner of the Superior Court

EXHIBIT 12–2

Sample request for production.

DOCKET NO. FA 96-123456	: SUPERIOR COURT
BRONSON, RODNEY	: JUDICIAL DISTRICT OF NEW HAVEN
V.	: AT NEW HAVEN
BRONSON, EVELYN	: SEPTEMBER 14, 2000

REQUEST FOR PRODUCTION

The plaintiff represents that certain documents material to the pending action, which are not privileged or within the possession of the plaintiff, whose production would be of assistance in the prosecution of the action, can be provided by the defendant with substantially greater facility than they could otherwise be obtained by the plaintiff and therefore requests that the defendant produce for inspection and copying the following:

1. Copies of any pension plan, retirement plan, profit sharing plan, stock option plan, deferred income plan, or other similar type plan, annuity, or fund.

2. Copies of all statements of accounts for the year 20___ through the present date which indicates the amount to your interest and contributions to all said plans, annuities, or funds.

THE PLAINTIFF,
RODNEY BRONSON

BY: _____
JUSTINE F. MILLER, ESQ.
HIS ATTORNEY
22 PARK PLACE
NEW HAVEN, CT 06511
(203) 861-4444
JURIS NO. 313133

ORDER

The foregoing motion having been heard, it is hereby ORDERED:

GRANTED/DENIED
THE COURT

BY: _____
JUDGE

CERTIFICATION

This is to certify that a true copy of the foregoing motion was mailed, postage prepaid, on this date to all counsel and pro se parties of record on this ____ day of _____, 2000, as follows:

Grace A. Luppino, Esq.
555 Main Avenue
New Haven, CT 06511

_____
Justine F. Miller, Esq.
Commissioner of the Superior Court

307

EXHIBIT 12–3
Sample request for medical examination.

DOCKET NO. FA 96-123456   : SUPERIOR COURT

BRONSON, RODNEY   : JUDICIAL DISTRICT OF NEW HAVEN

V.   : AT NEW HAVEN

BRONSON, EVELYN   : SEPTEMBER 14, 2000

REQUEST FOR PSYCHIATRIC EXAMINATION

The plaintiff, Rodney Bronson, requests the Court to order a psychiatric evaluation of the defendant, Evelyn Bronson. The plaintiff contends that the mother's ability to care for the children is at issue.

THE PLAINTIFF,
RODNEY BRONSON

BY: _____
     JUSTINE F. MILLER, ESQ.
     HIS ATTORNEY
     22 PARK PLACE
     NEW HAVEN, CT 06511
     (203) 861-4444
     JURIS NO. 313133

ORDER

The foregoing motion having been heard, it is hereby ORDERED:

GRANTED/DENIED
THE COURT

BY: _____
     JUDGE

CERTIFICATION

This is to certify that a true copy of the foregoing motion was mailed, postage prepaid, on this date to all counsel and pro se parties of record on this _____ day of _____, 2000, as follows:

Grace A. Luppino, Esq.
555 Main Avenue
New Haven, CT 06511

_____
Justine F. Miller, Esq.
Commissioner of the Superior Court

EXHIBIT 12–4
Sample request for admission.

DOCKET NO. FA 96-123456 : SUPERIOR COURT

BRONSON, RODNEY : JUDICIAL DISTRICT OF NEW HAVEN

V. : AT NEW HAVEN

BRONSON, EVELYN : SEPTEMBER 14, 2000

REQUEST FOR ADMISSION

The plaintiff hereby requests the defendant to admit the truth of the following statements:

That the defendant's employer provides health insurance coverage for all biological or adopted minor children of the insured employee, regardless of their place of residence.

THE PLAINTIFF,
RODNEY BRONSON

BY: _____

JUSTINE F. MILLER, ESQ.
HIS ATTORNEY
22 PARK PLACE
NEW HAVEN, CT 06511
(203) 861-4444
JURIS NO. 313133

ORDER

The foregoing motion having been heard, it is hereby ORDERED:

GRANTED/DENIED
THE COURT

BY: _____
JUDGE

CERTIFICATION

This is to certify that a true copy of the foregoing motion was mailed, postage prepaid, on this date to all counsel and pro se parties of record on this _____ day of _____, 2000, as follows:

Grace A. Luppino, Esq.
555 Main Avenue
New Haven, CT 06511

_____
Justine F. Miller, Esq.
Commissioner of the Superior Court

EXHIBIT 12–5

Sample notice of deposition.

DOCKET NO. FA 96-123456 : SUPERIOR COURT

BRONSON, RODNEY : JUDICIAL DISTRICT OF NEW HAVEN

V. : AT NEW HAVEN

BRONSON, EVELYN : SEPTEMBER 14, 2000

NOTICE OF DEPOSITION

The plaintiff, Rodney Bronson, hereby gives notice that his attorney intends to take the deposition of the defendant, Evelyn Bronson, regarding her knowledge of the above-captioned matter on October 22, 2000, at 11:30 a.m., before court reporters at the law office of the plaintiff's counsel located at 22 Park Place, New Haven, CT.

THE PLAINTIFF,
RODNEY BRONSON

BY: _____

JUSTINE F. MILLER, ESQ.
HIS ATTORNEY
22 PARK PLACE
NEW HAVEN, CT 06511
(203) 861-4444
JURIS NO. 313133

CERTIFICATION

This is to certify that a true copy of the foregoing motion was mailed, postage prepaid, on this date to all counsel and pro se parties of record on this _____ day of _____, 2000, as follows:

Grace A. Luppino, Esq.
555 Main Avenue
New Haven, CT 06511

_____
Justine F. Miller, Esq.
Commissioner of the Superior Court

EXHIBIT 12-6

Sample subpoena.

STATE OF CONNECTICUT
SUPERIOR COURT

SUBPOENA
FAMILY/JUVENILE
JD-FM-126   Rev. 4-89 (Old SJC-11A)
C.G.S. 52-143, 52-144, 52-280

INSTRUCTIONS

To be used only if the witness is being subpoenaed by the state in family or juvenile matters, including those subpoenas issued by the attorney general, or an assistant attorney general, or by any public defender or assistant public defender acting in his/her official capacity.
(For example, in family matters, use in conjunction with form JD-FM-124.)

NAME OF CASE

DOCKET NO.

NAME AND ADDRESS OF COURT *(No., street and town)*

TO

DATE AND TIME YOU ARE TO APPEAR

BY AUTHORITY OF THE STATE OF CONNECTICUT, you are hereby commanded to appear before the Superior Court in session at the above address on the date indicated above or to such day thereafter and within sixty days hereof on which the action named above is legally to be tried, to testify what you know in said action pending in the court.

YOU ARE FURTHER COMMANDED TO BRING WITH YOU AND PRODUCE:

HEREOF FAIL NOT, UNDER PENALTY OF THE LAW.

To any proper officer or indifferent person to serve and return.

NAME OF STATE AGENT ISSUING SUBPOENA

TITLE

SIGNED *(Clerk, Commissioner of Superior Court)*

ON *(Date)*

AT *(Town)*

NOTICE TO THE PERSON SUMMONED

You must report to the court at the time and address shown above and remain until this case is disposed of and you are discharged by the court. Present this subpoena when you report. Your statutory fees as witness will be paid by the clerk of the court where you are summoned to appear, if you give the clerk this subpoena on the day you appear. If you do not appear in court on the day and at the time stated, or on the day and at the time to which your appearance may have been postponed or continued by order of an officer of the court, the court may order that you be arrested. In addition, if you fail to appear and testify, without reasonable excuse, you shall be fined not more than twenty-five dollars and pay all damages to the aggrieved party.

RETURN OF SERVICE

JUDICIAL DISTRICT OF

ss.   , Connecticut

DATE

Then and there I made service of the within subpoena not less than eighteen hours prior to the time designated for the person summoned to appear, by reading the same in the presence and hearing/leaving a true and attested copy hereof in the hands/at the last usual place of abode of each of the within-named persons, viz:

FEES

COPY

ENDORSEMENT

SERVICE

TRAVEL *(Show miles and amount)*

The within is ☐ the original/☐ a true copy of the original subpoena.

ATTEST *(Signature of proper officer or indifferent person)*

TITLE *(If applicable)*

TOTAL

DISTRIBUTION: WHITE - Return to court after service   YELLOW - Witness   PINK - Retained by clerk

311

EXHIBIT 12–7
Sample motion for disclosure of assets.

DOCKET NO. FA 96-123456	: SUPERIOR COURT
BRONSON, RODNEY	: JUDICIAL DISTRICT OF NEW HAVEN
V.	: AT NEW HAVEN
BRONSON, EVELYN	: SEPTEMBER 14, 2000

MOTION FOR DISCLOSURE OF ASSETS

The plaintiff in the above-captioned matter hereby requests the Court to order the defendant to disclose her assets.

Wherefore, the plaintiff requests the Court to order the defendant to appear at the office of the undersigned on October 22, 2000, to disclose under oath during a deposition, all of her assets.

THE PLAINTIFF,
RODNEY BRONSON

BY: _____
JUSTINE F. MILLER, ESQ.
HIS ATTORNEY
22 PARK PLACE
NEW HAVEN, CT 06511
(203) 861-4444
JURIS NO. 313133

ORDER

The foregoing motion having been heard, it is hereby ORDERED:

GRANTED/DENIED
THE COURT

BY: _____
JUDGE

CERTIFICATION

This is to certify that a true copy of the foregoing motion was mailed, postage prepaid, on this date to all counsel and pro se parties of record on this _____ day of _____, 2000, as follows:

Grace A. Luppino, Esq.
555 Main Avenue
New Haven, CT 06511

_____
Justine F. Miller, Esq.
Commissioner of the Superior Court

EXHIBIT 12–8
Financial Affidavit

FINANCIAL AFFIDAVIT

JD-FM-6 Rev. 5-98
P.B. 25-30

STATE OF CONNECTICUT
SUPERIOR COURT

| COURT USE ONLY |
| FINAFF |

DOCKET NO.

| FOR THE JUDICIAL DISTRICT OF | AT (Address of court) | NAME OF AFFIANT (person submitting this form) |

NAME OF CASE

☐ PLAINTIFF ☐ DEFENDANT

| OCCUPATION | NAME OF EMPLOYER |

ADDRESS OF EMPLOYER

1. WEEKLY INCOME

A. WEEKLY INCOME FROM PRINCIPAL EMPLOYMENT (Use weekly average not less than 13 weeks)

DEDUCTIONS	AMOUNT/WEEK	DEDUCTIONS (Cont.)	AMOUNT/WEEK		
1.	$	4.	$	GROSS WKLY WAGE FROM PRINCIPAL EMPLOYMENT →	$
2.	$	5.	$	TOTAL DEDUCTIONS →	$
3.	$	6.	$	NET WEEKLY WAGE →	$

B. ALL OTHER INCOME (Include in-kind compensation, gratuities, rents, interest, dividends, pension, etc.)

SOURCE OF INCOME	GROSS AMT/WK	SOURCE OF INCOME	GROSS AMT/WK		
1.	$	2.	$	GROSS WEEKLY INCOME FROM OTHER SOURCES →	$
DEDUCTIONS	AMOUNT/WEEK	DEDUCTIONS	AMOUNT/WEEK	TOTAL DEDUCTIONS →	$
	$		$	NET WEEKLY INCOME FROM OTHER SOURCES →	$
	$		$		
	$		$	ADD "NET WEEKLY WAGE" FROM SECTION A, AND "NET WEEKLY INCOME" FROM SECTION B, AND ENTER TOTAL BELOW:	
	$		$		
	$		$	**A** TOTAL NET WEEKLY INCOME —	$

2. WEEKLY EXPENSES

1. RENT OR MORTGAGE	$			Gas/Oil	$	11. DAY CARE	$
2. REAL ESTATE TAXES	$	6. TRANSPORTATION		Repairs	$	12. OTHER (specify below)	
3. UTILITIES	Fuel	$		Auto Loan	$		$
	Electricity	$		Public Trans.	$		$
	Gas	$		Medical/Dental	$		$
	Water	$	7. INSURANCE PREMIUMS	Automobile	$		$
	Telephone	$		Homeowners	$		$
	Trash Collection	$		Life	$		$
	Cable T.V.	$	8. MEDICAL/DENTAL		$		$
4. FOOD	$	9. CHILD SUPPORT (order of court)		$		$
5. CLOTHING	$	10. ALIMONY (order of court)		$	**B.** TOTAL WEEKLY EXPENSES —	$

3. LIABILITIES

CREDITOR (Do not include mortgages or loan balances that will be listed under assets.)	AMOUNT OF DEBT	BALANCE DUE	DATE DEBT INCURRED	WEEKLY PAYMENT
	$	$		$
	$	$		$
	$	$		$
	$	$		$
	$	$		$
	$	$		$
C. TOTAL LIABILITIES (Total Balance Due on Debts) —	$	**D** TOTAL WEEKLY LIABILITY EXPENSE.	$	

(continued)

EXHIBIT 12–8
Continued

4. ASSETS	**A. Real Estate**	Home	ADDRESS		VALUE (Est.) $	MORTGAGE $	EQUITY $
		Other:	ADDRESS		VALUE (Est.) $	MORTGAGE $	EQUITY $
		Other:	ADDRESS		VALUE (Est.) $	MORTGAGE $	EQUITY $

		YEAR	MAKE	MODEL	VALUE $	LOAN BALANCE $	EQUITY $
B. Motor Vehicles	Car 1:	YEAR	MAKE	MODEL	VALUE $	LOAN BALANCE $	EQUITY $
	Car 2:	YEAR	MAKE	MODEL	VALUE $	LOAN BALANCE $	EQUITY $

C. Other Personal Property — DESCRIBE AND STATE VALUE OF EACH ITEM — **TOTAL VALUE** $

D. Bank Accounts — BANK NAME, TYPE OF ACCOUNT, AND AMOUNT — **TOTAL BANK ACCOUNTS** $

E. Stocks, Bonds Mutual Funds — NAME OF COMPANY, NUMBER OF SHARES, AND VALUE — **TOTAL VALUE** $

F. Insurance (exclude children)	NAME OF INSURED	COMPANY	FACE AMOUNT $	CASH VALUE $	AMT. OF LOAN $	**TOTAL VALUE**
			$	$	$	
			$	$	$	$

G. Deferred Compensation Plans — NAME OF PLAN (Individual I.R.A., 401K, Keogh, etc.) AND APPROX. VALUE — **TOTAL VALUE (less loans)** $

H. All Other Assets — **TOTAL VALUE** $

I. Total — E. TOTAL CASH VALUE OF ALL ASSETS — $

5. HEALTH INSURANCE	NAME AND ADDRESS OF HEALTH OR DENTAL INSURANCE CARRIER
	INSURANCE POLICY NO. — NAME(S) OF PERSON(S) COVERED BY THE POLICY

SUMMARY
(Use the amounts shown in boxes A thru E of sections 1-4.)

TOTAL WEEKLY INCOME (A)	$	**TOTAL CASH VALUE OF ASSETS (E)**	$
TOTAL WEEKLY EXPENSES (B + D)	$	**TOTAL LIABILITIES (C)**	$

CERTIFICATION
I hereby certify that the foregoing statement is true and accurate to the best of my knowledge and belief.

SIGNED (Affiant)	Subscribed and sworn to before me on	DATE	SIGNED (Notary, Comm. of Superior court)

JD-FM-6 Rev. 5-98 (Back)

REVIEW QUESTIONS

1. What is the purpose of the discovery process in a family law proceeding?

2. List and describe the five discovery tools and explain how each of these tools can be used in a family law proceeding.

3. What is the difference between an objection and a privilege raised in the discovery process?

4. List the privileges and objections that may be asserted to prevent disclosure of discovery information sought in a dissolution matter.

5. What types of interrogatories might be filed in a dissolution matter where the issue of child custody is contested?

6. What types of documents might either party request in a family law proceeding relating to a divorce matter for a modification of alimony, child support, or custody?

7. In what family law proceedings does the court require both parties to submit financial affidavits?

8. How may the paralegal assist in the preparation of interrogatories and production requests?

9. How may the paralegal assist in preparing responses to interrogatories and production requests?

10. If a party does not furnish adequate financial information and records in response to interrogatories and production requests, what other means may the opposing party employ to obtain this information?

11. What is the purpose of a motion to compel?

12. Are interrogatories and responses filed with the court?

13. Describe the paralegal's role in preparing requests for physical and mental examinations.

14. Describe the paralegal's role in assisting clients to comply with a court-ordered physical or mental examination.

15. What is the difference between a request and a motion?

16. What is a request for admission?

17. Give one example of when a party's attorney in a family law proceeding might decide to file a request for admission.

18. What is the paralegal's role in assisting a party in complying with a request for admission?

19. What is the legal term for the person being deposed in a deposition?

20. What are the advantages and disadvantages of employing depositions as a discovery tool in a family law proceeding?

21. What information must be contained in a notice of deposition?

22. What is the legal procedure for notifying a nonparty witness to appear at a deposition?

23. What is a subpoena *duces tecum*?

24. What is the paralegal's role at the deposition of the client and at the deposition of the opposing party?

25. Describe the paralegal's role in preparing a client's financial affidavit and list the types of documentation the paralegal should request and obtain from the client to ensure that the information provided is complete and accurate.

EXERCISES

1. Identify the form or format required by your jurisdiction for the filing of a financial affidavit. Prepare a financial affidavit for each spouse using this form or format.

2. Prepare a set of interrogatories and requests for production to be served by one of the two parties to a dissolution proceeding and prepare responses by the opposing party.

3. Check your jurisdiction's rules of court family matters section for rules governing discovery. List the section names and numbers and summarize each one.

4. At your local courthouse, obtain a copy of the short calendar listing upcoming motions. Circle ones that deal with discovery. Describe the nature of the various motions, why you think they were filed, and what the moving party hoped to achieve by bringing these matters before the court.

5. Prepare a motion or request for a medical or psychiatric examination that the other party is opposing using forms from your jurisdiction. In the text of the motion, list the compelling reasons why the court should grant the order.

6. Write an excerpt from a court reporter's transcript of a spousal deposition that covers one or two topics of dispute, such as the deponent's ability to have custody of the children, the deponent's assets and sources of income, or the deponent's physical and mental treatment of the spouse.

7. Prepare a bill from your law firm that details the time spent in connection with various forms of discovery, such as the work done and the costs of any related tools.

13

SEPARATION AGREEMENTS

KEY TERMS

Boilerplate	Proposal
Compromise	Proposal letter
Hold harmless provision	Separation agreement
Merger	Uncontested

Once discovery has been exchanged, reviewed, and analyzed, a picture of the marital estate emerges. The next step is for the parties to draft and exchange proposals. **Proposals** are formal written indications, from one party to the opposing party, that communicate what the first party is seeking in terms of a divorce settlement. Proposals are drafted after the attorney has consulted with the client. A client who is fully informed regarding the extent of the marital estate may determine, with the assistance of the attorney, what type of settlement he will seek. The **proposal letter** will detail the client's position on the various legal issues to be resolved: property division, alimony, child custody, visitation and support, maintenance of health and life insurance, distribution of debts and other liabilities, and, of course, counsel fees. Remember, the client determines what he is seeking in a divorce settlement, so any formal offer of settlement must be approved by the client before it is submitted to the opposing party. Similarly, any proposal or counterproposal received by an attorney should always be forwarded to the attorney's client for review and written approval before acceptance.

Many divorces are settled without a trial. With the help of their attorneys or mediators, many clients are able to resolve their issues through negotiation and compromise. Attorneys on opposing sides confer with each other and propose resolutions through telephone calls, meetings, and correspondence. The attorney's office communicates proposals to the client and the parties often come to a resolution. Sometimes the parties agree on some issues, but reach a stalemate on others. If this happens, the court will decide the unresolved issues after a trial.

Once the parties have reached a resolution, one of the parties undertakes the responsibility of reducing the agreement to a writing known as a **separation agreement.** In some jurisdictions, this writing is referred to as a *property settlement, settlement agreement,* or *marital settlement agreement.* A separation agreement is a contract between spouses who are in the process of obtaining a divorce or a legal separation. This agreement resolves the various legal issues that arise when a marriage dissolves.

Traditionally, the public policy of the states has been to encourage and preserve marriage. Marriage and the family unit are the very foundation on which our society has been built. At one time courts were very reluctant to accept separation agreements in divorce cases since these agreements promoted the breakdown of the family. Even today, courts will validate separation agreements only when entered into after one of both parties have instituted legal proceedings for divorce or for a legal separation. If the marriage has deteriorated with no hope of reconciliation, the courts will be more likely to accept the separation agreement. If the parties to a failed marriage have amicably agreed to the terms of their dissolution, it is in the best interest of all parties involved for the court to accept the separation agreement rather than forcing an agonizing divorce trial. The parties must indicate in their agreement that their marriage has broken down, there is no hope of reconciliation, and the parties intend to live separate and apart.

An agreement avoids the need for a contested divorce trial. The case will proceed as an **uncontested** matter. When a matter is uncontested, this means that neither party objects to the court granting a divorce and entering an order of marital dissolution. However, even when a divorce action is uncontested, most jurisdictions require a formal court proceeding at which at least the petitioning spouse must appear. This proceeding is relatively short. The parties will arrive at court on the date of the uncontested hearing with the signed separation agreement. The document will be submitted to the court. The judge will review the agreement and determine if it is fair and equitable and if it has been entered into voluntarily.

FIGURE 13–1
Many divorces are settled out of court with the help of attorneys or mediators.

MERGER OF SEPARATION AGREEMENT INTO THE COURT'S DECREE

As mentioned earlier, the separation agreement is a contract between the spouses. The language in the agreement will indicate if the parties want the agreement to *survive* as a contract or if the parties want it merged into the court's decree. If the agreement survives as a contract, the agreement cannot be modified unless both parties mutually consent. In the event that one of the parties fails to comply with the provisions of the agreement, the aggrieved party will be left with the traditional contractual remedies such as breach of contract and specific performance. If the agreement is instead merged into the court's decree, the **merger** is no longer a contract between the two parties, but rather a court order, which can be modified or enforced through contempt of court proceedings.

ADVANTAGES OF REACHING AN AGREEMENT

A successfully negotiated separation agreement reflects the best efforts of both parties and their respective attorneys. Legal professionals should encourage agree-

FIGURE 13–2
Reaching an agreement involves compromise on the part of both parties.

ments for many reasons. Agreements are quicker, more economical, and the parties are not subjected to an adversarial system that may destroy the little civility remaining between them. The ability to have some input regarding the resolution of the divorce affords the parties more control than they would have if the judge were to decide the case. Reaching an agreement, however, involves compromise on the part of both parties. **Compromise** involves meeting someone halfway or giving up a position in exchange for something else. By its very definition, compromising parties are generally not 100 percent satisfied with a separation agreement. The degree of noncompliance with separation agreements is very high. Even the most carefully scripted and negotiated agreement may result in noncompliance even before the ink has dried.

PARALEGAL'S ROLE IN DRAFTING THE SEPARATION AGREEMENT

Paralegals may be assigned the task of drafting a separation agreement under the attorney's supervision. To begin drafting the separation agreement, the paralegal must have a copy of the finalized proposal and a good understanding of the agreement between the parties. This is an essential element before commencing the initial draft.

The paralegal must next obtain a model separation agreement or several models to use in constructing one for the client. Standardized or **boilerplate** separation agreement forms or clauses may be available in the particular jurisdiction's practice book. Forms and clauses may also be found in loose-leaf legal publications specializing in family law. Model separation agreements may also be available in the local law library or in the law office library. In addition, the law office may maintain its own file of standard separation agreements, either on computer or as hardcopies. Paralegals may also review closed divorce files that contain previously drafted separation agreements.

The paralegal may need to draw from several resources to obtain the necessary language to draft the agreement. Whenever using standardized forms or previously drafted separation agreements as models, the paralegal must proceed with a great deal of caution. The agreement should contain the particular provisions applicable to the underlying case—it should not be merely an exercise in filling in the blanks. The paralegal should also check local practice rules and statutory and case law, which may require the inclusion of some mandatory provisions or language in order to make the agreement legally effective.

The paralegal may also have responsibilities related to reviewing an agreement drafted by the opposing party. In this case, the paralegal, under the attorney's supervision, reviews the separation agreement to make certain it reflects the agreement of the parties. If the document appears to depart from what was agreed to, the paralegal will bring this departure to the attorney's attention, and may also wish to offer suggested revisions to cure the discrepancies.

Whether on the drafting side or reviewing side, several drafts may be necessary to script an agreement that accurately reflects the intent of the parties. Separation agreements should be drafted with great care, because the parties to it will have to live with this agreement long after they have left the courthouse. Agreements drafted too hastily, without adequate review and reflection, by both attorneys and clients, set the stage for unnecessary future battles. Each party will hold the other to every letter, syllable, and punctuation mark in their agreement.

FIGURE 13–3
Paralegals may be
asked to draft a client's
separation agreement,
a task that must be
undertaken with care.

Therefore, it is necessary to draft them carefully, make them clear and readable, and spell out any definitions or terms that could later cause confusion.

FINALIZING THE SEPARATION AGREEMENT

Once the attorney has approved a final draft, an office appointment with the client should be scheduled. At this meeting the attorney carefully reviews the agreement with the client and thoroughly answers any and all questions the client poses. If the client approves the agreement and the opposing side does likewise, the case will proceed as an uncontested divorce matter. If the parties are still in dispute over various sections, renegotiation and revisions may be appropriate.

We cannot stress the importance of careful drafting. Sometimes when dissolution actions have been particularly draining, the attorneys and paralegals may hurriedly draft an agreement with very little thought or reflection. The trap is that this agreement may continue to haunt both client and attorney as various sections become disputed in postjudgment battles.

BASIC CLAUSES AND STRUCTURE OF THE SEPARATION AGREEMENT

The paralegal should delineate the various subjects covered by the separation agreement by dividing them into "articles" or "sections" and using roman numerals or cardinal numbers in numerical sequence. It is important to organize the agreement in this manner for quick reference and logical sequence.

HEADING

Every agreement should have a heading. As mentioned earlier, various headings can be used depending on your supervisor's wishes or the accepted local preference: <u>SEPARATION AGREEMENT</u>, <u>PROPERTY SETTLEMENT</u>, <u>PROPERTY SETTLEMENT AGREEMENT</u>, <u>MARITAL SETTLEMENT</u>, <u>MARITAL SETTLEMENT AGREEMENT</u>, <u>AGREEMENT</u>.

IDENTIFICATION

The identification clause identifies the parties, their respective residences, and the respective label that will be used to refer to each spouse throughout the agreement, avoiding the need to spell out full names each time one is used. It also indicates the date on which the agreement was executed.

EXAMPLE

SEPARATION AGREEMENT[1]

THIS AGREEMENT, made and entered into this 5th day of February, 2001, by and between RODNEY BRONSON of New Haven, Connecticut (hereinafter referred to as "Husband"), and EVELYN BRONSON (hereinafter referred to as "Wife"):

▽   ▽   ▽

RECITALS

The recitals section indicates the date and place of the marriage, names and ages of the minor children, grounds for the dissolution, a declaration that the parties are living separate and apart, the pendency of an action for dissolution, and the intent to settle the spouses' rights and obligations pursuant to this action. Each sentence is often preceded by the word "WHEREAS."

EXAMPLE

WITNESSETH:

WHEREAS, the parties married each other on March 28, 1986, at Woodbridge, Connecticut; and

WHEREAS, said parties have two minor children born issue of this marriage:

Marlise Bronson, born June 7, 1987

Sydney Bronson, Jr., born August 6, 1988

No other minor children have been born to the Wife since the date of the marriage;

WHEREAS, irreconcilable differences have arisen between the parties as a result of which the marriage of the parties has broken down irretrievably and they are now and have been living separate and apart; and

---

[1]The text of the separation agreement illustrated in this chapter has been constructed from provisions and portions of provisions of separation agreements that the authors of this book have accumulated during their years of practice and as such reflects the work of anonymous authors.

WHEREAS, the Husband has instituted an action against the Wife claiming a dissolution of marriage, and further relief, which case is currently pending in the Superior Court for the Judicial District of New Haven at New Haven.

WHEREAS, the parties wish to enter into an agreement under which they will continue living separate and apart and under which fair and reasonable provisions will be made for the support of each other and the minor children and for the settlement, adjustment and compromise of all property rights and obligations resulting from the marriage.

NOW THEREFORE, in consideration of the premises and the mutual promises and undertaking therein set forth and for other good and valuable consideration paid over by each party to the other, the receipt and sufficiency of which is hereby acknowledged, it is covenanted and agreed as follows:

IRRETRIEVABLE BREAKDOWN

This clause indicates that the marriage has broken down and there is no hope of the parties reconciling.

EXAMPLE

ARTICLE I

Irretrievable Breakdown

The marriage of the parties has broken down irretrievably, and there is no prospect of reconciliation.

▼   ▼   ▼

SEPARATION OF THE PARTIES

The parties intend to live separate and apart and will not interfere with each other. In addition each one is free to dispose of his or her property upon death as he or she sees fit.

EXAMPLE

ARTICLE II

Separation of the Parties

2.1 The parties may and shall at all times hereafter live separate and apart for the rest of their mutual lives. Each shall be free from interference, authority or control, direct or indirect, by the other as fully as if he or she were single and unmarried. Each may reside at such place or places as he or she may select. The parties shall not molest each other or compel or endeavor to compel the other to cohabit or dwell with him or her, by any legal or other proceedings for the restoration of conjugal rights or otherwise.

2.2 The Husband and Wife shall have the right to dispose of his or her property by will or otherwise in such manner as they may, in his or her uncontrolled discretion deem proper; and neither one will claim any interest in the estate of the other.

▼   ▼   ▼

ALIMONY

The alimony clause addresses the payment of alimony, maintenance, or spousal support. The agreement should clearly spell out the type of alimony, frequency and mode of payment, modifiability, and termination. If the parties are waiving alimony, it should be spelled out in the agreement.

EXAMPLE

ARTICLE III
Spousal Support

3.1 The Wife shall pay to the Husband as periodic alimony the sum of $450 per week, commencing February 5, 2001, for a period of 208 weeks/4 years, up to but not including the week ending February 5, 2004, unless terminated earlier as provided herein.

3.2 Said alimony shall terminate prior to February 5, 2004, upon the occurrence of the first of the following events: a) death of either party; b) remarriage of the Husband; or c) cohabitation of the Husband with an unrelated female over the age of 18 years. Cohabitation shall have the meaning from time to time, as per applicable Connecticut Statutes.

3.3 Said alimony payments shall be nonmodifiable by either party.

3.4 For federal and state income tax purposes, said spousal support payments shall be reportable as income by the Husband and deductible by the Wife.

REAL PROPERTY

The real property section deals with the parties' disposition of any real property owned. The most common asset to be dealt with is the marital home. The parties may agree to put the house up for sale and divide the proceeds after expenses have been paid. Another option is for one party to buy out the other party, or offset it with a pension. If the parties have minor children, the custodial parent may be allowed to live in the home until the emancipation of the children. Once the last child has reached age eighteen, the home can be sold.

EXAMPLE

ARTICLE IV
Real Property

4.1 The Wife shall quitclaim to the Husband all of her right, title and interest to the marital home located at 328 Sycamore Street, in New Haven, Connecticut, subject only to the existing mortgage, which shall be the sole responsibility of the Husband.

4.2 The Husband shall indemnify and hold the Wife harmless against any and all costs, expenses, losses, claims, and judgment, including attorneys fees, she may incur in connection with the failure of the Husband to fulfill his obligations under ARTICLE IV.

PERSONAL PROPERTY

In the personal property clause, the parties address the division of their personal property. This includes motor vehicles; bank, pension, and retirement accounts; household furnishings; and miscellaneous matters.

EXAMPLE

ARTICLE V
Personal Property

5.1 Motor Vehicles

The Wife shall have sole title, possession, and ownership of the 1987 Pontiac Grand Am.

The Husband shall have sole title, possession, and ownership of the 1995 Ford Taurus Station Wagon.

From and after the date of this Agreement, each party shall be responsible for any and all costs associated with said respective vehicles and shall indemnify and hold the other harmless for all said costs.

5.2 Individual Bank, Pension, and Retirement Accounts

The Wife shall retain sole right, title, and interest in and to the following:

a) New Haven Savings Bank checking account number 0060355276901, minimal balance;

b) IRA, approximate value $28,600.00.

The Husband shall retain sole right, title, and interest in and to the following:

a) Fleet Bank checking account number 3918840832 minimal balance;

b) New Haven Savings Bank checking account number 1395096600, minimal balance;

c) 401k, approximate value $20,000.00;

d) IRA, approximate value $10,000.00.

5.3 Furnishings at Marital Home

The Husband shall make available to the Wife for removal by the Wife from the Marital Home the following items of personal property as soon as possible but in any event on or before February 5, 2001:

a) exercise bike

b) foot massage machine

c) stereo system

d) quilt purchased at Martha's Vineyard at 1990 craft fair

e) compact disc collection

f) Guatemalan wall hanging

g) Elvis collector's plates

h) dried flower arrangement in foyer

i) maroon garment bag

j) vanity in master bedroom

k) green rug and matching curtains in family room

> *l) gourmet oriental food ingredients*
>
> *m) electric espresso machine*
>
> *n) pasta machine*
>
> *o) alarm clock in spare bedroom*

5.4 Miscellaneous Personal Property

The Wife waives any right, title, interest or claim in and to all proceeds, settlements, and judgments obtained by the Husband in connection with a personal injury action concerning his 1997 automobile accident.

▽   ▽   ▽

CUSTODY AND VISITATION

The issues considered in the custody and visitation section involve the type of custody (sole, joint, split) arrangement agreed to by the parties. Visitation is also addressed either by a "reasonable visitation" clause or by a more detailed schedule. In some situations, visitation with the child may be supervised. The success of a "reasonable visitation" arrangement will depend on how well the parties can arrange visits between themselves. A more detailed schedule may specify particular days, times, transportation, place of pickup and drop-off, holidays, summer vacations, and birthdays. A clause requiring the custodial parent to contact the noncustodial parent may also be included to cover certain situations such as medical emergencies.

The issue of relocation by the custodial parent should also be addressed in this section.

EXAMPLE

ARTICLE VI

Child Custody and Visitation

6.1 The parties agree that the Husband shall have sole custody of the minor children, subject to the Wife's rights of reasonable visitation.

6.2 The Husband agrees that he shall consult with the Wife on all major decisions regarding the upbringing, care, and education of the children. Whenever reasonable and possible under the circumstances, the Husband shall notify the Wife in the event of any major or extended illness of the children and shall consult with the Wife regarding such child's medical treatment.

▽   ▽   ▽

CHILD SUPPORT

The child support section should specify the amount of child support due and the date on which it is payable. It is very important to include the date on which the payments are to commence so as to avoid confusion.

Other matters that may be addressed in this section are whether support payments will extend beyond a child's majority. Some parties will agree to pay for a child's college education, which should be clearly expressed in the agreement and include any restrictions or conditions the parents may have regarding the choice of location or cost of the school.

This section should also address which parent will declare the children as dependants for federal and state income tax purposes.

EXAMPLE

ARTICLE VII
Child Support

7.1 Commencing with the calendar month of February 2001, the Wife agrees to pay to the Husband the sum of $600 per month, on the 10th day of each and every calendar month, for the support of the minor children of the parties.

7.2 The provision of this ARTICLE VII shall only remain in effect with respect to each child of the parties during such child's minority.

7.3 The Wife shall claim the children as her dependants on her state and federal income tax returns.

▼   ▼   ▼

Health Insurance

Many parties have health insurance coverage that is provided as a fringe benefit by their employer. Self-employed parties may carry their own health insurance and those who cannot afford coverage simply go without or apply for government benefits. The health insurance section should spell out the health insurance coverage for both spouses and the minor children. It should also cover payment of unreimbursed expenses and how the parties plan to pay such costs.

EXAMPLE

ARTICLE VII
Health Insurance

8.1 The parties agree that they each have available and shall maintain health insurance coverage through their respective employers.

8.2 The wife shall maintain health insurance coverage for the benefit of the minor children through her employer.

8.3 The parties shall equally share any unreimbursed medical expenses with respect to the minor children.

▼   ▼   ▼

Liabilities

The debts and liabilities of the parties and who will be responsible for their payment must be covered in the separation agreement. The liabilities section should also include a **hold harmless provision** whereby the spouses indemnify each other from any debt incurred by the other.

EXAMPLE

ARTICLE IX
Liabilities

9.1 The parties agree that they will each be responsible for the liabilities on their respective financial affidavits submitted in connection with this pending matter.

9.2 The Husband shall indemnify, defend, and hold Wife harmless from any and all other indebtedness, loans, obligations, claims, and causes of action that have, may now, or hereafter be made against Wife on her property as a result of any acts or omissions of Husband, judgments that may be obtained against Husband, debts, guarantees, or obligations incurred by Husband.

9.3 The Wife shall indemnify, defend, and hold Husband harmless from any and all other indebtedness, loans, obligations, claims, and causes of action that have, may now, or hereafter be made against Husband on his property as a result of any acts or omissions of Wife, judgments that may be obtained against Wife, debts, guarantees, or obligations incurred by Wife.

▽   ▽   ▽

TAXES

The filing of federal and state tax returns is an important issue to be addressed in the agreement. In addition, the question of how the parties will share a refund or pay for an assessment should be determined to avoid surprises later.

EXAMPLE

ARTICLE X
Taxes

10.1 With respect to the calendar year of 2000, the parties filed joint tax returns, both federal and state. Pursuant to these returns, the parties owed $0 in federal income tax and owed $750 in state income tax. The payment of $750 was tendered to the Connecticut Commissioner of Revenue Services, by the Husband and Wife.

10.2 The parties agree to equally pay any additional taxes which may hereafter be assessed in connection with either 1999 return and equally divide any refunds or rebates in connection with such returns.

10.3 For the calendar year of 2001, and thereafter, the parties shall file separate tax returns, both federal and state. Each party shall pay and be responsible for all taxes assessed against their respective separate incomes.

▽   ▽   ▽

DISCLOSURE

In the disclosure clause, the parties acknowledge that they have had the opportunity to fully discover any data regarding their spouse's income, assets, liabilities, and expenses and that they have accurately disclosed the same.

EXAMPLE

ARTICLE XI
Disclosure

11.1 The parties acknowledge that they have had the opportunity for full discovery of any and all pertinent data with regard to income, assets, liabilities, and expenses of the other and that each waives his or her right to further discovery based upon the other's representation that they have fully and accurately disclosed to each other all their respective assets, income, and liabilities as set forth in their financial affidavits.

▼   ▼   ▼

REPRESENTATION OF THE PARTIES

In the representation section, the parties acknowledge that they have been represented by independent counsel and indicate the name of each attorney. This section may also deal with the issue of attorney's fees and who will be responsible for their payment.

EXAMPLE

ARTICLE XII
Representation of the Parties

12.1 Each party to this AGREEMENT represents and acknowledges that he or she has been represented in negotiations for and in preparation of this AGREEMENT by counsel of his or her own choosing.

12.2 Each party has been fully advised by his or her respective attorney, Justine F. Miller, Esq., of New Haven, CT, for the Husband, and Grace A. Luppino, Esq., of New Haven, CT, for the Wife, as to their respective rights and liabilities, each against the other, and to and upon the property and estate of the other in regard to the dissolution of their marriage.

12.3 Each party has read this AGREEMENT and has had it fully explained to him or her.

12.4 Each party has agreed to pay their own respective attorney's fees in the present dissolution action.

▼   ▼   ▼

MISCELLANEOUS CLAUSES

The miscellaneous section addresses matters of a general nature that might be anticipated to arise such as questions of governing jurisdictional law, the parties' cooperation in executing documents necessary to facilitate the operation of the separation agreement, a waiver of rights in the other party's estate in the event of death, and provisions to address unexpected occurrences or events.

EXAMPLE

ARTICLE XIII
Miscellaneous

13.1 Except as provided herein, the Husband and Wife each hereby waives any right at law or in equity to elect to take against any last will made by the other, including all rights of power or of curtesy, and hereby waiver renounces, and relinquishes unto the other, their respective heirs, executors, administrators, and assigns forever, all and every interest of any kind or character which whether may now have or may hereafter acquire in any real or personal property of the other, whether now owned or hereinafter acquired by either.

13.2 Except for any cause of action for divorce, legal separation, or dissolution of marriage or any action or proceeding to enforce the provisions of their Agreement, each party hereby releases and forever discharges, and by this Agreement does for himself or herself and his or her heirs, legal representatives, executors, administrators and assigns, release and discharge, and releases the other, with respect to matters arising out of the marital relationship from any and all causes of action, claims, rights, or demands whatsoever in law or in equity, which either of the parties ever had or now has against the other.

13.3 The Husband and Wife agree that they will, from time to time, at the request of the other, execute, acknowledge, and deliver any and all further instruments that may be reasonably required to give full force and effect to the provisions of this Agreement.

13.4 A waiver of any provision of this Agreement shall be effective only if made in writing and executed with the same formality as this Agreement. The failure of either party to insist upon strict enforcement of any provisions of this Agreement shall not be construed as a waiver of such terms, and such terms shall nevertheless continue in full force and effect.

13.5 If any provision of this Agreement is held to be invalid and unenforceable, all other provisions shall nevertheless continue in full force and effect.

13.6 This Agreement shall be construed and governed in accordance with the laws of the State of Connecticut.

13.7 The parties hereto agree and intend that the Agreement shall be incorporated in full by reference or otherwise in the dissolution proceedings. This Agreement shall merge with any decree of any Court affecting the parties.

13.8 This Agreement shall not be modified or altered except by an instrument signed and acknowledged by the Husband and Wife.

13.9 This Agreement is simultaneously executed in five (5) counterparts and each of said counterparts shall be original and each of said counterparts shall constitute but one and the same instrument.

▽   ▽   ▽

SIGNATURE PROVISIONS

In the signatory section of the separation agreement, each party signs their legal signature, which should conform to the name used in the legal action before the court. Each party's signature is witnessed by two people.

EXAMPLE

IN WITNESS WHEREOF, the parties hereto have hereunto set their respective hands and seals on the day and year first above written.

_____	_____
Witness	*RODNEY BRONSON*
_____	
Witness	
_____	_____
Witness	*EVELYN BRONSON*
_____	
Witness	

▽   ▽   ▽

ACKNOWLEDGMENT

The acknowledgement section follows the signing and witnessing of the separation agreement. In this section, a notary public or an officer of the court, if allowed to do so in the jurisdiction, will take the acknowledgment of each party. This means that the notary public or court officer will acknowledge that the party signed the document in the presence of witnesses and acknowledge that he or she signed the document and did so freely and without coercion.

EXAMPLES

STATE OF CONNECTICUT)

)   ss. _____

COUNTY OF NEW HAVEN)

On this the 5th day of February, 2001, personally appeared RODNEY BRONSON known to me to be the person whose name is subscribed to the within instrument and acknowledged that he executed the same for the purposes therein contained, as his own free act and deed, before me.

IN WITNESS WHEREOF, I hereunto set my hand and official seal.

                        _____
                        JUSTINE F. MILLER,
                        Commissioner of the Superior Court

STATE OF CONNECTICUT)

)   ss. _____

COUNTY OF NEW HAVEN)

On this the 5th day of February, 2001, personally appeared EVELYN BRONSON known to me to be the person whose name is subscribed to the within instrument and acknowledged that she executed the same for the purposes therein contained, as her own free act and deed, before me.

IN WITNESS WHEREOF, I hereunto set my hand and official seal.

_____

GRACE A. LUPPINO,
Commissioner of the Superior Court

Appendix H includes the entire marital settlement agreement signed by entertainer Madonna and her former husband, Sean Penn.

▼   ▼   ▼

REVIEW QUESTIONS

1. What is a proposal?
2. Explain the purpose of a proposal letter.
3. What is a separation agreement?
4. How do family courts view separation agreements?
5. Explain the concept of a merger.
6. What is meant by the term *compromise?*
7. Describe the resources a paralegal might utilize when drafting a separation agreement.
8. What are boilerplate agreements and why should the paralegal proceed with caution when using them?
9. How should a paralegal structure a separation agreement?
10. List the basic clauses of a separation agreement.

EXERCISES

1. Go to your local law library and locate and list the various form books that illustrate boilerplate separation agreements and clauses.

2. Locate the statutes in your state that regulate the creation and enforcement of separation agreements.

3. Using the information in the Bronson family separation agreement, write a provision that will cover postmajority child support for the minor children in the form of college tuition and medical and dental coverage during their attendance at college.

14

THE DIVORCE TRIAL

KEY TERMS

Appeal	Judgment
Bench trial	Judicial pretrial
Bureau of Vital Statistics form	Merger
Claim for relief	Military affidavit
Contested hearing	Pretrial conference
Custody affidavit	Stipulation
Default trial	Testimony
Dissolve	Theory of the case
Divorce trial	Transcript
Document	Trial notebook
Final argument	Unconscionable
Financial disclosure affidavit	Uncontested hearing
Habeas corpus	Wage execution

The discovery process is now complete. The discovery material has been analyzed. The witnesses have been identified. The custody evaluation has been prepared. The parties have either reached an agreement or have identified areas of disagreement. The parties are now ready to proceed to the next step—the **divorce trial,** the process in which both parties present their case to the court for its final hearing. Divorce trials are for the most part **bench trials,** which means that the trial is conducted before a judge, not a jury. In some jurisdictions like New York and Texas, the parties can demand a jury trial in divorce cases. In a

FIGURE 14–1
Divorce trials are
generally bench trials,
in which there is no
jury. The judge acts as
both the trier of fact
and law.

bench trial the judge is both the trier of fact and law. The family court judge is knowledgeable in the area of domestic relations and his role is to apply the law, which includes statutory and case law, to the particular facts in the case before him and render a decision that is fair to both parties.

Divorce trials are open to the public so anyone can sit in and observe the case. Courtrooms may be sealed upon motion of the parties to protect children of the marriage when the trial issues are of a particularly sensitive nature. Divorce files are also open to the public and may be viewed in local courthouses at the clerk's office.

Divorce trials are either uncontested or contested. Whether the case is contested or uncontested, the paralegal must send a formal notice to the court indicating that the case is ready for the trial list. (See Exhibit 14–1.)

UNCONTESTED HEARING

In an **uncontested hearing,** the parties have either reached an agreement regarding the issues surrounding the dissolution of their marriage (i.e., alimony, property division, child custody and support, attorney's fees) or one party is defaulted for failure to appear. A **default trial** takes place when one of the parties to an action has failed to appear at the scheduled trial date even though she has received proper notice of the proceedings. In this case, the court will proceed with a default hearing and sever the marriage. It is important that the respondent/

defendant file a cross-complaint so in the event the petitioner/plaintiff does not appear, the court can proceed on the respondent/defendant's cross-complaint.

Most divorce cases proceed as uncontested matters. Many couples resolve their major issues through negotiations between themselves, through their respective attorneys, or with a professional mediator. The parties then preserve their agreement in writing. The case must then be put on the court calendar as an uncontested hearing.

Every jurisdiction has specific procedures for requesting a trial date in either an uncontested or contested dissolution matter. The paralegal should become familiar with his particular state's requirements for getting a case on the court calendar. In addition, some jurisdictions may also provide preprinted forms to facilitate this process.

Uncontested divorce trials are very brief in duration. The court will first confirm service of process on the defendant spouse. This means that the judge determines whether service of the divorce complaint/petition was adequately made on the defendant/respondent. In the case where there is a nonappearing defendant, the moving party must provide the court with a **military affidavit** in accordance with the Soldiers and Sailors Relief Act 50 USC §520 (1982) to prove that the defendant is currently not serving in one of the armed forces. (See Exhibit 14–2.) This requires contacting each branch of the military to determine whether or not the defendant is in the armed forces. (See Exhibit 14–3.) When requesting a military affidavit, the paralegal should provide the defendant's name, address, Social Security number, and date of birth. In addition, a small fee must accompany each request.

Some jurisdictions do not require the parties to appear in court if the divorce is uncontested or if there is a default. In these jurisdictions the parties are merely required to file the appropriate paperwork with the court.

In matters where the parties have worked out a settlement or separation agreement, the plaintiff/petitioner will be called to the witness stand and put under oath. The plaintiff's attorney will question her briefly on the allegations made in the complaint/petition, which is necessary to establish the statutory grounds for a dissolution of marriage. The judge may also direct some questions to the parties.

If the parties have executed the separation agreement, the original is presented to the court and reviewed by the judge. Separation agreements are usually approved by the court unless the terms of the agreement are deemed by the court to be **unconscionable,** unfair, or one sided. The court must determine if the parties are aware of the contents of the agreement, that they understand it, that it is their free and voluntary act, that it was not made under fraud or duress, and that the assets have been fully disclosed. Provisions regarding alimony and property division will not be scrutinized as carefully as those provisions dealing with child custody, support, or visitation. The court also has an interest in determining what economic position the parties will be left in after the divorce. If the court finds the agreement unconscionable, it will order the parties to go back to the drawing board and reconsider certain provisions.

If the court accepts the parties' agreement by finding it to be fair and equitable, the court will first dissolve the marriage, then the court, upon request of the parties, will incorporate the parties' agreement into the divorce decree. This is known as a **merger.** Once the settlement agreement has been merged with the divorce decree, the terms of the agreement are now considered court orders.

A merger affords the parties with the postjudgment remedies of contempt of court proceedings and modification. Without a merger, the settlement agreement is a contract between the parties, who will be left with contract remedies in order to enforce or change their agreement. If a spouse fails to comply with the terms of a separation agreement that has been merged into the divorce decree, the aggrieved spouse may seek contempt of court proceedings to enforce its provisions. A merger also allows parties to seek modification of certain provisions as long as they can prove that there has been a substantial change in circumstances since the entry of the original decree.

CONTESTED HEARING

Parties that have been unable to reach an agreement regarding issues of alimony, property division, visitation, and child custody and support will have to let the judge make those decisions. A disputed divorce trial is known as a **contested hearing.** Although contested trials give the client their "day in court," they can also be very stressful and their outcome uncertain.

Parties who have negotiated a settlement agreement are more likely to be content with the final results because they actually had some degree of participation in its formation and are more likely to cooperate with its terms because it was agreed to voluntarily. Once a case has been turned over to a judge, there is no telling what the result will be.

FIGURE 14–2
Although contested trials give clients their "day in court," trials can be stressful and their outcomes uncertain.

FIGURE 14–3
Pretrial conferences may be scheduled when it becomes apparent that a case will indeed go to trial.

Contested hearings may also increase the parties' hostility toward each other. This has a particularly devastating result when children are caught in the middle. Contested hearings can also be very expensive. Clients incur additional legal fees and expenses such as sheriff's fees, expert witness fees, court costs, transcript fees, appraisal reports, investigations, or evaluations prepared by third parties.

Why then, despite these consequences, do some divorces end up in a contested trial? The trial process provides a forum where opposing parties can vigorously litigate issues of law and fact before an impartial third party. Unfortunately, the hostility surrounding a broken marriage can often spill into the courts. Some parties find that a proposed settlement is unfair and refuse to accept it. The other spouse refuses to change or modify his position, hence the parties reach a stalemate. Sometimes clients have unrealistic expectations of what the legal system can do for them and insist on going to trial. Others wish to use the threat of trial to intimidate a spouse who may not wish to have every sordid detail of the marriage exposed in public. Others still play out their anger toward their spouse in the legal system by refusing to cooperate or compromise on anything and instead contest every single issue possible.

If the case cannot be settled and it looks like it will proceed as a contested matter, the appropriate forms must be filed to request a trial date.

Some jurisdictions require that parties in contested matters attend a **judicial pretrial** conference. The pretrial conference takes place before a judge. It is not a trial. The purpose of the judicial pretrial is to help parties come to an agreement. The judge's role is to tell the parties how she would rule if this matter were to be tried before her. If parties agree to the judge's proposal, an agreement will be drafted and the parties will bring the agreement before the court.

If the case cannot be resolved and instead heads for trial, a **pretrial conference** or mandatory settlement conference may be scheduled. (Exhibit 14–4 illustrates a notice to Melissa Carrey scheduling a settlement conference and ordering her and her attorney to have certain documents ready for trial.) The purpose of the pretrial conference is to streamline the trial process. At the pretrial conference, the parties will:

1. *Exchange witness lists.* This will assist the parties in preparation of cross-examination and impeachment of the opposing party's witnesses. It will also help anticipate witnesses' testimony.

2. *Disclose exhibits to be filed.* Parties can review in advance exhibits that will be entered as evidence and determine which exhibits may be entered into evidence by agreement and which ones will be opposed.

3. *Narrow the issues to be tried.* Even though the divorce is contested, there may be issues that the parties can agree on or can stipulate to.

4. *Establish if an interpreter is needed for the proceedings.* A party may not be able to speak or understand the English language or may require sign language to be used. The pretrial conference serves to give court personnel advance notice of such needs so they can make arrangements to have an interpreter present.

5. *Establish if a habeas corpus is needed.* A writ of **habeas corpus** may be necessary so that an incarcerated party may be transported by the states correction department for trial.

6. *Determine the role of the child's attorney.*

7. *Determine whether children will testify and under what circumstances.*

If disagreements still exist after a pretrial conference, a trial date will be scheduled. The goal of the trial process is to arrive at the truth. The way we arrive at the truth in our American system of jurisprudence is through the adversarial system. Both parties, represented by competent counsel, battle it out before an impartial third party known as a judge. The rules of evidence dictate which information can be admitted and which excluded so that evidence offered at trial is reliable and untainted. The problem with the adversarial system is that it assumes that both lawyers are equally competent, that the judge has no biases or prejudices, and that both sides have enough funds in their war chest to afford expert witnesses, evaluations, appraisals, investigators, and every legal maneuver available to present their case.

Unfortunately this is not always the case. Some attorneys are better than others and just because a judge puts on a black robe does not mean that he is saturated with the wisdom of Solomon. Clients do not always possess the funds to pay for the presentation of a perfect case and may have to settle for what is realistic.

As mentioned earlier, parties who go to trial take a risk when turning their decision-making power over to the judge. They have now lost the ability to control their destiny in terms of the dissolution of their marriage.

THE PARALEGAL'S ROLE IN TRIAL PREPARATION

The process of trial preparation begins on the day of the initial client interview. Only a clairvoyant will know whether or not a case will go to trial. Clients will, at times, inform the attorney that the parties have worked out an agreement and there are no problems. This, however, is never a sure thing. The amicable agreement of today can turn into the contested bloodbath of tomorrow.

The attorney will need to develop the theory of the case. The **theory of the case** is the legal justification for the client's position and for the relief she is seeking. A thorough review of the discovery materials will help formulate some type of case strategy.

Family court dockets can be extremely crowded and judges appreciate a well-prepared, well-researched, and well-organized case that does not take up time with matters that have already been resolved.

Once a theory of the case has been developed, the lawyer and paralegal must assemble the necessary evidence to present the client's case to the court. A client's case is proven by presenting evidence that will support the client's claim. The client's case is developed through the evidentiary vehicles of testimony and documents.

Testimony is often given during a divorce trial. A list of witnesses is prepared to determine who will testify at trial. In a divorce case, the client spouse will be the primary witness and he will tell his story to the court. Other witnesses may also be called to testify: expert witnesses such as physicians and mental health professionals, social workers, teachers, appraisers, accountants, and investigators. Lay witnesses such as family members, friends, neighbors, coworkers, employers, and/or supervisors may also testify.

When calling a witness other than a client, it is necessary for the party calling that witness to subpoena them to trial. A subpoena is a document ordering a witness to appear under penalty of law to provide testimony at a legal proceeding. (See Exhibit 14–5.) A paralegal may be in charge of preparing the subpoenas and arranging for service of these orders by a sheriff. The paralegal must also keep track of subpoenas to make sure they have been properly served. Failure to subpoena a party may result in her not appearing for trial. Records also need to be subpoenaed. Witnesses also need to be prepared by the attorney to testify.

Documents that may be used at trial include the following:

- Financial records of parties already produced through discovery,
- Any court-ordered evaluations that are part of the court file,
- Additional psychological or psychiatric reports that either party seeks to have admitted in support of their position, and
- Appraisals of assets, an independent financial evaluation of business interests, licenses, goodwill, and pensions.

Once the attorney has determined which types of evidence will be used at trial, the next step is to prepare the **trial notebook.** The trial notebook provides a way to organize materials important to the case in a manner that makes them readily available for use at trial. There is nothing more embarrassing for an attorney than having to fumble and leaf through stacks of unorganized documents during a trial. It gives the client and the court the impression that the attorney did not prepare adequately.

The trial notebook is not necessarily a physical notebook, although a notebook can be used if preferred. Some attorneys organize their trial notebooks by designating a series of file folders to contain certain information. These file folders will then be placed in a large folder or box to facilitate easy access during trial. Other attorneys may prefer to use commercially or self–prepared trial notebooks. The trial notebook may contain a variety of subfiles organized such that they facilitate easy access to the information.

The parties may also be required to submit certain documents to the court at the time of trial which may be prepared by the paralegal:

1. An updated sworn **financial disclosure affidavit,** indicating the income, expenses, assets, and liabilities of the client. (See Exhibit 14–6.)

FIGURE 14–4
Trial notebooks help
the attorney access
information in an
easy, timely manner.

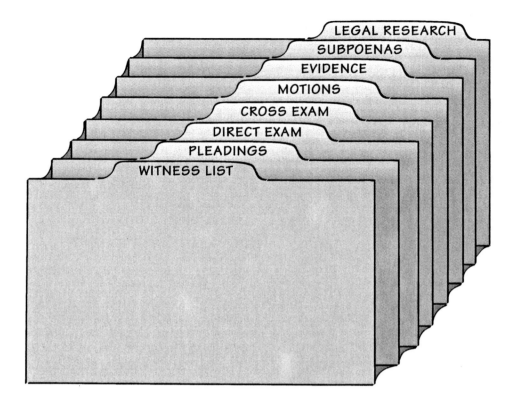

2. A **custody affidavit** indicating that there is no other proceeding pending in another court that affects the custody of the minor children. If a proceeding is pending, the paralegal must indicate where and the nature of the proceedings. (See Exhibit 14–7.)

3. A **claim for relief,** which is a statement filed by a party indicating what he wants in terms of a disposition in the case. (See Exhibit 14–8.)

4. **Wage execution** forms for the purpose of facilitating alimony and child support payments through automatic deductions from the obligor's paycheck. (See Exhibit 14–9.)

5. State-specific **Bureau of Vital Statistics forms** designed for the purpose of collecting statistical information on divorcing couples. (See Exhibit 14–10.)

6. **Stipulations,** which are written agreements where parties agree that certain facts are true or that certain procedures are to be followed.

The client should be notified by phone and then in writing regarding the trial date. The attorney should set up an appointment with the client prior to trial for the purpose of reviewing testimony and explaining the trial process to the client. The attorney should also review the exhibits she intends to introduce through the client so the client becomes familiar with them and prepared to testify. The client should be given directions either to the courthouse or to meet the attorney at the office. The client should also be informed to dress conservatively as if he or she were attending a religious service. A conservative appearance conveys reverence and respect for the court.

DAY OF THE TRIAL

Some attorneys allow their paralegals to assist at trial. Although a paralegal may not question witnesses, argue motions, make opening and closing arguments, or raise objections, paralegals can perform many important tasks at trial. At trial, the paralegal will sit at counsel table with the attorney and client. Remember that the paralegal's status must be communicated to the court so that neither the judge or opposing party is under the impression that the paralegal is an attorney.

The divorce trial will be heard by a judge, who will preside over the hearing. Parties may be referred to a hearing officer, referee, or a special master in courts that utilize these alternative decision makers to resolve the overflow of cases. As mentioned earlier, a divorce trial is open to the public unless the court has ordered the courtroom sealed to protect particularly sensitive cases, and in some jurisdictions, the parties can demand a jury trial.

The plaintiff or petitioner will be the first to put on his case and call his witnesses to the stand. The opposing party will then have the opportunity to cross-examine the plaintiff's witnesses. Once the plaintiff has rested his case, the defendant/respondent will be able to proceed with his case and present his witnesses. During the course of the trial, the paralegal may make notes during each witness's testimony. This is one of the most important functions of a paralegal during the trial. It is important that the lawyer focus his attention on the testimony in order to make the appropriate objections or argue with opposing counsel regarding the admission or exclusion of evidence. If the note-taking process is delegated to the paralegal, then the attorney can concentrate on the trial. Taking notes during testimony is essential for the purpose of preparing closing arguments and cross-examination. A paralegal may also assist at trial by dealing with the client. A client should be given a legal pad and pen and instructed to write down any questions or comments they may have during trial. This lets the client express himself without distracting the attorney.

The paralegal may also help keep track of exhibits, pass materials to the attorney, and deal with impatient witnesses waiting to testify. Paralegals may also run errands such as photocopying, make quick legal research trips to the court library, and make phone calls to witnesses or the office.

After testimony, each attorney argues why the court should rule in his or her client's favor. This is known as **final argument.** The court may decide the case immediately or render its decision at a later date. Sometimes court will require the parties to prepare briefs or memorandum of law on particular issues to assist the court in making its decision.

If the court renders its decision immediately after trial, the court must first **dissolve** the marriage, that is, declare that the spouses are no longer married. The court will then rule on the issues of child support, property division, alimony, attorney's fees, and debts. One of the parties will be ordered to prepare the judgment, which will be signed by the opposing party and the court. The **judgment** delineates the orders made by the court pursuant to the court's decision after trial and becomes a permanent part of the court file. (See Exhibit 14–11.)

A **transcript** of the trial may be necessary if the decision was rendered at the close of trial to facilitate the preparation of the judgment or the preparation of an **appeal** of the case to a higher court. The paralegal may have the responsibility of ordering the transcript and dealing with the court reporter's office that will be responsible for its preparation. The paralegal may also be required to draft the judgment in accordance with local rules.

EXHIBIT 14–1

Sample request for trial form.

Commonwealth of Massachusetts

THE TRIAL COURT
THE PROBATE AND FAMILY COURT DEPARTMENT

_____ Division   Docket No. _____

REQUEST FOR TRIAL — PRE-TRIAL ASSIGNMENT
THIS FORM SHOULD **NOT** BE USED FOR MARK-UP OF TEMPORARY ORDERS AND MOTIONS
Please print or type

Please assign
for hearing: _____

                                                    Plaintiff

                            v.

                _____

                                                    Defendant

TYPE OF CASE _____ TIME REQUIRED _____ HEARING AT _____

( ) Uncontested

( ) Contested

   ( ) Merits
   ( ) Custody
   ( ) Support
   ( ) Visitation
   ( ) 208, § 34
   ( ) Other_____

The following papers must be on file before
cases can be assigned for hearing:

( ) Summons or Return of Service
( ) Marriage Certificate
( ) Statistical Form R408
( ) Financial Statement (Supp. Rule 401)
( ) Affidavits of Both Parties (1A Divorces)
( ) Notarized Agreement (1A Divorces)

( ) **REQUEST FOR INTERPRETER SERVICES**

Has Discovery Been Completed ( ) Yes   ( ) No

Has This Case Been Pre-Tried ( ) Yes   ( ) No

I hereby certify that, in my opinion, this case is ready for trial.

Requested by: **Opposing Counsel:**

_____   Name   _____

_____   Address   _____
                                  and
_____   Phone No.   _____

- -

FOR REGISTER'S USE ONLY
ACTION

The above-entitled matter has been assigned for

_____ (Trial) _____ (Pre-Trial Conferen

at _____ OR _____ 20 ___ at _____

_____ . Returned without action.   Data Incomplete.   See above.

                                                    ┌──────────────┐
                                                    │   │
                                                    └──────────────┘
                                                    Clerk's Initials

Register of Probate
1/82

EXHIBIT 14–2
Sample military affidavit.

AFFIDAVIT CONCERNING MILITARY SERVICE
JD-FM-178 New 6-98
P.B. § 17-21

STATE OF CONNECTICUT SUPERIOR COURT

INSTRUCTIONS

Anyone who knows the military status of the defendant may complete the form below. You must swear that your statement is true and sign it in front of a court clerk, a notary public, or an attorney who will also sign and date the affidavit. Make one copy for yourself and give the original to the court clerk.

EXPLANATION: A military service affidavit is required in every case where the defendant has not filed an Appearance form with the court clerk's office by the time of the court hearing. The purpose is to protect men and women serving in the U.S. military from getting a court judgment against them without first receiving notice of the lawsuit and a chance to defend the case. The affidavit gives the court the necessary facts to find that the defendant is not in the U.S military.

JUDICIAL DISTRICT OF	AT *(Town)*	RETURN DATE *(Mo., day, yr)*	DOCKET NO.
PLAINTIFF'S NAME *(Last, first, middle initial)*		DEFENDANT'S NAME *(Last, first, middle initial)*	

certify that the following is true *(check all that apply and complete):*

☐   1.   The defendant is in the U.S. Military.

☐   2.   The defendant is not in the U.S. Military. I know this because:

     ☐ the defendant is working at _____

     ☐ the defendant currently lives at _____

     ☐ the defendant is _____ years old.

     ☐ other *(state reasons)* _____

☐   3.   I do not know whether the defendant is in the U.S. military service.

SIGNATURE	PRINT NAME	
SIGNED AND SWORN TO BEFORE ME *(Asst. Clerk/Notary Public/Comm. of Sup. Court)*	AT *(Town, State)*	DATE SIGNED

EXHIBIT 14–3

Contact information for determining whether a defendant is in the military.

Branches of the Military

Army

Army World-Wide Locator

U.S. Army EREC

8899 E. 56th Street

Indianapolis, IN 46249-5301

$3.50; check payable to Finance Officer

Navy

Bureau of Navy Personnel

PERS-02116 2 Navy Annex

Washington, DC 20370

(703) 614-3116

$5.20; check payable to U.S. Treasurer

Marines

HQMC MMSB 10

2008 Elliot Road, Room 201

Quantico, VA 22134-5030

$5.20; check payable to U.S. Treasurer

Coast Guard

Commander-CGPC-Adm3

U.S. Coast Guard Personnel Command

2100 Second Street S.W.

Washington, DC 20593–0001

(202) 267-2321

$5.20; check payable to U.S. Treasurer

Air Force

AFPC-MFIMDL

550 C Street West, Suite 50

Randolph AFB, TX 78150-4752

$5.20; check payable to U.S. Treasurer

EXHIBIT 14–4
Sample notice of trial date and pretrial conference.

```
1   NORMAN M. DOLIN, ESQ., SBN 30475
    LAW OFFICES OF NORMAN M. DOLIN
2   1925 Century Park East, Suite 2200
    Los Angeles, CA 90067-2723
3   Tel: (310) 552-9338

4   Attorney for Petitioner, JAMES EUGENE CARREY    FEB 18 1994

5                                          EDWARD _____ CLERK

6                                          BY _____ DEPUTY

7

8              SUPERIOR COURT OF CALIFORNIA

9             FOR THE COUNTY OF LOS ANGELES

10

11  In Re Marriage of:          )   CASE NO.  BD 135499
                                )
12  PETITIONER:  JAMES  EUGENE )   NOTICE   OF   TRIAL   DATE,
                 CARREY         )   MANDATORY    SETTLEMENT
13  and                         )   CONFERENCE DATE, AND ORDER
                                )
14                              )   Trial:
    RESPONDENT:  MELISSA  JANE )   Date:  May 11, 1994
15               CARREY         )   Time:  8:30 a.m.
                                )   Dept:  2B
16  _____)
                                    Mandatory   Settlement
17                                  Conference:
                                    Date:  April 21, 1994
18                                  Time:  8:30 a.m.
                                    Dept:  2
19

20  TO RESPONDENT, MELISSA JANE CARREY AND TO HER ATTORNEYS OF RECORD:

21       PLEASE TAKE NOTICE that trial in the above-captioned matter is

22  set for May 11, 1994, at 8:30 a.m., in Department 2B of the

23  Superior Court located at 111 North Hill Street, Los Angeles,

24  California.

25       PLEASE TAKE FURTHER NOTICE that the Mandatory Settlement

26  Conference in the above-captioned matter is set for April 21, 1994,

27  at 8:30 a.m. in Department 2 of the Superior Court located at 111

28  North Hill Street, Los Angeles, California.


    Carrey\NotTRI.MSC              1
```

EXHIBIT 14–4

Continued

1	PLEASE NOTE THE COURT HAS MADE THE FOLLOWING FURTHER ORDERS:
2	1. All discovery, including depositions of all experts,
3	shall be pursuant to the provisions of §2024 <u>Code of Civil</u>
4	<u>Procedure</u>.
5	2. At least seven (7) calendar days before the first trial
6	date, all counsel and parties in pro per shall exchange with each
7	other the following in writing:
8	a. A new trial brief discussing in detail the
9	disputed issues, approximate tax consequences.
10	b. Lists of names of all witnesses to be called at
11	trial. Except for good cause shown, failure to so disclose shall
12	preclude undisclosed witnesses from testifying.
13	c. Lists of exhibits as described in Los Angeles
14	Superior Court Civil Trials Manual Section 75. Except for good
15	cause shown, failure to so disclose shall preclude admission of
16	undisclosed exhibits.
17	3. Counsel and parties in propria persona are ordered to
18	premark their proposed exhibits in accordance with Section VIII
19	(Trial Preparation) of the Family Law Manual of Procedures.
20	4. Counsel or parties in propria persona are to comply with
21	CCP §2025(Q)(i) in identifying deposition transcripts to be used at
22	trial.
23	Dated: February 17, 1994 Respectfully submitted,
24	LAW OFFICES OF NORMAN M. DOLIN
25	
26	BY: _____
27	Norman M. Dolin Attorney for Petitioner,
28	JAMES EUGENE CARREY

Carrey\NotTR1.MSC   2

346

EXHIBIT 14–5
Sample subpoena.

SUBPOENA
FAMILY/JUVENILE
JD-FM-126   Rev. 4-89 (Old SJC-11A)
C.G.S. 52-143, 52-144, 52-260

STATE OF CONNECTICUT
SUPERIOR COURT

INSTRUCTIONS

To be used only if the witness is being subpoenaed by the state in family or juvenile matters, including those subpoenas issued by the attorney general, or an assistant attorney general, or by any public defender or assistant public defender acting in his/her official capacity. (For example, in family matters, use in conjunction with form JD-FM-124.)

NAME OF CASE	DOCKET NO.

NAME AND ADDRESS OF COURT *(No., street and town)*

TO

BY AUTHORITY OF THE STATE OF CONNECTICUT, you are hereby commanded to appear before the Superior Court in session at the above address on the date indicated above or to such day thereafter and within sixty days hereof on which the action named above is legally to be tried, to testify what you know in said action pending in the court.

YOU ARE FURTHER COMMANDED TO BRING WITH YOU AND PRODUCE:

HEREOF FAIL NOT, UNDER PENALTY OF THE LAW.

To any proper officer or indifferent person to serve and return.

NAME OF STATE AGENT ISSUING SUBPOENA	TITLE	
SIGNED (Clerk, Commissioner of Superior Court)	ON (Date)	AT (Town)

NOTICE TO THE PERSON SUMMONED

You must report to the court at the time and address shown above and remain until this case is disposed of and you are discharged by the court. Present this subpoena when you report. Your statutory fees as witness will be paid by the clerk of the court where you are summoned to appear, if you give the clerk this subpoena on the day you appear. If you do not appear in court on the day and at the time stated, or on the day and at the time to which your appearance may have been postponed or continued by order of an officer of the court, the court may order that you be arrested. In addition, if you fail to appear and testify, without reasonable excuse, you shall be fined not more than twenty-five dollars and pay all damages to the aggrieved party.

RETURN OF SERVICE

		DATE
JUDICIAL DISTRICT OF _____ ss. _____ , Connecticut		

Then and there I made service of the within subpoena not less than eighteen hours prior to the time designated for the person summoned to appear, by reading the same in the presence and hearing/leaving a true and attested copy hereof in the hands/at the last usual place of abode of each of the within-named persons, viz:

FEES

COPY

ENDORSEMENT

SERVICE

TRAVEL *(Show miles and amount)*

The within is ☐ the original/☐ a true copy of the original subpoena.

ATTEST (Signature of proper officer or indifferent person)	TITLE (if applicable)	**TOTAL**

DISTRIBUTION: WHITE - Return to court after service   YELLOW - Witness   PINK - Retained by clerk

EXHIBIT 14–6
Sample financial disclosure affidavit.

Commonwealth of Massachusetts

The Trial Court
_____ **Division**   **Probate and Family Court Department**   **Docket No.** _____

Financial Statement
(SHORT FORM)

_____ **v.** _____

Plaintiff/Petitioner   **Defendant/Petitioner**

INSTRUCTIONS: If your income equals or exceeds $75,000.000 you must complete the LONG FORM financial statement, unless otherwise ordered by the Court. All questions on both sides of this form must be answered in full or the word "none" inserted. If additional space is needed for any answer, an attached sheet may be filed in addition to, but not in lieu of, the answer. Information contained herein is confidential and only available to the parties and persons authorized under Probate and Family Court Department Supplemental Rule 401.

1. Your Name _____ Soc. Sec. No. _____

   Address _____
   (street and no.)   (city or town)   (state)   (zip)

   Age _____ Tel. No. (____) _____ No. of Children living with you _____
   Occupation _____ Employer _____
   Employer's Address _____
   (street and no.)   (city or town)   (state)   (zip)
   Employer's Tel. No. (____) _____ Health Ins. Coverage [ ] YES [ ] NO
   Health Insurance Provider _____ Cert. No. _____

2. **Gross Weekly income from All Sources (strike inapplicable words)**
   a) Base pay from salary, wages . . . . $_____
   b) Self Employment Income **(attach a completed Schedule A)** . . . . $_____
   c) Income from overtime-commissions-tips-bonuses-part-time job . . . . $_____
   d) Dividends - interest . . . . $_____
   e) Income from trusts or annuities . . . . $_____
   f) Pensions and retirement funds . . . . $_____
   g) Social Security . . . . $_____
   h) Disability, unemployment insurance or worker's compensation . . . . $_____
   i) Public Assistance (welfare, A.F.D.C. payments) . . . . $_____
   j) Rental from Income Producing Property **(attach a completed Schedule B)** . . $_____
   k) All other sources (including child support, alimony) . . . . $_____

   l) **Total Gross Weekly Income** (a through k) $_____

3. **Itemize Deductions from Gross Income**
   a) Federal income tax deductions (claiming _____ exemptions) . . . . $_____
   b) State income tax deductions (claiming _____ exemptions) . . . . $_____
   c) F.I.C.A./Medicare . . . . $_____
   d) Medical Insurance . . . . $_____
   e) Union Dues . . . . $_____

   f) **Total Deductions** (a through e) $_____

4. **Adjusted Net Weekly Income**
   2 (l) minus 3 (f) . . . . $_____

5. **Other Deductions from Salary**
   a) Credit Union (Loan Repayment or Savings) . . . . $_____
   b) Savings . . . . $_____
   c) Retirement . . . . $_____
   d) Other - Specify (such as Deferred Compensation or 401K) . . . . $_____

   e) **Total Deductions** (a through d) $_____

6. **Net Weekly Income**   4 minus 5 (e) $_____

7. **Gross Yearly Income from Prior Year** . . . . $_____
   (attach copy of all W-2 and 1099 forms for prior year)

EXHIBIT 14–6

Continued

8. **Weekly Expenses** (Do Not Duplicate Weekly Expenses - Strike inapplicable Words)
   - a) Rent - Mortgage (PIT) $_____
   - b) Homeowner's/Tenant Insurance $_____
   - c) Maintenance and Repair $_____
   - d) Heat (Type _____) $_____
   - e) Electricity and/or Gas $_____
   - f) Telephone $_____
   - g) Water/Sewer $_____
   - h) Food $_____
   - i) House Supplies $_____
   - j) Laundry and Cleaning $_____
   - k) Clothing $_____
   - l) Life Insurance $_____
   - m) Medical Insurance $_____
   - n) Uninsured Medicals $_____
   - o) Incidentals and Toiletries $_____
   - p) Motor Vehicle Expenses $_____
   - q) Motor Vehicle Loan Payment $_____
   - r) Child Care $_____
   - s) Other (attach additional schedule if necessary) $_____
   - _____ $_____
   - _____ $_____

   Total Weekly Expenses (a through s) $_____

9. **Counsel Fees**
   - a) Retainer amount(s) paid to your attorney(s) $_____
   - b) Legal fees incurred, to date, against retainer(s) $_____
   - c) Anticipated range of total legal expense to prosecute this action $_____ to $_____

10. **Assets** (Attach additional schedule for additional real estate and other assets, if necessary)
    - a) Real Estate _____
      - Location _____
      - Title _____
      - Fair Market Value $_____ – Mortgage(s) $_____ = Equity $_____
    - b) IRA, Keough, Pension, Profit Sharing, Other Retirement Plans
      List Financial Institution or Plan Names and Account Numbers
      - _____ $_____   _____
      - _____ $_____   _____
      - _____ $_____   _____
    - c) Tax Deferred Annuity Plan(s) . . . . $_____   _____
    - d) Life Insurance: Present Cash Value . . . . $_____   _____
    - e) Savings & Checking Accounts, Money Market Accounts, and CDs - which are held individually, jointly, in the name of another person for your benefit or held by you for the benefit of your minor child(ren). **List Financial Institution Names and Account Numbers**
      - _____ $_____   _____
      - _____ $_____   _____
      - _____ $_____   _____
    - f) Motor Vehicles
      - Fair Market Value $_____ – Motor Vehicle Loan $_____ = Equity $_____
      - Fair Market Value $_____ – Motor Vehicle Loan $_____ = Equity $_____
    - g) Other (such as - stocks, bonds, collections)
      - _____ $_____   _____
      - _____ $_____   _____
    - h) **Total Assets** (a through g) $_____

11. **Liabilities** (DO NOT list weekly expenses but DO list all liabilities)

	Creditor	Nature of Debt	Date of Origin	Amount Due	Weekly Payment
a)					
b)					
c)					
d)					
e)	**Total Amount Due and Total Weekly Payment**			$_____	$_____

12. **Number of Years you have paid to Social Security** _____ years

I certify under the penalties of perjury that my income and expenses, assets, and liabilities as stated herein are true to the best of my knowledge and belief. I have carefully read this financial statement and I certify the information is true and complete

Date _____   Signature _____

STATEMENT BY ATTORNEY

I, the undersigned attorney, am admitted to practice law in the Commonwealth of Massachusetts—am admitted pro hoc vice for the purposes of this case—and am an officer of the court. As the attorney for the party on whose behalf this Financial Statement is submitted, I hereby state to the court that I have no knowledge that any of the information contained herein is false.

Attorney's Signature _____   Date _____
Address _____   Tel. No. ( ) _____
B.B.O. # _____

EXHIBIT 14–7

Sample custody affidavit.

AFFIDAVIT DISCLOSING CARE OR CUSTODY PROCEEDINGS	TRIAL COURT OF MASSACHUSETTS	DOCKET NUMBER
Pursuant to Trial Court Rule IV	Name Of Case _____	_____

☐ Boston Municipal Court | ☐ District Court _____ Division | ☐ Juvenile Court _____ Division | ☐ Probate & Family Court _____ Division | ☐ Superior Court _____ Division

Section 1

I, _____, hereby declare, to the best of
NAME OF PARTY (PRINT)
my knowledge, information, and belief that all the information on this form is true and complete:

Section 2

The name(s) of the child(ren) whose care or custody is at issue in this case are:

A. _____ B. _____ C. _____
(LAST, FIRST) (LAST, FIRST) (LAST, FIRST)

Use only the letter appearing in front of the child's name above when referring to that child in completing the remaining sections.

Section 3

The party filing this affidavit may request certain addresses to be kept confidential if the address is a shelter for battered persons and their dependent child(ren), or the party filing this affidavit believes that he/she or the child(ren) are in danger of physical or emotional abuse, or the party is filing an action under G.L.c.209A. **If the party who completed this affidavit believed this provision applied to him/her, then the box at the right has been checked and sections 4 and 5 have not been completed.** ☐

Section 4

The address(es) of the above-named child(ren) whose care or custody is at issue in this case are:

Address(es)	Address(es) During Last 2 Years, If Different
CHILD A. _____	_____
CHILD B. _____	_____
CHILD C. _____	_____

Section 5

My address is: _____

Section 6

I ☐ have ☐ have not participated in and I ☐ know ☐ do not know of other care or custody proceedings involving the above-named child(ren) in Massachusetts or in any other state or country.

Certified copies of any pleadings or determinations in a care or custody proceeding outside of Massachusetts listed in sections 7 and 8 must be filed with this affidavit unless already filed with this court or an extension for filing these documents has been granted by this court.

Section 7

The following is a list of all pending or concluded proceedings I have participated in or know of involving the care or custody of the above-named child(ren):

Letter of Child	Court	Docket No.	Status of Case (Custody awarded to) (Date of award)	[W]itness [P]arty [O]ther [N]one
CHILD ____	_____	_____	_____	[ ]
CHILD ____	_____	_____	_____	[ ]
CHILD ____	_____	_____	_____	[ ]

Section 8

The names and addresses of parties to care or custody proceedings involving any of the above-named child(ren) or those claiming a legal right to these child(ren) during the last two years (not including myself) are:

Letter of Child	Name of Party/Claimant	Current (or last known) Address of Party/Claimant
CHILD ____	_____	_____
CHILD ____	_____	_____
CHILD ____	_____	_____

Section 9

If the box at the right is checked, this affidavit discloses the adoption of one or more of the above-named child(ren) and I am requesting the court to impound this affidavit. See instructions. ☐

This affidavit must be personally signed by the party listed in section 1 above, unless he/she is under 18 years of age or has been adjudged incompetent in which case the attorney of record must sign. A revised affidavit must be filed with the court if new information is discovered subsequent to this filing.

Signed this _____ day of _____, 20_____ under the penalties of perjury.

X_____
SIGNATURE OF PARTY OR ATTORNEY OF RECORD FOR INCOMPETENT/JUVENILE   PRINTED NAME OF PERSON SIGNING

_____
ADDRESS OF ATTORNEY OF RECORD FOR INCOMPETENT/JUVENILE

THE PARTY FILING THIS AFFIDAVIT MUST FURNISH A COPY OF IT TO ALL OTHER PARTIES TO THIS ACTION.

EXHIBIT 14–8

Sample claim for relief.

DOCKET NO. FA 96-123456 : SUPERIOR COURT

BRONSON, RODNEY : JUDICIAL DISTRICT OF NEW HAVEN

V. : AT NEW HAVEN

BRONSON, EVELYN : DECEMBER 8, 2000

DEFENDANT'S PROPOSED CLAIMS FOR RELIEF

1. **ALIMONY**—The parties each waive any right to alimony.

2. **REAL PROPERTY**—The marital home will be listed for sale and the parties shall divide the net proceeds equally.

3. **CUSTODY**—The parties shall share joint legal and physical custody of the minor children.

4. **PENSION**— The parties shall each retain their respective pensions.

> THE DEFENDANT,
> EVELYN BRONSON
>
> BY: _____
> GRACE A LUPPINO, ESQ.
> HER ATTORNEY
> 555 MAIN AVENUE
> NEW HAVEN, CT 06511
> (203) 333-3333
> JURIS NO. 160000

ORDER

The foregoing motion having been heard, it is hereby ORDERED:

> GRANTED/DENIED
> THE COURT
>
> BY: _____
> JUDGE

CERTIFICATION

This is to certify that a true copy of the foregoing motion was mailed, postage prepaid, on this date to all counsel and pro se parties of record on this _____ day of _____ , 2000, as follows:

Justine F. Miller
22 Park Place
New Haven, CT 06522

_____
Grace A. Luppino, Esq.
Commissioner of the Superior Court

EXHIBIT 14–9

Sample wage execution form for facilitating alimony and child support payments by means of automatic deductions.

STATE OF CONNECTICUT
SUPERIOR COURT

WITHHOLDING ORDER
FOR SUPPORT JD-FM-1 Rev. 9-91
Pr. Bk. Form 508.1 C.G.S. 52-362 P.A. 91-391

Name and mailing address of employer

To ⌐ ⌐

INSTRUCTIONS TO DEPENDENT OR ATTORNEY
1. Complete PART I and PART III.
2. Print or type original and 3 copies.
3. File original and 1 copy with the clerk.
4. If withholding order issues immediately against a non-appearing obligor, complete form JD-FM-70, Notice to Nonappearing Obligor.

"X" APPROPRIATE BOX(ES)

☐ NEW ORDER ☐ STIPULATION ☐ REISSUE

FROM (Name and address of court)	DOCKET NO.

Fold

NAME OF EMPLOYEE	ADDRESS OF EMPLOYEE	SOCIAL SECURITY NO.

MAKE CHECK PAYABLE TO (Name of individual, institution or agency to which checks are payable)

MAIL CHECK TO (Number, street, town, state and zip code of recipient)

PART I

DEPENDENT OR ATTORNEY TO COMPLETE PART A, AND IF THERE IS AN ARREARAGE COMPLETE B OR C ("X" applicable boxes)

SUPPORT/WEEK

☐ **A.** The Court ordered current support at . . . . $

ARREARAGE PYMT./WK.

☐ **B.** The Court ordered weekly payments on arrearage to be taken by way of a wage withholding at: $

until the total arrearage of $ _____ is paid in full.

ARREARAGE PYMT./WK.

☐ **C.** The Court did not order a specific payment on arrearage, therefore . . . . $

should be deducted until the total arrearage of $ _____ is paid in full. *This amount is determined by the greater of $10.00 per week or 20% of the current support order.*

TOTAL/WEEK

TOTAL WITHHOLDING ORDER . . . . $

PART II

TO ANY PROPER OFFICER: You are hereby ordered to make due service of this withholding order on the above-named employer according to law.

TO EMPLOYER: You are hereby ordered to deduct from the salary or wages due said employee and to make payable as prescribed above, the amount you must calculate on the reverse side. You are further ordered to comply with the requirements of Part IV of this order "Notice to Employer of Withholding Order".

	EFFECTIVE DATE	DATE OF COURT ORDER
EFFECTIVE DATE OF WITHHOLDING ORDER ▶		
SIGNED (Judge, Magistrate, Assistant Clerk)	DATE SIGNED	NAME OF JUDGE, MAGISTRATE

PART III

SUPPORT CATEGORY (Dependent or attorney to place an "X" in the appropriate box below)

☐ **A.** Obligor is supporting a spouse or dependent child other than the spouse or child with respect to whose support the order is issued.

☐ **B.** Obligor is not supporting a spouse or dependent child other than the spouse or child with respect to whose support the order is issued.

☐ **C.** Obligor is supporting a spouse or dependent child other than the spouse or child with respect to whose support the order is issued AND there is an arrearage of 12 weeks or greater in length.

☐ **D.** Obligor is not supporting a spouse or dependent child other than the spouse or child with respect to whose support the order is issued AND there is an arrearage of 12 weeks or greater in length.

PART IV   NOTICE TO EMPLOYER OF WITHHOLDING ORDER

You are being served with a withholding order, a court order requiring you to withhold nonexempt wages from a person employed by you. This notice is to inform you of the actions you must take in order to comply with the law regarding withholding orders. Please read each section carefully.

WITHHOLDING ORDER EFFECTIVE IMMEDIATELY—You must begin making deductions from your employee's wages from the Effective Date of Withholding Order shown above. Commencing no later than the first pay period that occurs after fourteen days following the date of service of this order for withholding and thereafter within ten days of the date the obligor is paid you must pay the sums withheld to the person or

(CONTINUED ON REVERSE SIDE)

EXHIBIT 14–9

Continued

PART IV NOTICE TO EMPLOYER
(CONTINUED)

agency in whose favor the withholding order was issued as set forth in the box "Make Check Payable To" above. If this withholding order is payable to the Bureau of Collection Services, you must specify the dates on which each withholding occurred and the amount withheld on those dates for the above-named employee.

PRECEDENCE OF WITHHOLDING ORDERS TO ENFORCE SUPPORT ORDERS—All orders for withholding issued to enforce a support order take precedence over other wage executions. Two or more support withholding orders may be levied at the same time, but if the total levy in any week exceeds the maximum permitted as calculated below as the Amount to be withheld, all sums due shall be allocated by the employer giving priority to current support.

MAXIMUM AMOUNT DEDUCTED—The computations you complete on this form will allow you to calculate the exact amount which should be withheld weekly from this employee's wages.

YOUR DUTY TO COMPLY WITH THIS WITHHOLDING ORDER—You have a legal duty to make deductions from your employee's wages and pay any amounts deducted as required by this withholding order. If you do not, legal action may be taken against you. If such an action is taken, you may be liable for the full amount not withheld since receipt of proper notice. You may also be subject to a finding of contempt by the court or family support magistrate for failure to honor any of the terms of this withholding order.

DISCIPLINE AGAINST YOUR EMPLOYEE—You must not discipline, suspend or discharge your employee because this withholding order has been served upon you. If you do unlawfully take action against your employee, you may be liable to pay him all of his lost earnings and employment benefits from the time of your action to the time that the employee is reinstated. In addition, a fine up to one thousand dollars may be imposed on any employer who discharges from employment, refuses to employ, takes disciplinary action against or discriminates against an employee subject to a support order for withholding because of the existence of such withholding order and the obligations or additional obligations which it imposes upon the employer.

The law allows you to take disciplinary measures against the employee if you are served with more than 7 withholding orders against your employee's wages in any calendar year.

TERMINATION OF EMPLOYMENT—You must promptly notify the dependent or the support enforcement division, as directed, when the employee terminates employment, makes a claim for workers' compensation benefits or makes a claim for unemployment compensation benefits and provide the employee's last known address and the name and address of the employee's new employer, if known.

COMPUTATION OF EMPLOYEE'S DISPOSABLE EARNINGS

Pursuant to General Statute 52-362, certain earnings of the employee cannot be withheld to satisfy this withholding order. First, only "disposable earnings" may be subjected to this withholding order. Disposable earnings for the purpose of this withholding order means "that part of the earnings of an individual remaining after deduction from those earnings of amounts required to be withheld for the payment of federal income and employment taxes, normal retirement contributions, union dues and initiation fees, and group life and health insurance premiums." Use the following table to compute your employee's disposable earnings each week.

1. Employee's gross compensation per week . . . . ————
2. Federal income tax withheld . . . . ————
3. Federal employment tax . . . . ————
4. Normal retirement contribution . . . . ————
5. Union dues and initiation fees . . . . ————
6. Group life insurance premium . . . . ————
7. Health insurance premium . . . . ————
8. Total allowable deduction (*Add lines 2-7*) . . . . ————
9. WEEKLY DISPOSABLE EARNINGS (*Subtract line 8 from line 1*) . . . . ————

COMPUTATION OF AMOUNT TO BE WITHHELD

10. Weekly Disposable Earnings Minus $135 . . . . ————

11. Refer to Part III Support Category on the reverse side and enter:

50% of Weekly Disposable Earnings if box A is checked
60% of Weekly Disposable Earnings if box B is checked
55% of Weekly Disposable Earnings if box C is checked . . . . ————
65% of Weekly Disposable Earnings if box D is checked

12. Amount available for withholding (*lesser of lines 10 and 11*) . . . . [ ]

The instructions below must be followed to determine the amount of weekly withholding. Refer to PART I on the reverse side and line 12 above.

13. Amount of withholding—to be computed weekly:

A. **ONE SUPPORT WITHHOLDING ORDER**

1. **If only A in PART I is completed**—deduct weekly the lesser of the amounts specified in PART IA and line 12.
2. **If A and B or A and C in PART I are completed**—add the amount of weekly support order in PART IA and amount of weekly arrearage order in PART IB or 1C and deduct weekly the lesser of such total and the amount in line 12. Upon payment of the total arrearage specified in PART IB or 1C deduct the amount of weekly support only.

B. **TWO OR MORE SUPPORT WITHHOLDING ORDERS (against same employee)**

1. Deduct weekly the amounts specified in PART 1A for each withholding order in the sequence in which the withholding orders were served provided that the total amount deducted is less than the amount specified in line 12.
2. If the amount withheld exceeds the sums specified in PART 1A for all withholding orders, the remaining amount, up to the maximum deduction specified in line 12, is to be applied to the amount specified in PART 1B or C on each withholding in the order in which the withholding orders were served.

EXHIBIT 14–9

Continued

ADVISEMENT OF RIGHTS

Re: Income Withholding

I. You have the right to present any evidence to the court as to why an order for withholding effective immediately should not be ordered.

II. EXEMPTIONS: If your income is subject to a withholding order, a portion of your income will not be withheld. Only disposable income is subject to a withholding order. Disposable income means that part of the income of an individual remaining after deduction from that income of amounts required to be withheld for the payment of federal, state and local income taxes, employment taxes, normal retirement contributions, union dues and initiation fees and group life and health insurance premiums. The amount withheld may not exceed the maximum amount permitted under section 1673 of title 15 of the United States Code: If you are supporting a spouse or dependent child other than the spouse or child with respect to whose support the order is issued, the maximum amount of your disposable income that may be withheld is 50% of such income, unless you are twelve weeks or more in arrears in which case the maximum is 55% of such income. If you are not supporting a spouse or dependent child other than the spouse or child with respect to whose support the order is issued, the maximum amount of your disposable income that may be withheld is 60% of such income unless you are twelve weeks or more in arrears in which case the maximum is 65%. In no event, however, under state law may you be left with less than $145 of disposable income.

III. You have the right to claim the exemptions listed above or any other applicable state or federal exemptions with respect to income withholding orders.

IV. The computation of the amount withheld will be done by the payer of the income based on information supplied by the court. If you believe that an incorrect amount of your income is being withheld due to incorrect information being supplied to the payer of the income and you would like the amount withheld modified, you must request a court hearing.

V. You have a right to seek a modification of, or raise a defense to, the support order by filing a proper motion with the court.

This is to certify that this document was read to me or read by me in a language that I understand. A copy of this statement has been given to me.

_____   _____
Signature   Date

This is to attest that the above document was signed in my presence.

_____   _____
Signature/Title   Date

Check the box below if the parties have completed the "Waiver" on the back/page 2 of this form.

☐ "Waiver of Right to Immediate Income Withholding Order" completed on back/page 2.

JD-FM-71 Rev. 2-98
C.G.S. 52-362, P.A. 97-7 (June Sp. Sess.), Sec. 28

EXHIBIT 14–9

Continued

WAIVER OF RIGHT TO IMMEDIATE INCOME WITHHOLDING ORDER

NAME OF CASE		DOCKET NO.	

The undersigned parties agree that a contingent and not an immediate income withholding order shall issue in this case.

OBLIGOR	DATE SIGNED	OBLIGEE	DATE SIGNED
OTHER	DATE SIGNED	OTHER	DATE SIGNED
WITNESS	DATE SIGNED	WITNESS	DATE SIGNED

JD-FM-71 (Back) Rev. 2-98

EXHIBIT 14–10
Sample form for collecting statistical information about divorcing couples.

LOCAL INDEX NUMBER _____

New York State
Department of Health
CERTIFICATE OF DISSOLUTION OF MARRIAGE

STATE FILE NUMBER

TYPE, OR PRINT IN PERMANENT BLACK INK

HUSBAND

1. HUSBAND – NAME: FIRST   MIDDLE   LAST
2. DATE OF BIRTH — Month | Day | Year
3. STATE OF BIRTH (COUNTRY IF NOT USA)

4 _____

4A. RESIDENCE: STATE   4B. COUNTY   4C. LOCALITY (CHECK ONE AND SPECIFY) ☐ CITY OF ☐ TOWN OF ☐ VILLAGE OF
4E. IF CITY OR VILLAGE, IS RESIDENCE WITHIN CITY OR VILLAGE LIMITS? ☐ YES ☐ NO IF NO, SPECIFY TOWN:

4D. STREET AND NUMBER OF RESIDENCE (INCLUDE ZIP CODE)

5A. ATTORNEY – NAME   5B. ADDRESS (INCLUDE ZIP CODE)

WIFE

9 _____

6A. WIFE – NAME: FIRST   MIDDLE   LAST   6B. MAIDEN NAME
7. DATE OF BIRTH — Month | Day | Year
8. STATE OF BIRTH (COUNTRY IF NOT USA)

9A. RESIDENCE: STATE   9B. COUNTY   9C. LOCALITY (CHECK ONE AND SPECIFY) ☐ CITY OF ☐ TOWN OF ☐ VILLAGE OF
9E. IF CITY OR VILLAGE, IS RESIDENCE WITHIN CITY OR VILLAGE LIMITS? ☐ YES ☐ NO IF NO, SPECIFY TOWN:

9D. STREET AND NUMBER OF RESIDENCE (INCLUDE ZIP CODE)

10A. ATTORNEY – NAME   10B. ADDRESS (INCLUDE ZIP CODE)

11 _____

11A. PLACE OF THIS MARRIAGE - CITY, TOWN OR VILLAGE   11B. COUNTY   11C. STATE (COUNTRY IF NOT USA)

12A. DATE OF THIS MARRIAGE — Month | Day | Year   12B. APPROXIMATE DATE COUPLE SEPARATED — Month | Year   13A. NUMBER OF CHILDREN EVER BORN ALIVE OF THIS MARRIAGE (SPECIFY)   13B. NUMBER OF CHILDREN UNDER 18 IN THIS FAMILY (SPECIFY)

15 _____

DECREE

14A. I CERTIFY THAT A DECREE OF DISSOLUTION OF THE ABOVE MARRIAGE WAS RENDERED ON — Month | Day | Year   14B. DATE OF ENTRY: — Month | Day | Year   14C. TYPE OF DECREE - DIVORCE, ANNULMENT, OTHER DISSOLUTION (SPECIFY)

14D. COUNTY OF DECREE   14E. TITLE OF COURT

23 _____

14F. SIGNATURE OF COUNTY CLERK ▶

CONFIDENTIAL INFORMATION

24 _____

HUSBAND

15. RACE: WHITE, BLACK, AMERICAN INDIAN, OTHER (SPECIFY)   16. NUMBER OF THIS MARRIAGE - FIRST, SECOND, ETC. (SPECIFY)   17. IF PREVIOUSLY MARRIED HOW MANY ENDED BY   A. DEATH NUMBER ☐ NONE   B. DIVORCE OR ANNULMENT NUMBER ☐ NONE   18. EDUCATION: INDICATE HIGHEST GRADE COMPLETED ONLY
ELEMENTARY 0 1 2 3 4 5 6 7 8 HIGH SCHOOL 1 2 3 4 COLLEGE 1 2 3 4 5+
00 01 02 03 04 05 06 07 08   09 10 11 12   13 14 15 16 17

25 _____

WIFE

19. RACE: WHITE, BLACK, AMERICAN INDIAN, OTHER (SPECIFY)   20. NUMBER OF THIS MARRIAGE - FIRST, SECOND, ETC. (SPECIFY)   21. IF PREVIOUSLY MARRIED HOW MANY ENDED BY   A. DEATH NUMBER ☐ NONE   B. DIVORCE OR ANNULMENT NUMBER ☐ NONE   22. EDUCATION: INDICATE HIGHEST GRADE COMPLETED ONLY
ELEMENTARY 0 1 2 3 4 5 6 7 8 HIGH SCHOOL 1 2 3 4 COLLEGE 1 2 3 4 5+
00 01 02 03 04 05 06 07 08   09 10 11 12   13 14 15 16 17

QR _____

23. PLAINTIFF - HUSBAND, WIFE, OTHER (SPECIFY)   24. DECREE GRANTED TO HUSBAND, WIFE, OTHER (SPECIFY)   25. LEGAL GROUNDS FOR DECREE (SPECIFY)

QS _____
DOH-2168 (4/94)

26. SIGNATURE OF PERSON PREPARING CERTIFICATE ▶ _____ ATTORNEY AT LAW

EXHIBIT 14–11

Sample judgment in a divorce trial.

1   At the *Matrimonial/IAS* Part _____
       of New York State Supreme Court at
2   the Courthouse, _____
3   County, on _____.

Present:
4   Hon. _____ *Justice/Referee*
       --X
5
6   Index No.:
                      Plaintiff,   Calendar No.:
       -against-
                                                JUDGMENT OF DIVORCE

7
                      Defendant.
       --X

8   This action was submitted to *the referee / this court* for consideration this date (on inquest
       of _____).

9   The Defendant was served   *personally/by publication/pursuant to court order dated*
       _____ *within/outside*   the State of New York.

10   Plaintiff presented a verified complaint.

11   The Defendant has   *not appeared and is in default   /   appeared and waived his or her*
       right to answer.

12   The Court accepted   *written/oral*   proof of non-military service.

13   The Plaintiff's address is _____, and social security
       number is _____. The Defendant's address is _____,
       and social security number is _____.

14   Now on motion of _____, the   *attorney for*   Plaintiff, it is:

15   ORDERED AND ADJUDGED that the Referee's Report, if any, is confirmed, and it is
       further

(Form UD-11)

EXHIBIT 14–11

Continued

16   ORDERED AND ADJUDGED that   *Plaintiff/Defendant*   shall have a judgment dissolving the marriage on the evidence found in the Findings of Fact and Conclusions of Law based upon DRL §170 subd. _____, and it is further

17   ORDERED AND ADJUDGED that   *Plaintiff/Defendant*   shall have custody of the children of the marriage, i.e.:

18   <u>Name</u>   <u>Date of Birth</u>

        _____   _____

        _____   _____

        _____   _____

        and it is further

19   ORDERED AND ADJUDGED that the existing Family Court Order(s) under Index No(s). _____ shall be continued.

20   ORDERED AND ADJUDGED that   *Plaintiff/Defendant*   shall pay to *Plaintiff/Defendant* the sum of _____ per *week/month* for maintenance commencing on _____ and on _____ *day of each week/the first day of each month*   thereafter, and it is further

21   ORDERED AND ADJUDGED that   *Plaintiff/Defendant*   shall pay to *Plaintiff/Defendant* the sum of _____ per *week/month* for child support commencing on _____ and on _____ *day of each week/the first day of each month*   thereafter, and it is further

22   ORDERED AND ADJUDGED that   *Plaintiff/Defendant*   shall pay to *Plaintiff/Defendant* the sum of _____ per *week/month* for child care expenses as follows:_____ _____, and it is further

23   ORDERED AND ADJUDGED that   *Plaintiff/Defendant*   shall pay to *Plaintiff/Defendant* the sum of _____ per *week/month*   for future reasonable health care as follows: _____, and it is further

(Form UD-11)

EXHIBIT 14–11
Continued

24   ORDERED AND ADJUDGED that *Plaintiff/Defendant* shall pay to *Plaintiff/Defendant* the sum of _____ per *week/month* for *present/future post-secondary / private / special / enriched* education for the children as follows: _____, and it is further

25   ORDERED AND ADJUDGED that this Judgment of Divorce shall serve as a Qualified Medical Support Order where a child support determination is being made, and it is further

26   ORDERED AND ADJUDGED that the minor children shall be enrolled and entitled to receive health insurance benefits as described below:

_____

_____

_____

27   ORDERED AND ADJUDGED that the relative legally responsible to supply health insurance benefits is:

_____

_____

_____

28   ORDERED AND ADJUDGED that the relative legally responsible to supply health insurance benefits is eligible under the following available group health plan or plans:

_____

_____

_____

_____

and shall provide health insurance benefits to the minor children *until the minor children reach the age of* _____ */ until* _____.

29   ORDERED AND ADJUDGED that the *agreement/stipulation* dated _____, a copy which is attached, and incorporated by reference into this judgment shall *survive and not*

(Form UD-11)

EXHIBIT 14–11
Continued

merge/not survive and merge   in this judgment, and the parties hereby are directed to comply with

every legally enforceable term and provision of such *agreement/stipulation;* and it is further

30   ORDERED AND ADJUDGED that the Family Court shall be granted concurrent jurisdiction

with the Supreme Court with respect to the issues of maintenance, child support, custody and

visitation, and it is further

31   ORDERED AND ADJUDGED that *(insert any transfers of monies, property or mandates*

*of the court that may need enforcement):*_____

_____

32   ORDERED AND ADJUDGED that either party may resume the use of a pre-marriage name

as follows _____.

33   Dated:

                                ENTER:

                                            _____
                                                    J.S.C./Referee

                                            _____
                                                    CLERK

(Form UD-11)

EXHIBIT 14–11
Continued

1 SUPREME COURT OF THE STATE OF NEW YORK
   COUNTY OF _____
   --X

2,3   Index No.:_____
                              Plaintiff.

       -against-   **NOTICE OF ENTRY**

4
                              Defendant.
   --X
   STATE OF NEW YORK   }
                                ss:
5 COUNTY OF_____   }

       PLEASE TAKE NOTICE that the attached is a true copy of a judgment of divorce in

6 this matter that was entered in the Office of the Clerk of the Supreme Court, _____

7 County, on the _____ day of _____,20____.

8 Date:_____
9
                                         _____
                                         Plaintiff

10   _____
                                         _____
                                         _____
                                         Address

11 TO:

   _____
   Defendant/Attorney for Defendant

   _____
   _____
   _____
         Address

(Form UD-12)

REVIEW QUESTIONS

1. Are divorce trials tried before a jury?
2. What is an uncontested hearing?
3. What is a default trial?
4. Explain the purpose of a military affidavit.
5. What is a contested hearing?
6. Explain the purpose of a judicial pretrial.
7. What type of information is exchanged between the parties at a pretrial conference?
8. What is the paralegal's role at the trial?
9. List five witnesses who may provide testimony at a divorce trial.
10. What is the purpose of a subpoena?
11. How does a trial notebook assist an attorney during a trial?
12. List the various documents that may need to be submitted to the court at the time of a divorce trial.
13. Explain the term *final argument.*
14. What is a judgment?
15. Why might it be necessary to obtain a transcript of the proceedings at the close of a trial?

EXERCISES

1. Make a list of the types of documents that must be filed with the family court in your jurisdiction on the day of trial. Obtain copies of any preprinted forms that are provided for documents on that list.

2. Contact the clerk's office of your local family court and ask when the next divorce trial is scheduled. See if you can arrange to observe this hearing. If you can, prepare a short paper on the matter at issue between the parties and the testimony provided by both sides in support of their arguments. If the judge entered a decision after the close of testimony, what was the court's ultimate resolution of the dispute?

3. Does your state family court provide alternatives to trials such as mediation services? If so, how are these services provided in your state? Are there any statutes or court rules that require mediation through the courts or through private agencies?

4. How are contested and uncontested matters scheduled for trial in your jurisdiction? Is there a special form that must be filed?

5. Locate the statutes that regulate divorce trials in your jurisdiction. Outline the requirements for both contested and uncontested matters.

15 CHAPTER

POSTJUDGMENT DIVORCE MATTERS

KEY TERMS

Arrearage
Modification
Contempt citation
Forum shopping
Motion for contempt
Motion to modify
Motion to modify alimony
Motion to modify child support
Motion to modify custody
Motion to modify visitation
Motion to open the judgment

Nonmodifiable
Order to show cause
Parental Kidnapping Prevention Act (PKPA)
Postjudgment matters
Substantial change in circumstances
Uniform Child Custody Jurisdiction Act (UCCJA)
Uniform Child Custody Jurisdiction and Enforcement Act (UCCJEA)

The entry of a final dissolution decree does not always end the litigation in a particular case. A spouse ordered to pay alimony or child support may cease making payments, either voluntarily or involuntarily. The circumstances of the party's may have also changed substantially since the date of the original divorce decree, thus requiring a change in the original order.

A large part of a family lawyer's practice involves **postjudgment matters.** Hence, this chapter focuses on postjudgment matters, which consist of **modifications** to an original order, enforcement of court orders, and motions to open the judgment. Appeals are also postjudgment matters, but because appeals are covered in basic civil litigation courses they are not addressed here.

The dissolution decree contains some provisions that constitute the final resolution of an issue and, hence, cannot be modified. Other provisions are modifiable and are subject to the court's continuing jurisdiction until certain events occur.

NONMODIFIABLE TERMS OF THE DISSOLUTION DECREE

A final decree of dissolution usually contains a section that deals with the distribution of marital assets or property. The separation agreement sets forth a final unappealable disposition of assets. Therefore, property distribution awards are **nonmodifiable.** If parties agree that one spouse will transfer all of his or her right and title to the family residence, once this agreement is made a part of the divorce judgment, the transferring party usually may not come back at a later date to modify or reverse this arrangement. Only if a spouse alleges and can prove fraud in the making of the divorce agreement will the court consider reopening and modifying the disposition of issues deemed final and nonmodifiable. This will require the aggrieved spouse to file a **motion to open the judgment,** requesting that a new trial be granted.

If alimony is awarded as a one-time lump sum and is labeled nonmodifiable in the divorce decree, then the spouse paying the lump sum is released from any future obligation to provide maintenance or support for the ex-spouse regardless of her future need for assistance, no matter how urgent. Lump-sum alimony is nonmodifiable even if it is to be paid in installments.

MODIFIABLE TERMS OF THE DISSOLUTION DECREE

Let's now take a look at the terms of a dissolution decree that can be modified.

MODIFICATION OF ALIMONY

In determining the modifiability of alimony, the parties must look to the original alimony award. The original award was either agreed on by the parties in a separation agreement or ordered by the court in a contested hearing where the parties could not agree on the issue of alimony. The court can modify alimony unless it is barred from doing so under the separation agreement or decree of dissolution.

If an order for alimony requires a spouse to pay the other spouse a fixed amount of money periodically, such as every week or every month, either the paying spouse or the receiving spouse may bring the matter back to the court to request either an increase or a decrease in the periodic amount ordered. In either case, the moving party will usually allege, as grounds, a change in their circumstances or a change in the other party's circumstances. The moving party must prove that since the date of the original order, there has been a **substantial change in circumstances** requiring a modification of the original order.

If either party waived alimony at the time of the dissolution, they are forever barred from returning to court and asking for alimony in the future. If a party was awarded nominal alimony of one dollar per year, this will allow the recipient spouse to return to court at a later date and request a modification of the original one-dollar alimony award. If a party was awarded rehabilitative alimony, either the separation agreement or court order after trial will indicate its modifiability. Reimbursement alimony is typically nonmodifiable since modifiability would defeat the purpose of "reimbursing" a spouse.

Arrearages, or amounts of unpaid alimony due to the recipient spouse, are nonmodifiable. A recipient spouse has a vested property right in the arrearage that cannot be changed by the court.

Motion to Modify Alimony

A party brings his or her request to the court's attention by filing a **motion to modify** the court's previous alimony order. (See Exhibit 15–1.) In this motion, the moving party alleges that a substantial change in circumstances has occurred since the date of the original decree, requiring the court to reopen the case and modify its original order.

In many jurisdictions, if a party files this motion within six months after the entry of the dissolution decree, the party need only file the motion with the court and serve, by mail, a copy of the motion to the attorney who represented the other spouse in the dissolution action. This avoids the need for service of the motion by a sheriff. The attorney must also serve by mail a copy on the attorney for the children if the children were represented by counsel in the action.

If more than six months has elapsed, the moving party must serve additional documents on the ex-spouse, along with the motion to modify. In many jurisdictions, the moving spouse must serve an **order to show cause** on the ex-spouse

FIGURE 15–1
Being laid off from a job may constitute enough of a "substantial change in circumstances" that a court would grant a motion to modify alimony.

(See Exhibit 15–1). This document must usually be personally served by a sheriff or other individual authorized to serve process. The **motion to modify alimony** will accompany the rule to show cause, which will already have identified a hearing date set by the court clerk. Some courts have preprinted forms and simplified procedures, allowing parties to appear pro se. (See Exhibit 15–2.)

After service is complete, the papers must be filed with the court and an entry fee must be paid, the amount of which depends on the jurisdiction. Sheriff's fees and attorney's fees must also be paid by the client. Therefore, bringing an action to modify parts of the divorce judgment can be costly.

Grounds for Modification of Alimony

Grounds for all modifications are broadly known as a substantial change in circumstance. What constitutes a substantial change? In matters relating to alimony, changed circumstances refers to an actual or assumed change in the financial status or capability of either party. For instance, if a spouse-husband was earning a high salary when the alimony order was entered and he subsequently loses his job and now works for a much lower rate, he can move to have the court lower the amount previously ordered based on his loss of ability to pay. Similarly, if a spouse-wife was receiving alimony and had a high-paying job that she had to leave because of illness, she may petition the court to increase the amount her ex-husband must pay to her.

When the court addresses a request to modify alimony, the court looks at the financial status of each of the parties and tries to make a decision that is reasonable under the circumstances. Both spouses are expected to provide for themselves according to ability to do so. If a spouse, male or female, has been making alimony payments consistent with the court order to an able-bodied nonworking spouse and the paying spouse suddenly, say, through a significant job promotion, experiences a large increase in earned income, the nonworking spouse may bring a motion to modify alimony upward. The court, however, may find that since the nonworking spouse never sought employment, the previous award sufficiently satisfied the spouse's financial need and that the other spouse should not be penalized because his or her ability and hard work has resulted in greater financial remuneration.

The change in circumstances must also be involuntary. If, for example, a husband ordered to pay alimony voluntarily quits his job and then shows up in court with a motion to modify alimony, the court will not be very sympathetic. If a recipient spouse runs up charges on a credit card, she cannot later come in to court and ask for a modification, since she created the financial problem.

The following circumstances may constitute sufficient grounds for modification of alimony:

  ▼ Deteriorating health of the payor or recipient spouse,
  ▼ Increased cost of living,
  ▼ Loss of employment,
  ▼ Remarriage or cohabitation of recipient spouse,
  ▼ Pay raises,
  ▼ Winning the lottery,
  ▼ Retirement,
  ▼ Employment changes (i.e., downsizing),
  ▼ Rehabilitation of recipient spouse, and
  ▼ Unforeseen economic circumstances.

FIGURE 15–2
An unforeseen change in a person's economic circumstances, such as an accident that prevents a spouse from performing a job and, hence, receiving a paycheck, would be considered by the court when deciding a motion to modify alimony.

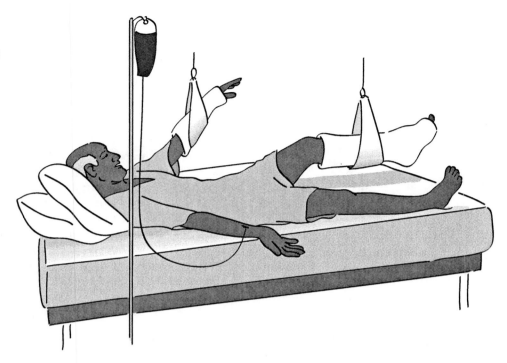

MODIFICATION OF CHILD SUPPORT

The court has continuing jurisdiction in child support matters and may entertain modifications until its jurisdiction ends. The family court has the right to order child support for each child until the child reaches the age of majority. As with alimony, a custodial parent may file a **motion to modify child support** if that spouse can prove a substantial change in circumstances since the date of the original order. A noncustodial parent paying child support may also move to modify an existing court order if he can prove a change in circumstances. The moving party must file motions similar to those discussed in the earlier section regarding modification of alimony. If a modification is warranted, the court will make the change in the child support award pursuant to that jurisdiction's child support guidelines. Child support arrearages, however, are unmodifiable.

When addressing a motion to decrease the amount obligated to pay, the court usually does not extinguish the arrearage and will order that continuing payments, whether the same or lower, include an additional amount to pay off any unpaid back alimony or child support. Alternately, the court may order that the total of the back amounts owed be paid to the recipient spouse within a reasonable time such as thirty or sixty days.

The following circumstances may constitute sufficient grounds for modification of child support:

▼ Cost of living increases—as children grow, their expenses increase (i.e., clothing, food, extra-curricular activities),

▼ Custody change—if the noncustodial parent moves for custody and prevails,

▼ An increase or decrease in either parent's income,

▼ Change in the child's health requiring unusual or extraordinary expenses, and

▼ Increased or onset of costs for special education, tutoring, or day care.

MODIFICATION OF CUSTODY AND VISITATION

Custody and visitation orders are always modifiable. The courts, however, will not disturb a custody or visitation order unless the moving party can prove that there has been a substantial change in circumstances *and* that a modification to the existing custody or visitation situation is in the best interest of the child or that the court did not have certain facts available at the time of entering the original order of custody. The substantial change of circumstances must have occurred after the date of the original order. The court will not entertain any evidence that has already been introduced at the divorce trial. New evidence must be such that justifies a **motion to modify custody** or a **motion to modify visitation;** the court will not tolerate a disgruntled parent retrying the custody matter through the mask of a modification.

The following circumstances may constitute sufficient grounds for modification of custody or visitation:

▼ The child becomes old enough to choose a custodian,

▼ Either parent's remarriage or cohabitation,

▼ A change in the child's needs,

▼ The parent's lifestyle adversely affecting the child,

▼ A parent's or child's health issues,

▼ Abuse or neglect, and

▼ The custodial parent's relocation.

RELOCATION OF CUSTODIAL PARENT

Because mobility is a characteristic of our society today, many dissolution decrees anticipate the possible relocation of a custodial parent and the consequences. Many dissolution decrees provide that a custodial parent may not move out of the jurisdiction without giving the noncustodial parent sufficient advance notice so that the noncustodial parent will have sufficient time if he or she desires to bring this proposed move to the attention of the court and object to this move as being contrary to the child's best interest. If the noncustodial parent brings such a motion before the court, the matter may be referred to the family relations division for a study and recommendation to the court. The noncustodial parent's chances of prevailing will be greater if that parent demonstrates the strength and value of the child's relationship with the noncustodial parent and with other significant individuals within the jurisdiction such as grandparents or uncles and aunts. On the other hand, if the noncustodial parent has played only an inconsistent and erratic role in the child's life, the court may not find that the child's best interests will be compromised by an out-of-state move.

In the past, in a decree for divorce or dissolution, a judge would sometimes order the custodial parent not to move out of the state with the children. While the parent was free to travel as they pleased, the children could not be moved out of the jurisdiction. Unfortunately, life isn't that simple and circumstances arise requiring a return to court to address the original order barring relocation. Let's say the mother is the custodial parent and her original decree states that she shall not remove the children from the state. Mother remarries and her new spouse is offered a job in another state. Mother must return to court to get permission to take the children out of the state or she will be in contempt of court. The court now must address the issue of relocation pursuant to a two prong test.

1) is the original decree modifiable?
2) if modifiable, is the relocation in the best interest of the children?

The court must look at the original decree and determine if the court ordered limitation on the custodial parent's freedom to relocate with the children is modifiable or whether the original order was a final, non-modifiable, non-appealable part of the judgment as is the case with the distribution of marital assets. While child custody is always modifiable, the issue of one parent relocating with the children may be limited by the court in that it deprives the other parent of contact and access to the children. The burden is on the moving party to prove to the court whether the original decree is modifiable. A review of the original decree and/or transcript may reveal that the issue is explicitly addressed and there is no dispute as to its modifiability. If the issue is unclear, then the court must make a decision based on the evidence offered and arguments of the parties. In the case illustrated above, if the decree is deemed unmodifiable, the relocation of the children is barred. If modifiable, then the court moves to the second prong of the test which is determining if the relocation is in the best interest of the children.

If the custodial parent prevails on the argument that the limitation on the custodial parent's freedom to have the child take up residence out of state is modifiable, then the burden falls on the noncustodial parent to demonstrate that such a move would not be in the child's best interest. At this point, the custodial parent may offer evidence to refute the noncustodial parent's evidence that such a move would compromise the child's best interest and the custodial parent may introduce evidence that such a move will enhance the child's best interest.

ENFORCEMENT OF COURT ORDERS

If the court has ordered a spouse to make periodic payments of alimony or child support and the spouse ceases to make these payments, the other spouse may file a motion for contempt to bring this matter to the court's attention. Enforcement of child support orders was addressed in Chapter 7.

If a party fails to make court-ordered payments, the receiving spouse should first write a letter to the paying spouse stating the arrearage owed and demanding payment of that arrearage. If that does not get a response and the party continues to fail to comply with a court order, the receiving spouse may bring this to the court's attention by filing a **motion for contempt** or **contempt citation.** (See Exhibits 15–3 and 15–4.) In family law disputes, common motions for contempt include motions for contempt for failure to pay alimony or child support or motions for contempt against the custodial parent for withholding visitation from the noncustodial parent, or motion for contempt against the noncustodial parent for not complying with visitation orders by bringing the child back late, picking the child up late, or engaging in inappropriate activities while the child is visiting.

Sometimes one or the other party may not be happy with the visitation arrangements under a court order that provided only for the "right of reasonable visitation." What is "reasonable" is a subjective judgment—what one party thinks is reasonable, the other party may not. Therefore, the unhappy party may not be successful in proving that the other party is in contempt of the court order. Therefore, a motion for contempt is not the appropriate legal vehicle to use in resolving this matter. Instead, one party or the other may file a motion to modify visitation and ask the court to modify its ruling from "reasonable visitation" to a definite schedule for weekly visitation and a specific visitation schedule for holidays, school year vacations, and summer vacations. This is usually needed when the parties are unable to resolve these types of issues on their own.

KIDNAPPING AND CROSSING STATE LINES

Occasionally, a parent flees with a child from the jurisdiction to parts unknown. A custodial parent may abruptly move out of state and fail to give the noncustodial parent information as to where the custodial parent and children are now living. Sometimes, a noncustodial parent may have the child legally in his or her possession during an agreed-on visitation period but then refuse to return the child at the end of the visiting period.

For instance, in one case a noncustodial father had the right to take his children to his residence in a neighboring state for a school vacation visitation. When the visitation period ended, the father refused to return the children. The mother sought legal counsel only to find that the father was not guilty of kidnapping because when he took the children, he had the legal right to do so. Instead, under the laws of the custodial parent's state, the noncustodial parent was merely guilty

FIGURE 15–3
Federal laws have been enacted to prevent the unlawful relocation of children from one state to another.

of a misdemeanor known as interference with custodial rights and the state would not seek extradition on such a minor criminal violation.

The custodial parent was forced to obtain the services of a lawyer in the neighboring state who had to bring an action there to enforce an out-of-state decree. The noncustodial parent countered by bringing a custodial action in that jurisdiction and a custody trial was held several months later in the neighboring state. During the entire period, the children remained with the parent who kept them away from the custodial parent and by the time of the trial had become so attached to that parent and the extended family members that they did not wish to leave that parent and the court deemed that it was in the children's best interest to remain where they were.

The advent of the **Uniform Child Custody Jurisdiction Act (UCCJA)** of 1968 changed this situation. Under this act, if a noncustodial parent took a child while under the custodial parent's control, and then failed to return the child after a visitation period ended, the custodial parent had the right to have law enforcement officials in the other jurisdiction arrest the noncustodial parent and arrange for the children's return to the custodial parent. This new law has resulted in fewer kidnapping and custodial interference cases—when the whereabouts of the noncustodial parent and children are known. However, where a noncustodial parent simply disappears, the custodial parent will receive no relief until the noncustodial parent and the children are located.

Many children who are kidnapped have been kidnapped by noncustodial parents. Alternately, sometimes a custodial parent and children will simply disappear or vanish to avoid having to deal with an abusive or difficult noncustodial parent. In several cases, mothers or fathers have disappeared with children when they believed that the noncustodial parent was sexually abusing the children. In at least one instance, a mother who came out of hiding with her child was willing to go to jail because her infraction had allowed her to successfully protect her child from the child's sexually abusive father.

All fifty states have adopted the UCCJA. As an additional response to the parental kidnapping dilemma, the federal government passed the **Parental Kidnapping Prevention Act (PKPA),** U.S.C. §1738A, in 1980. The PKPA was enacted by Congress because states had very different laws regarding the enforcement of another jurisdiction's custody decrees. Lack of a uniform system throughout the country encouraged parents dissatisfied with an original custody order to flee the jurisdiction and seek modification of the original order in another state. This is known as **forum shopping.** Under the PKPA, a new state court must give full faith and credit to a custody order entered in another state and cannot modify that order as long as one of the child's parents resides in that jurisdiction.

The PKPA and UCCJA had conflicting provisions that caused much confusion and litigation in the legal community. In 1997, the **Uniform Child Custody Jurisdiction and Enforcement Act (UCCJEA)** was drafted by the National Conference of Commissioners on Uniform State Laws in hopes of rectifying the inconsistencies between the PKPA and UCCJA. Some of the highlights of the UCCJEA include the following:

- Simplification of the procedures necessary for registering an original state's order in a new state,
- Prohibiting a new state (enforcing state) from modifying an original state's custody decision; the new state can only enforce the original order,

▼ A *habeas corpus* remedy requiring a return of the child by the parent violating a custody or visitation order,

▼ Granting the enforcing court the authority to issue a warrant to physically take the child into custody if there are fears that the parent will harm the child or flee the state, and

▼ Assistance of state prosecutors or attorney generals in the enforcement of the orders in civil proceedings and in locating the child. Prosecutors can pursue criminal actions if the parent violated a criminal law in the process.

Appendix I of this book includes the full text of the UCCJEA.

EXHIBIT 15–1
Sample Post Judgment Application and order to show cause to reopen and modify alimony.

DOCKET NO. FA 96-123456 : SUPERIOR COURT

BRONSON, RODNEY : JUDICIAL DISTRICT OF NEW HAVEN

V. : AT NEW HAVEN

BRONSON, EVELYN : JANUARY 5, 2001

POST JUDGMENT APPLICATION TO REOPEN AND MODIFY ALIMONY AND ORDER TO SHOW CAUSE

The defendant hereby requests that the above-referenced matter be reopened and modified and represents the following:

1. On (date of order), a Separation Agreement was entered into by the parties in the above-entitled matter;

2. Said Agreement stated that the Wife would pay to the Husband $100 per week as alimony;

3. Since that time there has been a substantial change of circumstances in that the Wife was involuntarily laid off from her job.

ORAL ARGUMENT REQUESTED
TESTIMONY IS REQUIRED

THE DEFENDANT,
EVELYN BRONSON

BY:_____
GRACE A. LUPPINO, ESQ.
HER ATTORNEY
555 MAIN AVENUE
NEW HAVEN, CT 06511
(203) 333-3333
JURIS NO. 160000

ORDER TO SHOW CAUSE

Upon the foregoing Post-Judgment Application to Reopen and Modify Alimony and Order to Show Cause, it is:

ORDERED, that Rodney Bronson, whose address is 328 Sycamore Street, New Haven, Connecticut, be cited to appear at the **Superior Court for the Judicial District of New Haven at New Haven, 235 Church Street, New Haven, Connecticut,** on the ____ day of _____ , 2001, at _____ o'clock in the forenoon, then and there to show cause, if he has any, why the Defendant's **Post Judgment Application to Reopen and Modify Alimony** should not be granted, and it is further ordered that notice of said Application and Motions and of this Order be given to said Rodney Bronson by some proper officer leaving with him in accordance with law, a true and attested copy of the Application and of this order, on or before the _____ day of _____ , 2001.

BY THE COURT

_____
JUDGE/ASSISTANT CLERK

DATED at New Haven, Connecticut, this ____ day of _____ , 2001.

EXHIBIT 15–1

Continued

SUMMONS

TO ANY PROPER OFFICER:

    BY AUTHORITY OF THE STATE OF CONNECTICUT, you are hereby commanded to serve a true and attested copy of the foregoing **POSTJUDGMENT APPLICATION TO REOPEN AND MODIFY ALIMONY AND ORDER TO SHOW CAUSE** on **RODNEY BRONSON,** whose address is 328 Sycamore Street, New Haven, Connecticut, in the manner prescribed by law for the service of civil process at least six (6) days before the date of the hearing.

    Herefor fail not, but due service make.

    DATED at New Haven, Connecticut this _____ day of _____ , 2001.

_____
GRACE A. LUPPINO
COMMISSIONER OF THE SUPERIOR COURT

ORDER

    The foregoing motion having been heard, it is hereby ORDERED:

    That the plaintiff-husband pay to the defendant-wife the sum of $_____ per _____ as alimony pendente lite.

    This order shall commence on _____ , 20___ .

The Court

By:_____
Judge

CERTIFICATION

    This is to certify that a true copy of the foregoing motion was mailed, postage prepaid, on this date to all counsel and pro se parties of record on this _____ day of _____ , 2001, as follows:

Justine F. Miller
22 Park Place
New Haven, CT 06522

_____
Grace A. Luppino
Commissioner of the Superior Court

EXHIBIT 15–2
Sample preprinted form for requesting a modification to a divorce decree.

MOTION FOR MODIFICATION
JD-FM-174 New 6-98
C.G.S. § 46b-88, P.B. §§ 25-26, 25-30, 25-57

STATE OF CONNECTICUT
SUPERIOR COURT

COURT USE ONLY
MFMOD

☐ **Before Judgment** *(Copy must be mailed or delivered to all parties/attorneys. Complete Certification on page 2/reverse.)*

☐ **After Judgment** *(Copy must be served on all parties with an Order to Attend Hearing and Notice on page 2/reverse.)*

JUDICIAL DISTRICT OF	AT *(Town)*	DOCKET NO.

PLAINTIFF'S NAME *(Last, first, middle initial)*	DEFENDANT'S NAME *(Last, first, middle initial)*

TYPE OF MOTION TO MODIFY

☐ CUSTODY ☐ VISITATION ☐ CHILD SUPPORT ☐ ALIMONY ☐ OTHER *(Specify):* _____

I am the ☐ PLAINTIFF ☐ DEFENDANT. I respectfully represent that:

1. This Court issued an order dated _____ directing the ☐ plaintiff ☐ defendant to:
   (Complete all that apply)

PAY CHILD SUPPORT IN THE AMOUNT OF:	PAY ALIMONY IN THE AMOUNT OF:	HAVE CUSTODY OF THE CHILD/CHILDREN: *(Check one)*
PER	PER	☐ JOINT ☐ SOLE
HAVE VISITATION OR PARENTING TIME AS FOLLOWS: *(Attach a copy of the visitation schedule if available)*		PRIMARY RESIDENCE WITH
OTHER:		

2. *(Check appropriate box(es) and explain)*

   ☐ Since the date of the order, the circumstances concerning this case have changed substantially as follows:

   _____

   ☐ The final order for child support is substantially different from the Child Support Guidelines as follows:

   _____

I ask the Court to modify the current order as follows: *(Check all that apply)*

CHILD SUPPORT *(You must file a Financial Affidavit (JD-FM-6) at least 5 days before the hearing. You must file an Affidavit Concerning Children (JD-FM-164) before the Court will act, and a completed child support and arrearage guidelines worksheet and an Advisement of Rights Re: Income Withholding (JD-FM-71) at the hearing.)*

☐ Increase ☐ Decrease the amount of child support to be paid. ☐ Order immediate income withholding.

ALIMONY *(You must file a Financial Affidavit (JD-FM-6) at least 5 days before the hearing. You must file an Advisement of Rights Re: Income Withholding (JD-FM-71) at the hearing.)*

☐ Increase ☐ Decrease the amount of alimony to be paid.

CUSTODY *(You must file an Financial Affidavit (JD-FM-6) and a completed child support and arrearage guidelines worksheet at the hearing. You must file an Affidavit Concerning Children (JD-FM-164) before the Court will act.)*

☐ Modify custody as follows:

_____

VISITATION *(You must file a Financial Affidavit (JD-FM-6) at the hearing. You must file an Affidavit Concerning Children (JD-FM-164) before the Court will act. You must file a completed child support and arrearage guidelines worksheet at the hearing.)*

☐ Modify visitation (parenting time) as follows:

_____

OTHER

☐ *(Please be specific):*

_____

SIGNATURE*	PRINT NAME	DATE SIGNED
ADDRESS *(No., Street, City, State, Zip Code)*		TELEPHONE NO.

(Continued...) *Check one: ☐ Superior Court ☐ Family Support Magistrate Division

375

EXHIBIT 15–2

Continued

CERTIFICATION *(Complete if motion if filed before judgment)*

I certify that I mailed or delivered a copy of this motion to:	NAME*	DATE MAILED/DELIVERED
ADDRESS *(No., street, city, state, zip code)**		

SIGNATURE	PRINT NAME	DATE SIGNED

If necessary, attach additional sheet with name of each party served and the address at which service was made.

ORDER TO ATTEND HEARING AND NOTICE *(Complete if motion is*

The Court orders that a hearing be held at the time and place shown below. The Court also orders the ☐ plaintiff ☐ defendant to give notice to the opposing party of the Motion and of the time and place where the court will hear it, by having a true and attested copy of the Motion and this Order served on the opposing party by any proper officer at least 12 days before the date of the hearing. Proof of service shall be made to this Court at least six days before the date of hearing.

BY THE COURT	,J/FSM.	ASSISTANT CLERK	DATE SIGNED

HEARING TO BE HELD AT →	SUPERIOR COURT, JUDICIAL DISTRICT OF	DATE
	COURT ADDRESS	TIME

SUMMONS

TO ANY PROPER OFFICER:

By the Authority of the State of Connecticut, you must serve a true and attested copy of the above Motion and Order to Attend Hearing and Notice on the below named person in one of the ways required by law at least 12 days before the date of the hearing, and file proof of service with this Court at least six days before the hearing.

PERSON TO BE SERVED	ADDRESS
CLERK/ASSISTANT CLERK	DATE SIGNED

ORDER

The court has heard this motion and orders it ☐ **GRANTED** ☐ **DENIED.**

BY THE COURT *(Judge/FSM/ Assistant Clerk)*	DATE SIGNED

FOR COURT USE ONLY

FEE FOR MOTION TO MODIFY: ☐ PAID ☐ WAIVED

JD-FM-174 (Back) New 6-96

EXHIBIT 15–3

DOCKET NO. FA 96-123456 : SUPERIOR COURT

BRONSON, RODNEY : JUDICIAL DISTRICT OF NEW HAVEN

V. : AT NEW HAVEN

BRONSON, EVELYN : JANUARY 5, 2001

APPLICATION FOR ORDER TO SHOW CAUSE

AND CONTEMPT CITATION

The defendant moves that the plaintiff be adjudged in contempt of court for violation of the terms of the judgment in this matter. In support thereof the defendant represents as follows:

1. On _____ , 20__ the Court (McVey, J.) dissolved the marriage of the parties and ordered that the defendant have reasonable rights of visitation.

2. The plaintiff is in contempt of court in that he refused to afford the defendant reasonable and flexible rights of access to and visitation with the children.

3. The plaintiff's violation of the Court's order is willful.

4. The defendant has incurred attorney's fees and costs in connection with the prosecution of this motion.

WHEREFORE, the defendant moves that:

1. The plaintiff be adjudged in contempt.

2. An appropriate visitation schedule be implemented.

3. The plaintiff be ordered to pay the defendant's attorney's fees and costs.

4. Such other and further relief deemed appropriate.

ORAL ARGUMENT REQUESTED
TESTIMONY IS REQUIRED

                              THE DEFENDANT,
                              EVELYN BRONSON
                              BY:_____
                              GRACE A. LUPPINO, ESQ.
                              HER ATTORNEY
                              555 MAIN AVENUE
                              NEW HAVEN, CT 06511
                              (203) 333-3333
                              JURIS NO. 160000

ORDER TO SHOW CAUSE

Upon the foregoing Post Judgment Application to Reopen and Modify Alimony and Order to Show Cause, it is:

ORDERED, that Rodney Bronson, whose address is 328 Sycamore Street, New Haven, Connecticut, be cited to appear at the **Superior Court for the Judicial District of New Haven at New Haven, 235 Church Street, New Haven, Connecticut,** on the _____ day of _____ , 2001, at _____ o'clock in the forenoon, then and there to show cause, if he has any, why the

EXHIBIT 15–3
Continued

Defendant's **Application for Order to Show Cause and Contempt Citation** should not be granted, and it is further ordered that notice of said Application and Motions and of this Order be given to said Rodney Bronson by some proper officer leaving with him in accordance with law, a true and attested copy of the Application and of this order, on or before the _____ day of _____ , 2001.

BY THE COURT

_____

JUDGE/ASSISTANT CLERK

DATED at New Haven, Connecticut, this _____ day of _____ , 2001.

SUMMONS

TO ANY PROPER OFFICER:

BY AUTHORITY OF THE STATE OF CONNECTICUT, you are hereby commanded to serve a true and attested copy of the foregoing **APPLICATION FOR ORDER TO SHOW CAUSE AND CONTEMPT CITATION** on **RODNEY BRONSON,** whose address is 328 Sycamore Street, New Haven, Connecticut, in the manner prescribed by law for the service of civil process at least six (6) days before the date of the hearing.

Therefore fail not, but due service make.
DATED at New Haven, Connecticut this _____ day of _____ , 2001.

_____
GRACE A. LUPPINO
COMMISSIONER OF THE SUPERIOR COURT

ORDER

The foregoing motion having been heard, it is hereby ORDERED:

That the plaintiff-husband allow the defendant-wife reasonable and flexible rights of access to and visitation with the children.

This order shall commence on _____ , 20___ .

The Court
By:_____
Judge

CERTIFICATION

This is to certify that a true copy of the foregoing motion was mailed, postage prepaid, on this date to all counsel and pro se parties of record on this _____ day of _____ , 2001, as follows:

Justine F. Miller
22 Park Place
New Haven, CT 06522

_____
Grace A. Luppino, Esq.
Commissioner of the Superior Court

EXHIBIT 15–4

MOTION FOR CONTEMPT
JD-FM-173 New 8-96
C.G.S. § 46b-87 P.B. § 25-27

STATE OF CONNECTICUT
SUPERIOR COURT

COURT USE ONLY
MFCONTP

☐ Before Judgment (pendente lite)   ☐ After Judgment

JUDICIAL DISTRICT OF	AT *(Town)*	DOCKET NO.

PLAINTIFF'S NAME *(Last, First, Middle Initial)*	DEFENDANT'S NAME *(Last, First, Middle Initial)*

PLAINTIFF'S ADDRESS *(No., street, city, state, zip code)*	DEFENDANT'S ADDRESS *(No., street, city, state, zip code)*

I, the ☐ PLAINTIFF ☐ DEFENDANT, respectfully represent that this Court issued an order on _____
directing the ☐ plaintiff ☐ defendant to *(complete all that apply)*:   *(month, day, year)*

PAY CHILD SUPPORT IN THE AMOUNT OF per	PAY ALIMONY IN THE AMOUNT OF per	TOTAL BALANCE OWED	AS OF *(Date)*
HAVE VISITATION OR PARENTING TIME AS FOLLOWS: *(Attach a copy of the visitation schedule if available)*			
PAY MEDICAL BILLS OR PROVIDE HEALTH INSURANCE AS FOLLOWS			
OTHER:			

The ☐ plaintiff or ☐ defendant has disobeyed the court order in the following ways: *(Please be specific. Include the amount of any arrears claimed due as of the date of this motion or a date specifically identified.)*

_____

_____

I ask the Court to find the ☐ plaintiff   ☐ defendant in contempt. I certify that the above information is true to the best of my knowledge.

SIGNATURE*	DATE

ORDER TO ATTEND HEARING AND NOTICE

The court orders ☐ the plaintiff ☐ the defendant to attend a hearing at the time and place shown below to show why you are not in contempt. The Court also orders the ☐ plaintiff ☐ the defendant to give notice to the opposing party of the Motion and of the time and place where the Court will hear it, by having a true and attested copy of the Motion and this Order served on the opposing party by any proper officer at least 12 days before the date of the hearing. Proof of service shall be made to this Court at least six days before the hearing.

BY THE COURT *(Judge/Assistant Clerk)*		DATE SIGNED	
HEARING TO BE HELD AT →	SUPERIOR COURT, JUDICIAL DISTRICT OF	DATE	TIME
	COURT ADDRESS	TELEPHONE NO.	

If you do not attend the court hearing, a civil arrest order (capias) may be issued against you.
SUMMONS

TO ANY PROPER OFFICER:
By the Authority of the State of Connecticut, you must serve a true and attested copy of the above Motion and Order to Attend Hearing on the below named person in one of the ways required by law at least 12 days before the date of the hearing, and file proof of service with this Court at least six days before the hearing.

PERSON TO BE SERVED	ADDRESS	
ASSISTANT CLERK	DATE SIGNED	

(CONTINUED ON REVERSE/PAGE 2)	*Check one: ☐ Superior Court ☐ Family Support Magistrate Division

EXHIBIT 15–4
Continued

ORDER

The Court has heard the above Motion and finds that the ☐ plaintiff ☐ defendant:

☐ **is not in contempt.**

☐ **is in contempt in the following way(s):**

  ☐ owes arrears as of _____ in the amount of _____ .

  ☐ other *(specify)*: _____

          _____

          _____

IT IS ORDERED:

  ☐ pay _____ current support and _____ on arrears by *(date)* _____

  ☐ income withholding in the amount of _____

  ☐ suspension of professional or driver's license with a 30-day stay

  ☐ post a surety bond

  ☐ incarceration

  ☐ attorney's fees

  ☐ other *(specify)*: _____

BY THE COURT *(Judge/FSM)*	SIGNED *(Assistant Clerk)*	DATE OF ORDER

RETURN OF SERVICE

I left a true and attested copy of the Motion for Contempt

  ☐ personally with the defendant ☐ personally with the plaintiff

  ☐ at the current home of the ☐ defendant or ☐ plaintiff at _____
                                  (Number, street, town or city)

The original Motion is attached.

NAME AND TITLE	COUNTY	DATE OF SERVICE

FEE INFORMATION:

        COPY _____

    ENDORSEMENT _____

      SERVICE _____

       TRAVEL _____

         TOTAL _____

JD-FM-173 (Back) New 6-96

REVIEW QUESTIONS

1. What parts of a dissolution decree are modifiable and what parts are not modifiable? Why are some parts modifiable and others not?

2. Discuss the facts that could constitute "changed circumstances" in terms of a modification of alimony or child support.

3. What are some changes in circumstances that could merit a modification of a custody order or a modification of a visitation order?

4. List the events that will precipitate an end to the payment of alimony.

5. What is a rule to show cause and when is it used in a postjudgment family matter?

6. What is the remedy available to an ex-spouse when the other ceases to pay alimony or child support?

7. What is an arrearage?

8. Discuss remedies available to a custodial parent when the noncustodial parent leaves the jurisdiction and ceases to pay child support.

9. Discuss the remedies available to a custodial parent when the noncustodial parent has fled the jurisdiction with a minor child.

10. Discuss the Uniform Child Custody Jurisdiction Act and the remedies it provides.

11. What factors does a court consider when allowing a custodial parent to move out of the jurisdiction with a minor child?

12. What is the difference between parental kidnapping and the misdemeanor known as custodial interference?

EXERCISES

1. In your jurisdiction's Rules of Court, in the family law section, find the rule or rules that authorize going back to court to modify a portion of the dissolution decree. List the section number and summarize the procedures.

2. In your local law library, locate case law in your state, if any, which states the rule governing out-of-state moves by a custodial parent. If there is no case law, see if any state statutes address this issue.

3. Prepare a motion for modification of visitation to be filed by a custodial parent. Use the format your jurisdiction requires.

4. Prepare a motion for modification of custody to be filed by a noncustodial parent. Use the format your jurisdiction requires.

5. Review a copy of the Uniform Child Custody Jurisdiction Act. Identify the section that an attorney would rely on to compel an out-of-state noncustodial parent to return the minor child to the jurisdiction after a legal visitation period has ended.

6. Prepare a paragraph in a separation agreement regarding alimony for a fixed time only and include appropriate language that will make this provision nonmodifiable.

7. Prepare a noncustodial parent's motion for a court order to prevent the custodial parent from moving out of the jurisdiction with the minor children. In the body of the motion, list specific facts and reasons why such a move would be detrimental to the children's best interests. Use the format for motions required by your jurisdiction.

16 CHAPTER

STATE INTERVENTION IN FAMILY MATTERS

KEY TERMS

Abuse	*Parens patriae*
Adoption	Petition to adopt
Child protection agency	Service (performance) agreement
Clear and convincing evidence	
Hot line	Specific steps (expectations)
Investigative child protection worker	Temporary custody
	Termination of parental rights
Mandatory reporter	Treatment worker
Neglect	

INTEGRITY OF THE FAMILY

The U.S. government has recognized the integrity of the family unit. In the Supreme Court case, *Stanley v. Illinois*, 405 U.S. 645, 92 S. Ct. 1208, 31 L. Ed. 2d 551 (1972), the Court maintained that family preservation is a priority and that the U.S. Constitution protects family integrity. However, this protection is not absolute. It must be balanced against States' obligations to protect children.

STATES' OBLIGATIONS TO PROTECT CHILDREN

In some instances, a child's health, safety, and physical and emotional well-being are in peril by virtue of being in an intact family. Sometimes one parent or both parents may behave in a neglectful or abusive manner toward a child or may simply allow or not attempt to prevent neglectful or abusive conditions. For instance, a parent may physically abuse a child by hitting and spanking the child in a way that inflicts physical injury on the child. Similarly, a parent may inflict mental abuse on a child by words or conduct that threaten and intimidate or ridicule and humiliate the child. Parents are neglectful of their children when they fail to adequately provide for the child's nutritional, medical, or educational needs or allow the child to live in conditions that are unsanitary or in a home that is uninhabitable due to the absence of heat, hot water, or electricity. A child left to sleep continuously on a urine-soaked, stained mattress in dirty bed clothes is a neglected child.

A parent is expected to take a child for regular physical examinations and make sure that the child's immunizations are up to date. A parent is expected to take a child to the doctor when the child has a serious illness, suffers a serious injury, or has a chronic health problem that requires periodic monitoring.

Parents must provide their children with adequate housing that is warm, clean, and large enough to accommodate all family members without excessive crowding in either living quarters or sleeping space.

DETECTING CHILD NEGLECT AND CHILD ABUSE

When parents fail to provide a safe and nurturing environment for their children, the state intervenes to protect the children. The state possesses the authority for such action under the legal doctrine of **parens patriae.** This Latin term is literally translated as the parent of the country. In reality, this doctrine gives the state the right to protect children and persons with disabilities when their parent or legal guardian has failed to do so. However, before the state acts, the state must have reason to believe that intervention is needed. The fact that a child needs protection must come to the state's attention, usually through a complaint or referral by a third party.

Every state has a **child protection agency** that is charged with intervening in a family unit when neglect or abuse is known or suspected. In many states, this agency is known as the Department of Children and Families (DCF), the Department of Children and Youth Services (DCYS), the Department of Health and Rehabilitative Services (HRS), or by a similar type of name.

The child protection agency receives complaints from a variety of sources. Certain professionals and paraprofessionals are **mandatory reporters**, meaning that by law, under penalty of law, they are required to report any signs of suspected child **abuse** or **neglect.** These persons include school personnel such as classroom teachers, school nurses, counselors, and social workers; and medical personnel, specifically pediatricians, general practitioners, emergency room personnel, medical social workers, and other hospital department staff. If a teacher sees a child with suspicious bruises or with inadequate clothing, the teacher must report this to the local child protection agency. Similarly if a child is brought to the emergency room with a suspicious injury or illness, the local child protection agency must be called.

Sometimes a neighbor or a family member will report suspected child neglect or abuse by calling the child protection agency's emergency **hot line.** States have established central hot lines that provide a twenty-four-hour toll-free number for reporting suspected child abuse. Occasionally, the caller to a hot line will identify himself or herself, especially if the caller is a blood relative and wants to serve as a placement resource for the child if removal from the home becomes an option. More frequently, the caller may wish to remain anonymous and refuse to give his or her name. If the anonymous caller sounds credible, the child protection agency will investigate the complaint.

INVESTIGATION OF A COMPLAINT OF CHILD NEGLECT OR CHILD ABUSE

When a child protection staff person decides that an incoming complaint warrants follow-up, an **investigative child protection worker** will visit the family, unannounced, and assess the physical living conditions and the emotional environment of the family. Through asking questions and observing the premises and condition of the children, the worker will decide whether or not the allegations can be substantiated.

If the allegations are not substantiated, no action is taken. However, the complaint is documented so that if another complaint is made in the future, knowledge of the previous complaint may alert the worker to move quickly and to conduct a more intensive investigation. If allegations are substantiated, the state will intervene. The type and degree of intervention will be determined by the seriousness of the situation.

SERVICE AGREEMENT APPROACH

If a worker goes to a home and finds that the children are at risk for not being properly cared for, the investigative worker may recommend that the children remain in the home but that a case be opened with the agency and that a **treatment worker** be assigned to the case and family. The treatment worker will meet with the parents and the children and communicate to the parents what they must do so that their children will not be removed from their home.

The worker may make a list of things that must be corrected. These items will be incorporated into a **service agreement** or **performance agreement** that the worker will ask the parent or parents to sign. For instance, the worker will indicate that the parents must take their children to the doctor and keep current with immunizations. If the parents indicates that they have a substance abuse problem, the worker will indicate that the parent must go to a treatment program; if food or clothing for the children is not sufficient, the worker may try to help the clients budget and also put them in touch with social service providers and government agencies for financial assistance, food stamps, medical insurance, and other benefits.

After the agreement is in place, the worker will visit the family regularly and if the problems are corrected and all is well, the case will be closed. As long as the worker has concerns, the case will remain open and if, at any time, the situation worsens and the risk to the children's health and safety increases, the worker may initiate a more intense intervention.

ORDER OF TEMPORARY CUSTODY

If at any time, a worker suspects that children may be in a situation of imminent harm or danger, the worker will seek authorization from his or her supervisor to apply to the child protection court for an order that gives the child protection agency **temporary custody** of the children. This order enables the worker to remove the children from the home and place them in temporary foster care. The parents are then notified that within five to seven days, a court hearing will be held to determine whether the children are to remain in the state's custody.

Frequently, at the same time the parents are notified of the impending court hearing, the parents are also served with a legal petition in which the child protection agency as the petitioner alleges that the children are being neglected and requesting the children be committed to the appropriate state agency for a statutorily mandated period of time. This petition usually contains a notice of a hearing on the neglect petition and the date of the hearing. This hearing date will be scheduled for a date after the date of the hearing on the order of temporary custody.

Prior to the temporary custody hearing, the child protection court appoints an attorney or guardian *ad litem* to represent the interests of the children. The parents are notified that they should obtain their own legal representation. If the parents cannot afford an attorney and if their income falls within certain guidelines, the court provides them with an attorney paid for by the judicial system.

At the temporary custody hearing, the attorney for the child protection agency, usually an attorney from the state's attorney general's office, has to prove that the children would be placed in immediate, imminent harm if they were to be returned to their parents at that time. The parents' attorney introduces evidence and testimony to rebut the state's arguments. The children's attorney has a chance to cross-examine the witnesses of both the state and the parents, and also may wish to present witnesses and evidence in support of either confirmation of the custody order or revocation, depending on what the children's attorney believes will best promote the children's interest.

After all evidence is presented and closing arguments are heard, the judge rules either to confirm the order of temporary custody or to revoke that order and allow the children to be returned to the parents. If the custody order is confirmed, the children will remain in the state's custody until the underlying neglect matter is adjudicated. If the order is revoked, the underlying neglect matter will remain. Although the children will be allowed to return home, the parents must return for further court proceedings, which may include a trial on the neglect petition. If the state prevails at the neglect trial or if the parents choose to forego their right to a trial and either admit or plead no contest to the allegations of neglect, the children will be adjudicated as neglected children. The court then makes a disposition that could result in the children being committed for a statutory period or in the children remaining in the home under state supervision for a period of several months.

EFFORTS FOR REUNIFICATION OF THE CHILD WITH THE PARENTS

When a court commits a child to the care and custody of the state's child protection agency, the court is frequently called on to order that specific requirements be met before the child may be returned to the parents. These requirements, which are often known as **specific steps** or **expectations,** are drawn up by the representative of the child protection agency. The parents sign the document containing these steps to acknowledge that they know what the court expects them to do and to acknowledge that they will participate in the activities the state requires in order to be reunified with their child.

SPECIFIC STEPS

The expectations or specific steps may include requirements such as the parent completing a substance abuse treatment program, attending parenting classes, or undergoing domestic violence counseling. The steps usually include general requirements such as the requirement that the parents visit their child as frequently as the child protection agency permits; that the parents keep their whereabouts known to the child protection agency and to their attorney; that the parents obtain a means of legal income and adequate housing; and that the parents have no involvement or no further involvement with the criminal justice system.

If a parent has completed all of the specific steps to the satisfaction of the child protection agency, the parent's attorney may bring a motion to revoke the commitment before the court before the statutory commitment period ends. If the state agrees that all expectations have been met or if the child's attorney demonstrates by a preponderance of the evidence that the parent has fulfilled all of the expectations, the court may revoke the commitment and order that arrangements be made to reunify the child and parent as soon as possible.

EXTENSION OF COMMITMENT

If a parent is unable to meet the requirements set for reunification within the statutory twelve-month commitment period, the child protection agency will file a motion or a petition to extend the period of custodial commitment for an additional statutory period. The parent may oppose this extension of commitment. Unless an agreement or compromise is reached between the state and the parent, the parent's attorney may request an evidentiary hearing on the motion for extension. At that hearing, the state presents evidence that the parent has not completed the specific steps needed to be fulfilled for reunification. The parent's attorney presents evidence to the contrary, which demonstrates that the parent has complied with the child protection agency's requirements and that the child's best interest will be served by reunifying parent and child.

If the court is persuaded that the parent has completed all requirements for reunification and if the court is persuaded that it will be in the child's best interest to return the child home, the extension will be denied and the child protection agency will have to reunify the child with the parents before the state's custodial commitment expires. Conversely, if the child protection agency proves that the parent has not complied with the court-ordered specific steps and has failed to fulfill the expectations required for reunification, the court will extend the commitment.

If following this period or perhaps even during this commitment period, the child protection agency has reason to believe that there is little chance that within a reasonable period of time the parent will be able to meet the conditions needed for reunification, the child protection agency will make a determination that reunification is no longer the agency's goal. At this point, the agency will look for other options. Such options include transferring of guardianship of the child to one of either of the parents' relatives; placing the child in a long-term foster care arrangement, especially if the child is older or has special needs and requires considerable therapeutic treatment; or terminating the natural parents' rights and the placement of the child in the agency's preadoption program. The most drastic option the child protection agency may elect is the bringing of an action to terminate the parent's parental rights to the child.

TERMINATION OF PARENTAL RIGHTS

A **termination of parental rights** is a court proceeding that severs the legal bond between a parent and his or her biological or legally adopted child. A court of appropriate jurisdiction may terminate or permanently remove all legal rights a parent possesses in connection with his or her child. Rights may be terminated as to both parents or only as to one parent. Specially, upon the effective date of termination, the parent will no longer have the following legal rights and responsibilities that are part of the parent/child relationship: The parent will no longer have a duty to support the child; nor will the parent have the right to inherit from the child or the legal right to participate in any decisions whatsoever regarding the health, education, or welfare of the child.

VOLUNTARY TERMINATION OF PARENTAL RIGHTS

A voluntary termination of parental rights occurs when a natural parent or an adoptive parent consents to having a court of appropriate jurisdiction terminate all legal rights a parent possesses regarding her relationship to a minor child. An individual's parental rights may be terminated only through a court proceeding. If the parent consents to the termination, the court proceeding is fairly short and uncomplicated. The judge asks the parent whether she wishes to have her parental rights severed. The judge canvasses the parent to make sure that the parent's consent is being freely given, without being pressured in any way to do so. The judge also informs the parent of each of the rights the parent will be relinquishing.

If the parent is represented by counsel in this matter, the judge may also ask the parent whether her attorney discussed the matter thoroughly with her and whether the parent is satisfied with the legal representation the attorney provided. Following this canvassing, the judge announces that the parent's rights have been terminated and the proceeding ends shortly thereafter.

INVOLUNTARY TERMINATION OF PARENTAL RIGHTS

An involuntary termination of parental rights proceeding involves a trial. The state or the child protection agency must bring a petition before the court seeking termination of parental rights. In this petition, the state will allege that one or more statutory grounds exist to provide the legal justification for the court to terminate the parent's rights.

GROUNDS FOR TERMINATION OF PARENTAL RIGHTS

Each state has its own set of statutory grounds for termination. Many states include grounds such as parental abandonment, absence of a parent/child relationship, and failure of the parent to rehabilitate to a degree where the parent can achieve a meaningful role in the child's care and upbringing. Parental consent is also usually a statutory ground. In order for the court to grant the state's petition for termination of parental rights, the state must prove at least one statutory ground by **clear and convincing evidence.** This term connotes a very high evidentiary standard of proof that requires a higher degree of certainty than the preponderance of the evidence standard required for a judicial finding of neglect.

CONSIDERATION OF THE CHILD'S BEST INTERESTS

If the court finds that the state has met its evidentiary burden and that one or more of the necessary grounds have been proven, the court must then go one step further and determine through the evidence whether it is in the child's best interest to terminate the parent's rights or whether additional time should be allowed to give the parent time to rectify whatever situations gave rise to the existence of the grounds for termination.

If the court decides to allow a parent a specific additional amount of time in which to do what is necessary for reunification with the child, the child protection agency will retain custody during this time period and the court will outline what requirements the parent will have to meet by the end of the additional time period. On the other hand, if the court decides that additional time is not warranted, the court will issue an order terminating the parent's rights. If the parental rights of both parents have been terminated, the child will be free to be adopted.

ADOPTION

Adoption is the legal procedure that makes a person or persons the legal parent or parents of a minor child that is not their natural child. In some states, the adoption procedure takes place in family court. In other states, the adoption is done in a court known as probate court or surrogates court.

AGENCY ADOPTIONS

There are two types of adoption agencies, public adoption agencies and private adoption agencies. Public agencies are usually a component of the state government's child protection agency. For instance, when parental rights to a minor child have been severed in response to a petition brought by a state's child protection agency, frequently, the child protection agency itself facilitates the child's adoption through the branch of the agency specializing in adoptions. When the parents voluntarily consent to termination of their parental rights and the state child protection agency is not directly involved, the adoption is often handled by a private agency, sometimes one that the parents themselves have selected.

PUBLIC ADOPTION AGENCIES

A public agency adoption usually addresses the adoption of children already committed to the state's custody. These children have been placed in foster care following court proceedings. Upon the termination of parental rights, the state becomes the statutory parent of the child and remains the child's statutory parent until the child is adopted. Sometimes, the child's foster parents may seek to adopt the child. If the foster parents meet the criteria for adopting the child, they are frequently given preference, especially if the child has been in their care for a period of time and has bonded with the foster family. If the foster family is unwilling or unable to adopt the child, the agency will transfer the child's file to the agency's preadoption unit and there an assigned worker will attempt to find suitable adoptive parents from the list of individuals and couples who have registered to be considered as adoptive parents.

Public agencies have many older children who have been in foster care for months or even years. Some of these children are available for adoption. A prospective adoptive parent who is willing to adopt an older child may face a shorter wait than the prospective parent who is seeking an infant or a very young child.

The children who are involuntarily committed to the care of a child protection agency are not available for adoption while the agency's goal for the child is reunification with the natural parents and, as discussed, the natural parents are usually given a reasonable period of time in which to complete the court-ordered steps required for reunification. Individuals seeking to adopt infants are more likely to have success by going to a private adoption agency or seeking out private adoption opportunities.

PRIVATE ADOPTION AGENCIES

A private adoption agency must be licensed and follow certain statutory and administrative regulations that govern the adoption process. Individuals and couples who register with either public or private adoption agencies must undergo rigorous examinations. Agency workers conduct home visits to assess the physical and emotional environment the prospective adoptive parents can provide for a child. Many agencies conduct intensive home studies to determine the appropriateness of placing a particular child with a particular family.

Once the decision is made to place a child with a family, the agency monitors the placement for several months to ensure that the placement meets the child's needs. When this provisional period ends and the agency approves the placement as permanent, the prospective adoptive parents file a **petition to adopt** or a similar document in probate or surrogates court. The court will request that the agency file a report. If the agency report is favorable and supports the adoption, the court will grant the adoption petition.

PRIVATE ADOPTIONS

A private adoption is an adoption that takes place without the intervention of an agency. In a private adoption, the child's natural parents agree voluntarily to sever their parental rights so that a particular person or couple may adopt their child. The adoption is frequently facilitated by an attorney or by the natural parents' doctor.

The private adoption must be approved by the court, and many states require that a state agency child protection worker investigate the proposed adoption and file a report with the court as to the advisability of permitting the adoption. The court reviews the report prior to making a decision and will usually not approve the adoption unless the report is favorable.

REVIEW QUESTIONS

1. Does the U.S. Constitution guarantee absolute protection of the integrity of the family?
2. Give some examples of child neglect.
3. What is the doctrine of *parens patriae?*
4. What is the function of a state child protection agency?
5. Define mandated reporter.
6. What is the state's social worker's role in investigating allegations of child abuse and neglect?
7. What is the purpose of an order of temporary custody?
8. What "specific steps" or "expectations" can be mandated by the court for a parent to be reunified with his or her child?
9. What are the legal grounds for terminating a parent's parental rights?
10. Define adoption.

EXERCISES

1. Research your state statute on mandatory reporters. What persons in your jurisdiction are required to report suspected child abuse and neglect?

2. What is the penalty in your state for the failure of a mandatory reporter to file a report of suspected child abuse or neglect? Must the report be in writing?

3. Research your state statute on termination of parental rights. Under what grounds may a parent's rights be terminated in your state?

4. Research your state adoption statute. What court in your state has jurisdiction over adoptions?

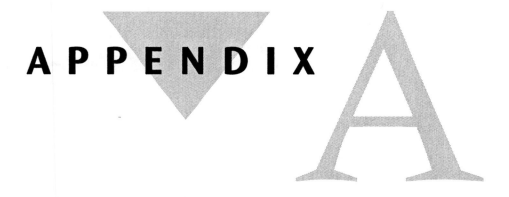

APPENDIX A

UNIFORM PREMARITAL AGREEMENT ACT

1. DEFINITIONS

As used in this Act:

   (1) 'Premarital agreement' means an agreement between prospective spouses made in contemplation of marriage and to be effective upon marriage.

   (2) 'Property' means an interest, present or future, legal or equitable, vested or contingent, in real or personal property, including income and earnings.

2. FORMALITIES

A premarital agreement must be in writing and signed by both parties. It is enforceable without consideration.

3. CONTENT

   (a) Parties to a premarital agreement may contract with respect to:

      (1) the rights and obligations of each of the parties in any of the property of either or both of them whenever and wherever acquired or located;

      (2) the right to buy, sell, use, transfer, exchange, abandon, lease, consume, expend, assign, create a security interest in, mortgage, encumber, dispose of, or otherwise manage and control property;

      (3) the disposition of property upon separation, marital dissolution, death, or the occurrence or nonoccurrence of any other event;

      (4) the modification or elimination of spousal support;

      (5) the making of a will, trust, or other arrangement to carry out the provisions of the agreement;

(6) the ownership rights in and disposition of the death benefit from a life insurance policy;

(7) the choice of law governing the construction of the agreement; and

(8) any other matter, including their personal rights and obligations, not in violation of public policy or a statute imposing a criminal penalty.

(b) The right of a child to support may not be adversely affected by a premarital agreement.

4. Effects of Marriage

A premarital agreement becomes effective upon marriage.

5. Amendment, Revocation

After marriage, a premarital agreement may be amended or revoked only by a written agreement signed by the parties. The amended agreement or the revocation is enforceable without consideration.

6. Enforcement

(a) A premarital agreement is not enforceable if the party against whom enforcement is sought proves that:

(1) that party did not execute the agreement voluntarily; or

(2) the agreement was unconscionable when it was executed and, before execution of the agreement, that party:

(i) was not provided a fair and reasonable disclosure of the property or financial obligations of the other party;

(ii) did not voluntarily and expressly waive, in writing, any right to disclosure of the property or financial obligations of the other party beyond the disclosure provided; and

(iii) did not have, or reasonably could not have had, an adequate knowledge of the property or financial obligations of the other party.

(b) If a provision of a premarital agreement modifies or eliminates spousal support and that modification or elimination causes one party to the agreement to be eligible for support under a program of public assistance at the time of the agreement, may require the other party to provide support to the extent necessary to avoid that eligibility.

(c) An issue of unconscionability of a premarital agreement shall be decided by the court as a matter of law.

7. Enforcement: Void Marriage

If a marriage is determined to be void, an agreement that would otherwise have been a premarital agreement is enforceable only to the extent necessary to avoid an inequitable result.

8. LIMITATION OF ACTIONS

Any statue of limitations applicable to an action asserting a claim for relief under a premarital agreement is tolled during the marriage of the parties to the agreement. However, equitable defenses limiting the time for enforcement, including laches and estoppel, are available to either party.

9. APPLICATION AND CONSTRUCTION

This [Act] shall be applied and construed to effectuate its general purpose to make uniform the law with respect to the subject of this [Act] among states enacting it.

10. SHORT TITLE

This [Act] may be cited as the Uniform Premarital Agreement Act.

This is the customary 'short title' clause, which may be placed in that order in the bill for enactment as the legislative practice of the state prescribes.

11. SEVERABILITY

If any provisions of this [Act] or its application to any person or circumstance is held invalid, the invalidity does not affect other provisions or applications of this [Act] which can be given effect without the invalid provision or application, and to this end the provisions of this [Act] are severable.

12. TIME OF TAKING EFFECT

This [Act] takes effect _____ and applies to any premarital agreement expected on or after that date.

13. REPEAL

The following acts and parts of acts are repealed:

(a)

(b)

(c)

Used with permission of National Conference of Commissioners on Uniform State Laws.

B APPENDIX

QUALIFIED DOMESTIC RELATIONS ORDER
(JIM CARREY)

Paul L. Basile, Jr.
(State Bar No. 050078)
Attorney at Law
11400 West Olympic Boulevard, Ninth Floor
Los Angeles, California 90064-1507
Telephone: (310) 478-2114

Special Tax Counsel

1
2
3
4
5
6
7

FILED
LOS ANGELES SUPERIOR COURT

JUN 1 4 1994

EDWARD M. KRITZMAN, CLERK

BY R. A. BELMONTE, DEPUTY

8 SUPERIOR COURT OF THE STATE OF CALIFORNIA

9 FOR THE COUNTY OF LOS ANGELES

10

11 In Re the Marriage of:

12 JAMES EUGENE CARREY,

13   Petitioner,

14   and

15 MELISSA JANE CARREY,

16   Respondent.

17

Case No: BD 135 499

STIPULATED QUALIFIED DOMESTIC RELATIONS ORDER RE AFTRA RETIREMENT PLAN

18   WHEREAS, Petitioner, JAMES EUGENE CARREY, and Respondent, MELISSA

19 JANE CARREY, were married to each other on March 28, 1987, and separated on June 15,

20 1993;

21   WHEREAS, this Court has personal jurisdiction over both Petitioner and

22 Respondent and jurisdiction over the subject matter of this Order and this dissolution of

23 marriage action;

24   WHEREAS, Petitioner, Respondent, and the Court intend that this Order

25 shall be a Qualified Domestic Relations Order (a "QDRO") as that term is used in the

26 Retirement Equity Act of 1984, P.L. No. 98-397 (the "Act"); and

27   WHEREAS, Petitioner and Respondent have stipulated that the Court shall

28 enter the following Order:

NOW, THEREFORE, IT IS HEREBY ORDERED BY THE COURT as follows:

1. As used in this Order, the following terms shall apply:

a. "Participant" refers to the Petitioner, JAMES EUGENE CARREY, whose last known address is c/o JOHN RIGNEY, RIGNEY/FRIEDMAN BUSINESS MANAGEMENT, 12400 Wilshire Boulevard, Suite 850, Los Angeles, California 90025, whose social security number is 000-00-0000, and whose date of birth is January 17, 1962.

b. "Alternate Payee" refers to the Respondent, MELISSA JANE CARREY, whose last known address is c/o JOHN RIGNEY, RIGNEY/FRIEDMAN BUSINESS MANAGEMENT, 12400 Wilshire Boulevard, Suite 850, Los Angeles, California 90025, whose social security number is 000-00-0000, and whose date of birth is July 8, 1960.

c. "Plan" refers to the AFTRA RETIREMENT PLAN, as amended, the Trustee of which is the Board of Trustees of the AFTRA RETIREMENT PLAN, and the assets of which are currently held by said Trustee.

d. "Plan Administrator" refers to the Board of Trustees of the AFTRA RETIREMENT PLAN.

2. The Alternate Payee is the spouse of Participant until the herein marriage has been dissolved.

3. This order is entered pursuant to the California Family Law Act, Section 2500 *et seq.* of the California Family Law Code.

4. The Alternate Payee shall be entitled to share in the benefits of the Plan as follows:

a. The Alternate Payee shall receive a monthly pension, commencing on the date when the Participant attains Normal Retirement Age (as defined in the Plan) in an amount equal to one-half (1/2) of the

- 2 -

396

Participant's accrued benefit as of the date of separation (June 15, 1993) to which the Participant would be entitled on normal retirement age computed on a single life annuity basis and multiplied by a fraction, the numerator of which is the number of months of the Participant's participation in the Plan between the date of marriage (March 28, 1987) and the date of separation (June 15, 1993), and the denominator of which is the total number of months of the Participant's participation in the Plan as of the Participant's Normal Retirement Age. If the Participant retires earlier than at Normal Retirement Age, the date of the Participant's actual retirement shall be used in the foregoing calculation in place of Normal Retirement Age.

b.   If the Participant dies before payments have commenced to the Alternate Payee, then, whether or not the Participant is survived by a spouse (other than the Alternate Payee) and whether or not the Participant has met the eligibility requirements for a pension, the Alternate Payee shall receive monthly payments in an amount equal to the monthly amount payable to a surviving spouse under the Plan, if any, multiplied by a fraction, the numerator of which is the number of months of the Participant's participation in the Plan between the dates of marriage and separation, and the denominator of which is the total number of months of the Participant's participation in the Plan as of the time of the Participant's death. The remainder of the monthly amount payable under the Plan, and no more, shall be paid to the Participant's spouse or designated beneficiary, as the case may be.

c.   With respect to the Alternate Payee's entitlements under Paragraph 4(a) above, the amount thereof shall be calculated on the basis of a single life annuity with the Participant's life as the measuring life, but the Alternate Payee may elect to have the Alternate Payee's share paid to the Alternate Payee in actuarially adjusted monthly amounts over the Alternate

Payee's lifetime. If the Alternate Payee does not so elect, payments to the Alternate Payee shall cease on the Participant's death. If the Alternate Payee does not so elect and the Alternate Payee predeceases the Participant, the remaining payments of the Alternate Payee's entitlement, if any, shall be made to the beneficiary designated by the Alternate Payee in writing and filed with the Plan Administrator, provided that any such beneficiary qualifies as an alternate payee of the Participant pursuant to ERISA §206(d)(3)(K). Similarly, if the Alternate Payee predeceases the Participant and dies before payments have commenced, the Alternate Payee's entitlement, if any, shall be paid to the Alternate Payee's designated beneficiary or beneficiaries and in the form designated by the Alternate Payee in writing and filed with the Plan Administrator, such payment to be made at the time it would have been made to the Alternate Payee if the Alternate Payee were still living, provided that any such beneficiary qualifies as an alternate payee of the Participant pursuant to ERISA §206(d)(3)(K).

      d.   Notwithstanding any provision of the Plan, payment of benefits to the Alternate Payee shall not be suspended by reason of the Participant's returning to covered employment after retiring.

      5.   At the Alternate Payee's election, the Alternate Payee may receive the Alternate Payee's benefits at the earliest time permissible under the Plan consistent with the methods set forth in this Order. If such election is made prior to the Participant's date of retirement, the date when the Alternate Payee makes the election shall be used in place of the Participant's date of retirement in calculating the denominator of the fraction expressed in Section 4(a) of this Order. If the Alternate Payee dies before making such election and before payments have commenced to the Alternate Payee, such election may be made by the Alternate Payee's designated beneficiary, provided that any such beneficiary qualifies as an alternate payee of the Participant pursuant to ERISA §206(d)(3)(K).

      6.   The Participant and the Alternate Payee shall be separately responsible

- 4 -

398

1 for income taxes attributable to the payments received by each of them under the Plan.

2   7.   This Order is intended to be a QDRO made pursuant to the Act, has

3 been determined to be a QDRO by the signature of the Plan Administrator below, and its

4 provisions shall be administered and interpreted in conformity with the Act. If the Act is

5 amended or the law regarding QDROs is otherwise changed or modified, then the parties

6 hereto shall immediately take such steps as are necessary to amend this QDRO to comply

7 with any such changes, amendments, or modification to the Act or laws regarding QDROs.

8   8.   The Court shall retain jurisdiction over this matter to amend this Order

9 in order to establish and/or maintain its qualification as a QDRO under the Act and to

10 carry out the terms and conditions of this Order.

12 Dated: _4/20/94_

13   JAMES EUGENE CARREY, Petitioner

14 Dated: _1/20/94_

15   MELISSA JANE CARREY, Respondent

16 APPROVED AS TO FORM AND CONTENT:

17 Dated: _5/26/97_   LAW OFFICES OF NORMAN M. DOLIN

19   By:_____
                                NORMAN M. DOLIN

20   Attorney for Petitioner,
                               JAMES EUGENE CARREY

21 Dated: _4/20/94_   SIMKE, CHODOS, SILBERFELD & ANTEAU, INC.

24   By:_____
                                RONALD W. ANTEAU,

25   Attorney for Respondent,
                               MELISSA JANE CARREY

-5-

Dated: 6-1-94

Board of Trustees of the
AFTRA RETIREMENT PLAN

By: _____
Plan Administrator

THE CLERK IS ORDERED TO ENTER THIS ORDER.

JUN 1 4 1994

Dated: _____

_____
JUDGE OF THE SUPERIOR COURT

JAMES D. ENDMAN
Judge Pro Tem

- 6 -

400

1 Paul L. Basile, Jr.
   (State Bar No. 050078)
2 Attorney at Law
   11400 West Olympic Boulevard, Ninth Floor
3 Los Angeles, California 90064-1507
   Telephone: (310) 478-2114
4
   Special Tax Counsel
5

FILED
LOS ANGELES SUPERIOR COURT

MAY 2 6 1994

EDWARD M. KRITZMAN, CLERK

BY R. A. BELMONTE, DEPUTY

6
7
8   SUPERIOR COURT OF THE STATE OF CALIFORNIA

9   FOR THE COUNTY OF LOS ANGELES

10
11 In Re the Marriage of:)   Case No: BD 135 499
)
12 JAMES EUGENE CARREY,   )   STIPULATED   QUALIFIED
)   DOMESTIC RELATIONS ORDER
13   Petitioner,   )   RE SCREEN ACTORS GUILD-
)   PRODUCERS PENSION PLAN
14   and   )
)
15 MELISSA JANE CARREY,   )
)
16   Respondent.   )
)
17
18   WHEREAS, Petitioner, JAMES EUGENE CARREY, and Respondent, MELISSA

19 JANE CARREY, were married to each other on March 28, 1987, and separated on June 15,

20 1993;

21   WHEREAS, this Court has personal jurisdiction over both Petitioner and

22 Respondent and jurisdiction over the subject matter of this Order and this dissolution of

23 marriage action;

24   WHEREAS, Petitioner, Respondent, and the Court intend that this Order

25 shall be a Qualified Domestic Relations Order (a "QDRO") as that term is used in the

26 Retirement Equity Act of 1984, P.L. No. 98-397 (the "Act"); and

27   WHEREAS, Petitioner and Respondent have stipulated that the Court shall

28 enter the following Order:

- 1 -

401

NOW, THEREFORE, IT IS HEREBY ORDERED BY THE COURT as follows:

1. As used in this Order, the following terms shall apply:

    a. "Participant" refers to the Petitioner, JAMES EUGENE CARREY, whose last known address is c/o JOHN RIGNEY, RIGNEY/FRIEDMAN BUSINESS MANAGEMENT, 12400 Wilshire Boulevard, Suite 850, Los Angeles, California 90025, whose social security number is 000-00-0000, and whose date of birth is January 17, 1962.

    b. "Alternate Payee" refers to the Respondent, MELISSA JANE CARREY, whose last known address is c/o JOHN RIGNEY, RIGNEY/FRIEDMAN BUSINESS MANAGEMENT, 12400 Wilshire Boulevard, Suite 850, Los Angeles, California 90025, whose social security number is 000-00-0000, and whose date of birth is July 8, 1960.

    c. "Plan" refers to the SCREEN ACTORS GUILD-PRODUCERS PENSION PLAN, as amended (a non-contributory defined benefit plan), the Trustee of which is the Board of Trustees of the SCREEN ACTORS GUILD-PRODUCERS PENSION PLAN, and the assets of which are currently held by said Trustee.

    d. "Plan Administrator" refers to BRUCE L. DOW, or his successor duly appointed by the Trustee.

2. The Alternate Payee is the spouse of Participant until the herein marriage has been dissolved.

3. This order is entered pursuant to the California Family Law Act, Section 2500 *et seq.* of the California Family Law Code.

4. The Alternate Payee shall be entitled to share in the benefits of the Plan as follows:

    a. The Alternate Payee shall receive a monthly pension, commencing on the date when the Participant retires under the Plan in an

402

amount equal to one-half (1/2) of the monthly pension to which the Participant would be entitled on that date computed on a single life annuity basis and multiplied by a fraction, the numerator of which is the number of years of Pension Credit (as defined in the Plan) earned by the Participant between the date of marriage (March 28, 1987) and the date of separation (June 15, 1993), and the denominator of which is the total number of years of the Participant's Pension Credit at the Participant's date of retirement. In computing the numerator, the Pension Credit for the year of marriage and the year of separation shall be prorated on a daily basis.

b.   With respect to the Alternate Payee's entitlement under Section 4(a) of this Order, the amount thereof shall be calculated on the basis of a single life annuity with the Participant's life as the measuring life and shall be paid to the Alternate Payee in actuarially adjusted monthly amounts over the Alternate Payee's lifetime. If the Alternate Payee dies before the Alternate Payee has received sixty (60) monthly payments, monthly payments shall be made to the beneficiary or beneficiaries designated by the Alternate Payee in writing and filed with the Plan Administrator until a total of sixty (60) monthly payments have been made. If no beneficiary declaration is on file at the Alternate Payee's death or if no designated beneficiary survives until the Alternate Payee's entitlement is paid in full, the unpaid balance of the Alternate Payee's entitlement shall be paid to the Alternate Payee's estate.

c.   If the Participant dies before payments have commenced to the Alternate Payee, then, whether or not the Participant is survived by a Qualified Spouse (as defined in the Plan), the Alternate Payee (or the Alternate Payee's designated beneficiary if the Alternate Payee shall have predeceased the Participant) shall receive an amount equal to one-half (1/2) of the Death Benefit (as defined below) multiplied by a fraction the

- 3 -

numerator of which is the same as the numerator expressed in Section 4(a) of this Order and the denominator of which is the total number of Pension Credit at the Participant's death. The Death Benefit shall be the amount described in Section 1(a) of Article V of the Plan if the Participant dies before attaining age sixty-five (65) or the amount described in Section 1(b) of Article V of the Plan if the Participant dies after attaining age sixty-five (65). In either case, the amount payable to the Alternate Payee (or the Alternate Payee's beneficiary) shall be paid in a lump sum or in monthly installments as the Alternate Payee (or the Alternate Payee's beneficiary) shall elect in accordance with said Sections of the Plan; provided, however, that if the amount of the Alternate Payee's entitlement is $3,500 or less, it shall be payable only in a lump sum.

5. Notwithstanding the provisions of Section 9 of Article VIII of the Plan, payment of benefits to the Alternate Payee shall not be suspended by reason of the Participant's returning to covered employment after retiring.

6. At the Alternate Payee's election, the Alternate Payee may receive the Alternate Payee's benefits at the earliest time permissible under the Plan consistent with the methods set forth in this Order. If such election is made prior to the Participant's date of retirement, the date when the Alternate Payee makes the election shall be used in place of the Participant's date of retirement in calculating the denominator of the fraction expressed in Section 4(a) of this Order. If the Alternate Payee dies before making such election and before payments have commenced to the Alternate Payee, such election may be made by the Alternate Payee's designated beneficiary.

7. The Participant and the Alternate Payee shall be separately responsible for income taxes attributable to the payments received by each of them under the Plan.

8. This Order is intended to be a QDRO made pursuant to the Act, has been determined to be a QDRO by the signature of the Plan Administrator below, and its provisions shall be administered and interpreted in conformity with the Act. If the Act is

- 4 -

amended or the law regarding QDROs is otherwise changed or modified, then the parties hereto shall immediately take such steps as are necessary to amend this QDRO to comply with any such changes, amendments, or modification to the Act or laws regarding QDROs.

9. The Court shall retain jurisdiction over this matter to amend this Order in order to establish and/or maintain its qualification as a QDRO under the Act and to carry out the terms and conditions of this Order.

Dated: 4/20/94

JAMES EUGENE CARREY, Petitioner

Dated: 4/20/94

MELISSA JANE CARREY, Respondent

APPROVED AS TO FORM AND CONTENT:

Dated: 4/26/94

LAW OFFICES OF NORMAN M. DOLIN

By: _____
NORMAN M. DOLIN
Attorney for Petitioner,
JAMES EUGENE CARREY

Dated: 4/20/94

SIMKE, CHODOS, SILBERFELD & ANTEAU, INC.

By: _____
RONALD W. ANTEAU,
Attorney for Respondent,
MELISSA JANE CARREY

Dated: 5/19/94

BRUCE L. DOW,
Plan Administrator

- 5 -

1 | THE CLERK IS ORDERED TO ENTER THIS ORDER.

2

3 | Dated: _____ MAY 2 6 1994 _____

JUDGE OF THE SUPERIOR COURT

4

5 | **JAMES D. ENDMAN**
Judge Pro Tem

6

7

8

9

10

11

12

13

14

15

16

17

18

19

20

21

22

23

24

25

26

27

28

A P P E N D I X C

STATE OF CONNECTICUT CHILD SUPPORT AND ARREARAGE GUIDELINES

State of Connecticut

Child Support
and
Arrearage Guidelines

Issued by the

**Commission for
Child Support Guidelines**

Pursuant to § 46b-215a of the
Connecticut General Statutes

Effective June 1, 1994

(4) "Child" means an unemancipated individual who has not attained the age of eighteen years, and includes "children" where the context so requires.

(5) "Child support guidelines" means the rules, principles, schedule, and worksheets established under these regulations for the determination of the appropriate level of current support for a child, to be used when establishing both temporary and permanent orders, whether in the initial determination of a child support order or a modification of an existing order.

(6) "Current support" means an amount for the ongoing support of a child.

(7) "Custodial parent" means the parent who provides the child's primary residence.

(8) "Dependent" means a spouse or child for whom an obligor is legally responsible pursuant to section 46b-215 of the Connecticut General Statutes.

(9) "Deviation criteria" means those facts or circumstances described in sections 46b-215a-3 and 46b-215a-5 of these regulations which, if specifically found on the record by the trier of fact, may be sufficient to rebut the presumption created by the child support and/or arrearage guidelines.

(10) "Effective self-support reserve" means the portion of the net income of a low-income obligor which, subject to section 46b-215a-3 of these regulations, is generally not obligated for current support payments. The amount represents a level of retained income greater than the minimum self-support reserve, and is incorporated in the schedule to ensure that at low income levels, as an obligor's income increases, the entire amount of additional earnings is not obligated for current support payments.

(11) "Gross income" means the average weekly income before deductions.

(A) Inclusions

Gross income includes, but is not limited to:

(i) salary and wages, including overtime

(ii) commissions, bonuses, tips and perquisites

(iii) rental income after deduction of reasonable and necessary expenses

(iv) estate or trust income

(v) royalties

(vi) interest, dividends, and annuities

- 2 -

(vii) social security (excluding Supplemental Security Income (SSI)), veterans, unemployment and workers' compensation, retirement, pension, and other benefits

(viii) net proceeds from contractual agreements

(ix) self-employment earnings, after deduction of all legitimate business expenses

(x) alimony being paid by an individual who is not a party to the support determination

(xi) unearned income from all sources

(xii) in-kind compensation (any basic maintenance or special need such as food, shelter, or transportation provided on a recurrent basis in lieu of salary).

(B) Exclusions

Gross income does not include:

(i) support received on behalf of a child who is living in the home of the parent whose income is being determined

(ii) federal, state, and local public assistance grants.

(12) "Imputed support obligation" means a theoretical obligation computed for given children in accordance with the child support guidelines, the amount of which is used in the calculation of arrearage payments under section 46b-215a-4 of these regulations.

(13) "Low-income obligor" means an obligor whose current support obligation is generally determined without considering the other parent's income (using the darker shaded area of the schedule), in order to ensure that such obligor retains a self-support reserve.

(14) "Minimum self-support reserve" means the portion of an obligor's net income which is generally not obligated for current support or arrearage payments under these regulations. The amount represents a minimal level of income to allow the obligor to provide for his or her own support, and is set at $145 per week.

(15) "Net income" means gross income minus allowable deductions.

(16) "Noncustodial parent" means a parent who does not provide the child's primary residence.

(17) "Obligor" means a parent who is ordered to pay current child support and/or arrearage payments in accordance with these regulations.

(18) "Schedule" means the Connecticut Child Support Guidelines Schedule of Basic Child Support Obligations included in section 46b-215a-2 of these regulations.

- 3 -

(19) "Shared custody" means a situation in which the parents share the physical care and control of the child.

(20) "Split custody" means a situation in which there is more than one child in common and each parent is the custodial parent of at least one of the children.

(21) "Title IV-D" means the provisions of the federal Social Security Act which require states to implement a child support enforcement program.

Section 46b-215a-2.   Child support guidelines

(a)   Applicability

This section shall be used in the determination of all child support award amounts within the state effective June 1, 1994.   When the parents' combined net weekly income exceeds $1,750, awards shall be determined on a case-by-case basis, and the amount of support prescribed at the $1,750 level shall be the minimum presumptive level.

(b)   Determining the amount of support

This subsection applies when one parent or a third party has primary custody of all children whose support is being determined, except as provided in subsection (c) in this section.   The line references throughout this subsection are to Worksheet A, which is intended for use with the following instructions.   Worksheet A is included in these regulations as Appendix A.   Use one worksheet in most cases.   When there is a third party custodian and either parent is a low-income obligor (as determined in this subsection), complete a separate Worksheet A for each parent.   All money amounts may be rounded to the nearest dollar.   When rounding, round up for amounts of 5 or more and down for amounts less than 5.

(1)   Determine the net weekly income of the noncustodial parent(s)

Follow the instructions in this subdivision to determine the net weekly income of the noncustodial parent.   Enter all amounts on Worksheet A in the column corresponding to the noncustodial parent.

(A)   Enter the gross income on line 1.

(B)   Enter the number of allowable exemptions on line 2.   Use this number to determine the appropriate income tax deductions.

(C)   Enter all allowable deductions on lines 3-9.   Add the amounts entered on lines 3-9 and enter the result on line 10.

(D)   Subtract the line 10 amount from the line 1 amount and enter the result on line 11.   This is the net weekly income of the noncustodial parent.

- 4 -

(2) Determine the basic child support obligation

Follow the instructions below in the order presented to determine the basic child support obligation using the Schedule of Basic Child Support Obligations found in subsection (d) of this section.

(A) Find the block in the schedule which corresponds to the income level of the noncustodial parent (rounded to the nearest ten dollars ($10.00)) and the number of children whose support is being determined.

(i) If this block is in the darker shaded area of the schedule and the amounts shown are not in parentheses, the noncustodial parent is a low-income obligor. The dollar amount shown in the block is the noncustodial parent's basic child support obligation. Enter this amount on line 13, place a check mark on line 14, and proceed to subdivision (3) in this subsection.

(ii) If this block is in the darker shaded area of the schedule and the amounts shown are enclosed in parentheses, the noncustodial parent is a low-income obligor. Proceed to subparagraph (B) in this subdivision to determine the basic child support obligation, unless the custodial parent has no income. In that case, follow step (i) above.

(iii) If this block is not in the darker shaded area of the schedule, the noncustodial parent is not a low-income obligor. Proceed to subparagraph (C) in this subdivision to determine the basic child support obligation.

(B) Determine the net weekly income of the custodial parent, following the same instructions as used to determine the net weekly income of the noncustodial parent. Add this amount to the noncustodial parent's net weekly income, and round to the nearest ten dollars ($10.00). The result is the combined net weekly income. Enter this amount on line 12. Find the block in the schedule which corresponds to the combined net weekly income and the number of children whose support is being determined. Compare the percentage shown in this block to the percentage shown in the block found in step (ii) of subparagraph (A).

(i) If the percentage shown in the darker shaded block is lower than the percentage in this block, the dollar amount shown in the darker shaded block is the noncustodial parent's basic support obligation. Enter this amount on line 13, place a check mark on line 14, and proceed to subdivision (3) in this subsection.

(ii) If the percentage shown in the darker shaded block is higher than the percentage in this block, proceed to subparagraph (C), immediately following.

- 5 -

(C) Determine the net weekly income of the custodial parent, following the same instructions as used to determine the net weekly income of the noncustodial parent. Add this amount to the noncustodial parent's net weekly income, and round to the nearest ten dollars ($10.00). The result is the combined net weekly income. Enter this amount on line 12. Find the block in the schedule which corresponds to the combined net weekly income and the number of children whose support is being determined.

The dollar amount shown in this block is the basic child support obligation of both parents for the support of all children. Enter this amount on line 13 and proceed to subdivision (3), immediately following.

(3) Determine the total child support obligation

Follow the instructions in this subdivision to determine the amount of the total child support obligation. Except in the case of a low-income obligor, the total child support obligation is the basic child support obligation obtained from the schedule plus the cost of health insurance premiums for coverage of the children whose support is being determined. In the case of a low-income obligor, the obligor's total child support obligation is the basic child support obligation reduced by the amount paid by such obligor for health insurance premiums for the subject children.

(A) Determine health insurance premium amounts

Determine the amount of any medical, hospital, dental, or health insurance premiums paid by either or both parents for coverage of the children whose support is being determined. Only amounts actually attributable to the subject children are considered. If any such amount is unknown or cannot be verified, the total cost of the premium is divided by the total number of persons covered by the policy and then multiplied by the number of subject children covered by the policy. The parent requesting an adjustment for health insurance premium costs shall submit proof that the children are enrolled in an insurance plan and proof of the cost of the premium. Enter the premium amounts in the appropriate columns on line 15.

(B) Add to basic obligation (parents other than low-income obligors)

Unless line 14 is checked, add the sum of the line 15 amounts to the line 13 amount and enter the result on line 16. This is the total child support obligation of both parents for all children whose support is being determined.

(C) Subtract from basic obligation (low-income obligors only)

If line 14 is checked, subtract the line 15 amount paid by the noncustodial parent (low-income obligor) from the line 13 amount and enter the result on line 16. This is the total child support obligation of the low-income obligor.

- 6 -

(4) Determine each parent's share of the total obligation

Each parent's share of the total obligation is determined by calculating each parent's share of the combined net weekly income, and multiplying the result for each parent by the total obligation.

(A) In the case of a low-income obligor, skip line 17, enter the line 16 amount in the noncustodial parent's column on line 18, and proceed to subdivision (6) in this subsection.

(B) Determine each parent's share of the combined net weekly income by dividing the line 11 amount for each parent by the line 12 amount. Enter the result (rounded to two decimal places) for each parent on line 17.

(C) Multiply the line 17 amount for each parent by the line 16 amount. Enter the result for each parent on line 18. These amounts are each parent's share of the total obligation.

(5) Adjust for payment of health insurance premiums

(A) Low-income obligors

In the case of low-income obligors, there is no adjustment for health insurance premiums since the cost was already deducted from the basic obligation in determining the total obligation in subdivision (3) in this subsection. In such cases, therefore, skip line 19 and proceed to subdivision (6).

(B) All other cases

In all other cases, enter on line 19 for each parent the same amount as was entered on line 15.

(6) Adjust for social security benefits

Enter on line 20 in the noncustodial parent's column the weekly amount of any social security benefits payable under such parent's account on behalf of the subject child.

(7) Determine the recommended support amount

The recommended support amount for each parent is determined by subtracting the adjustments for health insurance premiums and social security benefits from each parent's share of the total support obligation.

(A) Add the line 19 and line 20 amounts for each parent and enter the sum on line 21. These are the total adjustments for each parent.

(B) Subtract the line 21 amounts from the line 18 amounts for each parent and enter the results on line 22. These are the recommended support amounts for each parent.

- 7 -

(8) Determine the current support order

The current support order shall equal the recommended support amount for the noncustodial parent unless a deviation criterion applies.

(A) Enter the weekly current support order on line 23 in the noncustodial parent's column. If the line 23 amount differs from the line 22 amount, explain the difference in section VI of Worksheet A.

(B) The recommended support amount for the custodial parent is not established as an order and is not entered on line 23. The line 22 amount for the custodial parent is retained by the custodial parent and is presumed spent on the children.

(c) Determining the amount of support in split custody situations

In a split custody situation, as defined in section 46b-215a-1 of these regulations, separate obligations are computed for each parent in accordance with subsection (b) in this section, based on the number of children living with the other parent. A separate Worksheet A is used to compute each obligation. The separate obligations are then offset, with the parent owing the greater amount paying the difference to the other parent.

(d) Schedule of basic child support obligations

Following is the schedule to be used for determining the basic child support obligation in accordance with this section. Note that all obligation money amounts have been rounded to the nearest dollar in this schedule.

- 8 -

CONNECTICUT CHILD SUPPORT GUIDELINES
SCHEDULE OF BASIC CHILD SUPPORT OBLIGATIONS

NOTE: Noncustodial parent income only for darker shaded areas of schedule; combined parental income for the remainder of the schedule. Use amounts in parentheses only when the percentage in parentheses is lower than the percentage for combined parental income.

COMBINED NET WEEKLY INCOME	1 CHILD		2 CHILDREN		3 CHILDREN		4 CHILDREN		5 CHILDREN		6 CHILDREN	
	%	$	%	$	%	$	%	$	%	$	%	$
150	2.67%	4	2.67%	4	2.67%	4	2.67%	4	2.67%	4	2.67%	4
160	6.88%	11	6.88%	11	6.88%	11	6.88%	11	6.88%	11	6.88%	11
170	10.59%	18	10.59%	18	10.59%	18	10.59%	18	10.59%	18	10.59%	18
180	13.89%	25	13.89%	25	13.89%	25	13.89%	25	13.89%	25	13.89%	25
190	16.84%	32	16.84%	32	16.84%	32	16.84%	32	16.84%	32	16.84%	32
200	(20.00%	40)	20.00%	40	20.00%	40	20.00%	40	20.00%	40	20.00%	40
210	(22.86%	48)	22.86%	48	22.86%	48	22.86%	48	22.86%	48	22.86%	48
220	(25.45%	56)	25.45%	56	25.45%	56	25.45%	56	25.45%	56	25.45%	56
230	25.53%	59	(27.83%	64)	27.83%	64	27.83%	64	27.83%	64	27.83%	64
240	25.52%	61	(30.00%	72)	30.00%	72	30.00%	72	30.00%	72	30.00%	72
250	25.51%	64	(32.40%	81)	32.40%	81	32.40%	81	32.40%	81	32.40%	81
260	25.51%	66	(34.62%	90)	(34.62%	90)	34.62%	90	34.62%	90	34.62%	90
270	25.50%	69	(36.67%	99)	(36.67%	99)	(36.67%	99)	36.67%	99	36.67%	99
280	25.49%	71	37.57%	105	(38.57%	108)	(38.57%	108)	38.57%	108	38.57%	108
290	25.49%	74	37.56%	109	(40.34%	117)	(40.34%	117)	40.34%	117	40.34%	117
300	25.48%	76	37.56%	113	(42.00%	126)	(42.00%	126)	42.00%	126	42.00%	126
310	25.48%	79	37.55%	116	(43.55%	135)	(43.55%	135)	(43.55%	135)	43.55%	135
320	25.48%	82	37.54%	120	44.91%	144	(45.00%	144)	(45.00%	144)	(45.00%	144)
330	25.47%	84	37.53%	124	44.91%	148	(46.36%	153)	(46.36%	153)	(46.36%	153)
340	25.46%	87	37.52%	128	44.89%	153	(47.65%	162)	(47.65%	162)	(47.65%	162)
350	25.45%	89	37.49%	131	44.85%	157	(48.86%	171)	(48.86%	171)	(48.86%	171)
360	25.43%	92	37.46%	135	44.81%	161	49.51%	178	(50.00%	180)	(50.00%	180)
370	25.41%	94	37.44%	139	44.77%	166	49.47%	183	(51.08%	189)	(51.08%	189)
380	25.40%	97	37.41%	142	44.74%	170	49.44%	188	(52.11%	198)	(52.11%	198)
390	25.38%	99	37.39%	146	44.71%	174	49.40%	193	(53.08%	207)	(53.08%	207)
400	25.37%	101	37.37%	149	44.68%	179	49.37%	197	53.52%	214	(54.00%	216)
410	25.36%	104	37.34%	153	44.65%	183	49.34%	202	53.48%	219	(54.88%	225)
420	25.34%	106	37.32%	157	44.62%	187	49.31%	207	53.45%	224	(55.71%	234)
430	25.33%	109	37.30%	160	44.60%	192	49.28%	212	53.42%	230	(56.51%	243)
440	25.32%	111	37.28%	164	44.57%	196	49.25%	217	53.39%	235	57.13%	251
450	25.31%	114	37.26%	168	44.55%	200	49.22%	222	53.36%	240	57.10%	257
460	25.30%	116	37.24%	171	44.52%	205	49.20%	226	53.33%	245	57.07%	262
470	25.29%	119	37.23%	175	44.50%	209	49.17%	231	53.31%	251	57.04%	268
480	25.28%	121	37.21%	179	44.48%	214	49.15%	236	53.28%	256	57.01%	274
490	25.27%	124	37.19%	182	44.46%	218	49.13%	241	53.26%	261	56.98%	279

Combined Net Weekly Income	1 Child %	1 Child $	2 Children %	2 Children $	3 Children %	3 Children $	4 Children %	4 Children $	5 Children %	5 Children $	6 Children %	6 Children $
500	25.26%	126	37.17%	186	44.44%	222	49.11%	246	53.23%	266	56.96%	285
510	25.25%	129	37.16%	190	44.42%	227	49.09%	250	53.21%	271	56.93%	290
520	25.24%	131	37.14%	193	44.41%	231	49.07%	255	53.19%	277	56.91%	296
530	25.23%	134	37.13%	197	44.39%	235	49.05%	260	53.17%	282	56.89%	301
540	25.22%	136	37.11%	200	44.36%	240	49.02%	265	53.14%	287	56.85%	307
550	25.21%	139	37.09%	204	44.34%	244	48.99%	269	53.11%	292	56.82%	313
560	25.20%	141	37.07%	208	44.31%	248	48.97%	274	53.08%	297	56.79%	318
570	25.19%	144	37.05%	211	44.29%	252	48.94%	279	53.05%	302	56.76%	324
580	25.18%	146	37.04%	215	44.27%	257	48.92%	284	53.03%	308	56.73%	329
590	25.17%	148	37.02%	218	44.25%	261	48.89%	288	53.00%	313	56.71%	335
600	25.16%	151	37.01%	222	44.23%	265	48.87%	293	52.98%	318	56.68%	340
610	25.15%	153	36.99%	226	44.21%	270	48.85%	298	52.95%	323	56.66%	346
620	25.14%	156	36.98%	229	44.19%	274	48.83%	303	52.93%	328	56.63%	351
630	25.14%	158	36.96%	233	44.17%	278	48.81%	307	52.91%	333	56.61%	357
640	25.13%	161	36.95%	236	44.15%	283	48.79%	312	52.88%	338	56.58%	362
650	25.12%	163	36.93%	240	44.13%	287	48.77%	317	52.86%	344	56.56%	368
660	25.11%	166	36.92%	244	44.11%	291	48.74%	322	52.84%	349	56.54%	373
670	25.10%	168	36.90%	247	44.09%	295	48.72%	326	52.82%	354	56.51%	379
680	25.09%	171	36.89%	251	44.08%	300	48.70%	331	52.80%	359	56.49%	384
690	25.08%	173	36.88%	254	44.06%	304	48.69%	336	52.78%	364	56.47%	390
700	25.08%	176	36.87%	258	44.04%	308	48.67%	341	52.76%	369	56.45%	395
710	25.07%	178	36.85%	262	44.03%	313	48.65%	345	52.74%	374	56.43%	401
720	25.06%	180	36.84%	265	44.01%	317	48.63%	350	52.72%	380	56.41%	406
730	24.98%	182	36.72%	268	43.86%	320	48.46%	354	52.54%	384	56.22%	410
740	24.88%	184	36.58%	271	43.70%	323	48.28%	357	52.34%	387	56.01%	414
750	24.80%	186	36.44%	273	43.54%	327	48.11%	361	52.15%	391	55.80%	419
760	24.71%	188	36.31%	276	43.38%	330	47.93%	364	51.96%	395	55.60%	423
770	24.62%	190	36.19%	279	43.23%	333	47.77%	368	51.78%	399	55.41%	427
780	24.54%	191	36.06%	281	43.08%	336	47.60%	371	51.60%	403	55.22%	431
790	24.46%	193	35.94%	284	42.93%	339	47.44%	375	51.43%	406	55.03%	435
800	24.38%	195	35.82%	287	42.79%	342	47.29%	378	51.26%	410	54.85%	439
810	24.30%	197	35.71%	289	42.66%	346	47.14%	382	51.10%	414	54.67%	443
820	24.21%	199	35.57%	292	42.49%	348	46.96%	385	50.90%	417	54.46%	447
830	24.07%	200	35.37%	294	42.25%	351	46.69%	388	50.61%	420	54.15%	449
840	23.94%	201	35.17%	295	42.01%	353	46.42%	390	50.32%	423	53.85%	452
850	23.81%	202	34.98%	297	41.78%	355	46.17%	392	50.04%	425	53.55%	455
860	23.68%	204	34.79%	299	41.55%	357	45.92%	395	49.77%	428	53.26%	458
870	23.55%	205	34.60%	301	41.33%	360	45.67%	397	49.51%	431	52.97%	461
880	23.43%	206	34.42%	303	41.12%	362	45.43%	400	49.25%	433	52.69%	464
890	23.31%	207	34.25%	305	40.91%	364	45.20%	402	48.99%	436	52.42%	467
900	23.19%	209	34.07%	307	40.70%	366	44.97%	405	48.74%	439	52.16%	469
910	23.08%	210	33.91%	309	40.50%	369	44.74%	407	48.50%	441	51.90%	472
920	22.95%	211	33.71%	310	40.26%	370	44.49%	409	48.22%	444	51.60%	475
930	22.80%	212	33.50%	312	40.01%	372	44.21%	411	47.92%	446	51.28%	477
940	22.67%	213	33.30%	313	39.77%	374	43.94%	413	47.63%	448	50.97%	479
950	22.53%	214	33.10%	314	39.53%	376	43.68%	415	47.35%	450	50.66%	481
960	22.40%	215	32.90%	316	39.29%	377	43.42%	417	47.07%	452	50.36%	483
970	22.27%	216	32.71%	317	39.06%	379	43.16%	419	46.79%	454	50.07%	486
980	22.14%	217	32.52%	319	38.84%	381	42.92%	421	46.52%	456	49.78%	488
990	2201%	218	32.34%	320	38.62%	382	42.67%	422	46.26%	458	49.50%	490

Combined Net Weekly Income	1 Child %	1 Child $	2 Children %	2 Children $	3 Children %	3 Children $	4 Children %	4 Children $	5 Children %	5 Children $	6 Children %	6 Children $
1,000	21.89%	219	32.16%	322	38.40%	384	42.43%	424	46.00%	460	49.22%	492
1,010	21.77%	220	31.98%	323	38.19%	386	42.20%	426	45.75%	462	48.95%	494
1,020	21.65%	221	31.81%	324	37.98%	387	41.97%	428	45.50%	464	48.68%	497
1,030	21.54%	222	31.64%	326	37.78%	389	41.75%	430	45.26%	466	48.42%	499
1,040	21.42%	223	31.47%	327	37.58%	391	41.53%	432	45.02%	468	48.17%	501
1,050	21.31%	224	31.31%	329	37.38%	393	41.31%	434	44.79%	470	47.92%	503
1,060	21.21%	225	31.15%	330	37.20%	394	41.10%	436	44.56%	472	47.68%	505
1,070	21.15%	226	31.07%	332	37.10%	397	41.00%	439	44.44%	476	47.55%	509
1,080	21.10%	228	30.99%	335	37.00%	400	40.89%	442	44.33%	479	47.43%	512
1,090	21.04%	229	30.91%	337	36.91%	402	40.78%	445	44.21%	482	47.31%	516
1,100	20.99%	231	30.83%	339	36.81%	405	40.68%	448	44.10%	485	47.19%	519
1,110	20.94%	232	30.76%	341	36.72%	408	40.58%	450	43.99%	488	47.07%	522
1,120	20.89%	234	30.68%	344	36.63%	410	40.48%	453	43.88%	491	46.96%	526
1,130	20.84%	235	30.61%	346	36.54%	413	40.38%	456	43.78%	495	46.84%	529
1,140	20.79%	237	30.54%	348	36.46%	416	40.29%	459	43.67%	498	46.73%	533
1,150	20.74%	239	30.46%	350	36.37%	418	40.19%	462	43.57%	501	46.62%	536
1,160	20.69%	240	30.39%	353	36.29%	421	40.10%	465	43.47%	504	46.52%	540
1,170	20.65%	242	30.33%	355	36.21%	424	40.01%	468	43.37%	507	46.41%	543
1,180	20.60%	243	30.26%	357	36.13%	426	39.92%	471	43.27%	511	46.31%	546
1,190	20.55%	245	30.19%	359	30.05%	429	39.83%	474	43.18%	514	46.20%	550
1,200	20.51%	246	30.13%	362	35.97%	432	39.75%	477	43.08%	517	46.10%	553
1,210	20.47%	248	30.06%	364	35.89%	434	39.66%	480	42.99%	520	46.01%	557
1,220	20.42%	249	30.00%	366	35.82%	437	39.58%	483	42.90%	523	45.91%	560
1,230	20.38%	251	29.94%	368	35.74%	440	39.50%	486	42.81%	527	45.81%	564
1,240	20.34%	252	29.88%	370	35.67%	442	39.42%	489	42.72%	530	45.72%	567
1,250	20.30%	254	29.82%	373	35.60%	445	39.34%	492	42.64%	533	45.63%	570
1,260	20.27%	255	29.77%	375	35.54%	488	39.27%	495	42.57%	536	45.55%	574
1,270	20.23%	257	29.72%	377	35.48%	451	39.21%	498	42.49%	540	45.47%	578
1,280	20.20%	259	29.67%	380	35.42%	453	39.14%	501	42.42%	543	45.40%	581
1,290	20.17%	260	29.62%	382	35.36%	456	39.07%	504	42.35%	546	45.32%	585
1,300	20.14%	262	29.57%	384	35.30%	459	39.01%	507	42.28%	550	45.25%	588
1,310	20.10%	263	29.52%	387	35.25%	462	38.95%	510	42.21%	553	45.17%	592
1,320	20.07%	265	29.48%	389	35.19%	465	38.89%	513	42.15%	556	45.10%	595
1,330	20.04%	267	29.43%	391	35.13%	467	38.83%	516	42.08%	560	45.03%	599
1,340	20.01%	268	29.39%	394	35.08%	470	38.77%	519	42.01%	563	44.96%	602
1,350	19.98%	270	29.34%	396	35.03%	473	38.71%	523	41.95%	566	44.89%	606
1,360	19.95%	271	29.30%	398	34.97%	476	38.65%	526	41.89%	570	44.82%	610
1,370	19.93%	273	29.25%	401	34.92%	478	38.59%	529	41.82%	573	44.75%	613
1,380	19.90%	275	29.21%	403	34.87%	481	38.53%	532	41.76%	576	44.69%	617
1,390	19.87%	276	29.17%	405	34.82%	484	38.48%	535	41.70%	580	44.62%	620
1,400	19.84%	278	29.13%	408	34.77%	487	38.42%	538	41.64%	583	44.56%	624
1,410	19.81%	279	29.09%	410	34.72%	490	38.37%	541	41.58%	586	44.50%	627
1,420	19.79%	281	29.05%	412	34.67%	492	38.32%	544	41.53%	590	44.43%	631
1,430	19.76%	283	29.01%	415	34.63%	495	38.26%	547	41.47%	593	44.37%	635
1,440	19.74%	284	28.97%	417	34.58%	498	38.21%	550	41.41%	596	44.31%	638
1,450	19.71%	286	28.93%	419	34.53%	501	38.16%	553	41.35%	600	44.25%	642
1,460	19.68%	287	28.89%	422	34.48%	503	38.10%	556	41.29%	603	44.19%	645
1,470	19.65%	289	28.84%	424	34.43%	506	38.05%	559	41.23%	606	44.12%	649
1,480	19.62%	290	28.80%	426	34.38%	609	37.99%	562	41.18%	609	44.06%	652
1,490	19.60%	292	28.76%	429	34.33%	512	37.94%	565	41.12%	613	44.00%	656

418

COMBINED NET WEEKLY INCOME	1 CHILD		2 CHILDREN		3 CHILDREN		4 CHILDREN		5 CHILDREN		6 CHILDREN	
	%	$	%	$	%	$	%	$	%	$	%	$
1,500	19.57%	294	28.72%	431	34.28%	514	37.88%	568	41.06%	616	43.94%	659
1,510	19.54%	295	28.68%	433	34.24%	517	37.83%	571	41.01%	619	43.87%	663
1,520	19.52%	297	28.64%	435	34.19%	520	37.78%	574	40.95%	622	43.81%	666
1,530	19.49%	298	28.61%	438	34.14%	522	37.73%	577	40.90%	626	43.76%	669
1,540	19.47%	300	28.57%	440	34.10%	525	37.68%	580	40.84%	629	43.70%	673
1,550	19.44%	301	28.53%	442	34.05%	528	37.63%	583	40.79%	632	43.64%	676
1,560	19.42%	303	28.49%	445	34.01%	531	37.58%	586	40.74%	635	43.58%	680
1,570	19.39%	304	28.46%	447	33.96%	533	37.53%	589	40.68%	639	43.53%	683
1,580	19.37%	306	28.42%	449	33.92%	536	37.48%	592	40.63%	642	43.47%	687
1,590	19.34%	308	28.39%	451	33.88%	539	37.44%	595	40.58%	645	43.42%	690
1,600	19.32%	309	28.35%	454	33.84%	541	37.39%	598	40.53%	649	43.36%	694
1,610	19.30%	311	28.32%	456	33.79%	544	37.34%	601	40.48%	652	43.31%	697
1,620	19.27%	312	28.28%	458	33.75%	547	37.30%	604	40.43%	655	43.26%	701
1,630	19.25%	314	28.25%	460	33.71%	550	37.25%	607	40.39%	658	43.21%	704
1,640	19.21%	315	28.19%	462	33.64%	552	37.18%	610	40.30%	661	43.12%	707
1,650	19.16%	316	28.11%	464	33.55%	554	37.08%	612	40.19%	663	43.00%	710
1,660	19.11%	317	28.04%	465	33.46%	555	36.98%	614	40.09%	665	42.89%	712
1,670	19.06%	318	27.97%	467	33.37%	557	36.88%	616	39.98%	668	42.77%	714
1,680	19.01%	319	27.89%	469	33.29%	559	36.78%	618	39.87%	670	42.66%	717
1,690	18.96%	320	27.82%	470	33.20%	561	36.69%	620	39.77%	672	42.55%	719
1,700	18.91%	322	27.75%	472	33.12%	563	36.59%	622	39.67%	674	42.44%	722
1,710	18.87%	323	27.68%	473	33.03%	565	36.50%	624	39.57%	677	42.34%	724
1,720	18.82%	324	27.61%	475	32.95%	567	36.41%	626	38.47%	679	42.23%	726
1,730	18.77%	325	27.54%	476	32.87%	569	36.32%	628	39.37%	681	42.13%	729
1,740	18.73%	326	27.47%	478	32.79%	570	36.23%	630	39.27%	683	42.02%	731
1,750	18.68%	327	27.41%	480	32.70%	572	36.14%	632	39.17%	686	41.92%	734

Section 46b–215a–3. Child support guidelines deviation criteria

(a) Introduction

The amount of current support calculated under the child support guidelines is presumed to be the correct amount to be awarded. The presumption may be rebutted by a specific finding on the record that the application of such guidelines would be inequitable or inappropriate in a particular case. Any such finding shall state the amount of support that would have been required under the guidelines and include a justification for the variance. Only the deviation criteria described in this section establish sufficient bases for such findings.

(b) Criteria for deviation from child support guidelines

(1) Other financial resources available to a parent

In some cases, a parent may have financial resources which are not included in the definition of net income, but could be used by such parent for the benefit of the child or for meeting the needs of the parent. The following resources may justify a deviation from the guidelines amount:

(A) substantial assets, including both income-producing and non-income-producing property

(B) the parent's earning capacity

(C) parental support being provided to a minor obligor, which resource may only be considered for establishing a self-support reserve of less than $145 per week.

(2) Extraordinary expenses for care and maintenance of the child

In some cases, a parent may be incurring extraordinary expenses which are essential for the proper care and maintenance of the child whose support is being determined. The following expenses, when found to be extraordinary and to exist on a substantial and continuing basis, may justify a deviation from the guidelines amount:

(A) education expenses

(B) unreimbursable medical expenses

(C) expenses for special needs.

(3) Extraordinary parental expenses

In some cases, a parent may incur extraordinary expenses which are not considered allowable deductions from gross income but which are necessary for the parent to maintain a satisfactory parental relationship with the child, continue employment, or provide for the parent's own medical needs. The following expenses, when found to be extraordinary and to exist on a substantial and continuing basis, may justify a deviation from the guidelines amount:

(A) significant visitation expenses

(B) job-related unreimbursable employment expenses of individuals who are not self-employed

(C) unreimbursable medical expenses.

- 13 -

(4) Needs of a parent's other dependents

In some cases, a parent may be legally responsible for the support of individuals other than the child whose support is being determined. In such cases, it may be appropriate to deviate from the guidelines amount to permit the parent to assist in meeting the following needs, which shall include any extraordinary unreimbursable medical expenses for such individuals:

(A) those of children of prior unions residing with the obligor, or for whom the obligor is making verified payments

(B) those of children of subsequent unions for whom there is no support order, provided such needs may be used as a possible defense against an increase in the support order, but not as a reason for decreasing such order

(C) the significant and essential needs of a subsequent spouse, provided

(i) such needs may be used as a possible defense against an increase in the support order, but not as a reason for decreasing such order, and

(ii) the income, assets, and earning capacity of such spouse shall be considered in determining whether to deviate.

(5) Coordination of total family support

In some cases, the trier of fact may consider child support in conjunction with a determination of total family support, property settlement, and tax implications. When the trier of fact finds that such considerations will not result in a lesser economic benefit to the child, it may be appropriate to deviate from the guidelines amount for the following reasons:

(A) division of assets and liabilities

(B) provision of alimony

(C) tax planning considerations.

(6) Special circumstances

In some cases, there may be special circumstances not otherwise addressed in these regulations in which the court should have the discretion to deviate from the guidelines amount for reasons of equity. Following are such circumstances:

(A) Shared custody arrangements.

(B) When unreimbursed day care costs are incurred for the child whose support is being determined, the court may order an additional amount to cover such costs for as long as they are incurred, provided

    (i) such costs are reasonable,

    (ii) the payment of such costs fails to leave sufficient funds for the child's other needs, and

    (iii) day care is necessary for the parent to maintain or seek employment.

(C) When an obligor's support payment falls within the darker shaded area of the schedule, the obligor benefits from an effective self-support reserve greater than the minimum self-support reserve of $145 per week. In such cases, if the court finds that the custodial parent is employed but has a net income which is less than or equal to that of the obligor, the court may deviate from the guidelines amount by imposing an order which will reduce the obligor's effective self-support reserve to as low as the minimum self-support reserve.

(D) If, on a motion for modification, the trier of fact finds that the obligor is working more than 40 hours per week and has substantially increased the number of hours worked per week, by comparison with his or her work history at the time the order entered, the trier of fact may order child support from the increased income in an amount less than that which would otherwise be required by the guidelines.

(E) Best interests of the child.

(F) Other equitable factors.

Section 46b-215a-4. Arrearage guidelines

(a) Scope of section

This section shall be used in the determination of periodic payments on child support arrearages, effective June 1, 1994. The determination of lump sum payments remains subject to the discretion of the judge or family support magistrate, in accordance with existing principles of law.

(b) General rule

Subject to subsections (c), (d), and (e) of this section, the weekly order of payment toward any arrearage shall be twenty percent (20%) of the weekly current support order, rounded to the nearest dollar, provided:

(1) the sum of the weekly payments on current support and arrearages shall not exceed fifty-five percent (55%) of the obligor's net weekly income

- 15 -

(2) the sum of the weekly payments on current support and arrearages shall not reduce the obligor's retained net weekly income below the minimum self-support reserve of $145 per week

(3) an arrearage order of five dollars ($5.00) per week shall enter in the case of a low-income obligor provided such order will not reduce the obligor's retained net weekly income below the minimum self-support reserve of $145 per week

(4) where arrearages are owed to both the state and the family, five dollars ($5.00) per month of the arrearage payment calculated in accordance with this section shall be allocated for payment of the arrearage owed to the state, and the balance of such payment shall be allocated for payment of the arrearage owed to the family.

(c) Special rules for arrearages owed to the state

This subsection applies when a determination of the periodic payment on arrearages owed to the state is being made.

(1) Child under age eighteen

(A) Applicability

This subdivision applies when

(i) the child for whom the arrearage is owed is an unemancipated minor and

(ii) no current support order is in effect for such child

unless the custodial parent of such child has refused IV-D services in writing or the IV-D current support case has been closed in accordance with IV-D requirements.

(B) Special rule

When this subdivision applies, the weekly arrearage payment shall be twenty percent (20%) of the imputed support obligation for such child.

(2) No child under age eighteen

(A) Applicability

This subdivision applies when

(i) the child for whom the arrearage is owed is deceased, emancipated, or over age eighteen and

(ii) no child support arrearage is owed to the family.

- 16 -

(B) Special rule

When this subdivision applies, the weekly arrearage payment shall be fifty percent (50%) of the imputed support obligation for such child.

(d) Special rule for child living with the obligor

(1) Applicability

This subsection applies when the child for whom the arrearage is owed is living with the obligor. A child is deemed to be living with the obligor for purposes of this subsection if the circumstances in either (A) or (B) are found.

(A) The obligor is the child's legal guardian and is currently living in the same household with such child.

(B) The obligor is not the child's legal guardian, but the child has lived in the same household with the obligor for at least

(i) the six months immediately preceding the determination of the arrearage payment or

(ii) six of the twelve months immediately preceding such determination.

(2) Special rule

When this subsection applies, the weekly arrearage payment shall be:

(A) five dollars ($5.00) per month if the obligor's gross income is less than or equal to 250% of the poverty guideline for the obligor's household size, as published annually in the Federal Register by the Department of Health and Human Services

(B) twenty percent (20%) of the imputed support obligation for such child if the obligor's gross income is greater than 250% of the poverty guideline for the obligor's household size, as published annually in the Federal Register by the Department of Health and Human Services.

(e) Nominal payment

Notwithstanding subsections (b), (c), and (d) of this section, a nominal arrearage payment of five dollars ($5.00) per month shall be entered whenever the amount called for in this section is less than such amount, provided such payment shall not reduce the obligor's retained net income below the minimum self-support reserve of $145 per week.

- 17 -

(f) Use of the worksheet in arrearage determinations

Line references throughout this subsection are to Worksheet A, which is intended for use with the following instructions.

(1) Determine the total arrearage

Section III of Worksheet A is used to determine the total arrearage to be paid.

(A) Enter on line 24 the total of all delinquent amounts which have become due and payable under a current support order, but which have not been reduced to a judgment or an arrearage finding.

(B) Enter on line 25 the total of all unpaid support amounts which have been reduced previously to a judgment or arrearage finding.

(C) Enter on line 26 the total of all support amounts due for periods prior to the initial determination of a support order, calculated as provided in subparagraph (2)(C) of section 46b-215a-1 of these regulations.

(D) Enter on line 27 the sum of the line 24 through line 26 amounts. This amount is the total child support arrearage.

(2) Determine the arrearage payment

Section IV of Worksheet A is used to determine the periodic payment to be applied to the total arrearage determined in subdivision (1) of this subsection.

(A) Enter on line 28 either:

(i) the amount of the current support order from line 23 of the worksheet, or

(ii) the imputed support obligation for the child for whom the arrearage is owed if there is no current support order in effect for such child or the child is living with the obligor.

(B) Enter on line 29 either:

(i) twenty percent (20%) of the line 28 amount, or

(ii) fifty percent (50%) of the line 28 amount if there is no child under age 18.

(C) Enter on line 30 the noncustodial parent's net weekly income from line 11 of the worksheet.

(D) Enter on line 31 fifty-five percent (55%) of the line 30 amount.

- 18 -

(E) Subtract line 28 from line 31 and enter the result on line 32. This is the maximum arrearage payment that would not violate subdivision (1) of the general rule (subsection (b) in this section).

(F) Add $145 to the line 28 amount and enter the sum on line 33.

(G) Subtract line 33 from line 30 and enter the result on line 34. This is the maximum arrearage payment that would not violate subdivision (2) of the general rule (subsection (b) in this section).

(H) Enter on line 35 the recommended arrearage payment, as follows:

   (i) Unless the situations described in paragraphs (ii) or (iii) apply, enter the smallest of line 29, 32, and 34.

   (ii) If the child for whom the arrearage is owed is living with the obligor and the obligor's gross income is not more than 250% of the poverty level (see subsection (d) in this section), enter $5.00 per month.

   (iii) If the noncustodial parent is a low-income obligor, enter the lesser of $5.00 per week or the line 34 amount.

(I) Enter the amount of the arrearage payment order on line 36. This amount shall be at least $5.00 per month unless the line 34 amount is less than $1.00. If the order differs from the recommended payment, the deviation criterion applied shall be stated in section VI of the worksheet.

Section 46b-215a-5. Arrearage guidelines deviation criteria

(a) Introduction

The periodic payment on arrearages calculated under the arrearage guidelines is presumed to be the correct amount to be ordered. The presumption may be rebutted by a specific finding on the record that the application of such guidelines would be inequitable or inappropriate in a particular case. Any such finding shall state the arrearage payment that would have been required under the guidelines and include a justification for the variance. Only the deviation criteria described in this section establish sufficient bases for such findings.

(b) Criteria for deviation from arrearage guidelines

The arrearage order is based on the current support order and will already reflect consideration of the criteria for deviation from the child support guidelines. Therefore, the criteria for deviating from the arrearage guidelines are more limited. They are as follows:

(1) If the current support order was affected by the application of one or more deviation criteria, the trier of fact may consider adjusting the arrearage payment order upward or downward.

(2) Other equitable factors.

- 19 -

426

A P P E N D I X D

UNIFORM RECIPROCAL ENFORCEMENT OF SUPPORT ACT (AS AMENDED IN 1952 AND 1958)

PART I GENERAL PROVISIONS

SECTION 1. [*Purposes.*] The purposes of this act are to improve and extend by reciprocal legislation the enforcement of duties of support and to make uniform the law with respect thereto.

SECTION 2. [*Definitions.*] In this act unless the context otherwise requires:

(a) 'State' includes any state, territory or possession of the United States and the District of Columbia in which this or a substantially similar reciprocal law has been enacted.

(b) 'Initiating state' means any state in which a proceeding pursuant to this or a substantially similar reciprocal law is commenced.

(c) 'Responding state' means any state in which any proceeding pursuant to the proceeding in the initiating state is or may be commenced.

(d) 'Court' means the [here insert name] court of this state and when the context requires, means the court of any other state as defined in a substantially similar reciprocal law.

(e) 'Law' includes both common and statute law.

(f) 'Duty of support' includes any duty of support imposed or imposable by law, or by any court order, decree or judgment, whether interlocutory or final, whether incidental to a proceeding for divorce, judicial [legal] separation, separate maintenance or otherwise.

(g) 'Obligor' means any person owing a duty of support.

(h) 'Obligee' means any person to whom a duty of support is owed and a state or political subdivision thereof.

(i) 'Governor' includes any person performing the functions of Governor or the executive authority of any territory covered by the provisions of this act.

(j) 'Support order' means any judgment, decree or order of support whether temporary or final, whether subject to modification, revocation or remission regardless of the kind of action in which it is entered:

(k) 'Rendering state' means any state in which a support order is originally entered.

(l) 'Registering court' means any court of this state in which the support order of the rendering state is registered.

(m) 'Register' means to [record] [file] in the Registry of Foreign Support Orders as required by the court.

(n) 'Certification' shall be in accordance with the laws of the certifying state.

SECTION 3. [*Remedies Additional to Those Now Existing.*] The remedies herein provided are in addition to and not in substitution for any other remedies.

SECTION 4. [*Extent of Duties of Support.*] Duties of support arising under the law of this state, when applicable under Section 7, bind the obligor, present in this state, regardless of the presence or residence of the obligee.

PART II CRIMINAL ENFORCEMENT

SECTION 5. [*Interstate Rendition.*] The Governor of this state (1) may demand from the Governor of any other state the surrender of any person found in such other state who is charged in this state with the crime of failing to provide for the support of any person in this state and (2) may surrender on demand by the Governor of any other state any person found in this state who is charged in such other state with the crime of failing to provide for the support of any person in such other state. The provisions for extradition of criminals not inconsistent herewith shall apply to any such demand although the person whose surrender is demanded was not in the demanding state at the time of the commission of the crime and although he had not fled therefrom. Neither the demand, the oath nor any proceedings for extradition pursuant to this section need state or show that the person whose surrender is demanded has fled from justice, or at the time of the commission of the crime was in the demanding or other state.

SECTION 6. [*Conditions of Interstate Rendition.*]

(a) Before making the demand on the Governor of any other state for the surrender of a person charged in this state with the crime of failing to provide for the support of any person, the Governor of this state may require any [prosecuting attorney][1] of this state to satisfy him that at least [sixty] days prior thereto the obligee brought an action for the support under this act, or that the bringing of an action would be of no avail.

(b) When, under this or a substantially similar act, a demand is made upon the Governor of this state by the Governor of another state for the surrender of a person charged in the other state with the crime of failing to provide support, the Governor may call upon any [prosecuting attorney] to investigate or assist in investigating the demand, and to report to him whether any action for support has been brought under this act or would be effective.

---

[1]Where prosecuting attorney is set out in brackets, it is contemplated that the enacting state will insert the name of the proper officer.

(c) If an action for the support would be effective and no action has been brought, the Governor may delay honoring the demand for a reasonable time to permit prosecution of an action for support.

(d) If an action for support has been brought and the person demanded has prevailed in that action, the Governor may decline to honor the demand.

(e) If an action for support has been brought and pursuant thereto the Person demanded is subject to a support order, the Governor may decline to honor the demand so long as the person demanded is complying with the support order.

PART III CIVIL ENFORCEMENT

SECTION 7. [*Choice of Law.*] Duties of support applicable under this law [act] are those imposed or imposable under the laws of any state where the obligor was present during.the period for which support is sought. The obligor is presumed to have been present in the responding state during the period for which support is sought until otherwise shown.

SECTION 8. [*Remedies of a State or Political Subdivision Thereof Furnishing Support.*] Whenever the state or a political subdivision thereof furnishes support; to an obligee, it has the same right to invoke the provisions hereof as the obligee to whom the support was furnished for the purpose of securing reimbursement of expenditures so made and of obtaining continuing support.

SECTION 9. [*How Duties of Support Are Enforced.*] All duties of support, including arrearages, are enforceable by action irrespective of the relationship between the obligor and the obligee.

SECTION 10. [*Jurisdiction.*] Jurisdiction of all proceedings here under is vested in the [here insert title of court desired].

SECTION 11. [*Contents of [Complaint] for Support.*] The [complaint][2] shall be verified and shall state the name and, so far as known to the [complainant][2], the address and circumstances of the [respondent][2] and his dependents for whom support is sought and all other pertinent information. The [complainant] may include in or attach to the [complaint] any information which may help in locating or identifying the [respondent] such as a photograph of the [respondent], a description of any distinguishing marks of his person, other names and aliases by which he has been or is known, the name of his employer, his fingerprints, or Social Security number.

SECTION 12. [*Officials to Represent [Complainant].*] The [prosecuting attorney], upon the request of the court [a state department of welfare, a county commissioner, an overseer of the poor, or other local welfare official], shall represent the [complainant] in any proceeding under this act.

SECTION 13. [*Complainant for a Minor.*] A [complaint] on behalf of a minor obligee may be brought by a person having legal custody of the minor without appointment as guardian ad litem.

SECTION 14. [*Duty of Court of This State as Initiating State.*] If the court of this state acting as an initiating state finds that the petition sets forth facts from which it may be determined that the [respondent] owes a duty of support and that a

---

[2]Where complainant and respondent are set out in brackets, it is contemplated that the proper description of the parties and pleadings under local practice be inserted.

court of the responding state may obtain jurisdiction of the defendant or his property, it shall so certify and shall cause three copies of (1) the [complaint], (2) its certificate and (3) this act to be transmitted to the court in the responding state. If the name and address of such court is unknown and the responding state has an information agency comparable to that established in the initiating state it shall cause such copies to be transmitted to the state information agency or other proper official of the responding state, with a request that it forward them to the proper court, and that the court of the responding state acknowledge their receipt to the court of the initiating state.

SECTION 15. [*Costs and Fees.*] There shall be no filing fee or other costs taxable to the obligee but a court of this state acting either as an initiating or responding state may in its discretion direct that any part of or all fees and costs incurred in this state, including without limitation by enumeration, fees for filing, service of process, seizure of property, and stenographic service of both [complainant] and [respondent] or either be paid by the obligor or the [county, city, municipality, state or other political subdivision thereof].

SECTION 16. [*Jurisdiction by Arrest.*] When the court of this state, acting either as an initiating or responding state, has reason to believe that the [respondent] may flee the jurisdiction it may

(1) as an initiating state request in its certificate that the court of the responding state obtain the body of the defendant by appropriate process if that be permissible under the law of the responding state or

(2) as a responding state, obtain the body of the [respondent] by appropriate process

SECTION 17. [*State Information Agency.*] The [Attorney General][3] is hereby designated as the State Information Agency under this act, and he shall

(1) compile a list of the courts and their addresses in this state having jurisdiction under this act and transmit the same to the State Information Agency of every other state which has adopted this or a substantially similar act, and

(2) maintain a register of such lists received from other states and transmit copies thereof as soon as possible after receipt to every court in this state having jurisdiction under this act.

SECTION 18. [*Duty of the Court and Officials of This State as Responding State.*]

(a) After the court of this state acting as a responding state has received from the court of the initiating state the aforesaid copies the clerk of the court shall docket the cause and notify the [prosecuting attorney] of his action.

(b) It shall be the duty of the [prosecuting attorney] diligently to prosecute the case. He shall take all action necessary in accordance with the laws of this state to give the court jurisdiction of the [respondent] or his property and shall request the court [clerk of the court] to set a time and place for a hearing.

---

[3]The name of an appropriate official or agency may be inserted in place of the Attorney General.

SECTION 19. [*Further Duties of Court and Officials in the Responding State.*]

(a) The [prosecuting attorney] shall, on his own initiative, use all means at his disposal to trace the [respondent] or his property and if, due to inaccuracies of the [complaint] or otherwise, the court cannot obtain jurisdiction, the [prosecuting attorney] shall inform the court of what he has done and request the court to continue the case pending receipt of more accurate information or an amended [complaint] from the court in the initiating state.

(b) If the [respondent] or his property is not found in the county [judicial district] and the [prosecuting attorney] discovers by any means that the [respondent] or his property may be found in another county [judicial district] of this state or in another state he shall so inform the court and thereupon the clerk of the court shall forward the documents received from the court in the initiating state to a court in the other county [judicial district] or to a court in the other state or to the information agency or other proper official of the other state with a request that it forward the documents to the proper court. Thereupon both the court of the other county and any court of this state receiving the documents and the [prosecuting attorney] have the same powers and duties under this act as if the documents had been originally addressed to them. When the clerk of a court of this state retransmits documents to another court, he shall notify forthwith the court from which the documents came.

(c) If the [prosecuting attorney] has no information as to the whereabouts of the obligor or his property he shall so inform the initiating court.

SECTION 20. [*Procedure.*] The court shall conduct proceedings under this act in the manner prescribed by law for an action for enforcement of the type of duty of support claimed.]

SECTION 21. [*Hearing and Determination.*] If the [complainant] is absent from the responding state and the [respondent] presents evidence which constitutes a defense, the court shall continue the case for further hearing and the submission of evidence by both parties.

SECTION 22. [*Evidence of Husband and Wife.*] Laws attaching a privilege against the disclosure of communications between husband and wife are inapplicable to proceedings under this act. Husband and wife are competent witnesses [and may be compelled] to testify to any relevant matter, including marriage and parentage.

SECTION 23. [*Rules of Evidence.*] In any hearing under this law, the court shall be bound by the same rules of evidence that bind the [here insert the name of some court in the state that has relaxed the requirement that the technical rules of evidence must be followed, such as the Juvenile Court, the Domestic Relations Court].

SECTION 24. [*Order of Support.*] If the court of the responding state finds a duty of support, it may order the [respondent] to furnish support or reimbursement therefor and subject the property of the [respondent] to such order. [The court and [prosecuting attorney] of any county where the obligor is present or has property have the same powers and duties to enforce the order as have those of the county where it was first issued. If enforcement is impossible or cannot be completed in the county where the order was issued, the [prosecuting attorney] shall transmit a certified copy of the order to the [prosecuting attorney] of any county where it appears that procedures to enforce payment of the amount due would be effective. The [prosecuting attorney] to whom the certified copy of the order is forwarded shall proceed with enforcement and report the results of the proceedings to the court first issuing the order.]

SECTION 25. [*Responding State to Transmit Copies to Initiating State.*] The court of this state when acting as a responding state shall cause to be transmitted to the court of the initiating state a copy of all orders of support or for reimbursement therefor.

SECTION 26. [*Additional Powers of Court.*] In addition to the foregoing powers, the court of this state when acting as the responding state has the power to subject the [respondent] to such terms and conditions as the court may deem proper to assure compliance with its orders and in particular

(a) To require the [respondent] to furnish recognizance in the form of a cash deposit or bond of such character and in such amount as the court may deem proper to assure payment of any amount required to be paid by the [respondent].

(b) To require the [respondent] to make payments at specified intervals to the clerk [probation department] [bureau] of the court and to report personally to such clerk [probation department] [bureau] at such times as may be deemed necessary.

(c) To punish the [respondent] who shall violate any order of the court to the same extent as is provided by law for contempt of the court in any other suit or proceeding cognizable by the court.

SECTION 27. [*Additional Duties of the Court of This State When Acting as a Responding State.*] The court of this state when acting as a responding state shall have the following duties which may be carried out through the clerk [probation department] [bureau] of the court:

(a) Upon the receipt of a payment made by the [respondent] pursuant to any order of the court or otherwise, to transmit the same forthwith to the court of the initiating state, and

(b) Upon request, to furnish to the court of the initiating state a certified statement of all payments made by the [respondent].

SECTION 28. [*Additional Duty of the Court of the State When Acting as an Initiating State.*] The courts of this state when acting as an initiating state shall have the duty which may be carried out through the clerk [probation department] [bureau] of the court to receive and disburse forthwith all payments made by the [respondent] or transmitted by the court of the responding state.

SECTION 29. [*Proceedings Not to Be Stayed.*] No proceeding under this act shall be stayed because of the existence of a pending [action] for divorce, separation, annulment, dissolution, habeas corpus or custody proceeding.

SECTION 30. [*Application of Payments.*] No order of support issued by a court of this state when acting as a responding state shall supersede any other order of support but the amounts for a particular period paid pursuant to either order shall be credited against amounts accruing or accrued for the same period under both.

SECTION 31. [*Effect of Participation in Proceeding.*] Participation in any proceeding under this act shall not confer upon any court jurisdiction of any of the parties thereto in any other proceeding.]

[SECTION 32. [*Inter-County Application.*] This act is applicable when both the [complainant] and the [respondent] are in this state but in different counties. If the court of the county in which this petition is filed finds that the petition sets forth facts from which it may be determined that the [respondent] owes a duty of support and finds that a court of another county in this state may obtain jurisdiction of the [respondent] or his property, the clerk of the court shall send three copies of the [complaint] and a certification of the findings to the court of the county in which the [respondent] or his property is found. The clerk of the court of the county receiving these copies shall notify the [prosecuting attorney] of their receipt. The [prosecuting attorney] and the court in the county to which the copies are forwarded shall then have duties corresponding to those imposed upon them when acting for the state as a responding state.]

PART IV REGISTRATION OF FOREIGN SUPPORT ORDERS

SECTION 33. [*Additional Remedies.*] If the duty of support is based on a foreign support order, the obligee has the additional remedies provided in the following sections.

SECTION 34. [*Registration.*] The obligee may register the foreign support order in a court of this state in the manner, with the effect and for the purpose herein provided.

SECTION 35. [*Registry of Foreign Support Orders.*] The clerk of the court shall maintain a Registry of Foreign Support Orders in which he shall record [file] foreign support orders.

SECTION 36. [*Petition for Registration.*] The petition for registration shall be verified and shall set forth the amount remaining unpaid and a list of any other states in which the support order is registered and shall have attached to it a certified copy of the support order with all modifications thereof. The foreign support order is registered upon the filing of the [complaint] subject only to subsequent order of confirmation.

SECTION 37. [*Jurisdiction and Procedure.*] The procedure to obtain jurisdiction of the person or property of the obligor shall be as provided in civil cases. The obligor may assert any defense available to a defendant in an action on a foreign judgment. If the obligor defaults, the court shall enter an order confirming the registered support order and determining the amounts remaining unpaid. If the obligor appears and a hearing is held, the court shall adjudicate the issues including the amounts remaining unpaid.

SECTION 38. [*Effect and Enforcement.*] The support order as confirmed shall have the same effect and may be enforced as if originally entered in the court of this state. The procedures for the enforcement thereof, shall be as in civil cases, including the power to punish the [respondent] for contempt as in the case of other orders for payment of alimony, maintenance or support entered in this state.

SECTION 39. [*Severability.*] If any provision of this Act or the application thereof to any person or circumstance is held invalid the invalidity shall not affect other provisions or applications of the act which can be given effect without the invalid provision or application, and to this end the provisions of this act are severable.

SECTION 40. [*Repealer.*] The following acts are hereby repealed:

(Enumeration)

SECTION 41. [*Uniformity of Interpretation.*] This act shall be so construed as to effectuate its general purpose to make uniform the law of those states which enact it.

SECTION 42. [*Short Title.*] This act may be cited as the Uniform Reciprocal Enforcement of Support Act.

SECTION 43. [*Time of Taking Effect.*] This act shall take effect on
_____.

_____

Used with permission of National Conference of Commissioners on Uniform State Laws.

APPENDIX E

REVISED UNIFORM RECIPROCAL ENFORCEMENT OF SUPPORT ACT (1968)

PART 1 GENERAL PROVISIONS

SECTION 1. [*Purposes.*] The purposes of this Act are to improve and extend by reciprocal legislation the enforcement of duties of support.

SECTION 2. [*Definitions.*]

(a) 'Court' means the [here insert name] court of this State and when the context requires means the court of any other state as defined in a substantially similar reciprocal law.

(b) 'Duty of support' means a duty of support whether imposed or imposable by law or by order, decree, or judgment of any court, whether interlocutory or final or whether incidental to an action for divorce, separation, separate maintenance, or otherwise and includes the duty to pay arrearages of support past due and unpaid.

(c) 'Governor' includes any person performing the functions of Governor or the executive authority of any state covered by this Act.

(d) 'Initiating state' means a state in which a proceeding pursuant to this or a substantially similar reciprocal law is commenced. 'Initiating court' means the court in which a proceeding is commenced.

(e) 'Law' includes both common and statutory law.

(f) 'Obligee' means a person including a state or political subdivision to whom a duty of support is owed or a person including a state or political subdivision that has commenced a proceeding for enforcement of an alleged duty of support or for registration of a support order. It is immaterial if the person to whom a duty of support is owed is a recipient of public assistance.

(g) 'Obligor' means any person owing a duty of support or against whom a proceeding for the enforcement of a duty of support or registration of a support order is commenced.

(h) 'Prosecuting attorney' means the public official in the appropriate place who has the duty to enforce criminal laws relating to the failure to provide for the support of any person.

(i) 'Register' means to [record] [file] in the Registry of Foreign Support Orders.

(j) 'Registering court' means any court of this State in which a support order of a rendering state is registered.

(k) 'Rendering state' means a state in which the court has issued a support order for which registration is sought or granted in the court of another state.

(1) 'Responding state' means a state in which any responsive proceeding pursuant to the proceeding in the initiating state is commenced. 'Responding court' means the court in which the responsive proceeding is commenced.

(m) 'State' includes a state, territory, or possession of the United States, the District of Columbia, the Commonwealth of Puerto Rico, and any foreign jurisdiction in which this or a substantially similar reciprocal law is in effect.

(n) 'Support order' means any judgment, decree, or order of support in favor of an obligee whether temporary or final, or subject to modification, revocation, or remission, regardless of the kind of action or proceeding in which it is entered.

SECTION 3. [*Remedies Additional to Those Now Existing.*] The remedies herein provided are in addition to and not in substitution for any other remedies.

SECTION 4. [*Extent of Duties of Support.*] Duties of support arising under the law of this State, when applicable under section, bind the obligor present in this State regardless of the presence or residence of the obligee.

Part II Criminal Behavior

SECTION 5. [*Interstate Rendition.*] The Governor of this State may

(1) demand of the Governor of another state the surrender of a person found in that state who is charged criminally in this State with failing to provide for the support of any person; or

(2) surrender on demand by the Governor of another state a person found in this State who is charged criminally in that state with failing to provide for the support of any person. Provisions or extradition of criminals not inconsistent with this Act apply to the demand even if the person whose surrender is demanded was not in the demanding state at the time of the commission of the crime and has not fled therefrom. The demand, the oath, and any proceedings for extradition pursuant to this section need not state or show that the person whose surrender is demanded has fled from justice or at, the time of the commission of the crime was in the demanding state.

SECTION 6. [*Conditions of Interstate Rendition.*]

(a) Before making the demand upon the Governor of another state for the surrender of a person charged criminally in this State with failing to provide for the support of a person, the Governor of this State may require any prosecuting attorney of this State to satisfy him that at least [60] days prior thereto the obligee initiated proceedings for support under this Act or that any proceeding would be of no avail.

(b) If, under a substantially similar Act, the Governor of another state makes a demand upon the Governor of this State for the surrender of a person charged criminally in that state with failure to provide for the support of a person, the Governor may require any prosecuting attorney to investigate the demand and to report to him whether proceedings for support have been initiated or would be effective. If it appears to the Governor that a proceeding would be effective but has not been initiated he may delay honoring the demand for a reasonable time to permit the initiation of a proceeding.

(c) If proceedings have been initiated and the person demanded has prevailed therein the Governor may decline to honor the demand. If the obligee prevailed and the person demanded is subject to a support order, the Governor may decline to honor the demand if the person demanded is complying with the support order.

PART III CIVIL ENFORCEMENT

SECTION 7. [*Choice of Law.*] Duties of support applicable under this Act are those imposed under the laws of any state where the obligor was present for the period during which support is sought. The obligor is presumed to have been present in the responding state during the period for which support is sought until otherwise shown.

SECTION 8. [*Remedies of State or Political Subdivision Furnishing Support.*] If a state or a political subdivision furnishes support to an individual obligee it has the same right to initiate a proceeding under this Act as the individual obligee for the purpose of securing reimbursement for support furnished and of obtaining continuing support.

SECTION 9. [*How Duties of Support Are Enforced.*] All duties of support, including the duty to pay arrearages, are enforceable by a proceeding under this Act including a proceeding for civil contempt. The defense that the parties are immune to suit because of their relationship as husband and wife or parent and child is not available to the obligor.

SECTION 10. [*Jurisdiction.*] Jurisdiction of any proceeding under this Act is vested in the [here insert title of court desired].

SECTION 11. [*Contents and Filing of [Petition] for Support; Venue.*]

(a) The [petition] shall be verified and shall state the name and, so far as known to the obligee, the address and circumstances of the obligor and the persons for whom support is sought, and all other pertinent information. The obligee may include in or attach to the [petition] any information which may help in locating or identifying the obligor including a photograph of the obligor, a description of any distinguishing marks on his person, other names and aliases by which he has been or is known, the name of his employer, his fingerprints, and his Social Security number.

(b) The [petition] may be filed in the appropriate court of any state in which the obligee resides. The court shall not decline or refuse to accept and forward the [petition] on the ground that it should be filed with some other court of this or any other state where there is pending another action for divorce, separation, annulment, dissolution, habeas corpus, adoption, or custody between the same parties or where another court has already issued a support order in some other proceeding and has retained jurisdiction for its enforcement.

COMMENT

Wherever in this Act the word "petition" appears the word may be changed to "complaint" or "declaration" or the like and the word "petitioner" may be changed to "complainant" to conform to local usage.

SECTION 12. [*Officials to Represent Obligee.*] If this State is acting as an initiating state the prosecuting attorney upon the request of the court [a state department of welfare, a county commissioner, an overseer of the poor, or other local welfare officer] shall represent the obligee in any proceeding under this Act. [If the prosecuting attorney neglects or refuses to represent the obligee the [Attorney General] may order him to comply with the request of the court or may undertake the representation.] [If the prosecuting attorney neglects or refuses to represent the obligee, the [Attorney General] [State Director of Public Welfare] may undertake the representation.]

COMMENT

The first bracketed sentence is to be used in states where the Attorney General has supervisory powers over the prosecuting attorney; whereas, the second bracketed sentence is to be used if he does not have such powers.

SECTION 13. [*Petition for a Minor.*] A [petition] on behalf of a minor obligee may be executed and filed by a person having legal custody of the minor without appointment as guardian ad litem.

SECTION 14. [*Duty of Initiating Court.*] If the initiating court finds that the [petition] sets forth facts from which it may be determined that the obligor owes a duty of support and that a court of the responding state may obtain jurisdiction of the obligor or his property it shall so certify and cause 3 copies of the [petition] and its certificate and one copy of this Act to be sent to the responding court. Certification shall be in accordance with the requirements of the initiating state. If the name and address of the responding court is unknown and the responding state has an information agency comparable to that established in the initiating state it shall cause the copies to be sent to the state information agency or other proper official of the responding state, with a request that the agency or official forward them to the proper court and that the court of the responding state acknowledge their receipt to the initiating court.

SECTION 15. [*Costs and Fees.*] An initiating court shall not require payment of either a filing fee or other costs from the obligee but may request the responding court to collect fees and costs from the obligor. A responding court shall not require payment of a filing fee or other costs from the obligee but it may direct that all fees and costs requested by the initiating court and incurred in this State when acting as a responding state, including fees for filing of pleadings, service of process, seizure of property, stenographic or duplication service, or other service supplied to the obligor, be paid in whole or in part by the obligor or by the [state or political subdivision thereof]. These costs or fees do not have priority over amounts due to the obligee.

SECTION 16. [*Jurisdiction by Arrest.*] If the court of this State believes that the obligor may flee it may

(1) as an initiating court, request in its certificate that the responding court obtain the body of the obligor by appropriate process; or

(2) as a responding court, obtain the body of the obligor by appropriate process. Thereupon it may release him upon his own recognizance or upon his giving a bond in an amount set by the court to assure his appearance at the hearing.

SECTION 17. [*State Information Agency.*]

(a) The [Attorney General's Office, State Attorney's Office, Welfare Department or other Information Agency] is designated as the state information agency under this Act, it shall

(1) compile a list of the courts and their addresses in this State having jurisdiction under this Act and transmit it to the state information agency of every other state which has adopted this or a substantially similar Act. Upon the adjournment of each session of the [legislature] the agency shall distribute copies of any amendments to the Act and a statement of their effective date to all other state information agencies;

(2) maintain a register of lists of courts received from other states and transmit copies thereof promptly to every court in this state having jurisdiction under this Act; and

(3) forward to the court in this State which has jurisdiction over the obligor or his property petitions, certificates, and copies of the Act it receives from courts or information agencies of other states.

(b) If the state information agency does not know the location of the obligor or his property in the state and no state location service is available it shall use all means at its disposal to obtain this information, including the examination of official records in the state and other sources such as telephone directories, real property records, vital statistics records, police records, requests for the name and address from employers who are able or willing to cooperate, records of motor vehicle license offices, requests made to the tax offices both state and federal where such offices are able to cooperate, and requests made to the Social Security Administration as permitted by the Social Security Act as amended.

(c) After the deposit of 3 copies of the [petition] and certificate and one copy of the Act of the initiating state with the clerk of the appropriate court, if the state information agency knows or believes that the prosecuting attorney is not prosecuting the case diligently it shall inform the [Attorney General] [State Director of Public Welfare] who may undertake the representation.

SECTION 18. [*Duty of the Court and Officials of This State as Responding State.*]

(a) After the responding court receives copies of the [petition], certificate, and Act from the initiating court the clerk of the court shall docket the case and notify the prosecuting attorney of this action.

(b) The prosecuting attorney shall prosecute the case diligently. He shall take all action necessary in accordance with the laws of this State to enable the court to obtain jurisdiction over the obligor or his property and shall request the court [clerk of the court] to set a time and place for a hearing and give notice thereof to the obligor in accordance with law.

(c) [If the prosecuting attorney neglects or refuses to represent the obligee the [Attorney General] may order him to comply with the request of the court or may undertake the representation.] [If the prosecuting attorney neglects or refuses to represent the obligee, the [Attorney General] [State Director of Public Welfare] may undertake the representation.]

COMMENT

The first bracketed sentence is to be used in states where the Attorney General has supervisory powers over the prosecuting attorney; whereas, the second bracketed sentence is to be used if he does not have such powers.

SECTION 19. [*Further Duties of Court and Officials in the Responding State.*]

(a) The prosecuting attorney on his own initiative shall use all means at his disposal to locate the obligor or his property, and if because of inaccuracies in the [petition] or otherwise the court cannot obtain jurisdiction the prosecuting attorney shall inform the court of what he has done and request the court to continue the case pending receipt of more accurate information or an amended [petition] from the initiating court.

(b) If the obligor or his property is not found in the [county], and the prosecuting attorney discovers that the obligor or his property may be found in another [county] of this State or in another state he shall so inform the court. Thereupon the clerk of the court shall forward the documents received from the court in the initiating state to a court in the other [county] or to a court in the other state or to the information agency or other proper official of the other state with a request that the documents be forwarded to the proper court. All powers and duties provided by this Act apply to the recipient of the documents so forwarded. If the clerk of a court of this State forwards documents to another court he shall forthwith notify the initiating court.

(c) If the prosecuting attorney has no information as to the location of the obligor or his property he shall so inform the initiating court.

SECTION 20. [*Hearing and Continuance.*] If the obligee is not present at the hearing and the obligor denies owing the duty of support alleged in the petition or offers evidence constituting a defense, the court, upon request of either party, shall continue the hearing to permit evidence relative to the duty to be adduced by either party by deposition or by appearing in person before the court. The court may designate the judge of the initiating court as a person before whom a deposition may be taken.

SECTION 21. [*Immunity from Criminal Prosecution.*] If at the hearing the obligor is called for examination as an adverse party and he declines to answer upon the ground that his testimony may tend to incriminate him, the court may require him to answer, in which event he is immune from criminal prosecution with respect to matters revealed by his testimony, except for perjury committed in this testimony.

SECTION 22. [*Evidence of Husband and Wife.*] Laws attaching a privilege against the disclosure of communications between husband and wife are inapplicable to proceedings under this Act. Husband and wife are competent witnesses [and may be compelled] to testify to any relevant matter, including marriage and parentage.

SECTION 23. [*Rules of Evidence.*] In any hearing for the civil enforcement of this Act the court is governed by the rules of evidence applicable in a civil court action in the Court. If the action is based on a support order issued by another court a certified copy of the order shall be received as evidence of the duty of support, subject only to any defenses available to an obligor with respect to paternity (Section 27) or to a defendant in an action or a proceeding to enforce a foreign money judgment. The determination or enforcement of a duty of support owed to one obligee is unaffected by any interference by another obligee with rights of custody or visitation granted by a court.

SECTION 24. [*Order of Support.*] If the responding court finds a duty of support it may order the obligor to furnish support or reimbursement therefor and subject the property of the obligor to the order. Support orders made pursuant to this Act shall require that payments be made to the [clerk] [bureau] [probation department] of the court of the responding state. [The court and prosecuting attorney of any [county] in which the obligor is present or has property have the same powers and duties to enforce the order as have those of the [county] in which it was first issued. If enforcement is impossible or cannot be completed in the [county] in which the order was issued, the prosecuting attorney shall send a certified copy of the order to the prosecuting attorney of any [county] in which it appears that proceedings to enforce the order would be effective. The prosecuting attorney to whom the certified copy of the order is forwarded shall proceed with enforcement and report the results of the proceedings to the court first issuing the order.]

SECTION 25. [*Responding Court to Transmit Initiating Court.*] The responding court shall cause a support order to be sent to the initiating court.

SECTION 26. [*Additional Powers of Responding Court.*] In addition to the foregoing powers a responding court may subject the obligor to any terms and conditions proper to assure compliance with its orders and in particular to:

(1) require the obligor to furnish a cash deposit or a bond of a character and amount to assure payment of any amount due;

(2) require the obligor to report personally and to make payments at specified intervals to the [clerk] [bureau] [probation department] of the court; and

(3) punish under the power of contempt the obligor who violates any order of the court.

SECTION 27. [*Paternity.*] If the obligor asserts as a defense that he is not the father of the child for whom support is sought and it appears to the court that the defense is not frivolous, and if both of the parties are present at the hearing or the proof required in the case indicates that the presence of either or both of the parties is not necessary, the court may adjudicate the paternity issue. Otherwise the court may adjourn the hearing until the paternity issue has been adjudicated.

SECTION 28. [*Additional Duties of Responding Court.*] A responding court has the following duties which may be carried out through the [clerk] [bureau] [probation department] of the court:

(1) to transmit to the initiating court any payment made by the obligor pursuant to any order of the court or otherwise; and

(2) to furnish to the initiating court upon request a certified statement of all payments made by the obligor.

SECTION 29. [*Additional Duty of Initiating Court.*] An initiating court shall receive and disburse forthwith all payments made by the obligor or sent by the responding court. This duty may be carried out through the [clerk] [bureau] [probation department] of the court.

SECTION 30. [*Proceedings Not to Be Stayed.*] A responding court shall not stay the proceeding or refuse a hearing under this Act because of any pending or prior action or proceeding for divorce, separation, annulment, dissolution, habeas corpus, adoption, or custody in this or any other state. The court shall hold a hearing and may issue a support order pendente lite. In aid thereof it may require the obligor to give a bond for the prompt prosecution of the pending proceeding. If the other action or proceeding is concluded before the hearing in the instant proceeding and the judgment therein provides for the support demanded in the [petition] being heard the court must conform its support order to the amount allowed in the other action or proceeding. Thereafter the court shall not stay enforcement of its support order because of the retention of jurisdiction for enforcement purposes by the court in the other action or proceeding.

SECTION 31. [*Application of Payments.*] A support order made by a court of this State pursuant to this Act does not nullify and is not nullified by a support order made by a court of this State pursuant to any other law or by a support order made by a court of any other state pursuant to a substantially similar act or any other law, regardless of priority of issuance, unless otherwise specifically provided by the court. Amounts paid for a particular period pursuant to any support order made by the court of another state shall be credited against the amounts accruing or accrued for the same period under any support order made by the court of this State.

[SECTION 32. [*Effect of Participation in Proceedings.*] Participation in any proceeding under this Act does not confer jurisdiction upon any court over any of the parties thereto in any other proceeding.]

[SECTION 33. [*Intrastate Application.*]This Act applies if both the obligee and the obligor are in this State but in different [counties]. If the court of the [county] in which the [petition] is filed finds that the [petition] sets forth facts from which it may be determined that the obligor owes a duty of support and finds that a court of another [county] in this State may obtain jurisdiction over the obligor or his property, the clerk of the court shall send the [petition] and a certification of the findings to the court of the [county] in which the obligor or his property is found. The clerk of the court of the [county] receiving these documents shall notify the prosecuting attorney of their receipt. The prosecuting attorney and the court in the [county] to which the copies are forwarded then shall have duties corresponding to those imposed upon them when acting for this State as a responding state.]

SECTION 34. [*Appeals.*] If the [Attorney General] [State Director of Public Welfare] is of the opinion that a support order is erroneous and presents a question of law warranting an appeal in the public interest, he may

(a) perfect an appeal to the proper appellate court if the support order was issued by a court of this State, or

(b) if the support order was issued in another state, cause the appeal to be taken in the other state. In either case expenses of appeal may be paid on his order from funds appropriated for his office.

PART IV REGISTRATION OF FOREIGN SUPPORT ORDERS

SECTION 35. [*Additional Remedies.*] If the duty of support is based on a foreign support order, the obligee has the additional remedies provided in the following sections.

COMMENT

The language of the last sentence is permissive and so does not preclude other arrangements for the payment of the expenses of appeal. If it is thought desirable to spell out particular methods of payment this may be done.

SECTION 36. [*Registration.*] The obligee may register the foreign support order in a court of this State in the manner, with the effect, and for the purposes herein provided.

SECTION 37. [*Registry of Foreign Support Orders.*] The clerk of the court shall maintain a Registry of Foreign Support Orders in which he shall [file] foreign support orders.

SECTION 38. [*Official to Represent Obligee.*] If this State is acting either as a rendering or a registering state the prosecuting attorney upon the request of the court [a state department of welfare, a county commissioner, an overseer of the poor, or other local welfare officials shall represent the obligee in proceedings under this Part.

[If the prosecuting attorney neglects or refuses to represent the obligee, the [Attorney General] may order him to comply with the request of the court or may undertake the representation.] [If the prosecuting. attorney neglects or refuses to represent the obligee, the [Attorney General] [State Director of Public Welfare] may undertake the representation.]

COMMENT

The first bracketed sentence is to be used in states where the Attorney General has supervisory powers over the prosecuting attorney; whereas, the second bracketed sentence is to be used if he does not have such powers.

SECTION 39. [*Registration Procedure; Notice.*]

(a) An obligee seeking to register a foreign support order in a court of this State shall transmit to the clerk of the court (1) three certified copies of the order with all modification thereof, (2) one copy of the reciprocal enforcement of support act of the state in which the order was made, and (3) a statement verified and signed by the obligee, showing the post office address of the obligee, the last known place of residence and post office address of the obligor, the amount of support remaining unpaid, a description and the location of any property of the obligor available upon execution, and a list of the states in which the order is registered. Upon receipt of these documents the clerk of the court, without payment of a filing fee or other cost to the obligee, shall file them in the Registry of Foreign Support Orders. The filing constitutes registration under this Act.

(b) Promptly upon registration the clerk of the court shall send by certified or registered mail to the obligor at the address given a notice of the registration with a copy of the registered support order and the post office address of the obligee. He shall also docket the case and notify the prosecuting attorney of his action. The prosecuting attorney shall proceed diligently to enforce the order.

SECTION 40. [*Effect of Registration; Enforcement Procedure.*]

(a) Upon registration the registered foreign support order shall be treated in the same manner as a support order issued by a court of this State. It has the same effect and is subject to the same procedures, defenses, and proceedings for reopening, vacating, or staying as a support order of this State and may be enforced and satisfied in like manner.

(b) The obligor has [20] days after the mailing of notice of the registration in which to petition the court to vacate the registration or for other relief. If he does not so petition the registered support order is confirmed.

(c) At the hearing to enforce the registered support order the obligor may present only matters that would be available to him as defenses in an action to enforce a foreign money judgment. If he shows to the court that an appeal from the order is pending or will be taken or that a stay of execution has been granted the court shall stay enforcement of the order until the appeal is concluded, the time for appeal has expired, or the order is vacated, upon satisfactory proof that the obligor has furnished security for payment of the support ordered as required by the rendering state. If he shows to the court any ground upon which enforcement of a support order of this State may be stayed the court shall stay enforcement of the order for an appropriate period if the obligor furnishes the same security for payment of the support ordered that is required for a support order of this State.

SECTION 41. [*Uniformity of Interpretation.*] This Act shall be construed as to effectuate its general purpose to make uniform the law of those states which enact it.

SECTION 42. [*Short Title.*] This Act may be cited as the Revised Uniform Reciprocal Enforcement of Support Act (1968).

SECTION 43. [*Severability.*] If any provision of this Act or the application thereof to any person or circumstance is held invalid, the invalidity does not affect other provisions or applications of the Act which can be given without the invalid provision or application, and to this end the provisions of this Act are severable.

F APPENDIX

UNIFORM INTERSTATE FAMILY SUPPORT ACT (1996)

ARTICLE 1. GENERAL PROVISIONS

SECTION 101. DEFINITIONS. In this [Act]:

(1) 'Child' means an individual, whether over or under the age of majority, who is or is alleged to be owed a duty of support by the individual's parent or who is or is alleged to be the beneficiary of a support order directed to the parent.

(2) 'Child-support order' means a support order for a child, including a child who has attained the age of majority under the law of the issuing State.

(3) 'Duty of support' means an obligation imposed or imposable by law to provide support for a child, spouse, or former spouse, including an unsatisfied obligation to provide support.

(4) 'Home State' means the State in which a child lived with a parent or a person acting as parent for at least six consecutive months immediately preceding the time of filing of a [petition] or comparable pleading for support and, if a child is less than six months old, the State in which the child lived from birth with any of them. A period of temporary absence of any of them is counted as part of the six-month or other period.

(5) 'Income' includes earnings or other periodic entitlements to money from any source and any other property subject to withholding for support under the law of this State.

(6) 'Income-withholding order' means an order or other legal process directed to an obligor's employer [or other debtor], as defined by [the income-withholding law of this State], to withhold support from the income of the obligor.

(7) 'Initiating State' means a State from which a proceeding is forwarded or in which a proceeding is filed for forwarding to a responding State under this [Act] or a law or procedure substantially similar to this [Act], the Uniform Reciprocal Enforcement of Support Act, or the Revised Uniform Reciprocal Enforcement of Support Act.

(8) 'Initiating tribunal' means the authorized tribunal in an initiating State.

(9) 'Issuing State' means the State in which a tribunal issues a support order or renders a judgment determining parentage.

(10) 'Issuing tribunal' means the tribunal that issues a support order or renders a judgment determining parentage.

(11) 'Law' includes decisional and statutory law and rules and regulations having the force of law.

(12) 'Obligee' means:

    (i) an individual to whom a duty of support is or is alleged to be owed or in whose favor a support order has been issued or a judgment determining parentage has been rendered;

    (ii) a State or political subdivision to which the rights under a duty of support or support order have been assigned or which has independent claims based on financial assistance provided to an individual obligee; or

    (iii) an individual seeking a judgment determining parentage of the individual's child.

(13) 'Obligor' means an individual, or the estate of a decedent:

    (i) who owes or is alleged to owe a duty of support;

    (ii) who is alleged but has not been adjudicated to be a parent of a child; or

    (iii) who is liable under a support order.

(14) 'Register' means to [record; file] a support order or judgment determining parentage in the [appropriate location for the recording or filing of foreign judgments generally or foreign support orders specifically].

(15) 'Registering tribunal' means a tribunal in which a support order is registered.

(16) 'Responding State' means a State in which a proceeding is filed or to which a proceeding is forwarded for filing from an initiating State under this [Act] or a law or procedure substantially similar to this [Act], the Uniform Reciprocal Enforcement of Support Act, or the Revised Uniform Reciprocal Enforcement of Support Act.

(17) 'Responding tribunal' means the authorized tribunal in a responding State.

(18) 'Spousal-support order' means a support order for a spouse or former spouse of the obligor.

(19) 'State' means a State of the United States, the District of Columbia, Puerto Rico, the United States Virgin Islands, or any territory or insular possession subject to the jurisdiction of the United States. The term includes:

    (i) an Indian tribe; and

    (ii) a foreign jurisdiction that has enacted a law or established procedures for issuance and enforcement of support orders which are substantially similar to the procedures under this [Act], the Uniform Reciprocal Enforcement of Support Act, or the Revised Uniform Reciprocal Enforcement of Support Act.

(20) 'Support enforcement-agency' means a public official or agency authorized to seek:

    (i) enforcement of support orders or laws relating to the duty of support;

    (ii) establishment or modification of child support;

    (iii) determination of parentage; or

    (iv) to locate obligors or their assets.

(21) 'Support order' means a judgment, decree, or order, whether temporary, final, or subject to modification, for the benefit of a child, a spouse, or a former spouse, which provides for monetary support, health care, arrearages, or reimbursement, and may include related costs and fees, interest, income withholding, attorney's fees, and other relief.

(22) 'Tribunal' means a court, administrative agency, or quasi-judicial entity authorized to establish, enforce, or modify support orders or to determine parentage.

SECTION 102. TRIBUNAL OF STATE. The [court, administrative agency, quasi-judicial entity, or combination] [is the tribunal] [are the tribunals] of this State.

SECTION 103. REMEDIES CUMULATIVE. Remedies provided by this [Act] are cumulative and do not affect the availability of remedies under other law.

ARTICLE 2. JURISDICTION

Part 1. Extended Personal Jurisdiction

SECTION 201. BASES FOR JURISDICTION OVER NONRESIDENT. In a proceeding to establish, enforce, or modify a support order or to determine parentage, a tribunal of this State may exercise personal jurisdiction over a nonresident individual [or the individual's guardian or conservator] if:

(1) the individual is personally served with [citation, summons, notice] within this State;

(2) the individual submits to the jurisdiction of this State by consent, by entering a general appearance, or by filing a responsive document having the effect of waiving any contest to personal jurisdiction;

(3) the individual resided with the child in this State;

(4) the individual resided in this State and provided prenatal expenses or support for the child;

(5) the child resides in this State as a result of the acts or directives of the individual;

(6) the individual engaged in sexual intercourse in this State and the child may have been conceived by that act of intercourse;

(7) the individual asserted parentage in the [putative father registry] maintained in this State by the [appropriate agency]; or

(8) there is any other basis consistent with the constitutions of this State and the United States for the exercise of personal jurisdiction.

SECTION 202. PROCEDURE WHEN EXERCISING JURISDICTION OVER NONRESIDENT. A tribunal of this State exercising personal jurisdiction over a nonresident under Section 201 may apply Section 316 (Special Rules of Evidence and Procedure) to receive evidence from another State, and Section 318 (Assistance with Discovery) to obtain discovery through a tribunal of another

State. In all other respects, Articles 3 through 7 do not apply and the tribunal shall apply the procedural and substantive law of this State, including the rules on choice of law other than those established by this [Act].

Part 2. Proceedings Involving Two or More States

SECTION 203. INITIATING AND RESPONDING TRIBUNAL OF STATE. Under this [Act], a tribunal of this State may serve as an initiating tribunal to forward proceedings to another State and as a responding tribunal for proceedings initiated in another State.

SECTION 204. SIMULTANEOUS PROCEEDINGS IN ANOTHER STATE.

(a) A tribunal of this State may exercise jurisdiction to establish a support order if the [petition] or comparable pleading is filed after a pleading is filed in another State only if:

    (1) the [petition] or comparable pleading in this State is filed before the expiration of the time allowed in the other State for filing a responsive pleading challenging the exercise of jurisdiction by the other State;

    (2) the contesting party timely challenges the exercise of jurisdiction in the other State; and

    (3) if relevant, this State is the home State of the child.

(b) A tribunal of this State may not exercise jurisdiction to establish a support order if the [petition] or comparable pleading is filed before a [petition] or comparable pleading is filed in another State if:

    (1) the [petition] or comparable pleading in the other State is filed before the expiration of the time allowed in this State for filing a responsive pleading challenging the exercise of jurisdiction by this State;

    (2) the contesting party timely challenges the exercise of jurisdiction in this State; and

    (3) if relevant, the other State is the home State of the child.

SECTION 205. CONTINUING, EXCLUSIVE JURISDICTION.

(a) A tribunal of this State issuing a support order consistent with the law of this State has continuing, exclusive jurisdiction over a child-support order:

    (1) as long as this State remains the residence of the obligor, the individual obligee, or the child for whose benefit the support order is issued; or

    (2) until all of the parties who are individuals have filed written consents with the tribunal of this State for a tribunal of another State to modify the order and assume continuing, exclusive jurisdiction.

(b) A tribunal of this State issuing a child-support order consistent with the law of this State may not exercise its continuing jurisdiction to modify the order if the order has been modified by a tribunal of another State pursuant to this [Act] or a law substantially similar to this [Act].

(c) If a child-support order of this State is modified by a tribunal of another State pursuant to this [Act] or a law substantially similar to this [Act], a tribunal of this State loses its continuing, exclusive jurisdiction with regard to prospective enforcement of the order issued in this State, and may only:

    (1) enforce the order that was modified as to amounts accruing before the modification;

(2) enforce nonmodifiable aspects of that order; and

(3) provide other appropriate relief for violations of that order which occurred before the effective date of the modification.

(d) A tribunal of this State shall recognize the continuing, exclusive jurisdiction of a tribunal of another State which has issued a child-support order pursuant to this [Act] or a law substantially similar to this [Act].

(e) A temporary support order issued ex parte or pending resolution of a jurisdictional conflict does not create continuing, exclusive jurisdiction in the issuing tribunal.

(f) A tribunal of this State issuing a support order consistent with the law of this State has continuing, exclusive jurisdiction over a spousal-support order throughout the existence of the support obligation. A tribunal of this State may not modify a spousal-support order issued by a tribunal of another State having continuing, exclusive jurisdiction over that order under the law of that State.

SECTION 206. ENFORCEMENT AND MODIFICATION OF SUPPORT ORDER BY TRIBUNAL HAVING CONTINUING JURISDICTION.

(a) A tribunal of this State may serve as an initiating tribunal to request a tribunal of another State to enforce or modify a support order issued in that State.

(b) A tribunal of this State having continuing, exclusive jurisdiction over a support order may act as a responding tribunal to enforce or modify the order. If a party subject to the continuing, exclusive jurisdiction of the tribunal no longer resides in the issuing State, in subsequent proceedings the tribunal may apply Section 316 (Special Rules of Evidence and Procedure) to receive evidence from another State and Section 318 (Assistance with Discovery) to obtain discovery through a tribunal of another State.

(c) A tribunal of this State which lacks continuing, exclusive jurisdiction over a spousal-support order may not serve as a responding tribunal to modify a spousal-support order of another State.

Part 3. Reconciliation of Multiple Orders

SECTION 207. RECOGNITION OF CONTROLLING CHILD-SUPPORT ORDER.

(a) If a proceeding is brought under this [Act] and only one tribunal has issued a child-support order, the order of that tribunal controls and must be so recognized.

(b) If a proceeding is brought under this [Act], and two or more child-support orders have been issued by tribunals of this State or another State with regard to the same obligor and child, a tribunal of this State shall apply the following rules in determining which order to recognize for purposes of continuing, exclusive jurisdiction:

(1) If only one of the tribunals would have continuing, exclusive jurisdiction under this [Act], the order of that tribunal controls and must be so recognized.

(2) If more than one of the tribunals would have continuing, exclusive jurisdiction under this [Act], an order issued by a tribunal in the cur-

rent home State of the child controls and must be so recognized, but if an order has not been issued in the current home State of the child, the order most recently issued controls and must be so recognized.

(3) If none of the tribunals would have continuing, exclusive jurisdiction under this [Act], the tribunal of this State having jurisdiction over the parties shall issue a child-support order, which controls and must be so recognized.

(c) If two or more child-support orders have been issued for the same obligor and child and if the obligor or the individual obligee resides in this State, a party may request a tribunal of this State to determine which order controls and must be so recognized under subsection (b). The request must be accompanied by a certified copy of every support order in effect. The requesting party shall give notice of the request to each party whose rights may be affected by the determination.

(d) The tribunal that issued the controlling order under subsection (a), (b), or (c) is the tribunal that has continuing, exclusive jurisdiction under Section 205.

(e) A tribunal of this State which determines by order the identity of the controlling order under subsection (b)(1) or (2) or which issues a new controlling order under subsection (b)(3) shall state in that order the basis upon which the tribunal made its determination.

(f) Within [30] days after issuance of an order determining the identity of the controlling order, the party obtaining the order shall file a certified copy of it with each tribunal that issued or registered an earlier order of child support. A party who obtains the order and fails to file a certified copy is subject to appropriate sanctions by a tribunal in which the issue of failure to file arises. The failure to file does not affect the validity or enforceability of the controlling order.

SECTION 208. MULTIPLE CHILD-SUPPORT ORDERS FOR TWO OR MORE OBLIGEES. In responding to multiple registrations or [petitions] for enforcement of two or more child-support orders in effect at the same time with regard to the same obligor and different individual obligees, at least one of which was issued by a tribunal of another State, a tribunal of this State shall enforce those orders in the same manner as if the multiple orders had been issued by a tribunal of this State.

SECTION 209. CREDIT FOR PAYMENTS. Amounts collected and credited for a particular period pursuant to a support order issued by a tribunal of another State must be credited against the amounts accruing or accrued for the same period under a support order issued by the tribunal of this State.

ARTICLE 3. CIVIL PROVISIONS OF GENERAL APPLICATION

SECTION 301. PROCEEDINGS UNDER [ACT].

(a) Except as otherwise provided in this [Act], this article applies to all proceedings under this [Act].

(b) This [Act] provides for the following proceedings:

(1) establishment of an order for spousal support or child support pursuant to Article 4;

(2) enforcement of a support order and income-withholding order of without registration pursuant to Article 5;

(3) registration of an order for spousal support or child support of another State for enforcement pursuant to Article 6;

(4) modification of an order for child support or spousal support tribunal of this State pursuant to Article 2, Part 2;

(5) registration of an order for child support of another State for pursuant to Article 6;

(6) determination of parentage pursuant to Article 7; and

(7) assertion of jurisdiction over nonresidents pursuant to Article 2, Part 1.

(c) An individual [petitioner] or a support enforcement agency may commence a proceeding authorized under this [Act] by filing a [petition] in an initiating tribunal for forwarding to a responding tribunal or by filing a [petition] or a comparable pleading directly in a tribunal of another State which has or can obtain personal jurisdiction over the [respondent].

SECTION 302. ACTION BY MINOR PARENT. A minor parent, or a guardian or other legal representative of a minor parent, may maintain a proceeding on behalf of or for the benefit of the minor child.

SECTION 303. APPLICATION OF LAW OF STATE. Except as otherwise provided by this [Act], a responding tribunal of this State:

(1) shall apply the procedural and substantive law, including the rules on choice of law, generally applicable to similar proceedings originating in this State and may exercise all powers and provide all remedies available in those proceedings; and

(2) shall determine the duty of support and the amount payable in accordance with the law and support guidelines of this State.

SECTION 304. DUTIES OF INITIATING TRIBUNAL.

(a) Upon the filing of a [petition] authorized by this [Act], an initiating tribunal of this State shall forward three copies of the [petition] and its accompanying documents:

(1) to the responding tribunal or appropriate support enforcement agency in the responding State; or

(2) if the identity of the responding tribunal is unknown, to the state information agency of the responding State with a request that they be forwarded to the appropriate tribunal and that receipt be acknowledged.

(b) If a responding State has not enacted this [Act] or a law or procedure substantially similar to this [Act], a tribunal of this State may issue a certificate or other document and make findings required by the law of the responding State. If the responding State is a foreign jurisdiction, the tribunal may specify the amount of support sought and provide other documents necessary to satisfy the requirements of the responding State.

SECTION 305. DUTIES AND POWERS OF RESPONDING TRIBUNAL.

(a) When a responding tribunal of this State receives a [petition] or comparable pleading from an initiating tribunal or directly pursuant to Section 301(c) (Proceedings Under this [Act]), it shall cause the [petition] for pleading to be filed and notify the [petitioner] where and when it was filed.

(b) A responding tribunal of this State, to the extent otherwise authorized by law, may do one or more of the following:

(1) issue or enforce a support order, modify a child-support order, or render a judgment to determine parentage;

(2) order an obligor to comply with a support order, specifying the amount and the manner of compliance;

(3) order income withholding;

(4) determine the amount of any arrearages, and specify a method of payment;

(5) enforce orders by civil or criminal contempt, or both;

(6) set aside property for satisfaction of the support order;

(7) place liens and order execution on the obligor's property;

(8) order an obligor to keep the tribunal informed of the obligor's current residential address, telephone number, employer, address of employment, and telephone number at the place of employment;

(9) issue a [bench warrant; capias] for an obligor who has failed after proper notice to appear at a hearing ordered by the tribunal and enter the [bench warrant; capias] in any local and state computer systems for criminal warrants;

(10) order the obligor to seek appropriate employment by specified methods;

(11) award reasonable attorney's fees and other fees and costs; and (12) grant any other available remedy.

(c) A responding tribunal of this State shall include in a support order issued under this [Act], or in the documents accompanying the order, the calculations on which the support order is based.

(d) A responding tribunal of this State may not condition the payment of a support order issued under this [Act] upon compliance by a party with provisions for visitation.

(e) If a responding tribunal of this State issues an order under this [Act], the tribunal shall send a copy of the order to the [petitioner] and the [respondent] and to the initiating tribunal, if any.

SECTION 306. INAPPROPRIATE TRIBUNAL. If a [petition] or a comparable pleading is received by an inappropriate tribunal of this State, it shall forward the pleading and accompanying documents to an appropriate tribunal in this State or another State and notify the [petitioner] where and when the pleading was sent.

SECTION 307. DUTIES OF SUPPORT ENFORCEMENT AGENCY.

(a) A support enforcement agency of this State, upon request, shall provide services to a [petitioner] in a proceeding under this [Act].

(b) A support enforcement agency that is providing services to the [petitioner] as appropriate shall:

(1) take all steps necessary to enable an appropriate tribunal in this State or another State to obtain jurisdiction over the [respondent];

(2) request an appropriate tribunal to set a date, time, and place for a hearing;

(3) make a reasonable effort to obtain all relevant information, including information as to income and property of the parties;

(4) within [two] days, exclusive of Saturdays, Sundays, and legal holidays, after receipt of a written notice from an initiating, responding, or registering tribunal, send a copy of the notice to the [petitioner];

(5) within [two] days, exclusive of Saturdays, Sundays, and legal holidays, after receipt of a written communication from the [respondent] or the [respondent's] attorney, send a copy of the communication to the [petitioner]; and

(6) notify the [petitioner] if jurisdiction over the [respondent] cannot be obtained.

(c) This [Act] does not create or negate a relationship of attorney and client or other fiduciary relationship between a support enforcement agency or the attorney for the agency and the individual being assisted by the agency.

SECTION 308. DUTY OF [ATTORNEY GENERAL]. If the [Attorney General] determines that the support enforcement agency is neglecting or refusing to provide services to an individual, the [Attorney General] may order the agency to perform its duties under this [Act] or may provide these services directly to the individual.

SECTION 309. PRIVATE COUNSEL. An individual may employ private counsel to represent the individual in proceedings authorized by this [Act].

SECTION 310. DUTIES OF [STATE INFORMATION AGENCY].

(a) The [Attorney General's Office, State Attorney's Office, State Central Registry or other information agency] is the state information agency under this [Act].

(b) The state information agency shall:

(1) compile and maintain a current list, including addresses, of the tribunals in this State which have jurisdiction under this [Act] and any support enforcement agencies in this State and transmit a copy to the state information agency of every other State;

(2) maintain a register of tribunals and support enforcement agencies received from other States;

(3) forward to the appropriate tribunal in the place in this State in which the individual obligee or the obligor resides, or in which the obligor's property is believed to be located, all documents concerning a proceeding under this [Act] received from an initiating tribunal or the state information agency of the initiating State; and

(4) obtain information concerning the location of the obligor and the obligor's property within this State not exempt from execution, by such means as postal verification and federal or state locator services, examination of telephone directories, requests for the obligor's address from employers, and examination of governmental records, including, to the extent not prohibited by other law, those relating to real property, vital statistics, law enforcement, taxation, motor vehicles, driver's licenses, and social security.

SECTION 311. PLEADINGS AND ACCOMPANYING DOCUMENTS.

(a) A [petitioner] seeking to establish or modify a support order or to determine parentage in a proceeding under this [Act] must verify the [petition]. Unless otherwise ordered under Section 312 on disclosure of Information in Exceptional Circumstances, the [petition] or accompanying documents must provide, so far as known, the name, residential address, and social security numbers of the obligor and the obligee, and the name, sex, residential address, social security number, and date of birth of each child for whom support is sought. The [petition] must be accompanied by a certified copy of any support order in effect. The [petition] may include any other information that may assist in locating or identifying the [respondent].

(b) The [petition] must specify the relief sought. The [petition] and accompanying documents must conform substantially with the requirements imposed by the forms mandated by federal law for use in cases filed by a support enforcement agency.

SECTION 312. NONDISCLOSURE OF INFORMATION IN EXCEPTIONAL CIRCUMSTANCES. Upon a finding, which may be made ex parte, that the health, safety, or liberty of a party or child would be unreasonably put at risk by the disclosure of identifying information, or if an existing order so provides, a tribunal shall order that the address of the child or party or other identifying information not be disclosed in a pleading or other document filed in a proceeding under this [Act].

SECTION 313. COSTS AND FEES.

(a) The [petitioner] may not be required to pay a filing fee or other costs.

(b) If an obligee prevails, a responding tribunal may assess against an obligor filing fees, reasonable attorney's fees, other costs, and necessary travel and other reasonable expenses incurred by the obligee and the obligee's witnesses. The tribunal may not assess fees, costs, or expenses against the obligee or the support enforcement agency of either the initiating or the responding State, except as provided by other law. Attorney's fees may be taxed as costs, and may be ordered paid directly to the attorney, who may enforce the order in the attorney's own name. Payment of support owed to the obligee has priority over fees, costs and expenses.

(c) The tribunal shall order the payment of costs and reasonable attorney's fees if it determines that a hearing was requested primarily for delay. In a proceeding under Article 6 (Enforcement and Modification of Support Order After Registration), a hearing is presumed to have been requested primarily for delay if a registered support order is confirmed or enforced without change.

SECTION 314. LIMITED IMMUNITY OF [PETITIONER].

(a) Participation by a [petitioner] in a proceeding before a responding tribunal, whether in person, by private attorney, or through services provided by the support enforcement agency, does not confer personal jurisdiction over the [petitioner] in another proceeding.

(b) A [petitioner] is not amenable to service of civil process while physically present in this State to participate in a proceeding under this [Act].

(c) The immunity granted by this section does not extend to civil litigation based on acts unrelated to a proceeding under this [Act] committed by a party while present in this State to participate in the proceeding.

SECTION 315. NONPARENTAGE AS DEFENSE. A party whose parentage of a child has been previously determined by or pursuant to law may not plead nonparentage as a defense to a proceeding under this [Act].

SECTION 316. SPECIAL RULES OF EVIDENCE AND PROCEDURE.

(a) The physical presence of the [petitioner] in a responding tribunal is not required for the establishment, enforcement, or modification of an order or the rendition of a judgment determining parentage.

(b) A verified [petition], affidavit, document substantially complying with federally mandated forms, and a document incorporated by reference in any of them, not excluded under the hearsay rule if given in person, is admissible in evidence if given under oath by a party or witness residing in another State.

(c) A copy of the record of child-support payments certified as a true copy of the original by the custodian of the record may be forwarded to a responding tribunal. The copy is evidence of facts asserted in it, and is admissible to show whether payments were made.

(d) Copies of bills for testing for parentage, and for prenatal and postnatal health care of the mother and child, furnished to the adverse party at least [ten] days before trial, are admissible in evidence to prove the amount of the charges billed and that the charges were reasonable, necessary, and customary.

(e) Documentary evidence transmitted from another State to a tribunal of this State by telephone, telecopier, or other means that do not provide an original writing may not be excluded from evidence on an objection based on the means of transmission.

(f) In a proceeding under this [Act], a tribunal of this State may permit a party or witness residing in another State to be deposed or to testify by telephone, audiovisual means or other electronic means at a designated tribunal or other location in that State. A tribunal of this State shall cooperate with tribunals of other States in designating an appropriate location for the deposition or testimony.

(g) If a party called to testimony at a civil hearing refuses to answer on the ground that the testimony may be self-incriminating, the trier of fact may draw an adverse inference from the refusal.

(h) A privilege against disclosure of communications between spouses does not apply in a proceeding under this [Act].

(i) The defense of immunity based on the relationship of husband and wife or parent and child does not apply in a proceeding under this [Act].

SECTION 317. COMMUNICATIONS BETWEEN TRIBUNALS. A tribunal of this State may communicate with a tribunal of another State in writing, or by telephone or other means, to obtain information concerning the laws of that State, the legal effect of a judgment, decree, or order of that tribunal, and the status of a proceeding in the other State. A tribunal of this State may furnish similar information by similar means to a tribunal of another State.

SECTION 318. ASSISTANCE WITH DISCOVERY. A tribunal of this State may: (1) request a tribunal of another State to assist in obtaining discovery; and (2) upon request, compel a person over whom it has jurisdiction to respond to a discovery order issued by a tribunal of another State.

SECTION 319. RECEIPT AND DISBURSEMENT OF PAYMENTS. A support enforcement agency or tribunal of this State shall disburse promptly any amounts received pursuant to a support order, as directed by the order. The agency or tribunal shall furnish to a requesting party or tribunal of another State a certified statement by the custodian of the record of the amounts and dates of all payments received.

ARTICLE 4. ESTABLISHMENT OF SUPPORT ORDER

SECTION 401. [PETITION] TO ESTABLISH SUPPORT ORDER.

(a) If a support order entitled to recognition under this [Act] has not been issued, a responding tribunal of this State may issue a support order if:

    (1) the individual seeking the order resides in another State; or (2) the support enforcement agency seeking the order is located in another State.

(b) The tribunal may issue a temporary child-support order if:

    (1) the [respondent] has signed a verified statement acknowledging parentage;

    (2) the [respondent] has been determined by or pursuant to law to be the parent; or

    (3) there is other clear and convincing evidence that the [respondent] is the child's parent.

(c) Upon finding, after notice and opportunity to be heard, that an obligor owes a duty of support, the tribunal shall issue a support order directed to the obligor and may issue other orders pursuant to Section 305 (Duties and Powers of Responding Tribunal).

ARTICLE 5. ENFORCEMENT OF ORDER OF ANOTHER STATE WITHOUT REGISTRATION

SECTION 501. EMPLOYER'S RECEIPT OF INCOME-WITHHOLDING ORDER OF ANOTHER STATE. An income-withholding order issued in another State may be sent to the person or entity defined as the obligor's employer under [the income-withholding law of this State] without first filing a [petition] or comparable pleading or registering the order with a tribunal of this State.

SECTION 502. EMPLOYER'S COMPLIANCE WITH INCOME-WITHHOLDING ORDER OF ANOTHER STATE.

(a) Upon receipt of an income-withholding order, the obligor's employer shall immediately provide a copy of the order to the obligor.

(b) The employer shall treat an income-withholding order issued in another State which appears regular on its face as if it had been issued by a tribunal of this State.

(c) Except as otherwise provided in subsection (d) and Section 503, the employer shall withhold and distribute the funds as directed in the withholding order by complying with terms of the order which specify:

   (1) the duration and amount of periodic payments of current child-support, stated as a sum certain;

   (2) the person or agency designated to receive payments and the address to which the payments are to be forwarded;

   (3) medical support, whether in the form of periodic cash payment, stated as a sum certain, or ordering the obligor to provide health insurance coverage for the child under a policy available through the obligor's employment;

   (4) the amount of periodic payments of fees and costs for a support enforcement agency, the issuing tribunal, and the obligee's attorney, stated as sums certain; and

   (5) the amount of periodic payments of arrearages and interest on arrearages, stated as sums certain.

(d) An employer shall comply with the law of the State of the obligor's principal place of employment for withholding from income with respect to:

   (1) the employer's fee for processing an income-withholding order;

   (2) the maximum amount permitted to be withheld from the obligor's income; and

   (3) the times within which the employer must implement the withholding order and forward the child support payment.

SECTION 503. COMPLIANCE WITH MULTIPLE INCOME-WITHHOLDING ORDERS. If an obligor's employer receives multiple income-withholding orders with respect to the earnings of the same obligor, the employer satisfies the terms of the multiple orders if the employer complies with the law of the State of the obligor's principal place of employment to establish the priorities for withholding and allocating income withheld for multiple child support obligees.

SECTION 504. IMMUNITY FROM CIVIL LIABILITY. An employer who complies with an income-withholding order issued in another State in accordance with this article is not subject to civil liability to an individual or agency with regard to the employer's withholding of child support from the obligor's income.

SECTION 505. PENALTIES FOR NONCOMPLIANCE. An employer who willfully fails to comply with an income-withholding order issued by another State and received for enforcement is subject to the same penalties that may be imposed for noncompliance with an order issued by a tribunal of this State.

SECTION 506. CONTEST BY OBLIGOR.

(a) An obligor may contest the validity or enforcement of an income-withholding order issued in another State and received directly by an employer in this State in the same manner as if the order had been issued by a tribunal of this State. Section 604 (Choice of Law) applies to the contest.

(b) The obligor shall give notice of the contest to:

   (1) a support enforcement agency providing services to the obligee;

   (2) each employer that has directly received an income-withholding order; and

(3) the person or agency designated to receive payments in the income-withholding order or if no person or agency is designated, to the obligee.

(c) Upon receipt of the documents, the support enforcement agency, without initially seeking to register the order, shall consider and, if appropriate, use any administrative procedure authorized by the law of this State to enforce a support order or an income-withholding order, or both. If the obligor does not contest administrative enforcement, the order need not be registered. If the obligor contests the validity or administrative enforcement of the order, the support enforcement agency shall register the order pursuant to this [Act].

ARTICLE 6. ENFORCEMENT AND MODIFICATION OF SUPPORT ORDER AFTER REGISTRATION

Part 1. Registration and Enforcement of Support Order

SECTION 601. REGISTRATION OF ORDER FOR ENFORCEMENT. A support order or an income-withholding order issued by a tribunal of another State may be registered in this State for enforcement.

SECTION 602. PROCEDURE TO REGISTER ORDER FOR ENFORCEMENT.

(a) A support order or income-withholding order of another State may be registered in this State by sending the following documents and information to the [appropriate tribunal] in this State:

(1) a letter of transmittal to the tribunal requesting registration and enforcement;

(2) two copies, including one certified copy, of all orders to be registered, including any modification of an order;

(3) a sworn statement by the party seeking registration or a certified statement by the custodian of the records showing the amount of any arrearage;

(4) the name of the obligor and, if known:

(i) the obligor's address and social security number;

(ii) the name and address of the obligor's employer and any other source of income of the obligor; and

(iii) a description and the location of property of the obligor in this State not exempt from execution; and

(5) the name and address of the obligee and, if applicable, the agency or person to whom support payments are to be remitted.

(b) On receipt of a request for registration, the registering tribunal shall cause the order to be filed as a foreign judgment, together with one copy of the documents and information, regardless of their form.

(c) A [petition] or comparable pleading seeking a remedy that must be affirmatively sought under other law of this State may be filed at the same time as the request for registration or later. The pleading must specify the grounds for the remedy sought.

SECTION 603. EFFECT OF REGISTRATION FOR ENFORCEMENT.

(a) A support order or income-withholding order issued in another State is registered when the order is filed in the registering tribunal of this State.

(b) A registered order issued in another State is enforceable in the same manner and is subject to the same procedures as an order issued by a tribunal of this State.

(c) Except as otherwise provided in this article, a tribunal of this State shall recognize and enforce, but may not modify, a registered order if the issuing tribunal had jurisdiction.

SECTION 604. CHOICE OF LAW.

(a) The law of the issuing State governs the nature, extent, amount, and duration of current payments and other obligations of support and the payment of arrearages under the order.

(b) In a proceeding for arrearages, the statute of limitation under the laws of this State or of the issuing State, whichever is longer, applies.

Part 2. Contest of Validity or Enforcement

SECTION 605. NOTICE OF REGISTRATION OF ORDER.

(a) When a support order or income-withholding order issued in another State is registered, the registering tribunal shall notify the nonregistering party. The notice must be accompanied by a copy of the registered order and the documents and relevant information accompanying the order.

(b) The notice must inform the nonregistering party:

  (1) that a registered order is enforceable as of the date of registration in the same manner as an order issued by a tribunal of this State;

  (2) that a hearing to contest the validity or enforcement of the registered order must be requested within [20] days after notice;

  (3) that failure to contest the validity or enforcement of the registered order in a timely manner will result in confirmation of the order and enforcement of the order and the alleged arrearages and precludes further contest of that order with respect to any matter that could have been asserted; and

  (4) of the amount of any alleged arrearages.

(c) Upon registration of an income-withholding order for enforcement, the registering tribunal shall notify the obligor's employer pursuant to [the income-withholding law of this State].

SECTION 606. PROCEDURE TO CONTEST VALIDITY OR ENFORCEMENT OF REGISTERED ORDER.

(a) A nonregistering party seeking to contest the validity or enforcement of a registered order in this State shall request a hearing within [20] days after notice of the registration. The nonregistering party may seek to vacate the registration, to assert any defense to an allegation of noncompliance with the registered order, or to contest the remedies being sought or the amount of any alleged arrearages pursuant to Section 607 (Contest of Registration or Enforcement).

(b) If the nonregistering party fails to contest the validity or enforcement of the registered order in a timely manner, the order is confirmed by operation of law.

(c) If a nonregistering party requests a hearing to contest the validity or enforcement of the registered order, the registering tribunal shall schedule the matter for hearing and give notice to the parties of the date, time, and place of the hearing.

SECTION 607. CONTEST OF REGISTRATION OR ENFORCEMENT.

(a) A party contesting the validity or enforcement of a registered order or seeking to vacate the registration has the burden of proving one or more of the following defenses:

(1) the issuing tribunal lacked personal jurisdiction over the contesting party;

(2) the order was obtained by fraud;

(3) the order has been vacated, suspended, or modified by a later order;

(4) the issuing tribunal has stayed the order pending appeal;

(5) there is a defense under the law of this State to the remedy sought;

(6) full or partial payment has been made; or

(7) the statute of limitation under Section 604 (Choice of Law) precludes enforcement of some or all of the arrearages.

(b) If a party presents evidence establishing a full or partial defense under subsection (a), a tribunal may stay enforcement of the registered order, continue the proceeding to permit production of additional relevant evidence, and issue other appropriate orders. An uncontested portion of the registered order may be enforced by all remedies available under the law of this State.

(c) If the contesting party does not establish a defense under subsection (a) to the validity or enforcement of the order, the registering tribunal shall issue an order confirming the order.

SECTION 608. CONFIRMED ORDER. Confirmation of a registered order, whether by operation of law or after notice and hearing, precludes further contest of the order with respect to any matter that could have been asserted at the time of registration.

Part 3. Registration And Modification of Child-Support Order

SECTION 609. PROCEDURE TO REGISTER CHILD-SUPPORT ORDER OF ANOTHER STATE FOR MODIFICATION. A party or support enforcement agency seeking to modify, or to modify and enforce, a child-support order issued in another State shall register that order in this State in the same manner provided in Part 1 if the order has not been registered. A [petition] for modification may be filed at the same time as a request for registration, or later. The pleading must specify the grounds for modification.

SECTION 610. EFFECT OF REGISTRATION FOR MODIFICATION. A tribunal of this State may enforce a child-support order of another State registered for purposes of modification, in the same manner as if the order had been issued by a tribunal of this State, but the registered order may be modified only if the requirements of Section 611 (Modification of Child-Support Order of Another State) have been met.

SECTION 611. MODIFICATION OF CHILD-SUPPORT ORDER OF ANOTHER STATE.

(a) After a child-support order issued in another State has been registered in this State, the responding tribunal of this State may modify that order only if Section 613 does not apply and after notice and hearing it finds that:

    (1) the following requirements are met:

        (i) the child, the individual obligee, and the obligor do not reside in the issuing State;

        (ii) a [petitioner] who is a nonresident of this State seeks modification; and

        (iii) the [respondent] is subject to the personal jurisdiction of the tribunal of this State; or

    (2) the child, or a party who is an individual, is subject to the personal jurisdiction of the tribunal of this State and all of the parties who are individuals have filed written consents in the issuing tribunal for a tribunal of this State to modify the support order and assume continuing, exclusive jurisdiction over the order. However, if the issuing State is a foreign jurisdiction that has not enacted a law or established procedures substantially similar to the procedures under this [Act], the consent otherwise required of an individual residing in this State is not required for the tribunal to assume jurisdiction to modify the child-support order.

(b) Modification of a registered child-support order is subject to the same requirements, procedures, and defenses that apply to the modification of an order issued by a tribunal of this State and the order may be enforced and satisfied in the same manner.

(c) A tribunal of this State may not modify any aspect of a child-support order that may not be modified under the law of the issuing State. If two or more tribunals have issued child-support orders for the same obligor and child, the order that controls and must be so recognized under Section 207 establishes the aspects of the support order which are nonmodifiable.

(d) On issuance of an order modifying a child-support order issued in another State, a tribunal of this State becomes the tribunal having continuing, exclusive jurisdiction.

SECTION 612. RECOGNITION OF ORDER MODIFIED IN ANOTHER STATE. A tribunal of this State shall recognize a modification of its earlier child-support order by a tribunal of another State which assumed jurisdiction pursuant to this [Act] or a law substantially similar to this [Act] and, upon request, except as otherwise provided in this [Act], shall:

    (1) enforce the order that was modified only as to amounts accruing before the modification;

    (2) enforce only nonmodifiable aspects of that order;

(3) provide other appropriate relief only for violations of that order which occurred before the effective date of the modification; and

(4) recognize the modifying order of the other State, upon registration, for the purpose of enforcement.

SECTION 613. JURISDICTION TO MODIFY CHILD-SUPPORT ORDER OF ANOTHER STATE WHEN INDIVIDUAL PARTIES RESIDE IN THIS STATE.

(a) If all of the parties who are individuals reside in this State and the child does not reside in the issuing State, a tribunal of this State has jurisdiction to enforce and to modify the issuing state's child-support order in a proceeding to register that order.

(b) A tribunal of this State exercising jurisdiction under this section shall apply the provisions of Articles 1 and 2, this article, and the procedural and substantive law of this State to the proceeding for enforcement or modification. Articles 3, 4, 5, 7, and 8 do not apply.

SECTION 614. NOTICE TO ISSUING TRIBUNAL OF MODIFICATION.

Within [30] days after issuance of a modified child-support order, the party obtaining the modification shall file a certified copy of the order with the issuing tribunal that had continuing, exclusive jurisdiction over the earlier order, and in each tribunal in which the party knows the earlier order has been registered. A party who obtains the order and fails to file a certified copy is subject to appropriate sanctions by a tribunal in which the issue of failure to file arises. The failure to file does not affect the validity or enforceability of the modified order of the new tribunal having continuing, exclusive jurisdiction.

ARTICLE 7. DETERMINATION OF PARENTAGE

SECTION 701. PROCEEDING TO DETERMINE PARENTAGE.

(a) A tribunal of this State may serve as an initiating or responding tribunal in a proceeding brought under this [Act] or a law or procedure substantially similar to this [Act], the Uniform Reciprocal Enforcement of Support Act, or the Revised Uniform Reciprocal Enforcement of Support Act to determine that the [petitioner] is a parent of a particular child or to determine that a [respondent] is a parent of that child.

(b) In a proceeding to determine parentage, a responding tribunal of this State shall apply the [Uniform Parentage Act; procedural and substantive law of this State] and the rules of this State on choice of law.

ARTICLE 8. INTERSTATE RENDITION

SECTION 801. GROUNDS FOR RENDITION.

(a) For purposes of this article, "governor" includes an individual performing the functions of governor or the executive authority of a State covered by this [Act].

(b) The governor of this State may:

(1) demand that the governor of another State surrender an individual found in the other State who is charged criminally in this State with having failed to provide for the support of an obligee; or

    (2) on the demand by the governor of another State, surrender an individual found in this State who is charged criminally in the other State with having failed to provide for the support of an obligee.

(c) A provision for extradition of individuals not inconsistent with this [Act] applies to the demand even if the individual whose surrender is demanded was not in the demanding State when the crime was allegedly committed and has not fled therefrom.

SECTION 802. CONDITIONS OF RENDITION.

(a) Before making demand that the governor of another State surrender an individual charged criminally in this State with having failed to provide for the support of an obligee, the governor of this State may require a prosecutor of this State to demonstrate that at least [60] days previously the obligee had initiated proceedings for support pursuant to this [Act] or that the proceeding would be of no avail.

(b) If, under this [Act] or a law substantially similar to this [Act], the Uniform Reciprocal Enforcement of Support Act, or the Revised Uniform Reciprocal Enforcement of Support Act, the governor of another State makes a demand that the governor of this State surrender an individual charged criminally in that State with having failed to provide for the support of a child or other individual to whom a duty of support is owed, the governor may require a prosecutor to investigate the demand and report whether a proceeding for support has been initiated or would be effective. If it appears that a proceeding would be effective but has not been initiated, the governor may delay honoring the demand for a reasonable time to permit the initiation of a proceeding.

(c) If a proceeding for support has been initiated and the individual whose rendition is demanded prevails, the governor may decline to honor the demand. If the [petitioner] prevails and the individual whose rendition is demanded is subject to a support order, the governor may decline to honor the demand if the individual is complying with the support order.

ARTICLE 9. MISCELLANEOUS PROVISIONS

    SECTION 901. UNIFORMITY OF APPLICATION AND CONSTRUCTION. This [Act] shall be applied and construed to effectuate its general purpose to make uniform the law with respect to the subject of this [Act] among States enacting it.

    SECTION 902. SHORT TITLE. This [Act] may be cited as the Uniform Interstate Family Support Act.

COMMENT

Renaming the Act reflects the dramatic departure from the structure of the earlier interstate reciprocal support acts, URESA and RURESA.

    SECTION 903. SEVERABILITY CLAUSE. If any provision of this [Act] or its application to any person or circumstance is held invalid, the invalidity does not affect other provisions or applications of this [Act] which can be given effect without the invalid provision or application, and to this end the provisions of this [Act] are severable.

SECTION 904. EFFECTIVE DATE. This [Act] takes effect _____.

SECTION 905. REPEALS. The following acts and parts of acts are hereby repealed:

(1) _____

(2) _____

(3) _____

G APPENDIX

RESTRAINING ORDER (ROSEANNE)

TROPE AND TROPE
12121 Wilshire Blvd.
Suite 801
Los Angeles, CA 90025-1171
ATTORNEY FOR (Name) Petitioner

TELEPHONE NO. (310) 207-822
FOR COURT USE ONLY

ORIGINAL FILED

APR 1 8 1994

LOS ANGELES SUPERIOR COURT

SUPERIOR COURT OF CALIFORNIA, COUNTY OF LOS ANGELES
STREET ADDRESS 111 NORTH HILL ST
MAILING ADDRESS
CITY AND ZIP CODE LOS ANGELES CA 90012
BRANCH NAME CENTRAL

PETITIONER/PLAINTIFF: ROSEANNE CHERRIE ARNOLD

RESPONDENT/DEFENDANT: TOM DWAYNE ARNOLD

EX PARTE APPLICATION AND ORDER TO SHOW CAUSE FOR ☐ MODIFICATION

☐ Child Custody	☐ Visitation	☒ Injunctive Orders
☐ Child Support	☐ Spousal Support	☐ Other (specify):
☐ Attorney Fees and Costs		

CASE NUMBER:
BD155482

1. TO (name): TOM DWAYNE ARNOLD
2. YOU ARE ORDERED TO APPEAR IN THIS COURT AS FOLLOWS TO GIVE ANY LEGAL REASON WHY THE RELIEF SOUGHT IN THE ATTACHED APPLICATION SHOULD NOT BE GRANTED. *If child custody or visitation is an issue in this proceeding, Family Code section 3170 requires mediation before or concurrently with the hearing listed below.*

a. Date: 5-27-94 Time: 8:30 ☒ Dept: 20 ☒ Rm: 243

b. Address of court ☒ same as noted above ☐ other (specify):

3. IT IS FURTHER ORDERED that a completed Application for Order and Supporting Declaration, a blank Responsive Declaration, and the following documents shall be served with this order:

(1) ☐ Completed Income and Expense Declaration and a blank Income and Expense Declaration
(2) ☐ Completed Property Declaration and a blank Property Declaration
(3) ☐ Points and authorities
(4) ☐ Other (specify):

a. ☐ Time for ☐ service ☐ hearing is shortened. Service shall be on or before (date): ___
Any responsive declaration shall be served on or before (date): ___

b. ☒ You are ordered to comply with the temporary orders attached.
c. ☒ Other (specify): *Attorney for Respondent, Mackey Fried, has accepted service of the Petitioner and OSC on behalf of Respondent.* ROBERT SCHNIDE
JUDGE PRO TEM

Date: APR 1 8 1994 _____
JUDGE OF THE SUPERIOR COURT

Form Adopted by Rule 1285
Judicial Council of California
1285 (Rev. January 1, 1994)

ORDER TO SHOW CAUSE
(Family Law)

Gov Code § 26826
Family Code §§ 215, 271-272, 2030-2034, 2045, 2254, 4330-4339, 4350, 4370, 4455, 4801, 4809

EXHIBIT D

465

TEMPORARY RESTRAINING ORDERS
(Attachment to Order to Show Cause)

The person restrained in the first three orders is (name): TOM DWAYNE ARNOLD

Race White.................. Date of birth: 3/6/59........ Sex Male.......

THE RESTRAINED PERSON

1. [X] shall NOT contact, molest, attack, strike, threaten, sexually assault, batter, telephone, or otherwise disturb the peace of the other party, *and Petitioner shall not contact, molest, threaten, batter, telephone or disturb the peace of Respondent*

2. [ ] shall move out immediately and shall not return to the family dwelling at (address):

   [ ] taking only clothing and personal effects needed until the hearing

3. [X] a. must stay at least 100 .... yards away from the other party and the following places.

   (1) [X] Residence of (name): Roseanne Cherrie Arnold
   (address optional): 12916 Evanston Street, Los Angeles, CA 90049

   This order is without prejudice to the time of the OSC hearing. Each party is ordered to stay away from that person of the used exclusively by the other party.

   (2) [X] Place of work of (name): CBS/MTM Studios
   (address optional): Studio City, CA *not used exclusively by the other party.*

   Petitioner is ordered to stay 100 yards from

   (3) [X] The children's school (address optional): *Respondent and 10 yards from Wilshire House, 10001 Wilshire Bl., Los Angeles.*

   (4) [X] Other (specify): Residence of Bill Pentland
   This order without prejudice

   [ ] b. may make contact relating to pickup and delivery of children pursuant to a court order for visitation or a stipulation of the parties arrived at during mediation.

- Any person subject to any of these three restraining orders is prohibited by Penal Code section 12021 from purchasing or receiving or attempting to purchase or receive a firearm. Such conduct may be punishable by a $1,000 fine, imprisonment up to one year, or both.
- Taking or concealing a child in violation of this order may be a felony and punishable by confinement in state prison, a fine, or both.
- Other violations of these orders may also be punishable by fines, imprisonment, or both.

4. [X] **PROPERTY RESTRAINT**

   a. [X] Petitioner [X] Respondent is restrained from transferring, encumbering, hypothecating, concealing, or in any way disposing of any property, real or personal, whether community, quasi-community, or separate, except in the usual course of business or for the necessities of life.

   [ ] The other party is to be notified of any proposed extraordinary expenditures and an accounting of such is to be made to the court.

   b. [X] Both parties are restrained and enjoined from cashing, borrowing against, canceling, transferring, disposing of, or changing the beneficiaries of any insurance or other coverage including life, health, automobile, and disability held for the benefit of the parties or their minor child or children.

   c. [X] Neither party shall incur any debts or liabilities for which the other may be held responsible, other than in the ordinary course of business or for the necessities of life.

(Continued on reverse)

Form Adopted by Rule 1285.05
Judicial Council of California
1285.05 [Rev. July 1, 1992]

TEMPORARY RESTRAINING ORDERS
(Family Law)

Civil Code § 4359

EXHIBIT B

466

MARRIAGE OF (last name, first name of parties):	CASE NUMBER
ARNOLD, Roseanne and Tom	

TEMPORARY RESTRAINING ORDERS
(Family Law)

5 ☒ PROPERTY CONTROL

    a ☒ Petitioner ☐ Respondent is given the exclusive temporary use, possession, and control of the following property the parties own or are buying (specify): 12916 Evanston Street, Los Angeles, CA 90049

    b ☐ Petitioner ☐ Respondent is ordered to make the following payments on liens and encumbrances coming due while the order is in effect:

Debt	Amount of payment	Pay to

6. ☐ MINOR CHILDREN

    a. Neither party shall remove the minor child or children of the parties

        (1) ☐ from the State of California.

        (2) ☐ other (specify):

    b. ☐ Petitioner ☐ Respondent shall have the temporary physical custody, care, and control of the minor children of the parties, ☐ subject to the other party's rights of visitation as follows:

7. By the close of business on the date of this order, a copy of this order shall be delivered by the protected person to the law enforcement agency having jurisdiction over the residence of the protected person, who shall provide information to assist in identifying the restrained person. Proof of service of this order on the restrained person shall also be provided to the law enforcement agency. The law enforcement agency having jurisdiction over the plaintiff's residence is (name and address of agency): Los Angeles Police Department, West Los Angeles Division.

8. ☒ A copy of this order shall be given to the additional law enforcement agencies listed below as follows:

    a. ☐ Plaintiff shall deliver.   b. ☒ Plaintiff's attorney shall deliver.   c. ☐ The clerk of the court shall mail.

Law enforcement agency	Address
Los Angeles Police Department West Los Angeles Division	1663 Butler Avenue Los Angeles, CA 90025

9. This order is effective when made. The law enforcement agency shall enforce it immediately upon receipt. It is enforceable anywhere in California by any law enforcement agency that has received the order, is shown a copy of it, or has verified its existence on the California Law Enforcement Telecommunications System (CLETS). If proof of service on the restrained person has not been received, the law enforcement agency shall advise the restrained person of the terms of the order and then shall enforce it.

10. ☐ OTHER ORDERS (specify):

11 These orders expire on the date of the court hearing unless extended by the court.

Date APR 18 1994

        ►   JUDGE OF THE SUPERIOR COURT

ROBERT SCHNIDE
JUDGE PRO TEM

12 The date of the court hearing is (insert date when known):

EXHIBIT B

CLERK'S CERTIFICATE

467

MARRIAGE OF (last name, first name ____)
ARNOLD, Roseanne and Tc

(THIS IS NOT AN ORDER)

☒ Petitioner ☐ Respondent ☐ Claimant requests the following orders be made:

1. ☐ CHILD CUSTODY ☐ To be ordered pending the hearing
   a. Child (name and age)   b. Request custody to (name)   c. ☐ Modify existing order
                                                                (1) filed on (date):
                                                                (2) ordering (specify)

2. ☐ CHILD VISITATION ☐ To be ordered pending the hearing
   a. ☐ Reasonable
   b. ☐ Other (specify):
   c. ☐ Neither party shall remove the minor child or children of the parties
      (1) ☐ from the State of California. (2) ☐ other (specify):
   d. ☐ Modify existing order
      (1) filed on (date):
      (2) ordering (specify):

3. ☐ CHILD SUPPORT (A Wage and Earnings Assignment Order will be issued.)
   a. Child (name and age)   b. Monthly amount
                                (if not by guideline)
                                $
   c. ☐ Modify existing order
      (1) filed on (date):
      (2) ordering (specify):

4. ☐ SPOUSAL SUPPORT (A Wage and Earnings Assignment Order will be issued.)
   a. ☐ Amount requested (monthly): $
   c. ☐ Terminate existing order
      (1) filed on (date):
      (2) ordering (specify):
   b. ☐ Modify existing order
      (1) filed on (date):
      (2) ordering (specify):

5. ☐ ATTORNEY FEES AND COSTS a. ☐ Fees. $ b. ☐ Costs: $

6. ☐ RESIDENCE EXCLUSION AND RELATED ORDERS ☐ To be ordered pending the hearing
   ☐ Petitioner ☐ Respondent must move out immediately and must not return to the family dwelling at
   (address):
   ☐ taking only clothing and personal effects needed until the hearing.

7. ☒ STAY-AWAY ORDERS ☐ To be ordered pending the hearing
   a. ☐ Petitioner ☒ Respondent must stay at least 100... yards away from applicant and the following places
      (1) ☒ applicant's residence (address optional): 12916 Evanston Street, Los Angeles, CA 90049
      (2) ☒ applicant's place of work (address optional): CBS/MTM Studios, Studio City, CA
      (3) ☐ the children's school (address optional):
      (4) ☐ other (specify):
   b. ☐ Contacts relating to pickup and delivery of children pursuant to a court order or a stipulation of the parties
      arrived at during mediation shall be permitted.

8. ☒ RESTRAINT ON PERSONAL CONDUCT ☐ To be ordered pending the hearing
   ☐ Petitioner ☒ Respondent
   a. shall not molest, attack, strike, threaten, sexually assault, or otherwise disturb the peace of the other party
      ☒ and any person under the care, custody, and control of the other party
   b. ☒ shall not contact or telephone the other party.
   c. ☐ except that peaceful contacts relating to minor children of the parties shall be permitted.

(Continued on reverse)

Form Adopted by Rule 1285.20
Judicial Council of California
1285.20 (Rev. January 1, 1983)

**APPLICATION FOR ORDER
AND SUPPORTING DECLARATION
(Family Law)**

Case Code 8 <388

EXHIBIT B

468

9 ☐ **PROPERTY RESTRAINT** ☐ To be ordered pending the hearing

   a The ☐ petitioner ☐ respondent ☐ claimant be restrained from transferring, encumbering, hypothecating, concealing, or in any way disposing of any property, real or personal, whether community, quasi-community, or separate, except in the usual course of business or for the necessities of life

   ☐ and applicant be notified at least five business days before any proposed extraordinary expenditures and an accounting of such be made to the court.

   b ☐ Both parties are restrained and enjoined from cashing, borrowing against, canceling, transferring, disposing of, or changing the beneficiaries of any insurance or other coverage including life, health, automobile, and disability held for the benefit of the parties or their minor children.

   c ☐ Neither party shall incur any debts or liabilities for which the other may be held responsible, other than in the ordinary course of business or for the necessities of life.

10 ☒ **PROPERTY CONTROL** ☐ To be ordered pending the hearing

   a ☒ Petitioner ☐ Respondent be given the exclusive temporary use, possession, and control of the following property we own or are buying (specify): 12916 Evanston Street, Los Angeles, CA 90049

   b ☐ Petitioner ☐ Respondent be ordered to make the following payments on liens and encumbrances coming due while the order is in effect:

Debt	Amount of payment	Pay to

11 ☒ **LAW ENFORCEMENT AGENCIES** I request that copies of orders be given to the following law enforcement agencies having jurisdiction over the locations where violence is likely to occur.

Law enforcement agency	Address
Los Angeles Police Department West Los Angeles Division	1663 Butler Avenue Los Angeles, CA 90025

12 ☐ I request that time for service of the Order to Show Cause and accompanying papers be shortened so that they may be served no less than (specify number):............days before the time set for the hearing. I need to have the order shortening time because of the facts specified in the attached declaration.

13. ☐ **OTHER RELIEF** (specify):

14. ☒ **FACTS IN SUPPORT** of relief requested and change of circumstances for any modification are (specify):
   ☒ contained in the attached declaration.

I declare under penalty of perjury under the laws of the State of California that the foregoing is true and correct

Date April 16, 1994

ROSEANNE CHERRIE ARNOLD
(TYPE OR PRINT NAME)

_____
(SIGNATURE OF APPLICANT)

APPLICATION FOR ORDER AND SUPPORTING DECLARATION **EXHIBIT B**
(Family Law)

In re Marriage of ARNOLD   L.A.S.C. Case No. BD _____

DECLARATION OF ROSEANNE ARNOLD

I, ROSEANNE ARNOLD, declare as follows:

1.   I am the Petitioner in the instant action.   The facts stated herein are known by me to be true, and if called upon to testify, I could and would testify competently thereto.

2.   The Respondent and I married on January 20, 1990. Throughout our marriage, the Respondent has been physically and emotionally abusive toward me.   I now realize that I have been a classic battered and abused wife who has tolerated the conduct of the Respondent only because the Respondent has successfully lowered my self-esteem and reduced me into the realm of battered wife syndrome.

3.   Throughout our marriage, the Respondent hit me, struck me, has thrown objects at me, pinched me, and verbally abused me.   He also has pushed me against walls, while he screams and shouts at me, drowning out any possible plea that I might make for him to stop.

4.   I should note that the Respondent has a proclivity and character for violence.   He was arrested seven times for drunken and disorderly behavior, assaulting police, and other disorderly and violent conduct as a younger person.

5.   In recent months, the Respondent's pattern of violence has grown worse.   I am now extremely afraid of him and am extremely afraid for my physical safety.   I am gravely concerned that if the Respondent found out that I was filing for dissolution of marriage, and seeking these restraining orders, that he would

DECLARATION OF ROSEANNE ARNOLD   **EXHIBIT B**   Page 1

470

immediately seek revenge in the form of violent retribution against either me or some person who is important in my life. I am therefore requesting that personal conduct restraining orders be issued ex parte and without notice so as to minimize the possibility of such violent retribution.

6. Most recently, on April 15, 1994, I attempted to have the Respondent barred from access to the studio where I film my television program. I arranged for several security personnel to be present so as to prevent the Respondent from having access to this area. Notwithstanding these efforts, the Respondent gained access to the studio area and assaulted four people in a violent episode. He scratched and hit these individuals.

7. Also on April 15, 1994, the Respondent gained access to my personal residence located at 12916 Evanston Street, Los Angeles, California 90049. Although I have a security system at my residence, and attempted to prevent the Respondent from gaining access thereto, he nonetheless did gain access to the residence and threatened my children, none of whom are of my marriage to the Respondent. My children's names and ages are Brandi Brown (age 23), Jessica Pentland (age 19), Jennifer Pentland (age 17½), and James Pentland (age 15½), who reside with Bill Pentland. I called the police at approximately 3:00 p.m. on April 15, 1994 to seek their assistance in removing the Respondent from my property.

8. Respondent moved out of this residence approximately six months ago pursuant to an agreement we made at that time. He now resides in a condominium located at the Wilshire Towers on Wilshire Boulevard. Since he no longer resides at the residence,

TROPE and TROPE
ATTORNEYS AT LAW
·1·2· WILSHIRE BLVD
LOS ANGELES CA
90025-1171

DECLARATION OF ROSEANNE ARNOLD   **EXHIBIT B**   Page 2

I am requesting that I be granted exclusive use, possession and control of the residence located at 12916 Evanston Street. Since the Respondent has moved out and has a residence of his own, this will not pose any burden upon the Respondent.

9. On Saturday, April 9, 1994, my children, the Respondent, and I were driving in my limousine en route to a movie premiere. Without provocation, the Respondent grew angry and violent, and grabbed my calf and twisted it. This caused me severe pain and left a bruise. He did this in front of my children, which was the first time that he had displayed his violent behavior in front of my children.

10. A few days before that incident, we were in my residence and had an argument. As a result of this argument, he pushed me down on the bathroom floor, put his foot against my back, and pulled at my hair. I was screaming in desperation for him to relent, but he was screaming and shouting and ignoring my pleas. This episode lasted several minutes, and I was extremely frightened for my physical safety, if not my life.

11. Just a few days before this episode, he was in the residence and pushed me up against the wall. He pinned me against the wall and again was screaming loudly at me.

12. This type of pattern of violent and abusive behavior has been recurrent throughout our marriage. However, such episodes of violent and abusive behavior have become more frequent and more violent in recent months. I have finally come to the realization that I must not subject myself to his conduct. My life would be ruined if I continue in this abusive relationship.

DECLARATION OF ROSEANNE ARNOLD   **EXHIBIT R**   Page 3

13. The Respondent also has engaged in verbal abuse against me. He has constantly referred to me as a "fuckin' bitch" as well as other derogatory comments. He has a proclivity for attempting to humiliate me in public by inappropriately and unnecessarily revealing personal aspects of our life.

14. As a result of the foregoing, I am requesting that restraining orders be issued against the Respondent so that he cannot threaten, harass, annoy, or contact me. I am also requesting that restraining orders be issued to prevent him from coming near my residence or place of work. There is absolutely no reason why the Respondent need go to either of these locations. Again, I am also requesting that these restraining orders be issued on an ex parte basis with no notice, because of the very real possibility that the Respondent will seek violent revenge upon learning of my filing for dissolution and my seeking of these restraining orders.

15. I cannot overemphasize my grave fear of the Respondent and the fear that I have for my physical safety and well-being. This fear extends to individuals that are close to me. For example, Respondent has threatened a security person who works for me, Ben Thomas. He has literally threatened to kill Mr. Thomas.

16. I certainly realize that the revelations that I am making in this declaration will become a matter of public record and will no doubt be exploited by certain parts of the news media, in particular the tabloids. I have often been the subject of humiliating stories in tabloid newspapers. However, I must make

these revelations at this time because of the conclusion that I have reached that I cannot continue to live in a classic battered wife syndrome mentality. I am earnestly seeking the assistance of this court to separate myself from the Respondent and to remove his threatening and violent character from my life.

I declare, under penalty of perjury, under the laws of the State of California, that the foregoing is true and correct.

Executed April 16, 1994, at Los Angeles, California.

Roseanne Cherrie Arnold
ROSEANNE CHERRIE ARNOLD

TROPE and TROPE
ATTORNEYS AT LAW
12121 WILSHIRE BLVD
LOS ANGELES CA
90025-1176

DECLARATION OF ROSEANNE ARNOLD   **EXHIBIT B**   Page :

474

APPENDIX H

MARITAL SETTLEMENT AGREEMENT
(MADONNA AND SEAN PENN)

MARITAL SETTLEMENT AGREEMENT

THIS AGREEMENT, made and entered into _January 19_ , 1989, by and between SEAN PENN, hereinafter referred to as "Husband", and MADONNA CICCONE PENN, hereinafter referred to as "Wife":

WHEREAS, the parties hereto were lawfully married on August 16, 1985, and ever since then have been, and still are, Husband and Wife; and

WHEREAS, in consequence of unhappy differences and irreconcilable disputes which have arisen between Husband and Wife, as a result of which the parties have separated on December 31, 1988, and have not cohabited together since then, and are no longer living or cohabiting together as husband and wife; and

WHEREAS, there are no minor children who are the issue of the marriage of Husband and Wife; and

WHEREAS, it is the mutual wish and desire of both Husband and Wife to immediately effect, by way of a contract, a full, complete, and final settlement of all of their community property and quasi-community property interests, future and present, and, except as otherwise set forth herein, to irrevocably adjust and determine forever all legal obligations of any nature which may exist in respect to each other and by reason of their said

476

marriage, and to fully and completely resolve any and all issues relating to spousal support. This Agreement shall be effective irrespective of when or if a proceeding for dissolution of marriage is filed, a final decree of dissolution is entered, or this Marital Settlement Agreement is integrated into the decree of dissolution.

NOW, THEREFORE, by reason of the foregoing facts and in consideration of the mutual covenants and provisions hereinafter set forth, it is hereby agreed, by and between the parties, as follows:

PROPERTY AWARDED TO WIFE

FIRST: Husband hereby releases, sets over and assigns to Wife all right, title and interest and any claim to that certain real property located at _1 WEST 64th STREET_, in the City of New York, State of New York, the legal description of which is attached as Exhibit "A" hereto (herein the "New York Apartment"). Husband shall quitclaim to Wife all of his right, title and interest to the New York Apartment.

PROPERTY AWARDED TO HUSBAND

SECOND: Wife hereby releases, sets over and assigns to Husband all right, title and interest and any claim to that certain real property located at 22271 Carbon Mesa Drive, Malibu,

2

California the legal description of which is attached as Exhibit "B" hereto (herein the "Malibu Residence"). Wife shall quitclaim to Husband all of her right, title and interest to the Malibu Residence. ~~Husband shall pay to Wife, within 180 days from the date of execution of this Agreement, the sum of $_____ in order to equalize the difference in value between the Malibu property and the New York property.~~ Husband shall hold Wife harmless from, and pay all liens and encumbrances of record on the Malibu property and shall indemnify Wife from all claims connected with any such liens or encumbrances.

EXTENT OF COMMUNITY PROPERTY

THIRD: 1. The parties acknowledge that the only community property, quasi-community property or marital property owned by them is the Malibu Residence and New York Apartment. The parties have by other verbal agreement confirmed to each other their respective separate property interests in all other property owned by either of them. The parties further agree that the only community debt is the indebtedness on the Malibu residence secured by deeds of trust, which indebtedness (as between Husband and Wife) is expressly assumed by Husband.

3

478

PROPERTY WAIVER

FOURTH: 1.   Both parties voluntarily waive the right to require each other to account to the other for any use of funds and property each has received or managed during their marriage or to set out in this Agreement a description of their respective assets and liabilities.   Both parties voluntarily and expressly waive any requirement that the other provide a financial statement, or further information, in connection with this Agreement.

2.   To the extent that there exists any property of any kind or description, or any interest in any property in the name of either of the parties or under either of their control or held for the benefit of either of them that is not otherwise described and/or disposed of herein, that property, real or personal, wherever situated, is awarded to the party in whose name said property is held or for whose benefit said property is held.

3.   Each party hereby waives the right to investigate or value any property, or rights in and to property, either party has acquired during marriage or since the parties' separation.

4.   The parties acknowledge and agree that, to the extent that any opportunities to examine, audit and appraise books, records and accounts and business interests of either party

4

has not been exercised, the parties hereby, now and forever, expressly waive the right to do so.

SECTION 1041 OF INTERNAL REVENUE CODE

Fifth: The parties intend and agree that all transfers of property as provided for herein are subject to the provisions of Section 1041, Internal Revenue Code of 195486, as amended, entitled "Treatment of Transfers of Property Between Spouses or Incident to Divorce", that they shall be accounted for and reported on his or her respective individual income tax returns in such a manner so that no gain or loss shall be recognized as a result of the division and transfer of property as provided herein. Each party shall file his or her Federal or State tax returns, and report his or her income and losses thereon, consistent with the foregoing intent of reporting the division and transfers of property as a non-taxable event. In the event either party causes an adjustment to basis to be made to their property that gives rise to any actual or alleged claim or liability for taxes, state or federal, the party making such adjustment shall defend, hold harmless and indemnify the other with respect to any such claim or liability.

5

RELEASE FROM THIRD-PARTY CLAIMS

SIXTH: 1. Husband shall indemnify, defend and hold Wife harmless from any and all other indebtedness, loans, obligations, claims and causes of action that have, may now or hereafter be made against Wife on her property as a result of any acts or omissions of Husband, judgments that may be obtained against Husband, debts, guarantees or obligations incurred by Husband on his own behalf or on behalf of any company, owned or controlled by him.

2. Wife shall indemnify, defend and hold Husband harmless from any and all other indebtedness, loans, obligations, claims and causes of action that have, may now or hereafter be made against Husband or his property as a result of any acts or omissions of Wife, judgments that may be obtained against Wife, debts, guarantees or obligations incurred by Wife on her own behalf or on behalf of any company, owned or controlled by her.

SPOUSAL SUPPORT WAIVER

SEVENTH: Both parties warrant and agree that they have each, individually, consulted with their respective legal counsel concerning their rights to spousal support. Each party is self-supporting and waives the right to claim spousal support, temporary spousal support, family support, maintenance or alimony from the other, now or at any time.

6

ATTORNEY'S FEES, ACCOUNTANT'S FEES AND COSTS

EIGHTH: Each party shall bear his or her own attorney's fees, accountant's fees, appraiser's fees, and all other fees and costs incurred with respect to this Agreement or any action to dissolve the marriage of the parties.

INDEPENDENTLY BINDING

NINTH: This Agreement, and all of its terms and conditions, shall be absolutely binding upon the parties hereto, regardless of whether any action to dissolve the marriage of the parties is filed. The parties agree that this Agreement may be submitted in evidence in any action that may be brought to dissolve their marriage, but its effectiveness is not subject to Court approval. The executory terms hereof may be incorporated into a Judgment of Dissolution of Marriage. The parties declare it to be their intention that this Agreement shall be absolutely binding upon them, regardless of whether this Agreement is ever presented to any court or approved or disapproved by an court.

RELEASE OF CLAIMS

TENTH: Except as otherwise provided in this Agreement, Husband and Wife hereby release the other from any and all liabilities, debts, or obligations of every kind whatsoever

7

including any claims arising out of any tortious conduct, heretofore incurred or hereafter incurred, and from any and all claims and demands of any kind, nature and description.

Further, Husband and Wife agree that this Release extends to all claims of every nature or kind, known or unknown, suspected or unsuspected each may have against the other and each further waives all rights under Section 1542 of the California Civil Code, which provides:

> "A general release does not extend to claims which the creditor does not know or suspect to exist in his favor at the time of executing the release, which if known by him must have materially affected his settlement with the debtor."

RELEASE OF LIABILITY

ELEVENTH: A.   Husband hereby warrants to Wife that he has not incurred, and hereby covenants that he will not incur, any liability or obligation on which Wife is liable or may be liable and Husband hereby covenants and agrees that if any claim, action or proceeding shall hereafter be brought seeking to hold Wife liable on account of any debt, liability, act or omission of Husband, he will, at his sole expense, defend Wife against any such claim or demand, whether or not well-founded, and he will hold her free and harmless therefrom. HUSBAND is NOT RESPONSIBLE FOR PAYING FOR WIFES INDEPENDENT COUNSEL.

8

B.   Wife hereby represents to Husband that she
has not incurred, and hereby covenants that she will not incur, any
liability or obligation on which Husband is liable or may be liable
and Wife hereby covenants and agrees that if any claim, action or
proceeding shall hereafter be brought seeking to hold Husband
liable on account of any debt, liability, act or omission or Wife,
she will, at her sole expense, defend Husband against any such
claim or demand, whether or not well-founded, and she will hold him
free and harmless therefrom.

RELEASE OF ESTATES AND SURVIVOR BENEFITS

TWELFTH: A.   Husband and Wife hereby waive any and all
right to inherit the estate of the other at his or her death, or
to take property from the other by devise or bequest, unless under
a Will executed subsequent to the effective date hereof, or to
claim any family allowance or probate homestead, or to act as
administrator or administratrix of the estate of the other, except
as the nominee of another person legally entitled to said right,
or to act as the executor or executrix under the Will
of the other, unless under a Will executed subsequent to the
effective date hereof.

B.   Husband and Wife hereby waive any and all right
to receive surviving spouse benefits under any private, non-
governmental, pension or retirement plan in which either spouse is
a participant.

9

REPRESENTATION OF LEGAL COUNSEL

THIRTEENTH: Each party to this Agreement represents and acknowledges that he or she has been represented in negotiations for and in the preparation of this Agreement by counsel or his or her own choosing. Each party has read this Agreement and has had it fully explained to him or her.

PROPERTY ACQUIRED AFTER SEPARATION

FOURTEENTH: The parties have separated and have lived apart since December 31, 1988. It is hereby agreed that any and all property (except the Malibu Residence and the New York Apartment) acquired by Husband and Wife from and after August 16, 1986, ~~the effective date of the Post-Marital Property Agreement,~~ is and shall be the sole and separate property of the one so acquiring the same, and does hereby waive any and all right in or to such acquisitions, as well as future acquisitions made from and after the date of this Agreement and does hereby grant the other all such acquisitions and future acquisitions of property as the sole and separate property of the one so acquiring same.

10

485

ENTIRE UNDERSTANDING

FIFTEENTH: This Agreement constitutes the full and entire understanding of the parties with respect to the parties' community property, quasi-community property and marital property and any prior agreement, understanding or representation concerning the same is hereby terminated and cancelled in its entirety and is of no further force or effect. This provision is to not be understood to limit, or deny the effectiveness of, that certain Separate Property Agreement of even date herewith or the Post-Marital Property Agreement between the parties hereto. The parties hereto cannot alter and/or modify this Agreement, except by an instrument in writing executed by them and dated after the effective date hereof. This Agreement includes all of the representations of every kind and nature by the parties.

MODIFICATION

SIXTEENTH: No modification or waiver of any terms of this Agreement shall be valid as between the parties unless in writing and executed with the same formality of this Agreement; no waiver of any breach or default hereunder shall be deemed a waiver of any subsequent breach or default of the same or similar nature, no matter how made or how often occurring.

11

FREE OF COERCION

SEVENTEENTH: Each party hereto acknowledges that they are making this Agreement of their own free will and volition, and acknowledges that no coercion, force, pressure, or undue influence whatsoever has been employed against them in negotiations leading to or the execution of this Agreement, either by any other party hereto or by any other person or persons whomsoever, and declares that no reliance whatsoever is placed upon any representation other than those expressly set forth herein.

COUNTERPARTS

EIGHTEENTH: This Agreement may be executed in counterparts and each such counterpart shall be deemed to be an original.

EXECUTION OF DOCUMENTS AND RESERVATION OF JURISDICTION

NINETEENTH: The parties agree to perform all acts and to execute any documents necessary to effectuate and carry out the terms of this Agreement.

AGREEMENT SURVIVES INVALIDATION OF ANY PART

TWENTIETH: If any portion of this Agreement is held

12

to be illegal, unenforceable, void or voidable by any court, each of the remaining terms shall continue in full force as a separate contract.

RESOLUTION OF ALL ISSUES

TWENTY-FIRST: The parties acknowledge and understand that this Marital Settlement Agreement, and the Separate Property Agreement of even date ~~and the Post-Marital Property Agreement,~~ have resolved all issues between them.

CHANGES IN THE LAW

TWENTY-SECOND: Subsequent changes in California law, New York law or federal, through legislation or judicial interpretation, that creates or finds additional or different rights and obligations of the parties, shall not affect this Agreement.

PUBLIC RECORDS; INCORPORATION IN MARITAL PROCEEDING

TWENTY-THIRD: In the event that any court action is instituted concerning the subject matter of this Marital Settlement Agreement or in connection with a separation and/or dissolution of marriage, the parties agree that they will sign appropriate stipulations to cause this Marital Settlement Agreement and any and

13

all financial information of the parties to be placed under seal and not to be made public or part of any record. If the court directs that this Marital Settlement Agreement and said financial information to be made a part of the records, then the parties agree to request the court to place this Agreement and said financial information under seal and not allow this Agreement or said financial information to be seen read, reviewed or copied by anyone without the agreement of the parties, except as may be necessary to enforce the rights of either of the parties. The parties further agree that the court ~~shall be requested to approve this Marital Settlement Agreement as fair and equitable and to~~ may make specific orders requiring each party to do all of the things provided for in this Agreement and further agree that any executory provisions hereof shall be made a part of any decree entered by the court in a separation or dissolution proceeding. Notwithstanding incorporation or approval in any judgment or decree of this Marital Settlement Agreement or any of its terms, this Marital Settlement Agreement shall not be affected or altered in any way but shall continue to be fully independent and viable and enforceable to the same extent and by the same means and remedies as though such judgment had not been entered.

<u>MISCELLANEOUS</u>

<u>TWENTY-FOURTH</u>: This Agreement shall be binding upon, and shall enure to the benefit of the respective legatees,

14

devisees, heirs, executors, administrators, and assigns and successors in interest of the parties.

Each party agrees to not molest, harass, annoy, injure, threaten or interfere with the other party in any manner whatsoever or interfere with the use, ownership, enjoyment or disposition of any property now or hereafter owned or occupied by the other party.

"Property" as used herein is intended in its broadest and most comprehensive sense and includes real, personal and mixed real and personal property, tangible and intangible, and all earnings, interest, profits, appreciation and proceeds thereof and thereon, and insurance (and proceeds of insurance) thereon.

In the event any party hereto shall commence an action to enforce or receive damages or obtain any relief based on this Agreement, the prevailing party shall be entitled to recover, in addition to all other relief, reasonable attorneys fees fixed by the court in such action or in a separate action brought for that purpose.

IN WITNESS WHEREOF, the parties hereto have executed this Agreement as of the 19th day of January, 1989.

I, MADONNA CICCONE PENN, by my signature hereto, attest to my agreement to the terms and provisions of this Agreement. I have been advised as to the legal effect of the provisions of this Agreement by Michael K. Inglis, independent legal counsel chosen by me, and understand that I am, as a result of this Agreement, relinquishing certain rights as to properties which might and/or would, but for this Agreement, have been determined to be community

15

property, quasi-community property or marital property, or which I might have been entitled to receive had SEAN PENN died intestate or as dowry or its statutory equivalent or any other statutory share of a surviving spouse in the state or country in which he had died, owned property or was a resident or citizen. I understand all of the provisions of the Agreement and the rights which I am relinquishing as a result of the execution of the Agreement and the benefits I am receiving under the Agreement. I believe the benefits accruing to me under this Agreement are fair and reasonable. I have executed the Agreement without any influence on the part of SEAN PENN or any other party whomsoever and as a result of my own free volition. No oral statements or inducements, other than those contained herein, have been made as an inducement for me to sign this Agreement.

Madonna Ciccone Penn
MADONNA CICCONE PENN - "WIFE"

CAT. NO. NN00627
TO 1944 CA (1—83)

TICOR TITLE INSURANCE

(Individual)

STATE OF CALIFORNIA
COUNTY OF __LOS ANGELES__ } SS.

On __January 24, 1989__ before me, the undersigned, a Notary Public in and for said State, personally appeared __MADONNA CICCONE PENN__

_____, personally known to me or proved to me on the basis of satisfactory evidence to be the person__ whose name __is__ subscribed to the within instrument and acknowledged that __she__ executed the same.
WITNESS my hand and official seal.

Signature _Jill Napolitano_

STAPLE HERE

OFFICIAL SEAL
JILL M. NAPOLITANO
NOTARY PUBLIC - CALIFORNIA
LOS ANGELES COUNTY
My Comm. Expires Jan. 25, 1991

I, SEAN PENN, by my signature hereto, attest to my agreement to the terms and provisions of this Agreement. I have been advised as to the legal effect of the provisions of this Agreement by Robert Kaufman, independent legal counsel chosen by me, and understand that I am, as a result of this Agreement, relinquishing certain rights as to properties which might and/or would, but for this Agreement, have been determined to be community property, quasi-community property or marital property, or which I might have been entitled to receive had MADONNA CICCONE PENN dies intestate or as dowry or its statutory equivalent or any other statutory share of a surviving spouse in the state or country in which she died, owned property or was a resident or citizen. I understand all of the provisions of the Agreement and the rights which I am relinquishing as a result of the execution of the Agreement and the benefits I am receiving under the Agreement. I believe the benefits accruing to me under this Agreement are fair and reasonable. I have executed such Agreement without any influence on the part of MADONNA CICCONE PENN or any other party whomsoever and as a result of my own free volition. No oral statements or inducements, other than those contained herein, have been made as an inducement for me to sign the Agreement.

SEAN PENN - "HUSBAND"

492

GENERAL ACKNOWLEDGMENT

NO. 201

State of __California__

County of __Los Angeles__ } ss.

On this the __19th__ day of __January__ 19 __89__, before me,

__Tracie L. Marcelin__ ,

the undersigned Notary Public, personally appeared

__Sean Penn__ ,

☑ personally known to me
☐ proved to me on the basis of satisfactory evidence
to be the person(s) whose name(s) __is__ subscribed to the
within instrument, and acknowledged that __he__ executed it.
WITNESS my hand and official seal.

Tracie J. Marcelin

Notary's Signature

OFFICIAL SEAL
TRACIE L MARCELIN
NOTARY PUBLIC - CALIFORNIA
LOS ANGELES COUNTY
My comm. expires NCV 7, 1989

7110 122

NATIONAL NOTARY ASSOCIATION • 23012 Ventura Blvd. • P.O. Box 4625 • Woodland Hills, CA 91364

APPENDIX

UNIFORM CHILD-CUSTODY JURISDICTION AND ENFORCEMENT ACT (1997)

[ARTICLE] 1 GENERAL PROVISIONS

SECTION 101. SHORT TITLE. This [Act] may be cited as the Uniform Child-Custody Jurisdiction and Enforcement Act.

SECTION 102. DEFINITIONS. In this [Act]:

(1) 'Abandoned' means left without provision for reasonable and necessary care or supervision.

(2) 'Child' means an individual who has not attained 18 years of age.

(3) 'Child-custody determination' means a judgment, decree, or other order of a court providing for the legal custody, physical custody, or visitation with respect to a child. The term includes a permanent, temporary, initial, and modification order. The term does not include an order relating to child support or other monetary obligation of an individual.

(4) 'Child-custody proceeding' means a proceeding in which legal custody, physical custody, or visitation with respect to a child is an issue. The term includes a proceeding for divorce, separation, neglect, abuse, dependency, guardianship, paternity, termination of parental rights, and protection from domestic violence, in which the issue may appear. The term does not include a proceeding involving juvenile delinquency, contractual emancipation, or enforcement under [Article] 3.

(5) 'Commencement' means the filing of the first pleading in a proceeding.

(6) 'Court' means an entity authorized under the law of a State to establish, enforce, or modify a child-custody determination.

(7) 'Home State' means the State in which a child lived with a parent or a person acting as a parent for at least six consecutive months immediately before the commencement of a child-custody proceeding. In the case of a child less than six months of age, the term means the State in which the

child lived from birth with any of the persons mentioned. A period of temporary absence of any of the mentioned persons is part of the period.

(8) 'Initial determination' means the first child-custody determination concerning a particular child.

(9) 'Issuing court' means the court that makes a child-custody determination for which enforcement is sought under this [Act].

(10) 'Issuing State' means the State in which a child-custody determination is made.

(11) 'Modification' means a child-custody determination that changes, replaces, supersedes, or is otherwise made after a previous determination concerning the same child, whether or not it is made by the court that made the previous determination.

(12) 'Person' means an individual, corporation, business trust, estate, trust, partnership, limited liability company, association, joint venture, government; governmental subdivision, agency, or instrumentality; public corporation; or any other legal or commercial entity.

(13) 'Person acting as a parent' means a person, other than a parent, who:

(a) has physical custody of the child or has had physical custody for a period of six consecutive months, including any temporary absence, within one year immediately before the commencement of a child-custody proceeding; and

(b) has been awarded legal custody by a court or claims a right to legal custody under the law of this State.

(14) 'Physical custody' means the physical care and supervision of a child.

(15) 'State' means a State of the United States, the District of Columbia, Puerto Rico, the United States Virgin Islands, or any territory or insular possession subject to the jurisdiction of the United States.

[(16) 'Tribe' means an Indian tribe or band, or Alaskan Native village, which is recognized by federal law or formally acknowledged by a State.]

(17) 'Warrant' means an order issued by a court authorizing law enforcement officers to take physical custody of a child.

SECTION 103. PROCEEDINGS GOVERNED BY OTHER LAW. This [Act] does not govern an adoption proceeding or a proceeding pertaining to the authorization of emergency medical care for a child.

SECTION 104. APPLICATION TO INDIAN TRIBES.

(a) A child-custody proceeding that pertains to an Indian child as defined in the Indian Child Welfare Act, 25 U.S.C. 1901 et seq., is not subject to this [Act] to the extent that it is governed by the Indian Child Welfare Act.

[(b) A court of this State shall treat a tribe as if it were a State of the United States for the purpose of applying [Articles] 1 and 2.]

[(c) A child-custody determination made by a tribe under factual circumstances in substantial conformity with the jurisdictional standards of this [Act] must be recognized and enforced under [Article] 3.]

SECTION 105. INTERNAL APPLICATION OF [ACT].

(a) A court of this State shall treat a foreign country as if it were a State of the United States for the purpose of applying [Articles] 1 and 2.

(b) Except as otherwise provided in subsection (c), a child-custody determination made in a foreign country under factual circumstances in substantial conformity with the jurisdiction standards of this [Act] must be recognized and enforced under Article 3.

(c) A court of this State need not apply this [Act] if the child custody law of a foreign country violates fundamental principles of human rights.

SECTION 106. EFFECT OF CHILD-CUSTODY DETERMINATION. A child-custody determination made by a court of this State that had jurisdiction under this [Act] binds all persons who have been served in accordance with the laws of this State or notified in accordance with Section 108 or who have submitted to the jurisdiction of the court, and who have been given an opportunity to be heard. As to those persons, the determination is conclusive as to all decided issues of law and fact except to the extent the determination is modified.

SECTION 107. PRIORITY. If a question of existence or exercise of jurisdiction under this [Act] is raised in a child-custody proceeding, the question, upon request of a party, must be given priority on the calendar and handled expeditiously.

SECTION 108. NOTICE TO PERSONS OUTSIDE STATE.

(a) Notice required for the exercise of jurisdiction when a person is outside this State may be given in a manner prescribed by the law of this State for service of process or by the law of the State in which the service is made. Notice must be given in a manner reasonably calculated to give actual notice but may be by publication if other means are not effective.

(b) Proof of service may be made in the manner prescribed by the law of this State or by the law of the State in which the service is made.

(c) Notice is not required for the exercise of jurisdiction with respect to a person who submits to the jurisdiction of the court.

SECTION 109. APPEARANCE AND LIMITED IMMUNITY.

(a) A party to a child-custody proceeding, including a modification proceeding, or a petitioner or respondent in a proceeding to enforce or register a child-custody determination, is not subject to personal jurisdiction in this State for another proceeding or purpose solely by reason of having participated, or of having been physically present for the purpose of participating, in the proceeding.

(b) A person who is subject to personal jurisdiction in this State on a basis other than physical presence is not immune from service of process in this State. A party present in this State who is subject to the jurisdiction of another State is not immune from service of process allowable under the laws of that State.

(c) The immunity granted by subsection (a) does not extend to civil litigation based on acts unrelated to the participation in a proceeding under this [Act] committed by an individual while present in this State.

SECTION 110. COMMUNICATION BETWEEN COURTS.

(a) A court of this State may communicate with a court in another State concerning a proceeding arising under this [Act].

(b) The court may allow the parties to participate in the communication. If the parties are not able to participate in the communication, they must be given the opportunity to present facts and legal arguments before a decision on jurisdiction is made.

(c) Communication between courts on schedules, calendars, court records, and similar matters may occur without informing the parties. A record need not be made of the communication.

(d) Except as otherwise provided in subsection (c), a record must be made of a communication under this section. The parties must be informed promptly of the communication and granted access to the record.

(e) For the purposes of this section, 'record' means information that is inscribed on a tangible medium or that is stored in an electronic or other medium and is retrievable in perceivable form.

SECTION 111. TAKING TESTIMONY IN ANOTHER STATE.

(a) In addition to other procedures available to a party, a party to a child-custody proceeding may offer testimony of witnesses who are located in another State, including testimony of the parties and the child, by deposition or other means allowable in this State for testimony taken in another State. The court on its own motion may order that the testimony of a person be taken in another State and may prescribe the manner in which and the terms upon which the testimony is taken.

(b) A court of this State may permit an individual residing in another State to be deposed or to testify by telephone, audiovisual means, or other electronic means before a designated court or at another location in that State. A court of this State shall cooperate with courts of other States in designating an appropriate location for the deposition or testimony.

(c) Documentary evidence transmitted from another State to a court of this State by technological means that do not produce an original writing may not be excluded from evidence on an objection based on the means of transmission.

SECTION 112. COOPERATION BETWEEN COURTS; PRESERVATION OF RECORDS.

(a) A court of this State may request the appropriate court of another State to:
   (1) hold an evidentiary hearing;
   (2) order a person to produce or give evidence pursuant to procedures of that State;
   (3) order that an evaluation be made with respect to the custody of a child involved in a pending proceeding;
   (4) forward to the court of this State a certified copy of the transcript of the record of the hearing, the evidence otherwise presented, and any evaluation prepared in compliance with the request; and
   (5) order a party to a child-custody proceeding or any person having physical custody of the child to appear in the proceeding with or without the child.

(b) Upon request of a court of another State, a court of this State may hold a hearing or enter an order described in subsection (a).

(c) Travel and other necessary and reasonable expenses incurred under subsections (a) and (b) may be assessed against the parties according to the law of this State.

(d) A court of this State shall preserve the pleadings, orders, decrees, records of hearings, evaluations, and other pertinent records with respect to a child-custody proceeding until the child attains 18 years of age. Upon appropriate request by a court or law enforcement official of another State, the court shall forward a certified copy of those records.

[ARTICLE] 2 JURISDICTION
SECTION 201. INITIAL CHILD-CUSTODY JURISDICTION.

(a) Except as otherwise provided in Section 204, a court of this State has jurisdiction to make an initial child-custody determination only if:

(1) this State is the home State of the child on the date of the commencement of the proceeding, or was the home State of the child within six months before the commencement of the proceeding and the child is absent from this State but a parent or person acting as a parent continues to live in this State;

(2) a court of another State does not have jurisdiction under paragraph (1), or a court of the home State of the child has declined to exercise jurisdiction on the ground that this State is the more appropriate forum under Section 207 or 208, and:

(A) the child and the child's parents, or the child and at least one parent or a person acting as a parent, have a significant connection with this State other than mere physical presence; and

(B) substantial evidence is available in this State concerning the child's care, protection, training, and personal relationships;

(3) all courts having jurisdiction under paragraph (1) or (2) have declined to exercise jurisdiction on the ground that a court of this State is the more appropriate forum to determine the custody of the child under Section 207 or 208; or

(4) no court of any other State would have jurisdiction under the criteria specified in paragraph (1), (2), or (3).

(b) Subsection (a) is the exclusive jurisdictional basis for making a child-custody determination by a court of this State.

(c) Physical presence of, or personal jurisdiction over, a party or a child is not necessary or sufficient to make a child-custody determination.

SECTION 202. EXCLUSIVE, CONTINUING JURISDICTION.

(a) Except as otherwise provided in Section 204, a court of this State which has made a child-custody determination consistent with Section 201 or 203 has exclusive, continuing jurisdiction over the determination until:

(1) a court of this State determines that neither the child, the child's parents, and any person acting as a parent do not have a significant connection with this State and that substantial evidence is no longer available in this State concerning the child's care, protection, training, and personal relationships; or

(2) a court of this State or a court of another State determines that the child, the child's parents, and any person acting as a parent do not presently reside in this State.

(b) A court of this State which has made a child-custody determination and does not have exclusive, continuing jurisdiction under this section may modify that determination only if it has jurisdiction to make an initial determination under Section 201.

SECTION 203. JURISDICTION TO MODIFY DETERMINATION. Except as otherwise provided in Section 204, a court of this State may not modify a child-custody determination made by a court of another State unless a court of this State has jurisdiction to make an initial determination under Section 201(a)(l) or (2) and:

(1) the court of the other State determines it no longer has exclusive, continuing jurisdiction under Section 202 or that a court of this State would be a more convenient forum under Section 207; or

(2) a court of this State or a court of the other State determines that the child, the child's parents, and any person acting as a parent do not presently reside in the other State.

SECTION 204. TEMPORARY EMERGENCY JURISDICTION.

(a) A court of this State has temporary emergency jurisdiction if the child is present in this State and the child has been abandoned or it is necessary in an emergency to protect the child because the child, or a sibling or parent of the child, is subjected to or threatened with mistreatment or abuse.

(b) If there is no previous child-custody determination that is entitled to be enforced under this [Act] and a child-custody proceeding has not been commenced in a court of a State having jurisdiction under Sections 201 through 203, a child-custody determination made under this section remains in effect until an order is obtained from a court of a State having jurisdiction under Sections 201 through 203. If a child-custody proceeding has not been or is not commenced in a court of a State having jurisdiction under Sections 201 through 203, a child-custody determination made under this section becomes a final determination, if it so provides and this State becomes the home State of the child.

(c) If there is a previous child-custody determination that is entitled to be enforced under this [Act], or a child-custody proceeding has been commenced in a court of a State having jurisdiction under Sections 201 through 203, any order issued by a court of this State under this section must specify in the order a period that the court considers adequate to allow the person seeking an order to obtain an order from the State having jurisdiction under Sections 201 through 203. The order issued in this State remains in effect until an order is obtained from the other State within the period specified or the period expires.

(d) A court of this State which has been asked to make a child-custody determination under this section, upon being informed that a child-custody proceeding has been commenced in, or a child-custody determination has been made by, a court of a State having jurisdiction under Sections 201 through 203, shall immediately communicate with the other court. A court of this State which is exercising jurisdiction pursuant to Sections 201 through 203, upon being informed that a child-custody proceeding has been commenced in, or a child-custody determination has been made by, a court of another State under a statute similar to this section shall immediately communicate with the court of that State to resolve the emergency, protect the safety of the parties and the child, and determine a period for the duration of the temporary order.

SECTION 205. NOTICE; OPPORTUNITY TO BE HEARD; JOINDER.

(a) Before a child-custody determination is made under this [Act], notice and an opportunity to be heard in accordance with the standards of Section 108 must be given to all persons entitled to notice under the law of this State as in child-custody proceedings between residents of this State, any parent whose parental rights have not been previously terminated, and any person having physical custody of the child.

(b) This [Act] does not govern the enforceability of a child-custody determination made without notice or an opportunity to be heard.

(c) The obligation to join a party and the right to intervene as a party in a child-custody proceeding under this [Act] are governed by the law of this State as in child-custody proceedings between residents of this State.

SECTION 206. SIMULTANEOUS PROCEEDINGS.

(a) Except as otherwise provided in Section 204, a court of this State may not exercise its jurisdiction under this [article] if, at the time of the commencement of the proceeding, a proceeding concerning the custody of the child has been commenced in a court of another State having jurisdiction substantially in conformity with this [Act], unless the proceeding has been terminated or is stayed by the court of the other State because a court of this State is a more convenient forum under Section 207.

(b) Except as otherwise provided in Section 204, a court of this State, before hearing a child-custody proceeding, shall examine the court documents and other information supplied by the parties pursuant to Section 209. If the court determines that a child-custody proceeding has been commenced in a court in another State having jurisdiction substantially in accordance with this [Act], the court of this State shall stay its proceeding and communicate with the court of the other State. If the court of the State having jurisdiction substantially in accordance with this [Act] does not determine that the court of this State is a more appropriate forum, the court of this State shall dismiss the proceeding.

(c) In a proceeding to modify a child-custody determination, a court of this State shall determine whether a proceeding to enforce the determination has been commenced in another State. If a proceeding to enforce a child-custody determination has been commenced in another State, the court may:

  (1) stay the proceeding for modification pending the entry of an order of a court of the other State enforcing, staying, denying, or dismissing the proceeding for enforcement;

  (2) enjoin the parties from continuing with the proceeding for enforcement; or

  (3) proceed with the modification under conditions it considers appropriate.

SECTION 207. INCONVENIENT FORUM.

(a) A court of this State which has jurisdiction under this [Act] to make a child-custody determination may decline to exercise its jurisdiction at any time if it determines that it is an inconvenient forum under the circumstances and that a court of another State is a more appropriate forum. The issue of inconvenient forum may be raised upon motion of a party, the court's own motion, or request of another court.

(b) Before determining whether it is an inconvenient forum, a court of this State shall consider whether it is appropriate for a court of another State to exercise jurisdiction. For this purpose, the court shall allow the parties to submit information and shall consider all relevant factors, including:

(1) whether domestic violence has occurred and is likely to continue in the future and which State could best protect the parties and the child;

(2) the length of time the child has resided outside this State;

(3) the distance between the court in this State and the court in the State that would assume jurisdiction;

(4) the relative financial circumstances of the parties;

(5) any agreement of the parties as to which State should assume jurisdiction;

(6) the nature and location of the evidence required to resolve the pending litigation, including testimony of the child;

(7) the ability of the court of each State to decide the issue expeditiously and the procedures necessary to present the evidence; and

(8) the familiarity of the court of each State with the facts and issues in the pending litigation.

(c) If a court of this State determines that it is an inconvenient forum and that a court of another State is a more appropriate forum, it shall stay the proceedings upon condition that a child-custody proceeding be promptly commenced in another designated State and may impose any other condition the court considers just and proper.

(d) A court of this State may decline to exercise its jurisdiction under this [Act] if a child-custody determination is incidental to an action for divorce or another proceeding while still retaining jurisdiction over the divorce or other proceeding.

SECTION 203. JURISDICTION DECLINED BY REASON OF CONDUCT.

(a) Except as otherwise provided in Section 204 [or by other law of this State], if a court of this State has jurisdiction under this [Act] because a person seeking to invoke its jurisdiction has engaged in unjustifiable conduct, the court shall decline to exercise its jurisdiction unless:

(1) the parents and all persons acting as parents have acquiesced in the exercise of jurisdiction;

(2) a court of the State otherwise having jurisdiction under Sections 201 through 203 determines that this State is a more appropriate forum under Section 207; or

(3) no court of any other State would have jurisdiction under the criteria specified in Sections 201 through 203.

(b) If a court of this State declines to exercise its jurisdiction pursuant to subsection (a), it may fashion an appropriate remedy to ensure the safety of the child and prevent a repetition of the unjustifiable conduct, including staying the proceeding until a child-custody proceeding is commenced in a court having jurisdiction under Sections 201 through 203.

(c) If a court dismisses a petition or stays a proceeding because it declines to exercise its jurisdiction pursuant to subsection (a), it shall assess against the party seeking to invoke its jurisdiction necessary and reasonable expenses including costs, communication expenses, attorney's fees, investigative fees, expenses for witnesses, travel expenses, and child care during the course of the proceedings, unless the party from whom fees are sought establishes that the assessment would be clearly inappropriate. The court may not assess fees, costs, or expenses against this State unless authorized by law other than this [Act].

SECTION 209. INFORMATION TO BE SUBMITTED TO COURT.

(a) [Subject to [local law providing for the confidentiality of procedures, addresses, and other identifying information], in] [In] a child-custody proceeding, each party, in its first pleading or in an attached affidavit, shall give information, if reasonably ascertainable, under oath as to the child's present address or whereabouts, the places where the child has lived during the last five years, and the names and present addresses of the persons with whom the child has lived during that period. The pleading or affidavit must state whether the party:

   (1) has participated, as a party or witness or in any other capacity, in any other proceeding concerning the custody of or visitation with the child and, if so, identify the court, the case number, and the date of the child-custody determination, if any;

   (2) knows of any proceeding that could affect the current proceeding, including proceedings for enforcement and proceedings relating to domestic violence, protective orders; termination of parental rights, and adoptions and, if so, identify the court, the case number, and the nature of the proceeding; and

   (3) knows the names and addresses of any person not a party to the proceeding who has physical custody of the child or claims rights of legal custody or physical custody of, or visitation with, the child and, if so, the names and addresses of those persons.

(b) If the information required by subsection (a) is not furnished, the court, upon motion of a party or its own motion, may stay the proceeding until the information is furnished.

(c) If the declaration as to any of the items described in subsections (a)(1) through (3) is in the affirmative, the declarant shall give additional information under oath as required by the court. The court may examine the parties under oath as to details of the information furnished and other matters pertinent to the court's jurisdiction and the disposition of the case.

(d) Each party has a continuing duty to inform the court of any proceeding in this or any other State that could affect the current proceeding.

[(e) If a party alleges in an affidavit or a pleading under oath that the health, safety, or liberty of a party or child would be jeopardized by disclosure of identifying information, the information must be sealed and may not be disclosed to the other party or the public unless the court orders the disclosure to be made after a hearing in which the court takes into consideration the health, safety, or liberty of the party or child and determines that the disclosure is in the interest of justice.]

SECTION 210. APPEARANCE OF PARTIES AND CHILD.

(a) In a child-custody proceeding in this State, the court may order a party to the proceeding who is in this State to appear before the court in person with or without the child. The court may order any person who is in this State and who has physical custody or control of the child to appear in person with the child.

(b) If a party to a child-custody proceeding whose presence is desired by the court is outside this State, the court may order that a notice given pursuant to Section 108 include a statement directing the party to appear in person with or without the child and informing the party that failure to appear may result in a decision adverse to the party.

(c) The court may enter any orders necessary to ensure the safety of the child and of any person ordered to appear under this section.

(d) If a party to a child-custody proceeding who is outside this State is directed to appear under subsection (b) or desires to appear personally before the court with or without the child, the court may require another party to pay reasonable and necessary travel and other expenses of the party so appearing and of the child.

[ARTICLE] 3 ENFORCEMENT

SECTION 301. DEFINITIONS. In this [article]:

(1) 'Petitioner' means a person who seeks enforcement of an order for return of a child under the Hague Convention on the Civil Aspects of International Abduction or enforcement of a child-custody determination.

(2) 'Respondent' means a person against whom a proceeding has been commenced for enforcement of an order for return of a child under the Hague Convention on the Civil Aspects of International Child Abduction or enforcement of a child-custody determination.

SECTION 302. ENFORCEMENT UNDER HAGUE CONVENTION. Under this [article] a court of this State may enforce an order for the return of the child made under the Hague Convention on the Civil Aspects of International Child Abduction as if it were a child-custody determination.

SECTION 303. DUTY TO ENFORCE.

(a) A court of this State shall recognize and enforce a child-custody determination of a court of another State if the latter court exercised jurisdiction in substantial conformity with this [Act] or the determination was made under factual circumstances meeting the jurisdictional standards of this [Act] and the determination has not been modified in accordance with this [Act].

(b) A court of this State may utilize any remedy available under other law of this State to enforce a child-custody determination made by a court of another State. The remedies provided in this [article] are cumulative and do not affect the availability of other remedies to enforce a child-custody determination.

SECTION 304. TEMPORARY VISITATION.

(a) A court of this State which does not have jurisdiction to modify a child-custody determination, may issue a temporary order enforcing:

> (1) a visitation schedule made by a court of another State; or (2) the visitation provisions of a child-custody determination of another State that does not provide for a specific visitation schedule.

(b) If a court of this State makes an order under subsection (a)(2), it shall specify in the order a period that it considers adequate to allow the petitioner to obtain an order from a court having jurisdiction under the criteria specified in [Article] 2. The order remains in effect until an order is obtained from the other court or the period expires.

SECTION 305. REGISTRATION OF CHILD-CUSTODY DETERMINATION.

(a) A child-custody determination issued by a court of another State may be registered in this State, with or without a simultaneous request for enforcement, by sending to [the appropriate court] in this State:

> (1) a letter or other document requesting registration;
>
> (2) two copies, including one certified copy, of the determination sought to be registered, and a statement under penalty of perjury that to the best of the knowledge and belief of the person seeking registration the order has not been modified; and
>
> (3) except as otherwise provided in Section 209, the name and address of the person seeking registration and any parent or person acting as a parent who has been awarded custody or visitation in the child-custody determination sought to be registered.

(b) On receipt of the documents required by subsection (a), the registering court shall:

> (1) cause the determination to be filed as a foreign judgment, together with one copy of any accompanying documents and information, regardless of their form; and
>
> (2) serve notice upon the persons named pursuant to subsection (a)(3) and provide them with an opportunity to contest the registration in accordance with this section.

(c) The notice required by subsection (b)(2) must state that:

> (1) a registered determination is enforceable as of the date of the registration in the same manner as a determination issued by a court of this State;
>
> (2) a hearing to contest the validity of the registered determination must be requested within 20 days after service of notice; and
>
> (3) failure to contest the registration will result in confirmation of the child-custody determination and preclude further contest of that determination with respect to any matter that could have been asserted.

(d) A person seeking to contest the validity of a registered order must request a hearing within 20 days after service of the notice. At that hearing, the court shall confirm the registered order unless the person contesting registration establishes that:

(1) the issuing court did not have jurisdiction under [Article] 2;

(2) the child-custody determination sought to be registered has been vacated, stayed, or modified by a court having jurisdiction to do so under [Article] 2; or

(3) the person contesting registration was entitled to notice, but notice was not given in accordance with the standards of Section 108, in the proceedings before the court that issued the order for which registration is sought.

(e) If a timely request for a hearing to contest the validity of the registration is not made, the registration is confirmed as a matter of law and the person requesting registration and all persons served must be notified of the confirmation.

(f) Confirmation of a registered order, whether by operation of law or after notice and hearing, precludes further contest of the order with respect to any matter that could have been asserted at the time of registration.

SECTION 306. ENFORCEMENT OF REGISTERED DETERMINATION.

(a) A court of this State may grant any relief normally available under the law of this State to enforce a registered child-custody determination made by a court of another State.

(b) A court of this State shall recognize and enforce, but may not modify, except in accordance with [Article] 2, a registered child-custody determination of a court of another State.

SECTION 307. SIMULTANEOUS PROCEEDINGS. If a proceeding for enforcement under this [article] is commenced in a court of this state and the court determines that a proceeding to modify the determination is pending in a court of another State having jurisdiction to modify the determination under [Article] 2, the enforcing court shall immediately communicate with the modifying court. The proceeding for enforcement continues unless the enforcing court, after consultation with the modifying court, stays or dismisses the proceeding.

308. EXPEDITED ENFORCEMENT OF CHILD-CUSTODY DETERMINATION.

(a) A petition under this [article] must be verified. Certified copies of all orders sought to be enforced and of any order confirming registration must be attached to the petition. A copy of a certified copy of an order may be attached instead of the original.

(b) A petition for enforcement of a child-custody determination must state:

(1) whether the court that issued the determination identified the jurisdictional basis it relied upon in exercising jurisdiction and, if so, what the basis was;

(2) whether the determination for which enforcement is sought has been vacated, stayed, or modified by a court whose decision must be enforced under this [Act] and, if so, identify the court, the case number, and the nature of the proceeding;

(3) whether any proceeding has been commenced that could affect the current proceeding, including proceedings relating to domestic

violence, protective orders, termination of parental rights, and adoptions and, if so, identify the court, the case number, and the nature of the proceeding;

(4) the present physical address of the child and the respondent, if known;

(5) whether relief in addition to the immediate physical custody of the child and attorney's fees is sought, including a request for assistance from [law enforcement officials] and, if so, the relief sought; and

(6) if the child-custody determination has been registered and confirmed under Section 305, the date and place of registration.

(c) Upon the filing of a petition, the court shall issue an order directing the respondent to appear in person with or without the child at a hearing and may enter any order necessary to ensure the safety of the parties and the child. The hearing must be held on the next judicial day after service of the order unless that date is impossible. In that event, the court shall hold the hearing on the first judicial day possible. The court may extend the date of hearing at the request of the petitioner.

(d) An order issued under subsection (c) must state the time and place of the hearing and advise the respondent that at the hearing the court will order that the petitioner may take immediate physical custody of the child and the payment of fees, costs, and expenses under Section 312, and may schedule a hearing to determine whether further relief is appropriate, unless the respondent appears and establishes that:

(1) the child-custody determination has not been registered and confirmed under Section 305 and that:

(A) the issuing court did not have jurisdiction under [Article] 2;

(B) the child-custody determination for which enforcement is sought has been vacated, stayed, or modified by a court having jurisdiction to do so under [Article] 2;

(C) the respondent was entitled to notice, but notice was not given in accordance with the standards of Section 108, in the proceedings before the court that issued the order for which enforcement is sought; or

(2) the child-custody determination for which enforcement is sought was registered and confirmed under Section 304, but has been vacated, stayed, or modified by a court of a State having jurisdiction to do so under [Article] 2.

SECTION 309. SERVICE OF PETITION AND ORDER. Except as otherwise provided in Section 311, the petition and order must be served, by any method authorized [by the law of this State], upon respondent and any person who has physical custody of the child.

SECTION 310. HEARING AND ORDER.

(a) Unless the court issues a temporary emergency order pursuant to Section 204, upon a finding that a petitioner is entitled to immediate physical custody of the child, the court shall order that the petitioner may take immediate physical custody of the child unless the respondent establishes that:

(1) the child-custody determination has not been registered and confirmed under Section 305 and that:

> (A) the issuing court did not have jurisdiction under [Article] 2;
>
> (B) the child-custody determination for which enforcement is sought has been vacated, stayed, or modified by a court of a State having jurisdiction to do so under [Article] 2; or
>
> (C) the respondent was entitled to notice, but notice was not given in accordance with the standards of Section 108, in the proceedings before the court that issued the order for which enforcement is sought; or

(2) the child-custody determination for which enforcement is sought was registered and confirmed under Section 305 but has been vacated, stayed, or modified by a court of a State having jurisdiction to do so under [Article] 2.

(b) The court shall award the fees, costs, and expenses authorized under Section 312 and may grant additional relief, including a request for the assistance of [law enforcement officials], and set a further hearing to determine whether additional relief is appropriate.

(c) If a party called to testify refuses to answer on the ground that the testimony may be self-incriminating, the court may draw an adverse inference from the refusal.

(d) A privilege against disclosure of communications between spouses and a defense of immunity based on the relationship of husband and wife or parent and child may not be invoked in a proceeding under this [article].

SECTION 311. WARRANT TO TAKE PHYSICAL CUSTODY OF CHILD.

(a) Upon the filing of a petition seeking enforcement of a child-custody determination, the petitioner may file a verified application for the issuance of a warrant to take physical custody of the child if the child is immediately likely to suffer serious physical harm or be removed from this State.

(b) If the court, upon the testimony of the petitioner or other witness, finds that the child is imminently likely to suffer serious physical harm or be removed from this State, it may issue a warrant to take physical custody of the child. The petition must be heard on the next judicial day after the warrant is executed unless that date is impossible. In that event, the court shall hold the hearing on the first judicial day possible. The application for the warrant must include the statements required by Section 308(b).

(c) A warrant to take physical custody of a child must:

(1) recite the facts upon which a conclusion of imminent serious physical harm or removal from the jurisdiction is based;

(2) direct law enforcement officers to take physical custody of the child immediately; and

(3) provide for the placement of the child pending final relief

(d) The respondent must be served with the petition, warrant, and order immediately after the child is taken into physical custody.

(e) A warrant to take physical custody of a child is enforceable throughout this State. If the court finds on the basis of the testimony of the petitioner or other witness that a less intrusive remedy is not effective, it may authorize law enforcement officers to enter private property to take physical custody of the child. If required by exigent circumstances of the case, the court may authorize law enforcement officers to make a forcible entry at any hour.

(f) The court may impose conditions upon placement of a child to ensure the appearance of the child and the child's custodian.

SECTION 312. COSTS, FEES, AND EXPENSES.

(a) The court shall award the prevailing party, including a State, necessary and reasonable expenses incurred by or on behalf of the party, including costs, communication expenses, attorney's fees, investigative fees, expenses for witnesses, travel expenses, and child care during the course of the proceedings, unless the party from whom fees or expenses are sought establishes that the award would be clearly inappropriate.

(b) The court may not assess fees, costs, or expenses against a State unless authorized by law other than this [Act].

SECTION 313. RECOGNITION AND ENFORCEMENT.
A court of this State shall accord full faith and credit to an order issued by another State and consistent with this [Act] which enforces a child-custody determination by a court of another State unless the order has been vacated, stayed, or modified by a court having jurisdiction to do so under [Article] 2.

SECTION 314. APPEALS.
An appeal may be taken from a final order in a proceeding under this [article] in accordance with [expedited appellate procedures in other civil cases]. Unless the court enters a temporary emergency order under Section 204, the enforcing court may not stay an order enforcing a child-custody determination pending appeal.

SECTION 315. ROLE OF [PROSECUTOR OR PUBLIC OFFICIAL].

(a) In a case arising under this [Act] or involving the Hague Convention on the Civil Aspects of International Child Abduction, the [prosecutor or other appropriate public official] may take any lawful action, including resort to a proceeding under this [article] or any other available civil proceeding to locate a child, obtain the return of a child, or enforce a child-custody determination if there is:

   (1) an existing child-custody determination;

   (2) a request to do so from a court in a pending child-custody proceeding;

   (3) a reasonable belief that a criminal statute has been violated; or

   (4) a reasonable belief that the child has been wrongfully removed or retained in violation of the Hague Convention on the Civil Aspects of International Child Abduction.

(b) A [prosecutor or appropriate public official] acting under this section acts on behalf of the court and may not represent any party.

SECTION 316. ROLE OF [LAW ENFORCEMENT].
At the request of a [prosecutor or other appropriate public official] acting under Section 315, a [law enforcement officer] may take any lawful action reasonably necessary to locate a child or a party and assist [a prosecutor or appropriate public official] with responsibilities under Section 315.

SECTION 317. COSTS AND EXPENSES.
If the respondent is not the prevailing party, the court may assess against the respondent all direct expenses and costs incurred by the [prosecutor or other appropriate public official] and [law enforcement officers] under Section 315 or 316.

[ARTICLE] 4

MISCELLANEOUS PROVISIONS

SECTION 401. APPLICATION AND CONSTRUCTION. In applying and construing this Uniform Act, consideration must be given to the need to promote uniformity of the law with respect to its subject matter among States that enact it.

SECTION 402. SEVERABILITY CLAUSE. If any provision of this [Act] or its application to any person or circumstance is held invalid, the invalidity does not affect other provisions or applications of this [Act] which can be given effect without the invalid provision or application, and to this end the provisions of this [Act] are severable.

SECTION 403. EFFECTIVE DATE. This [Act] takes effect _____.

SECTION 404. REPEALS. The following acts and parts of acts are hereby repealed:

(1) The Uniform Child Custody Jurisdiction Act;

(2) _____

(3) _____

SECTION 405. TRANSITIONAL PROVISION. A motion or other request for relief made in a child-custody proceeding or to enforce a child-custody determination which was commenced before the effective date of this [Act] is governed by the law in effect at the time the motion or other request was made.

APPENDIX

GUIDES FOR DISTANCE LEARNING AND LEGAL RESEARCH

DISTANCE LEARNING

Distance learning presents you with wonderful opportunities for learning, growing, and expanding your personal and professional horizons. At the same time, it provides you with a number of unique challenges. The whole world is your classroom, yet you don't have the physical presence of classmates. The flexibility and excitement of this kind of learning can build your confidence while it develops your mind. However, it may sometimes seem overwhelming or lonely. We have included this appendix to help make your distance learning experience rewarding, invigorating, and successful.

Do's and Don'ts

▽ **DO** stay motivated. Write down your goals. Join Internet legal networks. Access on-line universities and associations. Keep a journal of your obstacles and successes. Reward yourself for work well done.

▽ **DO** become proficient in using the Internet. Really learn to navigate the World Wide Web. This technology provides abundant useful and free resources for your research. Learn how to use the search engines (particularly Yahoo, Infoseek, Snap, and Lycos). Utilize newsgroups; participate in forums.

▽ **DO** learn "netiquette"; for example, writing in all capital letters is considered yelling. A number of web sites will teach this (look up "netiquette" in Yahoo for a list of places that teach it). Remember that when you write your reader does not have the luxury of seeing your body language or hearing the tone of your voice.

▽ **DON'T** isolate yourself. Consider joining a local paralegal association, attending trials, and contacting your local courthouse for copies of forms.

- ▼ **DON'T** be afraid of new ideas—even radical new ideas.
- ▼ **DO** expect to feel overwhelmed or discouraged *sometimes*.
- ▼ **DON'T** give in to negative self-talk or challenging material. You can do it!
- ▼ **DO** make suggestions to your school. **DO** ask them for help when you need to.
- ▼ **DO** ask for support from your family and friends.
- ▼ **DO** be flexible, open-minded, willing to learn new ideas and "roll with the punches."
- ▼ **DO** have fun, be creative, and study well.

Distance Learning Support, Mentoring, and Study Aid Sites

Distance Learning Support and Mentoring

http://maxpages.com/edsupport

Provides help studying, note-taking, reading, and comprehending challenging material, test-taking, outlining, grammar, and writing skills. Includes advice on time management and balancing priorities. Offers virtual one-on-one tutoring and mentoring support for distance learners and nontraditional students. Check this one out!

Study Guides and Strategies

http://www.lss.stthomas.edu/studyguides/

Provides information on study preparation, studying, testing skills, writing skills, and reading skills.

Brain Dancing for Students

http://braindance.com/

Provides tips on how to enhance memory, improve reading, manage information, enhance mental clarity, and optimize web browsing. Great site!

Eggleston's Distance Education Resources

http://www.the-eggman.com

Provides extensive information about and links to distance learning support services, consultants, newsgroups, government resources, and more.

Study Guide for Distance Education

http://www.gwu.edu/~etl/deguide

Provides general information about distance education. Topics include "Fundamentals of Distance Education" and "The Distance Education Student."

Distance Learning on the Net

http://www.hoyle.com/distance

Provides descriptions of and links to distance education sites. Very user-friendly. Excellent guide.

Distance Education Clearinghouse

http://www.uwex.edu/disted/

Provides articles, bibliography, resources, and general information about distance education.

LEGAL RESEARCH

Hot Legal Web Sites

Take advantage of any links these sites provide. Cross-reference. Use keywords in general search engines (Yahoo, etc.) to find more! If you don't know where to find a particular search engine, use the default engine in your computer and type in the name of the search engine you're looking for. If your search does not reveal the site you are looking for, try typing the address without the *www* prefix or try adding the suffix *html* or *htm*.

LEGAL RESEARCH SITES

Nolo Press Self-Help Law Center

http://www.nolo.com

Discusses *how* to do legal research. A must see!

LawCrawler

http://www.lawcrawler.com

Use keywords to find documents for your subject. Provides links directly to sites.

Findlaw

http://www.findlaw.com

Allows user to search specific areas and continually narrow down and focus research.

Lawsource, Inc.

http://www.lawsource.com

Lets you research by jurisdiction. Includes Canada and Mexico.

Law Journal Extra!

http://www.ljx.com

Contains electronic versions of print periodicals, employment information, law firm listings.

Substantive Law on the World Wide Web

http://www.mother.com/~randy/law

Provides links to state and federal statutes and case law. Links to specific areas of law (bankruptcy, family, criminal, etc.).

Law Guru

http://www.lawguru.com

Provides links to specific areas of legal research.

FastSearch

http://www.fastsearch.com

Includes four search engines—be sure to click on "the law engine."

UNIVERSITIES AND LAW SCHOOLS

Chicago–Kent College of Law: http://www.kentlaw.edu
Cornell Law School: http://www.law.cornell.edu/library
Emory Law Library: http://www.law.emory.edu/law/refdesk/reference/legal

COURTS, COURT INFORMATION, AND GOVERNMENT AGENCIES

Court Decisions on the Web

http://www.stanford.edu/group/law/library/how/web-courts

Allows user to choose jurisdiction and find decisions. Provides state, national, and international data.

The Courthouse

http://www.ljextra.com

Provides access to circuit court database (Supreme, federal, and state).

Internal Revenue Service Home Page

http://www.irs.ustreas.gov/prod/cover

Home of the IRS. Can access general tax information and specific treasury regulations.

Legal and Government Forms

Online legal forms from Versuslaw:
http://www.versuslaw.com/versuslaw/forms

Findlaw's forms collections and indexes:
http://www.findlaw.com/16forms/index

The 'Lectric Library's forms room: http://www.lectlaw.com

PROFESSIONAL ASSOCIATIONS

American Bar Association: http://www.abanet.org

Association of Legal Administrators: http://www.alanet.org

National Association of Legal Assistants: http://www.nalanet.org

National Federation of Paralegal Associations: http://www.paralegals.org

LEGAL EMPLOYMENT

Law Journal Extra! Law Employment Center

http://www.lawjobs.com

Draws from ads in various law journals. Regional focus (New York, New Jersey, Connecticut, Massachusetts).

LawJobs WWW

http://www.lawlib.wuacc.edue/postlaw/joblists.htm

Features various list and listserv links.

The Legal Employment Search Site

http://www.legalemploy.com

Connected to employment section of Yahoo.

K APPENDIX

FINDING STATE LAW

State	Court Opinions	State Statutes
Alabama	http://www.alalinc.net/	
Alaska	http://www.alaska.net/~akctlib/	http://www.legis.state.ak.us/
Arizona		http://www.azleg.atate.az.us/
Arkansas	http://www.state.ar.us/supremecourt/	http://www.uark.edu/~govninfo/PAGES/
California	http://www.courtinfo.cagov/opinions/	http://www.leginfor.ca.gov/
Colorado	http://www.cobar.org/coappcts/	http://www.state.co.us/gov_dir/stateleg
Connecticut		http://www.cslnet.ctstateu.edu/statutes
Delaware		http://www.state.de.us/govern/governor/signed
Florida	http://www.justice.courts.sate.fl.us/	http://www.leg.state.fl.us/
Georgia	http://www.statega.us/Courts/Supreme	http://www.ganet.state.ga.us/services
Hawaii	http://www.hsba.org/Hawaii/Court/Curr/courin	http://www.hawaii.gov/lrb/dig/digdoc
Idaho	http://www.state.id.us/judicial/	http://www.state.id.us/legislat
Illinois	http://www.state.il.us/court/Opinions	http://housegop.state.il.us/illconst
Indiana	http://www.indiana.edu/law/incourts/	http://www.law.indiana.edu/law/research
Iowa		http://www2.legis.state.ia.us/Indices/
Kansas	http://www.law.ukans.edu/kscourts	http://www.ink.org/
Kentucky		http://www.lrc.state.ky.us/
Louisiana	http://www.gnofn.org/~lasc	
Maine	http://www.courts.state.me.us/	http://www.state.me.us/legis
Maryland	http://www.mec.state.md.us/mec/	
Massachusetts	http://www.socialaw.com/	http://www.state.ma.us/legis
Michigan	http://www.sado.org/	http://www.umich.edu/~icle/
Minnesota	http://www.courts.state.mn.us	http://www.leg.sate.mn.us/leg/
Mississippi	http://www.mslawyer.com	http://www.mslawyer.com
Missouri	http://www.state.mo.us/sca	http://www.house.state.mo.us/
Montana		http://www.mt.gov/leg/
Nebraska	http://www.nol.org/legal/	http://unicam1.lcs.state.ne.us/

State	Court Opinions	State Statutes
Nevada		http://venus.optimis.com/
New Hampshire	http://www.state.nh.us/courts/	http://www.state.nh.us/gencourt/
New Jersey		http://www.njleg.state.nj.us/
New Mexico		http://www.nm.org/legislature
New York	http://www.law.cornell.edu/ny/ctap/	http://assembly.stateny.us/ALIS
North Carolina	http://www.nando.net/insider/	http://www.legislature.state.nc.us/
North Dakota	http://sc3.court.state.nd.us/	http://www.state.nd.us/lr/
Ohio	http://www.sconet.ohio.gov/	http://winslo.ohio.gov/stgvleg
Oklahoma	http://www.ou.edu/okgov/	http://www.onenet.net/oklegal/statutes
Oregon	http://www.willamette.edu/~ccrowell/law/	http://www.leg.state.or.us/bills
Pennsylvania	http://www.cert.net/penna~courts	
Rhode Island		http://www.state.ri.us/wwwenact
South Carolina	http://www.law.sc.edu/opinions/	http://www.eginfo.state.sc.us/
South Dakota	http://www.sdbar.org/opinions/	
Tennessee	http://www.tsc.state.tn.us/opinions/	
Texas	http://www.window.state.tx.us/txgovinf/	http://lamb.sos.state.tx.us/
Utah	http://courtlink.utcourts.gov/	http://info.law.utah.edu/
Vermont	http://dol.state.vt.us/WWW_ROOT/	
Virginia	http://leg1.state.va.us/	http://senate.state.va.us/
Washington	http://www.wa.gov/courts	http://www.leg.wa.gov/
West Virginia	http://www.scusco.wvnet.edu/www/	
Wisconsin	http://www.wisbar.org/WIS/	http://badger.state.wi.us/agencies
Wyoming	http://courts.state.wy.us/	http://legisweb.state.wy.us/

GLOSSARY

abode residence

abuse physically harmful treatment

administrative enforcement action by a state or federal agency, rather than a court

Administrative Procedure Act a federal statute that allows a person appearing before a federal administrative agency to be represented by an attorney or, if the agency permits, "by other qualified individual"

adoption a legal procedure that makes a person or persons the legal parent or parents of a minor child who is not their natural child

adultery voluntary sexual intercourse of a married person with a person other than the offender's spouse; one of the legal grounds to establish fault in a divorce proceeding

affidavit a signed, sworn statement

affidavit of publication a signed, sworn statement that a legal notice was printed

alienation of affection where a husband or wife contends that a third party has become romantically or sexually involved with his or her spouse and interfered with or broken up the marriage

alimony a sum of money, or other property, paid by a former spouse to the other former spouse for financial support, pursuant to a court order, temporary or final, in a divorce proceeding; also known as spousal maintenance or spousal support

alimony in gross a support payment made in one single payment; also known as lump sum alimony

allowable deductions taxes, debts, and allowable expenses that must be deducted from a spouse's gross income to determine net income

annulment a judicial decision that a valid marriage does not exist or never existed between a person and another party

answer a document in which each of the allegations contained in the numbered paragraphs of a complaint is responded to

antenuptial agreement a contract entered into by the prospective spouses regarding their rights during the marriage and in the event of a divorce; also known as a premarital or prenuptial agreement

appearance a document which states that a person has come into a court action as a party or an attorney representing a party

application for a prejudgment remedy where a party asks the court to take some action before a judgment in the case is rendered

arrearage amounts due by court order but unpaid; also known as back alimony

attorney client privilege the ethical rule which states that attorneys cannot disclose information related to the representation of a client, with certain exceptions

attorney's fees the amount charged by a lawyer to a client for undertaking his or her case

authorized practice of law general criteria for obtaining a license to practice law required by state statute

bench trial a trial conducted before a judge, not a jury

beneficiary the person for whom a trustee holds legal title to property

best interest of the child standard which opened the contest for custody not only to fathers but also to other potential caregivers when the child's well-being or interests could be best served by such a custody determination

billable hours the amount of time expended on a particular case, which can later be billed to that client

body the part of a complaint that contains the necessary factual information that establishes the jurisdiction of the court and identifies the grounds on which the divorce is being sought

boilerplate standardized agreement forms or clauses

breach of promise to marry where a man promises to marry a woman to gain favor and then fails to do so

Bureau of Vital Statistics form a form that is filled out and sent to the state in order to keep track of certain information regarding divorcing couples

buyout where the pension of one spouse is valuated and the employee spouse gives cash to the nonemployee

517

spouse in exchange for any interest the nonemployee spouse may have in the employee spouse's pension

canon law   the church's body of law or rules that determine man's moral obligations to man, to woman, and to God

capias   a document empowering a sheriff to arrest a nonappearing, noncustodial parent and bring him or her to jail and to court

caption   the initial section of a complaint which contains the names of the parties, the name and division of the court, the docket number or the return date of the action, and the date the complaint was drawn up

certification   page accompanying a court document which states that a copy of the document was sent on a specific date to all counsel of record and *pro se* appearing parties (if any)

child protection agency   a state agency charged with intervening when abuse or neglect is known or suspected

child support guidelines   statutorily enacted formulas for determining the amount the noncustodial parent must pay for the support of each child

church courts   courts that had the jurisdiction to hear some matters that could also be heard in the general state courts; however, they had exclusive jurisdiction over all family-related legal matters; also known as ecclesiastical courts

civil code   the system of Spanish and French concepts of marital property law existing on the European mainland; also known as the *code civile*

claim for relief   a statement filed by a party indicating what he or she wants in terms of a disposition in the case

clear and convincing evidence   a high evidentiary standard of proof which requires a higher degree of certainty than the preponderance of evidence standard required for a judicial finding of neglect and lower than the beyond a reasonable doubt standard required in criminal matters

COBRA   see *Consolidated Omnibus Budget Reconciliation Act*

code   a set of written rules that establishes the guidelines for attorneys in their interactions with clients, courts, staff, and their obligations to the general public

cohabitation   unmarried parties living together as if married

cohabitation agreement   contracts entered into by unmarried persons who live together or plan to live together

combined net income   the figure arrived at when each parent's net income is added together to determine child support; also known as total net income

community property   a system of property division that assumes that both husband and wife contributed to the accumulation of marital assets

competency   the duty to exercise a reasonable degree of care and skill commonly used by other attorneys engaged in a similar area of practice

complaint   a grievance filed with a disciplinary body against an attorney; also, a document that commences an action when the opposing party is served; also known as a petition

compromise   meeting someone halfway or giving up a position in exchange for something else

concurrent ownership   when property is held by two or more persons together; also known as joint ownership

confidential   information that is privileged; that is, not everyone is allowed access to it

confidentiality   the ethical rule that protects communications between attorneys and their clients

confidentiality agreement   an arrangement between an attorney and a client that certain information the client may divulge will be kept secret

conflict of interest   any activity which may divide the attorney's loyalty and compromise his or her independent judgment

Consolidated Omnibus Budget Reconciliation Act 26 USC sec. 4980B(f) (COBRA)   a federal law that enables a nonemployee spouse to continue his or her health insurance coverage provided by his or her spouse's employer for a period of three years after a divorce, as long as the nonemployee spouse pays the premium

constructive trust   trust imposed by the court to avoid unjust enrichment when there is no intent between the parties

contempt   where one party in an action does not comply with the court's order

contempt proceeding   a civil proceeding that a party may commence to force the payor spouse to comply with the court's order when the party entitled to alimony is not paid

contested   a disputed divorce trial

contingent fees   an arrangement that entitles attorneys to a percentage of the financial outcome of the case, be it a judgment or settlement

cooling-off period   the statutorily mandated time period following the initiation of divorce proceedings during which no final decree may be entered

cost of living clause   provides for increases in the alimony payments due to the increase of payor's income and an increase in the cost of living, which obviates the need for the parties to go back to court for modifications; also known as an escalation clause

costs of litigation include filing fees, sheriff's fees, deposition costs, expert witness fees, excessive photocopying and mailing costs

counterclaim an allegation presented by the defendant against the plaintiff

court calendar a small printed booklet or a set of pages that contains a number of cases listed according to parties and docket number and indicates the order in which cases will be heard

court-entry fee an amount of money required to file a complaint in court; also known as a filing fee

creditor a party to whom a sum of money is owed; also known as an obligee

cross-claim where the defendant-spouse assumes the role of a plaintiff by bringing a cross-action or countersuit for dissolution in which the party makes allegations and asks the court to grant him or her the relief of a dissolution or divorce and orders regarding custody, child support, alimony and property division; also known as a cross-complaint

cross-complaint see *cross-claim*

cross-examination when the opposing party's lawyer has the opportunity to question the opposing party

custodial parent the parent with whom the child primarily resides

custody affidavit an affidavit indicating that there is no other proceeding pending in another court that affects the custody of the minor children

debt a sum of money owed to another party

debtor the party responsible for the money that is owed; also known as an obligor

deep pocket the term applied to characterize the defendant in a lawsuit who has the financial resources to absorb a civil suit for monetary damages

default judgment where one party "wins" the dissolution or divorce suit by failure of the other party to act

default trial where one of the parties to an action has failed to appear at the scheduled trial date even though he or she has received proper notice of the proceedings; the court proceeds with a hearing and severs the marriage

defendant the party against whom an action is brought

deny in a court proceeding, where the judge refuses to grant the motion of one of the parties

deponent the person who is being questioned at a deposition

deposition a procedure in which one party's attorney orally questions an opposing party or a nonparty witness who has sworn under oath to answer all questions truthfully and accurately to the best of their knowledge and ability

desertion where one spouse abandons his or her duties toward the other; one of the legal grounds to establish fault in a divorce proceeding

deviation from the guideline when the parties agree between themselves that one or the other will pay more or less of the statutorily determined amount

direct examination the initial questioning by the party's own attorney

disciplinary board bodies that may sanction or punish attorneys for engaging in conduct that violates the state's code of professional conduct

disclosure the process of the parties revealing the full extent and current values of all their assets

discovery the process or stage in a civil litigation matter during which information is gathered by each party for use in their case against the other party

discovery tools ways in which an attorney may gather information for use in their case against another party

discretion of the court where the court has the power to make the alimony decision and an appellate court will not reverse that decision unless the judge somehow abused his or her discretion

dissipation depletion of the marital assets by waste

divorce the complete severance of the marital relationship allowing the parties to go their separate ways, including the right to remarry; also known as divorce *a vinculo matrimonii*

divorce *a mensa et thoro* divorce from bed and board, which did not sever the marriage, but just enabled the spouses to live separate and apart; also known as divorce

divorce *a vinculo matrimonii* the complete severance of the marital relationship allowing the parties to go their separate ways, including the right to remarry

divorce trial a trial in which both parties present their case to the court for its final hearing

docket control system a system of one or more calendars that helps an attorney keep track of the various court dates and deadlines

documents the papers associated with a case

domestic partnership an arrangement between couples who choose not to marry, but live together just like a married couple

duplicative referring to discovery, something that has already been asked for

earned retainer   amount from the retainer which the attorney may keep in proportion to the amount of work expended on the client's file

ecclesiastical courts   courts which had the jurisdiction to hear some matters that could also be heard in the general state courts; however, they had exclusive jurisdiction over all family-related legal matters; also known as church courts

Employee Retirement Income Security Act(ERISA) a federal statute passed in 1974 to protect employees and their pensions in case the employer declared bankruptcy or went out of business

equitable distribution   a system allowing family courts to distribute property acquired during marriage on the basis of fairness, as opposed to ownership

equity   the fair market value of the property minus any encumbrances

ERISA   see *Employee Retirement Income Security Act*

escalation clause   provides for increases in alimony payments due to the increase of payor's income and an increase in the cost of living, obviating the need for the parties to go back to court for modifications; also known as a cost of living clause

ethical wall   when a paralegal cannot discuss a case with anyone in the office or have access to the file because of the possibility of conflict of interest

expert witness   a person with specialized knowledge who is called to testify in court

express contract   an agreement between the parties regarding the specific terms

expressed trusts   a trust in which the terms have been negotiated by the parties

fair market value   the price a buyer is willing to pay a seller in exchange for a property

family relations unit   trained social workers who work for the court and conduct studies and applied child development and child psychology concepts to make custody and visitation recommendations; also known as the family services division

family services division   see *family relations unit*

family support payments   the term given to regular, periodic payments a payor spouse makes to the other spouse for the financial maintenance of both the ex-spouse and children

fees   the amount the attorney will charge the client, based on the skill and experience of the attorney, the simplicity or complexity of the client's matter, cost of similar service in the community, the result obtained, the repu-

tation of the attorney and whether the matter is contested or uncontested

filing fee   an amount of money required to file a complaint in court; also known as a court entry fee

final argument   where each attorney argues why the court should rule in his or her client's favor

financial affidavits   a sworn statement that enumerates the party's sources of income, earned and unearned, the party's expenses, necessary and optional, and all of the party's assets and liabilities

financial disclosure affidavit   a sworn statement indicating the income, expenses, assets, and liabilities of a client

financial worksheet   focuses on the client's income, expenses, assets, and liabilities, be they joint or separate; enables the attorney to begin assessing the extent of the marital estate

fixed schedule   definite dates and time frames set aside for the purpose of allowing a noncustodial parent to visit with a child

flat fee   an arrangement whereby a fixed dollar amount is agreed on and charged for the entire case

former client–current opponent   upon an attorney or paralegal switching jobs, discovering that his or her new employer is representing the opponent in a former client's case

freelance paralegal   independent contractor who works for a number of attorneys on an as-needed basis

front loading   where the majority of property settlements in a divorce case are made in the first three years after the divorce

full faith and credit clause   part of the United States Constitution that states that all states must honor the public acts, records, and judicial proceedings of every other state

fundamental right   a right either expressed in the Constitution or one which the Supreme Court has stated may be inferred (implied) from the existing rights

grant   in a court proceeding, when the judge decides to allow a party's request or motion

grievance   a complaint filed with a disciplinary body against an attorney

grievance committees   state bar associations that regulate the legal profession through disciplinary bodies

gross income   the sum of all available sources of income

habeus corpus   a document that allows an incarcerated party to be transported by a state's correctional department for trial

habitual intemperance where one party frequently and repeatedly becomes intoxicated; one of the legal grounds to establish fault in a divorce proceeding

hold harmless clause part of a separation agreement that indicates that a particular spouse will be responsible for a debt incurred during the marriage, that he or she will be solely responsible for its payment, and the other spouse shall be free and clear of any obligation regarding that debt

hotline twenty-four-hour telephone number established for the reporting of suspected child abuse and neglect

hourly basis billing the client for each hour of time spent working on a client's file, including, but not limited to, research, drafting documents, phone calls, travel, office visits, trial preparation, interviewing witnesses

implied-in-fact contract an agreement in which the intention of the parties is inferred by their conduct

implied partnership in the case of a cohabitating couple that works on a business enterprise owned by one of the parties, the court recognizes an implied partnership

implied trust a legal relationship in which the trustee holds legal title to property for the benefit of the beneficiary

incarceration in a penal institution confinement in a jail or prison; one of the legal grounds to establish fault in a divorce proceeding

incompatibility the no-fault ground for divorce; may be also be referred to as irreconcilable differences, irretrievable breakdown, or irremediable breakdown

initial client interview the first meeting between a client and an attorney or paralegal at which basic information to start work on a case is gathered

institutionalization for mental illness confinement to a sanitarium or asylum; one of the legal grounds to establish fault in a divorce proceeding

integrated bar associations affiliations of state bar associations where membership is mandatory

interrogatories requests for disclosure of all real and personal property owned by a spouse either in his or her own name or owned jointly with the spouse or with another person or entity

investigative child protection worker social worker representing the state child protection agency who makes the initial investigation of suspected child abuse or neglect and determines whether the state should take further action to protect the child

irreconcilable differences the no-fault ground for divorce; may be also be referred to as incompatibility, irretrievable breakdown, or irremediable breakdown

irrelevant not having anything to do with the matter at hand

irremediable breakdown the no-fault ground for divorce; may be also be referred to as incompatibility, irreconcilable differences, or irretrievable breakdown

irretrievable breakdown the no-fault ground for divorce; may be also be referred to as incompatibility, irreconcilable differences, or irremediable breakdown

IRS recapture rule applies when the parties do not wish to have alimony taxed as income or deducted; should be indicated in the settlement agreement

joint custody arrangement in which parents are equally responsible for the financial, emotional, educational, and health-related needs of their children

joint ownership when two or more persons hold property together; also known as concurrent ownership

joint tenancy with rights of survivorship where each party owns equal interests in property and at the death of one of the joint tenants, his or her interest automatically passes to the remaining parties

judgment the orders made by a court pursuant to the court's decision after trial; orders become a permanent part of the court file

judicial pretrial a conference that takes place before a judge, not a trial, to help the parties try to come to an agreement before the trial starts; also known as a pretrial conference

juris number the attorney's license number

legal advice advising a client of his or her specific legal rights and responsibilities, and either predicting an outcome or recommending that the client pursue a particular course of action

legal custody where both parents are the children's legal guardians and, as such, have the right to make decisions regarding their children's health, education, and welfare

legal grounds prior to the passage of no-fault divorce laws, where a spouse seeking a divorce was required to have facts proving that the other spouse was at fault

legal separation an action brought by a spouse who wishes to avoid the legal, social, or religious ramifications of a divorce but nevertheless wishes to live apart from his or her spouse

living expenses any monies for client's personal use that may not be advanced to a client by the attorney

lump sum alimony a support payment made in one single payment; also known as alimony in gross

malpractice negligent legal representation; representation that is below the standard of the professional community and could result in damage to the client

mandatory reporter a professional who is required by state statute to report suspected child abuse or neglect

marital assets the property acquired during a marriage

marital debts the liabilities incurred by either spouse during a marriage

marital settlement agreement a contract between spouses who are in the process of obtaining a divorce or a legal separation resolving the various legal issues that arise when a marriage is dissolving; also known as a property settlement, separation agreement, or settlement agreement

marriage statute a law passed by a state legislature which indicates who may marry

Married Women's Property Acts statutes that eliminated the disadvantages of married women and gave them the right to control their own earnings, bring lawsuits, be sued, own their own property, enter into contracts, and function in a legal capacity

mediation where the parties meet and attempt to resolve the pending issues surrounding their dissolution of marriage action with the assistance of a trained third party, either court-provided and free, or privately engaged and paid

memorandum of law a written document presented to the court that states a party's argument in a case and supports that argument with specific case law and statutes

mental cruelty where one spouse tries to cause psychological harm to the other; one of the legal grounds to establish fault in a divorce proceeding

merger an agreement that is no longer a contract between the two parties, but rather a court order, which can be modified or enforced through contempt of court proceedings

military affidavit a sworn statement that serves as proof that the defendant is currently not serving in one of the armed forces

miscegenation laws statute that prohibited interracial marriages

Model Rules of Professional Conduct a prototype for attorney's ethics written by the American Bar Association as a model for states that wish to adopt them

modification a change or adjustment to a previous court order

modification of alimony the issue of whether spousal support may be either increased or decreased after the original order has been entered due to a substantial change in one spouse's circumstances

motion a written document that asks the court to take some type of action

motion day one or two days of the week that courts set aside to hear motions brought before the court; also known as the short calendar

motion for alimony, *pendente lite* where a party to a dissolution proceeding asks the court to grant support payments to him or her for the duration of the case

motion for child support, *pendente lite* where a party to a dissolution proceeding asks the court to have the other party pay child maintenance for the duration of the case

motion for contempt a document that alerts the court to the other party's failure to comply with the court's earlier order and requests that the court provide relief

motion for custody, *pendente lite* where a party to a dissolution proceeding asks the court to have possession of the children for the duration of the case

motion for disclosure of assets requests disclosure of all real and personal property owned by a spouse either in his or her own name or owned jointly with the spouse or with another person or entity

motion for exclusive possession of the marital home, *pendente lite* where a party to a dissolution proceeding asks the court to allow him or her to stay in the home, without the other party, for the duration of the case

motion for modification where a party asks that orders entered by the court be changed when there has been a substantial change in the one of the party's circumstances from the time the original order was entered; also known as a motion to modify

motion for modification of child support a document requesting the court to order the noncustodial parent to pay higher periodic child support payments, so that less of the custodial parent's income will be needed for the child

motion for payment of mortgage payments and insurance premiums, *pendente lite* where a party to a dissolution proceeding asks the court to have the other party pay for certain bills for the duration of the case

motion for protective order where a party asks the court to prevent the other party from coming in contact with him or her

motion for use of the automobile, *pendente lite* where a party to a dissolution proceeding asks the court to have sole use of the couple's automobile for the duration of the case

motion to compel examination a document that asks the court to force the opposing party to submit to an examination

motion to freeze marital assets where a party asks the court to stop any transactions of the marital property from taking place

motion to modify where a party asks that orders entered by the court be changed when there has been a substantial change in one of the party's circumstances from the time the original order was entered; also known as a motion for modification

motion to modify alimony where a party asks that orders for spousal support entered by the court be changed when there has been a substantial change in one of the party's circumstances from the time the original order was entered; also known as a motion to modify support

motion to modify custody where a party asks that orders regarding child custody entered by the court be changed when there has been a substantial change in one of the party's circumstances from the time the original order was entered

motion to modify support where a party asks that orders for spousal support entered by the court be changed when there has been a substantial change in one of the party's circumstances from the time the original order was entered; also known as a motion to modify alimony

motion to modify visitation where a party asks that orders for child visitation entered by the court be changed when there has been a substantial change in one of the party's circumstances from the time the original order was entered

motion to restrain party from entering marital residence where a party asks the court to order that the other party be forbidden to enter the home where that party is living

moving party the person bringing the motion to court

multiple representation where one lawyer is hired to represent both parties to a case

National Association of Legal Assistants (NALA) voluntary national, state, and local paralegal association that has established its own ethical codes

National Federation of Paralegal Professionals (NFPA) voluntary national, state, and local paralegal association that has established its own ethical codes

neglect the failure of a parent to adequately provide for the child's nutritional, educational, or medical needs, or allowing a child to live in conditions that are unsanitary or dangerous

net income the dollar amount remaining after allowable deductions are subtracted from the gross income

no-fault divorce where one of the parties only has to allege that the marriage has broken down and that there is no hope of reconciliation in order for the court to dissolve a marriage

no-fault divorce laws a modification of existing divorce laws to include the ground that the marital union or marital relationship had broken down irretrievably

nominal alimony a very small award of alimony, usually one dollar, which allows the recipient spouse to go back to court in the future, if necessary, to have the award modified

noncustodial parent the parent who does not have the child living with him or her on a full-time basis

nonmodifiable orders issued by a court that cannot be changed, regardless of the circumstances

nonvested in an employee pension plan, when the right to the employer portion of the funds has not yet attached

notice of deposition a document that alerts a party that he or she will be required to submit to examination by the opposing attorney

notice of filing of interrogatories a document which alerts the court that a party has asked the opposing party to answer a set of written questions

notice of responding to and/or objecting to interrogatories a document that alerts the court that the answering party has either answered the written questions or objects to one or more of the questions

notice to appear for a deposition to disclose assets a document which requires a party to appear in order to be questioned, under oath, on the previous disclosure to determine whether it completely revealed all of the party's assets

objection a document used when a party is in opposition to an action the court or the opposition has taken

obligee a party to whom a sum of money is owed; also known as a creditor

obligor the party responsible for money that is owed; also known as a debtor

offset when an employee-spouse agrees to transfer his or her interest in other marital assets in exchange for the full ownership of his or her pension benefits

order a statement that sets forth the judge's decision on a particular motion before the court

order of temporary custody a court order enabling the state to remove children from their home and place them in relative or foster care, when they are in imminent danger

overbroad too general; not specific enough

padding unjustifiably increasing the number of hours actually spent on a client's case

partnership during a marriage, when the efforts and personal and financial resources of the parties are pooled for the benefit of the marriage

paternity action where the petitioning party, usually the child's mother but occasionally the father, requests that the court hold a hearing to establish whether a particular man is the child's biological father

patria potestas in ancient civilizations, where fathers possessed absolute right to the possession of their children and could even sell the children or put them to death if desired

pendancy period the time during court proceedings before judgment is rendered

pendente lite **alimony** payments made during the pendency of the divorce with the purpose of providing temporary financial support for the spouse; also known as temporary alimony

pendente lite **motion** a motion granting relief only for the duration of the court action, before judgment is rendered

pension a retirement benefit acquired by an employee

periodic alimony term applied to court-ordered payments that are to be made to a spouse on a regular basis

permanent alimony the term applied to court-ordered payments that are to be made to a spouse on a regular and periodic basis and that terminate only on the death, remarriage, or cohabitation of the other spouse or on court order

personal property anything other than real property that can be touched and is movable

petition a document that commences the action when the opposing party is served; also known as a complaint

petitioner the party who brings a court action against another; also known as the plaintiff

physical cruelty actual personal violence of one spouse toward another; one of the legal grounds to establish fault in a divorce proceeding

physical custody when a parent has actual bodily possession of the children

plaintiff the party who brings a court action against another; also known as the petitioner

pleading documents that state the plaintiff's claims giving rise to the dissolution action and the defendant's responses or defenses to such claims

postmajority support agreements that frequently address payment for college tuition or other postsecondary education; payment for the maintenance of postmajority adult children with special needs; and payment of medical and dental insurance coverage for dependent adult children while they are students or when they are newly employed but not yet eligible for coverage at work

postnuptial agreement agreements made *after* the marriage has been performed in which the elements are similar to those of prenuptial agreements

prayer for relief the plaintiff's request for a dissolution and for court orders, when appropriate, regarding property distribution, alimony, child custody, and support of the minor children

premarital agreement a contract entered into by the prospective spouses regarding their rights during the marriage and in the event of a divorce; also known as an antenuptial agreement or prenuptial agreement

premium a monetary sum paid on an annual or installment basis for malpractice insurance coverage

prenuptial agreement a contract entered into by the prospective spouses regarding their rights during the marriage and in the event of a divorce; also known as an antenuptial agreement or premarital agreement

prereturn date relief where a plaintiff spouse needs and may seek immediate relief or court intervention as soon as the complaint is served

pretrial conference a meeting that takes place before a judge, not a trial, to help the parties try to come to an agreement before the trial starts; also known as a judicial pretrial

primary caregiver the individual who has done most of the significant parenting of the child since birth or for the several preceding years

privilege a court-conferred right permitting parties in a lawsuit to keep confidential any information exchanged between themselves and another person in instances where there was a special type of relationship between themselves and the other person that promoted an expectation of trust, confidentiality, and privacy

pro hac vice where a state may grant an attorney special permission to handle one particular case

pro per individuals who represent themselves in court; also known as *pro se*

pro se see *pro per*

property settlement a contract between spouses who are in the process of obtaining a divorce or a legal separation resolving the various legal issues that arise when a marriage is dissolving; also known as a marital settlement agreement, separation agreement, or settlement agreement

proposal a formal written indication, from one party to the opposing party, that communicates what the first party is seeking in terms of a divorce settlement

proposal letter details the client's position on the various legal issues to be resolved, such as property division, alimony, child custody, visitation and support, maintenance of health and life insurance, distribution of debts and other liabilities, and counsel fees

psychological parent the parent who has had the child since the child's birth and/or who has spent the most meaningful time with the child, has bonded most fully with the child, and who has provided the most psychological nurturing of the child

public policy a belief generally held by a majority of the public as to the desirability or rightness or wrongness or certain behavior

Qualified Domestic Relations Order (QDRO) a court order served on the pension administrator ordering the plan to distribute a specified portion of the pension funds to the nonemployee spouse

quasi-contract contractual obligations that are imposed on the parties by the court, but no actual contract has been entered into by the parties

REA see *Retirement Equity Act*

real property land and anything affixed to it

reasonable rights of visitation a very flexible arrangement that requires the parties to work out their own schedule for visitation with children

reciprocity where one state may extend to attorneys in a different state the right to practice law in its jurisdiction in exchange for the other state's granting the same privilege to attorneys in their state

redirect after cross-examination, where the party's attorney may question the witness on any subject covered in the cross-examination testimony

rehabilitative alimony spousal support that is awarded for a limited period of time to give the spouse the opportunity to become self-sufficient

reimbursement alimony where a nondegreed spouse may be compensated for his or her contribution to the student spouse's attainment of an advanced degree that results in an enhanced earning capacity

release a document that indicates the client has given his or her attorneys the permission to disclose information to another party

request a document that asks the court to take some type of action; it is automatically granted by the court thirty days after filing, absent the opposing party's objection

request for admission where a party formally asks that an opposing party admit the truth of some fact or event that will inevitably be proved at trial

request for an order attacking known assets a document asking the court to freeze the opposing party's property in order to prevent dissipation of those assets

request for production of documents where a party formally asks that the other party present certain papers for use in a case

requesting party the party asking the court to take some action

requests for physical and mental examination where a party formally asks that the other party have a physical and/or psychiatric examination

respondeat superior the doctrine that states an employer is responsible for negligence and other torts committed by his or her employees when the acts are committed during the scope of their employment

respondent the party against whom an action is brought

responding party the party who must produce discovery documents

resulting trust where only one party provides the funds for property, while title is in the other party's name

retainer payment made in advance to an attorney

retainer agreement a contract between the law firm and the client whereby the law firm agrees to provide specified legal services in exchange for monetary compensation; also known as a retainer letter

retainer letter see *retainer agreement*

Retirement Equity Act of 1984 (REA) a federal statute determining the manner in which states may divide a pension at the time of divorce

return date a date in the near future by which the complaint must be returned to the court clerk's office and filed with the court

Revised Uniform Reciprocal Enforcement Act of 1968 (RURESA) where a custodial parent may ultimately obtain child support from the noncustodial parent residing in another state by instituting certain procedures

rule to show cause a document commanding a party to appear and argue as to why his or her motion should be granted

rules of court a jurisdiction's official publication containing the procedural codes of the jurisdiction

rules of ethics standards of conduct that a profession demands from its members

RURESA see *Revised Uniform Reciprocal Enforcement Act*

same-sex marriage marriage between two people of the same gender

sanctions punishment issued to attorneys for engaging in conduct that violates the state's code of professional conduct

second glance doctrine consideration of what circumstances exist at the time of enforcement of a prenuptial agreement in order to protect spouses from changes in circumstances that occurred since the date of the formation of the prenuptial agreement

secular courts courts administered by the state, as opposed to church, or ecclesiastical, courts

separate maintenance an action that affirms the continuation of a marriage and enforces the legal obligations of each spouse in the marriage

separate property property acquired by a spouse *prior* to the marriage, or after the marriage by a gift, inheritance, or will, designated to that particular spouse alone

separation agreement a contract between spouses who are in the process of obtaining a divorce or a legal separation resolving the various legal issues that arise when a marriage is dissolving; also known as a marital settlement agreement, property settlement, or settlement agreement

service by publication when a sheriff puts a legal notice in the newspaper in the city, town, or general area where the defendant was last known to reside, or where the defendant is now thought to be residing

service or performance agreement a document signed by a parent or parents in a child protection case in which the parent agrees to accomplish certain tasks

settlement the practice of negotiating areas of disagreement and, through compromise, reaching an agreement to present to the court

settlement agreement a contract between spouses who are in the process of obtaining a divorce or a legal separation resolving the various legal issues that arise when a marriage is dissolving; also known as a marital settlement agreement, property settlement or separation agreement

shared custody arrangement where a child resides with one parent for a certain number of days a week and a certain number of days with the other parent

sheriff's return a signed statement from a sheriff stating that he or she made proper service of a court document

short calendar one or two days of the week that courts set aside to hear motions brought before the court; also known as motion day

sole custody where one parent has exclusive custody of a child

sole ownership property owned by an individual alone

solicitation actively seeking persons in need of legal services, either by mail or in person, unless there already exists an attorney–client relationship or a family relationship

special defenses part of a defendant's answer in which he or she cites unusual or extraordinary circumstances as part of his or her defense

split custody arrangement where one parent has sole custody of the child for a part of each calendar year, and the other parent has sole custody for the remaining portion of the year

spousal maintenance a sum of money, or other property, paid by a former spouse to the other former spouse for financial support, pursuant to a court order, temporary or final, in a divorce proceeding; also known as alimony or spousal support

spousal support see *spousal maintenance*

standing a term that describes whether a party has a legal right to request an adjudication of the issues in a legal dispute

stipulations written agreements where parties agree that certain facts are true or that certain procedures will be followed

subpoena a legal document signed by an officer of the court that requires the person receiving it to appear under penalty of law at the time, date, and place indicated on the document

subscription part of a court document that confirms the truth and accuracy of allegations and confirms the veracity of the party making these allegations; also known as the verification

substantial change in circumstances an actual or assumed alteration in the financial status or capability of either party

summons a one-page preprinted form on which the names and addresses of parties and the name and address of the court are inserted and which directs the defendant to appear in court and answer allegations in a complaint

tax-deferred when taxes on the income produced by the pension will not be paid until the monies are withdrawn

temporary alimony payments made during the pendency of the divorce with the purpose of providing temporary financial support for a spouse; also known as *pendente lite* alimony

tenancy by the entirety a form of co-ownership which can only exist between a husband and wife and cannot be severed by either co-owner

tenancy in common where each party owns an undivided interest in certain property, has equal rights to its use and enjoyment, and may dispose of their share by gift, will, or sale

tender years doctrine the theoretical justification for the placing of children with their mother

termination of parental rights a court proceeding that severs the legal bonds between a parent and his or her biological child

testimony evidence given by a witness under oath or affirmation

theory of the case the legal justification for a client's position and for the relief he or she is seeking

third-party intervenor a party who is not one of the main parties in a dispute

time sheet a record of work performed on behalf of a client that will be billed to the client on a periodic basis; also known as a time slip

time slips see *time sheet*

title a party's ownership interest in property

total net income the figure arrived at when each parent's net income is added to determine child support; also known as combined net income

transcripts an official copy of the record of proceedings in a trial or hearing

transmutation the transformation of separate property to marital property

treatment worker social worker representing the state child protection agency who works with the family on a long-term basis by putting essential services in place and visiting the family on a regular basis

trial notebook a method of organizing the materials prepared for trial in a manner that makes them readily available for use at trial

trustee a person who holds legal title to property for the benefit of another

UIFSA see *Uniform Interstate Family Support Act*

unauthorized practice of law (UPL) when a nonattorney engages in any activity that the state UPL statute prohibits. Anyone engaging in the unauthorized practice of law can be prosecuted in criminal court

unconscionable something that is so wrong as to go against public policy

uncontested where neither party objects to the court granting a divorce and entering an order of marital dissolution

unearned retainer any part of a retainer left over after the attorney has completed his or her work that must be returned to the client

Uniform Interstate Family Support Act (UIFSA) where the noncustodial parent's state must honor the original support and may not enter a new order or modify the existing order to conform to its guidelines for determining the amount of support

Uniform Premarital Agreement Act act that many states have adopted which sets forth the criteria for drafting a valid premarital agreement

Uniform Reciprocal Enforcement Act (URESA) where a custodial parent may ultimately obtain child support from the noncustodial parent residing in another state by instituting certain procedures

unity of spouses the English common law system used to determine the division of marital property on dissolution of a marriage, which stated that, on marriage, a husband and wife merged into a single legal entity—the husband

UPL see *unauthorized practice of law*

value what the marital property is worth

verification part of a court document that confirms the truth and accuracy of allegations and confirms the veracity of the party making these allegations; also known as the subscription

vested in an employee pension plan, entitles the employee to the employer's contribution portion provided that the employee has worked for the employer for an enumerated number of years

vicarious liability where an employer is responsible for negligence and other torts committed by his or her employees when the acts are committed during the scope of their employment

visitation the time allotted for the noncustodial parent to spend with the child

wage execution serves the purpose of facilitating alimony and child support payments through automatic deductions from the obligor's paycheck

waiver where the parties agree not to seek an alimony award in a divorce case

willful contempt when the recipient spouse proves that the payor spouse has the means to make weekly payments but purposefully and deliberately fails to do so

work product the notes, materials, memoranda, and written records generated by an attorney, as well as the written records of the attorney's mental impressions and legal theories concerning a case

INDEX